W9-CEW-763

Television Criticism:
An Introduction to Reading, Writing and Analysis

Kimberly B. Massey, Ph.D.

Kimberly B. Massey, Ph.D.

Stanley J. Baran, Ph.D.

Stanley S. Baran, Ph.D.

KENDALL/HUNT PUBLISHING COMPANY
4050 Westmark Drive   Dubuque, Iowa 52002

Copyright© 1994, 1996 by Kendall/Hunt Publishing Company

ISBN 0–7872-2474-x

All rights reserved. No part of this publishing may be reproduced,
stored in a retrieval system, or transmitted, in any form or by any
means, electronic, mechanical, photocopying, recording, or otherwise,
without the prior written permission of the copyright owner.

Printed in the United States of America

10 9 8 7 6 5 4 3 2 1

For our best co-production,

Simmony Margaret Baran

CONTENTS

Chapter 10: News and Reality-based Television 211

Chapter 11: Music Television 245

Chapter 12: Television Sports 275

Chapter 13: Commercials   311

Chapter 14: Talk Shows   337

Epilogue   367

Index   369

CONTENTS

BY CRITICAL APPROACH

HISTORICAL CRITICISM

IDEOLOGICAL ANALYSIS

NARRATIVE ANALYSIS

READER-ORIENTED CRITICISM

"Terrorism and the Media: A Rhetorical Genre" *by Ralph E. Dowling*

"Sitcoms, Seriously" by *Tad Friend*

"Some Structural Characteristics of Music Television Videos" by *Donald L. Fry and Virginia H. Fry*

"Soap Opera Bridal Fantasies" by *Lauren Rabinovitz*

"How Nothing Relates to Everything: The World of Seinfeld" by *Mark Rudkin*

"Television Talk and Ritual Space: Carson and Letterman" by *Bernard Timberg*

RHETORICAL CRITICISM

"Terrorism and the Media: A Rhetorical Genre" by *Ralph E. Dowling*

SEMIOTICS

"The Dialectic of the Feminine: Melodrama and Commodity in the Ferraro Pepsi Commercial" by *Mary Ellen Brown*

SOCIOLOGICAL CRITICISM

"Counterfeiting the News" by *Jeffrey Chester and Kathryn Montgomery*

"Sitcoms, Seriously" by *Tad Friend*

"Battle for Your Brain" by *John Leland*

"Television and Democracy" by *Elayne Rapping*

"TV's Talking Headaches" by *Janet Steele*

"Race and the Transformation of Culture: The Making of the Television Miniseries *Roots*" by *Lauren Tucker and Hemant Shah*

PREFACE

If you're like the vast majority of people in America today, you watch a lot of television. The statistics have nearly become cliches, but they're still true: in a typical home, the set is on for more than seven hours a day and large numbers of us spend more time watching television than we do any activity other than sleeping. And yet, if you're like most folks, you spend almost no time at all *thinking about* what you're watching. We hope to change that because there's no hope of improving television unless we think about, comment on, analyze and criticize what we watch.

So, this is a book about television criticism. But it's also a book of television criticism. That means that in its pages you will find not only information on how to engage in good television criticism, but you'll also come across many fine examples of criticism written by others. Our goal is to provide you with a framework to guide your own critical analyses when:

- you watch television programming;
- you write television criticism, popular and/or academic; and,
- you read television criticism.

We will try to accomplish our goal in four steps:

First, **we will introduce you to criticism and critical theory**. There are a lot of different ways to evaluate not only the medium as a whole, but even individual programs.

Second, **we will discuss the process of criticism, that is, how to do it**. Sure, everyone's a critic, but not everyone can raise his or her analyses above "that stinks." There's griping and then there's criticism. The former may make you feel better for a moment or two, but the latter makes you a better viewer and works to improve the medium at the same time. We'll offer advice from past and current television critics as well as our own instructions.

Third, **we will detail the structure of the television industry that produces the "texts" that we will evaluate**. More than any other form of artistic expression, television content is inextricably shaped and molded by the economics, technologies, and production practices of a large industry. You'll need to understand how these interact to produce what ends up on television screens in millions of homes.

Fourth, **we will begin the act of criticism**. Using identifiable genres as our basis of organization, we will introduce you to analyses of Sports, News, Soap Operas, Drama, Comedy, Commercials, Game Shows, Talk Shows, and Music Television. We will offer an overview of each genre's development, examine some contemporary issues surrounding each, and discuss each form relying mainly on historical and genre criticism, but often employing other critical perspectives introduced throughout the book. As all critics must, we will make decisions about which approach or approaches will be most instructive. You may disagree with our choices. In fact, we hope you do. When it come to criticism, each of us is our own best judge.

Even though we will apply different critical approaches to the different genres, each section will follow a set format. We'll begin with a "What is..." discussion. Here we'll tell you what genre we'll be examining and how we defined it. Then we'll move to a brief history of the genre—criticism without historical perspective is pointless. From there we will go to the heart of each section: Our discussion of different critical issues germane to the genre under study. Finally, we will offer our comments on the examples of criticism that follow the discussion.

Typically we will offer two or three examples of other critics' work. For each genre you will find a piece of academic criticism and a piece of journalistic criticism. Each piece of academic criticism will reflect one of the critical perspectives detailed in Chapter 5. In addition, we may also include a third essay, one written by a television criticism student. Our intention here is to allow you to not only familiarize yourself with what others are saying about television, but to give you the opportunity to compare and contrast different types and levels of criticism, from detailed academic analyses to criticism written by people like you.

Some of the criticism you will like. Some you won't. But isn't that the way it is with television programming itself? The goal is to open you up to new ways of understanding television's content, to guide you to become more critical viewers, to give you the tools you'll need to be a better writers of television criticism and better "readers" of our culture's dominant literature: television programming.

We'd like to thank several people who have helped us prepare this book. First, we'd like to acknowledge one of our favorite criticism teachers, Dr. Chris Oravec, who actually sparked Kim's interest in the discipline. We'd also like to thank the following individuals who provided photographs for us: Gary A. Rosen from *Hard Copy* (Paramount), George D. Faber from *Matlock* (Viacom Entertainment), and Robert Anderson from KNTV-TV Channel 11 *The San Jose News Channel*.

On a more personal note, Barbara Stahl accomodated our hectic book-writing schedule with flexible (but always cheerful) child-care arrangements. And finally, we'd like to mention our loving parents who began our self-reflexive concern for watching television by telling us if we sat too close to the screen, we'd go blind.

We must also mention two issues we faced in preparing this text that may be of importance to you. First, we use gender-neutral language throughout this book. We think this is necessary in contemporary writing to make it most inclusive. However, many of the critics we quote in the following pages were writing at a time when the masculine form of most pronouns was proper. We experimented with including "her," "she," "herself," and so on in brackets after the original authors' "his," "he," "himself," and so on. But too often the ideas that made the quote important enough to include became lost in a syntactical jumble. So where you see sexist or exclusionary language in a quote, forgive the original author and hope she (or he) now knows better.

The second issue has to do with the student essays. You'll notice that many chapters do not include student writing. You and your teacher can help rectify this sad state of affairs. If you think your criticism is as good as the student work we do present, ask your instructor to send it to us. There is a submission letter at the end of this preface to use when you submit your writing. We'll read your essay and, if we use it in the next edition of this book, we'll not only send you a copy of the text, but you will for all time be a published television critic.

We all know that television can be frustrating, but that it can also be very rewarding and satisfying. We hope to convince you that the same can be said for television criticism. Have fun reading, watching and writing!

K.B.M & S.J.B., San Jose, CA

Kimberly B. Massey, Ph.D.
Department of Theatre Arts
San Jose State University
San Jose, CA 95192-0098

Dear Professor Massey:

Please consider this essay, written by student _____,

for inclusion in the next edition of *Television Criticism: An Introduction to Reading, Writing and Analysis.*

This critique was written in the _____ semester of 19 _____.

We believe that other television criticism students will not only enjoy it, but that they will learn something from it.

I grant permission for this essay's publication in any editions of *Television Criticism.*

If under 18, parent or guardian must sign.

We look forward to your reactions.

Sincerely

_____   _____
Instructor's signature   Student's signature

_____   _____
Instructor's name (print)   Student's name (print)

Student information:

College or university   _____

Major   _____

Class standing: Fr.   So.   Jr.   Sr.   Grad.

CHAPTER 1

THE ACT OF CRITICISM

Kill your television.

—Anonymous

Most of us have seen this popular bumper sticker and, if we're honest with ourselves, we'd have to admit that our first reaction was probably, "Yeah!" At one time or another we've all become angry with television, saying things like, "TV stinks," "It's the boob tube," "It's an idiot box," "They're couch potatoes," "I hardly ever watch," and most frustratingly, "There's nothing on." But television wouldn't make us so mad if it wasn't so important to us.

Imagine if we did kill our televisions. There would be no Super Bowl, World Series, or NBA Championships. No *Star Trek*, *Star Trek: The Next Generation*, *Star Trek: Deep Space 9*. No *Seinfeld*, *Cheers*, *Saturday Night Live*, or *Cosby*. There would be no *Sesame Street*, no Clarence Thomas vs. Anita Hill Senate Judiciary Committee Hearings or Watergate Hearings or Iran Contra Hearings. No more *Married . . . With Children* or *Simpsons*. And all of the cable specialties would be gone too. No more HBO, MTV, Cinemax, Discovery Channel, Showtime, Bravo, A&E, Encore and Comedy Central. Perhaps some programs wouldn't be missed as much as others, shows like *My Mother the Car*, *The Pat Sajak Show*, *Punkey Brewster*, *Alf*, and those early Sunday morning public affairs talk shows to satisfy licensing obligations.

Yes, everyone dislikes something on television at one time or another, and television can often present the trivial and the ridiculous. But we would no more condemn "the movies" industry for the likes of *Ishtar* or *Spaceballs* than we would a bookstore for stocking a volume we don't like; so why is our judgment of television different, and so often negative? The answer rests somewhere between former FCC Chairman Mark Fowler's characterization of television as "a toaster with pictures" (1982) and critic Tony Schwartz's "the second god" (1981).

Of course, television is much more than an appliance and, hopefully, much less than a deity. But for every one of us, it is an important part of our lives. Even non-viewers (an infinitesimally small number of individuals) live in a world where everyone else watches television. And it is this centrality that makes us so ambivalent about television. Every one of us has complained about television, but virtually all of us watch it. Every one of us has something to say about the medium, but that doesn't necessarily make us television critics.

1

Overview

In this chapter we will see how notable critics from many major art forms define criticism . . . what it is and what it isn't. We will discuss the responsibilities of the critic, the role of the critic, the purpose of criticism, and the audiences for whom critics write, again using the words of working critics. We make so much use of the critics' own explanations because, as you'll see, there is some disagreement between many critics as to what criticism actually is. So rather than tell you what we think it is, we will let several of those who engage in formal criticism lay out for you their own experiences and biases. Eventually, though, *our* bias will show, because when such a universal medium (or art form) as television is the focus of interest, the most valuable perspective on criticism may well be the most inclusive view: **informed talk about matters of importance**.

What Criticism Is . . . And Isn't

Complaining isn't criticism. Griping isn't criticism. Neither is throwing the remote control on the floor and cursing the cable company. Criticism is often difficult to define, as we can see in the following comments from three noted literary critics:

> *Critics hold and debate widely differing views as to what criticism is or should be (John M. Ellis, 1981, p. 15).*

> *What is criticism, then? Criticism is nothing determinate, no one thing, no collection of things. In the abstract, as some thing to be grasped either as now present or as some future goal, criticism simply isn't (Wayne C. Booth, 1981, p. 163).*

> *For there is no defining criticism, at least not in any detailed terms, because criticism does not exist in any absolute or stable fashion. As a social activity conducted by and within some living community, criticism always goes on in some specific context, with respect to some specific body of art, some specific group-*

ing of artists, audiences, and critics, some specific social and institutional structure. Its concerns and methods vary along all these lines (Mary Pratt, 1981, p. 177).

What these writers want us to understand is that criticism is what *we* make it. There are as many definitions of criticism as there are critics; it isn't any one thing and it's different things in different situations. This makes the act of criticism, then, an exciting and liberating one. But it doesn't mean that there are no rules for criticism; because although there is no uniform definition of criticism, there is agreement on what makes *good* criticism when it does happen in whatever form.

Good criticism is a method of systematic organization, observation and interpretation. It offers description, evaluation, analysis, contextualization and understanding. It is developing an informed opinion and sharing it, either orally or in writing, with others. It is having something of interest and importance to say about something that you and your reader (watcher or listener) care about; or, as rhetoricians Phil Wander and Steven Jenkins wrote, criticism is "informed talk about matters of importance" (1972, p. 450). Drama critic Rustom Bharucha (1984, p. 10) fleshes out this definition, but we'll soon see that not all critics agree with him:

1. **Criticism is an objective scrutiny of facts.** It can't be personal, though it may be (and frequently is) opinionated.

2. **Criticism is not creative.** It does not have a life of its own. Its function is to remain faithful to what has already been produced.

3. **Criticism is logical.** It can't go off on tangents or circumlocute or digress.

4. **Criticism is serious business.** It should help us to live, and therefore, it cannot tolerate any play of thought. At best, it can be . . . a "superior amusement."

Speaking specifically of media criticism, Scodari and Thorpe (1992, p. 3) offer their apparently thorough definition: "legitimate media criticism involves the intellectual, subjective analysis and/or evaluation of media artifacts, policies, technologies, and/or institutions by 'disinterested' persons who do not stand to personally profit as a consequence of their specific criticism." But as you can see, they differ immediately with Bharucha. Where he says criticism should be objective, they say it should be subjective. There's also a hint in their definition of one of the special aspects of media criticism. They make clear that media critics (this includes television critics) can or even must involve themselves with much more than the basic artifact. This means that in the case of television, the "text" available for critical scrutiny goes well beyond the program or programs. To them, "media policies, technologies, and/or institutions" are fair game for the critic: the text can be more than the artwork itself. We'll revisit this issue in Chapter 2.

Finally, criticism should also be fun. Literary critic Emanuel Carnevali enthused, "Criticism is hellfire, death and destruction, war and revolution, and all the fun there is in rockets and gas bombs and smoke screens and camouflage, butchery and a danse macabre of ghosts, of murdered kings and princes gone mad withal, that's what criticism is" (1985, p. 39).

The Responsibilities of the Critic

Engaging in good criticism, however, places certain obligations on the critic—obligations to oneself, to the artform in question, and to the reader. Once again there is disagreement between critics—this time regarding how these obligations should be prioritized.

Film and drama critic John Simon of *Esquire* and *New York Magazine* (Searle, 1974, pp. 6-7) writes, "Like any other artist, [the critic's] responsibility is first and last to himself, to the high standards and the requirements of discriminating taste that he sets for himself, and to enlighten himself about the play or whatever it is that he's writing about." New York *Times* drama critic Clive Barnes concurs, saying the critic's duty is "merely the expression

of his own tastes" (Searle, 1974, p. 5).

Village Voice drama critic John Lahr sees the responsibility to the artform as paramount, "The only responsibility a critic has is to be good, and he has no responsibility, really, I believe, to his readers, but to the art" (Searle, 1974, p. 6). And literary critic Wallace Martin (1981) views this duty as mediation "between literature and culture . . . to turn the work of art into a cultural acquisition" (p. 83). But in helping the artform better reach its consumers, the critic obviously has a responsibility to them as well. Readers of good criticism "are to be provided a piece of reading that will be pleasurable enough for them to enjoy as a piece of reading," explains John Simon (Searle, 1974, p. 7).

The Audience for Criticism

But just who are these readers of criticism? Generally speaking, there are three audiences for criticism. One is the *academic audience,* that is, students and scholars of the artform under examination. These folks typically exist in colleges and universities. A second is the artforms' *creators.* These are the authors of the books, the writers and directors of the plays, the givers of the speeches, the sculptors of the statues, the painters of the paintings and, in the case of television, industry practitioners. And while most critics of the more traditional artforms like music, drama and literature would claim that their writing has little effect on the work of the creators they examine (see Hernandi, 1981 and Searle, 1974 for example), television criticism may be different. Washington *Post* and National Public Radio television and film critic Tom Shales believes it is. "You chastise people; you try to humiliate them," he said. "Aaron Spelling (*Charlie's Angels* and *Beverly Hills, 90210*) cannot be shamed but Grant Tinker (*Lou Grant*) can be" (Traub, 1987, p. 42). Finally, there are the *consumers* of the artform, the playgoers, readers, moviegoers, listeners and viewers; that is, the public.

These three audiences differ in the kinds of criticism they usually read. Students and scholars of an artform typically consume "scholarly," "interpretive" or *academic* criticism, while creators and the public most often read "popular" or *journalistic* criticism (Newcomb, 1986). Scodari and Thorpe (1992) further break journalistic *media* criticism down into two categories: *consumer-oriented media reviews* and *social critiques*. The former is self explanatory. As for social critiques, they say (p. 9), "Such pieces spring from an ethical or philosophical position and have as their primary purpose the forging of a connection. . . . The connection in question might be *mimetic*— that is, the media are considered as a mirror of society. Or, the connection might be *influential*—that is, the media are seen as having, or not having, a specific effect on society or human behavior."

What differentiates academic and popular criticism is not only where each usually appears (scholarly journals and books for the former, newspapers, magazines, and trade journals for the latter), but the "amount of supporting argumentation, the range and amount of supporting evidence, and the extent to which the theoretical assumptions underlying the critique and the method used to arrive at the critical proposition are explicitly laid out for the reader" (Vande Berg & Wenner, 1991, p. 8). We'll have much more to say about this in Chapter 5.

The Role of the Critic/The Purpose of Criticism

Although critics disagree on what responsibilities they may have, and although any one critic will probably never fulfill all the various roles identified as appropriate for a critic, and although no one piece of criticism can ever satisfy all the purposes of criticism, there is general agreement among critics on what the role of the critic and the purpose of criticism *should* be. We'll list them here and, again, let our collection of noted critics explain.

1. Critic as Teacher/Interpreter

Good critics help create a critical climate for the consumption and enjoyment of the artform in question. The critic provides services that we typically associate with teachers: explanation, interpretation, and education. Critic Simon says , "They (readers of criticism) are to be taught something by it, if possible. In other words, educated somewhat in matters theatrical by way of elucidation, by way of explication, by way of all things that come under the heading of education, teaching" (Searle, 1974, p. 7).

2. Critic as Guide and Judge

Clive Barnes calls a good critic the readers' "guide, philosopher, and friend" (Searle, 1971, p. 14). And while this seems straightforward enough, some critics disagree about this aspect of the critic's role. Is it possible to guide and *not* judge? If it *isn't*, is judging (making evaluations) an appropriate task for critics? Literary critic Monroe Beardsley (1970, p. 39) argues that if the critic "is a discriminating guide . . . he cannot avoid evaluations." And F. V. N. Painter (1903) concurs that "the critic ought to be a person of sound judgement . . . should have the power to divest himself of prejudice; and, like a judge upon the bench, should decide every question by law and evidence" (pp. 4–5).

But drama critic Alfred Emmet disagrees, "None would deny that criticism, in part at least, must be an expression of personal opinion, and the whole must be coloured by the personality of the writer. But it does not follow that this is a good thing. It is inevitable, but not necessarily desirable. Because the critic must unavoidably write in some degree of himself, or at least from a personal viewpoint, it does not follow that his function is to write primarily about himself, or even that it is permissible for him to emphasize the personal aspect in his writing. Because there is some water in beer, it is not an *et sequitur* that the best beer has no hops" (1973, p. 3). Fellow drama critic Michael Kirby agrees, "There are two aspects to criticism: the passing of value judgments and analysis. . . . Indeed, the word 'criticism' [should] be used to refer specifically to the act of publishing statements of value. (One definition given by Webster is 'a finding fault; censuring; disapproval.') Thus, the evaluative and analytical functions [should] be considered as separate and distinct; 'analysis' [is] opposed to 'criticism' rather than being included in it. In these terms, it is not merely a change that [should] be asked of criticism. Criticism as value judgment is a harmful anachronism and should be eliminated completely" (1974, p. 59).

Yet most critics would argue (Peckham, 1981) that good criticism cannot help but be evaluative, because it *should* combine

- interpretational statements;
- judgements of competence; and,
- ascriptions of value.

This is because if an artform is important enough to be the subject of critical evaluation, it is important enough to be judged evaluatively . . . otherwise, why should anyone care? Even the very guide-like role of reviewer is not without its evaluative value. Literary critic Pratt writes that reviews play

> *an important role in the critical process of working out community consensus of judgement and interpretation of art—which is why people read and discuss reviews after having taken in the work, or even when they don't intend to take it in. A preoccupation with entertainment value obviously does not preclude serious consideration of art. Entertainment and leisure are serious matters (1981, p. 182).*

3. Critic as Historian/Recorder

Good critics record contemporary judgments of specific works. They fix for all time what at least one person, they themselves, thought of the work. In this way, good criticism *contextualizes* a piece of work by setting it in time—political time, economic time, social time, cultural time, aesthetic time—that may or may not be evident in the work itself. The critic helps create the "backdrop" against

which a piece can be judged and enjoyed. Literary critic Northrop Frye explains this role: "Criticism . . . is to art what history is to action and philosophy is to wisdom: a verbal imitation of a human productive power which itself does not speak. And just as there is nothing which the philosopher cannot consider philosophically, and nothing the historian cannot consider historically, so the critic should be able to construct and dwell in a conceptual universe of his own" (1957, p. 12).

4. Critic as Analyst

Clive Barnes explained that a critic's role is to try "to describe and catch the essence of a work's spirit and . . . to explain what the artist was attempting" (Searle, 1974, p. 6). Speaking specifically of television, critic Horace Newcomb explained this role this way: "television is so smooth, so carefully disguised, that the role of the critic is essentially that of de-mystifer. So well has television done its job that no one *but* the critic can strip away the mask" (1986, p. 223–224). It isn't that those who consume various artforms are incapable of their own definitions, interpretations and evaluations; it's just that the critic should have a deeper understanding and awareness of the form in question. But the inevitable question arises, "So what? Why should anyone, especially those enjoying a musical performance, a book, a play, a movie, a television show, need or even want this 'help' from an 'outsider?'" The answer is imbedded in Wander and Jenkins' definition of criticism (informed talk about matters of importance) and Bharucha's reminder that criticism is "important business . . . it should help us to live." Therefore, the most valuable purpose of criticism, the most important role of the critic, is as a . . .

5. Critic as Catalyst for Reflection

Critic Simon said, "The critic should use the work of art as a springboard for philosophical speculation about life, about existence, about what it means to be a human being" (Searle, 1974, p. 7). Increasingly, we know our world and our place in it through the eyes of others— the author, the film-maker, the journalist, the poet, the dramatist, the composer, and the television producer. Good criticism, then, should move us to think not only about the work under examination, but about the artist who created it, the particular set of circumstances that allowed and shaped that creation, the political/social/cultural environment that colored its consumption and interpretation by the public, the "deeper truths" obscured by Newcomb's "mask."

This is especially and crucially true in the case of television. The creations illuminated on its phosphorescent screen are today's dominant form of literature, today's dominant mode of entertainment, today's dominant source of information—in short, today's dominant way of knowing. Literary critic (and no fan of television) John Gardner offers an example, "Sympathetic black actors on TV have more power than bussing laws. . . . (I)deals expressed in art can effect behavior in the world" (1978, p. 27). Therefore, to remain less reflective of television's grammar, economics, structures, operations, and impact than we might otherwise be is to remain less culturally literate than we might otherwise be. To be less aware of the culture that shapes us and our experiences than we might otherwise be is to be less human than we can be. Again, John Gardner:

> We need to stop excusing mediocre and downright pernicious art, stop "taking it for what it's worth" as we take our fast foods, our overpriced cars that are no good, the overpriced houses we spend all our lives fixing . . . our schools thrown up like barricades in the way of young minds, our brainless fat religions, our poisonous air, our incredible cult of sports, and our ritual fornicating with all pretty or even horsefaced strangers. We would not put up with a debauched king, but in a democracy all of us are kings, and we praise debauchery as pluralism (1978, p. 100).

Put somewhat less dramatically (and less angrily), *a good critic turns others into good critics.*

These notions of critic as teacher, judge, guide, historian, analyst and catalyst for reflection reinforce the prerequisite that critics must know their subject—and know it well—in order for them to be considered reliable sources of information, no matter what role they assume. This is not to say that someone must first work in the television industry or produce a television program in order to be a good television critic. At the same time, however, just because you watch a lot of television doesn't make you a critical expert either.

What we are suggesting is that in order to be a good television critic, you must understand all of the facets of television: the structure of the industry, the economics of the business, the goals of the producers, etc. Because it is these things that ultimately affect the products of television—programming and its impact on audiences—which are typically the subject of television criticism.

Services Provided by the Critic

Legendary author and critic T. S. Elliot (1957, p. 117) writes, "The critic to whom I am most grateful is the one who can make me look at something I have never looked at before, or looked at only with eyes clouded by prejudice, set me face to face with it and then leave me alone with it."

It seems that Elliot believes that critics render valuable service to their audiences. But what kind of value? Why do we need criticism, especially of something as common as television?

If we take into consideration the various roles that a critic can assume, then there should be a number of services a critic can provide. The following list highlights some of the values found in criticism. Some are more broadbased than others. Some overlap with others. And, of course, criticism can encompass any number of these at any time although rarely does any critic accomplish all of them at once.

Among the valuable services a successful critic can provide are:

1. to present an alternate perspective in which to consider the work;

2. to render additional information about a work that is not commonly known;

3. to guide the viewer through the experience and understanding of the work;

4. to teach the audience to understand and appreciate the complexities of the work, whether they find favor in it or not;

5. to reconstruct a historical context for the work, that is, provide an explanation of the work according to the time in which it was originally produced;

6. to provide a comparison of the work—presenting what makes the work the same as or peculiar from others that share history, form or content;

7. to judge or assess value to the work on a macro level—highlighting the generalities that make the work important, or on a micro level—concentrating on the specifics or details that make the work unique;

8. to help the reader of the criticism interpret the work in a specific way (never *the only* way).

Yet, as we mentioned earlier, audiences are not the only ones served by enlightenment at the hands of the critic. Peter Orlik writes,

Also of substantial importance, however, is how the critic assists the creator or (particularly in radio/television) the multiple creators of the work in question. . . . By opening up the lines of communication and understanding between creator and consumer, the critic makes it easier for each to comprehend the need of the other. In the short term, creators thereby learn what their audience desires now while, for the long term, the audience can be coaxed into a positive anticipation of the more profound expressions of which the creator may be capable (1988, p. 13).

Orlik thinks that, ideally, this bridging of creator and audience can lead to positive change, stimulate creativity and lead to new techniques and works from the broadcast industry.

And so to our previous list of eight valuable services provided by critics we now add three more:

9. to act as a mediator between audience and media producer;

10. to provide suggestions for positive change by the television industry; and,

11. to stimulate new ideas in the future.

Obviously these "valuable services" that critics might provide the creators and consumers of television paint a very positive picture of the critic. It almost seems as if we are suggesting that the *only* way to fully experience, understand, judge, create or change television content is by allowing the critic to lead us through the process. Some readers of criticism bristle at the thought of having a critic's interpretations imposed upon them to the exclusion of their own perceptions.

In fact, we are suggesting that a critic's evaluation of any of television's many texts **should not** *take the place of* your own. Rather, we think that criticism can be used uniquely by individuals to enhance their understanding and enjoyment. This is the value of criticism although it is certainly not achieved by every piece of criticism ever written. For example, John Gardner (1987) expresses great frustration about contemporary criticism. He writes,

Though more difficult than ever before to read, criticism has become trivial. The trivial has its place, its entertainment value. I can think of no good reason that some people should not specialize in the behavior of the left-side hairs on an elephant's trunk. Even at its best, its most deadly serious, criticism, like art, is partly a game, as all good critics know. My objection is not to the game but to the fact that contemporary critics have for the most

*part lost track of the point of their game. . . .
Fiddling with the hairs on an elephant's nose
is indecent when the elephant happens to be
standing on the baby. At least in America art
is not thought capable, these days, of tromping
on babies. Yet it does so all the time, and what
is worse, it does so with a bland smile (p. 4).*

Criticism for criticism's sake is a waste. Only when criticism enhances the television experience is it valuable. Otherwise, it's only complaining. It's only griping. You might as well throw the remote control on the floor and curse the cable company.

Exercises

John Gardner's Frustration

Do you share Gardner's frustration? What do you think makes so much criticism trivial? Do different things make journalistic criticism trivial than make academic criticism trivial? Do you believe that American art (especially television) "tromps on babies?" Given this emotional passage, what role or roles do you think Gardner sees as most important for the good critic?

Trivial criticism occurs when critics write abashedly. To just insult a performer with no substance is unnecessary. Journalistic criticism leans towards what people (general public) want: exciting? fun? entertaining? whereas academic criticism focuses more on aspects of the medium itself a what it represents —

Do you think some roles are more important than others? Using the box provided below, place the roles of the critic (Teacher/Interpreter, Guide/Judge, Historian/Recorder, Analyst, and Catalyst for Reflection) in hierarchical order that reflects your judgement of the their importance.

ROLES OF THE CRITIC	
Critic's Role	**Why do you feel it is important?**
1. T/I 2. Reflection 3. Guide 4. His/R 5. Analyst	

Talking About Criticism

In this chapter Rustom Bharucha lists his four part definition of criticism. But this noted drama critic also had this to say about critics: "Critics are, not infrequently, cretins . . . What makes them different from other spectators? Knowledge, a way with words, disinterestedness, taste— qualities, more imagined than real, that conjure up the perfect critic who does not exist" (1984, p. 9).

The "perfect" critic may not exist, but it is obvious that many competent if less than perfect ones do. What characteristics and qualities do you see in yourself that would make you a good critic? What characteristics or failings do you see in yourself that might make you a "cretin" critic? What can you do to improve your strengths and overcome your weaknesses?

SELF EVALUATION AS A TELEVISION CRITIC	
Strengths	**Ways to Improve**
1. well-rounded 2. perceptive 3. intelligent 4. . 5.	

Weakness	**Ways to Overcome**
1. very strong opinions 2. don't like particular genres 3. 4. 5.	

References and Resources

Beardsley, M. C. (1970). *The Possibility of Criticism.* Detroit, MI: Wayne State University Press.

Bharucha, R. (1984). Confessions of an itinerant critic. *Performing Arts Journal, 8,* 9–27.

Booth, W. C. (1981). Criticulture: or, why we need at least three criticisms at the present time. In P. Hernadi (Ed.). *What Is Criticism?* Bloomington, IN: Indiana University Press.

Brock, B. L., Scott, R. L. & Cheseboro, W. E., (Eds.). (1990). *Methods of Rhetorical Criticism: A Twentieth-Century Perspective.* Detroit, MI: Wayne State University Press.

Carnevali, E. (1985). Noted with pleasure. *New York Times Book Review,* January 6, p. 39.

Elliot, T. S. (1957). The frontiers of criticism. In T. S. Elliot, *On Poetry and Poets.* London, Faber and Faber, 117.

Ellis, J. M. (1981). The logic of the question "what is criticism." In P. Hernadi (Ed.). *What is Criticism?* Bloomington, IN: Indiana University Press.

Emmet, A. (1973). A short view of dramatic criticism. *Theatre Quarterly, 3,* 3–5.

Fowler, M. S. & Brenner, D. L. (1982). A marketplace approach to broadcast regulation. *Texas Law Review, 60,* 205–254.

Frye, N. (1957). *Anatomy of Criticism.* Princeton, NJ: Princeton University Press.

Gardner, J. (1978). *On Moral Criticism.* New York: Basic Books.

Hernadi, P. (Ed.). (1981). *What is Criticism?* Bloomington, IN: Indiana University Press.

Kauffmann, S. (1971). *Figures of Light: Criticism and Comment.* New York: Harper & Row.

Kirby, M. (1974). Criticism: four faults. *The Drama Review, 18,* 59–68.

Martin, W. (1981). Critical truth as necessary error. In P. Hernadi (Ed.). *What is Criticism?* Bloomington, IN: Indiana University Press.

Newcomb, H. (1986). American television criticism 1970–1985. *Critical Studies in Mass Communication, 3,* 217–228.

Orlik, P. B. (1988). *Critiquing Radio and Television Content.* Boston, MA: Allyn and Bacon, Inc.

Painter, F. V. N. (1903). *Elementary Guide to Literary Criticism.* Boston, MA: Ginn and Company.

Peckham, M. (1981). Three notions about criticism. In P. Hernadi (Ed.). *What is Criticism?* Bloomington, IN: Indiana University Press.

Pratt, M. (1981). Art without critics and critics without readers *or* Pantagruel versus The Incredible Hulk. In P. Hernadi (Ed.). *What is Criticism?* Bloomington, IN: Indiana University Press.

Schwartz, T. (1981). *Media: The Second God.* New York: Random House.

Scodari, C. & Thorpe, J. (1992). *Media Criticism: Journeys in Interpretation.* Dubuque, IA: Kendall/Hunt.

Searle, J. (1974). Four drama critics. *The Drama Review, 18,* 5–23.

Traub, J. (1987). Who's afraid of Tom Shales? *Channels,* February, pp. 36–42.

Vande Berg, L. R. & Wenner, L. A. (1991). *Television Criticism: Approaches and Applications.* New York: Longman.

Wander, P. & Jenkins, S. (1972). Rhetoric, society, and the critical response. *Quarterly Journal of Speech, 58,* 441–450.

CHAPTER 2

CRITICISM AND POPULAR CULTURE

The clearest case of a gap in criticism at the moment is television, a medium whose very invention took place after criticism's move into the university, and whose only critical tradition is the Nielsen ratings, doubtless the crudest critical tool ever conceived. In recent years, a gap has been opening between TV programmers and viewers right where criticism ought to be. Far from being bound to each other in a mindless consumer orgy, the television viewing audience and programming establishment have by now . . . so fallen out of touch with each other that a crisis of sorts has been acknowledged. . . . The networks respond with a frenzy of wasteful production, trying out series after series, pilot after pilot, special after special, in hopes that something will click. Viewers seem able to communicate only what they don't want to watch, not what they do; networks seem unable to explain their successes and failures except individually and in terms of scheduling, weather, raw chance, or perhaps the price of oil.

—Mary Pratt

Critic Pratt's (1981, p. 180) implication should be clear: Good criticism can help make better viewers and better television. But before we can begin discussing television, we must acquaint ourselves with another factor affecting criticism of that medium; we must examine the emergence and impact of the mass media on the world of the critic-to-be. In doing this, we will find that criticism of mass media is very different from criticism of the more traditional forms of artistic expression (as we hinted in Chapter 1). We must adapt our critical tools to the job at hand, and while the task of a television critic and an art critic, for example, may look the same, there are some significant differences.

Overview

We'll lead up to our discussion of television criticism with a look at the roots of our culture's view of that medium and of popular culture in general. The introduction of mass media, beginning with the printing press in the Fifteenth century, brought new forms of entertainment to people whose choices had previously been very limited. In the days before mass media, two forms of "art" or communication were fairly easily identified and differentiated—High (or Elite) art and Folk art. The rise of Mass art (or popular culture) was wonderful for the rapidly-growing middle class, but posed problems for critics.

In dealing with mass media, critics have new questions to ask—questions with no simple answers: How can the mass media text in general, and the television text in particular, be identified? Who is the creator of mass media, "assembly-line" presentations? Who is the audience for mass media presentations? How does the audience "read" mass media texts? Do the mass media teach audiences behavior, or do the mass media reflect culturally determined behavior patterns? Do the mass media *reflect* cultural beliefs or *create* them?

Popular culture critics must deal with the fact that most people don't want to think about the mass media, choosing instead to consume them unself-consciously. Some people consider them beneath notice, not worthy of comment or so dangerous they should be swept under a cultural rug and forgotten. Still, none of the questions above is unanswerable, none of the problems insurmountable. In the chapters which follow, we'll provide answers and solutions but, in the end, critics must deal with these issues on their own.

Communication Changes

When considering the more traditional art forms—painting, music, sculpture, literature, often even film—determining the text and context of your critical endeavor is relatively simple. In these more traditional arts, the work is generally created by an individual artist (although to be sure there have been important artists who have worked with apprentices and collaborators). And these artworks are designed to express the hopes, feelings, beliefs, or desires of their creators.

The audience is rarely a factor in determining either the subject matter or its treatment (although, again, artists working in any form must, on occasion, submit to the demands of patrons and supporters in order to ensure their supply of materials, money and meals).

All that's necessary to create a novel is a PC, some paper and a writer with an idea; all that's necessary to create a painting is a canvas, some paint, and again, an artist with a vision. The critical text which results from these sorts of processes is, more or less, easily identified. In dealing with the Mona Lisa, for example, we can easily place ourselves within the narrative context by simply looking at and thinking about the Mona Lisa. There it is, a painting hanging on a wall in a museum, waiting for us. We can also easily place ourselves within the creative context and know, beyond a doubt, that this is the work of Leonardo Da Vinci. In other words, the creator, text and context are, for all intents and purposes, spelled out for us.

The introduction of mass media—modes of communication designed specifically to reach large numbers of people—complicates this relatively simple critical process. What we have been referring to as the "traditional arts" underwent major changes during the period in history called the *Industrial Revolution,* and these changes are of great importance to us as critics and consumers of mass media content. Industrialization changed the very nature of communication, changed virtually every art form, changed the size, definition, and role of the audiences for those art forms, and changed the ways in which critics must deal with those forms and audiences. And it all began with the printing press.

Before Johann Gutenberg introduced moveable type and the modern printing press in 1440, communication was conducted primarily face-to-face. Someone with a message delivered it directly to those for whom it was intended. A speaker spoke to one or, at most, a few people at a time. Plays existed only for those who could see them performed live. Music existed only for those within earshot of the musicians. Books were rare, with each volume having to be laboriously copied by hand. A painter created a work on canvas and only those wealthy enough to commission that work (or fortunate enough to know one of these rich patrons) had the opportunity to see that painting.

Before print came along, communication was by voice or manuscript, both very limiting. At most, a person could verbally address only a few hundred people at a time and a writer only the very few who could physically hold a scroll or letter and know how to read it. Print made it possible for communication to be duplicated endlessly. Marshall McLuhan suggested the importance of this development when he argued that the single most important invention in the history of architecture was the printing press because it allowed for the construction of interior walls in buildings, as communication no longer had to be face to face.

Print was the first method for duplicating information and disseminating it to large numbers of people but it was certainly not the last. Since the late Nineteenth Century we have seen the introduction of several mass media that make it possible for artists and other communicators to reach even larger audiences: radio, motion pictures, and television.

The implications of this newfound ability to duplicate and distribute an artwork, almost endlessly, are many for the artist, critic, audience and society itself. Among the most immediate and far-reaching changes wrought by the invention and diffusion of the printing press was the *increased importance accorded the written (printed) word.* Before Gutenberg's marvel, history, business transactions, stories, customs, laws—all vital to the development and maintenance of a culture—were expressed orally and then committed to memory, at least among the lower classes. The very wealthy could afford only handwritten documents and books, and even these were deemed a luxury.

The printing press eventually brought such written memory aids within range of a much larger portion of the population. But like the written materials themselves, education, especially the ability to read, was limited to those who could afford it. The cost of an education, in time and money, made reading a very expensive luxury available to few. With the spread of printing, however, came the need for education among the lower and

middle classes. As written records became more common, *the ability to read became less of a luxury and more of a necessity.* So more people learned to read.

Two other factors that increased the importance of printing as a cultural force were *industrialization* and the *increase in leisure time that* its machines made possible. Machines reduced the amount of time necessary to complete work and this, of course, increased the amount of free time for workers. But industrialization had another effect. As more and more people left their sunrise-to-sunset jobs in agriculture, the crafts and the trades to go work in the factories, not only did they have more time, but they had more money. Farmers, clam diggers, and carpenters had to put their money back into their jobs. Factory workers walked home with a paycheck—more or less discretionary money. Combine increases in leisure time and expendable cash with the spread of literacy and the result is a growing audience for written (or printed) *entertainment*, an audience much larger than ever possible in the pre-printing world. *Printing gave people the time and ability to read, leading to an increased demand for enjoyable things to read.*

For the first time, a mass audience and the means to reach it existed. So in the five hundred years following the introduction of the printing press, a new kind of artist emerged, one dedicated not necessarily to the expression of some inner vision or to the satisfaction of some patron's tastes, but one committed to reaching the new mass audience. New media such as photography, the phonograph, movies, radio and television, extended the artist's reach. As the audience for mass-mediated entertainment steadily grew in size, a new entrepreneurial spirit overtook the arts, which changed them by shifting the emphasis from the artist to the audience. The new artist/ entrepreneurs, rather than expressing their own hopes, fears, desires and beliefs, actively worked to determine and then satisfy the hopes, fears, desires and beliefs of the growing (remember industrialization) middle class, hoping to attract the largest possible paying (again, remember industrialization) audience.

Giving the people what they wanted (or believed they wanted) became the goal of the new mass art.

The emergence of mass art, for example mass produced books and reproduced paintings, prints and pictures, did not happen overnight, but over the course of centuries. Eventually, though, this form of cultural artifact, this mass art, sometimes called *popular culture*, came to dominate the cultural lives of the vast majority of people in the industrialized world.

Only Entertainment?

The emergence of the mass audience and the growth of mass arts to serve its needs require a bit more comment. It may not be immediately obvious what developments over the last five centuries have to do with television and the way we evaluate its content, but in fact this history has much to tell us. Many of our attitudes about television were debated and/or formed long before anyone could have imagined instantaneous electronic communication. Our current attitudes are not much different from earlier critics' attitudes toward other mass media. Our assessment of the quality of television programming is not much different that their assessments of the quality of past media presentations.

Television is not the first medium to be attacked and blamed for our social ills. Virtually every form of mass art or popular culture has been similarly vilified, denigrated and, paradoxically, consumed. Here, for example, are samples of what critics had to say about movies, talking pictures and radio in their infancy:

The version of life presented to him in the majority of moving pictures is false in fact, sickly in sentiment, and utterly foreign to the Anglo-Saxon ideals of our nation.

Outlook, *July 26, 1916*

And if the speech recorded in the dialogue (of talking pictures) is vulgar or ugly, its potentialities for lowering the speech standard of the country are almost incalculable. The fact that it is likely to be heard by the less discriminating portion of the public operates to increase its evil effects.

Commonweal, *April 10, 1929*

Is radio to become a chief arm of education? Will the classroom be abolished, and the child of the future stuffed with facts as he sits at home or even as he walks about the streets with his portable receiving set in his pocket?

Century, *June, 1924*

If all new forms of mass entertainment are similarly reviled, we may be able to learn something about television and our contemporary attitudes toward it by tracing the development of mass culture itself. To do this, we must distinguish it from its apparent opposite, elite or high culture.

Before the advent of mass media there were thought to be two dominant forms of culture: *elite* (or high) *art* and *folk art*. Elite art was the art of the upper classes, the art of the educated and the powerful. It was created by known, acknowledged, or self-designated artists—individuals of genius. High art is therefore *creator-oriented*. What dominated is the artist's message, intention and/or execution. Little thought was given to the impact of the work of art on its audience because, generally speaking, the audience was simply not a consideration in the work's creation.

Elite art was (and is), in the words of critic Russell Nye (1970, p. 3), "Produced by known artists within a consciously aesthetic context and by an accepted set of rules, its attainment (or failure) judged by reference to a normative body of recognized classics. The subjective element, that is, the presence of the creator or performer, is vital to its effectiveness." Elite art, then, is subjective, exclusive, and individualistic or, as Nye wrote, "Its aim is the discovery of new ways of recording and interpreting experience."

Before the Industrial Revolution and before the development of our modern mass media, these works of art were created by a particular kind of artist, working in a particular social and political setting. Gans (1975) noted that high art was supported by city-dwelling elites—the court, the nobility, the Church, and merchants who had the time, education, and resources for entertainment and art. These elites could subsidize a number of creative people to produce the kinds of entertainment and art they wanted. These artists were therefore close to the sources of power and obviously shared their prestige and privileges.

Gans identified several important characteristics of elite art:

- the urban nature of elite art (at a time when most people—the masses to be—lived an agrarian lifestyle);
- the importance of power and education in defining art (art is what those in power say it is);
- those in power set the standards for all the rest; and,
- by setting standards of judgment and appreciation of art, the powerful solidified their positions of power; artists, intellectuals, and critics had much to gain by accepting and perpetuating the aesthetic standards imposed by the powerful—it ensured them work.

Still, artists and critics did have some choice available to them; they were not forced to follow unquestioningly the dictates of their wealthy patrons. They could work in accepted forms and in conventional, accepted ways or they could break with prevailing norms, break new ground. Of course, choosing the path of independence ensured starvation for lack of a wealthy patron, but at least these artists and critics had the freedom to make that choice. The vast majority of people in pre-industrial society had no choices open to them at all; they were excluded from the process of artistic expression; they had no place in the dominant cultural dialogue. And this is just as the powerful wished it to be.

It might be difficult for us to imagine a world with no radio, no television, no movies, no records, tapes and CDs, no videos and photographs, and for the vast majority of people, no paintings, books, magazines or newspapers. But this is precisely the world in which most people found themselves in the pre-industrial era. Most people's art experiences, such as they were, had little in common with the experiences of the upper classes. The art of the lower classes in pre-industrial society is called folk art.

Folk art is generally less concerned with conscious aesthetic manipulation and, therefore, is typically considered simpler than elite art. Messages and the stories that convey them are, in other words, presented in as straightforward a manner as possible (though latent or hidden meanings may be less obvious, even to the folk artists themselves). Folk art (which we define as, among other things, the tales of a wandering story-teller, the drawings of a sidewalk artist, the folk songs handed down from generation to generation, and even circus acts and posters) exists at the opposite extreme from elite art. Folk art is unsophisticated and localized. It concerns itself directly with the concrete and familiar world of its audience. Folk art is, then, the art of peasants, of the countryside. It is not concerned with creating new ways of seeing the world, but with preserving traditional links with old ways.

These two forms of culture existed side by side for centuries and, in fact, still exist today. Operatic aria and folk song, ballet and clog dance, paintings in museums and spray-painted graffiti on walls—all still exist. Today, however, the relationship between the two forms of culture is a bit more complicated; and, it is a relationship that is not an unimportant one.

Machine-age Art

The complicating factor is industrialization: the impact of machines on the arts and on the communication processes. Machines made possible the speedy and efficient production and distribution of cultural artifacts—books, paintings (and later, music, movies, and television programs)—which had previously been denied to all but the wealthiest and most powerful people. The development of mass entertainment media turned the art world on its head, giving rise to a new audience, as we have already seen, and new forms of art and entertainment to meet that audience's needs and desires.

Industrialized arts, or mass media, came to dominate the cultural lives of ever greater numbers of people over the last five centuries, particularly in the lower and middle classes; groups which had been effectively disenfranchised by the ruling elites in the pre-industrialized era. These mass media brought into being a hybrid form of entertainment, neither elite art nor folk art. There was a blurring of the traditional distinctions between elite and folk art. The resulting hybrid is sometimes called *mass culture* or *mass-mediated culture*, and sometimes simply *popular culture*.

Popular culture, embodying such forms of communication as movies, television, magazines, posters, comic books, popular music, and best-selling novels, is generally designed to reach and appeal to the greatest number of people possible. Artists working in these fields have a radically different approach than creators of elite or folk art works. Russell Nye's book *The Unembarrassed Muse* remains one of the most cogent analyses of popular culture years after its initial publication. It provides a concise examination of the rise of this new breed of popular artist:

> *The growth of a large popular audience, increasingly accessible through the mass media, caused in turn a demand for artists to satisfy its cultural needs. To these artists success lay not in pleasing a rich patron and his small, aristocratic, cultural circle, but in satisfying an increasingly broad popular audience. By the middle of the eighteenth century a large number of artists, especially novelists and dramatists (genres most adaptable to mass consumption) aimed their work directly at this new general audience. The popular artists had to make his own tradition by investigating his market, calculating its desires, and evolving devices (many of which he adapted from folk art) for reaching it. He became a kind of professional...who created for profit the kind of art that the public wanted (1970, pp. 2-3).*

This audience-orientation is a primary characteristic of popular culture in all its forms. Other characteristics of this form of culture are bound up in its subject matter, which may be drawn from folk art, high art, or any combination of the two.

Drawing its subject matter from a variety of sources, one would expect mass media content to be more, rather than less, complex than either elite or folk art. In fact, this is a hotly debated subject. Until very recently, most critics agreed that, as in folk art, popular culture content tends to be simple, at least in the sense that no special knowledge or training is required in order to make sense of it. Recently, critics have begun to explore in more detail the narrative and structural complexity which makes popular culture artifacts so accessible.

We'll have more to say about this issue in later chapters; for now, suffice it to say that mass culture's tendency to borrow from and mix together elements of all levels of cultural creation is problematic. How we approach this issue may well determine our attitude toward the mass media.

Another characteristic of popular art is the manner in which popular culture artifacts are created. They are, in fact, created in a very different manner than those of elite or folk art. Generally speaking, popular art is not so much created by an artist as it is the end-product of an industrial process; popular culture creation is often likened to an assembly-line, a fact which, in the eyes of many, dooms mass culture artifacts to an inferior status.

Such assembly-line artifacts are, to some, beneath notice, not worthy of serious study or consideration. The profit orientation, the inevitable homogenization of a standardized product, the transformation of the creator into a cog in the machinery of cultural creation, all of these diminish popular culture to such a degree that "cultured" people ought not to acknowledge even the possibility that the popular arts might have the capacity to enrich the lives of those who partake of them (which is to say, all of us).

Critiques of Mass Culture

But the widespread acceptance of popular art has never been questioned. From dime novels to radio to television, the mass audience has easily embraced each new mass medium. Critics, on the other hand, as the discussion above indicates, are another story entirely. Until very recently—the last thirty years or so—the vast majority of serious observers rejected the notion that the mass media have something to tell us about the world we have built. This rejection has come in the form of a more or less standard critique which one scholar, Herbert Gans (1975), has broken down into four component parts. We have touched on each these in passing; they deserve further attention and some kind of response.

The first component of the archetypal mass culture critique identified by Gans is bound up in the systems which create mass media artifacts. Unlike high culture, Gans observes, popular culture is doomed to "undesirability" or worse, simply because it is created by "profit-minded entrepreneurs" for the sole purpose of gratifying a paying audience. In other words, it just doesn't matter how "good" a television program or best-selling novel is—the profit-motive underlying their creation dooms them to inferiority when compared with the least painting created by a "recognized" artist.

The second component of mass culture criticism as it existed for so many years concerns the effect of mass culture on high culture. It has long been feared that popular art forms, in borrowing styles, themes, and subjects from elite art, debase and dilute traditional art forms.

Further, the money to be made in the popular culture arena lures many potential artists from more "artistic" pursuits, thus depleting the elite arts' reservoir of talent.

The third oft-stated mass culture critique concerns the negative effects of popular works on those consuming them. This consumption, mass culture critics argue, at best produces unnecessary gratifications, and at worst is emotionally and psychologically harmful to the audience. This is perhaps the most widely disseminated component of the mass culture critique. How often have we all read or heard how bad television or comic books or video games are for us?

Growing out of this concern is the final component of the mass culture critique. Mass culture is harmful not only to individuals who consume it, but to society as a whole. The distribution of "inferior" works—works which bastardize and dilute the efforts of acknowledged artists, and which produce only spurious gratifications—has far-reaching effects. The claim is that the distribution of popular culture not only reduces the level of cultural quality of the society, but it also encourages totalitarianism by creating a passive audience unable to defend itself against the techniques of persuasion and propaganda used by demagogues.

Each of these critiques, echoed in one form or another by countless critics, can be answered. Taken at face value they do little but offer an excuse to ignore the mass media. But this is antithetical to the concept of criticism as we have defined it in Chapter 1.

The first criticism of popular culture—the negative character of its industrial nature, or its profit-orientation, and of its mass audience—is rather easily answered. All of these are simply characteristics of the mass media and are, in and of themselves, neutral—neither good nor bad.

The system of creation becomes a factor only inasmuch as that system affects the artifacts, or artworks, or programs created. And the plain truth of the matter is that many popular artists manage to be quite creative working within the undeniable structures imposed by the arts industries. Does it take more skill to please a small, sophisticated audience than it does to please a large heterogeneous one? And who would deny the aesthetic delights of a film like Steven Spielberg's *Schindler's List* or a television program like *Northern Exposure*? Yet each was created within industrialized systems of mass culture creation.

The second critique—that popular culture's undeniable and continuous borrowing from high art debases elite culture—is equally easy to answer. This view is based on the nostalgic, rose-tinted recollection of a bright, shining, unspoiled yesterday which, if the truth be known, never actually existed. All previous cultures, including the most classical and revered, have had their cultural failings.

It's simple to look to the past and see only the best. The dregs of past cultural epochs—the crass, the vulgar, the trite, the boring—all these have long since disappeared. When we look to the past, to the glories of ancient Greece or of the Renaissance, when we look backwards to any period in the history of humankind, we are left with only the very best of high culture (or at least what has been defined and presented that way) and perhaps some romanticized aspects of folk culture.

Scholars and educators, as part of their social function, serve to weed out those elements of past cultures which seem less valuable or interesting than others. This is a job academicians have done remarkably well, leaving today's scholars with little alternative but to see the past as somehow better than the present. We see our own culture, our own time, for what it is, warts and all. We see the past as one might see a heavily retouched photograph. Of course the totality of current (or recent) media presentations seem less worthy of serious consideration than a carefully selected sample from days gone by. It's inevitable. But compare the best of today's mass media artifacts with the best of the past, and the qualitative chasm between elite arts and mass-mediated arts may not be as wide as some critics believe.

The third objection to popular culture, that mass media have a negative effect on audience members, is less easily answered. This is a troublesome issue, one which has been much debated from the introduction of novels as a viable form of expression, to the increasing popularity of comic books, to the introduction of television. Whatever mass medium happens to be dominant at any given point in time is sure to be blamed for every upsurge in crime, for rampant sexuality, and for just about any other social ill we can name.

Social scientists have spent the better part of this century conducting tests, experiments, and surveys to determine just what sorts of effects the mass media, particularly television, have on those who partake of them. Clearly, the media have some sort of impact on viewers, listeners, or readers. The weight of evidence indicates that under certain circumstances, some people may be affected by the mass media in harmful ways. Proof of direct negative effects is, however, difficult to come by. And given the competing interests involved (i.e., industry, advertisers, government, public interest groups), the possible existence of these effects is still open to much debate as is demonstrated by arguments surrounding television violence that have reemerged in the last two years.

The fourth critique of mass media, that they have a negative effect on civilization in general, and that they create "passive" consumers, is also difficult to answer. Again, proof of this sort of macro- or societal level effect is difficult to come by. Still, the idea that the very existence of the mass media (or the poor quality of mass media presentations) can have such sweeping effects is based on a skewed view of popular culture. Look at the average or bad in any medium of expression—elite, folk, or popular—and we can infer negative effects on the quality of civilization. But as we have already pointed out, it is much more sensible at least to consider the best that any medium has to offer before condemning those media out of hand.

The passive audience critique is equally problematic and has been much debated. One of the characteristics of the mass media is that audiences need no special training in order to understand (at some level) what they see and hear. Stories are, apparently, told in as simple a manner as possible. In later chapters we may find that the mass media tell us more complex stories than we ever suspected. Assuming narrative simplicity, however, it is easy to conclude that audience members do nothing but consume this simple fare as it is served up to them by profit-minded entrepreneurs. The mass media, it is said, require no thought or effort on the part of consumers.

This idea has been challenged in recent years by critics who see the audience's role as a more active one than anyone had dreamed in the past. These critics see mass media content as being only superficially simple. In fact, they say, the texts offered us by the mass media are multi-layered; audiences must negotiate these texts—accepting some of what they are told, rejecting other bits of information. Some critics even go so far as to say that television programs and other media presentations are, in a sense, created in the minds of the viewers.

The Massness of the Mass Media

Each of the critiques cited by Gans begins with the "massness" of the mass media. From Gutenberg's time to the present, the mass media have imposed certain requirements on artists working in them and on the audiences consuming them. The mass media ensured that art would no longer be created solely at the whim of an artist; pen would no longer be committed to paper only when a writer had something of significance to say. The introduction of mass media of communication led, seemingly inevitably, to the demand for regular, periodic publication. In other words, the introduction of mechanization and the subsequent creation of a mass audience in need of satisfaction, made regular, unalterable, scheduled release of cultural artifacts necessary.

The entrepreneurial spirit which infused the mass media demanded a steady stream of mass-mediated items, rather than the occasional, irregular, inspired efforts of traditional artists. This first "requirement" of the new mass media was matched by another: the need to fill what has often been described as a gargantuan amount of space and time.

With the rise of the mass media came the need to satisfy the greatest number of people, the need to meet a regular production schedule, and the need to beat out one's competition (in other words, to attract a larger portion of the potential audience than other mass media creators). All of these were new concerns, concerns no artist had ever had to worry about before. All of these became "requirements" only because of the size of the mass media audience.

For our purposes then, what differentiates the popular arts from the elite arts is not the inherent quality of their respective artifacts but rather divergent systems of creation and varying attitudes toward their respective audiences. This being the case, the means by which mass media creators attract audience members becomes of paramount importance.

Many explanations have been offered for the popularity of the mass media. Three are particularly important to our discussion. First, it has been suggested that the mass media offer audiences books, discs, movies, and television programs that appeal to the *lowest common denominator*. Second, it has been suggested that mass media presentations are designed to offer *multiple points of access*. And finally, it has been suggested that mass media presentations offer some sort of *cultural forum*. Let's look at each of these possible explanations individually.

Elite artists, working primarily for themselves or perhaps for an educated, wealthy patron, consequently can create for themselves. They can afford to create works which appeal to a small group of people—people with needs and desires quite similar to those of the artist or, at least, whose needs and desires are well-known to the artist. The elite work can be tailor-made to appeal to the specific needs of a specific audience.

The popular artist, whose success depends on the greatest number of sales, or the greatest number of viewers, cannot afford this luxury. In the words of Nye (1970, p. 6): "The popular audience expects entertainment, instruction, or both, rather than an 'aesthetic experience.' To create for such an audience means that the popular artist cannot take into consideration the individualities and preferences of minority groups. Since the popular arts aim at the largest common denominator, they tend to standardize at the median level of majority expectation."

Programming in the mass media can't be aimed at the best-educated, most sophisticated audience members. To produce works aimed primarily at this audience could mean that the vast majority of people in the potential mass media audience would be unable to understand what was going on. Mass media creators, the argument goes, have to produce works which can be understood by anyone—from the most educated person down to the least sophisticated audience member. This is what is meant by lowest common denominator programming: producing down to the level of the least sophisticated audience member.

This is one way of looking at the popular arts. There are, however, other perspectives. Some critics believe that the media provide multiple points of access. That is, each best-seller, each television program, each top-grossing motion picture, offers viewers, readers, or listeners all sorts of information. They are full of ideas—often contradictory ones—which allow the audience member to pick and choose, seeing and accepting whatever fits his or her world view, rejecting whatever does not.

The success of the television program *All in the Family* provides an excellent example of what is meant by multiple points of access.

Archie Bunker's ranting and raving, the cries of a loud-mouthed bigot, were enjoyed by millions of television viewers—old, young,

liberal, conservative. Different viewers "read" this particular "text," the television series *All in the Family*, in different ways. Conservatives may have identified with Archie; liberals may have thought him a fool and identified instead with his ultra-liberal son-in-law, Mike; women might have related to Archie's wife Edith or his daughter Gloria. The program provided enough material that viewers could read it in a variety of ways. *All in the Family* is an obvious example supporting this explanation for the popularity of mass media presentations, but we can see the same broad appeal at work in other programs (if to a lesser degree) as well. Was *Charlie's Angels* a step forward for the medium in 1976, an early feminist program in which women assumed job roles typically reserved for men? Or was it just another example of television's exploitative use of attractive females who, regardless of their harrowing profession, were still controlled by and working for "the man?" Is *Beavis and Butthead* poking fun at the deadhead Generation X or catering to its tastes?

Proponents of the multiple-points-of-access view of the mass media tend to see the consumer playing an active role in interpreting mass-mediated information, creating stories, like jigsaw puzzles, out of the pieces provided by the producers. In contrast, the most extreme proponents of the lowest common denominator approach see the mass media consumer as essentially passive, accepting whatever producers deem fit for the "lowest" of them.

Before turning our attention to television criticism *per se*, we must deal with one other possible explanation for the incredibly broad appeal of mass media, especially television. Some critics have proposed that the mass media provide a cultural forum, a place where issues of cultural importance are discussed, argued, accepted, discarded. Many critics believe that the work of popular artists is successful especially and primarily because it embodies or expresses the values of the culture in particularly effective and direct ways.

This idea of the mass media—the view which

holds that media provide a forum in which culture is created, maintained, and repaired—is associated primarily with European critics, though Americans are turning to this view with increasing frequency. Old school American critics held tight to the notion that communication processes can best be explained through an analysis of information transmitted from producer to audience. If one accepts this *transmission model of communication* it is a logical next step to ask what effect the ideas transmitted have on consumers.

This is surely a valid approach to mass media study but it isn't the only one. The *ritual model of communication* leads critics to view the communication process differently and to ask different kinds of questions about that process. Communication is not viewed as a means of influence and by extension, control. Producers do not offer content to be soaked up by audience members. Instead, communication is seen as a process through which cultural beliefs are negotiated. This approach sees producers and consumers acting in concert (though not always at a conscious level) to "discuss" issues and attitudes toward those issues.

In this view, movies, television, popular songs, and other forms of popular culture express and test acceptable and unacceptable behavior, appropriate and inappropriate responses to everyday situations, and/or appropriate and inappropriate sexual and racial roles. Those situations and roles may be highly stylized or distorted, but both producer and audience understand these deviations from real-world experience. Information is not so much transmitted as it is shared and then debated and, in a sense, voted upon.

Thus far in this chapter we have discussed briefly many of the debates which have centered around the mass media. We have examined some of the questions raised by critics over the years concerning the function of the audience, the role of the mass media in general, and some of the possible reasons for the incredible appeal of mass-mediated entertainment. There are no answers, no right and wrong, in these debates—at least not so far as we know at this point in time—but it is important to be aware of the multiplicity of approaches to criticism, the audience, and to the media themselves. All that we have said thus far may appear to be only peripherally related to television and television criticism. In fact, the issues discussed provide a necessary foundation for all that follows.

Television Criticism

Television, as a medium of mass communication and as a force in American life, is just forty or so years old. That may sound like a lot, but compared with the history of literature, dance, painting, or even motion pictures, this is a very brief span of time. Television criticism is, of course, even younger than television.

To be sure, as long as there has been television there have been television critics; there have even been some whose primary concern was understanding and enlightenment rather than judgement or condemnation. Popular writers like Robert Lewis Shayon, John J. O'Connor, Michael Arlen, Gary Deeb, Ron Powers, Tom Shales, Harlan Ellison, and a handful of others, though "dourly negative" at times, have made some headway in establishing television as a subject worthy of serious consideration even among the enlightened intelligentsia who (claim they) wouldn't be caught dead watching the Tube. But critics of this sort have been few and far between in the area of television study. Only recently (within the last twenty years or so) have academicians discovered television. This is not an unimportant concern. Caughie (1984, p. 119) explains,

The absence of history from academic and journalistic writing about television seems to me to be critical. The insistence on history, and the concern about its absence, is not simply an academic whine about gaps in research or an antiquarian fascination with the past, but is part of a desire to be able to understand the movements of television and the continual re-workings and re-shapings of its relationship to the wider culture.

There are a variety of reasons for this historic lack of critical attention paid to television. For one thing, the dominant mass medium of any era is rarely accorded anything but passing critical notice—and, generally, what attention is paid to such a medium is in the form of condemnations. Newcomb (1976, p. xxi) explained it this way: "Because television has not been given attention by those whose professed purpose is the serious concern for education in its fullest sense, it has developed no respected place in the culture."

Compounding this historical problem is the fact that television just doesn't seem to offer much that is new and unique. Television has traditionally been treated (when it has been treated at all) as a new means of transmitting works designed for, or imitative of, previously existing media. Radio comedian Fred Allen once said, "Imitation is the sincerest form of television." Though his tone was flip, his message summarizes much of the critical attention given television.

Television has most often been viewed as an amalgamation of all the mass media, combining elements of the motion picture ("It's just movies on a small screen"), radio ("It's just radio with pictures"), and theater ("It's just a stage on the small screen."). Bogart (1956, pp. 42-43) wrote, "the underlying assumption is that television functions largely to project information or to communicate experience already well developed either by the traditional art forms or by the other popular arts....Theater, film and television are all branches of the same art."

You might think it odd that we quote a critic writing in the 1950s to make a point about current critical attitudes. The fact is, however, that these attitudes remain prevalent in many circles of criticism. Only in recent years has the notion of television's lack of originality been challenged. Today, there is a growing feeling that television must be treated as television. For example, critics now argue that there are significant differences between viewing a television program (for free, in the privacy of your own home, on a small screen) and

paying to watch a movie (in public, on a big screen).

It may be that we are more willing to accept mediocre entertainment—when we don't have to pay for it. It may be that we are more receptive to transmitted visual images—in the comfort of our own homes. It may be that we are more willing to argue back, to disagree with what we are "told" on television because we're in familiar surroundings. Critics are only recently beginning to address these possibilities, to examine the viewing experience as an integral part of the communication process. Whatever answers we may find, it is clear that television's originality (or lack of it) is a red herring, a non-issue. Critical approaches developed for dealing with other media may not be suitable for the task of dealing with television.

Who's Asking the Questions?

For many years, only the social scientists raised their voices when questions about television were asked. Those who were concerned about the possible impact or importance of television—primarily the government and the television industry itself—asked specific questions and demanded equally specific answers: What effect does television have on individual viewers? How can a program maximize its appeal and reach the largest audience? How can a commercial be positioned within an evening's programming in order to reach the people for whom the advertised product was designed? These are all questions which seem to lend themselves best to testing using quantitative (or statistical) methods.

As television has grown in popularity and sophistication, the range of questions to which individuals, special interest groups, and scholars desire answers has broadened. In recent years, scholars and critics from a variety of fields—film studies, literary criticism, history, sociology, anthropology, and many others—have begun to turn their attention to that most significant, yet neglected medium of mass communication: television.

Critical methods developed for dealing with a variety of media are being adapted, blended together, tested, and applied to the study of television. Critics have remained conscious of older forms of criticism but they have also tried to design new forms, new approaches, better suited to television studies. Here we begin to bring into sharper focus many of the issues touched upon earlier, relating them specifically to television, rather than to mass media in general.

The critic of television faces a variety of unique and troubling problems. Not the least of these is the disdain with which television is sometimes held in American society. As already discussed, it is generally felt that television programs, like the products of all mass media, are less worthy of serious attention, and serious criticism, than are the works of literature, drama, painting, or any of the elite arts. The medium is almost universally reviled (if even more universally watched) and considered to be "transparent": Anyone can "read" television's texts without serious thought and, certainly, without any formal training.

Television viewers who want to become more thoughtful, more aware consumers of the medium—who, in other words, want to become critics—must confront this problem at some point along the road to critical expertise. But television critics (and those viewers who feel the need to assess the place of television in their lives) face more serious problems than a possible lack of support for their endeavors.

For one thing, defining the object of study— the *text* and *context* of one's critical approach— is more problematic when dealing with television than with any other medium of communication. Further complicating matters is the primacy of commerce, of business, in shaping television's content. The critic who ignores the business of television risks weakening his or her arguments about television programming. Finally, the role of the audience is the subject of some controversy. Let's look at each of these inherent problems a bit more closely.

Defining text and context would seem to be simple enough. All a critic has to do is decide whether to examine a television program, or the television audience, or some other aspect of broadcasting. Then he or she needs only to decide, according to his or her individual interests or skills, how to examine that particular text. In fact, television is too complex to fit a model as simple as this.

The critic must ask: Do we watch (and should we study) individual programs—the way we read most books, look at most paintings, and watch most plays and movies? That is, should each episode of a particular series be taken as a potential text? Can we come to an understanding of any television program—or television as a medium—on the basis of a single viewing of a single series episode?

Common sense dictates that viewers must be too familiar with a series—its characters, its setting, its basic conventions—to take each individual episode at face value. It follows then, that a television critic might do well to look elsewhere in defining the critical test: Do we "read" an entire series, rather than individual episodes? And should the television series itself, taken as a whole, be the critic's text?

This is an approach which must be given some thought, but there exists the possibility of yet another critical text, one some critics see as truer to the viewing experience than other conceptions of textuality. A critic might examine television in terms of *strips* of programming, that is, a viewer's individual "television consumption session." Allen (1987, p. 3) explains, "Our experience of television is usually not of isolated works but of chunks of time filled with multiple texts carefully linked together so that they flow almost unnoticed one into another." This strip of television (the text) might include not only the individual programs watched, but the commercials, station IDs and promos, trailers, interruptions for breaking news, all the possible elements that might come to the screen in the viewer's viewing session.

This strip text is intriguing because it forces

critics to take note of the actual viewing experience, possibly bringing criticism more in line with reality; it acknowledges the possibility that the messages of television, so hotly debated, and the effects of television may not be as easily discovered, measured, and interpreted as many think; it puts some measure of power and control back in the hands of the viewers; it recognizes the fact that people don't just watch a single television program in a single viewing experience but may, in fact, sit and watch all sorts of programs—and all sorts of program interruptions—during the course of an evening. And this doesn't even begin to take into account the complications created when a viewer changes channels in the middle of a program. What happens to the neat and tidy critical text when a viewer switches from, for example, *Married...With Children* to the *News Hour With Jim Lehrer*?

Further complicating matters is the possibility that people watch, and critics could analyze, all of the programs created by a particular producer. Thus, the text could be the works of Mary Tyler Moore Productions, for example, or the works of Aaron Spelling. Or perhaps it is the genre that provides the most revealing text. A *genre* is a group of works which share a set of more or less identifiable and generally agreed upon characteristics or conventions; thus a critic might apply a generic approach to television and study Situation Comedies, or Westerns, or Crime Dramas.

Another possibility is worth considering. The television text may be bigger than an evening's programming, the work of a single producer, or even all Westerns or some other genre. It may be that we as viewers "simply" read Television, sucking in all sorts of programs as a huge, undifferentiated flow. This raises the possibility that critics should make some attempt to deal with the totality of television programming.

This complex decision that critics must make about which aspects of television should be chosen for analysis as texts might be simplified if we stop and think about the various components of the television communication process. Earlier in this chapter we discussed the ritual model of communication where message meanings are negotiated by the audience and creators within the context of society and culture. The model below demonstrates the various points in the process where critics might stand to provide analysis.

We've provided the small television symbol ▨ at all of the places where a critic may come to the television communication process and provide analysis. The model also represents some "truths" about television that are central to contemporary criticism (and which we will discuss in detail in Chapter 5). Among them is the idea that meaning is/can be made not only on the source side of the process, but on the receiver side as well. Another is that the source and receiver can and often do negotiate meaning. It should also be obvious that the operation of the television communication process and any subsequent meaning-making occur within the framework of the larger culture or society and that both sources and receivers must ultimately deal with the messages, however defined, of an industry. As we've said throughout, good television criticism is a challenge. This model also suggests that no critical stance, no one place of entry, is any better than another; however, critics need to be sure and accumulate appropriate evidence (within the appropriate text) to support their specific arguments.

The problems involved in delineating critical tests and contexts as they relate to television might also become clearer if we look at the center of the model, the "message." We'll suggest some of the critical possibilities inherent in a single program—*All in the Family*. We might examine an individual episode from the series' twelve year network run; a critic or sensitive viewer could do an in-depth analysis of the episode in which Edith Bunker died, for example. And then, bear in mind, the critic would still have to decide which context in which to operate. Still, in this case, a single episode becomes the critical text. This sort of analysis is little different than the literary or art critic who analyzes a single book or painting. Simple enough.

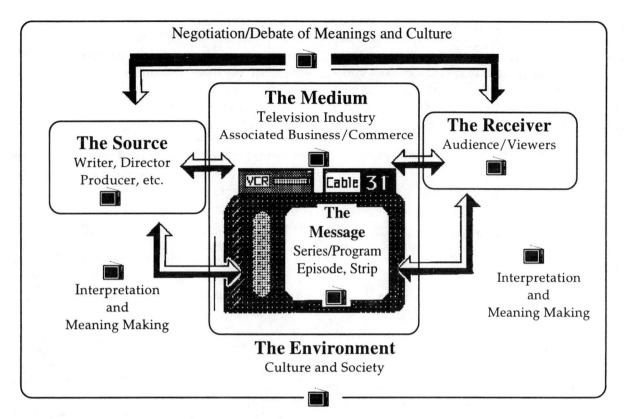

Ritual Model of Communication as an Ongoing Process

On the other hand, a critic could begin with the assumption that viewers tune-in to a particular program—in this case, *All in the Family*—week after week. This would surely color that critic's approach to the series. With this as a starting point the critic might be inclined to take a more general view of the series as it changed (or didn't change) over the years. Here we see a different conception of the text, and the individual episode becomes important only insofar as it exemplifies (or proves to be an exception to) what the critic observes about the series as a whole.

Another critic might apply the strip-as-text approach, discussing a particular episode of *All in the Family* as it relates not to other episodes in the same series, but rather to programs, commercials, and news breaks aired that same evening. Such a critic would suggest possible viewer readings for juxtaposition of, for example, the death of Edith Bunker and a Nike "Just Do It" commercial and a news flash about a drive-by shooting. These individual elements have a meaning (for viewers and critics) primarily because they stand in a unique, non-repeatable relationship with one another. The relationship, content, and timing of these elements could be a critic's main concern

Another critic might approach *All in the Family* from the viewpoint that it exemplifies the work and world view of its producer, Norman Lear. Yet another might look at the program as an example of the Situation Comedy, and examine the series' impact on that particular genre.

The point of this discussion is to make clear the myriad ways of evaluating television. Though several of the choices and problems described above are common to the criticism of any medium, television poses its own, unique problems as well. The television text is remarkably ill-defined and the potential critic has to make some crucial decisions before he or she begins any critical inquiry of television programming. This has, in fact, proved to be a major stumbling block in the development of television studies. Critics themselves seem unable to articulate just what they see as their text. Confusion about textuality makes communication between critics difficult, if not impossible. And if critics can't communicate with one another, then surely the poor viewer is left completely out in the cold.

One Text or Many?

To bring some order to this chaotic situation, some critics now suggest that we rethink the very notion of textuality. It may be that the mass media in general, and television in particular, just don't operate according to the same story-telling rules as literature, painting, or the other accepted arts. It has been suggested that the most profitable way of dealing with television may be to realize that what television provides is not a single, discrete, easily recognized text, but rather many texts: There is, first, the text *conceived* by the program producer. All television programs begin with an idea, a concept, a vision. The first "layer" of television textuality is this conceived text. The second layer is the program as it is *produced*; here we have to deal with the actual program, not some producer's conception. Next is the program as it is *transmitted*; here the produced text is modified, in a sense, by its placement in a network, station or channel's schedule, as well as by the placement of commercials, news bulletins, and promotional announcements within it.

Moving still deeper through layer after layer of textuality we come to the *received* text, or the program as individual viewers see it; here we deal not only with the personalities and biases of individual viewers (remember the myriad ways one could interpret Archie Bunker's character), but with channel flipping, surfing and cruising, discussions about the program among family members and friends, and even with dinner burning in the microwave—all of which may affect viewers' perceptions of a given program.

Finally, there is the *recalled* text, the deepest

layer of textuality; what do viewers remember of a given program? What do they say about the program the next day at school or work? What do they say about it to researchers seeking some clue about television's effects or to television executives attempting to gauge the impact of a particular program?

All of these are viable critical texts. All of these affect the way we, as viewers, perceive individual programs as well as how they affect us and touch our daily lives. The important thing is not which text a critic or thoughtful viewer chooses to examine; the important thing is that a choice be made in the first place and then acknowledged by the viewer or clearly articulated to readers of a piece of criticism.

As if an ill-defined text wasn't enough, the television critic is faced with still more problems. Most important of these is the questions of authorship in television production: Who is responsible for what we see and hear on television? Who creates the television text (however we define it)?

In elite arts, in folk arts, even in most popular arts, identifying the author of a work is simple. Look for the author's name on the cover of a book; look for an artist's signature on a painting; look for a composer's name on a piece of sheet music or on a concert program. Leonardo Da Vinci created the Mona Lisa; Herman Melville created *Moby Dick*; Tchaikovsky created "The 1812 Overture." Authorship is simply not a problem for critics working in most areas. Television (like movies and a select few other media) is another story.

Who is responsible for an episode of *Cheers*? Should we assign authorship to the series' producers, Glen Charles, Les Charles, and James Burroughs, as some critics have suggested? Should we assign authorship to the writer of a particular episode's screenplay, or to the director (the person who determines the images offered to viewers and coaches actors in the performance of their roles)? What should we make of the contributions of camera crew, actors, lighting technicians, and the dozens of people who bring their skills to bear on the creation of a television program? And what of the input provided by producers and network executives? The operative words in describing television are "collective creation" and "collaborative production."

Television is a complex system of checks and balances—the desires of each individual held in check by the input of a host of competing individual and organizational imperatives. Television programs are the product of business decisions and assembly-line production procedures.

This brings us to the subject of our next chapter—the business of television and the systems that create the sorts of programs we watch. The primacy of commerce, of business considerations, colors the forms of television programming we see and so, are of concern to television critics.

Chapter Exercise

Television Programming: The Product of an Industry

Choose one of your favorite television programs. Research its production background by finding out the following information:

PROGRAM TITLE
Who produces the show?
Is there one central director or different ones for different episodes?
Is there one central writer or group of writers or do the writers change from episode to episode?
Who distributes the program?
List five members of the production crew and their contributions. 1. 2. 3. 4. 5.

References and Resources

Abrams, M. H. (1972). Orientation of critical theories. In D. Lodge (Ed.). *Twentieth Century Literary Criticism.* London: Longman.

Allen, R. C. (1987). Introduction: talking about television. In R. C. Allen, (Ed.). *Channels of Discourse: Television and Contemporary Criticism.* Chapel Hill, NC: University of North Carolina Press.

Barthes, R. (1972). *Mythologies.* London: Hill and Wang.

Bedell, S. (1981). *Up the Tube.* New York: Viking Press.

Blonsky, M., (Ed.). (1985). *On Signs.* Baltimore, MD: The Johns Hopkins University Press.

Bogart, L. (1956). *The Age of Television.* New York: Frederick Ungar.

Caughie, J. (1984). Television criticism: 'a discourse in search of an object.' *Screen, 25,* 109–121.

Culler, J. (1975). *Structuralist Poetics.* Ithica, NY: Cornell University Press.

Davis, D. K. & Baran, S. J. (1981). *Mass Communication and Everyday Life: A Perspective on Theory and Effects.* Belmont, CA: Wadsworth.

Davis, R. E. (1976). *Response to Innovation: A Study of Popular Argument About New Mass Media.* New York: Arno.

Davison, P., Meyersohn, R. & Shils, E., (Eds.). (1978). *Culture and Mass Culture.* Cambridge, Eng.: Chadwyck-Healey.

Fiske, J. & Hartley, J. (1978). *Reading Television.* London: Methuen.

Gans, H. (1975). *Popular and High Culture: An Analysis and Evaluation of Taste.* New York: Basic Books.

Grealy, J. (1977). Notes on popular culture. *Screen Education, 22,* 5-11.

Gurevitch, M., Bennett, T., Curran, J. & Woollacott, J., (Eds.). (1982). *Culture, Society and the Media.* London: Methuen.

Hall, S., Hobson, D., Lowe, A. & Willis, P., (Eds.). (1986). *Culture, Media, Language.* London: Hutchinson.

Hammel, W., (Ed.). (1972). *The Popular Arts in America.* New York: Harcourt Brace Jovanovich.

Handy, B. (1995). The real golden age. *Time,* October 30, pp. 87-90.

Lentricchia, F. (1983). *Criticism and Social Change.* Chicago, IL: University of Chicago Press.

Mander, J. (1978). *Four Arguments for the Elimination of Television.* New York: Morrow Quill.

Marc, D. (1984). *Demographic Vistas: Television in American Culture.* Philadelphia, PA: University of Pennsylvania Press.

Newcomb, H. (1976). *TV: The Most Popular Art.* Garden City, NY: Anchor/Douleday.

Newcomb, H., (Ed.). (1993). *Television: The Critical View.* New York: Oxford University Press.

Newcomb, H. & Hirsch, P. M. (1983). Television as a cultural forum: implications for research. *Quarterly Review of Film Studies, 8,* 45–56.

Nye, R. (1970). *The Unembarrassed Muse: The Popular Arts in America.* New York: The Dial Press.

Pratt, M. (1981). Art without critics and critics without readers *or* Pantagruel versus The Incredible Hulk. In P. Hernadi (Ed.), *What is Criticism?* Bloomington, IN: Indiana University Press.

Schramm, W. (1973). *Men, Messages, and Media: A Look at Human Communication.* New York: Harper & Row.

Seldes, G. (1957). *The New Mass Media: Challenge to a Free Society.* Washington, DC: American Association of University Women.

Swanson, D. L. (1977). A reflective view of the epistemology of critical inquiry. *Communication Monographs, 44,* 207–219.

THE BUSINESS OF TELEVISION PROGRAMMING

We don't read week by week which cars sell best, which barber is shaving more faces, but we do read what show is attracting more viewers. Television is berserk with that, the crawling around like crazed insects scrambling to climb this tree to be number one. In such a system there is no room for innovation and for creativity.

—Norman Lear

The creator of *All in the Family, Maude, Good Times, The Jeffersons, Mary Hartman, Mary Hartman*, and *One Day at a Time* would surely admit that there is *some* room for innovation, but his point is obvious . . . television is a business (Newcomb, 1983, p. 194).

Overview

Business considerations determine who "makes it" in television and who doesn't, which programs reach the air and which do not, which shows stay on long enough to become classics and which ones die after one broadcast. Understand the business of television and you understand the medium. In this chapter we'll examine those aspects of the television industry that directly affect programming. But we must warn you at the outset that advances in technology, changes in broadcast regulation, and the state of the national economy also impact television programming;

they threaten to so dramatically alter the business of television that within a few years of the time you read this book, all of what we are about to discuss may no longer be true. But for now, *television is still defined in terms of the commercial television networks*, even with the ascendence of cable, the rapid diffusion of VCRs, the emergence of viable direct broadcast satellite (DBS), the standardization of High Definition Television (HDTV), the on-going governmental debates about de- and re-regulation, and the networks' dwindling audiences (and therefore dwindling advertising revenues).

The Networks and Their Affiliates

From its earliest days, television has been dominated by three centralized production, distribution, decision-making organizations called networks. Although these "Big 3" have recently been joined by the Fox Television

Network, The United Paramount Network and The Warner Brothers Network, and although cable has introduced us to dozens of new channels like ESPN, MTV, Comedy Central and Lifetime, most programs that come to mind when we think of television were either conceived, approved, funded, produced and/or broadcast by the Columbia Broadcast System (CBS), the American Broadcasting Company (ABC) or the National Broadcasting Company (NBC).

This doesn't mean, however, that the networks air their programs on stations that they own across the country. In fact, each of the four commercial networks owns very few stations (typically no more than five each). Most of our best known and best liked television programs are aired by the networks because most of the television stations in the U.S. are *local affiliates* of those networks. A station that remains independent of network affiliation is called an *independent station* and this is a good example of how the business of television is invariably defined in terms of the networks.

Network affiliates in virtually every city of any size in America yield or *clear* air-time for network programming rather than produce their own programs. According to the *Broadcasting & Cable Yearbook 1995* (pp. G61-G67), ABC has 204 affiliates, NBC has 209, CBS has more than 200, Fox has 140, and PBS has over 340.

Local affiliates carry the networks' programs for a number of reasons—all financial. Affiliates benefit in five direct ways:

1. **Networks make direct payments to affiliates for carrying their programs.** CBS actually pays your local CBS affiliate *compensation* for airing *60 Minutes*.

2. **Networks allow their affiliates to insert locally sold commercials into a certain number of specified spots in their programs.** That's why you'll see an ad for your local dry cleaner next to a national McDonald's spot on ABC's *Monday Night Football*. And yes, the affiliate keeps all the money it makes from the local spots.

Moreover, the affiliate can charge more for local ads inserted into network programming than it could for one placed in a show it produced itself.

3. **Affiliates don't risk their own money making programs which might or might not be successful.**

4. **Affiliates bask in their networks' prestige.** Affiliates can generally turn this to their financial advantage. Not only can they command higher advertising rates for the local programming that abuts a network offering (for example, *Eyewitness News at 6* that immediately follows *CBS Evening News With Dan Rather*), but it can generally get more for local spots at other times of the day than can independent stations in the same market.

5. **Affiliates get network-quality programming.** These shows, combined with benefits 1 through 4 listed above, constitute a wonderful deal for affiliates. Few local stations can match the promotional efforts of the networks; few locally produced programs can equal the budget, the glamour, and the audience appeal of network programming.

Affiliation, then, ensures a local station's profits. This, in turn, gives the networks a great deal of power and a large measure of control over them. In fact, only recently have affiliates truly begun to "flex their muscle." The changes that are buffeting the business of television (and which we will detail in this chapter) have caused the networks to become increasingly desperate for viewers. So now, when networks attempt to dictate *exact* programs and *exactly when* they will be shown, affiliates are increasingly emboldened with the counter threat of *pre-emption* (refusing to clear time for the network programs and scheduling something else in their place). Pre-emption obviously causes the networks to lose additional viewers which means further loss of revenue.

Nevertheless, affiliates still need the networks much more than the networks need any individual affiliate. The network can argue that a station that pre-empts too much must not really *want* to be exclusively affiliated in their market. The network can easily break its tie with that station and even more easily find another independent station that would love to become affiliated if given the opportunity. Consequently, affiliated stations, on the most part, still toe the network line, almost invariably accepting whatever programming comes to them, regardless of its suitability for viewers in their broadcast areas. They accept network programming despite the federally mandated obligation to serve the viewers in their license area because there is no equally profitable alternative to network affiliation.

This has important implications for viewers and, therefore, critics. Since approximately 85% of all commercial stations in America are affiliates of the three big networks, audience members have few alternatives when making their viewing selections . . . that is, they *had* few alternatives before cable, Fox and the flowering of the independents. But the reality is this: even though cable, Fox and the increasingly successful independent stations have increased the *number* of alternatives, it is still programming that makes it on the networks that dictates what comes to and succeeds on these alternative outlets. Of course there are exceptions, we'll discuss them in a few pages, but half-hour comedies and action adventure shows are staples on Fox, and the majority of independent stations and cable channels, from Nick at Night to The Family Channel to A&E, fill their schedules not only with network-type programming, but with shows that earned fame on the networks themselves (most people call them *re-runs*; the industry prefers the term *off-network*). There are many reasons for this; *availability* is one of the main factors. A second is that the *production and distribution* mechanisms that have served the Big 3 for so long are well entrenched and serve these new outlets just as well as they did NBC, CBS and ABC. A third important reason why programming on the alternative channels looks more or less like the fare on the commercial networks is *the audience*. The formats we have become comfortable with, our television tastes and expec-

tations, have been and continue to be developed on the networks. Again, there are exceptions, (Comedy Central's *Mystery Science Theater 3000*, for example), and again, this situation will no doubt change in the next few years. But for now, recall the favorite shows of your childhood. Ask your parents to do the same. Probably most (if not all) will be network or have been network programming at one time or another.

Television and Program Producers

The networks not only control what appears on the majority of local television stations (and by extension, what is on most channels), but for decades the Big 3 have held as much, if not more power over program producers. Technology, regulation and finances are rapidly altering this state of affairs, so to best understand the program production process as it exists today we need to take a brief look at the history of program production and the networks' role in it.

In the early days of television, advertisers exercised the greatest amount of power over television programming. Advertisers and advertising agencies often produced the programs themselves; programs made by independent producers would be sold to advertisers who would then buy time for these shows from the networks.

So producers had many potential buyers for their programs—companies that advertised on television and ad agencies whose clients could be persuaded to use the new medium. Theoretically, this plethora of buyers assured producers that they could find a market for any program, no matter how different or controversial. Variety in television programming was assured—theoretically.

In reality there were neither numerous markets for nor great variety in early programming. The ad agencies relied heavily on in-house production facilities, ignoring the independent producers. In addition, ad agency executives, as well as the heads of their client companies, could be as risk-aversive as the most conservative network programmer. But the point remains, in the medium's infancy the networks served as *time brokers*. Outside agencies provided the programs and commercials, the networks provided the air time and the distribution system (the affiliates). This system had been developed during the "Golden Age" of radio and had worked well for many years. The television networks, having been developed and nurtured by the existing radio networks, saw no reason to change.

But the television networks were forced to change in 1959. Or so they said. In that year a scandal involving independently-produced, advertiser-sponsored quiz shows erupted. The television industry was shaken. The quiz show scandal forced the networks to eliminate the advertisers and ad agencies from the production/distribution process. The networks argued that because audiences held them responsible for what appeared under their name, they were obligated to control their schedules themselves. This they have done ever since, but there is another version of this history. It says that the networks, realizing the wealth that could be realized from *spot* or *magazine-style commercial sales*, were already planning to remove the advertisers from the arrangement and they used the scandal as their excuse. Either way, the networks now ran the show.

Some observers argue that this change killed the "Golden Age of Television," because if a sponsor was going to attach its name to a program, *Alcoa Presents* or the *Texaco Star Theater* for example, that show had better be the very best. They claim that the new fangled way, network salespeople offering 10, 30 and 60 second spots to a variety of sponsors, not only reduced the demand for quality (no one sponsor had a reputational stake in any given show), but also reduced the networks' willingness to try innovative or different types of content (familiarity and predictability combine to maximize the number of potential advertisers). The counter argument is that once the networks' own profits became tied to the success of the programming they aired, they themselves became more concerned with the quality of that content; thus lifting the medium out of its dull infancy, remembered now as the "Golden Age" only by those intellectual snobs wealthy enough to have one of the few sets available back then and who were enamored with heavy, character-based, dreary dramas and esoteric, egg-head humor.

Nevertheless, from the time of the scandals until just recently, thirty or so years, virtually all programming decisions were made at the network level. Though they had the ability and the facilities to produce their own programs, the networks rarely used them (sports and news being the obvious exceptions). Instead they turned directly to independent producers. This meant that the networks needed the producers just as these independent producers needed them—theoretically. In fact, power rested solidly in the checkbooks of the networks: If it were not for the networks as buyers, production companies would have no outlet for their wares.

But just as the 1959 quiz show scandal altered the network/producer equation in favor of the "Big 3," several forces are now at work that have already begun to weaken the networks' domination of that formula. As already mentioned, they are technology, regulation and finances. But before we can talk about how these are changing the business of television, we must discuss how a program typically gets on the air—because, in fact, it is on this process where those forces are having the greatest impact.

How a Program (Typically) Gets on the Air

Each year ABC, CBS, NBC, and Fox will receive somewhere around 4000 proposals for television series. Fewer than 100 of these will advance to the point where a pilot is shot. Of these, approximately 20 will be scheduled, fewer than half of these will survive 13 weeks and, in a very, very good year, maybe 3 or 4 will be big enough successes to be called "hits."

How this process unfolds, a program matur-

The Business of Television Programming 39

ing from idea to premiere, has changed very little over the decades of the networks' rule of the medium. We'll describe this route and then discuss how it's changing.

First, an independent producer (or someone who works for him or her) has an *idea*. That idea is then *shopped*, more than likely to one of the three big commercial networks. The producer hopes that the first network pitched buys the idea, because it is very rare (*All in the Family* and *Family Ties* being notable exceptions) that a series rejected by one network is bought by another. What executive, say from NBC, will pick up an idea rejected by either ABC or CBS, knowing full well that fewer than one in one hundred ideas that are bought ever make it to the air? The chances of proving the competition wrong are vastly outweighed by the possibility that they could be right.

If the producer has a good track-record (that is, has been successful in series television in the past), the networks will probably listen. Newcomers have a much smaller shot. But let's say the pitch is heard and the network is persuaded: it *buys the option*.

The network asks for a written *outline* in which the producer refines the original idea. If still interested, the network will order a *full script*. If it approves of that script, the network will order the production of a *pilot* and then subject that one episode to rigorous testing by its own and independent audience research organizations. It is not rare that, based on this research, the network will demand changes, for example, writing out characters who "tested" poorly or beefing up story lines that the test-audiences particularly liked.

If the network is *still* interested, that is, if it believes that the show will be a hit, it orders a set number of episodes and *schedules* the show. In television's early days, an order might be for 26 episodes (a full 52 weeks of programming, assuming one re-run of each episode). But as production costs climbed and the life expectancy of prime-time entertainment shows declined (*Gunsmoke's* 20 year run will never be matched), 13 episodes became the norm, al-

though untested program ideas or not fully established producers might only get orders for 2 or 3 episodes. CBS even has a name for this practice, "short ordering."

At any point in this process, the network can call it quits. But this doesn't seem to be a problem because *at least* the producer has made some decent money on the script, pilot, and those first few episodes. Right?

Actually, just the opposite is true. In fact, the network invests very little of its own money during the developmental stages of a program. And even when it does order a package of episodes, including those for an established hit that has been on for years, it typically pays the producer only *one half* of the show's entire production costs. That's correct: the producer *loses* money throughout the developmental process and continues to lose even more money the longer his or her show stays on the network's schedule. *Hill Street Blues*, for example, saddled its producers with an annual loss of nearly $1.5 million.

The reason why television program producers participate in this apparently foolhardy enterprise is because of the vast amounts of money they can potentially make in *syndication*, the sale of their programs to stations on a market-by-market basis. Even though the network controls the process from idea to scheduling and decides how long a show stays in its line-up, the producer continues to *own the rights* to that program. The producer, once enough episodes are made (generally about 50, the product of four years on the network), can sell the syndicated package to the highest bidder in each of the country's 210 television markets, keeping all the revenues for him or herself.

The price of a syndicated off-network program depends on the market size, the level of competition between the stations in the market, and the age and popularity of the program itself. The station buys the right to a specified number of *plays* for a specified period of time. After that, the rights return to the syndicator (the producer or the company to whom he or she has sold the rights) to be sold again . . . and again . . . and again.

A program that has survived at least four years on one of the networks has obviously proven its popularity, has been around long enough to attract a loyal following, and has accumulated enough individual episodes so that local stations can offer weeks of daily scheduling without too many re-runs. That means it's a money maker. MCA Television's president, Don Menchel, has predicted that *The Bill Cosby Show* will ultimately make a half billion dollars in syndication (The State . . . , 1987). It is anticipated that *M*A*S*H* will earn its producers nearly that much.

How does a producer ensure a long enough network run to enter the lucrative syndication market? Many critics argue that it is the answer to this question that has kept television a medium, neither rare nor well done. Here is what the producer must do:

- **Develop an idea that will attract network interest.** Something similar to what is already doing well is a safe bet. Maybe a sort of *Cheers* kind of show but with the warmth of *Home Improvement* but with the edge of *NYPD Blue*.

- **Write first an outline and then a script that maintains the network's interest.** See above.

- **Produce a pilot for which the network has put up only half the money and which will be tested in an artificial research setting by viewers who will have one opportunity to pass judgment on your work.**

- **Produce 13 episodes, again losing money all the time**, and hope that the show isn't cancelled after one year. Thirteen episodes can't be easily syndicated.

- **Stay on the network long enough to accumulate the necessary number of episodes** keeping in mind that not only do the idea and program have to be "safe enough" to satisfy network executives and test audiences throughout the development period, but the program must continue to be "safe enough" to ensure those second, third and fourth years.

- **In other words, the program that is created and produced right now must be acceptable to audiences years and years into the future,** because that's when the syndication money will come rolling in. In short, a network signs a program that has yet to be produced, asking the independent producers to assume all the financial risk while making a television series for an audience that, in some cases, hasn't even been born yet.

Consequently, there isn't much incentive to gamble with characters or story-lines; there is little profit in pushing the aesthetic boundaries of the medium. But remember, we said that this is how a program *typically* gets on the air.

Big Changes In the Process and In the Near Future

In 1978 the Big 3 commercial networks had a 92% share of all prime-time television viewers. Ten years later, they owned 70% of that audience. Today, their share hovers around 60%. These numbers are both the product and the cause of the profound changes that are occurring in television programming. As we've mentioned, technology, regulation, and money are transforming the television production and distribution landscape. We'll discuss them individually, but as we'll see, they are inextricably wedded.

Technology

Cable and VCRs are primarily responsible for the decline in network television viewing. The impact of the VCR is obvious and straightforward. According to Arbitron (the ratings company) at least one VCR sits in over 77% of American homes (some areas, like Flagstaff, AZ, have penetration rates in excess of 97%); and with annual revenues for videocassette sales and rentals exceeding $12 billion, it is obvious that many people often choose to watch something other than network fare.

The impact of cable television in less obvious but arguably more damaging. Introduced in the Forties by a television salesman whose business was hampered by reception problems in his rural Pennsylvania, *cable television* is now wired into over 61.4% of all American homes, representing 56 million cable households, or 147 million viewers. The *pass-by rate* is 77% (the percentage of homes that have access to one of the country's 11,588 cable systems that actually take the service). And where the pre-cable television audience had very few choices (three commercial networks, possibly public television, and an independent station or two sitting way out on the end of the UHF dial that played old movies and poorly-produced local shows), today's cable audience has anywhere from 30 to 60 channel options. Moreover, with the increased diffusion of *fiber optic cable* (signals carried by light beams over glass fibers), 500 channel cable systems are becoming technologically feasible. So, much like VCR, part of cable's influence on declining network audiences is that, by its mere existence, it offers alternatives that were not otherwise available. But there's more.

When the *Federal Communications Commission (FCC)* presented its blueprint for television station allocation to the public in 1952, it made specific types and numbers of channels available to most cities based, more or less, on size. This report, the *6th Order and Report*, prescribed not only how many channels an area could sustain, but how many should be VHF (channels 2 through 13) or UHF (14 through 83). Very rare is the city with more than three VHF stations. More typical is an allocation of just that, three VHF channels. Because television sets at the time were not required to have UHF receivers, the VHF stations obviously became more popular and, therefore, more likely to win network affiliation and, therefore, more likely to be more popular. The UHF stations, relegated to the distant (and unreceivable) end of the tuner, remained independent and barely watched. *All-channel legislation*, passed by Congress in 1963 and requiring that all sets produced in or

imported into the country be capable of picking up all channels, helped UHF somewhat, but not much . . . the audience's tastes and habits were firmly set. Cable changed that by making all channels equal, at least technologically. The fact that network affiliate Channel 4 might appear as cable channel 11 and that it sits next to independent Channel 44 (located on cable channel 12) erases possible dial-location advantage. The fact that the affiliate station is now only one of dozens of options further diminishes the distinction between it and its independent neighbors. Cable, in other words, has enriched and empowered the independent stations. Where there were only 73 independent stations on the air in 1972, today there are over 240. This has fueled not only the syndication business, but the *first-run syndication business*, encouraging the appearance of high-quality, first-run prime-time fare, *Baywatch* or *Deep Space 9* for example, drawing even more viewers away from the Big 3.

Cable has also allowed for the birth and success for the Fox, UPN, and WB Networks, again, providing additional alternatives to the Big 3. In the early days of television there were other commercial networks (DuMont and Mutual, for example) but the ABC, CBS, NBC triumvirate survived and it was their domination of the airwaves that had fueled speculation about a "fourth commercial network" for decades. The development of that fourth network was fatally hampered by the lack of available VHF channels (remember, UHF has always been unpopular). But once cable eradicated the distinction between VHF and UHF, Australian Rupert Murdoch was quick to move. Although it's the new kid on the television network block, Fox's affiliates have won viewers away from its competitors with innovative and popular programming like *The Simpsons*, *In Living Color*, *Married . . . with Children*, and *The X Files*.

The cable channels have also provided numerous new outlets for innovative, first-run series like HBO's *The Larry Sanders Show* and *Dream On*, the Disney Channel's *Still the Beaver*, and Showtime's *Brothers*. This last example suggests why the networks may be poorly matched in their competition for audiences. *Brothers* was a program about a homosexual man and his siblings that aired in the mid-1980s. Near the same time that *Brothers* was on television, NBC scheduled the critically acclaimed *Love, Sidney*, a ground-breaking series about a conservative, gay, commercial artist which starred Tony Randall. When the network cancelled *Love, Sidney* in 1984, according to Randall, "Grant Tinker [then network president] said to me—and these are his exact words—'Bluntly, Tony, we've got to go for the crap.' I wished him luck, but he got the luck he deserved" (Shister, 1984, p. 4C). Randall's "luck he deserved" comment referred to NBC's last place position in the ratings.

The traditional broadcasters' luck may get even worse if affordable DBS using small receiving dishes can capture viewers' loyalty. DirecTv began just such a service in spring of 1994, offering 150 channels (but no over-the-air stations). It is too soon to tell if the $700 installation fee and an additional monthly charge will allow DBS to be successful.

Even without a well established DBS system, the networks' loss of viewers to other channels means a loss of revenues to those channels as well. Increased revenues for the alternatives means that they, too, can buy and produce programming. The networks' monopoly over television programming has been destroyed.

Money

Technology and money cross paths again at an unlikely spot: at the remote control, currently in about 80% of American homes. With the power to change channels just a finger-flick away, people are increasingly *flipping* (moving from one program to another, perhaps when a show breaks for commercial), *grazing* (watching several programs simultaneously) and *channel surfing* or *cruising* (moving through the dial for the minute or two that a commercial is on, returning to the show when the spot is over). In any case, this spells more financial bad news for the networks because what they

sell to advertisers is viewers for their commercials. But if viewers don't stay around for those spots (ad agencies estimate at least half the audience moves around during commercial breaks), the networks have nothing to sell. This means that, increasingly, advertisers are directing their expenditures (their money) to those alternatives that offer programming that attracts a more loyal, and therefore presumably more stable audience than does typical mass-appeal network fare. This *narrowcasting*, aiming programs at smaller but more loyal audiences that are of interest to specific advertisers, is now occasionally attempted by the networks. For example, *Tour of Duty* in the late 1980s and *NYPD Blue* in the 1990s may not have achieved huge ratings, but they were very popular among young males, television's most active flippers, grazers, cruisers and surfers. But the facts of economic life say this is easier and less expensive to achieve on the smaller, less mass-oriented cable and independent channels.

As the non-network channels attract more money, they can buy more programming; and this has led to important changes and great expansion of the television syndication business. In describing the annual convention of the National Association of Television Program Executives (NATPE) in Miami Beach in 1994, critic Tom Jicha wrote, "Almost every TV program not supplied by ABC, CBS, NBC and Fox is introduced at the meeting. Then the shows return each year to line up renewals and cajole for better time periods. It is also where the successful major network series come after three or four years to arrange their rerun afterlife. In short, this meeting is where the real money is in TV" (p. 5E).

As we've seen, syndicated programming is packages of shows sold on a station-by-station/market-by-market basis. And in the era of network domination of television content, most syndicated content was either movie packages, game and talk shows for non-prime-time, and reruns of series that were once hits on one of the Big 3. But syndicated programming is coming into viewers' homes in several new and important ways. In the era of network domination of content, first-run syndication (except for game and talk shows) was rarely ever attempted and, when it was, it showed in a low quality look that was definitely non-network. Where *Space 1999* failed in first run syndication twenty years ago, *Star Trek: The Next Generation* airs, often more than once a week, on 220 stations, it has spawned its own syndicated spin-off, *Deep Space 9*, and is headed for the big screen movie theatres. MCA took the 22 episodes of *Charles In Charge* that were aired before network cancelation and combined them with newly produced first-run episodes and sold them into syndication.

There is another common form of first-run syndication that is made possible by one of the technologies that has cut into the networks' audience—satellite. *Hard Copy*, *Inside Edition*, and *Entertainment Tonight* are only three examples of the reality (or tabloid) shows that

are distributed daily by satellite to the hundreds of stations that have bought them. They are inexpensive to make, inexpensive to distribute, easily *stripped* (broadcast at the same time five nights a week) and easily promoted ("Tonight, did the high school teacher lure her teen-age lover into killing her husband? Tune in at seven-thirty."). They offer an inexhaustible number of episodes without ever airing the same show twice. And they're popular with audiences—perfect syndicated programming.

Another form of syndicated programming that is appearing increasingly on the tube is *barter syndication*. Typically, a producer sells several but not all commercial spots in his or her first-run show and then either gives the package to local stations or sells it to them at very low rates. The local station then sells the remaining spots and pockets the income. In

Hard Copy. Co-anchored by Barry Nolan and Terry Murphy, is a nationally syndicated, first-run news magazine that premiered in 1989. The program, which was named one of *Time Magazine's* Ten Best Television Shows of 1993, is seen on over 160 stations across the country.

this way, the producer, advertisers, and the local stations share the financial risk. Mutual's *Wild Kingdom* is an example of a barter program that is literally given to stations (as long as they agree to leave the Mutual commercials in place). *Fame*, after it left the network, is one example of a barter show that was sold with a variety of commercials already in place.

For the networks, money is changing the programming balance of power even more directly than by encouraging/allowing the growth of syndicated alternatives. For example, as *Cheers* came to the end of its run on NBC in the early 1990s, its producers demanded 100 percent of their production costs from the network. The network was mired in last place in the ratings war behind its two long-time foes. Even though the show's producers and distributor were assured syndication success (it was already successful in syndication even as it ran on the network), they knew that they had the advantage over the ratings-hungry third-place NBC. The network relented, keeping Sam and his friends in the Thursday night line-up for an additional two years.

Two other interesting twists on the usual program production system exist as well. Fox has experimented with having pilot episodes of possible comedy series produced live, on stage in front of an audience, keeping costs down and speeding up the process, allowing it to consider a greater number of new shows. The second change is the growing practice of shooting pilots either in a 15 minute format (reducing costs) or in a two hour format, allowing the pilot to stand alone as a made-for-TV-movie, a movie for video-tape rental, or as a movie for foreign distribution, allowing the producers to recap their money should the program not otherwise make it to the air.

Aspiring television critics would be wise to monitor these changes in the production/distribution system to see their effects on content, but there is an even more dramatic alteration in the programming process that demands their attention, one that has arisen at the juncture of money and regulation.

Regulation

For more than 60 years, broadcasting has been regulated by the Federal Communication Commission which was created by the *Communications Act of 1934*. That Act prohibited the FCC from meddling in matters of content (Section 307) but demanded that it award licence renewals based on broadcasters' performance (Section 325), which is obviously manifested in the content it airs. This apparent inconsistency has been the focus of many lawsuits and court cases. The two most notable cases are the Supreme Court's 1943 *NBC Decision* where it ruled that the FCC had a duty to be more than a "traffic cop" directing the technical flow of broadcast waves, and the 1969 *Red Lion Decision* where the Supreme Court declared that the Commission had a right to regulate content because when a broadcaster's and a listener's (or viewer's) rights clash, it is the listener's rights that "are paramount."

One way that the FCC walks this fine line is to make rules that, while dealing directly with technical or non-programming issues, will ultimately impact content in what it hopes will be some beneficial way. For example, we've already seen the all channel legislation which regulated the manufacture and importation of TV sets, but its real goal was to boost the fortunes of UHF and independent stations by creating a greater number of alternatives to network television and thereby injecting what it hoped would be greater diversity in television programming.

In 1970 the Commission attempted to increase the variety and diversity of television content through regulation—not of a technical matter—but of a financial matter. Concerned that the three networks (before Fox) held a virtual monopoly over content (they could produce their own shows, air them to the exclusion of independent producers, and sell them into a syndication market that held no real competition because only their shows had the advantage of a network run), the FCC passed its *Financial Interest and Syndication Rules* or *Fin-Syn*. It limited the three networks' ownership of the entertainment shows they aired, hoping that many independent producers would bring before them a more diverse array of programming. The networks would serve primarily as distributors of the work of the independent producers.

Much to the chagrin of the Big 3, these Fin-Syn rules were suspended for the Fox network when it first emerged. The new network was allowed to air programs, most of which had been produced by its parent company, 20th Century Fox. Why was Fox allowed to do this? The FCC argued that certain concessions must be allowed for budding companies in order to insure fair competition. Fox probably would not have survived had it been required to purchase all of its programming while trying to set up the network. Also, Fox wasn't "on the air" enough hours per week to be considered a bona fide network according to the FCC's definition.

In 1983, the networks, because they were losing audiences to the alternatives we've been talking about in this chapter, lobbied the Commission for change. Of course the program producers were also lobbying—but to keep Fin-Syn in place. A set of compromise rules was passed in that year, implemented on a trial basis, and eventually formalized ten years later, in 1993. Now the networks can produce and own the syndication rights to up to 50% of their prime-time entertainment fare. The Big 3 are disappointed that the Fin-Syn rules will not give them an even greater stake in the shows they air; the independent producers scream that they will now be ruined.

Just as the change from ad agency to network ownership of programming after the Quiz Show Scandals dramatically altered what we saw on our screens, Fin-Syn will do the same. But the question is, "How?" The networks claim that content will get better because when it is their "up-front" production money and potential syndication profits that are at risk, they will be more likely to stay with a high quality or innovative yet lowly rated show until it finds an audience. The producers, on the other hand, argue that they will become "little more than robots responding to the

whims of networks. Without being able to anticipate full revenues from syndication . . . they would have no incentive to swallow losses on offbeat new shows" (DeMott, 1983, p. 47).

In February, 1996, President Bill Clinton signed into law the *Telecommunications Act of 1996*, the first major communication legislation since the *Communications Act of 1934*. This new Act was particularly focused on new, emerging technologies in terms of establishing fair competition mandates (i.e., ownership limitation, barriers to entry, etc.); technological standards; and universal access for consumers. In the television broadcasting arena, the new law presents several changes that will affect the programming we watch and/or critique:

The FCC modified its rules for ownership. The number of television stations that a person or entity can directly or indirectly own, operate, or control (nationwide), formerly was limited to 12 stations total. The 1996 Act eliminated the restrictions and increased the national audience reach limitation for television stations to 35 percent (up from 25%), regardless of how many stations are owned. Critics contend that this policy places content decision-making in the hands of fewer and fewer "players" which ultimate must affect quality.

The establishment of a television rating code. The 1996 Act requires the FCC to establish an advisory committee to create a system that will identify and rate video programming that contains sexual, violent, or other indecent material about which parents should be informed *before* it is displayed. It requires distributors of video programming to transmit the ratings in order for parents to block the programming if they determine it is inappropriate for their children. Critics speculate that such a ratings system will affect content in at least two ways: 1) some broadcasters will use the ratings code as an invitation to create *more explicit or graphic* content over-the-air because they will be "protected" by an "R" rating; or 2) some broadcasters will be overly conservative in their censorship of questionable content which might adversely affect artistic or First Amendment freedoms.

The "V" Chip or similar technology. The 1996 Act requires television sets sold in the U.S. (with 13 inch screens or larger) to be manufactured or equipped with a feature designed to enable viewers to block display of all programs with a common rating. This technology, dubbed the violence or "V" chip, has been described as a personalized way for viewers (specifically parents) to take control of the viewing situation.

Broadcasters are uneasy about these provisions set by the new *Telecommunications Act of 1996*. They question *who* will determine the definitions for the various ratings categories in the system and *how* various content will be pigeon-holed into these predetermined slots. For example, would the violence on *Schlindler's List* be considered the same as violent portrayals on *ER* or *NYPD Blues* or a *Batman* cartoon? As a first-strike strategy, broadcasters have been meeting (most recently with President Clinton, himself) to establish definitions or specific boundaries for a rating system. It seems that broadcasters are attempting to self-regulate *before* the FCC does it for them. Some critics contend that broadcasters might simply be concerned about loss in viewership (and subsequent revenues) because of the ratings system or "V" chip technology.

As we can see, the *Telecommunications Act of 1996*, as well as the other forces we've been discussing, promise to change the television programming landscape in interesting and exciting ways. As we said at the start of this chapter, it is a fascinating time to engage in evaluation of the medium, that is, to be a television critic.

STONE

Rolling Stone TV critic Laurie Stone offers a wonderful critique of one of the most innovative and interesting programs of the post-network dominance era, *The Larry Sanders Show*. What is particularly interesting is that she examines a show that is on a prime network competitor, HBO; a program that probably could only have appeared on a competitor because the networks wouldn't have aired it; and, a program that deals with life at the network during these perilous (for networks) times. Note her comparison of *Sanders* to *Murphy Brown* and *Seinfeld*, network comedies that are themselves considered innovative.

Garry Shandling looks pained. Chronically. He's ordered a rare burger, and it's well-done. His girlfriend says he's remote. His favorite jacket . . .well, there's grease on the lapel. From the burger. Sigh. Not to mention the ozone layer and mortality. The pain is mostly in the mouth, with its fleshy, disappointed lips. And in the eyes, poised for a wince. Shandling understands this face, knows how the fear of humiliation can turn into a bludgeon-knows how good it feels to sneer and pull ahead in the power derby and how bad it feels, too, how pointless. Shandling has used this insight to surmount his anger and doubt, turned them into subjects rather than merely copping to them in order to indulge them. The result is *The Larry Sanders Show* (HBO)—a shrewd satire of talk shows with a dazzling ensemble cast-which may well be the hippest, funniest take ever on the pecking order.

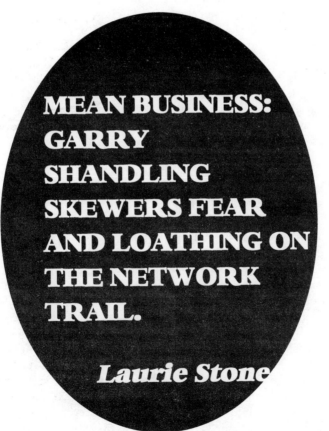

MEAN BUSINESS: GARRY SHANDLING SKEWERS FEAR AND LOATHING ON THE NETWORK TRAIL.

Laurie Stone

Like Richard Pryor's concert movies, *Sanders* is charged with giddy license, a sense of possibility arising not from stagy shocks but from simple truths that are ordinarily suppressed. The series—its cameras poised to pounce on un-

guarded moments—is a wildly unmuzzled gloss on repression and on the devil-brokered bargains and slipping authority behind it. *Sanders* is HBO's most exuberant fuck-you to the networks, a dance on the grave of centralized power—no more Kremlin, no more almighty big-three networks, no more Carson. This show couldn't have been made five years ago; the players wouldn't have risked biting the only hands with kibble.

When it debuted in August, the series, cocreated with Dennis Klein, inspired raves. Now, after 13 episodes, an expansive, cohesive vision has emerged. Ten installments will rerun from December 7 through 11 and from December 14 through 18, at 11 p.m. Twenty-two new episodes have been ordered for next year.

Larry Sanders, played by Shandling, is the golden-boy/lackey at an unnamed network owned by Unideck Electronics—

read Letterman, pampered/dissed by NBC, minion of GE. He jousts for ratings in the post-Carson frontier, a mediascape at once lawless and energized, a breeding ground for paranoia and the hunger to stay alive. His trademark is holding out an invisible remote control and urging, "Do not flip around." When the show's producer, Artie (Rip Torn), hears mention of CNBC, he grouches: "What the hell is that? What does that mean? My TV stops at 13, where it's supposed to."

Most of the action unfurls behind the scenes; *Sanders* is a show biz confidential, its nose trained on power, its characters archetypes worthy of Moliére. Atop the show's pyramid hunkers distant-father Larry. On the air, he isn't as irascible as Letterman, rather closer to Leno, blanding himself out in his monologues, curbing his hostility to and competitiveness with his guests (who are real celebrities, playing themselves and hyping actual projects). He is cripplingly self-conscious, a man who worries that his ass looks fat, a creature struggling to be decent but who would always sell out for a punch line. Not sex, not money, not intimacy—nothing makes him feel as alive as a laugh. He can simulate connection *only* before cameras; during commercials, he sinks into stony silence, stranding the gulls on his couch to stare bleakly into space. He's so terrified of self-exposure, he's never invited longtime ally Artie to his home. When his wife, Jeannie (Megan Gallagher), arranges a dinner and informs him, "It's at your house," Larry gets a hunted look and wishfully asks, "What is that, a new Chinese restaurant?"

As for sidekick Hank (Jeffrey Tambor), there is no turd he will not swallow with a rueful grin. Hank—former cruise director and current endorsement junkie/bimbette hunter—is the Ed McMahon who guffaws as Carson

ridicules his drinking while obscuring his own, who plays the sport in a feigned friendship requiring he accept barbs.

Head writers Jerry (Wallace Langham) and Phil (Jeremy Piven) are geeks turned tormenters. Among themselves, they curse Larry's delivery for blunting their brilliance, then separately draw him aside to backbite each other. When Larry has William Shatner on the phone, they challenge, "Get him to say 'Klingon,'" then huddle around the speaker phone so their snickers can be heard.

This world is Animal House, *Sanders* pointedly documents. When Jon Lovitz and his female satellite dine *chez* Sanders, the men relive their club gigs, oblivious that the women are sitting by silent and glum. The female regulars, in addition to Jeannie, include Larry's assistant, Beverly (Penny Johnson), Hank's assistant, Darlene (Linda Doucett), and the talent booker, Paula (Janeane Garofalo)—team players lacking even parking space on the influence totem pole. Darlene, an aerobicized mommy, is Hank's ideal, but overworked Paula and Beverly, the only African American on staff, shoot off smart mouths in private.

With the least at stake, they are the least snowed, functioning as the show's chorus. One night before a taping, a depressed Jeannie says to Larry, "Do you know that I sleep all day?" And Beverly, feeling implicated, remarks to Paula, "We fetch for him all day. We create the atmosphere he takes home to her." When at last a woman with clout does enter-network exec Melanie Parrish (Deborah May)—she's so desperate to measure up in the locker room, she hurls threats and insults (shades of Leno's Helen Kushnick?), outcruding even the actual pale penis people.

Paranoia saturates the atmosphere. In almost every episode, someone's head rolls or a character

fears being replaced. Everyone feels tangential, assumes that pod replicants are waiting in the wings. Their egos stroked one minute and clobbered the next, the characters are unable to gauge their sizes, seeing themselves one minute as scurrying rodents and the next as gigantic talents. "I'm a day away from being the funny weatherman in Tucson," Larry whines, serious enough to hawk Garden Weasels when the sponsor insists. On another show, he returns from a two-week vacation after three days, a nail-biting interval during which guest host Dana Carvey has raked in big ratings.

Fear of the ax distracts the characters from taking stocks, but when, occasionally, the buzzing quiets, they are filled with melancholy. Cynicism, they see, doesn't protect them from midlife malaise. The inanities of talk shows are continually paraded: bits with wild animals, the youngest X and the oldest Y, banter about last night's audience. Yet this gig is the brass ring for Larry, Artie, and Hank, men who sense their mediocrity but have no urge for more challenge. When Larry complains that, since he doesn't own a Garden Weasel, endorsing it would be unethical, Artie's eyes fill with weltschmerz and he cautions, "Don't start pulling on that thread, or our whole world will unravel!"

With all its unmasking, though, *Sanders* doesn't come off mean-spirited. It is generous, permissive, overflowing with antic detail. Even when it snarls at the real people, the targets are padded with status and fame. Most shows would settle for one plot line per episode; this one routinely weaves together three. The writers—including Shandling, Paul Simms, and Maya Forbes—are reference junkies far from recovery. Artie keeps replaying Larry's flirting with Mimi Rogers, and Larry gripes, "Christ, it's like making me watch the Rodney King tape." Hank auditions for substitute host, and Artie counsels a network chief: "Go easy and don't mention Rupert Pupkin." When Artie says the network is pushing Donna Mills, Larry groans, "Donna Mills, even Kiss is working without makeup."

The dished and dishers alike dive into the candor. It's as if Hollywood has waited its lifetime to flash underbelly—even to look unattractive. Family man Billy Crystal admits putting business first. Robin Williams screws up his timing and dies. Nicegirl Carol Burnett, prodded to do a Tarzan sketch, bitches to her assistant about Larry's bad acting, and, during a commercial, she whispers loud—"Get a longer loincloth. I saw your balls."

Even innovative sitcoms—*Murphy Brown, Seinfeld*—present cartoons with shtick that's repeated over and over. On *Sanders*, doubleness rules, and the characters are drawn with increasing richness in seemingly marginal exchanges. During Burnett's appearance, Larry freaks out, killing two tarantulas that have been placed on his arm. Afterward, we see Artie weave his devilish spell: "You finally got to do a sketch with Carol," Larry (miserably): "It wasn't a sketch. It was a massive, spastic fuck-up." Artie: "Tomato, tom*aa*to, it was broad physical comedy. It made the Ed Ames tomahawk throw look like a big piece of shit." Larry: "Really?" Artie (sadistic glee washing over his face): "Until you sent that poor creature to a fiery death." Larry: "But in a funny way." Artie: "Very funny." Larry: "Want to watch the tape again?" Artie: "Atta boy."

Hank generally crouches on Larry's other shoulder, piping up as conscience. When Larry bumps David Spade for appearing on Leno's show first, Hank reminds him of his own scrabbling days. When Larry admits, "I've turned into an asshole," Hank responds, "Have a good time with it," causing Larry's face to freeze in dismay. But poignance never turns maudlin here; it always remains laced with gritty truth. Hank finally explodes at Larry for his sniggering; "What about the time I chipped my tooth on the bathroom urinal? What the fuck is comical about that?" Larry is tempted to be a mensch, but his resolve melts. Slowly, he exhales, "It was a back took, Hank. Don't know how you did it."

Shandling himself is straddling excitement and anxiety when I reach him by phone. "I'm glad the series was picked up," he enthuses, then worries, "but now we have to deepen the characters, especially Larry, find out why he even *has* a personal life, since he keeps running away from it." Shandling measures his words, as if each is a bubble he wants to examine. Unlike Larry, he doesn't sniff extensively before revealing his thoughts. He's evasive only once, halfway through the conversation; "Er, I'm going to call you back on another phone. In five minutes," I think: "He's getting in his car. He's reluctant to look like an L.A. cliche." The phone rings. "Are you in your car?" Shandling: "Behind an Arrowwood truck, on my way to an agent."

A part of Shandling would like to store the praise he's received and live off it, go camping or something, because exploring Larry means that his source, Garry, goes back on the couch. That he's will-

ing is what distinguishes him from his creation. Shandling understands that exposure is funnier than protecting himself, and he wants to dramatize the struggle.

Shandling: "Next season, Larry has to look at what he is or the show won't be interesting. He surrounds himself with yes men, and there are a lot of other temptations. You get all this recognition, and the pay is great, and it's not exactly digging ditches. But when I was hosting *The Tonight Show*, I got to a point where I had to ask myself: 'Do you really want this as a career, dealing with momentous decisions like whether Michael Bolton is going to do one number or two?'"

Stone: "Larry lets in the truth when he absolutely has to, like when his job is on the line."

Shandling: "He's going to feel that urgency with women. He's unhappy enough to ask why he would choose a wife like Jeannie. It's very common in show biz, women without lives of their own who devote all their attention to their husbands. So many men need women to revolve around them. But it's not just that Jeannie is frustrated with Larry, I think he resents *her*, and he will think about why. I want to bring back Melanie Parrish. She's a good authority figure for Larry to clash with, and we can explore what makes a woman become that angry."

Stone: "What does Larry really think of Hank?"

Shandling: "He believes Hank is the best man for the job. He loves him."

Stone: "*Loves* him? When he constantly mocks him?"

Shandling: "Oh, come on, you can be mean to anyone."

Chapter Exercise

You Be the Program Director

Prepare a one-page memo to the network VP of your choice, suggesting how you would change one of these shows as it moves channels (*Friends* or *Seinfeld* to HBO or *The Larry Sanders Show* to either CBS, ABC, NBC or Fox). Defend your decisions!

MEMORANDUM

To: Bruce Friedberg, Vice President for Comedy at
(circle one): NBC or CBS or ABC or Fox or HBO

From: _____
(Print your name here)

Re: Moving a hit to our network.

I've been assured by the producers of (Pick one):

Friends or *Seinfeld* or *The Larry Sanders Show*
that they are ready to make a move to a different network. Of course, I will need to "fine-tune" the show to fit the special needs and character of our network. Here's what I have in mind . . .

Let's take lunch on Thursday to rap about my ideas. Ciao Baby!

References and Resources

Boddy, W. (1979). The rhetoric and economic roots of the American broadcasting industry. *Cinetracts, 6,* 37–54.

Broadcasting & Cable Yearbook 1995. (1995). New Providence, NJ: R. R. Bowker.

DeMott, J. (1983). Sharing that syndication gravy. *Time,* August 15, p. 47.

Jicha, T. (1994). It's a big deal, all these TV folks together. San Jose *Mercury News,* January 27, p. 5E.

MacDonald, J. F. (1993). *One Nation Under Television: The Rise and Decline of Network TV.* Chicago, IL: Nelson-Hall.

Newcomb, H. (1994). *Television: The Critical View.* New York: Oxford University Press.

Newcomb, H. & Alley, R. S. (1983). *The Producer's Medium: Conversations With Creators of American TV.* New York: Oxford University Press.

Shister, G. (1984). Randall resents television. San Jose *Mercury News,* August 23, p. 4C.

The state of syndication. (1987). *Channels, 7,* 72–73.

Tuchman, G., (Ed.). (1979). *The TV Establishment: Programming for Power and Profit.* Englewood Cliffs, NJ: Prentice-Hall.

Sterling, C. H. & Kittros, J. M. (1990). *Stay Tuned: A Concise History of American Broadcasting.* Belmont, CA: Wadsworth.

CHAPTER 4

COMMERCIALS, RATINGS AND THE ROLE OF THE AUDIENCE

So I figured the least I could do, for television, was be an Arbitron household. This involves two major responsibilities: 1. Keeping track of what you watch on TV. 2. Lying about it. At least that's what I did. I imagine most people do. Because let's face it: Just because you watch a certain show on television, that doesn't mean you want to admit *it.*

—Dave Barry

Humorist and columnist Dave Barry, who himself became the topic of a network situation comedy in 1993, doesn't like to admit he watches the least objectionable program (1990, p. 23). For him and for many critics and viewers, the least objectionable program doesn't necessarily provide the most entertainment; but for most television executives and program producers, it does ensure the largest audience. And to these executives and producers, that's what television is all about: audiences attract advertisers, who provide commercials and pay dearly to get those commercials aired for audiences to watch. Commercials are the lifeblood of television. Viewers may determine which shows, of all those offered, remain on the air, but it is advertising dollars that pay television's bills and, in a real sense, keep our favorite programs coming to us night after night, week after week.

This has been true since the earliest days of television. Back then—before the quiz show scandals—it was common for a single advertiser to sponsor a whole program. A company would "buy" a program and only that particular company's commercials would appear during the program. After the scandals, with the networks firmly in control of programming, the whole notion of program sponsorship changed. The old, familiar phrase, "Brought to you by . . . " was heard less and less frequently, as the single sponsor program became increasingly rare. Today, advertisers buy spot announcements (rather than programs) which can be placed in a program the way an ad is positioned in a magazine. Just as very few magazines are supported by a single advertiser, few television programs of today are "brought to you by" a single sponsor. Magazine-concept advertising (multiple-sponsorship) now dominates commercial television, with advertisers paying various amounts of money for *spots* differing in length from 10 to 60 seconds.

The amount of money paid for a spot varies with its length, surely. But even more importantly, the price varies with the size and "quality" of the audience that is delivered at any

55

given time by any given program. For this to be the case, it follows that broadcasters and cablecasters (and potential advertisers) must be kept aware of just how big the audience is at different times and for different shows. Accurate measurement of the audience and a reasonably precise picture of what sorts of people watch television are essential if the medium is to survive as a commercial entity. This audience measurement is related in terms of *ratings* and *shares*—two very important terms in understanding television and why it looks the way it does.

Overview

How we as critics understand television's audience determines to a great extent our attitude toward television and television programming. It is crucial that we begin to place ourselves, self-consciously and openly, somewhere along the continuum between viewing the audience as *passive* (simply the product delivered by television to its advertisers), or viewing the audience as *active* (meaning-making consumers of television texts). As critics, we may even want to reconcile these two views.

The audience may well be the television industry's true product, but the programming is the delivery system; a fact reflected by the industry's reliance upon audience measurement techniques—like the ratings—in determining the worth of a particular program. It is important to ask how this delivery system works. Regardless of the viewers' relative power in the television scheme of things, producers and networks must still offer programs people want to watch in order to deliver those people to advertisers. It is this interaction between audience and programming that is the focus of this chapter. We will examine both the product and the delivery system—however we choose to define those terms—because neither, standing alone, gives us a complete picture of the communication process. No single model can explain a process as complex as communication, a business as complex as television, or a form of communication as complex as the television program.

The Ratings

We all have some awareness of the ratings, some knowledge of what they are and the kind of impact they have on television programming. We wonder what the Number One show is, and we complain when our favorite programs are driven from the air by "low ratings." Newspapers report the top-rated shows for each week and when a program or special—*60 Minutes*, the "who shot JR" episode of *Dallas*, the finalé of *Cheers* or the Super Bowl, for example—garners especially high ratings, the news is sure to be featured in the channel's promotions and in stories carried in newspapers and magazines across the country.

Many viewers (as well as many industry observers and executives) assume that the ratings have something to do with a show's popularity or quality. Sadly, this just isn't so. Put simply, the ratings are a measurement of audience size, *not* of audience opinion. As we shall see, the ratings services typically count sets on and sets off; they determine the channel to which sets are tuned; and while they do make some attempt to measure viewer satisfaction, the results of these surveys are often suspect.

Just as a magazine or newspaper sets its advertising rates according to the size of the audience (subscribers) it reaches and the sorts of people who make up that audience, so, too, do television stations and networks use the ratings—their measures of "circulation"—to determine the amount of money an advertiser must pay for a commercial. These measures of circulation are provided primarily by one market research firm: The A. C. Nielsen Company. A second company, Arbitron, reacting to the changing face of the medium, withdrew from the television rating business in 1994 to focus its resources on radio ratings and on what it calls qualitative audience measurement. "The company is . . . moving forward in developing its 'personal portable meter' and is continuing to explore new options to measure local cable television audiences" (Arbitron, 1993, p. 1; see the ratings box for details).

A. C. Nielsen offers a variety of services; the best known of these is the Nielsen Television Index (also known as the NTI, or simply, "the ratings"). In compiling this index, the Nielsen Company selects 1200 households representative of the entire American viewing audience. Each of these households is provided with a device called an audimeter which records when the television set is turned on, the frequency to which it is tuned (in other words, which station is on), and the time of day. The information recorded by the audimeter is transmitted via telephone lines to the Nielsen Company. From this information, Nielsen can determine the program being watched and the amount of time each household spent with that program.

The audimeter (and, therefore, the Nielsen ratings) can't measure whether anyone was actually watching the television set at any given time, or if anyone was paying close attention, much less if anyone likes what's on. It can't indicate if the program was being used as background noise for eating or studying. It can only measure, in the most mechanical fashion, whether or not the set was turned on and tuned-in to a specific channel.

In order to give potential advertisers a more complete picture of the viewing situation, A. C. Nielsen conducts diary surveys of viewing patterns. Rather than recording viewing patterns mechanically, diaries are distributed to sample households. Viewers are asked to write down which programs they watch and who in the family is watching them.

The diary system offers a more complete picture of viewing patterns but it is far from perfect. In the first place, it requires active participation on the part of those being surveyed. Lack of interest, forgetfulness, and even lying enter the picture when diaries are used to measure audience size. In any event, the structure of the diaries offers viewers little opportunity to reveal their likes and dislikes. Its purpose is to record numbers of viewers and a bit of pertinent information about who watches different programs.

The ratings come in for quite a bit of derision from critics of television. The fact that they measure viewers rather than program quality is one such complaint; and the shortcomings of the diary system have been documented.

THE RATINGS SYSTEM

Ratings (and shares) determine which programs survive and which die, so they are obviously of interest to programmers, to advertisers, and (should be) to critics and viewers. They are so important that broadcasters and advertisers are constantly seeking new ways to improve their speed and accuracy.

One way is through the use of overnights. Nielsen augments its metered and diary ratings with data gathered from homes connected to its computers by telephone lines. Approximately 535 homes in New York, 530 in Chicago, 535 in Los Angeles, 440 in San Francisco, 345 in Philadelphia, 335 in Detroit, 315 in Boston and 390 in Washington, D.C. all provide Nielsen with instant ratings.

These overnights are useful, but they do have a drawback. When Mary Tyler Moore premiered her new show, *Mary*, in 1985 it scored very highly in the overnights, winning its time-slot. But when the data were gathered from the remainder of the nation's television markets (most far less urbane than those listed above), the family oriented *Highway to Heaven* proved to be the true ratings winner.

The greater need for precision demanded by ever-rising advertising time and production costs as well as the problem of audiences tuned to cable and VCR have forced the ratings people to experiment with even newer ways of counting and evaluating viewers. All of these refinements have been tried and are or have been in full use:

People Meters. Combining the precision of the audimeter with the detail of a diary, this device allows individual members of a household to press buttons on a small box to record their personal viewing. Parents or guardians are responsible for registering the viewing habits of small children or others who might be incapable.

Ratings for Commercials. Using the technology of the People Meter, these ratings can be used to measure audience loss due to viewers leaving the room during commercial spots or because of grazing or surfing (using remote control to cut away from a commercial).

Electronic Monitoring of Commercials. Every commercial has a video and audio "information pulse" at the beginning of the announcement which gives signature information about the spot (sort of the way the little UPC bar codes work on products at the grocery store). Nielsen developed a way to electronically read these commercial "signatures" in order to report overall advertising activity, in all markets, for an entire year. This provides a reliable index of aired commercials that, when coupled with People Meters, could allow ratings of commercials.

Single-Source Data Base. Arbitron developed a system called Scan America that allows viewers to pass an electronic wand over the UPC code on products that they buy. The data that are produced are then matched against the viewing patterns of that household allowing broadcasters and advertisers to see if a given spot in a given program resulted in the purchase of a specific product.

Personal Portable Meters. Arbitron is currently testing a system that requires people to wear a receiving mechanism (in the form of a wrist watch or a type of beeper box which is clipped onto a belt) that detects and records radio and television transmission information. So no matter where you go or what you do, it will be able to establish whether or not you were in the vicinity of a broadcast signal and what station was emitting that signal. Again, even this sophisticated technology can't ascertain what amount of attention is paid to the broadcast or whether the consumer liked it or not.

There are other critiques of the ratings system as well. The most common complaint is that a sample of 1200 households is insufficient to reflect the viewing patterns of millions of Americans. Your instincts may tell you this is a valid complaint, but from a statistical point of view the sample is large enough, and selected in a manner carefully enough, to ensure a high degree of accuracy. In fact, Nielsen is accurate to within plus or minus 3 percentage points. This means that a program with a rating of 20 (meaning 20% of all the households with television are tuned to that show) may actually be attracting only 17% of the households with television, or as many as 23% of those households. This is sufficiently accurate, at least for the purposes of television executives and potential advertisers, to warrant television's reliance on the ratings in setting advertising rates.

The Share

In addition to supplying the ratings, Nielsen provides another, perhaps even more important, measure of television's audience—the share. The share is a more direct reflection of a particular program's competitive position. It doesn't measure a program's viewers as a percentage of *all* television households (as the rating does) but rather, measures a program's audience as a percentage of the television *sets in use* at the time the program airs. The share tells us what percentage of the actual (as opposed to the potential) audience a program attracted. Two simple formulae may make the distinction between a rating and a share a bit more clear:

$$\text{Rating} = \frac{\text{Households Tuned In}}{\text{Total \# of Households With TV (all } \textit{possible} \text{ viewers)}}$$

$$\text{Share} = \frac{\text{Households Tuned In}}{\text{Households Using Television (HUT)}}$$

The share is a more meaningful reflection of a program's success than the rating (despite the fact that the general public hears more about the ratings than any other measure of program success). The share tells broadcasters and advertisers how well a particular program is doing on its given night, in its time slot, against its competition. The *Late Show With David Letterman* illustrates the difference between rating and share and the significance of the latter in determining advertising rates. Generally speaking, this CBS show gets terrible ratings, usually no more than 7 or 8 percent of the total (potential) television audience. But since it is on late at night and many fewer people are awake to watch television than at an earlier hour, it attracts approximately 40% of the actual audience—the people who are awake and watching television. Thus, its share is very high and the network in 1993 was more than happy to pay its star $42 million for three years.

In order for a television program to remain on the air it must be more than successful. Given television's pervasiveness, even a low-rated program with a relatively small share of the available audience reaches many more people than all but the most popular movies, books, and records. Even a low-rated show is, to some extent, a "success," reaching millions of people simultaneously. Still, the networks cancel shows right and left for not being ratings smashes (although remember that cable channels and the independents may apply a different standard, one more demographically based).

Generally speaking, before the decline of the networks' audience, a prime-time program (one aired between 8 p.m. and 11 p.m. EST and PST; 7 p.m. and 10 p.m. CST) needed to achieve ratings of 17 to 20 and a share between 25 and 30 to stay on the air. That meant that in order to just survive, approximately one television household in every five must have been tuned-in to the program and one out of every three households in which the set was actually turned on while the show was airing must have been tuned to that show. Today, such numbers make a show a smash. For example, the number one show in the 1977 / 78 season was *Laverne & Shirley* with an average annual rating of 31.6. The number 25 program that year was the *ABC Monday Night Movie* with a rating of 20.3. Now consider the Nielsen figures for the first week of March, 1996 below.

Even though *Friends*, the second highest rated program that week, wouldn't have cracked the top 25 in the pre-cable/VCR era, it still attracted nearly 18 million households. Yet, the fact remains, on network television it's not enough to be loved by millions; you have to be loved by enough millions. A rating of 10 might mean nine or so million homes tuned-in, but more than likely that simply isn't enough to satisfy prime-time network programmers.

The power of the ratings in the television world is enormous—programs of quality can, in the words of Les Brown (1979), be cancelled for "forfeiting audience" to the competition. Moreover, programs which even the broadcasters and advertisers don't like can be saved by big numbers. *Maude*, produced by Norman Lear and disliked intensely by advertisers and

affiliates, survived for six seasons because of strong ratings (typically about a 25).

Demographics

The ratings services provide network programmers and advertisers with data far beyond ratings and shares; they also provide detailed audience member breakdowns, offering information to potential advertisers about the average age, sex, education, and income of those people viewing television programs— all potential viewers of commercial messages. Demographics of this sort are of ever-increasing importance to everyone involved in television.

In the early days of television, demographics didn't carry as much weight as they do today. It wasn't until Paul Klein (then head of research for Doyle, Dane, and Bernbach—an advertising agency), reassessed *I Love Lucy*, the biggest hit on television at that time. Klein advised Philip Morris (the cigarette company which sponsored the program) to drop its

RANK/SHOW	RATING*
1. *Seinfeld*	21.7
2. *Friends*	18.7
3. *Caroline in the City*	16.7
3. *ER*	16.7
5. *Home Improvement*	16.6
6. *Single Guy*	16.2
7. *60 Minutes*	15.2
8. *20/20*	14.4
9. *Frasier Special*	13.8
10. *Seinfeld Special*	13.4

*(one ratings point equals 958,525 TV homes)

support of the phenomenally successful show. He saw that *Lucy* appealed primarily to (or was, at least, watched by) children and older women—not exactly heavy smokers. Klein felt that Philip Morris could do better sponsoring a lower-rated show, *Medic*, which, though viewed by fewer people, reached an audience that was much more likely to buy cigarettes. This was a revolutionary idea, one whose time was slow in coming.

Toward the close of the 1960s, CBS was at the top of the ratings. The network had several big hits, but lagged behind NBC in attracting urban viewers. Advertisers began to turn to NBC in order to reach the highly-valued urban audience. CBS, in response to lost advertising revenue, turned around and dropped many of its top shows. Between 1968 and 1970 it jettisoned *The Beverly Hillbillies* (rated 18th at the time), *Gomer Pyle, USMC* (the second highest rated show in the country), *Green Acres* (19th), *Mayberry R.F.D.* (4th), and *Family Affair* (12th). Other popular shows also removed from its schedule were *Hee Haw, Petticoat Junction, The Red Skelton Hour* and *The Jackie Gleason Show*. The failing of these programs: they appealed primarily to a non-urban audience and, what's more, to children and "over-50s."

Advertising rates, then, are set according to the size of a program's audience, but also by the *perceived quality of that audience* based upon demographic characteristics. Top rates are charged for programs appealing to people between the ages of 18 and 34 who are prime buyers of kitchen and cosmetic products as well as automobiles and over-the-counter drugs—all products that are heavily advertised on television. After this group, rates drop. The next most valuable commodity a show can deliver is an audience between the ages of 18 and 49, typically comprising young, often upwardly-mobile families. The lowest rates are charged for time on programs appealing to young children and those over 50 years of age. High and low rates are relative terms; just because commercial time on children's television costs less than a popular prime-time sitcom doesn't mean it is cheap to purchase. Buying time on television is nearly always an expensive enterprise; but it is "worth it" when you consider how many people the advertising message can potentially reach.

Keep in mind that advertising rates based on demographics will change as buying patterns change. Whatever age-group does the most buying at any given point in time will command the highest rates.

Why Take Risks?

Dependence on the ratings in determining which programs remain on the air, and even more, the use of demographics in setting advertising rates, have profound effects on the content of television programming. The surest way to make a profit in broadcasting is to produce and air programs with proven capacity to attract the most desirable audience, thus guaranteeing the highest possible advertising rates. Why air a program which will appeal to the elderly when advertisers pay so little for that audience? The same air time, devoted to a show appealing to young people, brings in many more dollars. Everyone in television realizes this, as do all the advertisers and all the producers, and this knowledge leads to startling conservatism. The amount of money spent on program production and on star salaries and on syndication deals may seem anything but conservative, but as we saw in the last chapter, these vast sums of money are spent to assure even greater income down the line.

The Audience—Up Close and Personal

We have spent a great deal of time talking about the audience. When we discuss the ratings and demographics, when we talk about virtually every aspect of the television business, we end up talking about the audience somewhere along the way. The entire broadcasting structure is set up to deliver programs to audiences . . . and audiences to advertisers. We would, then, do well to look a bit more closely at the television audience.

How we view the position, role, and power of the television audience is of vital concern as we think about television programming. Different conceptions of the audience inevitably lead to different conclusions about television. Some critics view the audience as essentially passive, as accepting whatever programs broadcasters see fit to provide. Taking this perspective, we see the audience as giving little thought to the information, the messages, inherent in these programs. Other critics see the audience as taking a more active role both in determining program content (through the indirect feedback mechanism of the ratings) and in negotiating the information (meaning) offered by those programs. In this formulation, viewers somehow use the information they glean from television programming to assist in understanding and functioning in the everyday world.

On one level, the adherents of these two positions (and those whose fall somewhere between these two extremes) are asking: Do we get what we want from television or are we content to take what we can get? On a still more fundamental level, however, the question becomes more intriguing: We must ask who is the true consumer of television? Is the audience the consumer of television's product (and therefore the most powerful and central element in the production process)? Is the viewer the person everyone in the television business really has to please, or is the true consumer of television to be found somewhere else? And if we determine that the audience isn't the ultimate consumer of television, just who is? And what implications does this discovery have for critics and viewers? If the producers and telecasters aren't out to please the public at large, just who are they out to please?

Predictably enough, the television industry, at all levels—from producer, to network, to affiliate station, to independent, to cable channel—argues that the audience is central to any and all programming decisions. In other words, they say, we get what we want—no more, no less. We vote with our channel changers. The audience, they say, is television's prime con-sumer and ultimate judge. Thus, when confronted with the oft-expressed opinion that television programs are less interesting, less worthwhile, or less stimulating than works produced in other media, the industry's response is predictable: We can't buck public opinion; we've got to give the public what it wants. In other words, if television programs are perceived by the public as bad, that public has no one to blame but itself. The broadcasters determine the wishes and needs of viewers through the ratings. If a viewer doesn't like a program, he or she need not watch it. The simple act of turning a program off (or not watching it to begin with) is acknowledged in the program's overall rating or its share of the viewing audience and, if enough people vote "NO" on a program it goes off the air (and, in all likelihood, so will other programs similar to it).

For adherents to this model, the quality of television programming may be irrelevant. At the very least, it isn't the responsibility of the programmers or production companies, since the viewer—the ultimate consumer of television programming—selects (in the same direct way as in any other business) what sorts of products he or she wants. This, in turn, determines the product types (or, in narrative terms, the genres) offered in the future.

In the case of network television, this model of programming is based on a classic American business model. It proposes that the "production-through-consumption" process is a never-ending, circular cycle, with the consumer (in this case, the viewer) holding the single most important position.

AMERICAN BUSINESS MODEL

PRODUCER
creates a

PRODUCT
that is disseminated by a

DISTRIBUTOR
to outlets called

RETAILERS
that get the product to the

CONSUMERS
who respond to the product by way of

FEEDBACK
to the

PRODUCER

The model works reasonably well with products like soap, cereal, and automobiles. With these products, the purchaser buys the product and consumes it or makes direct, obvious, use of it. There is no question about what the product is or who the consumer is (since the consumption process is literal). The person who buys a bar of soap and washes with it is clearly the consumer of that bar of soap; the person who purchases a box of cereal, eats that cereal.

The purchase of a product is registered with the producer in the form of direct income—the purchase of a bar of soap results in a precise and invariable amount of money for that producer. The number of purchases is tallied. This determines the viability of the product. If enough people buy soap (or cereal or cars), the product producer stays in business and, in all likelihood, competitive manufacturers offer similar products based on the success of the original.

Applying this model to television (as the industry itself and some critics do), the process seems just as straightforward. A program is aired; its popularity with the audience is gauged; it succeeds or fails on the basis of its popularity. If a particular program or format seems to show up again and again—think of all the nearly interchangeable *Star Trek* rip-offs or soap operas you've seen—this is a direct indication of the wants and needs of the audience. It doesn't mean program producers and network executives lack creativity. The network executives can sit back and relax, secure in the knowledge that they're giving the public what it wants. Critics, taking this idea a step further, can try to make sense of what it is the public seems to want, as reflected in television programming.

AMERICAN BUSINESS MODEL
(FOR CONSUMER PRODUCTS)

PRODUCER — PROCTER & GAMBLE
creates a

PRODUCT — ZEST SOAP
that is disseminated by a

DISTRIBUTOR — ACME DISTRIBUTING
to outlets called

RETAILERS — SAFEWAY STORES
that get the product to the

CONSUMERS — US
who respond to the product by way of

FEEDBACK — MONEY PAID FOR ZEST
to the

PRODUCER — PROCTER & GAMBLE

AMERICAN TELEVISION BUSINESS MODEL

PRODUCER — TELEVISION PRODUCTION COMPANY
creates a

PRODUCT — TV PROGRAM
that is disseminated by a

DISTRIBUTOR — NETWORKS
to outlets called

RETAILERS — AFFILIATES
that get the product to the

CONSUMERS — US, THE AUDIENCE
who respond to the product by way of

FEEDBACK — THE RATINGS
to the

PRODUCER — TELEVISION PRODUCTION COMPANY

What Does This Have to do With Criticism?

The television audience is almost unimaginably large and more diverse than one might think. Speaking of "an" audience or "the" audience is only superficially accurate. On a typical night, more than 100 million people are apt to be watching television. That amounts to nearly one half the population of the United States. This audience is comprised of people from all walks of life, from all racial and ethnic groups, all age groups, all levels of education. Given the size and diversity of "the" television audience, many critics feel secure in discussing television programming as a reflection of cultural concern (albeit something of a funhouse mirror reflection) and as a forum for the airing of cultural issues—a safe place to air unresolved issues and dirty cultural laundry.

A belief that television programming decisions are made with the audience's desires uppermost in the minds of executives (and with, at the very least, strong indirect input from the audience itself) provides the basis for this approach to television. If millions of people of all ages, races, genders and education- levels choose to watch a particular program, then we can assume that that program's particular view (or views) of society, of social structures, of personal and professional relationships, represents a particularly potent expression of broad cultural attitude.

From this perspective, television texts, for all their apparent realism, should be read less literally and more *symbolically*. We don't accept Greek myths as literal statements of fact, but as symbolic restructurings of real-world concerns. Just like Greek myths, television (despite its undeniable, uncanny resemblance to reality as we experience it day to day) can be "read" as a symbolic recreation of the real world; television programs can be examined for what they have to say about us as a people.

Television programs are both reflections of and reflections on the culture in which they are produced and of which they are a part.

Culture is an on-going process; it's not conscious or premeditated or planned. But somehow we, all of us, reach unspoken agreements on virtually every aspect of our lives—the fact that we don't belch in public and that we stop at red lights; the fact that we wear nice clothes to job interviews and raise our hands before speaking in class. These are all cultural "decisions." We don't learn them in school; we absorb them through experiencing the real world, through living, through reading and, yes, through watching television. Television, as the most pervasive of the mass media, speaks to the greatest number of us. It can then be seen as the most accurate reflector not of reality, but of our constantly shifting, culturally determined negotiation of reality.

In the stories we, as a culture, tell ourselves (and in this view of television we, the audience, determine which stories are told) we can see the ebb and flow of ideas; we can see accepted beliefs and unacceptable ones in conflict. We can see the limits of acceptable behavior stretched and defined. We can see American Culture, in a sense, talking to itself, asking, "What do you believe? Are you ready for this yet? Is this belief still valid?" We can see all these things if (and it's a big if) we accept the premise that the audience is the central consideration in programming decisions.

Taking this view, the audience is the consumer of television and the determiner of television content. Individual programs may best be seen as the end-result of a process of "cultural creation" and less the product of an individual creator like a David Lynch, Norman Lear or Grant Tinker, or the expression of a particular broadcast executive's taste. A vast cross-section of the American people, in "casting their vote" for a particular distortion of their real world experience, tells the programmer (and the critic) it wants more of the same.

This is clearly a view with a certain amount of validity, and we would be wise to bear it in mind when we begin to evaluate television programming. But this idea is not without its problems and opponents. Some critics see the audience not as consumers of television programming, but as the product of television—a product to be delivered to advertisers. Advertisers, then, are viewed as the true consumers in the revised model below.

It's common knowledge that television is a commercial medium, supported by advertising revenues. For many critics, this immediately and radically alters the production process. Who is the "purchaser" or "consumer" of television programming? Clearly, in at least one sense, it isn't the viewer. The audience is provided with programming (apparently) without cost. It is the advertiser who, in this view, constitutes the sole source of revenue for the broadcasters and, therefore, for program producers. The advertiser is, then, the only "audience" that really needs to be satisfied.

And how may advertisers be satisfied? Simply by delivering the largest possible audience and/or the right demographic profile. A. Frank Reel, author of *The Networks: How They Stole the Show*, wrote:

> The advertiser on television wants us to buy his deodorant or detergent or automobile; that is, he hopes we will enter into a financial transaction with him in the future. But before we receive his message, a number of purchases have already occurred. The key one involved that same advertiser's paying thousands or hundreds of thousands of dollars in order to get the advertisement to us. Looking at that financial transaction, it becomes obvious that we, the television audience, are the commodity that is sold, the product that is bartered. We are examined, analyzed, and dissected—squeezed like the toilet paper, weighed like the steak, tested like the laundry soap (1979, p. 4).

This situation has profound implications for the critic (as well as for broadcasters at all levels). In this formulation, programs are not the product of television but rather they are "the machines" that manufacture the industry's *real* product: Audiences. Therefore, the successful program is not the one which is original, ground-breaking, or aesthetically daring; the successful program is the one which "manufactures" the most people by whatever means possible. If aesthetic or cultural audacity brings in viewers, that's all well and good; if not, turn up the violence and sex to keep viewers glued to the screen.

AMERICAN TELEVISION BUSINESS MODEL
(AN ALTERNATIVE VIEW)

PRODUCER — THE NETWORK
buys or produces television programs which "manufacture" the

PRODUCT — US, THE AUDIENCE
that is sold to the

CONSUMERS — ADVERTISERS
who respond to the product (audience) by way of

FEEDBACK — THE ADVERTISING DOLLARS PAID
to the

PRODUCER — THE NETWORK

In this view of the audience-programming relationship, programs are viewed less as reflections of cultural concerns, and more as a risk-free means of insuring that a particular product (the audience) will be delivered to the consumer (the advertiser) in as efficient and inexpensive a manner as possible. Why bother being imaginative and creative, both of which imply a certain amount of risk, when an old formula, spruced up a bit, will attract the same audience?

Adherents to this model go further than simply denying the possibility that the audience is the determiner of television program content. They even deny the democratic nature of the medium. The ratings may register "votes," and may be a factor in programming decisions, but in the world of television, all votes don't carry equal weight. The television audience, at least that portion of the audience that counts in the business of television, is seen as a very distinct group, rather than the cultural cross-section of our earlier discussion. Any demographic group whose members cannot be counted on to purchase enough of an advertiser's goods, or whose members cannot be assembled in large enough numbers, are effectively disenfranchised. They may (and in fact do) watch television programs, but their "vote," their voice in the ratings, is of little importance. Programs are designed to meet the needs (or at least the desires) of those members of our culture who fit the advertisers'—the consumers'—demographic needs. The 1992 NBC cancellation of *In the Heat of the Night* is a case in point. Highly rated, it was the 29th most popular series for the entire year, the Peacock Network dropped it from its schedule, according to its own executives, because they were trying to air programs "that appeal to the younger audiences preferred by advertisers" (O'Connor has . . . , 1992, p. 4A). The award winning program was quickly picked up by CBS.

Les Brown (1979, pp. 24–25) asserts that broadcasters' claim (echoed by some critics) that they are at the mercy of public wishes stems from an inability to differentiate between the culture at large and that portion of the general public that most interests advertisers:

> *Broadcasters have displayed a tendency to use the terms "audience" and "public" interchangeably, as though they were synonymous. This bit of flawed semantics has fathered the industry's claim that television is a cultural democracy, a medium in which programs succeed or fail by the public vote (the "vote" being expressed, however, in audience ratings). It has also created a confusion in the broadcaster's mind about the meaning of "public interest." A great many broadcasters are satisfied to define the public interest as "what the public is interested in."*

Television, in this view, is democratic only to a point. The right to "vote" is extended to all, but only the votes of a select few are counted.

A critic who accepts this model of the television production through consumption process would, quite naturally, attribute the apparent lack of variety or quality in television programming to the broadcasters. Such a critic might be inclined to see television as an uncreative, repetitive, and unimaginative medium. This critic might also be inclined to view the medium as inherently manipulative, in that program producers and television executives will do whatever is necessary to deliver viewers to advertiser (even present empty symbols and false myths).

If, in fact, television has any effect on viewers (and though specific effects may be debated, the basic notion that television is an effective medium should no longer be in doubt), the concerned critic who adopts this model must hold the broadcasters—who are accountable to advertisers, rather than viewers—responsible.

And again, someone who subscribes to our first model—one who feels, in other words, that the public is the final arbiter of the content of television programming—would, almost without questions, come to different conclusions about the television industry and about the medium in general. Placing responsibility for program content on the shoulders of the viewing audience removes responsibility from the broadcasters, program producers, and advertisers. If, then, television affects us in significant ways—inuring us to violence or making us more likely to use violence in solving problems, encouraging the use of alcohol, smoking, or promiscuous sex—we, the viewers, are to blame.

If television's effects, whatever they may be, are in any way a result of our own choices, then an examination of the choices we make is imperative. But if our choices are restricted or limited by the broadcasters' advertiser-demanded and ratings-driven choices, can we honestly argue that the viewers' tastes and interests are paramount? But does it matter at all who the ultimate arbiter of available content really is? Either way, the audience, as a whole, watches the same finite set of programs, the equivalent of our nation's literature. But now the question resurfaces. Whose myths fill that literature? But individual audience members read or interact with these shows in more-or-less idiosyncratic ways, making meaning and pleasures for themselves. So don't they create their own understandings, regardless of whose myths are told and retold in television's stories?

So, here we are again, television critics with more questions than answers. The next chapter will help, not by offering the correct answers, but by presenting a variety of approaches or frameworks that can assist each of us in developing her or his own critical stance. This won't reduce the number of questions (in fact, it should have just the opposite effect), but it will move us toward the kind of answers that make for good television criticism.

Chapter Exercise

Defining the Audience

On the continuum provided here place a mark at the spot that you think best represents the audience's true role in the American television system. Defend your response. Can you speculate on what happens to the quality of programming as your mark moves either to the right or the left?

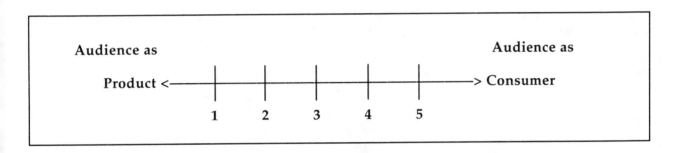

Reference and Resources

Adams, W. J. (1993). TV program scheduling strategies and their relationship to new program renewal rates and rating changes. *Journal of Broadcasting & Electronic Media, 37,* 465-489.

Arbitron discontinues syndicated television & cable ratings service. (1993). Press release, October 18.

Barry, D. (1990). It's Howdy Duty time. *West Magazine,* March 18, p. 23.

Brown, L. (1982). Are the networks dinosaurs? *Channels,* June/July, pp. 26–29.

Brown, L. (1979). *Keeping Your Eye on Television.* New York: Pilgrim Press.

Brown, L. (1971). *Television: The Business Behind the Box.* New York: Harcourt Brace Jovanovich.

Coe, S. (1991). Networks limit risk for reward of season win. *Broadcasting,* June 3, p. 35.

Coe, S. (1991). Quality TV: Hollywood's elusive illusions. *Broadcasting,* November 18, p. 3.

Essline, M. (1982). *The Age of Television.* San Francisco, CA: W.H. Freeman and Company.

O'Connor has words for NBC. (1992). San Jose *Mercury News,* July 4, p. 4A.

Reel, A. F. (1979). *The Networks: How They Stole the Show.* New York: Charles Scribner's.

CHAPTER 5

WRITING TELEVISION CRITICISM

No one can become a functioning critic overnight; and those who try . . .
generally embarrass all concerned by educating themselves in public.
In general, fly-by-night critics tend to have no real purpose, which means
not only no credo but also no consistency of either interest or opinion.

—Richard Kostelanetz

Noted art critic Kostelanetz (1967, p. 17) makes it clear that learning to become a good critic is not necessarily an easy task. Literary critic Mary Pratt agrees (1981, p. 187), arguing that the critic of popular culture has relatively few traditions on which to depend: "The concepts of mass art and mass culture oversimplify . . . a highly complex range of cultural activities about which we know very little, in comparison with the knowledge and understanding we have achieved of elite art."

Both observations have important implications for those who would write television criticism. They not only warn us of the risks of this enterprise, but they offer the promise of a good challenge. What appears to be a rather simple, accessible text and what most people know as an everyday, in-the-home medium may together pose a rich field of inquiry for those of us who attempt to analyze and understand them.

Overview

In Chapter 2 we introduced some of the difficulties faced by the television critic, for example the traditional lack of serious attention paid to television, an ill-defined text, multiple texts, and questions of authorship. In this chapter we will discuss the various forms of both academic and journalistic criticism that can overcome these (apparent) problems. We will then demonstrate how to write different types of television criticism, taking into consideration the nature of the audience and text.

Types of Television Criticism: Journalistic

As we saw in Chapter 1, journalistic (or popular) television criticism typically takes one of two forms: consumer-oriented reviews and social critiques. We saw, too, that many critics believe that reviews, if they are to have any real value to the reader, should include at least some social critique. This is obviously the case in television criticism as can be seen in these *aspects of journalistic criticism* offered by Cohen (in Watson, 1985, p. 67):

1. **Evaluation,** judgments of program quality. She said, "People have many reasons for seeking out a critic's opinion of a work's worth—perhaps chief among them is the question, 'Is it worth investing one's time and/or money to see or hear it?'"

2. **Reporting,** detailing the nature of the program(s) "in a thoughtful, well informed manner. The critic is in the unique position of being able to let a large number of people know what something is about, that is, not whether they've missed something good, but what the work was . . . its style, means of expression, story, manner of presentation." The reporting function of the television critic does not mean, however, that he or she should *be* a reporter. New York *Times* critic John J. O'Connor explains, "There's the possibility of an inherent conflict of interest between the two functions. Not only that you might play one off against the other, the critic and reporter saying . . . you give me an exclusive and I'll review your program . . . But a reporter has to deal differently with the industry. A reporter has to cultivate contacts, do a lot of socializing . . . and meet people on a different level than a critic. . . . I try to stay as independent as possible" (in Himmelstein, 1981, p. 60).

3. **Attention-caller,** making both regular and less frequent viewers know about programs they otherwise might miss or ignore. Or, as *Time* magazine media critic William Henry III explained, "One of the things the critics may be able to do, simply because they're paid to sit and think all day, is recognize some of this quality maybe a bit sooner and help guide the public to shows while they're there [on television]" (in Watson, 1985, p. 73).

4. **Documentation,** a critic's writing forms a record of the history of television. This function has not necessarily changed with the advent of VCR. Cohn explains, "The first performance of the Beatles on Ed Sullivan can easily be retrieved from a video library, but only criticism from that time can construct what the event meant to its viewers."

5. **Illumination,** because beyond the critic's judgment, "the analysis contained in a review may offer readers insights into the nature of the work being discussed . . . its cultural or political relevance, its connections to other works of the same or similar ilk, and so on." Long-time television writer Bernie Harrison, suggests two more aspects of journalistic criticism (in Himmelstein, 1981):

6. **Education,** because the viewing public's knowledge of the economic, business and policy/regulatory aspects of television most typically comes from the popular, rather than academic or industry, press.

7. **Entertainment,** to offer writing that is, in and of itself, a pleasure for the reader.

Montgomery (1985, p. 78) adds an eighth and final aspect:

8. **Watch dog.** She writes, "Those who write about television in the popular press can raise questions about the nature of the television medium, its institutional processes, its political and social impact, the meaning of its programming, and the degree of its power. Television critics have the power to turn the public into more critical viewers, and to encourage more active participation on policy issues. They can, from time to time, influence changes within the industry."

These aspects of journalistic criticism harken back to the five roles of the critic forwarded in Chapter 1. The teacher/interpreter would no doubt provide education and engage in the task of reporting and calling attention to specific television content. An analyst would illuminate "insights into the nature of the work being discussed." A guide or judge would evaluate program quality. An historian or recorder would present documentation or a record. And a catalyst for reflection might serve a watchdog function by raising questions for consideration.

The one aspect of journalistic criticism presented here but not in Chapter 1 as a role for the critic is that of providing entertainment. In fact, entertainment is one of the most obvious elements that separates journalistic criticism from academic criticism. This is not to say that academic criticism *can't* be entertaining to read. But entertainment isn't one of its primary purposes. Journalistic criticism, on the other hand, is more of a mass media, commercial enterprise in that it is typically located in periodicals that are consumed by the general public. One of the key goals of this type of writing is to be accessible to as many people as possible. In order to *appeal* to the public it helps to be entertaining while you communicate your critical message.

But what is the critical message? And how do you go about communicating your critique effectively? Just because you might have an opinion about or interpretation of a television program does not make you a critic. Lawrence Rosenfield writes,

Simple capacity *to render commentary is not yet criticism. The expert-spectator who relishes the events he observes but does not relate his appreciation to others is not a critic, for "criticism" normally refers to the critic's verbal commentary on the event. Criticism is therefore the special variety of discourse which results when a person who has adopted a critical posture makes assertions, i.e., statements by an expert about "the way things are" (1968 p. 32).*

If we define *discourse* as the communication of ideas and information or the formal treatment of a subject in speech or writing, how can you tell the difference between critical discourse and other, more general discourse?

Originally, formal criticism emerged during the Romantic period as a way to evaluate literary works and illuminate readers about possible author intentions and hidden meanings. The goal was to help consumers appreciate or appropriately respond to the works—to define and develop "good taste." After the turn of the 20th Century, the thrust of criticism changed from "elaboration" to expressions of the "genius" of the authors, as critics remained true to the idea that elite or high art was the only form of expression worthy of serious investigation. This orientation was followed into the 1950s by a different approach, one which shifted the primary focus from the authors to the texts themselves. Largely as a result of the coming of television, mass communication studies became less interested in *expression*. Instead, the inquiry was typically scientific evaluation of messages as agents of *persuasion* or effects, as the transmissional model of communication (see Chapter 2) dominated.

As we've already seen, television critics had a very difficult time conducting their work because many people thought the medium wasn't worthy of critical consideration. As Richard Stonesifer writes,

I decided that I have little sympathy for those of my critical colleagues who think that probing studies of such things as broadside ballads or the "realism" of Daniel Defoe constitute proper concerns for the literary analyst, but who are inclined to snort in derision at the idea that television merits any critical concern. . . . I have some logical difficulty in separating the antics of a country booby in an 18th-century play and the farce of The Beverly Hillbillies, *in elevating the one as an object worthy of a student's attention (perhaps largely because of its antiquity) and in condemning the other wholly as prefabricated trash cooked up for something called the tasteless Mass Man of our own time, and so beneath notice. . . . And the evidence simply cannot be shrugged aside that, speaking broadly, popular culture since 1900 has been a slowly maturing culture. Or that the best of what appears in the mass media constitutes something of a new art form, falling between what is usually called "folk" and "high" culture and thus helping to form a desirable continuum between them (1971, pp. 208–209).*

As television became more and more embedded in the fabric of our culture, it became increasingly apparent that, as valuable as it was in helping us understand television's effects, the prevailing criticism—quantitative, empirical and "objective"—left many, many questions about people's relationship to the medium unanswered. As Allen wrote,

> *What scientific law explains the curious relationship we have with fictional television programs, for example? We know that the characters and situations presented to us are not "real," that a character that "dies" on a soap opera is played by an actor that will go home at the end of the day and have dinner just like always. And yet those characters and situations are endowed with sufficient "real-seemingness" that they can move us to anger or to tears . . . What will the observable behavior of viewers or their responses to a survey questionnaire tell us about our willingness to "suspend our disbelief" every time we enter the narrative worlds of Dallas or General Hospital? (1987, p. 11).*

Therefore, contemporary criticism treats television as very worthy of serious attention. It sees the text—whether industry, strip, series, genre, or individual program—not as something that does something to the audience, but as something with which the audience interacts. In other words, the audience member is now increasingly central to modern criticism.

The point of presenting this brief historical look at the various "critical postures" that have been assumed over the years is to make you understand that at the most basic level, criticism always has been and still is simply *an assertion that is supported by arguments.* This is what separates criticism from other forms of discourse. Not only do critics provide information about a subject, they take their analysis one step further by making some sort of evaluation, interpretation or judgement *about* that information. What separates critical dis-

course from simple opinion is that the critic is an expert supporting his or her assertions by formulating arguments based upon accumulated evidence or data. And as you will see, these assertions and arguments come in many different forms.

Writing Journalistic Television Criticism

Due to the demands of documentation and proof (see Chapter 2), written academic television criticism tends to follow a relatively strict format. However, there is much variation in the style and content of popular television criticism because these writers cover a number of medium-related issues and are read by a wide variety of audiences who consume a tremendously broad range of publications. Still, there are general guidelines that can be used to structure this work. Of course, individual imagination and creativity (not to mention the text under consideration) can take the popular critic beyond this format as you'll see in the examples of journalistic criticism (written by both professionals and students) that follow the next several chapters. As you begin to follow the format outline, you should keep in mind these overall basic writing tips:

1. **Present a clear, well-defined question or issue.** Make your reader want to continue.

2. **Organize your presentation as an argument.** This will provide your criticism with shape or form. This will also maintain the piece as a subjective interpretation based upon evidence (which characterizes criticism) rather than an assertion of fact which characterizes journalistic reporting.

3. **Polish for style and effect: re-read to challenge your own logic; test your own assumptions.**

4. **Proofread!** One of the easiest ways to lose the confidence of your reader is sloppy writing. It gets in the way of otherwise good communication.

GENERAL FORMAT FOR JOURNALISTIC TELEVISION CRITICISM

I.   **Introduction**

    A.   Call or grab attention

    B.   Provide necessary background information

    C.   Introduce your critical question

    D.   Sketch, review or describe the text (if it is content)
         Characterize or describe the text (if it is an issue)

II.   **Thesis**

What is your judgment or evaluation of the text (content);
What is your conclusion (issue)?

III.   **Argument—the body of your paper**

    A.   Premise
         What standards of judgment or evaluation are you applying?

    B.   Evidence
         Your offering of elements in and related to the text (content) that sup-
         port your position; can be descriptions of scenes, dialogue, plot, etc.;
         your offering of data (issue) that support your position; can be statistics,
         facts, quotes, quotations

    C.   Intermediate Judgment
         Your restatement of your thesis now that you have moved your reader
         toward your conclusion; subordinate conclusions that lead logically to
         your . . .

IV.   **Final or formal conclusion**
       This can be a restatement or summary

Types of Television Criticism: Academic

Himmelstein argued that,

The academic critic has a major advantage over the journalist in that he does not have to participate in the producer-consumer relationship that day-to-day affects the contemporary world of art salesmanship. However, this distancing factor may sometimes prove a hindrance, for this critic's writing may become anachronistic by ignoring contemporary reassessments of traditional evaluations of art works (1981, p. 23).

The academic critic must also face the challenge of strict demands of evidence; proof or documentation; a relatively rigid format; and an often-time antagonistic audience of peers. The variations in style and content for journalistic criticism are typically the result of the text under consideration, the publication where it is published and the audience for which it is written. The variations in style and content for academic criticism result more from the *different aspects of our personal relationship or our culture's relationship with television.* In other words, given the text and question under consideration, *a specific critical approach* provides the framework for the analysis. Allen (1987) identifies several forms of what he calls "contemporary criticism," as do Vande Berg and Wenner (1991). Taken together and allowing for different labels for similar types we've combined their lists and offer 11 critical approaches: semiotics, narrative analysis, genre criticism, reader-oriented criticism, ideological analysis, gender criticism, auteur criticism, historical criticism, sociological criticism, rhetorical criticism, and dialogic criticism. These approaches share several assumptions:

1. Television is a, if not the central medium of our culture.

2. Television is not a mere sender of information (the transmissional perspective), but rather is a medium whose complex texts are among the primary, if not the primary means through which we experience and know the world.

3. Television is not a "mirror" on the world, but rather constructs, with its viewers, its own picture or *representation* of things in that world through the operation of its own rules, aesthetics and conventions.

4. To know our world, we must understand these rules, aesthetics and conventions.

In order to help focus criticism (or combinations of criticism) in terms of what should be studied and how that analysis should unfold, different critics organize the many forms of contemporary academic television criticism into different overarching, metacritical categories. Though disagreeing at times, Vande Berg and Wenner (1991), Newcomb (1986), and Gronbeck (1984) offer useful divisions such as hermeneutics, cultural studies, structuralism and semiotics to "umbrella" specific types of criticism.

Cultural Studies (sometimes referred to as British cultural studies because that is where it was developed) is a division used to describe critical approaches (or combination of approaches) concerned with identifying components of television that create, recreate, reflect, distort or contribute to the culture. This categorization clearly reflects the ritual model of mass communication discussed in Chapter 2.

The **Hermeneutic** metacritical approach is more concerned with interpretive criticism which focuses on the structures and processes that television uses to disseminate particular meanings *to* society and how those meanings can possibly be interpreted *by* society. Typically television (as a medium) or television programming (as a whole) is the object of critical concern (the critical text) rather than concentrating on specific episodes or programs that seemingly can't function outside the overall television context.

Two additional metacritical approaches called *Structuralism* and its sibling *Semiotics* are concerned with how meanings are put together (or *structured*) in television texts through the use of signs and sign systems (the study of signs is called *semiotics*). The goal is to identify signs and analyze their connection to the object or concept they represent, then provide an explanation of the political, social or cultural ramifications of such representations.

These metacritical approaches provide descriptive tools and theories of communication that can be used by virtually any critic (using any approach) to identify meanings that support his or her critical argument. Again, there is some disagreement between critics as to which specific approaches should be placed under which "umbrella" metacritical category because deciding what should be emphasized and how to proceed with analysis can be a very subjective choice. But for our purposes, we will list and define, free from categorization, the types of academic criticism most commonly practiced and offer an example of a question that might be asked in each. Keep in mind that our list is not an exhaustive one; there are other critical approaches and some of them are made from combining two or more.

Auteur Criticism, a source-based critical method, examines the style, conventions, philosophies, and/or ideologies of a single television creator (most often a producer or director but sometimes a writer as well) across a number of texts for the purpose of better understanding this artist and his or her relationship to the medium, to the audience or to the culture. Basically, the critic using the auteur approach searches for an affinity between the texts that concretely bonds them with their maker. It could be the composition of shots including lighting, color, movement, editing, sound, or timing. And similarities could also exist in story lines, dialogue, characterization, or themes. But recognizing these commonalities is only the first step of the analysis: remember that criticism is an assertion. Therefore, critics must provide an interpretation of the meaning or a value judgement of the artist's stylistic contribution.

Question: How do the politics of Bill Cosby shape *The Cosby Show* and *Fat Albert and the Cosby Kids*?

Ideological Analysis examines television as a forum or arena where various elites and publics compete for power and influence to better understand how the culture arrives at its interpretations of itself. Ideological criticism is rooted in neo-Marxist theories of culture. These are based on Karl Marx's idea that elites dominate common people through their ownership of the means of production (the base) and their control of culture (the superstructure). Ideological analysis, then, examines the ways in which a cultural artifact—like television—creates certain types of knowledge, power and positions for viewers. The critic's job, then, is to identify the interests of the dominant ideology that are being presented (or perpetuated) by television or to identify other ideologies that are being subordinated by the dominant/ruling ideology. The dominant ideology may manifest itself as a political agenda, a position on a controversial issue, or even a philosophical perspective. The term *hegemony* has been used to describe the process by which the dominant class controls society by presenting its own dominant interests as "the best," "most normal or natural," and "most acceptable." Ideological conflict is seen as a struggle for hegemony—that is, which ideas will be seen as the prevailing, common-sense view.

Question: Why did television news label the turmoil in South Central Los Angeles a riot rather than a rebellion after the Simi Valley jury acquitted the policemen who beat Rodney King?

Gender Criticism is a specific kind of ideological criticism because it examines the representation of gender in television programming to shed light on our culture's construction of what it is to be women or men. This approach isn't concerned with biological differences but rather focuses on the social construction of gender in terms of defined "appropriate" behaviors, physical attributes and societal roles. Once gender portrayals have been identified, the critic should interpret them to provide insight into the cultural ramifications of those representations. The critic tries to unravel the gender power hierarchy to reveal any subordination or oppression as well as to debunk prevailing unequal or unfair circumstances which are being presented as "normal," "natural" or "the way things should be." *Feminist criticism* is the most common type of gender criticism; it works to illuminate the defining and positioning of women within the dominant patriarchal order.

Question: Are women presented as subordinate to men in television commercials?

Dialogic Criticism examines the "conversation" or dialogue between the different ideological and value systems presented in a text as personified by the television characters' looks, words and deeds—especially in terms of interaction with other characters. In this way, the critic provides insight into the culture's various or competing sets of values in and of themselves and in terms of one another.

Question: What ideological viewpoints of race relations are personified in the Lt. Fancy and Detective Sipowicz characters on *NYPD Blue*? How does Fancy's position evolve after he hears Sipowicz use the "N–word?"

Genre Study examines categories or genres of television content to better identify and understand their particular structural and convention similarities. For example, westerns can be identified by their recurring style, form and plot lines such as: set in southwestern U.S. in the 1800s, cowboys, Indians (Native Americans), horses, covered wagons, saloons, posses, good guys wear white hats and always win the gunfights and the women's hearts, bad guys wear black hats and usually die, riding off into the sunset at the end, etc.

Question: Is *Space: Above and Beyond* an advance of the western genre? Is it a

step backward; or are its generic conventions a parody of the form?

Historical Criticism examines, analyzes and/or describes television texts in their historical contexts to better understand those texts and times. The critic's task, then, is to be the time machine that transports the reader back to the time and circumstances in which the text was produced by providing additional historical background and description. Thus, readers can interpret the text based on their own experience *and* they can interpret the text from an alternate experience of a different time.

Question: What factors in American society in the late Seventies and early Eighties fueled the proliferation of humiliation game shows like *The Gong Show* and *The Cheap Show*?

Narrative Analysis examines television as our primary storyteller to better understand the culture's values and beliefs as articulated in the organization, plots, characters (heros and villains) and conventions of its content. The narrative (or story-telling) device is used constantly by television, most obviously in program formats such as soap operas and sit-coms. However, narratives can also be found in less obvious formats such as news, game shows and music television. For example, when it is time to cover the Olympic Games, news coverage could present the events, report the scores and declare the winners. However, the Olympics are transformed into a story by including background or personal profiles of participants, the history of their athletic careers, the politics of their native countries, etc. These types of information are used to create a story line complete with the narrative components of plot, characters and conventions. This changes the coverage from simple, straightforward information to "dramatic portraits of the struggles of competition."

The critic using this perspective must identify the narrative components found in the text and then draw conclusions about why these stories are being told and what connections and meanings they share with our culture which consumes them. These narrative components can be found in various forms such as characters (heroes and villains and their motivations); the plot (what happens); the story line (how it happens); the scene (where it happens); character motivations (why it happens); and even production conventions that move the story along (the way it happens, i.e., flashbacks, use of a narrator, breaking the "fourth wall" to talk to the audience). Another narrative component that is often used to enhance the story is the adding of "extra" meaning through *intertextuality*—when one text makes an implicit or explicit reference to another.

Question: What different versions of "the American family" are being presented by the Cosbys and the Simpsons?

Reader-Oriented Criticism, an audience-based approach, examines television as a medium and/or as an industry that tells its stories to viewers and is comprehended by those viewers in specific ways. This analysis allows us to better understand the nature of the relationships we forge with television itself and its various texts. It analyzes the meanings and pleasures that individuals and groups of viewers take/make from television. The critic using this approach concentrates on the audience and how it perceives and interacts with the text (what occurs during the process of reading a text) and what this behavior might say about the culture.

Question: Why is the *Beavis and Butt-head* program so popular with teenagers?

Rhetorical Criticism examines television as an essentially persuasive medium to better understand how to maximize that power (presumably for good reasons) or to protect ourselves from it. This is not to say that every decision made in producing television content (what story, what characters, what script, what colors, what lighting, what music, etc.) is consciously contrived to persuade the audience to do something. Rather, rhetorical criticism focuses on what choices were made and the possible ramifications of those choices (intended or not) that might emerge from the presentation of the content. Rhetorical critics probe into: 1) the way in which meanings are presented (through choices) by the producers of content; 2) the potential impact of these meanings when they are received (through interpretation) by the audience; 3) what ramifications these activities might have on our culture.

Question: How does the cartoon series *Batman* distinguish between good and evil and how might these portrayals be perceived by children?

Semiotics examines television content very specifically as a complex system of signs that "stand for" specific meanings. Rather than providing the interpretation of the sign systems presented in the text (through symbols, objects, sound, words, etc.), the critic, in a sense, works backwards to deconstruct *how* meanings are created through the signs or combinations of signs (often referred to as structuralism). This process promotes better understanding of how viewers "read" texts by exposing the way meaning is constructed.

Question: Is *Charlie's Angels* a step forward for women because it presents the Angels as capable of "men's work," or is it the same old subordination of the gender, as the three do the bidding of the faceless, distant Charlie?

Sociological Criticism examines television's representation of the social processes that support our culture (e.g., politics, business, relationships, race). This approach is concerned with exposing these social representations in terms of: 1) how they are defined; 2) how closely they resemble "reality;" 3) where they are positioned in the power hierarchy; 4) how they are presented interacting with other social representations; and finally, 5) what social influence/effects (if any) they will have on television viewers who watch them.

Question: Does television advertising's constant portrayal of product consumption as the means to happiness disrupt important social roles and relationships between people?

It should be apparent from reading even these very brief descriptions that these are not discrete categories of analysis. They are not meant to be. For example, the question about *Charlie's Angels* posed under semiotics might be approached from a gender (feminist) point of view. Or inasmuch as no text can really be separated from the era in which it was created, another critic might choose to take a historical look at the Angels as products of their time, the Seventies. Obviously, the possibilities are countless and in the examples that follow the next several chapters we'll see how some very fine academic critics mix and match their critical perspectives to move us to a fuller understanding of the medium of television. We'll also see that much of the thought behind academic television criticism has made its way into journalistic television criticism. A separate table of contents (found at the beginning of the book) indicates where you can find examples of each critical approach among the essays that follow the next nine chapters.

Writing Academic Television Criticism

As we mentioned before, writing academic criticism requires more formality and adherence to certain generalized rules. This does not mean you cannot be creative in your critical writing. Nor does it mean that you are limited in your freedom to choose a topic, critical approach (or combination of approaches), or personal writing style. Your job is not to persuade readers to your viewpoint nor is it to tell them what their interpretation should be (there aren't many of us who enjoy being told what to think). Simply put, your job is to know enough about your topic to be an informed "expert" (so your readers will trust that your work is worth reading) who is making an argument or assertion about some specific television content.

Regardless of the perspective utilized, academic criticism should be judged on four criteria described by Vande Berg and Wenner (1991, p. 37):

1. **Internal Consistency**—do the thesis, arguments, evidence, and conclusions of the analysis flow logically? It will be a waste of your time (and your reader's time) if your criticism can't be comprehended by anyone but you.

2. **Propriety and Sufficiency of Evidence**—is the supporting evidence of sufficient amount and appropriately applied to move the reader to accept the arguments and conclusions?

3. **Value or Significance**—does the analysis convincingly make clear its cultural, critical, practical or theoretical importance?

4 **Acceptance and Reflection**—does the analysis move the reader to accept, not necessarily the "truth" of the criticism, but at least its reasonableness and plausibility and does it cause the reader to reflect on his or her own values, beliefs and/or interpretations?

Based upon these criteria, the outline should provide some guidance on how to structure your academic critique. Don't feel compelled to follow the exact order; however, at some point, all applicable components should be addressed in your writing in order to make your critique complete.

Stay close to the text. The point is that you are providing an analysis. Avoid going off on tangents that can't be supported by the text. Don't think you must explain every detail of your critical approach; you might overkill and damage your argument. Instead, let the text suggest the parts of the approach that are most applicable or important to your critique. At the same time don't describe the text for the sake of description; make your critique more interesting by interweaving analysis with description. Feel free to use ideas from other

GENERAL FORMAT FOR ACADEMIC TELEVISION CRITICISM

I. **Introduction**

    A.   Introduce your critical question. This is the interpretation or value statement you are making about a specific text.

    B.   Describe the significance of the critique. Give your readers a justification for reading it.

    C.   Introduce your topic and explain why it is important enough to warrant your critical consideration. Give enough information about the television text you've chosen so your readers can understand your analysis even if they have never seen the programs themselves.

    D.   Introduce the critical approach (or combination of approaches) that you will be using and why you decided to use them for this critique.

    E.   Provide a brief literature review. That is, report on other critiques or articles that have been written on your topic and explain what your critique will add to this already existent body of work. What are you saying that hasn't already been said before?

II. **Argument—The body of your paper**

    A.   Premise
        What standards of judgment or evaluation are you applying? Thoroughly explain the critical approach(es) you have chosen and how you will use them to analyze your text.

    B.   Evidence
        Your offering of elements in and related to the text (content) that support your position; can be descriptions of scenes, dialogue, plot, etc.; your offering of data (issues) that support your position; can be statistics, facts, quotes.

    C.   Intermediate judgment
        Your restatement of your thesis now that you have moved your reader toward your conclusion; subordinate conclusions that lead logically to your . . .

IV. **Final or formal conclusion**

    A.   This can be a restatement or summary of your critical evaluation—making the final connection between your value statement, your premise and your evidence/data.

    B.   Include the possible implications of the conclusions you've drawn for:

        1.   the producers of the content
        2.   the content
        3.   the audience consuming the content
        4.   our culture or society
        5.   the critical approach(es) you used

critics to help support your argument. If you do use specific or complex terminology or concepts make sure you explain them thoroughly and/or provide an example. And just as you should do in all of your writing, be sure to: organize your presentation; polish for style and effect; and, proofread for any mistakes.

ARLEN

The Arlen essay offers insight into a gifted critic. Note how he uses his criticism to talk about American morality, war, economics. It's clear that he sees the "catalyst for reflection" role of the critic as most important. Can you find other instances where he attempts to move his reader beyond the issue of television *per se*? This is a learned critic. He infuses his essay with allusions to political science, economics, and physics. Do you think this helps or hurts his criticism? Who do you think is his primary readership?

What is his view of television as "realistic?" Do you share it?

Which television industry defense (of its practices) does Arlen's Moby Dick theory challenge? With whom do you agree? Why?

Can you relate what he had to say about television's performance in covering the Viet Nam War to the medium's success or failure in covering the 1991 Gulf War?

Arlen's overall point in this essay is that critics should write and speak of television "as if it mattered." What does that mean? How can you, as a critic, do this in a readable and meaningful manner?

My approaches to television represent one writer's attempts to get around what seems to be the chief obstacles in the way of writing usefully about contemporary television: that is, how to take the overall subject seriously, when the content of individual programs or performances belies seriousness? How to write about American television as part of American life, without being so practical or professional that one never sees beyond the imperatives of the television

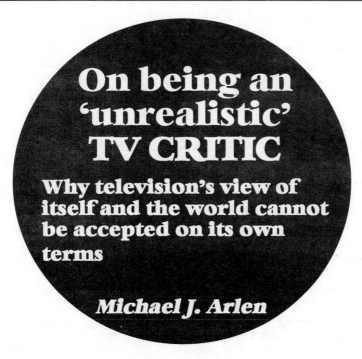

On being an 'unrealistic' TV CRITIC

Why television's view of itself and the world cannot be accepted on its own terms

Michael J. Arlen

industry? This last matter has been the most troublesome, and I note —with no perverse satisfaction at all—that the most frequent comment my essays (especially on the subject of news) have received from people within the television industry has been that they are "unrealistic." I think I understand the comment, though I also think that it is wrong and in a way indicates the nature of the problem that faces not merely critics but viewers. At the source of the disagreement, if one

---

Michael J. Arlen writes about television for *The New Yorker*. This article is excerpted from the introduction to a collection of his writing, The View from Highway 1. Copyright © 1974–1975. 1976 by Michael J. Arlen. By permission of Farrar, Straus & Giroux, Inc.

Reprinted from the *Columbia Journalism Review*, Nov/Dec © 1976.

might call it that, is the supposition—advanced generally by the television industry—that commercial television somehow is a willing, or at least a neutral, servant of the public. Thus, the world view or life view expressed by television is bound to be "realistic," according to conventional notions of reality, or else—as runs an argument which was advanced for many years, until the consumer revolution, by American manufacturers—the public would not accept it; and any challenges to these expressions of so-called conventional reality are thereby "unrealistic."

It seems to me that there are two key flaws to this supposition. The deepest of these has to do with the fact that surely one of the most visible lessons taught by the twentieth century has been the existence, not so much of a number of different realities, but of a number of different lenses with which to see the same reality. Consider: America is primarily an industrial and business-oriented nation, and businessmen are said to be mainly concerned with matters of profit, trade, financial stability, and so forth; such concerns, one might say, represent the conventional reality of a major segment of the country. For roughly the past ten years, however—a period dominated by the Vietnam war—the lenses through which so many Americans scanned the landscape of their nation and the world proved to be so short-sighted and out of focus that tens of thousands of American lives were lost in Asia, apparently to no purpose, and a poisonous and highly unstable division was allowed to appear in American life, such as had not been seen since the Civil War; and on top of that, as a result of the inflationary armament expenditures under two presidents, the once-vaunted American economy was seriously weakened and was propelled into a decline from which it is only now allegedly

beginning to emerge, albeit with immense intervening loss of profits, and loss of the domestic social legislation which might have made the underpinnings of a mercantile nation more secure.

Television was only one of the lenses through which Americans were offered a view of this supposed "reality" of Vietnam, but I think many people are agreed that, in its commissions and omissions, it was a crucial view. In short, the television cameras helped America march into Vietnam in the middle 1960s, and attended each evening, year after year, while America marched farther in, and farther in, and *farther* in. . . . And then suddenly, or so it appeared, with the national spirit in shambles, and the national economy already beginning to collapse, and with the war nowhere nearer to being won than it had ever been, television—aligning itself with, and so authoritatively expressing, a new shift in conventional reality—now told its public that the war was wasteful and ill-advised (save, temporarily, for the prisoner-of-war issue, which was soon forgotten), and, by implication, that it had been of no importance. With one or two minor exceptions, at no time during the period of the major American involvement in Vietnam did the television networks employ their vast financial resources in an honest attempt to discover the actual reality of the Vietnam situation. Even in the fading reign of an American president, Lyndon B. Johnson (whose own political insecurity was such that he virtually resigned from office—at least from a second term—as the result of antiwar protest), at no time did the networks appear willing to encourage even their own correspondents in pursuing an independent, and perhaps "unrealistic," course in charting the strange and deadly geography of the war. In such a fashion, during a crucial, communications—dominated pe-

riod of American history, was "reality" presented to the American public.

One difficulty, then, that I have had in accepting television's view of its performance is not that it serves a mass audience but that it serves this audience so badly. To whose benefit, after all, was the reporterlike promotion and acquiescence in a lengthy war which gained no objective and which seriously undermined (among other things) even the mercantile basis of a mercantile nation? When, in 1967-68, the networks glamorized the air-bombing of North Vietnam while noticeably refraining from following up reports (as well as stories published in reliable journals) of the wasteful and pointless destruction of South Vietnamese land and life that was then taking place as a result of American military policy, in what way could such a glimpse of the war be said to have been viewed through a "realistic" lens, and who gained by it? Surely not the mass audience (many among whom lost their sons, and later their jobs), which the commercial television establishment has been in the habit of exploiting by professing to regard the public's silent acceptance of triviality and trivialization as if this were the same thing as an enthusiasm or appetite for the second-rate, and indeed, by constantly asserting the very notion that a homogeneous, monolithic mass of the public somewhere exists, when it has become abundantly clear that, despite the pressures of national advertising, the populace continues to be composed of innumerable regional, political, and ethnic groupings whose definition is at least as vivid as that of any abstract "mass."

For the second flaw in the argument on behalf of American television's intrinsically "real" or benign basis in American life has to do with the television industry's own shortsighted and delusive relationship with the public. Here the allegation persists that commercial television exits as a kind of neutral provider of "what the public wants," whether it be entertainment, sports, news, or advertising: a sturdily profit-minded storekeeper who would as gladly furnish marmalade as motorcars, who would as soon display a Durer woodcut, or a bowl of Jell-O, or a comedy series about a talking horse, depending only on the public's preference—a preference increasingly determined by the taking of polls and "samplings." It seems to me that there are several rejoinders that can be made to such an important assertion, though admittedly none of them is likely to be entirely satisfactory in an age which shies from making intuitive judgments, even on deeply felt issues, unless accompanied or transformed by scientific-like evidence.

Even so, speaking of science, it seems to run markedly counter to one of the principal laws of modern physics (to say nothing of plain reason) to insist that an institution is, so to speak, what it says it is. Since the formulation of Einstein's special theory of relativity, the world has had to accept the notion that the position of any object is relative to the position of the observer. In this case, one might say that the American television industry is the "object," and that the position it claims for itself is that of a neutral provider of entertainment, information, and advertising. And clearly, this simply cannot generally or necessarily be so. That is, for each viewer there is bound to be a different, and sometimes a very different, relationship with television, and more importantly: in a majority of instances the position or role of television has increasingly become that of an authority. In recent years, to be sure, there have been attempts by various observers to play down television's authoritarian role, with one writer,

in a popular disclaimer, characterizing television as being merely "another utility, like the telephone." Aside from the fact that the utilities are not notably alike or neutral even in *their* roles, this cozy, matter-of-fact view of television seems disingenuous. Statistical-minded journalists, I know, have shown that despite the expenditure of x amount of money for y minutes of air time, a certain candidate has still not been elected to public office, but to argue from this that television is nonauthoritarian in its influence seems to me to be countering one simplistic view with another. Television, to take one example, seems indubitably authoritarian in the position it has assumed in this country (as in most) of delegating *to itself* the majority as well as the minority expressions of politics, culture, or even sensibility in the nation. The television set transmits *its* version of our Yeas and *its* version of their rebuttal: our Nays. It seems fair to say that while some writers in the past have overstated the demonological implications of television's role, this most definitely does not rule out the larger fact that television *does* have a role and that it is virtually impossible for this role to be matter-of-fact or neutral.

But whenever a critic, armed not only with the evidence of his eyes and ears but with a passing, school-text acquaintance with the laws of nature, points out that television, despite its pronouncements as to its own fixed position, is certain to be in a variable and dynamic (rather than passive) relationship with its viewers, what usually happens is that a member of the television elite announces that, though a certain dynamism may well exist, this dynamism is rigorously shaped and even controlled by the viewers himself. Thus, television managers, it is said, far from being arbitrary or self-serving autocrats, disseminate their broadcast messages at the

mercy of the polls, and consequently of the public.

This is a trickier terrain for a critic to maintain his footing upon, for the recent generation, while perhaps being less scientifically creative than its immediate predecessors, has nonetheless advanced the new technics of measurement to their greatest heights. We have measured the speed of the electron and the distance between ourselves and Betelgeuse; why should it be so implausible that one might measure the preference of a man for eggs and apples? Common sense is usually a help in these matters, and common sense here at least tells one that, given the complexity of the human brain, one cannot merely ask someone what he or she wants, and then give it to them, and then, having given it to them, count on having done very much by the overall possibilities. This is perhaps a corollary of what might be called the *Moby Dick* theory: namely, if a reader cannot, in advance, conceive of *Moby Dick* on his own, how should he ask the culture somehow to provide such a work? It also strikes me that maybe the distant voice of another great physicist, Werner Heisenberg, has something to communicate in this regard, though admittedly less by the intended application of his equations than through a more philosophic inference that might be drawn from some of them. For it was Heisenberg who in 1927 formulated the influential uncertainty principle, which has to do not so much with states of mind as with the behavior of subatomic particles and the uncertainty—even employing the best measuring devices imaginable—with which they can be effectively measured. In essence, the uncertainty principle states that it is impossible to "specify or determine simultaneously" both the position and the velocity of a particle with full accuracy, and from this it goes on to declare that even the act of measuring these tiny elements of the universe inevitably alters their disposition and behavior: that is, one cannot ever ascertain their exact position because the very act of observation or examination invariably will change the pattern. What is true for subatomic particles admittedly may not be precisely true for humans, though often it seems that there is a general consistency in nature which envelops some unlikely components. One of the distant messages of Werner Heisenberg, then (or so it seems to me), is one of *modesty:* the need for a certain reserve or caution in asserting the exactitude and meaning of certain measurements—for example, of units as volatile and complicated as exist within the minds of men and women. As perhaps too glib or early a confirmation of this conjecture, I noticed, in the course of the much-troubled and much-measured 1975–76 television season, a report by *The New York Times*'s television reporter Les Brown which commented not merely on a sudden, unexpected

drop in the public's viewing hours but also on a new disparity which seemed to be appearing between the responses the public was making to the attempts to measure what it liked to watch or wished to watch—and what, if fact, it actually did watch, or not watch, in the relative privacy of its homes.

Even so, for all the marshaling this way or that way of supposedly factual argument, in the end the point seems to be that ours is predominantly a moral society—whether conforming to the physical laws of Copernicus, Newton, or Einstein, and whether disagreeing among ourselves, or with other societies, as to the precise nature of desirable morality—and that, at present, the tension of American television with—or, one might say, against—American society is primarily a moral tension: a conflict of competing moral views of life and of its possibilities. On the one hand, armed with vast, concentrated resources of power and organization, and clutching official-looking certificates insisting that it is

really the *servant* of the people, stands the television industry, motivated and shaped by the well-ordered and articulated morality of business, with its short-term, close-focused, tidy dynamism of annual sales and growth and profits. On the other hand stands, or rather sprawls, the public—that untidy multitude that lurks behind the "mass"—with scant organization, a most diffuse and unrealized power, and not so much armed with, as often merely occupied by, a far vaguer, longer-term morality of human existence: that most bewildered, and perhaps most noble, dream of living through one's life as if it mattered. The critic, I think, must choose his own place on this new terrain, and must learn to speak of television as if it were part not only of a world of facts and measurements but of a larger, changing world of untold possibilities—not the least of which would be for it to truly serve its audience. In other words, he should speak of television as if it mattered.

Chapter Exercises

Critiquing the Critic

Do you identify with Michael Arlen as a television critic? How would you rate him in terms of his contribution to television criticism, to improving television, to enlightening the audience, and to entertaining the audience? If you had to sit backstage or behind the scenes at your favorite television show with him, how might your conversation go?

Critiquing the Critic

Formulating Critical Questions

Before you read another page in this book, choose a television text (a series, a single episode, a commercial, the strip, the industry, etc.) that you think might interest you. Now list below as many different critical questions that you can think of. Challenge yourself even further and see how many of those questions you can associate with an appropriate critical approach or combination of approaches.

POSSIBLE CRITICAL QUESTIONS FOR A SINGLE TEXT	
What is your text? _____	
Critical Questions	**Applicable Approach(es)**
1.	
2.	
3.	
4.	
5.	
6.	
7.	
8.	
9.	
10.	

Matching Critical Questions with Approaches

Obviously, whatever critical approach you choose will depend on what aspect of television you are analyzing. Still some approaches seem to be "tailor-made" for certain subjects. Take another look at our model of the process of television communication from Chapter 2. Based upon what you have read in this chapter, place each of the listed critical approaches at a place on the model where you think the approach would most typically be utilized. The example we have provided is: Auteur Criticism focuses on the source of television communication. You may find that some approaches (or combination of approaches) fit well in many different positions.

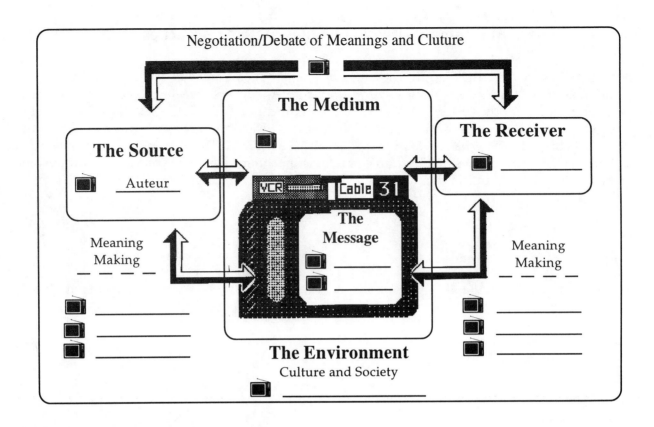

1. Auteur Criticism

2. Ideological Criticism

3. Gender (Feminist) Criticism

4. Historical Criticism

5. Narrative Analysis Criticism

6. Reader-Oriented Criticism

7. Rhetorical Criticism

8. Semiotics/Structuralism

9. Sociological Criticism

10. Dialogic Criticism

11. Genre Criticism

References and Resources

Adler, R. & Cater, D., (Eds.). (1975). *Television as a Cultural Force*. New York: Praeger.

Adorno, T. W. (1976). Television and the patterns of mass culture. In H. Newcomb (Ed.). *Television: The Critical View*. New York: Oxford University Press, pp. 239–259.

Alvarado, M. (1979). Teaching television. *Screen Education, 31*, 25-28.

Arato, A. & Gebhardt, E., (Eds.). (1978). *The Essential Frankfurt School Reader*. New York: Urizen Books.

Arlen, M. J. (1976). *The View From Highway 1: Essays on Television*. New York: Farrar, Straus and Giroux.

Arlen, M. J. (1981). *The Camera Age: Essays on Television*. New York: Farrar, Straus and Giroux.

Arlen, M.J. (1982). *The Living Room War*. Middlesex, Eng.: Harmondsworth.

Attallah, P. (1984). The unworthy discourse: situation comedy in television. In W. D. Rowland, Jr. & B. Watkins (Eds.). *Interpreting Television: Current Research Perspectives*. Beverly Hills, CA: Sage.

Baron, D. E. (1974). Against interpretation: the linguistic structure of American drama. *Journal of Popular Culture, 7*, 946–954.

Barrett, M. *et al.*, (Eds.). (1979). *Ideology and Cultural Production*. New York: St. Martin's Press.

Barthes, R. (1968). *Elements of Semiology*. New York: Hill and Wang.

Barthes, R. (1972). *Mythologies*. New York: Hill and Wang.

Batra, N. D. (1987). *The Hours of Television: Critical Approaches*. Metuchen, NJ: The Scarecrow Press.

Bazalgette, C. (1976). Reagan and Carter, Kojak and Crocker, Batman and Robin? *Screen Education, 20*, 54-65.

Ben-Horin, D. (1977). Television without tears: an outline of the Socialist approach to popular television. *Socialist Revolution, 7*, 7–35.

Bennett, T., Boyd-Bowman, S., Mercer, C. & Woollacott, J. (Eds.). (1981). *Popular Television and Film: A Reader*. London: British Film Institute/Open University Press.

Berger, A. A. (1978). The hidden compulsion in television. *Journal of the University Film Association, 30*, 41–46.

Berger, A. A. (1976). *The TV-guided American*. New York: Walker Publishing Company.

Berger, A. A. (1980). *Television as an Instrument of Terror: Essays on Media, Popular Culture and Everyday Life*. New Brunswick, N.J.: Transaction Books.

Black, P. (1973). Can one person criticize the full range of television? *Journal of the Society of Film and Television Arts, 2*, 4–5.

Bledhill, C. (1984). Developments in feminist film criticism. In M. A. Doane, P. Mellencamp & L. Williams (Eds.). *Re-Vision: Essays in Feminist Criticism*. Los Angeles: American Film Institute.

Bleich, D. (1978). *Subjective Criticism*. Baltimore, MD.: Johns Hopkins University Press.

Bloom, H. (1973). *The Anxiety of Influence: A Theory of Poetry*. Oxford: Oxford University Press.

Booth, W. C. (1961). *The Rhetoric of Fiction.* Chicago: University of Chicago Press.

Bordwell, D. (1985). *Narration in the Fiction Film.* Madison, WI: University of Wisconsin Press.

Branston, G. (1984). TV as institution. *Screen, 25,* 85–94.

Breen, M. & Corcoran, F. (1982). Myth in the television discourse. *Communication Monographs, 49,* 127–36.

Brown, L. & Walker, S. W., (Eds.). (1983). *Fast Forward: The New Television and American Society: Essays From Channels of Communications.* Kansas City, MO: Andrews and McMeel.

Browne, N. (1984). The political economy of the television (super) text. *Quarterly Review of Film Studies, 9,* 174–82.

Burton, H. (1973). Criticism at the receiving end. *Journal of the Society of Film and Television Arts, 2,* 12–14.

Carpenter, R. (1969). Ritual, aesthetics and TV. *Journal of Popular Culture, 3,* 251–59.

Caughie, J. (1984). Television criticism: 'a discourse in search of an object.' *Screen, 25,* 109–121.

Cawelti, J. (1968). Beatles, Batman and the new aesthetic. *Midway, 9,* 49–70.

Chatman, S. (1978). *Story and Discourse: Narrative Structure in Fiction and Film.* Ithaca, NY: Cornell University Press.

Chodorow, N. (1978). *The Reproduction of Mothering: Psychoanalysis and the Sociology of Gender.* Berkeley, CA: University of California Press.

Clarke, S. *et al.* (1980). *One-Dimensional Marxism.* New York: Allison and Busby.

Cohn, W. H. (1976). History for the masses: television portrays the past. *Journal of Popular Culture, 10,* 280–289.

Corcoran, F. (1984). Television as ideological apparatus: the power and the pleasure. *Critical Studies in Mass Communication, 1,* 131–45.

Coward, R. & Ellis, J. (1977). *Language and Materialism.* London: Routledge and Kegan.

Culler, J. (1975). *Structuralist Poetics.* Ithaca, NY: Cornell University Press.

Culler, J. (1981). *The Pursuit of Signs: Semiotics, Literature, and Deconstruction.* London: Routledge and Kegan Paul.

Curran, J. *et al.,* (Eds.). (1979). *Mass Communication and Society.* Beverly Hills, CA: Sage.

D'Agostino, P., (Ed.). (1985). *Transmission: Theory and Practice For a New Television Aesthetics.* New York: Tanam Press.

Davis, D. & Simmons, A., (Eds.). (1977). *The New Television: A Public/Private Art.* Cambridge, MA: The MIT Press.

Day-Lewis, S. (1973). The specialization issue and other problems for the critic. *Journal of the Society of Film and Television Arts, 2,* 6–8.

de Lauretis, T. (1982). *Alice Doesn't: Feminism, Semiotics, Cinema.* Bloomington: Indiana University Press.

de Saussure, F. (1966). *Course in General Linguistics, Trans. Wade Baskin.* New York: McGraw-Hill.

Deming, R. H. (1985). Discourse/talk/television. *Screen, 26,* 88–92.

Deming, R. H. (1985). The television spectator—subject. *Journal of Film and Video, 37,* 49–63.

Doane, M.A., Mellencamp, P. & Williams, L., (Eds). (1984). *Re-vision: Essays in Feminist Criticism.* Los Angeles: American Film Institute.

Downing, J. (1985). Communications and power. *Socialist Review, 15,* 111–127.

Drummond, P. & Paterson, R., (Eds.). (1985). *Television in Transition.* London: British Film Institute.

Eco, U. (1976). *A Theory of Semiotics.* Bloomington, IN: Indiana University Press.

Eco, U. (1977). *The Role of the Reader.* Bloomington, IN: Indiana University Press.

Eco, U. (1979). Can television teach? *Screen Education, 31,* 15–24.

Elliott, P., Murdock, G. & Schlesinger, P. (1983). "Terrorism" and the state: a case study of the discourses of television. *Media, Culture, and Society, 5,* 155–177.

Ellis, J. (1982). *Visible Fictions: Cinema, Television, Video.* London: Routledge and Kegan Paul.

Ellison, H. (1970). *The Glass Teat: Essays of Opinion on the Subject of Television.* New York: Ace Books.

Ellison, H. (1975). *The Other Glass Teat.* New York: Pyramid Books.

Esslin, M. (1982). *The Age of Television.* San Francisco, CA: W.H. Freeman and Company.

Feuer, J. (1983). The concept of live television: ontology as ideology. In E.A. Kaplan (Ed.). *Regarding Television—Critical Approaches: An Anthology, American Film Institute Monograph Series, vol. 2.* Frederick, MD: University Publications of America.

Fish, S. (1980). *Is There a Text in This Class?* Cambridge, MA: Harvard University Press.

Fiske, J. & Hartley, J. (1978). *Reading Television.* London: Methuen.

Fiske, J. (1978). Television: the flow and the text. *Madog, 1,* 7–14.

Fiske, J. (1986). Television and popular culture: reflections on British and Australian critical practice. *Critical Studies in Mass Communication, 3,* 200–216.

Flitterman, S. (1981). Woman, desire and the look: feminism and the enunciative apparatus of cinema. In J. Caughie (Ed.). *Theories of Authorship.* London: Routledge and Kegan Paul.

Fowles, J. (1982). *Television vs. Media Snobs: What TV Does for People.* New York: Stein and Day.

Freeman, D. (1978). *Eyes as Big as Cantaloupes: An Irreverent Look at TV.* San Diego, CA: Joyce Press.

Freeman, D. (1980). *In a Flea's Navel: a Critic's Love Affair With Television.* New York: A. S. Barnes and Company.

Garnham, N. (1982). Film and media studies: restructuring the subject. *Film Reader, 5,* 177–183.

Genette, G. (1980). *Narrative Discourse: An Essay in Method.* Trans. J. E. Lewin. Ithaca, NY: Cornell University Press.

Giles, D. (1985). Television reception. *Journal of Film and Video, 37,* 12–25.

Gitlin, T. (1977). Spotlights and shadows: television and the culture of politics. *College English, 38,* 789–801.

Gitlin, T. (1978). Media sociology: the dominant paradigm. *Theory and Society, 6,* 205–253.

Gitlin, T. (1985). *Inside Prime Time.* New York: Pantheon.

Gledhill, C., (Ed.). (1986). *Women and Melodrama.* London: British Film Institute.

Goethals, G. T. (1981). *The TV Ritual: Worship at the Video Altar.* Boston: Beacon Press.

Gronbeck, B. E. (1984). *Writing Television Criticism.* Chicago, IL: Science Research Associates.

Grossberg, L. (1984). Strategies of Marxist cultural interpretation. *Critical Studies in Mass Communication, 1,* 392–421.

Hall, S. (1974). Deviancy, politics and the media. In P. Rock & M. McIntosh (Eds.). *Deviance and Social Control.* London: Tavistock, pp. 261–305.

Hall, S. *et al.,* (Eds.). (1980). *Culture, Media, Language.* London: Hutchinson.

Hall, S., Hobson, D., Lowe, A., & Willis, P., (Eds.). (1980). *Culture, Media, Language.* London: Hutchinson.

Halloran, J. D. (1975). Understanding television. *Screen Education, 14*, 4–13.

Hawkes, T. (1977). *Structuralism and Semiotics.* Berkeley: University of California Press.

Hoy, D. C. (1982). *The Critical Circle.* Berkeley, CA: University of California Press.

Hyde, M. J. & Smith, C. R. (1979). Hermeneutics and rhetoric: a seen but unobserved relationship. *Quarterly Journal of Speech, 65*, 347–363.

Hazard, P. D., (Ed.). (1966). *TV as an Art: Some Essays on Criticism.* Campaign, IL.: National Council of Teachers of English.

Heath, S. & Skirrow, G. (1977). Television: a world in action. *Screen, 18*, 7–59.

Hernadi, P. (1981). *What is Criticism?* Bloomington, IN: Indiana University Press.

Hilmes, M. (1984). The television apparatus: direct address. *Journal of Film and Video, 37*, 27–36.

Himmelstein, H. (1981). *On the Small Screen: New Approaches in Television and Video Criticism.* New York: Praeger.

Himmelstein, H. (1984). *Television Myth and the American Mind.* New York: Praeger.

Holland, N. (1975). *5 Readers Reading.* New Haven, CN: Yale University Press.

Holub, R. D. (1984). *Reception Theory: A Critical Introduction.* London: Methuen.

Honeyford, S. (1980). Women and television. *Screen, 21*, 49–52.

Horkheimer, M. & Adorno, T. W. (1972). *Dialectic of Enlightenment, Trans. John Cuming.* New York: Seabury Press.

Houston, B. (1984). Viewing television: the metapsychology of endless consumption. *Quarterly Review of Film Studies, 9*, 183–95.

Irigary, L. (1985). *This Sex Which is Not One.* Trans. Catherine Porter & Carolyn Burke. Ithaca, NY: Cornell University Press.

Jameson, F. (1981). *The Political Unconscious: Narrative as a Socially Ssymbolic Act.* Ithaca, NY.: Cornell University Press.

Kaminsky, S. M. & Mahan, J. H. (1985). *American Television Genres.* Chicago: Nelson-Hall.

Kaplan, E. A. (1983). Theories of melodrama. *Women and Performance, 1*, 40–48.

Kaplan, E. A. (1983). *Women and Film: Both Sides of the Camera.* London: Methuen.

Kaplan, E. A., (Ed.). (1983). Regarding television— critical approaches: an anthology. *American Film Institute Monograph Series,* vol. 2. Frederick, MD: University Publications of America.

Kellner, D. (1979). TV, ideology and emancipatory popular culture. *Socialist Review, 9*, 13–53.

Kristeva, J. (1981). Women's time, trans. Alice Jardine & Harry Blake. *Signs, 7*, 13–35.

Kuhn, A. (1982). *Women's Pictures: Feminism and Cinema.* London: Routledge and Kegan Paul.

Kuhn, A. (1984). Women's genres. *Screen, 25*, 18–28.

Lemert, J. B. (1989). *Criticizing the Media: Empirical Approaches.* Newbury Park, NJ: Sage.

Levinson, R. M. (1975). From Olive Oyl to Sweet Polly Purebred: sex role stereotypes and televised cartoons. *Journal of Popular Culture, 9*, 561–572.

Lovell, T. (1980). *Pictures of Reality.* London: British Film Institute.

Lovell, T. (1982). Marxism and cultural studies. *Film Reader, 5*, 184–191.

MacDonald, J. F. (1983). *Blacks and White TV: Afro-Americans in Television and Video Criticism.* Chicago: Nelson-Hall.

Macherey, P. (1978). *A Theory of Literary Production, Trans. Geoffrey Wall.* London: Routledge and Kegan Paul.

Mailloux, S. (1982). *Interpretive Conventions: The Reader in the Study of American Fiction.* Ithaca, NY: Cornell University Press.

Manvell, R. (1973). Why television criticism differs from other forms of criticism. *Journal of the Society of Film and Television Arts, 2,* 1–3.

Marc, D. (1984). *Demographic Vistas: Television in American Culture.* Philadelphia: University of Pennsylvania Press.

Martin, W. (1986). *Recent Theories of Narrative.* Ithaca, NY: Cornell University Press.

Mayer, M. (1972). *About Television.* New York: Harper and Row.

McRobbie, A. (1982). Jackie: an ideology of adolescent femininity. In B. Waites, T. Bennett & G. Martin (Eds.). *Popular Culture: Past and Present.* London: Croom Helm, pp. 263–283.

Meehan, D.M. (1983). *Ladies of the Evening: Women Characters of Prime-time Television.* Metuchen, NJ: Scarecrow Press.

Metz, C. (1974). *Film Language: A Semiotics of the Cinema, Trans. Michael Taylor.* New York: Oxford University Press.

Metz, C. (1974). *Language and Cinema, Trans. Donna Umiker-Sebeok.* The Hague: Mouton.

Moi, T. (1986). *Sexual/Textual Politics: Feminist Literary Theory.* London: Methuen.

Montgomery, K. (1985). Writing about television in the popular press. *Critical Studies in Mass Communication, 2,* 75–80.

Morley, D. (1980). *The Nationwide audience: structure and decoding.* London: British Film Institute.

Morse, M. (1985). Talk, talk, talk—the space of discourse in television. *Screen, 26,* 2–15.

Neale, S. (1980). *Genre.* London: British Film Institute.

Newcomb, H. (1984). On the dialogic aspects of mass communication. *Critical Studies in Mass Communication, 1,* 34–50.

Newcomb, H. (1986). American television criticism 1970–1985. *Critical Studies in Mass Communication, 3,* 217–228.

O'Connor, J. E., (Ed.). (1983). *American History/American Television: Interpreting the Video Past.* New York: Frederick Ungar.

Palmer, R. E. (1969). *Hermeneutics.* Evanston, IL: Northwestern University Press.

Pratt, M. (1981). Art without critics and critics without readers *or* Pantagruel versus The Incredible Hulk. In P. Hernadi, (Ed.). *What is Criticism?* Bloomington, IN: Indiana University Press.

Ray, W. (1983). *Literary Meaning: From Phenomenology to Deconstruction.* Minneapolis, MN: University of Minnesota Press.

Requena, J. G. (1981). Narrativity/discursivity in the American television film. *Screen, 22,* 38–42.

Rose, B. G. (1985). *TV genres.* Westport, CT: Greenwood Press.

Rosenfield, L. W. (1968). The anatomy of critical discourse. *Speech Monographs, 35,* 50–69.

Schatz, T. (1981). *Hollywood Genres.* New York: Random House.

Silverman, K. (1983). *The Subject of Semiotics.* New York: Oxford University Press.

Silverstone, R. (1976). An approach to the structural analysis of the television message. *Screen, 17,* 9–40.

Silverstone, R. (1981). *The Message of Television: Myth and Narrative in Contemporary Culture.* London: Heinemann.

Silverstone, R. (1984). Narrative strategies in television science—a case study. *Media, Culture, and Society, 6,* 377–410.

Sklar, R. (1980). *Prime-time America.* New York: Oxford University Press.

Stam, R. (1983). Television news and its spectator. In E. A. Kaplan (Ed.). *Regarding Television—Critical Approaches: An Anthology, American Film Institute Monograph Series, vol. 2.* Frederick, MD: University Publications of America.

Stonesifer, R. J. (1971). A new style for TV criticism. In B. Rosenberg & D.M. White (Eds.). *Mass Culture Revisited.* New York: Van Nostrand Reinhold.

Suleiman, S. & Crossman, I., (Eds.). (1980). *The Reader in the Text: Essays on Audience and Interpretation.* Princeton, N.J.: Princeton University Press.

Tompkins, J. P., (Ed.). (1980). *Reader-Response Criticism: From Formalism to Post-Structuralism.* Baltimore, MD.: Johns Hopkins University Press.

Vande Berg, L. R. & Wenner, L. A. (1991). *Television Criticism: Approaches and Applications.* New York: Longman.

Watson, M. A. (1985). Television criticism in the popular press. *Critical Studies in Mass Communication, 2,* 66–75.

White, M. (1985). Television genres: intertextuality. *Journal of Film and Video, 37,* 41–47.

White, M. (1986). Crossing wavelengths: the diegetic and referential imaginary of American commercial television. *Cinema Journal, 25,* 51–64.

Williams, R. (1975). *Television: Technology and Cultural Form.* New York: Schocken Books.

Williams, R. (1976). *Keywords.* New York: Oxford University Press.

Williams, R. (1980). *Problems in Materialism and Culture.* London: Verso.

Williams, R. (1981). *Culture.* Glasgow: Fontana.

Winship, J. (1981). Handling sex. *Media, Culture and Society, 3,* 6–18.

Wolff, J. (1984). *The Social Production of Art.* New York: New York University Press.

Woollacott, J. (1982). Messages and meanings. In M. Gurevitch, T. Bennett, J. Curran & J. Woollacott, (Eds.). *Culture, Society and the Media.* London: Methuen, pp. 91–111.

Wright, J. L. (1974). TUNE-IN: the focus of television criticism. *Journal of Popular Culture, 7,* 887–894.

CHAPTER 6

SITUATION COMEDIES

121,624,000 people

That's the number of folks who tuned in to the farewell episode of *M*A*S*H* in 1983. That makes it the fifth most watched program in television history and the only non-Super Bowl among the medium's all-time Top 10 rated shows. For all of the abuse and ridicule that situation comedies receive from viewers and critics alike, this genre represents the most popular and oldest programs on television. The much maligned *I Love Lucy* in fact, is the one program most responsible for the medium's evolution from live shows to filmed programs.

Situation comedies are the staple of the four commercial networks' success. The early 1970s Saturday night CBS line up of *All in the Family*, *M*A*S*H*, *The Mary Tyler Moore Show*, and *The Bob Newhart Show* is legend and those programs are now immortalized in syndication. When ABC developed a strong stable of situation comedies in the mid-Seventies, *Laverne & Shirley*, *Happy Days*, *Welcome Back Kotter*, *Barney Miller* and others, it unseated CBS as the number one rated network, a position that the latter broadcasting company had enjoyed since the very beginning of network television in the 1940s. And NBC, never able to produce a lineup of successful situation comedies in that period, fell to the number three place only to move toward number one in the ratings race in the mid-1980s largely on the strength of its sitcom lineup of *Cheers*, *Family Ties*, and *The Cosby Show*. Fox established itself with *The Simpsons* and *Married . . . With Children* and succeeded with comedy like *Roc* and *Herman's Head*.

Overview

Television comedy has been popular with both programmers and viewers for decades. Originally developed for radio, the situation comedy easily moved to television during the medium's early days. The limitations of live television helped give the form much of its character, but Lucille Ball was to soon refine it. When Lucy moved to the West Coast to produce her *I Love Lucy* on film, she not only changed the shape of television comedy, but she made possible reruns and syndication.

The half hour television comedy has two dominant formats that sometimes overlap:

1. In *domestic comedy* the humor is inherent in the relationships of the characters; and

2. In *situation comedy* the humor derives from the oftentimes outlandish situations in which the characters find themselves.

Whether domcom or sitcom, half-hour televised comedy typically follows a set format and each relies on a specific set of character types. As with most television genres, the comedy is evolving in the face of technological and economic change in the broadcasting world. What we will examine in some detail in this chapter is the nature of half hour comedy, the advantages and disadvantages of its format and character conventions, and its possible evolution in the new television environment.

The Early Days

Situation comedies have always been popular with viewers as well as with programmers. At the end of any given season, it is almost guaranteed that more than half of the top twenty rated programs will be situation comedies. Comedies dominate the schedules of the four commercial networks and a few even appear in the lineups of the cable channels, for example HBO's *Dream On* and *The Larry Sanders Show*.

1949 was the beginning of the situation comedy's long history on television. *The Aldrich Family* came from radio to NBC that year and featured Henry Aldrich, his high school buddies, and a "typical American Family." Also making the move that year from radio (where they lived for twenty years) to television was CBS's *The Goldbergs*, featuring a middle-class Jewish family living in the Bronx. Jackie Gleason brought Chester Riley from radio to television in NBC's original *Life of Riley*. *Mama*, based on the play and movie, *I Remember Mama*, came to the small screen in 1949, as did radio's famous *Amos 'n Andy*.

The formula for successful situation comedies, as demonstrated by these television comedy pioneers, was established early in the medium's life and depended largely on already successful radio formats: seemingly everyday people, in family or group settings, dealing with the family or group situations created by the setting. The dominant technical ingredient in that formula was the setting—

the one room or at most a very few rooms—which was mandated by the limitations of live television. Live television demanded minimum movement between scenes and minimum action within scenes.

It remained for Lucille Ball, however, to free the form from those strictures and to shift the emphasis in television comedy from humor based upon the *interaction* of the family and group members to humor created by *situations* in which the cast members embroil themselves. Lucy took television comedy from what could be called "family comedy" to what she called "physical comedy."

In 1951, CBS approached Lucy with plans to move her successful radio program, *My Favorite Husband*, to television. Lucy wanted to make the switch to the tube and asked that her real-life husband, Desi Arnez, be allowed to play the role of her television spouse. The network refused (there is much dispute about this point; CBS denies it balked at televising an interracial marriage). Lucy had other requests as well. She wanted the program staged before a live audience, like a play, and filmed by three movie cameras recording simultaneously, like live television. Editors could then review the three sets of film and edit them together to give the best combination of action and reaction shots. Lucy also asked that the production take place in Hollywood, the nation's film capital, instead of New York, the country's television center at the time.

The network refused these requests as well, but Lucy was undaunted. She and Desi borrowed the necessary money and produced *I Love Lucy* on their own, selling the broadcast rights to CBS, assuring it Monday night primetime ratings dominance for decades.

Lucy's insistence was to shape the future of the medium once it became apparent that *I Love Lucy* would be successful. For one thing, reruns were now possible where they had not been practical with live television and this, in turn, helped create the syndication business.

Weekly series could now be produced relatively inexpensively and quickly. Live television shows had to be produced at the same time that they were broadcast; that's what made them "live." But because shows were now being done on film, even though some were in front of live audiences, the production of a thirty-nine week series could be done in six months. The films for the last episodes were simply held in the can until their scheduled air date. This made for less expensive production because actors, crew, equipment, and facilities did not have to be assembled and maintained for thirty nine weeks. In addition, stock shots could be used across a number of episodes, but in live television every shot had to be live for every show.

Lucy's most important contribution to television, however, may be that she gave definition to what was to become the medium's staple, the situation comedy.

The Form Takes on Style

Lucille Ball's innovation altered the television comedy genre. Before *I Love Lucy*, half hour comedies were centered around the humor inherent in domestic family life. Because they were live, the shows could accommodate very little physical humor. For example, there was no allowance for re-shooting a failed sight gag like there was with film production. After Lucy, the comedy revolved around funny situations encountered by people who happen to be members of a family or, in many cases, around institutional "pseudo" families such as the military or law enforcement agencies (for example, *The Phil Silvers Show* and *Car 54 Where Are You?*)

In domestic comedies or *domcoms*, family or group members served a purpose: they were the source of the humor. In the situation comedies or *sitcoms*, the purpose of the characters was less central; they served as foils to or victims of the situational zaniness.

In the four decades since Lucy premiered, situation and domestic comedies have existed side by side on network schedules, *Mr. Ed* and *The Dick Van Dyke Show* on CBS for example. There have been periods when one form has seemed dominant. The 1960s were ripe with situation comedies like *I Dream of Jeannie*, *Bewitched*, and *The Munsters*, while the 1970s boasted domcoms like *All in the Family*, *The Mary Tyler Moore Show*, *The Jeffersons*, and *Good Times*. The Eighties and Nineties seem to have emerged with a nice combination of the two comedy types. Some examples of contemporary domcoms are *Cheers*, *The Days and Nights of Molly Dodd*, *Roc*, *Mad About You*, *The Cosby Show*, *Seinfeld*, *Wings*, *Roseanne*, *Frasier*, and HBO's innovative contributions, *The Larry Sanders Show* and *Dream On*. Some examples of contemporary sitcoms might include *Martin*, *Married . . . With Children*, and *The Critic*.

There have always been programs that are not easily categorized as one or the other, *Soap*, *Herman's Head*, *The Odd Couple*, and the three Bob Newhart comedies, *The Bob Newhart Show*, *Newhart*, and *Bob*, for example. And, in fact, a program's categorization is often the product of the individual viewer's perception of and affection for a show and its characters. *Friends* may be one person's domcom and another's sitcom.

Newcomb (1974) offered a detailed analysis of these sibling television forms. Situation comedies, he wrote, are dependent on a strict formula. It includes one room sets (Lucy's living room, Sgt. Bilko's motor pool, the Bundy's den). Movement from scene to scene is accomplished by fading in and out of adjacent scenes. We rarely see Hogan walk from his heroes' bunk quarters to Colonel Klink's office, that movement is performed by fade. Characters are usually middle or upper-middle class— Dobie Gillis' family owned a grocery store, Samantha Stevens' husband was an advertising executive and *I Dream of Jeannie's* primary bread-winner was an astronaut.

The action in a situation comedy also conforms to a specific formula.

1. **Establishment of the Situation.** A situation comedy typically begins with the establishment of the situation, the presentation of a broad outline of events that will follow from the episode's particular funny situation.

In some situation comedies, the funny situation is built in—the wife is a witch (*Bewitched*); the family members are hillbillies from the mountains trying to cope with the modern and rich ways of Beverly Hills (*The Beverly Hillbillies*); the African-American young man from the poor side of Philadelphia moves to his rich uncle's home in a ritzy part of Los Angeles (*The Fresh Prince of Bel-Air*).

In others situation comedies, the situation befalls the hapless protagonist—in *I Love Lucy*, Lucy purchases 500 pounds of meat but the freezer she bought for its storage is broken; in *Car 54 Where are You?* Toody and Muldoon wreck patrol car 54 and have to keep it a secret from Captain Block until after inspection; and in *Martin*, Martin has to call a plumber to fix his toilet while he and his buddies go to a big basketball game.

2. **Complication.** A witch, a hillbilly family, 500 pounds of meat about to spoil, a wrecked police car and a broken toilet are not in and of themselves particularly funny. The situation comedy formula, then, requires some complication of the situation to heighten the humor.

The husband has a candy maker as one of his advertising clients but the witchly wife resents the manufacturer's portrayal of ugly witches on his Halloween candy advertising billboards. The hillbillies are told that they cannot harbor animals in their backyard even though they think that the pool is a watering hole. Ricky is bringing a big star home, but the meat is laying all around the house. The paint that Officer Muldoon has used to turn car 51 into car 54 comes off when Officer Toody decides to wash the substitute vehicle. When Martin returns home he finds the plumber dead on the floor; he and his friends panic because they feel they'll be held responsible.

3. **Confusion.** The humor of the situation is compounded by confusion; confusion that is usually the result of the characters' unwillingness to choose the most logical solution to their predicament. This confusion also allows the writers to fill their allotted half hour.

The witch's husband is fired from his job for refusing to use ugly witches in his campaign and the wife's witch colleagues hold a sit-in in the manufacturer's bedroom. The hillbillies hide their animals in the living room, but the daughter has a gentleman caller coming. Lucy is caught by the butcher as she tries to sell the meat out of a baby carriage while pretending to shop in his market. Toody and Muldoon wreck car 51, newly designated Car 54, on their way to inspection. Martin and his friends try to hide the body before any one discovers it but it turns out the plumber isn't dead; he simply has a sleeping disease.

4. **Reduction of Confusion, or Resolution.** Comedy demands a happy ending, so the situation is resolved, all returns to normal, but there is no learning. Next week's episode occurs as if this week's never existed. This is the biggest difference between situation comedy and domestic comedy; there is no history in situation comedy, the characters learn nothing and are not changed because of the situation and its resolution. Lucy will no doubt buy more meat and another freezer. On *All in the Family*, on the other hand, Edith Bunker decides to report a rapist's attack because her daughter Gloria counsels her to do so. Gloria recalls being raped (seasons before) and not reporting it. Gloria feels guilty because of her own cowardice and doesn't want her mother to go through the same. These characters clearly learn and reflect upon past experiences which are used to allow the characters to grow and change.

The reduction of confusion, then, only has meaning for that particular situation. On *Bewitched*, the candy maker finally likes the idea of a beautiful witch instead of an ugly one for his product's logo, but Samantha will still intrude into Darrin's business next week. Elly May's suitor turns out to be a veterinarian who loves animals, but Jed and Granny will still fish in the watering hole on *The Beverly Hillbillies*. Ricky will coincidentally have to feed not only his band, but also the band of the big star that he is escorting and the meat saves the day, but Lucy will forever embark on zany money-making schemes. The officers of Car 54, in their second wreck, stop a burglary, but they will misadminister justice for another half hour, same time, same station, next week. Things may have turned out well for Martin, but he will still think with his fear and not his head in future episodes.

Characters are central to the situation comedy, for it is their antics that bring viewers back week after week. They are usually unchanging, predictable. Lucy will always be Lucy, Sgt. Schultz will always trade information for chocolate and say, "I zee nothing ... I hear nothing!" when confronted with Hogan's duplicity.

Situation comedies usually revolve around the machinations of the "Star"—Lucy, of course; Sister Bertrille (Sally Field) in *The Flying Nun*; Ed (voice supplied by the old time cowboy actor Allan "Rocky" Lane) in *Mr. Ed.*

Other people are necessary, however. They are needed to add to the confusion. They can be the regular supporting cast. These characters serve as foils for the star's antics—Ricky and Mr. Mooney, Mother Superior, and Wilbur Post. Other characters appear in the form of non-regulars, people like bank tellers and store owners who serve as a sort of audience for the star, offering humor through their amazement and naiveté.

The situation comedy, then, is a thirty minute gag that, when played out, is good for a laugh. Problems are solved, relationships are not altered, things remain the same.

Domestic comedies, on the other hand, are more realistic than situation comedies. They are not dependent on the confused and confusing antics of the star, but like *The Goldbergs*

before Lucy and *M*A*S*H* and *Leave It To Beaver* after, they depend on the interaction that develops between the characters. The humor depends not on situations, but on people. An episode of *One Day at a Time* can center around something as non-zany as the mother counseling her oldest daughter on the issue of virginity. *M*A*S*H* offers viewers several shows that are devoid of any solvable situation, programs in which Hawkeye or B. J., in a letter home, simply describe the members of the 4077th. *Seinfeld*, in fact, is famous for having entire episodes, if not seasons, about absolutely nothing (nothing other, of course, than the relationship between Jerry, Kramer, Elaine and George).

It is this sense of family, this warmth of character interaction, from which Newcomb draws the name "domestic comedy." He identified three types of characters that populate domcoms, the *authoritative father*, the *reassuring mother*, and the *troublesome child*. A domestic comedy, however, need not have a family in the traditional sense. In fact, to avoid any gender or age bias of these labels altogether, it might be clearer to think of these roles as the *authoritative character*, the *reassuring character* and the *troublesome character*. Keep in mind that characters don't necessarily maintain the same role all of the time. In *The Mary Tyler Moore Show*, for example, Mr. Grant is often the authoritative figure who guides Mary or Murray. But Mary often assumes that role, when Mr. Grant's wife left him, for example, or when married Murray fell in love with another woman. At times, Murray plays the reassuring character to Mary or Lou Grant and there are episodes when even Ted Baxter drops his troublesome-character role to aid one of his WJM-TV colleagues.

It is the interaction, the warmth and growth of these relationships, that carries the humor and action in domestic comedy. The problems that are encountered—the death of a homosexual cousin on *All In The Family*, the consequences of lying on *Leave It To Beaver*—are emotional and mental, not situational. This allows for more ambiguity and complexity of character than does the situation comedy.

There is, however, still a certain predictability in domcoms, but it is a predictability of role rather than of character. We can always predict Lucy's next move, just as we can predict the actions of a dramatic comedy's troublesome character. We cannot, however, predict which character will play that role in a given episode, how that role will be manifested, or how that episode's main problem will be resolved.

Predictability is also part of the domcom formula because we always know that the problem will be solved. The characters will learn and grow from their encounter with the problem. The relationships between characters may even change as a result. It may even take two or more episodes to resolve the matter; but it is indeed solved.

Is this predictability necessarily a bad thing, something for which situation and domestic comedies should be criticized? Does it mean that television comedy, as a form of expression, should not be taken seriously? Of course not. For one thing, many viewers simply enjoy familiar characters in familiar settings. For example, when 1952 presidential candidate Adlai Stevenson interrupted *I Love Lucy* to campaign against eventual winner Dwight Eisenhower, he was inundated with angry mail. "I love Lucy. I like Ike. Drop dead!" wrote one fan furious that her weekly visit with her "friend" had been disturbed.

There is a second, more significant reason that the formula of comedy may be one of its greatest assets as opposed to one of its flaws. If we view the formula and viewers' familiarity with it as a means of imposing communication efficiency, then the television comedy can be seen as a rich source of entertainment and insight. Free from the requirement of having to establish each character's role and free of the obligation of building and illuminating a variety of plot lines, the creators of television's comedies are able to devote more of their talents to delighting or challenging us.

Situation comedies like *Three's Company* and *Lucy* may well generate easy laughs for that very reason: the characters and situation are so familiar that the jokes flow without much effort. Domestic comedies like *The Cosby Show*, *M*A*S*H*, and *Frasier* quite adroitly move our emotions as well as they do possibly because we need to spend little intellectual effort "positioning" characters and situations. There is little inherently funny in buying 500 pounds of meat and bigotry is rarely enlightening. But Lucy Ricardo and Archie Bunker have used each respectively to produce effective television comedy.

Both forms of television comedy, however, are popular because they make us laugh. Regardless of the silliness or seriousness of the predicament—Lucy nearly drowning in a vat of grapes or Archie addicted to pills—comedy demands resolution, and television comedy gives it to us.

A Changing Staple

Viewers, critics and industry insiders can see some subtle and not so subtle alterations in the nature of television comedy as it evolves. Themes change, programming conservatism entrenches and is challenged, and production techniques and schedules are altered.

Themes. Even the most casual viewer can't help but notice that television comedy themes seem to follow certain patterns and that those themes reflect their times.

The first half of the 1960s were good years for the hayseed comedy. In a time of ever growing urbanization and modernization, the American public could enjoy such throwbacks to the good old days as *Petticoat Junction*, *Green Acres*, *The Real McCoys*, *The Beverly Hillbillies*, *Andy of Mayberry*, *The Farmer's Daughter*, and *Gomer Pyle U.S.M.C.* A constant theme throughout these series was the goodness of home-spun rural values.

One dominant theme from the second half of that decade was the fantastic comedy. The world was beginning to become complicated. There were moon shots, the space and arms race with the Russians, war in the middle east, and someplace called Viet Nam was being discussed in Congress. Viewers could turn their attention away from these confusing, troublesome issues and lose themselves in a totally unreal selection of comedies—*My Mother the Car, The Flying Nun, My Favorite Martian, The Munsters, The Addams Family, I Dream of Jeannie, Get Smart, Bewitched,* and *Mr. Terrific.*

The Seventies, as Americans began to come to grips with the changing world, saw the birth and predominance of the relevant comedy, *All in the Family, The Mary Tyler Moore Show, Maude, Sanford and Son, The Jeffersons, Good Times, One Day at a Time, Hot l Baltimore,* and *M*A*S*H.*

As that decade ended and the 1980s dawned, the dominant theme seemed to be non-relevancy, a return to the largely situational and physical comedies of the Lucy era—*Happy Days, Laverne & Shirley, Mork and Mindy, Three's Company, Gimme A Break, Jennifer Slept Here, Mr. Smith.* Relevancy no longer was selling in the post-Watergate/Viet Nam era. But as the Eighties progressed and became the Nineties, there was a drift back toward relevancy, but relevancy of home, family and relations—a shift that reflected tough times for people trying to deal with the situations dealt them by fate. *Cheers* with reformed alcoholic Sam, unemployed Norm and professionally frustrated Rebecca; the *Designing Women* dealing with running a small business and facing divorce, sexism, and breast cancer; the *Golden Girls* working to maintain dignity in their latter years; *Roc,* a working-class man and his family struggling against racism and economic barriers; another reformed alcoholic, *Murphy Brown,* confronting the travails of contemporary broadcast journalism and single motherhood, are all notable examples.

Of course, trends are just that, trends. Programs like *Taxi* and *M*A*S*H* existed side by side with *What's Happening. The Donna Reed Show* shared the air with *I Dream of Jeannie;* and *Wings* and *Herman's Head* premiered around the same time.

Programming conservatism. Many television observers argue that the move toward non-controversial issues in the post-relevance 1980s is the result of industry conservatism brought on by an over concern for ratings and profitability. This concern with fiscal matters stems in part from the spiraling cost of producing television comedy. In 1980 it cost $300,000 an episode to make *Archie Bunker's Place,* $475,000 an episode for *Happy Days,* and $400,000 an episode for *M*A*S*H.* A single episode of *Cheers* in its last season cost a reported $2 million.

Many critics feel there is an irony in this outgrowth of programming conservatism. It has led to an increase in television comedy's reliance on sex for its humor. *All in the Family, Good Times,* and the other relevant comedies dealt with controversial issues, among them sex and sexual issues—rape, loss of virginity, homosexuality and menopause. When the 1980s came, Americans were "tired of Watergate, tired of Viet Nam," so program producers, eager to draw on the success of the relevancy shows, latched onto sex as a dominant source of humor. The problem is that realistic comedic presentations of sex were replaced by titillation.

In 1953, when Lucille Ball was pregnant in real life, the producers were forced to write that condition into the show, they couldn't hide her changing shape on the air. But CBS censors would not allow the use of the word "pregnant" (they substituted "enceinte"), and went as far as to have the program dealing with her pregnancy previewed by a priest, minister, rabbi, and judge to make sure that it would not offend. At the end of the 1960s, Mrs. Drysdale of *The Beverly Hillbillies* was going to a reducing farm that had as its motto, "Leave your fat behind in Tucson." Paul Henning, the producer, took the line out, even after it passed the network censor, because "it might have offended somebody."

In the 1980s, however, television comedy like *Three's Company* featured a man living with two women and feigning homosexuality. Their apartment was managed by two sex-starved middle aged men: first Stanley Roper and then later, Mr. Fernley. *The Ropers* was a spin-off from *Three's Company* and its humor revolved almost exclusively around Stanley's sexual failings and his wife's sexual deprivation. Sexual innuendo and humor are normal—almost required—ingredients of most contemporary television comedy. These types of programs, despite some criticism, continue to be highly rated and much enjoyed on the networks and in syndication.

Another product of the trend toward programming conservatism is the growing lack of distinction between situation and domestic comedy. Many critics feel that this mixing of the elements of situation and domestic comedy, this "domestication of the situation," is a positive step for television comedy. Critics think the inclusion of more realistic characters and interactions than are normally found in situation comedy enriches the form. Traditional sitcoms such as *Laverne & Shirley* and *Happy Days* introduced physically challenged people into their casts and often dealt with their feelings and adjustments. *Mork and Mindy*, a fantastic comedy in the mold of *My Favorite Martian* and *Bewitched*, tackled issues like the meaning of friendship, the problems of loneliness, and the value of family, themes seemingly better suited for domestic comedies like *M*A*S*H* and *Leave It To Beaver*.

The related phenomenon, the situationalization of the domestic comedy, however, is not so well appreciated by most critics. When Archie Bunker moved from *All in the Family* to *Archie Bunker's Place*, many observers felt that he moved from the prototypic domcom to a program that exhibited many elements of situation comedy. Several of the Fox comedies, *Married . . . With Children* and *The Simpsons*, are attacked for this "sin" of cheapening the domcom formula.

The trend toward programming conservatism, toward increased dependence on the ratings and financial success, has also resulted in television comedy that exhibits a quality of sameness. The increased lack of distinction between domestic and situation comedies can be seen as one aspect of that sameness, but there are others. One is the growth of the spin off, programs that develop as a direct outgrowth of a popular character moving from one comedy to another of his or her own. *Three's Company* spawned *The Ropers*. *The Mary Tyler Moore Show* gave us *Phyllis, Lou Grant* and *Rhoda*. *Alice* spun off *Flo*. *Happy Days* gave us *Laverne & Shirley, Mork and Mindy*, and *Joanie Loves Chachi*. And finally, *Cheers* begat *The Tortellis* and *Frasier*.

Another aspect of the problem is the rip-off. How many *Friends* clones can you name?

Many industry insiders see the homogenization of television comedy as the result of fiscal conservatism. Norman Lear, creator of *All in the Family, Maude*, and the rest, complains that television programming is the prisoner of a "total winner mentality" with a concept's potential for immediate high ratings the prime determinant of its "airworthiness." The way that this mentality produces sameness in programming, Lear says, is that programmers are afraid to take chances. New ideas and talents are ignored.

And yet the argument that competition and the winner mentality overcome innovation is challenged by the likes of *Seinfeld, The Garry Shandling Show, Brothers, Dream On* and *The Larry Sanders Show*. It can be argued that the first show only made it to the network schedule because Seinfeld had already achieved success and notoriety as a stand-up comic. It can also be argued that last four only made it to television because of cable channels. Nonetheless, comedy is much less predictable than many critics claim.

Decreased Production Schedules. Another trend in television comedy that gained momentum as the medium moved through the Eighties into this decade is also related to business or financial concerns. In the early days of television comedy, circa Lucy, 39 shows a season were produced. The trend now is toward doing fewer new episodes per season, twenty to twenty four at most, and toward heavier reliance on reruns to fill out the year's schedule. The production of twenty or so new episodes has become standard for proven programs like *Alice* or *One Day at a Time* during their network runs. Newer comedies may have as few as thirteen new episodes produced for a season. A brand new comedy may produce even fewer episodes (only two or three.) This allows producers to minimize their losses if the program fares badly. CBS calls this their "Short Order" policy. Critics contend, however, that this retards the development of television comedy because new ideas are not given an opportunity to develop an audience. They point to *M*A*S*H*, *The Mary Tyler Moore Show*, and *All in the Family*, all programs that were departures from comedy already on the air, and all programs that were slow in finding audiences. If they were allowed only two episodes to win a following, they would have disappeared from television.

Changes in Production Techniques. Two technological trends that began in the mid-Seventies now seem firmly entrenched in television comedy—the use of videotape instead of film and the production of the show on a stage, before a live studio audience.

In 1971 Norman Lear turned the production of television comedy back to the days of *I Love Lucy* by taping his *All in the Family* in front of a live audience and utilizing several videotape (as opposed to Lucy's film) cameras. Videotape production was less expensive than film and because it gave the viewer the feeling of live television (as in sports and news), it heightened the sense of reality. This sense of immediacy was important to a program like *All in the Family*, whose staple was topicality.

Lear's experiment was a success. With the exception of *M*A*S*H* and *House Calls*, almost all important and successful contemporary television comedy is produced in the Lear style, either filmed or videotaped in front of a live audience. *The Simpsons* and *The Critic*, for obvious reasons, are exceptions, as are *The Larry Sanders Show* and *Dream On*.

The demise of canned laughter is a secondary result of the Lear production revolution. With live audiences present (and presumably laughing), there is little need for the boffo laugh track, although it lives on in many syndicated reruns. This is not to say, however, that no augmentation of the audience's laughter occurs, just that canned laughter has given way to sweetening, the electronic enhancement of actual studio audience reaction added to the finished tape after the episode is completed.

But there is no sweetening of our laughter at home. Most of us just enjoy television comedy. In the early 1960s, several critics were taken with *The Beverly Hillbillies*. One wrote, "It is a contribution to social criticism. Its primary magnetism inheres in its unendurable challenge to our money oriented value system." Another wrote that the show had a moral: that innocence "triumphantly survives the possession of riches." Still others attributed reduced sexual and status anxieties in this country to Granny and the gang. The show's writers, however, saw it differently. They were writing a program, they said, "to be thigh-slapping funny." From the thigh-slapping Hillbillies to programs with very different intentions like *M*A*S*H*, television comedy is a disparate form that will endure and evolve as financial pressures, technological advances, audience expectations, and the times change. As long as there are prime-time half hours to be filled by network comedies and local half hours to be filled by syndicated shows, the situation comedy will remain a favorite television form.

MERRITT

The first essay that follows this chapter is a fine example of auteur criticism. Merritt's goal, and the singular mark of auteur study, is to see if "past situation comedies produced by Cosby share commonalities" with *The Cosby Show*.

Note her arguments defending the notion of television producers as auteurs. What commonalities does she find to support her claim of auteurship for Cosby? Do you find her evidence of a "Cosby signature" compelling? What is that signature?

Bill Cosby: TV Auteur?

Bichetta D. Merritt

In the 25 years Bill Cosby has been in show business, he has simultaneously entertained "adults with dry humor and captured the imaginations of children with his almost magical sense of the ridiculous."[1] From executive producer to product spokesperson, American television audiences have been exposed to Cosby for over twenty years. If the 1950s garnered the title, "decade of the westerns," the 1980s might easily be remembered as the "Cosby Show" and his acceptance as a product representative for companies such as Coca Cola, Jello Pudding, Ford Motor Company and Del Monte qualify him for that accolade.

Starting in 1964 with the Emmy award winning *I Spy*, Cosby's most popular series' include *The Bill Cosby Show* and *Fat Albert and the Cosby Kids*. He experienced only one minor setback in his television career when *The New Bill Cosby Show* was cancelled in 1973 fol-

lowed by *Cos* in 1974. Cosby's forte as a producer is the half-hour comedy and when he ventures outside that formula his efforts do not prove successful. The above shows, both variety programs, did not succeed and MacDonald attributes these failures to their genre.[2] A series of comedy-variety programs starring blacks premiering from 1972–74 met the same fate and did not survive the ratings test. About this same time in his career, however, commercials began to interest the actor/comedian and eventually Cosby developed into one of the most respected and believable product spokespersons in television.[3] Not only did this lucrative venture strengthen his appeal to the masses but helped him achieve more financial stability.

Cosby's audience appeal and financial security contribute to the

---

Reprinted by permission of *Journal of Popular Culture*. Article by Bichetta Merritt.

success of his newest series, *The Cosby Show,* but are these factors, though important, the only reasons for the show's large weekly viewership? Do past situation comedies produced by Cosby share commonalities with this current program? What is the benefit of studying them collectively? And, is there an established set of criteria to measure an individual's impact on a medium as diverse as television? To begin to answer these questions three of the series were chosen for analysis—*The Bill Cosby Show, Fat Albert and the Cosby Kids (Fat Albert)* and *The Cosby Show.* These programs were selected on the basis of their common genre, content, Nielsen ratings and executive producer or executive consultant-Bill Cosby. Though *The Bill Cosby Show* aired only two years, media historian J. Fred MacDonald named it one of the most popular shows (with a black central star) of the late 1960s, basing this selection on audience approval supported by Neilson ratings.[4] In addition, the program is syndicated and aired on cable in several markets across the country. For the above reasons, *The Bill Cosby Show* was considered a successful program. *Fat Albert* and *The Cosby Show* qualify because of their longevity on television and high ratings.

Background

Research indicates that television has been analyzed utilizing various critical methods. Some include the use of the tenets of mythology, signification, the comparison of television to the "dreamworld" espoused by Freud and genre analysis.[5] Genre analysis, for example, categorizes television shows and series within a conceptual system from which the critic can draw similarities and make critical judgements. Problems surface using this method when programs within the same genre bear little meaningful resemblance. For example, *The*

Outcasts and *Gunsmoke,* are both westerns, but share no other distinctions. In film, *Silverado* and *Heaven's Gate* are both westerns, yet again no further similarities exist. Whether the medium is television or film, genre analysis becomes cumbersome when the critic must differentiate within formats.[6]

Genre criticism may take another approach. The critic may elect to focus on one episode within a series. This method narrows the scope, and creates another problem, breadth of analysis. Alternatively, a critic may choose to evaluate the entire series by utilizing one element. For example, Wanders' study of "put-down" humor in *Maude.*[7] Media researchers Davis and Marc write, however, that a model exists that would allow for in-depth analysis and make the appropriate distinctions by form and type between various programs.[8] Such a system, holistic in design, is used in film criticism and would facilitate analysis of television on a number of levels. It is the "auteur" theory.

What components constitute the "auteur" approach to film criticism and how should this critical method be applied to television? Based on three concepts, this theory avoids isolating a director's work into compartments. A film undergoes evaluation as part of the director's entire creative output. Generally, excluded from inclusion in the study are first films, yet no director's films exist in a vacuum nor should be barred from scrutiny.[9] A new film, analyzed in relation to the others, is investigated by exploring the themes followed, whether the director exhibited any artistic growth, and whether the director attempted and succeeded in accomplishing his/her goal with the film. An artistic context, when established using the above standards, allows for broad in-depth analysis of the particular work.[10] Secondly, each film is analyzed for the per-

sonality, style or as Sarris writes, the "signature" of a specific director. Finally, the third and "ultimate premise" concerned with the film as art—the interior meaning of a film, distinguishes one director from another. This meaning can be detected in tempo, rhythm and pacing of the film. More difficult to describe than the first two concepts, the third may be defined as the "soul" of the director. "Soul," Sarris writes may be defined as that "intangible difference between one personality and another, all other things being equal. . . . [T]his difference is expressed by no more than a beat's hesitation in the rhythm of film."[11] If one were to diagram the three concepts of the auteur theory, three concentric circles should be drawn with "the outer circle representing technique; the middle circle, personal style; and the inner circle, interior meaning."[12] "Auteur" status is granted according to Davis, therefore, when a director in film demonstrates technical competence, familiarity with the medium and creative growth from film to film.[13] What distinguishes one creator of film from another are those recurring charactersistics of style, process and technique. Hitchcock, for example, became known for his very effective use of stairways. In addition, his blond heroines, who at times meet unpleasant ends, were often a Hitchcock trademark, along with his cameo appearances. Other directors whose film technique and competence qualify them for auteur status are John Ford and Charlie Chaplin. Their films bear the distinguishing marks of their creative genius.

Then, how does this theory apply to television or a study of Bill Cosby? The creative center of film is the director. In television the producer has that role. Cantor[14] and Marc[15] note that producers are powerful individuals in shaping television series, while Newcomb and Alley[16] consider producers the creative forces in television. As in film, television auteurs possess characteristics that are above all distinguished by the themes they follow in a group of shows supported by their artistic progress, "signature" or style, and their technique and procedural tendencies. Marc considers the most meaningful way to determine television authorship is to find the thematic continuity in a group of shows produced by the same personality. "Surprise" endings are the signature of *Twilight Zone* episodes written by Rod Serling, whereas laws-and-order politics dominate the series' *Adam-12* and *Dragnet* produced by Jack Webb.[17]

Setting a style that would dominate situation comedy and leave a permanent imprint on the genre are the comedies of Norman Lear. The flagship series *All in the Family,* followed closely by *Sanford and Son,* then *Maude, Good Times, One Day at a Time,* and *The Jeffersons* revolutionized sitcoms. His characters were so universal, the audience feels a part of the families being presented. Though loud and argumentative, these families coalesced during stressful situations. Lear's trademarks include episodes that discuss real-life issues relating to the family, generational conflict, and frank political dialogue that contrast to the traditional sitcom setting and structure. Instead of conversing on such topics as school grades and the necessity of purchasing a second car, the Bunkers debate racism, poverty, women's liberation, and transportation. In addition to Lear, other television producers elevated to "auteur" status are Quinn Martin, Aaron Spelling, James Brooks and Allan Burns, and Garry Marshall.[18] These persons attained their status because the shows they produced reflect their distinctive look and vision.

Bill Cosby, though not categorized as a producer with the individuals listed above, has served as executive producer and executive consultant for his successful television series' *(The Bill Cosby Show, Fat Albert,* and *The Cosby Show).* His creative technique, style, personality and "signature" are evident in each series. Therefore this paper utilizes the criteria ascribed to the auteur method of analysis to determine whether Cosby (and his work) qualify him as a television "auteur."

Cosby as Auteur

The Bill Cosby Show, Fat Albert, and *The Cosby Show* share several common characteristics. Each of the series is a trend-breaker, each includes characters surrounded by family and friends, and each specializes in plots with universal themes and multidimensional characters. For the purposes of this paper, the terms, trend-breaker, universal themes and multidimensional characters require definition. The Cosby shows are *trend-breakers* because each series either presents a different view of blacks in situation comedies by breaking previously held stereotypes, or creates an innovative method to handle content in an established genre. Chet Kincaid *(The Bill Cosby Show)* defied the image to the typical "clenched fist" black man depicted on television in the 1960s, by exuding his blackness in more subtle, nonverbal ways. *Fat Albert* is the first cartoon show to include value-laden messages instead of the slapstick humor used in cartoons to that time. *The Cosby Show* discontinues using mechanical plots, disrespectful children, and generational conflict and presents the two-parent black family where both partners work as professionals.

To ensure that *universal themes* are depicted (situations presented where the entire television audience could identify; those slice-of-life scenarios), Cosby hires professionals to serve as consultants and to review scripts. Gordon Berry assumed that role for *Fat Albert* and Alvin Poussaint for *The Cosby Show.* "My job is to ensure all the situations presented in the program are possible in real-life families and that the content focuses on what one can rather than cannot accomplish," asserts Poussaint.[19] The three series, seeking to tell an American story, appeal to as ethnically broad an audience as possible.[20] Cosby has been quoted as saying. "I don't think you can bring the races together by joking about the differences between them. I'd rather talk about the similarities, about what's universal in their experiences."[21]

Multidimensional characters are those that reveal their resourcefulness, intelligence, sensitivity *and* human frailties and weaknesses. Not one character is all good or all bad. All characters possess angelic and mischievous traits. Characters on the Cosby shows portray a wide range of personality differences, qualifying them for multidimensional status.

Trend-breaker

Cosby, the first black person to co-star in a network dramatic series *(I Spy),* created Chet Kincaid, the featured character in *The Bill Cosby Show,* very differently from the way other blacks were depicted on television during the late 1960s. Although a middle-class professional, living in an integrated environment, Cosby's Kincaid was strikingly different from Diahann Carroll's Julia who shared many of the same characteristics. Unlike *Julia,* a program criticized for the shallowness of its central character and saccharine dialogue, *The Bill Cosby Show,* evolved into a series extracted from the black experience.[22] The characters' blackness subtly integrated into the plots and dialogue, created a unique black man for that era. Kincaid listened to black music, had pictures of Martin Luther King, H. Rap Brown and prints by black artist Charles White hanging on the walls of his home. He worked with less privileged children, wore dashikis, and ordered "soul" food in black restaurants. Starting with the opening music by Quincy Jones, *The Bill Cosby Show* created a black ambiance totally missing in *Julia,* says MacDonald.[23]

Kincaid did not use stereotypical language and mannerisms, but let the nonverbal props chosen to complete the scenes help to reflect his cultural identity. A physical education teacher living in San Francisco and moonlighting to earn more money, Chet contradicted another black image of that period—the riotous rebellious black. In the series Cosby portrayed a black man who had not deserted his roots, but moved effectively in all circles. He tutored students in history, recruited athletes for this track team, attempted to settle arguments between his aunt and uncle, had friends over to watch basketball and encouraged another to stop smoking. The program did not rely on old stereotypes or the tendency to present blacks in roles that avoided any association with black life and culture like *The Leslie Uggams Show* and *Julia.*[24]

Fat Albert also broke tradition when the half-hour cartoon about friends from a Philadelphia neighborhood began airing on CBS in 1972. Cosby rejects slap-stick comedy and violence, therefore strenuous behind-the-scenes work was necessary to convince CBS executives the series would garner an audience which would appreciate the program and its educational storylines.[25] Used as a vehicle to teach social values, judgment and personal responsibility, the show precipitated the major realignment of Saturday morning programming at CBS, as well as presented its black characters in a positive light. The Cosby kids, though black and living in a poor neighborhood, do not display offensive behavior. They are innocent children, making the best of life and learning from experiences.[26]

After the success of *Fat Albert,* CBS added other children's shows to its Saturday morning line-up *(Valley of the Dinosaurs, Shazam,* for example) that also communicated value-laden messages. Most of these cartoons and children's programs were eventually cancelled, but *Fat Albert* continues on the network. ABC and NBC, inspired by the popularity and appeal of *Fat Albert,* introduced their own set of message shows for children. Included were *The Big Blue Marble, Zoom,* and *Kids are People.* Program content initiated in the episodes of *Fat Albert* and adopted by the above shows became the primary subject matter of children's programs.[27]

Breaking tradition a third time, *The Cosby Show* rejects the use of contrived plots, gag lines, and generational putdowns (the latter a characteristic of Norman Lear comedies). "The over utilized characteristics of previous black-oriented comedies with stereotyped black adults *(Good Times, Stanford and Son)* or wise-cracking black children *(Diff'rent Strokes, Webster)* with white parents were also missing," according to television critic Tom Shales.[28] The Huxtables—Clair, Cliff and the Children (Sondra, Denise, Theo, Vanessa and Rudy), expose audiences to a two-parent, successful, upper middle-class, cohesive black family without the self-deprecation of series like *The Jeffersons* or *Good Times. The Cosby Show* avoids this brand of humor and other negative characteristics (isolated, matriarchal, violent, and conflict prone), observed in black television families of the 1970s.[29]

As in *The Bill Cosby Show,* the black experience on *The Cosby Show* emerges through subtle references. Black artist Varnette Honewoods' pictures hang on the walls along with posters of Frederick Douglass and signs to "end-apartheid." The children

dance and listen to black music while discussing whether to attend black schools like Howard University or Talledega College. Storylines develop, according to critic Sally Smith, from life's small humorous moments that viewers recognize, not contrived situations that offer cliff-hangers before each commercial.[30]

Not only was *The Cosby Show* instrumental in the revitalization of situation comedies but it helped NBC become the number one rated network for the first time in thirty years.[31] During the series' first season, ABC and CBS unsuccessfully counter-programmed the show, and then during the second season, created clones *(Charlie & Co.* and *Growing Pains),* and reshuffled the lineups in an attempt to offset its popularity. Interestingly enough, Cosby fought the same battle he encountered with *Fat Albert* to get the Huxtable family on the air. Additionally, ABC and CBS rejected the program anticipating the continued unpopularity of situation comedies.[32]

In one way or another each series set a standard in the treatment of black people or black situations by not acquiescing to old stereotypes of behavior or subject matter. Television programming has been affected by the trends set by *Fat Albert* and *The Cosby Show.* Derivatives of these series fill the programming schedules of American television *(Electric Co., Kids Break, Smurfs, Growing Pains,* and *227).*

Characters Surrounded by Family and Friends

In addition to the role of trend-breaker, a second distinguishing feature of the Cosby programs is the presentation of characters surrounded by family and friends. Never isolated from the larger community, the characters in the Cosby shows do not exist in a vacuum but have families that provide support, continuity, and generational links to past and present. Characters frequently mention ancestors whose lives have been inspirational or who passed along family remedies or keepsakes. The audiences for *The Bill Cosby Show* were introduced to Chet Kincaid's mother, siblings and extended family. Fat Albert, Bill, Rudy, Mushmouth, Russell and the other Cosby kids regularly spend time with their parents. However rare the moments, specific episodes highlight these parent-child relationships. The Huxtable family circle, enriched not only by paternal and maternal grandparents, enjoys the pleasure of friends who visit their New York brownstone. This particular characteristic, often absent from previous black television families, is an integral element in *The Cosby Show*. Video audiences were rarely introduced to the extended families or ancestors of the Evans' of *Good Times* or those of Louise and George Jefferson. From inception, the Cosby programs included family members. Kincaid lived next door to his sister. Rudy's *(The Cosby Show)* friend Peter visits her regularly from his home across the street. With *Good Times* and *The Jeffersons,* for example, audiences only caught glimpses of family members.

Universal Themes and Multidimensional Characters

A third characteristic shared by the Cosby shows are their dependence on plots utilizing universal themes and characters with multidimensional personalities. Audiences, through identification, relate to the experiences unfolding before them on the television screen. This process is nothing new to television. However, Cosby's characters and the situations in which they appear depict people with a distinct ethnic background coupled with universal appeal.[34]

Chet Kincaid of the *The Bill Cosby Show* had experiences that placed him in varied situatuations and settings that contribute to the developement and portrayal of a well-rounded character. Not confined to his apartment or classroom, Chet moved about San Francisco shopping for groceries, visiting his sister, and auditioning for a commercial. These activities placed him in contact with his students' parents, old classmates and people in his neighborhood. Occasionally guest stars appeared on the program as members of the Holmes High School staff or as romantic interest for Kincaid (Cicely Tyson).

Situations depicted him stuck in an elevator overnight at his high school, exhausted after sleepless nights caused by barking dogs in his neighborhood, and frustrated after delivering papers for his sick nephew to all the wrong homes. Kincaid was pictured as a colleague, friend, teacher, and member of a close supportive family unit. Audiences experienced his failures and successes in coping with life's everyday occurrences and see themselves or what they'd like to be reflected in Kincaid. A teacher in New Fairfield, Connecticut assigned the program to her students for homework. They were required to watch the show every Sunday night. Impressed with the type of teacher Cosby portrayed and the ideals he presented, she felt the show set an example modern teachers should be required to follow when communicating to students.[35]

Drawing from his experiences growing up in Philadelphia, Cosby created "Fat Albert" as an extension of his childhood. Cosby's voice, in its many variations, is the one most frequently used by the characters. Plots feature Fat Albert and the kids playing, going to school, and sharing experiences that provide the back-drops for the inclusion of pro-social messages. These messages, fused with entertainment, offer the young audiences the opportunity to be exposed to values and concepts applicable to their age and experience in life.[36]

The main center of action is the junk yard and the club house, but occasionally the children wander home where their parents offer discipline and counsel. Major characters include Fat Albert and the Kids joined by different persons whose problems or personalities help introduce the message for that particular episode. The Brown Hornet, the children's favorite television hero; Mudfoot, an elderly gentleman from the neighborhood; and Bill Cosby, who appears between scenes to focus the messages, complete the cast. In certain episodes Mudfoot delivers his particular form of advice while the Brown Hornet's adventures serve as vehicles to introduce additional subject matter.

Fat Albert, generally cast as the "good angel," provides the strength and backbone of the gang, while Rudy often cast as the "Bad angel," assumes the role of his foil, while the others fall somewhere in between. All the children develop skills, learn, and expand their levels of knowledge and understanding as the series unfolds. Even Fat Albert loses his halo once when he drives his father's car without permission; and Rudy gains one when he saves a friend from drowning. The multidimensionality of the Cosby Kids is reflected in the range of personalities represented by each child and in the manner in which they accept, internalize and mature emotionally from the problem-solving tasks they share and the lessons they learn in each episode.

Just as Chet Kincaid and the Cosby Kids portray their frailties and personality traits, the Huxtables follow this Cosby tradition by depicting imperfect, but likeable people in realistic situations. Borrowing heavily from experiences with his real-life family (as he did with his childhood with *Fat Albert*), Cosby helps create plots audiences easily recognize.[37] Norment considers the storylines ones with which viewers of the eighties can easily identify. Episodes present the overworked mother; the unmechanical husband who insists on making home repairs; the teen daughter who frustrates her parents by dating boys with earrings; the pre-teen who one moment is frightened by horror movie and the next discovers boys; and the son who hates homework, exams and cleaning his room. One or all of these situations conceivably occurs in real families. With the age of the siblings, spanning primary school to college, children easily identify with their counterparts in the series.[38] For example, a *Washington Post* article from November 1986 includes interviews of five families with different incomes, ethnic backgrounds and composition, who all acknowledge they relate to a situation or character on *The Cosby Show.* Cliff goes to the refrigerator and takes out an empty carton of orange juice. Jim McEachien, director of operations for the distribution division of National Public Radio and father of three is quoted as saying, "That happens every day." "Someone goes to the fridge and takes out an empty orange juice carton that someone's put back in."[39] Harvard Psychiatrist Robert Coles asserts, "I hear white working class families quoting 'The Cosby Show' as though it were the last church sermon they heard. . . . It's a pastoral quality."[40]

The personalities of each family member reveal people who are resourceful, intelligent, sensitive, and yet have human fragilities. The Huxtables, though imperfect, show fear, pain, rejection, and betrayal, qualifying each of them as multidimensional people. Children and parents in the television audience share the same problems, have similar faults and personality quirks, and conceivably see themselves in each episode of the program, comments media analyst Mary Helen Williams.[41] Cosby succeeds

in presenting universal themes, multidimensional characters, and adds to the trend of narrowcasting to capture specific audiences by "broadcasting" to appeal to a mass audience.[42]

The Cosby "Signature"

The Cosby "signature" evolves from his use of raceless humor in his role as comic storyteller. This trait, central to each of his series from *I Spy* to *The Cosby Show,* and evident in his act as a stand-up comedian, developed into the Cosby trademark. Once Cosby began appearing on television in *I Spy* he vetoed the use of racial messages in the dialogue and, when he became an executive producer, this technique was maintained. Cosby solidifies this concept of raceless humor in his television series' by his presence, and influence.[43] Script-writers are challenged to satisfy Cosby's image of how the individual characters should be created, the plots developed and the humor fused into the dialogue of the episodes. The writing staffs, therefore, translate Cosby's ideas into stories crafted around his comedic style.

Cosby creates this style based on situations and storytelling, not racial jokes. When he first appeared in clubs, Cosby imitated Dick Gregory's brand of humor. He soon discovered "there was room for only one Dick Gregory" and created a mode of comedy he could master.[44] His "colorblind" humor, therefore, developed as an outgrowth of this realization. Cosby's "humor for everyone" cast him as a humorist commenting from a personal point of view on the experiences of life, rather than a comedian. Often compared to Mark Twain, Cosby creates stories that grasp the funny side of life yet echo a subtle seriousness based in reality.[45]

Cosby structures his work similarly to jazz musicians playing a

melody. A joke translates into a musical tune with a beginning, middle, and an end. Cosby assumes the soloist role and his chord changes evolve into punch lines that make people laugh. Once he masters the melody, improvisation follows and the same story develops, taking many turns before it ends.[46] For Cosby, a very simple story can be embellished by simply changing the "melody" to accommodate the audience or situation.

Breaking the mold of verbal insults and "put down" humor utilized by sitcoms like *Sanford and Son* and *The Jeffersons,* Cosby also includes in his comedy style the communication mode defined in black verbal behavior as narrative sequencing. Dating back to an African past, this method of storytelling takes the form of a concrete narrative and relates general abstract observations about life, people and love. The storyteller uses his voice and body movements to bring the story to life.[47] Cosby's brand of raceless humor, influenced by this linguistic style in the black community and his exposure to the words of Mark Twain, his love of jazz, his childhood in Philadelphia and his life as a father, are his signature. Cosby's allegiance to his code of raceless humor does not waver, even when critics label Alexander Scott of *I Spy* as "second banana" to Robert Culp's Kelly Robinson; Chet Kincaid, a black man trying to play white; and, The Huxtables, *Leave it to Beaver* in blackface.[48]

Conclusion

Acquiring auteur status indicates a producer communicates successfully with the audience, creates innovative themes that challenge tradition, advances the medium through artistic and technical competence and demonstrates the ability to sustain a "signature" from series to series. Auteurs are the creators of programming history and have the power to significantly influence and restructure programming aired by the networks. For, in television, success very often breeds imitation. In considering the discussion on the preceding pages and the definition of an auteur in the above sentences, one question remains: Does Bill Cosby merit the title, television auteur?

Cosby is a ground breaker. His technical competence and familiarity with television, evident by the success and longevity of his series', influence the medium. *Fat Albert* and *The Cosby Show* have significantly altered television programming. Value-laden cartoons laced with humor grace the Saturday morning network offerings as a direct result of *Fat Albert and the Cosby Kids.* Further, situation comedies, thought to be a dying genre by network decision makers, were salvaged when *The Cosby Show* first aired and reversed that trend. *The Bill Cosby Show* presents a different, more realistic image of the black male than the accepted portrayal utilized frequently in television during the 60s.

Cosby goes against the stereotype and does not create blacks as sterile, white reproductions like *Julia* or place them in abject poverty, performing odd jobs for survival *(Good Times).* His characters are accepted or rejected because they depict real people not "types." The people and situations he creates for television emanate from his own experience, not through reading the pages of eighteenth century literature or viewing old tapes of *Amos 'n Andy.*

As a creative artist, Cosby's forte is the half-hour comedy. His application of universal themes and multidimensional characters create situations common to audiences of all ages and races. In addition, Cosby subtly introduces unique elements of black culture to his audiences. With *The Cosby Show,* a standard is set by which all television portrayals of black characters and culture will be compared.

Cosby's creative technique and "signature" of raceless humor, apparent in each series, have their base in the black communication mode of narrative sequencing. Never a comedian who found humor in verbal insults or the "put down," Cosby maintains his standard by never acquiescing to the criticism his series' garner concerning their authenticity or "blackness." Cosby states, "I want to share the happiness within our people. I want to show that we have the same kind of wants and needs as other American families. I'm going to take this show *[The Cosby Show]* and make it last as long as I can show black people that they have something to be proud of."[49]

The Bill Cosby Show presented a different image of the black male while *Fat Albert* and *The Cosby Show* have significantly influenced television programming and its audiences' image of the black family. Cosby's personal style is stamped on all his products. His creative technique and "signature" are reflected in each series, and his shows influence the medium, thus qualifying him as a television auteur.

Notes

1. Cynthia Griffin and George Hill, "Bill Cosby: In Our Living Rooms for 20 Years," *Ebony Images: Black Americans and Television* (Los Angeles: Daystar Publications, 1986), p. 97.

2. J. Fred MacDonald, *Blacks and White TV: Afro-Americans in Television Since 1948* (Chicago: Nelson-Hall, 1983), p. 189.

3. William Greider, "On Television, Race no Longer Divides Us," *The Washington Post,* 12 April 1978, p. A12.

4. MacDonald, p. 114.

5. Robert Sklar, *Prime-time America: Life on and Behind the Television Screen* (New York: Oxford University Press, 1980). See also Robert R. Smith, *Beyond the Wasteland: The Criticism of Broadcasting* (Annandale, Virginia: Speech Communication Association, 1980).

6. Donald David, "Auteur Film Criticism as a Vehicle for Television Criticism," *Feedback* 26 (1984), 14.

7. Philip Wander, "Was Anyone Afraid of Maude Finlay," *Understanding Television: Essays on Television as a Social And Cultural Force,* Robert Adler, Ed. (New York: Praeger, 1981), pp. 225–230.

8. Donald Davis, p. 15 see also David Marc, "TV Auteurism," *American Film* (1981), 52–53.

9. Andrew Sarris, "Notes on the Auteur Theory in 1962," *Film Theory and Criticism,* Gerald Mast and Marshall Cohn, Eds., (New York: Oxford University Press, 1974). p. 511.

10. Donald Davis, p. 14.

11. Andrew Sarris, pp. 512–513.

12. Andrew Sarris, pp. 512–513.

13. Donald Davis, p. 15.

14. Muriel Canton, *The Hollywood TV Producer* (New York: Basic Books, 1971), p. 8.

15. David Marc, p. 53.

16. Horace Newcomb and Robert Alley, *The Producer's Medium: Conversations with Creators of American TV* (New York: Oxford University Press, 1983).

17. David Marc, p. 53.

18. Horace Newcomb and Robert Alley. See also Donald Davis, pp. 16-17. David Marc, pp. 54–55.

19. Alvin Poussaint, personal interview, March 1 1985, Cambridge, Massachusetts.

20. Ann Feltman, "Laughing and Learning with Bill Cosby," *Parent's Magazine* (1974), 48.

21. Bill Cosby, personal interview by Larry Linderman, *Playboy* (1985), 75–92.

22. J. Fred MacDonald, p. 118.

23. J. Fred MacDonald, p. 118.

24. J. Fred MacDonald, pp. 117, 119.

25. Audrey Wright, "Cosby on Comedy: What it's Like Being Number One!" *Right On Special* (1985), p. 40.

26. J. Fred MacDonald, p. 195.

27. J. Fred MacDonald, p. 196.

28. Tom Shales, "NBC's Cosby, the Pick of the Fall Crop," *Washington Post,* 20 September 1984, sec. C, p. 6.

29. Gordon Berry, "Research Perspectives on the Portrayals of Afro-American Families on Television, *Black Families and the Medium of Television,* Jackson, Ed. (Ann Arbor: The University of Michigan, 1982), pp. 47–59. See also Barry Greenberg and Kimberly Neuendorf, "Black Family Interactions on TV," *Life on Television,* Barry Greenberg, Ed. (New Jersey: Ablex, 1980), pp. 173–181. Pilar Baptista-Fernandez and Barry Greenberg, "The Context, Characteristics and Communication Behaviors of Blacks on Television," *Life on Television,* Barry Greenberg, Ed. (New Jersey: Ablex, 1980), pp. 13–21.

30. Sally Smith, "Cosby Puts His Stamp on a TV Hit," *New York Times,* 18 November, 1984.

31. Harry Waters, "Cosby's Fast Track," *Newsweek,* September 2, 1985, p. 52. See also Jeff Jarvis, "TV and Family," *Elle,* September 1987, pp. 152–153. Richard Zoglin, "Cosby, Inc," *Time,* 28 September 1987, p. 60.

32. Audrey Wright, p. 40.

33. Bill Davidson, "I Must be Doing Something Right," *McCall's,* May 1985, P. 147.

34. Sally Smith. See also Tom Shales, p. 1C. Harry Waters, p. 54.

35. Muriel Davidson, "Command Performance." *Good Housekeeping,* June 1971, p. 50. See Muriel Davidson, "Bill Cosby" The Man, His Work, His World." *Good Housekeeping,* March 1970, p. 26.

36. Ann Feltmann, p. 47.

37. Alvin Poussaint, personal interview. Also Lynn Norment, "The Cosby Show: The Real-Life Drama Behind Hit TV Show About a Black Family," *Ebony,* April 1985, p. 28.

38. Lynn Norment, p. 30.

39. Lynn Norment, p. 30.

40. Richard Zoglin, p. 56.

41. Mary Helen Williams, "How to Make Cosby Even Better." *TV Guide,* 22 March 1986, p. 5.

42. Paula Matabane, personal interview, March 7, 1986. Howard University. Washington, D.C.

43. Richard Zoglin, pp. 58, 60.

44. "Right." *Newsweek, 17* June 1963, p. 89.

45. "Color-Blind Comic." *Newsweek*, 20 May 1968, pp. 92–93, see also Lawrence Christon, "Bill Cosby—A Family Style." *Calendar,* 2 May 1982, p. 57. Ross Daniels, "Inside Cosby." *US*, 6 May 1985, p. 43.

46. Bill Cosby, personal interview by Lawrence Linderman, p. 89.

47. Geneva Smitherman, *Talking and Testifying: The Language of Black America* (Boston Houghton Mifflin Company, 1977), pp. 147–166.

48. Melvin Moore. "Blackface in Prime Time," *Small Voices and Great Trumpets: Minorities and the Media.* Bernard Rubin Ed. (New York: Praeger, 1989), p. 130. See also Muriel Davidson, p. 26. John Leonard, "Leave it to Cosby," *New York*, 22 October 1984, p. 154.

49. Bill Cosby, 1958 quoted by Lynn Norment. p. 30, see also Cynthia Griffin and George Hill, p. 105. Richard Zoglin, p. 60.

FRIEND

This essay is an excellent example of valuable journalistic criticism in that it offers readers an interesting yet thorough examination of "television's defining form." But it is also instructive because it is informed by several academic critical approaches. Genre analysis is most obvious. But can you identify hints of historical analysis? Reader-oriented criticism? Sociological criticism? Narrative analysis? Ideological criticism? Any others?

Sitcoms, Seriously

Tad Friend

A Brady Bunch dream the other night. I was a Brady Kid, in the sunken living room with Greg, Marcia, Peter, Jan, Bobby, and Cindy. We were fighting over the lead in the school play, or who could drive the car—something, anyway—when Mike Brady lolloped in. Our father wore bell-bottoms and a totally boss Qiana shirt and was grooving to a Walkman. Scattered laugh-track chuckles, perhaps at the anachronistic personal stereo. We all shouted, "Hey, Dad, we've got a problem!" Mike bopped on.

Kids: Hey, Dad!

Mike: What?

Kids: You can't hear us. You've got a Walkman on!

Mike: What?

Kids: You can't hear us. You've got a Walkman on!

Mike: I'm sorry, kids, I can't hear you—I've got a Walkman on!

The laugh track roared, and I awoke, lunging out of the sheets. It's spooky to have a Brady dream, particularly one with a laugh track. Spookier still to have my sleep troubled by lame sitcom dialogue. Weren't there some deep-seated

childhood conflicts to work out?

Since then I've slowly come to realize that the Brady dream did express a childhood conflict. This was clarified for me one recent evening when I sat on the beach with a dozen friends, enjoying the stars, the salty tang of the incoming tide, the moon glowing over the white carpet of water. Inspired, we took turns naming *Brady Bunch* episodes and recalled 107 before someone stumped. They only made 116.

By my own estimate I have spent

eleven thousand hours of my life, many of them the golden afternoons of youth, watching television sitcoms. They were often idiotic; I loved them anyway. Nowadays, as more or less a grown-up, I view sitcoms with a mixture of irony, nausea—many of them really do suck—and, still, deep affection. So, I'm conflicted. Something new has happened to the generations born since *The Goldbergs,* the first sitcom, aired on CBS forty-four years ago. Those of us under forty-five grew up whelmed in sitcoms as minnows are whelmed in the sea, in thrall to a new mass art form, a transcontinental, trans-societal in-joke that reaches up to 30 million people every half hour. Critics charge that even the wittiest sitcom bypasses the brain and spears the emotions, that sitcoms are really meant for children, or the child lurking in adults. They're right. We are cradled in sitcoms, rocked in their warm lap, nursed from what Harlan Ellison calls "the glass teat."

"Who needed friends when we had chums like Dobie and Maynard, Margie and Mrs. Odettes. Walter

Reprinted by permission of *International Creative Management,* Inc. © 1993 by Ted Friend.

Denton and Eddie Haskell?" writes Rick Mitz in *The Great TV Sitcom Book*. "I'm not a freak; I'm not so different. I'm just an average member of a generation that was weaned on the nineteen-inch screen." (TV has come to understand its role as wet nurse: Whereas in the early '60s *The Beverly Hillbillies's* Granny mistook a television for a newfangled washing machine, now the opening credits of *The Simpsons, Dream On,* and *The Jackie Thomas Show* present their characters hungrily eyeing the set.)

The sitcom is television's defining form. Although only one of the top ten top-rated shows in 1952 was a sitcom and three of ten in 1972 were sitcoms, seven of the top ten in 1992 were sitcoms. Sitcoms are on the networks during prime time, on local channels early in the morning and late at night, on Turner Broadcasting, Christian Broadcasting, the Family Channel, and Nick at Nite. If you have cable in New York City, you can (try to) watch thirty-two and a half hours of sitcoms a day. The reason the weird Dan Quayle-*Murphy Brown* fracas got such play, that Bill Clinton chose Harry Thomason and Linda Bloodworth-Thomason—creators of *Designing Women* and *Evening Shade*—to shape his media image, and that movies based on *The Addams Family, The Beverly Hillbillies, Dennis the Menace, The Flintstones,* and *The Brady Bunch* are in the works or already out is that sitcoms have become our most pervasive, powerful, and cherished form of media output. They flow into every corner of our lives.

And what have we learned from electronic Mom? Not much, say "adults," who denounce sitcoms for turning us into Chance the Gardener. As long ago as 1961, FCC chairman Newt Minnow declared sitcoms "formula comedies about totally unbelievable families;" more recently Steven Spielberg, of all people, called *Cheers, Roseanne,*

and *The Cosby Show* part of "a wasteland of homogenized milk." And certainly when I ponder how contentedly I watched *Hogan Heroes's* Sergeant Schultz shake his strudel-fed face and protest for the thousandth time, "I know *nuthing,*" the suspicion occurs that he wasn't kidding.

The dismissive adult view of sitcoms is loudest espoused by highbrow cultural guardians like Neil Postman and the late Allan Bloom, who want to build a fire wall around the popular art forms they claim will destroy us with their damnable intent to cause pleasure and laughter. (They'd be vixed if we pointed out that sitcoms are to an extent, old wine in a new bottle: Aristophanes and Moliere wrote the sitcoms of their times.) The adult view says that sitcoms fail to meet traditional highbrow standards: Great art should kidnap its auditors, knock them on the head and drag them through the cobbled streets, shake the snowy globe of the world and let the flakes fall where they may.

Okay, sitcoms don't have this effect. But so what? Sitcoms must be judged by a different standard—not lower, necessarily, just different. Those of us who've swum in the cathode sea since birth experience sitcoms in a new way and expect them to serve a different purpose than *Madame Bovary* and Schubert's Eighth Symphony—we expect them to show us our place in the world, not disturb it.

Sitcoms, like pop songs, seep into memory through reruns, filtering home while we think we're paying attention to something else. Reruns, which collapse time into the eternal present, are how we best appreciate television; a show's early episodes can't be experienced as classics because we don't yet really know and love the characters—early episodes gain density over the years. Watching for the third time an encore episode of *The*

Wonder Years, with its nostalgic emphasis on old TV and old Herman's Hermits and James Taylor songs, is the Ur—sitcom experience.

The average American watches more than twenty-eight hours of television a week, and according to a 1989 study, even the Luddite 8 percent who insist they never watch average ten hours a week; TV, as Camille Paglia notes, is "a hearth fire in the modern home. . . . It is simply on all the time"—seeping in. So while velvet clown paintings and steamy drugstore novels trip a few cortical synapses and vanish forever, endlessly repeated songs like "Brandy (You're a Fine Girl)" and the entire *Sanford and Son* oeuvre remain in memory Ziplocfresh. Seep, I should note, is the process by which we discover that we're mired in complex family relations, that we're in love, or that we're getting flabby and short of breath. Seep is how we learn jugular truths.

It's important to make a distinction here that most critics omit as they blitzkrieg across popular culture, using *Three's Company* as the propaganda equivalent of the Reichstag Fire. There are actually two basic sitcom varieties: highconcept comedies, like *Three's Company* and *Welcome Back, Kotter,* which feature farcical characters, absurd mishaps, and double entendres; and character-driven comedies, like *Seinfeld,* which seek to illuminate emotional truths.

It's hard to defend *Three's Company* too strenuously, because it is pure formula (four lame misunderstandings, eight pratfalls, twelve gay jokes, thirty-four boob and boinking gags).

But it and shows like it have a certain limited worth; the pure sitcom formula, honed by generations of writers from the *I Love Lucy* and *Honeymooners* models, is valuably predictable, particularly for children. Love outweighs queasiness when I think about a bad high-concept comedy like *The Brady Bunch* for the same reason love outweighs queasiness when I think about my old toy bunny. The cocoon of *The Brady Bunch's* repetitious plots (Jan has allergies; Jan feels unloved; Jan's dream guy falls for Marcia; Jan's so depressed she gets a wig; Jan's jealous of Marcia; Jan's too vain to wear glasses; Jan's worried how she'll look when she's old; Jan wants her siblings dead; Jan fails at ballet, tap-dancing, and baton-twirling, then can't get the lead in the school play—*but she perseveres and triumphs through foreseeable plot twist and robotic parental guidance*) conjured the world as a safe place, as warm and fuzzy and remote-controllable.

We feel affection for bad children sitcoms because we needed that message then, needed a cathode pacifier. We are also fond of them because we use sitcoms as triangulation points to chart our growth from the child who watched with wonder to the adult who watches with doting irony. Wed to that childhood moment, and to our changing perspective on it, we don't particularly care to see Bobby Brady in a wheelchair in the 1990 adult-oriented sequel, *The Bradys,* and we scoff at bad sitcoms that come along later—for me, at age thirty, the *Blossoms* and *Mr. Belvederes*—because to an adult they proclaim the world not so much harmless as pointless.

On the other hand, the classic character-driven comedies—*The Honeymooners, The Dick Van Dyke Show, All in the Family, The Mary Tyler Moore Show, Taxi, Cheers, Roseanne, The Simpsons*—admit that life is too much for us. These shows face death and despair, combat them with man's best existential weapon—sharp wit—and suggest that in a cruel and possibly meaningless world, a soft bower awaits. Thus *Cheers* weaves maladjusted barflies into a charmed

circle; and even a lesser show like *The Golden Girls* assures us we'll still have friends when we're old and our spouses have died. "A great half hour is like having a wonderful dinner with friends," says *Roseanne* and *Home Improvement* creator Matt Williams. "You have an afterglow—you feel glad to be part of the human race."

For me, now even hearing *The Mary Tyler Moore Show* theme song on Nick at Nite is fiercely exalting. It's partly because the shows are weekly time capsules (remember Betty Ford's appearance?) and because they conjure up those family Saturday nights, watching MTM when I was freshly bathed, in my flannel pj's, and angling not to be sent to bed. And because I had a monster crush on Mary.

But it's mostly because MTM was so well written, well acted, and funny that it subconsciously schooled me through seep. I knew those people better than I knew anyone outside my family, and I understood them better than I understood most people in my family. So I believed that my friends, too, would get married and give birth in my apartment, that coffee sobers a drunk, that bald people are especially witty, and that women look sexy in flared slacks. Sadly, this information turned out to be false.

But MTM also taught me, by implication, that loneliness, separation, divorce, and death can be borne and that life is a hard journey eased by love. If these sound like fairy-tale truths, they should: Great character-driven sitcoms have become our fairy tales (whereas high-concept comedies and bad character-driven sitcoms—those that coerce us with sermons and life lessons—are our fables. I'll expand on this distinction later).

Just as a child insists on hearing fairy tales read the same way every night, so we delight in reruns. Like fairy-tale formulas and stock characters—the three wishes, the

wicked stepmother—character-driven sitcom formulas and stock characters are deeply satisfying. A fairy tale, Bruno Bettelheim notes in *The Uses of Enchantment,* "simplifies all situations. Its figures are clearly drawn" and polarized: "One brother is stupid, the other is clever. One sister is virtuous and industrious, the others are vile and lazy. One is beautiful, the others are ugly."

And fairy tales, like great sitcoms, show us our place in life, in the family we'll grow into: They "provide the modern child with images of heroes who have to go out into the world all by themselves and who, although originally ignorant of the ultimate things, find secure places in the world by following the right way with deep inner confidence."

That perfectly describes Mary Richards, who set out in her car toward Minneapolis in 1979 alone and uncertain and ended seven years later clustered in a warm rugby scrum with her TV family—Murray, Ted, Sue Ann, Georgette, Mr. Grant. In the final episode Mary made explicit the message encoded in all great sitcoms: "I thought about something last night. What is a family? And I think I know. A family is people who make you feel less alone and really loved. Thank you for being my family."

In the highbrow view anyone who enjoys watching this scene has debased standards and perhaps even debased morals. Viewing " is a private act, an act that we perform by ourselves and with ourselves," Michael Arlen has written. "What it resembles most, I think, is masturbation." Actually, *writing* about sitcoms most resembles masturbation. Watching them most resembles adoption.

We watch, in other words, to join a surrogate family. Yet our link to these substitute families is uneasy, because we supply so much of the love. "That song in *Cheers*—

'Sometimes you want to go/Where everybody knows your name'—is very comforting, but it's completely untrue," notes Andy Borowitz, cocreator of *The Fresh Prince of Bel Air*. "We know their names, we know Sam and Woody and Norm, but no one on the show knows your name. In fact, you're really all alone out there."

Probably without having thought about it much, we all know what a sitcom is: a bunch of people who love one another, either a family or a familylike gang of coworkers and friends, and twenty-two minutes of funny things that happen to them at work and at home. Time has brought some changes: *All in the Family* introduced social issues and bedroom topics; and with *The Simpsons, Married . . . with Children,* and *Shaky Ground,* Fox established a new pop-psych paradigm: the dysfunctional family (loser dad teasing and being teased by his budding-loser children). Sitcoms have also increasingly incorporated purely dramatic moments, as on a recent *Wonder Years* about a Vietnam veteran's difficult readjustment at home—yet these plots are always balanced by a jokey subplot or leavened with cheer at the end.

Through all these thematic changes, the basic sitcom structure has remained remarkably constant. Its narrative arc is usually divided into two "acts" comprising three or four scenes each. A recent *Cheers* illustrates the armature:

Problem: Cliff's old girlfriend, Maggie, is back in town.

Cliff-hanger near the act break: She's pregnant, calls Cliff "Daddy."

Crisis moment early in the second act: After taking "you stud" congratulations all around, Cliff confides to Sam that he never had sex with Maggie.

Increased jeopardy: Maggie admits the child is really her ex-boyfriend Jerry's; Cliff says he'll marry her anyway.

Resolution: Maggie calls Jerry to tell him, and he says he wants her back after all; Cliff's off the hook.

Denouement: Turns out Maggie and Cliff did have sex once, only he was drunk and forgot. "You were great!" she assures him.

Classic sitcom structure "turns" the story every seven pages and has three jokes per page, or a joke at least every twenty-eight seconds. Characters can evolve over the years (Edith Bunker learns to stand up for herself; *The Bob Newhart Show's* Howard Borden becomes more than just an absent minded dunderhead—he becomes a nuanced absentminded dunderhead), but to maintain the show's core dynamic, most episodes, like the *Cheers* above, must end where they started. If Roseanne inherits a million dollars, she must lose it; if Jethro meets a Bel Air babe, nineteen minutes later she's revealed as a gold digger, maniac, or robot hermaphrodite.

"In real life, Alex Keaton is now doing pro bono work for women's-rights groups," says *Family Ties* creator Gary David Goldberg, "but the audience would never have let us do that. They wanted purity, not real-life change. Michael [J. Fox] said to me. 'What do I care that Mallory talks on the phone? How can I still care?' And he was right—we did 180 *Family Ties* and the last 100 we were fighting the format."

But, as with the sonnet, a lot can be packed into a confining structure. Sitcoms have developed their own emotional shorthand: For instance, that we never see Buddy's wife, Pickles, on *The Dick Van Dyke Show;* Phyllis's husband, Lars, on *The Mary Tyler Moore Show;* or Norm's Wife, Vera, on *Cheers* speaks volumes about those marriages. And most sitcoms ring changes on about ten plots. This has been decried as unimaginative; in fact, it's exemplary structural purity. Sitcoms plots, after all, are really just vehicles allowing the characters to be vengeful, vexed,

perplexed, conniving, or goofy—whatever they do best.

The characters who inhabit these story lines—the ensemble of lovable eccentrics—are as typical as Punch and Judy or commedia dell'arte figures. Among many other types there's the blond bimbo (Chrissy Snow, Elly May Clampet, Kelly Bundy); the crusty-but-lovable boss (Lou Grant, Mr. Mooney, Louie De Palma); the kooky-but-cuddly foreigner/alien (Latka, ALF, Mork); and the all-powerful servant (Benson, Mr. French, Ann B. Davis as Alice).

"The stupid guy, the wiseass, the sex maniac, the fat guy, the saucy wench, the bitch, the fob, and the distaff fop—that describes the cast of *Cheers,* says Susan Borowitz, cocreator of *Fresh Prince*. "That one-line *TV Guide* blurbiness is necessary for people to recognize the show, to clearly understand what's going on." This singleness of intent is underscored by signature expostulations: *"Ayyy!"; "Dyn-o-mite!";* "To the moon, Alice!"; Stifle yourself!"; "Kiss my grits!"; "oh, *Ro-o-ob!";* and "Don't have a cow, man!"

The characters and their desires must be blueprint clear: we never have to infer motivations as we do with novels and films—in twenty-two minutes, there's no time for guesswork. "In every sitcom I've worked on, if we're having trouble clarifying characters' attitudes or sharpening opposing points of view—telling the audience what's at stake—we apply the Ralph Kramden test," says Matt Williams, the *Roseanne* and *Home Improvement* creator. "We go back through the scene to figure out where Ralph would say, 'Alice, you take that job and you're out of my life!' or 'Alice, if your mother comes through that door and calls me fat one more time, I'm throwing her out the window!' *Knock, knock.* 'Hi, Mom.'"

Good character-driven sitcoms have at least one character, like Ralph, with an extreme point of view. Thus Lucy, who desperately wants to break into show business; Archie, who fears "coons," "spiks," and "hebes"; and Hawkeye, a zealous pacifist surrounded by war. Bad shows have characters with quirks and traits; good shows have characters with a world view.

"Great sitcoms are character-driven," says former Warner Brothers comedy executive Scott Kaufer, echoing many in Hollywood. "A mistake even experienced writer-producers make is to pitch occupations and locales—'How'd you like a comedy set in a firehouse?' You want people to pitch Archie Bunker and Mike Stivic."

What we treasure about a show is not jokes and plot points but characters and relationships—people we'd like to be like, friendships we'd like to be in. I was always skeptical about *Bewitched* because when Dick Sargent replaced Dick York as Darrin, the characters pretended nothing had happened, while I felt as one might toward a new stepfather. (Only years later did I realize Samantha was much too smart and creative for either dimwit Darrin.)

People don't care about people who don't care, so even the most abrasive characters must hide a heart of gold. We needn't love them—we don't love George Jefferson or *Coach's* Hayden Fox—but we must empathize. Miles Drentell of *thirtysomething,* perhaps television's most interesting character, couldn't have survived on a half-hour comedy: Erratic and unfathomable, he would have made a sitcom seem . . . unsafe.

"A series is like a dinner guest," says Gary David Goldburg. "If you're scintillating but you open a wound, you won't get invited back. You must be nonthreatening. Early on, the audience didn't understand how Alex felt about Mallory when

he teased her, and they weren't laughing. So we did a show in which Alex, instead of going to his Princeton interview, comforts her when she's been dumped by her boyfriend. We had to say, 'Hey, he really does love her.'"

The characters' love—or anger or ambition, their strong drives—must be expressed within a family or surrogate family, socialized lest it undermine the core group. (Even in Fox's dysfunctional-family sitcoms, the family goes everywhere together and its members always support one another in the end.) In the early, unsteady going of *Happy Days,* Arthur Fonzarelli was the hood with no real connection to Richie's family. "I knew that if I could get him [living over the Cunninghams'] garage," *Happy Days* creator Garry Marshall has said, "I could get him into the kitchen; he could become a member of the family." The Fonz moved in; the show went to number one.

This sort of development enacts the truth that the French express as *tout comprendre, dest tout excuser*—if you really get to know a character, if you really understand someone like Louie De Palma, you will excuse him completely, as his fellow characters do. In good sitcoms the malcontent, brat, loner, lout, clodpoll, or witch creates disorder, then gets slowly drawn back, redomesticated, through the love of others and the private dawning of wisdom. Lucy, Ralph, Sam Malone, and Bart Simpson—the child characters, the raging ids—are shown the error of their disruptive ways, and we can identify with both the high jinks and the penitence.

The danger of this dynamic was well expressed by Nabokov, who warned that easy psychological identification with fictional characters gives way to sentimentality and dulls your sense of the work as a whole. The mistake we sometimes make while watching a sitcom

is to think that because we're watching a sitcom (which we know is meant to be nonthreatening), characters who feel emotionally minatory must really be hiding a heart of gold, so it's okay to identify with them. Sometimes they're not and it's not.

Bad sitcoms make their malcontents comform not through love but through sermon and coercion; anyone with a variant idea is mercilessly mocked. Critic Mark Crispin Miller rightly pillories the jeering dynamic on *The Cosby Show,* citing an episode in which Cliff Huxtable ridicules some verses Denise has written for the school choir ("I walk alone...I walk alone"); Denise does a rewrite ("My mother and father are my best friends. . . . Their love is real, their love is real") and receives a big kiss. Cliff "strikes his children as a peach," Miller writes, "until they realize, years later and after lots of psychotherapy, what a subtle thug he really was."

"What Bill said was often mean and unacceptable on the page," says Matt Williams, who wrote for *Cosby.* "He would verbally abuse his kids, lie to them, hide things from them—but the audience knew he loved them." Did he really, or were we just hoping?

Do we so love the very idea of the sitcom family that we'll watch terrible shows because we know the characters right off the bat, because we've seen them a dozen times before on other shows? "There are a lot of cynical people [in Hollywood] manufacturing just the right dose of warmth," says Conan O'Brian, a writer for *The Simpsons.* "Watching it starts to make you feel like a lab ape. The networks want a mother and father who are good-looking and in their late thirties to appeal to baby boomers. They have some money because people like seeing nice possessions but not too much money because then people can't identify.

Their cute teenage daughter is just starting to date, which appeals to teenage girls and guys. There's a bratty kid like Bart—kids love kids who can get away with stuff—and, look, there's a little black kid who hangs around, because old people and little black kids love little black kids. And they have a big, furry dog."

In the last decade alone that recipe reasonably describes *Who's the Boss, Growing Pains, Diff'rent Strokes, Gimme a Break!, Family Ties, Webster,* and *The Cosby Show.* It's fair to wonder who's running whose maze to get a food pellet.

Many such sitcoms end episodes with "the warm moment"—"the hug." Everyone embraces and we learn a lesson: Prejudice is bad; sharing is good; slow and steady wins the race. Thus, in the Big Lie plot, the wiseacre invariable learns the biblical proverb that a stone will come back upon him who starts it rolling. This, like most such epiphanies, illuminates one of the core sitcom truths: Don't Rock the Boat. The other core sitcom truth is Just Be Yourself, which would seem to contradict Don't Rock the Boat, except that you should be yourself only insofar as it doesn't rock the boat.

Just Be Yourself is also something of a sly disclaimer, because the networks are skittishly aware that millions tune in to learn who they are and how they should behave. "A lot of latchkey kids are watching alone," says Gary David Goldberg, "and, frighteningly, you are many people's closest friend. So you avoid certain ambiguities. I will not make a casual drug joke. I will not show teenagers drinking. I will show kids doing the chores and Dad cooking dinner without anyone remarking on it. Or when you start a scene, someone's reading. Or when someone goes out, you have someone say, 'Put your seat belt on.'"

"The sitcom has taken the place of church, of religious training," says Susan Borowitz. "If an episode is just a romp or a farce, the audience isn't as satisfied. Sitcoms work better if they're little sermons or parables." (In his novel *Generation X,* Douglas Coupland defines tele-parablizing as "morals used in everyday life that derive from TV sitcom plots: That's just like the episode where Jan lost her glasses!") In many families, watching sitcoms together is an almost sacred obligation: When the set goes on, the couch becomes a pew.

But sermons—the deus ex telemachina descent of poetic justice—mark a craven sitcom, a point made deftly on a *Simpsons* episode. In "Blood Feud," Bart donates life-saving blood to Homer's boss, Mr. Burns, who presents the family with an ugly stone head.

MARGE: The moral of this story is, A good deed is its own reward.
BART: We got a reward; the head is cool.
MARGE: Well, then, I guess the moral is, No good deed goes unrewarded.
HOMER: Wait a minute, if I hadn't written that nasty letter we wouldn't have gotten anything.
MARGE: Well, then, I guess the moral is, The squeaky wheel get the grease.
LISA: Perhaps there is no moral to this story.
HOMER: Exactly, it's just a bunch of stuff that happened.

"A lot of people loved Homer's line," says *Simpsons* executive producer Mike Reiss. "They all got the joke."

The sermon gap between bad and good sitcoms is precisely the distinction between fables and fairy tales. "The question for the child is not 'Do I want to be good?' but 'Whom do I want to be like?'" Bruno Bettlehiem writes. Fairy tales inspire the latter question, whereas "fables demand and threaten—they are moralistic—or they just enter-

tain. The fable always states a moral truth; there is no hidden meaning, nothing is left to our imagination."

Fables—whether via Aesop or CBS—are hackwork, no matter how sitcom producers gussy them up with highbrow claims. "There's a lot of underlying philosophy to the characters on *Gilligan's Island,*" its creator, Sherwood Schwartz, has said. "They're really a metaphor for the nations of the world, and their purpose was to show how nations have to get along together or cease to exist." So I guess Mr. Howell, overdressed and fussy, would be France; Gilligan, underfed and disaster-prone, would be Bangladesh. . . .

Compare *Gilligan's Island* with the famous "Chuckles Bites the Dust" episode of *The Mary Tyler Moore Show.* While leading a parade, WJM's kiddie-show host Chuckles the Clown is killed by a rogue elephant that tries to shell him out of his Peter Peanut costume. First Murray, then Lou, then Sue Ann, relieve their astonished grief with wisecracks.

LOU: This could have happened to any of us, Ted.
MURRAY: Somewhere out there, there's an elephant with your name on it.

Mary is shocked and priggish: At the funeral, she says, "A man has died. We came here to show respect—not to laugh." Many a sitcom would stop with that lesson. But when Reverend Burns gives his eulogy and mentions Billy Banana, Mary has to stifle a snicker. When he reminds the congregants how Chuckles's character "Mr. Fee-Fi-Fo would always pick himself up, dust himself off, and say: 'I hurt my foo-foo,'" she giggles. Everyone glares, and she pretends she's coughing. Then Reverend Burns mentions Chuckles's ditty, "A little song, a little dance, a little seltzer down your pants," and Mary can't restrain a loud cackle. The reverend asks her to stand and "laugh out loud. Don't you see, nothing could have made Chuckles happier? He lived to make people laugh. Tears were offensive to him, deeply offensive. He hated to see people cry. So go ahead, my dear—laugh for Chuckles." Mary bursts out crying.

First of all, "Chuckles" was hilarious. When Ted says, "If it were my funeral, this place would be packed," we laugh. Cut to Murray, and we chuckle anticipating. "That's right, Ted," he says, "it's just of matter of giving the public what they want." Another laugh. This familiar byplay between antagonists, this three-laugh transaction, is like the chorus of a great popular song to which we can all sing along.

"Chuckles" also went against type. By this, her sixth season, we'd spent more than sixty hours with Mary and had come to understand her in a way possible only on a long running sitcom and we knew she'd be mortified to laugh at a funeral. "Chuckles" also risked making Mary unlikable when she primly reproved her friends. And the episode flaunts—indeed, comments on—MTM's empathy encouraging verisimilitude: Its characters laugh when other characters say funny things, as they would in life, instead of saying "What?" or ignoring the line, as they would on *Full House.*

Furthermore, the lines aren't necessarily written to be funny on the page. "One of the definitions of a great sitcom is that you can't repeat the jokes out of context for a friend," says MTM writer Treva Silverman. "You have to explain, 'Murray is coming into the newsroom and Ted is reading his script and Mary has been feeling sad and she's wearing a red dress with green buttons.'" In great sitcoms, lines are funny only because a specific character is saying them.

Contrast that with these two-and three-beat gags:

WOMAN: Is there something you don't like about my cooking?
MAN: Yeah—eating it.
And
MAN: You made sponge cake the other night and used a real sponge.
WOMAN: But you ate all of it.
MAN: Yeah—but it was the best thing you ever cooked.

The jokes come from *The Jeffersons* and *Good Times;* they could come from anywhere.

Finally, "Chuckles" offers no lesson, only the same implicitly socializing example found in fairy tales. (e.g., We make up our own minds what it means that Little Red Riding Hood dallies on the way to her grandmother's house, enjoys a sexy interlude with the wolf, gets eaten up, and is rescued by the fatherly hunter.) We are subtly encouraged to consider how these people we love deal with life's absurd affronts. We are permitted to discover, if we care to, that Mary's glossy perfection hides a deep fear of death. But because it's Chuckles who died, not, say, Rhoda (who just got canceled), we aren't threatened. Great sitcoms address our deepest dilemmas with immense tact.

Sitcom writers are fond of depressing themselves by reciting a catechism that goes something like this: "'Chuckles'-is-great-it's-the-best-we-can-do-but-is-it-great-art?-I-think-not." They see themselves being well paid to crank out a commercial product that they believe—or profess to believe—is beneath their true talents. They bemoan the straitjacket buckles of their form—the need to keep things fundamentally light; the need to goose the studio audience with easy jokes; the up to twenty ads per half hour that deflate the gathering joy with pitches for marshmallows and incontinence underpants; the timid frettings of the networks; the actors' interference (according to writers' legend, *My Favorite Mar-*

tian star Roy Walston once vetoed his lines, explaining. "A martian would never say that"); the Sisyphean demand for new episodes, many of which are written in a week and completely rewritten in three days; and the Tony Danza Syndrome—likability, likability, likability.

"I used to have such grand designs," says Matt Williams. "I thought every half hour could be a one-act play revealing a deep truth about the human condition. The truth is, it's twenty-two minutes, you're constantly interrupted by commercials, the phone's going to ring, and the dog's going to pee on the carpet. The most you can do is entertain and scrape the surface, be artful. If you want to delve deep into the human condition, go write a novel, or a film script no one will make."

Williams is judging sitcoms by the old standards of great art. But his capitulation is too profound. Even if, for the sake of argument, we allow traditional standards to frame the debate, it seems clear that great sitcoms both instruct and entertain: Aristotle's two criteria for art. What they don't do is threaten our deepest beliefs; they confirm rather than confront. If the world were like sitcoms, sitcoms wouldn't be necessary. They exist as a response to pain, a palliative to ease and smooth our path. Our laughter is how we speak back to TV, how we thank it for helping us. Even if we sometimes feel abandoned by our TV families, our laughter reconnects us with the community, with the millions of people who think that Rob Petrie tripping over a hassock or Archie Bunker being kissed on the cheek by Sammy Davis Jr. is funny.

Sitcoms aren't great art because great art is, in some way, more than we can bear—it is awesome or terrible, it daunts and dares, it asks us to be more than we are. Great art is admirable, and it can be loved, but it can never be fully lovable. Good art, because it is human and frail, is lovable. Great character-driven sitcoms should be judged not by the standards of great art but by the standards of fairy tales. These, our lovable modern fairy tales, are good art, because they provide life examples and seek to assuage our needs and fears. They ask us not to be more than we are but simply to be ourselves.

The strength of our collective hunger to be ourselves yet feel approved of by others is astonishing and a little alarming. But good art that reaches 30 million people and makes them feel connected may have more to offer us now than great art that reaches three thousand people and makes them feel more or less alone. In our time the standards for art have changed, expanded. The future belongs to Bart Simpson.

RUDKIN

Senior television student Mark Rudkin of Sam Houston State University wrote this essay on *Seinfeld* for criticism instructor Dr. Chris White. Can you find indications of both narrative analysis and reader-oriented criticism?

What do you think of his lengthy "set up," that is, his explanation of why television should be taken seriously? Do you think the critic should remind his or her readers of this or should the critic simply assume that most people interested in television already believe this? Are there critics who fail to see television's significance?

Could someone who has never seen *Seinfeld* appreciate this essay? What devices does Rudkin employ to include *Seinfeld* fans and non-watchers alike?

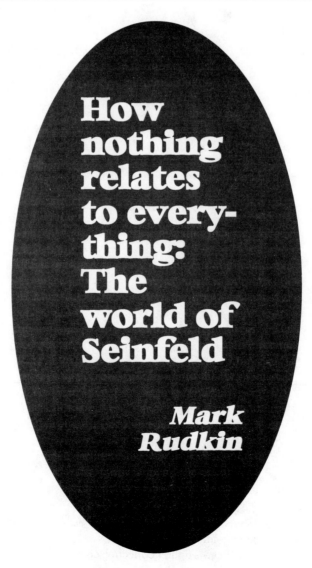

How nothing relates to everything: The world of Seinfeld

Mark Rudkin

It has long been the belief of many that television is a waste of time and nothing more than a mindless masturbation of otherwise worthwhile neurons. But what is TV? Is TV a reflection of our culture? Will post apocolyptic archeologists find these glowing altars of light to be the basis of our belief system or will the TV and all it stands for be tossed aside in favor of the more appealing hand blender? It is my belief that our little flickering dream boxes are not only entertainment tools, but magical mirrors that can tell us more than Alice's looking glass could ever concoct.

There are some who are opposed to the mass pilgrimage that each of us makes to the TV. And yes, it has become almost a ritual or religion for many, often attended to more than any real religion (Wober, 1988). Critics tend to intellectualize the content and condemn the entire medium for what little meaning some shows contain. It is easy to condemn TV in this manner. But those critics who usually put down TV are those who spend twenty-three hours working and find little pleasure in anything that entertains (Grube, 1984). So what kind of people watch this strange non-active, all-encompassing medium an average of three or four hours a day? Karl Marx would insist that TV is nothing more than a scheme for those who own to brainwash those who don't. There are no conspiracies, though. TV is just cheap entertainment. According to Jim Fowles (1982), author of *Television Viewers vs. Media Snobs*, the highly educated watch just as much television, and often the same shows as their less affluent counterparts. If ever you have the grand opportunity to confront one of these "snobs," however, you will find a certain amount of hesitation in their reply. Sure "Cop Rock" is melodic and mildly entertaining but what college professor, bank executive or supreme court judge would admit to watching it?

Then there is the beloved critic, interpreter of meaning, divine magistrate of what is good and what is bad. He is not necessarily a member of the upperclass snob club, yet sometimes he is quick to announce his displeasure of media. It seems that at any given time, in any given periodical, for any given reason, the critic is voicing his dislike of sitcoms being too silly, his abhorance of soap operas being too far fetched, his detestment of the cop shows being too violent (Shayer, 1971). The critic may gain stature in his or her own circles through these statements but sometimes this criticism could not be further from the truth. Certain shows, however, can never be appreciated for full value unless they are seen in a different environment, an environment unlike the laboratory motif many critics are accustomed to.

Finding true value in television can sometimes be an arduous endeavor. It may take the same amount of time to find cultural value in a show like "American Gladiators" as it would deciphering DNA. But there is something in there, behind the fanciful costumes, harkening back to middle ages and the impossible obstacle courses sponsored by your favorite breakfast cereal.

Television is not meant to be a fine art. Da Vinci may have invented the helicopter, painted the Mona Lisa and been a great doctor, but he sure as hell wouldn't have had the gall to write an episode of "Married . . . with Children." If television had to be compared to an art movement, the work of the bauhaus movement in pre-nazi Germany would be the best counterpart. TV is a highly industrialized, cheap art form that can be cranked out, often faster than Twinkies. Its form meets its function: to entertain and babysit a demographic so that the commercials can do their

job. After realizing this staggering fact, it is now possible to see just what is so damn entertaining about this medium and why we are so compelled to hold our need to answer nature's call just to find out how our favorite character reacts to the fact that the non-fat yogurt actually has fat in it (this week's episode of Seinfeld). This is a strength of television—the ability to make viewers negate their own needs in order to fulfill a sponsor's.

Television has strength. Television can muscle around any other medium because it is so real to us. Why are the images so real? Because that luminescent metal frame in our living rooms tells us about ourselves. What does society think of unwed mothers? What should we think of the upcoming vote in congress over this NAFTA thing? Does Bill Clinton really eat that many french fries? Television answers all of these questions and allows society to create a norm for any given topic.

Television also allows us to vent our emotion. Imagine the countless masses who will turn into a soap opera to compensate for their own deprived social lives. How many people turn on "COPS" just to reassure themselves that they are protected. Drama and comedy have become a socially acceptable means of agressive release for the viewer (Fowles, 1982). The main strength of television is its ability to mirror the beliefs of a given culture during a given time. Watch an episode of "Father's Knows Best." Study how the characters talk, how they dress, what morals they present. Although this may not be what the society was actually like, it does show what the Americans of the 1950s strived to become. With this in mind, it becomes clearer and clearer as to what fears, hopes and dreams a given culture may posses.

This make the shows on TV artifacts and though you may not be seeing an exhibit of Beavis and Butt-head's lighter collection com-

ing to your nearest metropolitan museum, you can see Cliff Claven's postal uniform at the Smithsonian. This is why television must be looked at not as a worthless piece of mind trash but as a genuine article of viable data as to what a given generation was thinking as the Gulf War was televised on CNN or what the popular attitude was toward Senator Packwood's naughty diaries way back in the 1990s.

An example of one such artifact that reflects society as it is now can be viewed on Thursday nights on NBC. Although "Seinfeld" the show, with Seinfeld the man, may not be the great orator Churchill, Lincoln and Caesar were, both say something about our society. The inner meaning and cultural implications of Seinfeld and what he says are the topic of this treatment.

"Seinfeld," is a half hour show that airs weekly and is centered around the life of Jerry Seinfeld. Jerry, who narrates the beginning and ending in a biographical manner, is a comedian who plays himself, a single, thirty-something male who leads a near-normal life. Each show is seasoned by the pack of friends that Jerry has accumulated. These friends include George, an out-of-work man with low self-esteem who lives with his parents. He is Jerry's best friend. Kramer is a neighbor who enters Jerry's apartment at will and is the origin of most of the zany plotlines. And finally, there is Elaine, Jerry's exgirlfriend who advises him on his sex life and other related matters. Although the show has been very popular and has done very well as a sitcom, it really isn't a sitcom. Rather it is a forum from which one man can reinact his own personal pet peaves, much to the chagrin of those who cause them in the show. Seinfeld is different.

From the stand-up routine at the beginning of the show, through the elaboration of the same routine at the end, these differences soon become evident. The stand-up usually deals with some part of the show's stream-of-thought plot, meaning we see the show not as a drama being performed, rather we see it as it unravels before the eyes of the characters, conversely allowing us to feel the narrative momentum of the show. This later becomes apparent to the viewer when the actual adventure begins.

This "adventure" into nothingness occupies most of the show. Similar to most shows, "Seinfeld" has characters reacting with one another, forming bonds and dealing with life. But, unlike most shows, there is no plot, just a series of incidents which in time validate the reasoning in Seinfeld's pet peaves introduced in the stand-up portions beginning and ending the show. Seinfeld himself says the shows are about nothing. Instead of focusing on a definite storyline, "Seinfeld" dances around main ideas, and displays the type of stream-of-thought vehicles that made writers who incorporated this same narrative pattern, like Faulkner, so unique. This uniqueness is what allows us to see through the eyes of the characters and experience these everyday nothings.

Not many sitcoms have ever spent a full thirty minutes determining the problems in understanding people who talk too softly or the difficulty one brings upon himself when faking an injury. Seinfeld confirms the universal beliefs of our society by making us think, "Well, what would I do in that same situation?" or "Yes! that has happened to me to....I hate it when that happens."

Because of this comprehensive treatment of the insignificant, "Seinfeld" has been able to turn the everyday event into an unusual, original media text. Through this particular show, the cultural beliefs of a given socio-economic group, of a given decade and of a given week may be probed.

Semioticians, critics and historians alike can learn where the popular pulse of our society rests.

In each show, several different occurances that might happen to anyone in a given day are magnified, dissected and resolved with the morals, beliefs and common sense "Seinfeld's" demographic would most likely agree upon. The linguistic style between the members of the show's "Family" reflects the ideas of the current pop culture. The continual reflection that the show has on itself is self-centered, much like many of those who view it weekly. Important details that normally would not have great meaning eventually become the intertwining ties that hold the show together. This type of material in a show brings not only unity among its viewers but an underlying confidence that "the way I do things is all right."

In one episode Jerry thinks his current girlfriend (he goes through them faster than Captain Kirk), is cheating on him with his cousin. He questions the word of George, based on whether or not George's glasses were "stolen" and if he could see or not. These became the deciding factors on the validity of George's word. This episode does not attempt to solve the theft in its plot, rather it focuses on an idiosyncracy that many people have who wear glasses: that when the corrective lenses are not on, they tend to squint in a failing effort to improve their impaired sight. During the remainder of the show, George attempts to prove through self-inflicted tests of visual acuity that he can indeed see objects that may appear larger in his imagination.

During this time, Jerry, faced with a scientific dilemma, conducts his own tests to see if his girlfriend is actually cheating on him. He twice outwardly accuses her of messing around with his cousin to no avail. The truth that squinting

really doesn't help surfaces when George grabs for an apple in Jerry's refrigerator and ends up biting into an onion. The show exhibits even more human nature when George, attempting to make it seem like he grabbed the white bulb on purpose, continues to engulf the tear-inflicting ball of crunchy sourness to the befuddlement of his peers.

In another episode, Seinfeld and Elaine come to suspect that the fat-free yogurt that they have been consuming at incredible levels isn't actually fat-free because Kramer tells each of them that they are plumping up. By the end of the show, competing mayoral candidates for the city of New York, where the foursome live, base their platforms on the fight against yogurt that claims to be fat-free but really isn't. In the same episode, George encounters a friend from the past who seems to look down on him. George forewarns Jerry of the approaching friend and nudges him with his elbow each time the friend talks down to George. The friend, who coincidently is an advisor for New York Mayor Dinkens, notices this unusual twitch and inquires as to why George is moving his elbow so much. George explains that is a nervous injury from a desk-bumping earlier and the friend advises George to seek medical help. As the show progresses, George eventually ends up in a doctor's office, at his friends' urging, and is called a fake by the practitioner. In a fit of anger, George actually bumps his elbow on the doctor's desk and, for the remainder of the show, actually suffers from an elbow twitch. "Seinfeld" offers a perspective into the psyche of the average man in a twisted way that eventually ends up making us look at the show and see ourselves.

The show's philosophy, on love, sex, and life, isn't that of society in general. Few men continue to be friends with their ex's. Seinfeld does. Few friends talk openly about masterbation, the ability to have an orgasm, or the thought of your parents having sex and owing your existence to them "having too much wine for dinner" (Kaplan, 1992). Seinfeld does. So why does this show do things that we, its audience, seldom do? Because it is not only a vehicle used to show us what we are, but in some respect, it is also a viable guide of what our ideology should be.

And so tomorrow night, television may seem to continue to be nothing more than an electric lobotomy, but thousands of years from now, it will be our scrolls, our heiroglyphics and our cave drawings. And although Seinfeld himself may not be the most attractive legacy, he and his show will allow future students of history to look inside the mind of a yuppy comic, to understand the fear of relationships we have, and to experience through these media texts the morals, thoughts and fears of the last decade in the twentieth century. Our descendents will celebrate with a confetti of magnetic tape and wonderment of our bizarre remote channel switching contraptions as they learn who we are and why we left them the artifact we call T.V.

Works Cited

Fowles, Jim. *Television Viewers vs. Media Snobs,* Stein and Day Publishers, New York, 1982.

Grube, Joel. *The Great American Values Test,* Collier, McMullin Publishers, London, 1984.

Kaplan, David. "Seinfeld Makes Angst Enjoyable", *The Houston Post,* Thursday, November 26, 1992

Shayer, Robert. *Open to Criticism,* Beacon Press, 1971

Wober, Mallory. *Television and Social Control,* St. Martin's Press, New York, 1988.

Chapter Exercises

Categorizing Comedies

Using the table provided below, position ten contemporary television comedies where you think they belong on the continuum between domestic comedy and situation comedy. We've provided two examples to get you started. Then, explain your answer using examples or descriptions from the programs.

SITCOM			DOMCOM
I Love Lucy			
		Soap	
			Everyone Loves Ray
	Will + Grace		
	Veronica's Closet		
Cheers			
		King of Queens	
		Friends	
		Frasier	

Identifying Comedy Conventions

Does your favorite 30 minute comedy fit the television comedy format conventions discussed in this chapter? Why or why not?

NAME OF SHOW _____
ANALYSIS

References and Resources

Alder, R. (1979). *All in the Family: A Critical Appraisal.* New York: Praeger.

Boyd-Bowman, S. (1985). The MTM phenomenon. *Screen, 26,* 75–87.

Bryant, J. (1979). Emma, Lucy and the American situation comedy of manners. *Journal of Popular Culture, 13,* 248–255.

Butsch, R. (1992). Class and gender in four decades of television situation comedy: *plus ca change? Critical Studies in Mass Communication, 9,* 387–399.

Feuer, J., Kerr, P. & Vahimagi, T. (1984). *MTM: Quality Television.* London: British Film Institute.

Finke, N. (1989). The blue-collar backgrounds behind a blue-collar hit. Los Angeles *Times,* 26 January, pp. 6/10.

Freeman, L. (1992). Social mobility in television comedies. *Critical Studies in Mass Communication, 9,* 400–408.

Gray, H. (1986). Television and the new black man: black male images in prime-time situation comedy. *Media, Culture, and Society, 8,* 223–242.

Grote, D. (1983). *The End of Comedy: The Sit-Com and the Comedic Tradition.* Hamden, CN: Shoe String Press.

Homans, P. (1983). Psychology and popular culture: ideological reflections on *M*A*S*H. Journal of Popular Culture, 17,* 3–21.

Hilmes, M. (1990). Where everybody knows your name: *Cheers* and the mediation of cultures. *Wide Angle, 12,* 64–73.

Kagan, N. (1975). *Amos 'n' Andy*: twenty years late, or two decades early? *Journal of Popular Culture, 9,* 71–76.

Kerr, P. (1983). Situation comedies. *Screen, 24,* 71–74.

Lee, J. (1992). Subversive sitcoms: Roseanne as inspiration for feminist resistance. *Women's Studies, 21,* 87–102.

Lynch, J. (1973). Seven days with *All in the Family*: case study of the taped TV drama. *Journal of Broadcasting, 17,* 259–274.

Mayerle, J. (1991). *Roseanne*—how did you get inside my house? A case study of a hit blue-collar situation comedy. *Journal of Popular Culture, 24,* 71–78.

Mellencamp, P. (1985). Situation and simulation: an introduction to *I Love Lucy. Screen, 26,* 30–40.

Mitz, R. (1983). *The Great TV Sitcom Book.* New York: Perigree Books.

Newcomb, H. (1974). *TV: The Most Popular Art.* New York: Anchor Press.

Parker, P. (1987). *Literary Fat Ladies: Rhetoric, Gender, Property.* New York: Methuen.

Rowe, K .K. (1990). Roseanne: unruly woman as domestic goddess. *Screen, 31,* 408–419.

Williams, C. T. (1974). It's not so much "you've come a long way baby"—as "you're gonna make it after all." *Journal of Popular Culture, 7,* 981–989.

Zoglin, R. (1990). Home is where the venom is; domestic life takes a drubbing in TV's anti-family sitcoms. *Time,* 16 April, pp. 85–86.

CHAPTER 7

TELEVISION DRAMA

Why does your newspaper every Tuesday highlite [sic] "NYPD" on ABC Television in your entertainment television guide? This show reflects values that go against several major creeds & cultures. It glorifies violence as entertainment. And you promote it.
Unless you stop promoting irresponsible network programming, I will give you violence and damage every one of your corner vending machines. I mean it. We all share this planet; let's have some respect for each other. Killing people is not entertainment. "NYPD" is pornagraphy [sic]. Don't promote "NYPD."

—Anonymous

The spelling-impaired author who sent this postcard to the San Francisco *Examiner* didn't think much of the innovative, highly popular police drama. A good question would be: Did this person even watch the program? If so, why would he or she have watched such "glorification of violence" in the first place? And what about the 21 million viewers a week that did tune-in to see characters, plots, and moral challenges equal, many critics feel, to the best that movies and stage offer? One, the critic who released the text of the threatening postcard, Joyce Millman (1992, p. D-6), wrote, "This is an exemplary anti-violence drama, a powerful, moving cop show with a conscience . . . The message of *NYPD Blue* is clear—in an armed society, no one is really safe. Advocating restraint, opposing vigilantism, clearly showing the consequences of violence . . . the Oct. 12 episode was the essence of the deglamorization-of-violence."

It's interesting that such comments would be used to describe a network television series. It's also remarkable that the series was de-

fended and aired by the network despite two overwhelming obstacles: 1) an organized mail campaign against the show before its first episode ever aired, and 2) the refusal of 57 affiliates to clear it. The program ultimately achieved a Top 20 rating (despite the absence of those 57 markets) and it became the highest rated new drama of the season. *NYPD Blue* may well represent the future of commercial television drama: producers unafraid to use and twist the genre's conventions to challenge an audience they respect, viewers willing to be challenged in exchange for quality, and a network willing to fight for innovation in an increasingly channel and content cluttered world of television.

Overview

Television drama, once it left its Golden Age of serious, live performances produced in New York, has settled into a well defined set of character and format conventions. But no matter how these elements are presented (traditionally, as in *Dragnet*, or more imaginatively, as in *NYPD Blue* or *The Rockford Files*), drama, by definition, must rely on conflict. The "human against human" conflict is most typical of what appears on our home screens and we will examine the reasons for this as well as the various forms the genre has taken in the face of a changing television industry.

The Early Days

Although most of us probably aren't as familiar with television's early dramatic series as we might be with some of its early comedies, we probably would have found them just as enjoyable. Viewers in 1948 and 1949 watched dramatic programs like CBS's *Roar of the Rails*. This live adventure show had actual railroad workers dramatize the excitement of railroad life using model trains and a terrain of miniature tunnels, mountains, and bridges. The DuMont Network gave its followers *The Plainclothesman*, a program in which everything was viewed from "the Lieutenant's" perspective. The viewer saw the action as if he or she were the star. If the Lieutenant was knocked down, the camera looked up to the ceiling. If he lit a cigarette, the match approached the television screen and smoke wafted up in front of the action.

Of course, there were other early dramatic series. NBC's *Martin Kane, Private Eye*, a live detective/mystery show, had a five year network run and DuMont's prime-time children's action drama, *Captain Video and His Video Rangers*, aired for six years in spite of horrendously cheap props and sets, eventually perishing with its network in 1955.

There were fewer dramatic series in these first few years, however, than there were comedies because: 1) television was live and live television left little room for high-scale action; 2) the half hour format left little time for detailed drama and, therefore, was more conducive to live comedy than drama; and, 3) the television audience was limited at the time and did not warrant the large expenditures necessary to create the kind of dramatic action stories that audiences had become accustomed to at the movies. Consequently, the fledgling industry had relatively small amounts of money available for anything other than the simplest of productions and the medium's early dramatic programs usually depended on gimmicks. Two things changed that, however.

One was caused by the Masked Man himself. In 1934, when radio station WXYZ in Detroit shared its popular program, *The Lone Ranger*, with stations in New York City, Chicago, and Cincinnati, the Mutual Broadcast System was born. This first radio network still exists. Ironically, *The Lone Ranger* became important to the early television industry as well. It was the first and clearly the most popular filmed action program on the new medium.

Not only had the western series been introduced to television, but drama began its move from the live New York studios to the back lots of Hollywood when *The Lone Ranger* demonstrated in 1949 that filmed half hours (minimovies in a sense) could be popular and profitable. Soon, half-hour filmed dramas became a television staple, from *Sky King* to *Sea Hunt*.

The second factor that would influence the direction of television drama were the live *anthology series* (programs that presented different stories and characters each week) that dominated the medium's early years, a time now viewed as the Golden Age of Television.

The Kraft Television Theatre debuted on NBC in 1947 and was so successful in its attempt to bring live drama to American audiences that for two years it appeared on ABC as well as on NBC. Kraft did 650 live one-hour dramas for television. NBC also aired *Robert Montgomery Presents* and *The Philco Television Playhouse*. CBS offered its viewers *Westinghouse Studio One* and ABC had *The U.S. Steel Hour*. A dozen other 60 and 90 minute anthologies were on the air in the late 1940s and 1950s, all broadcast live from New York. These series gave viewers stories like *Days of Wine and Roses*, *The Comedian*, *Marty*, *The Caine Mutiny Court Martial*, *Judgement at Nuremburg*, and *Requiem for a Heavyweight*.

Actors like Sidney Poitier, Martin Balsam, Mickey Rooney, Charlton Heston, Tab Hunter, Ralph Bellamy, Steve McQueen, Ed Wynn, Claude Raines, Paul Newman, Joanne Woodward, E. G. Marshall, and Robert Culp all toiled in the studios of the Golden Age. Directors of the calibre of Sidney Lumet (director of such films as *The Verdict, Dog Day Afternoon*, and *Serpico*), George Roy Hill (*The Sting, Butch Cassidy and the Sundance Kid*), Arthur Penn (*Bonnie and Clyde, Little Big Man*), and John Frankenheimer (*Manchurian Candidate, Seven Days in May*) brought the original scripts of writers Paddy Chayesfky (*Network*) and Rod Serling (*The Twilight Zone*) to life.

When *Playhouse 90* left CBS in September of 1961, live dramatic series disappeared altogether from network television. Their legacy is an important one, however. In addition to bringing many fine stories and talents to the home screen, they established some significant precedents. Through them the television industry learned that television audiences would sit for more lengthy dramatic shows. Thirty minutes had until then been the norm for filmed action and adventure drama. Characters could be painted in shades other than black and white and still capture viewers. And, the action and adventure in a drama could be psychological and verbal as well as physical.

But still, many factors combined to chase live drama from the air. As audiences became more accustomed to the conventions of filmed drama, the live studio presentations began to appear less sophisticated. Filmed television simply could present drama, physical as well as psychological, more effectively for most television viewers.

As the number of TV sets in use grew, so did the size of the audience; the larger the audience became, the proportion that enjoyed or appreciated live, sophisticated drama steadily decreased.

Television, unlike the movies or the stage, was in the home and viewed nightly. It was a medium better suited for the presentation of

regular series with recurring, identifiable characters like Perry Mason, Sgt. Friday, and Matt Dillon and as already noted, in the anthology presentations of live television drama, characters never reappeared in the next week.

Finally, there were the inevitable technological and financial concerns. More efficient and portable film equipment meant that more adventure and action could be built into filmed drama than was possible in the live dramas; and, as television became a more expensive medium, ratings became increasingly important. Regular series featuring big name stars seemed to insure high ratings, and the stars and film studios were more readily available in California than they were in New York. Where *Hallmark Hall of Fame* and *Omnibus* once characterized television drama, *The Adventures of Rin Tin Tin* and *The Life and Legend of Wyatt Earp* eventually came to carry that banner.

The Television Drama Format

Television drama, from the implausible plots of *The Incredible Hulk* to the gritty realism of *NYPD Blue* to the science-fiction wonder of *Star Trek: The Next Generation*, closely follows a strict formula.

1. **Posing of the plot and problem and the introduction of the essential characters.** The standard opening of *The Rockford Files*, for example, shows the telephone ringing and the caller leaves a message on the tape recorder, "Listen, Jimmy, it's me, Angel. You see, I owe this guy in Fresno some bread and . . . well, he wants to waste me, Jimmy." *Star Trek: The Next Generation* invariably begins with one of the officers (most frequently Captain Picard) reciting the situation faced (e.g., "After three months on a geological survey mission to the Twadus sector, the crew has earned shore leave on Reisa 3") into that day's log, accompanied by the appropriate stardate. Most programs, however, are not as straightforward in their posing of the plot and introducing the characters, but before the first com-

mercial, we usually will meet the good guys, the bad guys, and the victims and we will be told how and why they are brought together.

2. **Posing the solution or laying the strategy for the resolution of the problem faced.** The thirty or sixty minute format does not leave much time for detailed character development, so the already-introduced characters quickly develop a plan for resolving the problem. Jim Rockford decides that Angel's one-time benefactor needs to be paid and the officers of the Enterprise quickly and efficiently swing into their different leisure pursuits.

3. **Thickening of the plot.** Drama, however, is not documentary; something more than a simple recitation of problem posed/problem solved is necessary. Drama demands that the plot be thickened. This can happen in one of two ways: character twists or plot twists. In the former case, the man that Rockford wants to pay-off in order to protect Angel turns out to be the head of all the West Coast Mob. In the latter case, Picard becomes romantically involved with a beautiful adventurer but is plagued by suspicious and possibly evil pursuers.

4. **Climax and resolution.** As the story moves forward from introduction, through strategy and subsequent plot thickening, we are headed for the climax—the resolution of the problem in some dramatic or action-packed way. Rockford and Angel engage in an exciting car chase followed, after the vehicles have spectacularly crashed, by a fist-fight and the final apprehension of the mob leader. Picard's pursuers and his new friend are after rare artifacts and these smugglers attack and torture him until he uses his wiles and the Federation's technology to defeat them.

5. **Outcome.** In traditional drama, this would be called *denouement*. It is the explication of the final result of the story.

The police thank Rockford for bringing the mobster to custody; it seems they've been after this bad guy for years. But they still tell Rockford to stay out of police business in the future. Captain Picard returns to the Enterprise safe and sound. He joins his crew in the ship's bar, 10 Forward, for drinks and a debriefing on one another's vacations. Outcomes are almost always happy.

Violation of the formula usually means a short network run. NBC's critically acclaimed *Police Story*, which ran in the mid-1970s, often had very non-climatic, non-resolved climaxes and just as often, unhappy or depressingly realistic outcomes. It was not uncommon to see a crooked cop ruined and alone at the end of the sixty minutes. Because it was an anthology and not dependent on returning characters, it could do this. Yet, despite its critical laurels, it ended its four year run never once making the annual top twenty and consistently being outrated by traditional police dramas like *The Streets of San Francisco*.

The television drama formula not only requires specific elements, it also precludes others. One "unnecessary" factor is any in-depth attempt to deal with the personality or psychological make-up of characters. The thirty and sixty minute format of television renders this quite difficult, although there have been some notably successful attempts such as *I'll Fly Away*, *Picket Fences*, *Star Trek: Next Generation*, and *NYPD Blue*. Programmers tend to believe that character ambiguity doesn't promote dedication to a series and interferes with continued, regular viewing.

Typically, then, characters—even the heroes—tend to be stereotypic, although this particular aspect of the formula is in the greatest danger of change as television drama increasingly adopts the conventions of other genres, most notably domestic comedies (Chapter 6) and soap operas (Chapter 9). *Hill Street Blues* and *St. Elsewhere* are two early examples of televised drama presenting multi-dimensioned characters. *NYPD Blue* and *Picket Fences* are currently quite successful doing the same.

Change may also be coming for another of television drama's traditional characteristics: the lack of sophisticated drama (in the sense of stage drama). In the past, concerns of time limitations and the need to attract the largest possible audience prohibited more intellectual drama. But due to the challenge by a host of cable and VCR alternatives, broadcasters have become more aware of the value of demographic or niche broadcasting to highly specific audiences. This, in combination with television drama's adoption of the soap opera's flexibility of time, is changing in the depth of drama seen on the television screen. Again, *Hill Street* and *St. Elsewhere* are good early examples; and more contemporarily there is *Northern Exposure*, *NYPD Blue*, *I'll Fly Away*, and *Star Trek: Deep Space 9*.

Nonetheless, depth of drama is still somewhat limited by the need to structure the story around commercial breaks. To insure that the viewer returns after the commercial, each twelve minute (or so), between-commercial segment must build its own suspense. The suspense heightens to the point that, although interrupted by the station break, the viewer wants to return to see its resolution. It's the tried and true "girl on the railroad tracks" device. Even the best structured television drama, when cut into several of these mini-dramas in order to meet the medium's demands, cannot reach the levels of sophistication of stage and film drama, both unfettered by these limitations.

Character in Television Drama

One of the things that doomed live television drama and accounts for the relatively few anthology series that we have seen over the years is their lack of strong, identifiable, recurring characters. Programmers believe that these are the characters that bring viewers back week after week and help build ratings— Picard, Captain Kirk, Cagney or Lacey, the Bionic Woman, Christie Love, Captain Furillo, JR Ewing, Mannix, Sgt. Friday.

The most obvious character type is the *hero*.

The strong, fearless, independent hero has a long history in American culture. But where other media, especially books and film, have enriched their heroes with believable characteristics that take them beyond the stereotypic bounds of All-Americanism, television has typically been at a loss to follow. Early live television drama did portray heroes with feet of clay, sometimes lacking in courage, strength, and independence, but those portrayals are often cited as one of the reasons that this television form disappeared. The medium was and is much better suited to recurring, easily understood, predictable heroes. As is the case with the lack of depth in television drama plots, time—thirty and sixty minutes—does not allow the presentation of complex personalities.

Television heroes, then, are a relatively uniform lot. Heroes are usually male. They can be either singular heroes—Marshall Dillon, Matlock, Columbo, Marcus Welby, Dr. Quinn. Or they can be multiple heroes—Cagney and Lacey, Starsky and Hutch, Ponch and John (*CHiPs*) the crew of the Enterprise. Singular or multiple, male or (the rare) female, television heroes perform the same function. They solve the episode's conflict or problem.

Depending on the type of program, detective or medical for example, heroes represent or symbolize hope, justice, science, right or goodness. Dr. Quinn does not simply cure illness, she demonstrates for us the power of medicine and the strength of a good person. Detective John Kelly does not simply solve crimes on *NYPD Blue*, he is strength, cunning, and rightness personified. Quincy personifies diligence and dedication. Matlock exudes justice.

Television heroes share a common psychological profile as well. They are independent, moral, innately good, and they combine in the proper balance both reason and emotion. Columbo, for example, has a superior officer, but operates independently of that superior's control. Starsky and Hutch report to Captain Dobey, but they solve crimes free of any meaningful input from him. In fact, their "getting around the book," and enforcing the law in ways the captain would disapprove, was a continuing sub-theme in that series.

As for the heroes' basic morality, the thought of Trapper John (from *Trapper John M.D.*, a spin-off of *M*A*S*H*) prescribing pills unnecessarily or Tom Magnum (*Magnum, P.I.*) taking a pay-off is absurd. Heroes may have been imprisoned like Lovejoy, Alexander Munday and Jim Rockford. They may have a touch of innocent larceny in their hearts like the Maverick brothers. But they are clearly and unequivocally moral, innately good people.

Too much reasoning renders a hero too cold and impersonal. Too much emotion renders him or her too volatile, unpredictable, and unsuited for weekly series television. Drama heroes balance head and heart in the way we wish our parents did. Ironside despises the mass murderer who kills only beautiful women. He seethes with ill will, but he uses reason to apprehend him. Even Capt. Furillo, hard bitten chief of *Hill Street Blues*, often wrestles with feelings of love and hate, as does Commander Cisco on *Deep Space 9*.

Heroes need *side-kicks*. They are the second dominant character type in television drama. There is less homogeneity within this group because their function is less central to the plot and our continued identification with them is less influential to a show's success.

Side-kicks can be male or female, young or old, but they usually perform one or more of the following functions in television drama. They can provide comic relief and dialogue (Matt Dillon's Chester in *Gunsmoke*, Eric Catchpole and Tinker on BBC import *Lovejoy*). They can be the hero's helper or assistant (James West's Artemus Gordon on *Wild Wild West*. Steve Keller, younger partner to Mike Stone on *Streets of San Francisco*). Side-kicks can provide moral or physical support (Captain Picard's Number 1, Commander Riker, Arnie's assistant Roxanne on *L.A. Law*). They can sometimes serve as accidental troublemakers or accidental trouble resolvers (Jim Rockford's Angel, Quincy's Sam Fujiyama, Commander Cisco's Major Kira). Finally, they

can function as suppliers of information or insight (as Spock does for Captain Kirk on *Star Trek*, as Counselor Troi does for Captain Picard on *Star Trek: The Next Generation*, and as Betty and J. R. Jones do for *Barnaby Jones*.)

Side-kicks are much freer to vary in their characters. Their usual nature—emotional, with strong consciences subject to human flaw—can lead them into a wider variety of behaviors than is available to the hero who must remain always heroic. In *Star Trek: Deep Space 9*, Doctor Baschire can be foolish in one episode, brave in action in the next. Lieutenant Kira can be a loyal Federation officer one week and return to her Bajorian, rebel roots in the next. Ferengi merchant Quark can be weak one day, hard as nails the next. But Commander Cisco must always run DS9 as the heroic officer.

The third class of characters that populates television drama is the *enemy*. Enemies can be individuals—a murderer; a group—the Cardasians on *Next Generation* and *Deep Space 9*; or institutional—the Mob (as you see on *The Untouchables)* or polluting industries (as seen on *Baywatch)*. They can be one time villains or they can be recurring, like *Hawaii Five-O's* Wo Fat and *Next Generation's* Q.

Psychologically the villains are immoral, selfish, often insane and evil-driven. The television audience can experience little satisfaction at the apprehension or destruction of a thoughtful, sympathetic bad guy. The thirty and sixty minute format does not allow that sort of dramatic depth. So enemies remain evil in order to be crushed by the hero.

One function of the enemy is simple, to cause the conflict that moves the plot. A second function, however, is less obvious. Television villains symbolize doubt, badness, and wrong. Unlike the hero (the definition of heroism is relatively constant in our society), evil changes. Therefore, the enemy's character is flexible, changing with the pressing evils and issues of the day—revolutionaries, money hungry and insensitive corporations, polluters, drug dealers, the CIA, nuclear power plants, and so on.

Conflict in Television Drama

What makes drama dramatic is conflict. A series like *The Rockford Files* defies most of the precepts of television drama and it's often very funny, but it is at root a drama because of its weekly presentation of conflict. *Dynasty* offers its viewers weekly conflict, although familial and psychological rather than physical.

Television writers recognize that there are several areas of conflict that can be utilized in drama. One is *humans vs. nature*, but because of the large-scale time and financial demands of such drama, it is better suited for the movies. *The Poseidon Adventure*, *Towering Inferno* and *Earthquake* were not made for television. Realistic natural disaster is simply too expensive to effectively bring to the small screen.

Human vs. God is a second traditional form of dramatic conflict. But it is too philosophical, intellectual and controversial for television. What use to audiences is a villain who cannot be seen, who is representative to most people of the ultimate good, and who can never be dispatched? *Waiting for Godot* and *Job* are not likely to become television series.

A *human vs. himself* or herself does not offer the medium enough visual action. This conflict remains too psychological and it defies heroics. An individual's battle with him or herself has no clear hero or villain, no clear winner or loser. *Equus* and *Elephant Man* are better suited for the stage, novels, and movie screens.

The form of dramatic conflict that finds its way most often to television, then, is *human vs. human*. This type of conflict is relatively easy to write, relatively inexpensive to produce, replete with visual excitement, easily comprehended by the audience, and populated by easily identifiable heroes, side-kicks, and villains. These conflicts put people in jeopardy and that jeopardy makes for good television drama.

Forms of Television Drama

Television drama employs this conflict in a wide variety of forms. Some have remained throughout television's first fifty years, some have disappeared altogether, and some continue to resurface after periodic absences from the screen.

One traditional dramatic form that had a brief life on television and that has vanished probably forever is the war series. From 1962 to 1967, *Combat* raged on ABC and *The Lieutenant* held forth on NBC for two years, 1963 and 1964. But when war began to lose its glamour with the intensification of the conflict in Viet Nam and as the heroism of World War II faded into memory, so did televised stories of military men. War, unlike the Old West, offered fewer opportunities for video heroism as people began to question the heroics of warfare altogether. *M*A*S*H*, of course, is an anti-war series and technically a comedy, so it doesn't classify as war drama. And *China Beach*, despite superb writing and excellent acting, lasted only a few seasons.

The same fate has befallen the spy or espionage drama. In the 1950s, 60s and 70s, when the "Reds" were thought to be better dead, there were several spy dramas on network television—*Mission Impossible*, *I Spy*, *Danger Man*, *The Man From U.N.C.L.E.*, *The Girl From U.N.C.L.E.*, *The Hunter*, and *Espionage*. *I Led Three Lives* was a rare first-run syndication success in those years. All left the air at about the same time it was revealed that our government was supporting many of the evil regimes that the spies in these shows worked so hard to destroy. And then Pepsi, Coke and McDonalds opened shop in the two great evil empires, the Soviet Union and Red China. You couldn't tell the good guys from the bad. It became increasingly difficult to show heroics in an arena that was growing increasingly difficult for people to comprehend.

Science-fiction, a long-time traditional American dramatic form, has made occasional comebacks throughout television's history and its recent resurgence speaks volumes about the power of independent stations and the financial influence of the syndication market.

Science-fiction was one of the earliest dramatic action formats. *Captain Video* and *Buck Rogers* were two of the medium's earliest dramatic shows, but science fiction disappeared from the screen for several years. One reason was that it was perceived as children's fare, largely as a result of the poor production quality and the simple story lines of programs like these two early shows. In addition, as the television audience grew, the proportion of science-fiction fans among that group began to shrink.

In the late 1960s, however, science-fiction reappeared in prime-time in the persons of Mr. Spock and Captain Kirk in *Star Trek*. What is often overlooked however, is that despite the large cult following that the show now enjoys as it lives on in syndication, at the time it was—at best—a marginally successful program in prime-time. It lasted only three years on NBC and was cancelled in 1969 as a result of declining ratings. What audience it did have, mostly youngsters and science-fiction fans, was insufficient to maintain advertiser interest. Never once did it rate in the top twenty programs for any year of its network run. Science-fiction, after *Star Trek*, disappeared again.

The late 1970s saw a small rebirth, as programs based on successful movies made brief network appearances. *Battlestar Gallactica* was aired by ABC hot on the heels of the *Star Wars* movie success. *Buck Rogers in the 25th Century* was on NBC soon after the success of the movie of the same name, and CBS had *Logan's Run*, also based on a feature film. But it was in the mid-Eighties that two forces came together to fuel a sci-fi renaissance. Sophisticated computer techniques made good-looking science-fiction economically feasible for television and the financial strength of the independent and Fox channels opened a lucrative market for high-class first-run syndication. *Star Trek: The Next Generation* was born, soon to be followed by its own offspring, *Star Trek: Deep Space Nine*. *Babylon 5* and NBC's *seaQuest DSV* are

two more sci-fi programs that have recently emerged, only to be joined by *Island City*, *Time Trax*, and *The X-Files*.

Another form that has occasionally succeeded in prime time is the fantasy drama. Programs like *Wonder Woman*, *The Bionic Woman*, *The $6 Million Man*, *Knight Rider*, *Lois & Clark: The New Adventures of Superman*, *Spiderman*, *MANTIS* and *The Incredible Hulk* all have or have had network lives of varying length and success. Although presenting heroic heroes and heroines and clearly evil villains, their appeal is not as strong as that of the more usual dramatic programs because their heroes are a little too far out of the ordinary for viewer identification. More important, the relatively youthful age of their fans is distressing to advertisers who want to parade their products before the buying nineteen to forty year old audience.

The form that has been most characteristic of prime-time television drama is the western. Where else can heroic adventurers so easily do battle with evil villains surrounded by a century of romance and tradition?

The western persisted so long on television because it was the perfect vehicle for drama on that medium. The western easily fit the thirty and sixty minute format because it needed no explanation. The hero was good because he/she was the good guy. The villain was bad because he/she was the bad guy. Little explanation was necessary, so more of those valuable thirty and sixty minutes could be devoted to the action.

The western too, was its own world, or at least it was a world that we created and believed in. There were none of the problems of today (i.e., Marshal Dillon never had to read anybody their rights, he just whupped 'em good). For decades, then, viewers could immerse themselves in western drama and escape the rigors of their everyday world.

Westerns were among the first dramatic programs on television. The DuMont Network had regular Sunday night western movies as early as 1946 and *The Lone Ranger*, television's first western series, followed in 1949.

Programs like *The Lone Ranger*, *The Cisco Kid*, and *Hopalong Cassidy* were typical of television's early westerns, better suited for children than for the growing adult, prime-time audience. Television westerns changed, however, with the 1955 debut of *Gunsmoke* and *The Life and Legend of Wyatt Earp*. These series, unlike their predecessors, displayed a more realistic, gritty picture of the west rather than the white-hat/black-hat fantasy of the Masked Man and Tonto.

In 1954 there were two westerns in prime-time, *The Lone Ranger* and *The Adventures of Rin Tin Tin*. In 1955, there were five. A year later there were nine. In 1957, there were eighteen. In 1958 there were twenty-four and eleven of the top twenty shows for that year were westerns. This pattern persisted throughout the 1950s and into the 1960s, but the popularity of the western began to wane in the 1970s.

One reason that the western began to lose some of its attraction in the 1970s was television's demand for "relevancy" in that decade. Two notable but short-lived attempts at relevancy in westerns were *Alias Smith and Jones* from 1971 to 1973 and *Nichols* in 1971 and 1972. *Bonanza* and *The Big Valley* were two westerns that made successful attempts to bridge the old and new western forms. But it seemed that the wild west did not accommodate social commentary very well. In fact, when television westerns began to move away from their fastest-gun-in-town themes to more contemporary concerns, no less an expert than John Wayne gave this evaluation. In traditional, pre-relevancy television westerns, he noted, the problems were solved by shooting the bad guy. In the new westerns, villains are talked to death.

Talk did not play well against the plains. In 1975, then, *Gunsmoke* was cancelled. It had been a top rated program for several years and the continuing series with the longest run (twenty years) in network television history. Other than the family-western, *Little House on the Prairie*, there were no longer any "shoot 'em ups" on television. When the 1980s opened, the situation remained the same, although James Garner was very briefly back in Maverick's saddle in the 1981-1982 season. The 1994 network schedules and the offerings of the first-run syndication producers contain only two westerns, *Dr. Quinn, Medicine Woman* and *The Adventures of Briscoe County, Jr.* Still, several heroes of the Old West, most notably Matt Dillon and Maverick, live on in syndication.

One form that has persisted and prospered is the professional drama, series about people engaged in heroic struggles as part of their jobs—doctors, lawyers, police, and private eyes.

Cops and P.I.s have been around from the beginning, easily making the move from radio and movies to television. They were present in the live anthology drama and in weekly series like *The Plainclothesman* and *Hands of Mystery*. They have remained on the air because, unlike the Western, they are contemporary and more able to accommodate changes in viewer preference and taste.

The cops and P.I.s of the '50s and '60s were simply transplanted western marshals, All-American, unswerving, always right—Sgt. Friday on *Dragnet*, Eliot Ness of the *Untouchables*, Lt. Mike Parker of *Naked City*.

This tradition held into the mid-1960s, as Steve McGarrett fought island crime on *Hawaii Five-O* and Inspector Lewis Erskine served *The F.B.I.* well. But they began to share the air with a new breed of cop and P.I., one more realistic in personality and job performance—*Homicide, Columbo, The Streets of San Francisco, Kojak, Ironside, Cannon, Barnaby Jones, Hill Street Blues, In the Heat of the Night, Picket Fences, NYPD Blue,* and *Police Story*. These shows are contemporary programs, presenting modern people fighting modern crime in modern cities.

Doctors, too, have been well represented in television drama. Although medical drama was present on the networks as early as the mid-1950s when *Medic* aired, it became established as a television staple with the premiere, in 1961, of both *Ben Casey* and *Dr. Kildare*. Good scripts, realistic life or death drama, handsome leading men (Vince Edwards and Richard Chamberlain), and excellent supporting actors (Sam Jaffe and Raymond Massey), made doctor shows a standard. *The Bold Ones, Birdland, Marcus Welby, M.D., St. Elsewhere, Picket Fences, Northern Exposure, Medical Center, Medical Story, ER, Chicago Hope* and *Trapper John, M.D.* have all maintained the Hippocratic Oath in prime-time.

"Doctor drama" is perfect for the medium, it allows for all the standard television drama elements—heroic doctors and nurses fighting identifiable and defeatable enemies like time, disease, ignorance, drug pushers and evil hospital administrators.

Lawyer drama benefits from this same characteristic. Legal drama has been another television standard that has changed a great deal over time. In the 1960s, Perry Mason could solve a crime with the witness/perpetrator on the stand while *Judd for the Defense*, *The Defenders*, and *The Bold Ones* tried cases that came from the day's headlines. During the 1970s, *Rosetti and Ryan*, *Petrocelli*, and *Kaz* turned their attention to simple violent crime once again. And through the 80s to now *Law and Order*, *Matlock*, and *L.A. Law* again practice relevant courtroom law.

Other occupations have received some television drama exposure, but these series, too, have put emphasis on conflict—teachers (in *Room 222* and *The White Shadow*,) newspaper people (in *Lou Grant*,) and long-distance truck drivers (in *B. J. and the Bear*). These professions, though, may not have the longevity of doctors, lawyers, and law enforcement professionals. They tend to come and go with the headlines. *Room 222* was popular in the days of Lyndon Johnson's massive social programs. *Lou Grant* came to the air following the new esteem bestowed on the press after Watergate, and *B. J. and the Bear* made it to the screen when the long-distance trucker emerged as something of a modern cowboy during the truckers' strikes of the late 1970s and the boon in popularity of CB radios.

Matlock, one of network television's longest running series, exemplifies the courtroom drama that has long been a staple of the medium.

A Changing Genre

When talking about television, it's often risky to discuss trends. Who could have predicted in the halcyon days of the western, the late 50s and early 60s, when as many as twenty "shoot 'em ups" dotted the network schedules in a single season, that when the 1980s opened, not one western would appear on the network prime-time schedule? Moreover, with the introduction of new technologies like cable, satellite, and videocassette recorders, old programs are resurrected, new programs live forever, and programmers with concerns and pressures different from those of the traditional networks have come into being. All these combine to make comments on trends and predictions of the future somewhat of a gamble.

Nevertheless, there are some changes in the traditional form of television drama that deserve note. We opened this chapter with a brief discussion of one break-through program, *NYPD Blue*. But there are others that paved the way for it. One change in typical television drama that was evident at the close of the 70s that has reached full bloom in this decade is the development and success of a new form, the domestic drama. Series like *James at 15*, *Little House on the Prairie*, *The Waltons*, *Family*, *Brooklyn Bridge*, *I'll Fly Away*, *Palmerstown, U.S.A.*, *The Family Holvak*, *The Byrds of Paradise* and *Picket Fences* do not offer traditional conflict, heroes, or villains. Instead they present realistic families in conflict with poverty, puberty and other family pressures. Their presence on the air may have been the result of the anti-TV violence movement of the late 70s. The success of the realistic Norman Lear comedies no doubt also helped. But the staying power of this dramatic form is dependent on the production of fine scripts, good stories, and excellent acting. *The Waltons*, in fact, has been hailed as a modern classic of our culture. Quality scripts, stories and acting, however, take time and money, two things seemingly in short supply in the television business. With the demise of the critically acclaimed *Family Tree* in 1982, domestic drama disappeared for a while, leaving prime-time drama dominated by relatively inexpensive, quick and easy-to-produce, car-chase, action shows like *The Dukes of Hazzard*, *The A Team*, and *Knight Rider*. Largely through the "we've got nothing to lose" attitude of the number three rated network, NBC, as well as the success of the prime-time soap operas like *Dynasty* and *Dallas*, the domestic drama resurfaced in the form of serialized ensemble drama like *Hill Street Blues* and *St. Elsewhere*. The families may be more a function of a situation (a police station and a hospital) than blood, but they are families nonetheless.

Underlying these and other changes in the form is an undeniable trend: sharply rising production costs. Programs like *Dallas* cost more than a million dollars an episode. *SeaQuest DSV* costs two million dollars an episode; *The Young Indiana Jones Chronicles* cost $1.7 million per show. Even a simple program like *Charlie's Angels*, set in Los Angeles and having no special effects, cost over three quarter of a million dollars a show in its last year. Production costs are rising at over 40 percent a season and it's having an effect on programming. It may be one reason, for example, that sex is replacing violence. Car chases and shootings may not be exorbitantly expensive, but *Northern Exposure's* sometimes steamy dialogue and situations are still cheaper.

As costs go higher, then, series drama is being joined by other forms, some related and some not, such as mini-series (abbreviated dramatic series), made for television movies, and "reality programming." Made for television movies cost about the same to produce, minute for minute, as do series dramas, but producers' expenses can be recouped in syndication. A failed or short lived series has no syndication value, but a made-for-television movie can be syndicated as part of a package of films or even made available for video rental. These made-for-television movies can also be sold overseas as feature films, especially after the inclusion of spicy, non-television scenes. In addition, these one-time television films are not bound by the limitations of series dramas and as a result, they can deal with more diverse and controversial issues than can regular series in an attempt to draw a large audience (for example, incest, rape, Viet Nam, nuclear war).

So called reality programming—*I Witness Video, Code 3, Rescue 911, America's Most Wanted, Missing Persons*—are very inexpensive, by television standards, to produce—often as little as one fourth the cost of a dramatic series. They look like home movies, but they are cheap. A program that pays no actors, needs no sets, and has the look of a local news magazine show may not be in the best tradition of the Golden Age of Television but it is affordable and people do tune-in.

If the trend toward higher costs is not slowed, many industry insiders feel that regular weekly dramatic series may go the way of the live anthology drama of the 1950s. When 1994 opened, there were fewer than 20 hour-long dramatic shows on television's regular sched-

ule, and several of those were first-run syndication programs (*Kung Fu: The Legend Returns, The Untouchables*) and one, *I'll Fly Away*, was re-running on PBS after its cancellation by NBC.

As the amounts of money involved in series television grow, many critics argue that a kind of programming conservatism inevitably develops. Fewer and fewer gambles are taken as the stakes get higher and higher. New and different ideas are more frequently rejected by the networks; old ideas tend to be recycled (*Viper* is more than a program-length commercial for an Oldsmobile, it is *Knight Rider* redone for the Nineties). Yet other critics point to *NYPD Blue, Picket Fences, Northern Exposure*, and *In The Heat of the Night* and argue that as the stakes get higher, the networks, especially, are willing to rise to the challenge to attract viewers who increasingly have many, many choices.

TUCKER AND SHAH

The "reality" of slavery and racism in the miniseries *Roots* forms the core of the Tucker and Shah essay. An overarching critical question drives their analysis: what happens when a book "about slavery told from a slave's point of view—an essentially African-American perspective" is transformed to the screen by white people courting white advertisers and viewers?

The authors see the myths about slavery and race held by white Americans as impediments to a fuller understanding of the true nature of these twin evils. Moreover, they argue that those myths deflect most people from an appreciation of the strengths in African traditions and values that made it possible for a people who were ripped from their homes and treated as a commodity to maintain their culture in the face of unimagined horror.

Because they pose their arguments within the framework of capitalism and race relations, their critique is best viewed as sociological criticism. But it is easy to identify, especially toward the essay's conclusion, arguments drawn from ideological and structural criticism. This is not surprising, because the implicit question that Tucker and Shah weave throughout the piece is: "At what price?" Is a "flawed" *TV Roots* that brings at least some of the reality of slavery and racism to an otherwise unaware white audience better than no *TV Roots* at all?

Do you think that people of different ethnic and racial backgrounds might answer this question differently? Do you think that the majority television audience would have been more accepting of a *TV Roots* that was truer to Alex Haley's book than were the series' producers and ABC? Why or why not? What does your answer say about your own view of the television audience? Of American television? Of American society?

Race and the Transformation of Culture: The Making of the Television Miniseries Roots

Lauren R. Tucker and Hemant Shah

First published in 1976, Alex Haley's *Roots* symbolized the cultural, social, economic, and political experience of the black community in America, an experience profoundly shaped by the brutality of slavery. *Roots* was a story about slavery told from a slave's point of view—an essentially African-American perspective. When ABC acquired the broadcast rights to Haley's epic slave story, however, *Roots* the television program (*TV Roots*) became a creation of an institution dominated largely by whites. *TV Roots* was produced, written, and directed by whites (with the exception of Gilbert Moses, who directed one episode), broadcast over a network whose programming was dominated by white characters, and shown to a predominantly white audience. As a result, Haley's novel was transformed from a critique of slavery and exposition of white cruelty and indifference into one that diluted, in many ways, the horror, complexities, and seriousness of slave holding.

Discrepancies between *Roots* and *TV Roots* resulted from specific creative choices that were influenced by concerns of the program's makers about reaction of the largely white audience to a story about slavery in America told from a black perspective. These considerations about race took place not in a vacuum but rather in the context of a complex process of producing television content—a process that itself took place in a specific understanding of social relations between black and white Americans. The transformation of *Roots* to *TV Roots* provides clues about how the U.S. television establishment views race in America.

Mass media represent important channels for cultural expression. They produce and spread symbols and images that describe and explain how and why the world works. Among the many representations of the social world mass media

Lauren R. Tucker is a Ph.D. candidate and Hemant Shah is an assistant professor at the School of Journalism and Mass Communication at the University of Wisconsin-Madison. The authors contributed equally to this article. They would like to thank James F. Tucker, Cora Marret, Jo Ellen Fair, and anonymous reviewers for their useful comments on earlier drafts.

Race the Transformation of Culture: the Making of the Television Miniseries Roots. *Critical Studies In Mass Communication*, Vol. 9. 1992, pp. 325–336. Used by permission of the Speech Communication Association.

create is a perspective on race—what the term means, who it refers to, and how it will be understood (Omi & Winant, 1986, pp. 68–69). The key ideas embodied within the prevailing understanding of race in the United States are that a high level of homogeneity exists within a racial group, that there is a hierarchy of races (with whites at the top and other races and ethnic groups hovering at or near the bottom), and that the culture and sensitivities of blacks and other ethnic groups are subordinate to those of whites (see Fredrickson, 1988, pp. 189–205; Miles, 1989, pp. 42–50; Omi & Winant, 1986). By examining the discrepancies between *Roots* the novel and *TV Roots*, we can discover how and to what extent ideas about race informed creative choices made during the production process and are reflected in the program.

The Production of Television Content

The study of how television (and other mass media) content is produced, which generally comes under the rubric of "production of culture" research, has been informed and shaped by theories and methods used in the study of complex organizations. The general goal of production of culture research was laid out by Peterson (1976). This traditional approach focuses on the organizational structures, functions, and processes by which "creation, manufacture, marketing, distribution, exhibiting, inculcation, evaluation and consumption" of mass media content are undertaken and accomplished (p.10).

In the traditional approach, television content is seen as the result of decisions made by powerful producers and a handful of associates. A variety of factors, of course, may affect those decisions. The research literature on the production of television programming suggests that factors at three levels—industrial/

institutional, organizational, and individual (Ettema, Whitney, & Wackman, 1987)—have an impact on the program decisions and, ultimately, on material coming out of mass media organizations. The *industrial/institutional level* refers to factors such as market considerations and competition with other media organizations. At the *organizational level,* production techniques, product conventions, and casting decisions are some important factors. Television networks, like other businesses, try to reduce uncertainty in their production process. By routinizing certain creative decisions, networks bring control and stability to the creation of television programs. At the *individual level,* important factors include the perceptions, attitudes, and ideas of writers, directors, producers, and others involved in creating the television program.

Although far from mutually exclusive, these three levels can be conceptualized as a hierarchy, with the institutional/industrial level at the top, the organizational level in the middle, and the individual level at the bottom. Interaction among factors at various levels is complex, and it is not always easy to trace the impact of a particular factor at one level to a second factor at another level. But, generally, influence flows in a top-down fashion. Factors at the top level influence factors at the middle level, and top-level and middle-level factors influence bottom-level factors. This "trickle-down" process affects decision making and, ultimately, television content.

Although the traditional approach to production of culture is essentially apolitical in that it "would hold in abeyance the evaluation of cultural forms and focus on the mechanisms that reproduce these forms" (Ettema, Whitney, & Wackman, 1987, p. 748), it is far from non-ideological. Tuchman (1983), for example, has criticized

this approach for taking for granted contemporary capitalism and thus obscuring the fact that cultural products emerge from specific sociopolitical and economic relations and tend to reinforce the status quo. By ignoring this dimension of the production of culture, the traditional approach leaves unquestioned and unexamined the relationship between the process of cultural production and the cultural products themselves, and the implications of that relationship for understanding race relations and other social phenomena.

By ignoring American capitalism, the traditional approach to the production of culture also ignores questions about race. One need only look at the importance of slavery to the economic strength of the southern United States in the nineteenth century (Williams, 1944), at the massacre of American Indians in the name of manifest destiny (Steinberg, 1989), and at interpretations of naturalization laws in the 1920s that prohibited Asian Indians from applying for U.S. citizenship (Helweg & Helweg, 1990; Takaki, 1989) to be convinced that the development of American capitalism is inextricably linked to views about race. By ignoring race, a traditional production of culture approach cannot fully explain how the processes involved in the transformation of Haley's novel into *TV Roots* resulted in the marginalization of the black cultural experience and the elevation of the white perspective on the black American experience. The most powerful and illuminating strategy for studying the production of culture, and specifically the transformation of *Roots* to *TV Roots*, is to combine the traditional approach, with its emphasis on the mechanisms and procedures of production, with a close examination of how ideas about race are embedded in the production process and are then reflected in cultural products.

From *Roots* to *TV Roots:* Race and the Transformation of Culture

Led by executive producer David Wolper, the predominantly white production team made creative choices and manufactured content that reflect the dominant understanding of race in the United States. In his book *The Inside Story of TV's "Roots"* (Wolper & Troupe, 1978), Wolper goes into edifying detail concerning the timidity of ABC network executives in developing *Roots* for network television. A dramatic series featuring a predominantly African-American cast had never been successful on American television. In addition, the story of Kunta Kinte and his family required more air time than was usually allotted to a network movie. Ultimately, network executives questioned whether Wolper could make a movie about an African slave acceptable to conservative advertisers and the predominately white audience. After three months of negotiations and Wolper's assurances, ABC finally agreed to finance the project (Wolper & Troupe, 1978).

For Haley, *Roots* symbolized more than one black family's struggle to maintain continuity and identity in the shadow of the dehumanizing institution of slavery. Haley's *Roots* offered an interpretation of American history that connected black Americans with a unique history, identity, and cultural experience that began in Africa. Haley's vision provides black America a connection not only with its past, but also with its present and future. In short, Haley's vision of the black American cultural experience is solidly rooted in the black, African-American perspective of the cultural experience of the black American community. When David Wolper and the network executives at ABC initiated negotiations for the television rights to *Roots*, Haley's vision began to be fundamentally altered.

Although thousands of black Americans viewed *TV Roots,* its producers primarily were concerned about attracting white viewers (Fishbein, 1983, pp. 288-289; Wolper & Troupe, 1978). ABC executive Larry Sullivan stated, "Our concern was to put a lot of white people in the promos. Otherwise, we felt the program would be a turnoff" (quoted in Bogle, 1988, p. 339). Brandon Stoddard, then in charge of ABC's novels for television, stated, "We made certain to use whites viewers had seen a hundred times before [Ed Asner, Lorne Greene] so they would feel comfortable" (quoted in Bogle, 1988, p. 340).

Transforming White Characters

Concern about the predominantly white audience (an institutional/industrial-level factor) motivated many of the changes that occurred during the transformation of Haley's novel into the television series. Some of these changes resulted in production decision (organization- and individual-level factors) that led to the softening of the personalities of the white characters. During the opening episode of *TV Roots,* the sharp division between the white world of the slaveship captain and the pastoral world of Kunta Kinte's Gambia foreshadows how Haley's vision would be profoundly compromised throughout the production process.

Captain Davies, the slaveship captain portrayed by Asner, is introduced as an honorable, innocent, and naive participant in the thriving slave trade of the 1750s. The captain is characterized as a deeply religious family man and intelligent and capable sailor, who begins his voyage on the Sabbath because it "seems the Christian thing to do."

His conscience-stricken demeanor is artfully contrasted with that of his godless and depraved first mate, Slater. Slater, no stranger to the slave trade, offers Davies the benefit of his expertise and experience. As they tour the lower decks where the slaves will be chained in a "loose pack" formation, each man evaluates the other's commitment to the task at hand. Viewing his first mate with a mixture of disgust and deference, Davies inquires about the number of times Slater has made the voyage. Upon hearing that Slater has participated in 18 such voyages, Davies responds, "Eighteen! That's seventeen more than I've made. So I'd be willing to admit Mr. Slater that below decks, let's say, you're the expert."

The interaction between Davies and Slater exemplifies the way in which the producers of *TV Roots* manufactured characterizations and content throughout the series to appeal to what they perceived were the needs and desires of white audience members. The inhumanity of Slater, and of the institution of slavery itself, is made more palatable by the humanity of Davies. Even when, longing for home and human warmth, he puts aside his morals and succumbs to temptation with a young African girl brought to him by Slater, Davies is made to appear even more human in his vulnerability and fallibility. Wolper and Troupe (1978) quote William Blinn, the head writer on the *TV Roots* project, offering his rationale for the Davies character:

"For our purposes, he was certainly not a sympathetic man. An understandable man yes—but it is clearly absurd to have a likable slaveship captain. It was equally unwise, we thought, to do four hours of television without showing a white person with whom we could identify." (p. 48)

In his reference to "a white person with whom *we* could identify," Blinn, who is white, clearly is alluding to his concern for the sensibilities of white audience members, which then apparently guided his characterization of Davies.

However, Davies, as the conscience-ridden slaveship captain of *TV Roots*, is in sharp contract to the nameless, faceless "toubob" or white man that Haley (1976) describes in Kunta Kinte's first encounter with the slaveship crew:

"One of the new toubob was short and stout and his hair was white. The other towered over him, tall and huge, and scowling, with deep knife scars across his face, but it was the white-haired one before whom the slatees and the other toubob grinned and all but bowed. . . . Looking at them all, the white-haired one gestured for Kunta to step forward, and lurching backward in terror, Kunta screamed as a whip seared across his back. . . . The white-haired toubob calmly spread Kunta's trembling lips and studied his teeth." (pp. 169–170)

Clearly, a slaveship captain with a conscience is not a part of Haley's narrative.

Blinn's characterization of Davies commences the profound alteration of the images conceived by Haley. Perhaps to accommodate the white television audience, the makers of *TV Roots* added substance and depth to many of the white characters, giving them complex personalities and important positions within the narrative. They also added white characters who did not appear in Haley's novel. Throughout *TV Roots*, white culture and community is given the substance and definition that Haley reserved for his African and black American subjects. The slave's perspective, central to Haley's novel, was subordinated in *TV Roots* so that multidimensional portrayals of white characters with whom the white audience could identify and empathize could be added to the story.

Transforming Black Characters

While expanding the content and characterizations of the white char-acters, the makers of *TV Roots* narrowed and consolidated many of the black characters developed by Haley. During the first two episodes, many of the black characters were eliminated, reduced, or homogenized by the miniseries' creators. The members of Kunta Kinte's TV family seem to be mere icons compared to the rich characterizations Haley developed. In the novel, Kunta Kinte's relationship with his parents, especially Binta, his mother, plays a significant role in his development. As a woman in a male-oriented society, Binta struggles with the difficult task of maintaining discipline and structure in her son's life without disrupting the social structure. The tension between the two grows as Kunta becomes a man and Binta faces the inevitability of his leaving home. However, Binta's character in *TV Roots*, played by Cicely Tyson, remains flat. Although the makers of *TV Roots* maintain the tension between Kunta Kinte and his mother, they do not provide the depth of characterization or context in which this tension makes logical sense.

According to Haley, Kunta Kinte's African heritage and history form the connective tissue between his homeland and his new home on the American continent. By not giving adequate time or attention to the full development of Kunta Kinte's life in Juffure, the makers of *TV Roots* broke the connection between Kunta Kinte's cultural experience in Africa and his subsequent experience as an American slave. As a result, the series' creators dismissed the uniqueness and complexity of Kunta Kinte's identity and heritage, and, on a broader level, the identity and heritage of all black Americans.

Once the series' makers consolidated and homogenized many of the black characters created by Haley, the rich diversity of slave life and culture described in the novel was lost. For example, the character of Fiddler in the television series was actually a composite of three of Haley's characters— the carriage driver Samson, the gardener, and the Fiddler. In Haley's narrative, each of these characters played a significant role in helping Kunta Kinte to manage life as a slave. In addition, each represented the variety of ways in which slaves adapted to the realities of the "peculiar institution." Each in some way revealed to Kunta different perspectives on slavery from the slaves' point of view.

The makers of *TV Roots* manufactured additions in content that are inconsistent with those portions of the series that remain faithful to the novel. The beauty of Haley's narrative lies in the way in which he intertwines the slave's crucial awareness of the white world with the routines of slave culture. Through their actions and conversations, the members of the slave population reveal their deep understanding of the social, political, and personal influence of slavery on their lives. By contrasting the white slave owners' general ignorance and fear of the activities of the slave population with the slave community's ability to obtain voluminous and insightful information concerning the white masters' world, Haley demonstrates with painstaking care that surviving life as an American slave required constant vigilance and informed awareness of white culture.

In the novel and the series, Kunta Kinte quickly comes to the important realization that a successful escape could be possible only through cautious observation of the white world and the careful control of his own behavior. Kunta Kinte learns to manage the duality of living in the white world and the slave world. However, in episode three, the producers add content that reveals their profound lack of understanding of Kunta Kinte's slave world. In this episode, Kunta Kinte plans the last of his many escape attempts, during which he wastes valuable time and energy by running to the next plantation to find his first love, Fanta, with whom he made the middle passage. The Fanta character loudly rebuffs Kunta Kinte's plea for her to escape with him. Her loud cries alert the slave catchers to Kunta Kinte's presence and, eventually, lead to his anguishing return to slavery.

But Haley's characterization of slave culture does not provide the logic for Fanta's behavior. As a monologue by Fiddler illustrates, the slaves in Haley's novel were painfully aware of the cruel sanctions awaiting those who forgot for a moment the repressiveness of the surrounding white world:

"Looka here, don't start me on white folks' laws. Startin' up a new settlement, dey firs' builds a courthouse, fo' passin' more laws. . . . It's a law niggers can't carry no gun, even no stick that look like a club. Law say twenty lashes you get caught widdout a travelin' pass, ten lashes if'n you looks white folks in dey eyes, thirty lashes if'n you raises your hand 'gainst a white Christian. Law say no nigger preachin' less'n a white man dere to listen; law say can't be no nigger funeral if dey think it's a meetin'. Law say they cut your ear off if'n white folks swear you lied, both ears if dey claim you lied twice. Law say you kill anybody white, you hang; kill 'nother nigger, you jes' gits whipped. Law says reward a Indian catchin' a 'scaped nigger wid all de tabacco dat Indian can carry. Law 'gainst teachin' any nigger to read or write, or givin' any nigger any book. Dey's even a law 'gainst niggers beatin' any drums—any dat African stuff." (Haley, 1976, p. 274)

Thus, Fanta's loud outburst clearly is inconsistent with Haley's view of slave culture, and the scene has little credibility. Although the

structure of Haley's narrative could have allowed for Fanta's presence (in the novel there is a woman named Fanta in the village of Juffure), the hysterical nature of Fanta's television character is clearly more akin to that of the character played by Butterfly McQueen in *Gone with the Wind* than to the wary and discreet characters developed by Haley. According to critic Donald Bogle:

"She was simply on television to titillate the viewer. . . . When she loudly argued with Kunta the morning after their night together, her idiotic explosion that led to this entrapment seemed blatantly fake because the very thing other parts of *Roots* pointed out (most notably with the characters Fiddler and Belle [sic]) was that the slave population never made a move without terrifying awareness of the surrounding white world." (1988, p. 340)

Thus, in one of the rare instances in which the makers of *TV Roots* added a black character to the story line, they did so in a way that revealed a lack of understanding of and sensitivity for the slave culture Haley described. Kunta's sensational romance with Fanta represents one of the many production techniques characteristic of the family of television spectaculars of which *TV Roots* was a member. Sex, greed, violence, and a star-studded cast comprise much of the recipe by which miniseries continue to be made. Bogle (1988) argues that these techniques aimed to attract and maintain the white viewer throughout the series. Manufactured by whites for whites, these enhancements compromised the cultural integrity of Haley's vision.

Casting Choices

The producers of *TV Roots* made careful casting choices designed to attract and maintain the white audience. Brandon Stoddard, the ABC executive, admitted that the network executives and the producers of *TV Roots* made a conscious deci-

sion to stack the supporting cast with well-known white actors as a means to attracting the white audience. The vast majority of these actors, such as Edward Asner, Lorne Greene, Sandy Duncan, Chuck Connors, Ralph Waite, and Robert Reed, were at the time strongly associated with the positive, good-natured television personas they had developed as the stars of regular television series. The audience's strong identification of these stars with their positive television personas became a cushion between the audience members and the characters portrayed by these stars. Robert Reed was recognized as the nice father of *The Brady Bunch,* who, for the moment, was portraying a slave master. Temporarily playing a slaveship captain, Edward Asner still seemed the gruff but loveable Lou Grant from *The Mary Tyler Moore Show.* The star status of these actors served as a means of putting psychological distance between white audience members and the negative white characters engaged in the cruel business of the slave trade.

The use of popular black actors served much the same purpose. With the exception of the young Kunta Kinte, played by the then unknown LeVar Burton, the majority of the black characters were portrayed by easily identifiable actors such as John Amos, Lou Gossett, Jr., Ben Vereen, and Leslie Uggams. Although no one can quarrel with the powerful, quality performances offered by the majority of *TV Roots* actors, black and white, the star factor played an important role of distancing the audience from the cruel realities of slavery. A star's popularity provided a screen through which the audience could view a character's suffering or depravity. For this very reason, the makers of *TV Roots* chose not to cast a big-name star in the role of the young Kunta Kinte. According to ABC's Stoddard, "From a purely casting standpoint it was essential that Kunta Kinte be seen not as an actor being Kunta Kinte but this *being* Kunta Kinte, which is exactly what happened" (Quoted in Fishbein, 1983, p. 288).

Transforming Africa

The makers' perceptions of their white audience, as well as their own white backgrounds, probably motivated the use of certain direction techniques as well. Although Haley's description of Africa approached a mythological ideal, his detailed description of African life, community, work, religion, and economy provided definition to Kunta Kinte's history and, ultimately, to the history of all black Americans. In contrast, *TV Roots* presented Africa as an American abstraction (the Africa scenes were filmed in Savannah, Georgia), more representative of an exhibit at the Smithsonian Institution than the living, breathing, thriving community Haley describes. The sparseness of the set, the isolation of the village, the primitiveness of the villagers' activities and conversations, and the limited amount of television time devoted to developing this part of Kunta Kinte's life offer viewers only a superficial glimpse of an African community, ignore the humanity and civility that Haley emphasizes in his novel, and trivialize and subordinate Africa and Africans.

The makers of *TV Roots* offered white audience members an image of Kunta Kinte's village that did not counter the audience's cultural perspective of Africa as the primitive and ancient dark continent (Fishbein, 1983). In his novel, Haley describes the thrill and consternation of Kunta and his classmates as they take on their school masters' rigorous challenges. Kunta also engages in the close observation of his village's civic and cultural life as he becomes more conscious of his role as a leader. However, the audience of *TV Roots* sees

only the images of African children herding goats or running through the woods. As a result, Africa remains an uncivilized place, a place of natives and tribes, to which America seemed, naturally, a better alternative.

According to Stoddard, the tourist-eye-view of Gambia was necessary to maintain the attention of an ethnocentric white American audience: "What seems to interest Americans most are Americans. . . . In *Roots,* we got out of Africa as fast as we could. . . . I knew that as soon as we got Kunta Kinte to America we would be okay" (quoted in Fishbein, 1983, p. 289). As this and other statements suggest, the main goal of *TV Roots* was to capture the interest of white Americans. As a result, the scenes of Kunta Kinte's Africa met the requirements of the world view of the white audience members.

The plot emphasis and the direction of *TV Roots* offer additional insight into the efforts to make the series palatable to the white audience. In his novel, Haley draws strong connections between African culture and the cultural characteristics exhibited by the slaves. Frequently in the book Kunta Kinte notes with bewilderment and some degree of satisfaction the similarity between the slave community and Juffure:

"These heathen blacks wouldn't understand drumtalk any better than the toubob. Kunta was forced to concede though—if only with great reluctance—that these pagan blacks might not be totally irredeemable. Ignorant as they were, some of the things they did were purely African, and he could tell that they were totally unaware of it themselves. For one thing, he had heard all his life the very same sounds of exclamation, accompanied by the very same hand gestures and facial expressions. . . . And Kunta had been reminded of Africa in the way that black women here wore their hair

tied up with strings into very tight plaits. . . . Kunta also saw Africa in the way that black children here were trained to treat their elders with politeness and respect." (Haley, 1976, p. 243)

The miniseries' creators deemphasized the theme of African identity and community found within the slave culture in favor of highlighting the lives and activities of the white characters. Certainly, the development of the slave community's African identity would take additional airtime and require further effort. But just as the slave owners sought to erase the Africanness from Kunta Kinte, the makers of *TV Roots* sought to reduce the story's African focus to meet the perceived desires and needs of the white audience.

TV Roots clearly reflects the key ideas outlined earlier associated with the dominant understanding of race in the United States. The white producers of *TV Roots*, catering to a predominantly white audience, had little problem with adding white characters to the story or with giving them depth and agency not found in the novel. Black characters, on the other hand, movingly and intelligently sketched in Haley's novel, were either consolidated or eliminated altogether from the television series. Inevitably, the slave's perspective of slavery, much bally-hooed in ABC's promotional campaign for the miniseries, was subordinated in favor of the white interpretation of the black cultural experience and heritage in America.

Discussion

The foregoing analysis leads to several observations about the creation of *TV Roots*. The significance of Haley's story about the enslavement, freedom, and eventual success of a black family in America, all the while keeping alive its African heritage, was one that the white producers of *TV Roots* apparently did not fully grasp. Rather than a story that revealed how slaves kept a measure of dignity and self-esteem, and the social and cultural mechanisms they used to survive in the face of inhuman oppression, *TV Roots* became a generic tale of the classic immigrant success story in America (see Fishbein, 1983). What could be more appealing and understandable to American whites, in the audience and on the *TV Roots* production team, than a story about immigrant success in a new land? The story of Kunta Kinte's descendants is vintage rags-to-riches genre: His daughter Kizzy is sold to an unknown slave owner; his grandson Chicken George becomes an expert cock-fight trainer and eventually wins his freedom; his great-grandson Tom Moore earns respect as a skilled blacksmith and finally takes his family to Tennessee to live in freedom on their own land. But while Haley's novel presents the story as one of success in *spite* of the oppressive social system in which the family lived, *TV Roots* downplays the family's effort and determination and seems to attribute its success to the social system. In the context of the television production, the family couldn't have done it without the effort and sympathy of understanding whites.

TV Roots does little to enhance understanding of the black experience or the immigrant experience in America. By presenting the experience of Kunta Kinte's family as an immigrant story, *TV Roots* denies that slavery forced onto African blacks was a unique cultural experience different from that of most white immigrants, who came to the United States voluntarily (Fredrickson, 1988). White skin and the circumstances under which they arrived in America enabled white immigrants to assimilate into the mainstream of American life with relative ease (Steinberg, 1989). On the other hand, blacks, even after emancipation, remained outside the mainstream.

Part of the lore of the immigrant story is suffering and hard times in the new environment. Casting the story of slavery and freedom for blacks as an immigrant story, therefore, rationalizes the suffering of blacks as an inevitable step toward acceptance. In addition, because the suffering is set in the past, it does not impinge on contemporary white sensibilities (Willett, 1980).

TV Roots also "naturalized" slavery and the slave experience. The television drama masquerades as reality but describes conditions without analyzing the social context in which institutions such as slavery develop (Willett, 1980). Thus, slavery appears to be a naturally occurring phenomenon, an acceptable, inevitable, logical—and not at all peculiar—part of American history. By not examining social and economic conditions, both domestic and international, underlying the development of slavery, *TV Roots* appears to exonerate whites and white institutions of any moral or ethical responsibility for the exploitation and suffering of black slaves. In fact, by creating and emphasizing white characters who are caring and sensitive—kinder, gentler slave owners—*TV Roots* portrays slavery as not all that bad.

One of Haley's goals in writing *Roots* was to correct what has been termed a political amnesia about slavery in America (Fishbein, 1983). Popular, stereotypical images of slave life have downplayed the horror and cruelty associated with whites' treatment of black slaves (see Dates & Barlow, 1990; Wilson & Gutierrez, 1980; Woll & Miller, 1987). In his book, Haley provides an alternative understanding of slavery and slave life. His narrative offers an image of the black experience in America that counters the dominant American understanding of race.

Conclusion

Despite similarities of plot, themes, and focus, Haley's novel and *TV Roots* offer competing myths or cultural explanations of American slavery and race relations. The fundamental difference between Haley's *Roots* and the television series begins with the difference in the ideological perspective from which each was developed. In his novel, Haley presents the black American cultural experience as a distinct thread in the fabric of American and world history. Haley attributes most, if not all, of the success of Kunta Kinte, his family, and ultimately all black Americans to the resiliency and vitality of their African heritage. In his characterizations, content, and dialogue, Haley portrays the institution of slavery as a singular crime against humanity, clearly created and perpetuated by the white Euro-Americans for economic and social gain. Within the context of his epic slave narrative, Haley reveals his understanding of slavery as the forge that fashioned a unique yet tragic social, historical, and cultural experience that continues to affect the black community and the character of American race relations to the present day.

In the case of *TV Roots*, the white producers and network executives made several structural changes during the production process that altered the original characterizations, content, and theme of Haley's story in such a way as to promote an entirely different social meaning and ideology. By placing the black experience in the context of the classic immigrant story, the creators ignore the distinctiveness of Kunta Kinte's struggle—and the struggle of all black Americans—against the institution of slavery and oppression in favor of an emphasis on the idea of universal assimilation implicit in the immigrant myth.

Although the popular perspective of myth emphasizes the falsity of society's stories, a more useful view promotes the cultural role that myths play in conceptualizing historical or social events and relationships within a particular ideological framework (Fiske, 1990). For example, the pre—Civil Rights myths supported an ideology of race relations that favored racism and discrimination (see Omi & Winant, 1986). Fostered by works such as *Gone with the Wind* and D. W. Griffith's *Birth of a Nation*, a hierarchy of race was transmitted in terms of heroic, aristocratic whites, servile, contented black servants, and savage, lustful black freedmen. Against these images, which continued to linger in the media consciousness of the 1970s, Haley attempted to dramatically redefine and recode the black American experience from a black American perspective.

Once Haley's novel was adapted by the predominantly white television establishment, the explanation of slavery and race relations began to take on a different mythic flavor, reflecting the perspectives of the white producers and executives who controlled the production process. Content and characterizations were altered by the series' creators, obscuring any connection between Haley's collective indictment of the white establishment responsible for slavery and the identity of the white audience. The classic immigrant myth perpetuated by *TV Roots* invites white audience members to identify with the struggles of Kunta Kinte's family while relieving them of the responsibility to acknowledge the social and political contradictions underlying race relations in the United States.

References

Bogle, D. (1988). *Blacks in American films and television: an encyclopedia.* New York: Garland.

Dates, J. L. & Barlow, W. (1990). *Split image: African American and the media.* Washington, D.C.: Howard University Press.

Ettema, J. S., Whitney, D. C. & Wackman, D. B. (1987). Professional mass communicators. In C. R. Berger and S. H. Chaffee (Eds.), *Handbook of communication science* (pp. 747-780), Newbury Park, CA: Sage.

Fishbein, L. (1983). *Roots:* Docudrama and the interpretation of history. In J. O'Connor (Ed.), *American history, American television: Interpreting the video past* (pp. 279-305). New York: Frederick Ungar.

Fiske, J. (1990). *Introduction to communication studies* (2nd ed.). London: Routledge.

Fredrickson, G. M. (1988). *The arrogance of race: Historical perspectives on slavery, racism and social inequality.* Middletown, CT: Wesleyan University Press.

Haley, A. (1976). *Roots: the saga of an American family.* New York: Dell.

Helweg, A. W. & Helweg, U. M. (1990). *An immigrant success story.* Philadelphia: University of Pennsylvania Press.

Miles, R. (1989). *Racism.* London: Routledge.

Omi, M. & Winant, H. (1986). *Racial formation in the United States from the 1960s to the 1980s.* London: Routledge.

Peterson, R. A. (1976). The production of culture: A prolegomenon. *American Behavioral Scientist. 19*, 7-22.

Steinberg, S. (1989). *The ethnic myth: Race, ethnicity and class in America.* Boston: Beacon Press.

Takaki, R. (1989). *Strangers form a different shore: A history of Asian Americans.* Boston: Little, Brown.

Tuchman, G. (1983). Consciousness industries and the production of culture. *Journal of Communication, 33(3),* 330-341.

Willett, R. (1980). Twisting the roots: Fiction, faction and recent TV drama. *UMOJA, 4,* 11-20.

Williams, E. (1944). *Slavery & capitalism.* Chapel Hill, NC: University of North Carolina Press.

Wilson, C. R. & Gutierrez, F. (1980). *Minorities and media: Diversity and the end of mass communication.* Beverly Hills: Sage.

Woll, A. L. & Miller, R. M. (1987). *Ethnic and racial images in American film and television: Historical essays and bibliography.* New York: Garland.

Wolper, D. & Troupe, W. (1978). *The inside story of TV's "Roots,"* New York: Warner Books.

MILLER

The Ron Miller review of a controversial episode of *NYPD Blue* is an example of the critical value inherent in a well-conceived piece of journalistic criticism. In the course of his thirteen or so paragraphs, he touches on an important social issue (racism); an important judicial issue (police attitudes and behaviors); and he discusses genre conventions (character and story development).

How many of the eight aspects of journalistic television criticism can you find in this brief piece? Do you find Miller's succinctness a plus or minus in his critical effort? Do you agree or disagree that reviews such as this inevitably serve the functions of criticism? How good a job does he do of using examples from the show itself as evidence for his arguments?

In tonight's turbulent episode of ABC's "NYPD Blue," Detective Andy Sipowicz (Dennis Franz) uses the word "nigger" while booking a black suspect and winds up in a serious clash with his boss, Lt. Arthur Fancy (James McDaniel).

It may be the most powerful episode yet of the cutting-edge police series, this time taking on the controversial issue of the racial attitudes of urban white cops and their explosive use of the same word that sparked a national furor when it surfaced in the O.J. Simpson murder trial.

Though the fiery Sipowicz uses the word only after the suspect uses it first, he makes his racial attitudes clear when he goes on to suggest the mass shooting incident he's investigating is typical behavior for blacks.

The suspect promises to make Sipowicz pay for every racist act he's ever suffered from white cops. When Lt. Fancy demands an explanation, Sipowicz accuses him of taking sides with the black suspect because he's also black. He admits the word isn't new to him and "I've thought it lots of times," even if he's never used it on the job before. He says part of why Fancy is on his case is "just to see me sweat."

"So this is about me?" Fancy snarls. "I'm the racist?"

Sipowicz gets no support from his Latino partner, Bobby Simone (Jimmy Smits), who witnesses the confrontation— along with a white liberal reporter. Later, when he explains the affair to his wife,

Reprinted with permission from the *San Jose Mercury News.* © January 24, 1994.

Sylvia, he shows her the hand sign cops often use to indicate the "n-word," so they don't have to say it aloud. She's deeply bothered.

Asked about involving a leading character in "NYPD Blue" in the same pattern of behavior that destroyed the credibility of Los Angeles Detective Mark Fuhrman in the Simpson Trial, executive producer Steven Bochco said, "I think when you're doing these kinds of shows, these kinds of stories are absolutely appropriate. They're legitimate to the environment. These are exactly the kinds of conflicts that exist in the department and are sort of a paradigm for the society at large."

Though Sipowicz's racial attitudes have been revealed before in "NYPD Blue" and he's already clashed with Lt. Fancy over the subject, putting the "n-word" into such a major character's mouth seems a monumental risk for what it may mean to viewer attitudes.

"That's the character," Bochco said. "We aren't arbitrarily grafting something onto him. This has been the character really from the onset of the series. What you're seeing here is very much a part of the development and evolution of Andy Sipowicz. You don't forgive him for that. It's more complicated than that. He's a lot of things—cop, father, husband, friend—and perhaps his biases reside a little closer to the surface than they do in others. I think you just tell that story and let the people judge for themselves how they feel about this guy."

While still a top-rated show, "NYPD Blue" has dropped a few points in the ratings this season. Some speculate the "softening" of Sipowicz, who married last season and is now about to become a father again, may have contributed to the decline. Recent episodes have begun restoring his raw edges, but tonight's show really challenges his likability.

On another subject, Bochco said he was confident ABC will stick by his sagging "Murder One" serial drama despite low ratings for its Jan. 8 return to the air in a new Monday night time period. He expects all 23 episodes to air as planned.

However, Bochco conceded it was a mistake to start the series with a concept that included secondary story lines that detracted from he main story—a seasonlong murder trial. He said the secondary story lines were dropped as of the Jan. 8 episode and won't return.

On the other hand, Bochco doesn't blame ABC for sabotaging the show by scheduling it opposite NBC's blockbuster hit "ER" last fall. He said ABC had no other viable time periods open and he knew "ER" probably would clobber the series most critics acclaimed as the new season's best newcomer.

GRAY

San José State University senior Radio-TV-Film major Leslie Gray combines genre and feminist criticism in this analysis of *Dr. Quinn, Medicine Woman*. How well do you think she does in making her readers aware of the necessary genre conventions to ensure their understanding? What might you have done differently? Because she discusses issues of gender, does that necessarily mean that this is *feminist* criticism? Why or why not?

Popularity of Western Genre

When you think of television westerns, what is the first image that comes to mind? If it is bad guys in black hats shooting up the town, and good guys in white hats shooting the bad guys, you are not alone.

In the 1950s, westerns were the dominant program fare on network prime-time. In 1958, the western had reached its zenith. There were twenty-four westerns being shown on television, of which eleven were ranked in the top twenty. Westerns remained a constant form of network programming until the 1970s when audiences grew weary of one-dimensional characters who encountered situations of little relevance to modern viewers.

People used to flock to the movies on Saturday afternoon to watch their favorite western heroes such as Gene Autry, Roy Rogers and John Wayne. Today, families gather together in front of the television on Saturday night to watch their new hero, Dr. Quinn, Medicine Woman. With the continual decline of the western as a viable genre for television, why is *Dr. Quinn, Medicine Woman* so popular?

From Boston to the Rocky Mountains

Dr. Quinn, Medicine Woman, a sixty-minute drama which features an ensemble cast, can be seen on CBS at 7:00 p.m. on Saturday night. What makes this program unique among westerns? First and foremost, a woman is the hero of this series. Michaela Quinn M.D., who was born and educated in Boston, answers an ad in the paper for a position as a doctor in the small, rural community of Colorado Springs in the 1860s.

Another interesting facet of Dr. Quinn is that the citizens of Colorado Springs are given a great deal of depth and breadth in the script. The bad guys are not all bad and the good guys are not all good. As in real-life, these characters are muted in various shades or gray.

Dr. Quinn, who is greeted by these townfolk with suspicion and alarm, must convince them that she is a capable and professional doctor. One of her first patients, a woman with three children, dies of a rattlesnake-bite and Dr. Quinn vows to care for the trio of orphans, Matthew, Colleen and Brian.

Thus, Dr. Quinn becomes a single parent who must now provide for a family. Yet, all this adversity seems to strengthen her resolve to succeed. Dr. Mike, which is Dr. Quinn's newly-acquired moniker, demonstrates many skills and abilities as the new town doctor. She proves especially adept when acting as healer, philosopher, egalitarian, psychiatrist, peacekeeper, politician, or activist.

Most of the other female characters in the series have careers. This is rare in a western because women's roles are consistently relegated to that of homemaker, teacher or saloon girl. The prominence of women in this series is probably due to the vision of its creator/writer/executive producer, Beth Sullivan. In the first season, the town's wealthiest citizen is a benevolent woman everyone calls Miss Olive. Miss Olive helps an African-American woman named Grace become the proud and hardworking owner of a café. Then there is Dorothy, who is the town reporter/editor who behaves in an alternately noble and neurotic fashion. Perhaps the most engaging female is Dr. Quinn's adopted daughter, Colleen, who has aspirations of going to medical school and assists Dr. Quinn at the clinic in the interim. This suggests the value and significance of a positive role model.

The community of Colorado Springs as a whole is wary of strangers, Indians, and anyone who is different. The townfolks will do anything to you if you are an insider, but they can be a xenophobic, unenlighted and illiterate bunch. For example, they have burned books containing controversial themes and have threatened to lynch a man simply for looking strange (he was a burn victim). This is where the hero, Dr. Quinn, comes to rescue the locals from their own ignorance. Usually, something is lost before something is gained; the books are destroyed before a lesson in tolerance and diversity is learned and the man's faith in humanity is shaken to the core before he witnesses the community reach out in kindness.

Dr. Mike is the town's conscience. She is outspoken in the face of injustice, prejudice and inhumanity—all of which run rampant in the wild west. She understands that fear and ignorance can be overcome with patience, understanding and knowledge. This is not to say that she is perfect. Michaela is engaged to Byron Sully who is the strong, silent type and a friend of the nearby Cheyanne tribe. Yet, Dr. Quinn is overly-modest and can be blinded by convention and propriety. She is chaste and easily embarrassed when discussing man/woman relations. She could not bear to hear Sully read a Walt Whitman poem aloud because of its overt sensuality. However, this vulnerability actually seems to make her more endearing, if a bit prudish.

Critical Reviews

Most reviewers praise the show for its solid script writing, well-liked cast and superior production values. While some feel the show is too sentimental and Dr. Quinn herself anachronistic, they admit that the series is relevant and pleasurable. *Time Magazine* critic, Richard Zoglin, said that the town characters are colorful and the series has sweep and moral heft. He added that treacle like this goes down easier because the storytelling is confident and plainspoken (Time, 1993). *Variety* critic Tony Scott said that "Dr. Quinn" could work into a workable family Saturday evening practice (Variety, 1992).

One aspect of *Dr. Quinn, Medicine Woman* reviewers neglect to mention is the educational angle. The 1860s were a tumultuous and rapidly changing era. The transcontinental railroad was about to be completed, bringing about the industrial revolution which would turn America from an agrarian to a mechanized society. There were many issues surrounding Native Americans, efforts on their behalf and the tyranny they were ultimately subjected to. These and other historically significant issues have been brought to life in an accurate as well as entertaining fashion.

Positive Female Role Models Wanted

Since at least half the population of the United States is female, reason and common-sense would dictate that about half the lead characters on television programs would or should be women or girls. Sadly, the television industry is remiss in its efforts to portray women as capable and professional. According to the a 1990 study by the National Commission on Working Women and Women in Film, the bulk of women's roles are written for those who are white, under 40 and who work as clerks, homemakers or act as helpmates to lead male characters. After more than 20 years of feminist struggle, this is clearly unacceptable. How do we know that people want to see more positive roles for women?

One method is to examine the Nielsen Ratings which systematically measure audience viewing habits. When *Dr. Quinn* debuted, the television executives were ecstatic because people were watching it and sponsors were lining up to buy commercial time. Polaroid Corp., a *Dr. Quinn* sponsor, said that because the show is wholesome, family-oriented and very popular, many advertisers are trying to jump on the bandwagon. In fact, *Dr. Quinn* had the highest TvQ rating of any show ever on television, a 45 TvQ score (Advertising Age, 1993). TvQ rating refers to the ratio of people who like a show to the total number of people who are familiar with it.

Share is another way of measuring audience response. It tracks how many people watch a given program out of all the programs available in a certain time-slot (Ziegler, 1991). The share for *Dr. Quinn* on a national level is a 25. This means that 25% of all the people watching television on Saturday nights at 7:00 p.m. were watching *Dr. Quinn, Medicine Woman* (Advertising Age, 1993).

Another set of ratings for *Dr. Quinn* were obtained from local station KPIX–San Francisco. That station's data indicate that women and children make up about 80% of *Dr. Quinn's* audience (KPIX, 1994). This demonstrates that this is a family show. *Dr. Quinn* offers something for everyone, but identifies most closely with women and children.

Inside "*Dr. Quinn*"

Dr. Quinn, Medicine Woman has been on the air for two years. In that time a myriad of subjects has been covered. However, there are some themes that are worthy of repetition. Some of those message remind even adults of simple truths such as: be yourself, always be honest, be more compassionate and empathetic and find out all the information you can about a person or issue before you make a judgement. It's surprising to discover that even the kindest people sometimes forget these valuable lessons.

In one episode, Dr. Quinn received a large shipment of her father's books. With the help of the town she opens a library. But then some books are deemed unfit for the good citizens of Colorado Springs. After an emergency town meeting, many books are confiscated from the patrons' homes in the middle of the night. Among them were Goethe's *Faust*, a collection of Walt Whitman's poetry and *The Scarlet Letter*. When Dr. Quinn decides to retrieve the books and loan them out privately, the town unloads the books and ar-

ranges them into a pile. The books are set on fire in dramatic fashion. At church the next day she tells the Reverend he forgot one book. She explains it has violence, wars, wanton sex, satan and disobedience. When the congregation wants to know the name of this book that contains such vile content, Dr. Quinn replies, *The Holy Bible*. This may be a melodramatic representation, but here in the 1990s, schools all over the United States are banning books from school libraries. Dr. Quinn told her young son that he should find out about everything he could before he made up his mind and that is wise and sage advice indeed.

The Importance of *Dr. Quinn, Medicine Woman*

Because television is advertiser-driven, and *Dr. Quinn, Medicine Woman* is commercially successful, this could open the door for more programming of relevant interest to the audience.

Successful television programs are somewhat rare, so when one succeeds, viewers are bound to see several more like it by the next season. Television producers have a way or trying to reproduce the elements that made a series popular.

With this in mind, it is possible that producers will see the benefit or presenting more women as positive role models and strong lead characters. Women have come a long way since the 1860s when a doctor named Edward H. Clarke said that higher education was destroying the health and capacities of women. He argued that their energy was needed to develop their reproductive organs, and they were depleting that energy by building up their brains (Dorenkamp, 1985).

The popularity of *Dr. Quinn* may encourage producers and writers to deliver scripts which contain pro-social messages. American family-life is rich and diverse, it may be possible to bridge the education

gap if families talk about the television programs they watch together. Since television is the main storyteller in our culture, we need to make sure that the stories we tell have substance and are not simply designed to extract maximum profits.

Bibliography

Advertising Age. "Dr. Quinn" Could Cure CBS blues on Saturday by Joe Mandese. February 15, 1993, pp. 3–4.

Advertising Age. Saturday Night Audience is Ripe for the Picking by Monte Williams. May 24, 1993, p. 218

Baran, S. J., Davis, D. K. (1995) *Mass Communications Theory; Foundations, Ferment and Future*. Belmont, CA: Wadsworth, p. 305.

Dorenkamp, A., McClymer, J., Moynihan, M., Vadum, A. *Images of Women in Popular American Culture*. Orlando, FL: Harcourt Brace Jovanovich, p. 43.

Time Magazine. "Dr. Quinn." Reviewed by Richard Zoglin. March 1, 1994. pp. 63–64.

Variety Magazine. "Dr. Quinn." Reviewed by Tony Scott. December 21, 1992.

Wilson, S. L. (1993). *Mass Media/Mass Culture: An Introduction*. New York: McGraw-Hill, Inc., p. 262.

Ziegler, S. K. (1991) *Broadcast Advertising*. Ames, Iowa. Iowa State University Press, pp. 248-249.

Chapter Exercises

Comparing Drama Formats

As we've seen, television drama follows a strict format. Choose one episode each from your favorite science fiction, police, and family dramas. In the space provided in the box below, briefly describe how each program fulfills the various aspects of the formula.

TELEVISION DRAMA FORMAT COMPARISON

List the names of the programs you have chosen: _____

Science Fiction drama: _____

Police drama: _____

Family drama: _____

How does each program fulfill the components of the dramatic formula?

1. **Posing of the plot / Introduction of the characters**

   Science Fiction _____

   Police _____

   Family _____

2. **Posing the solution / Laying the strategy for resolution**

   Science Fiction _____

   Police _____

   Family _____

3. **Thickening of the plot**

   Science Fiction _____

   Police _____

   Family _____

4. **Climax and Resolution**

   Science Fiction _____

   Police _____

   Family _____

5. **Outcome**

   Science Fiction _____

   Police _____

   Family _____

Using the Dramatic Formula

Based on your descriptions from question #1, what conclusions can you draw about each form's use of the dramatic formula?

DRAMATIC FORMULA ANALYSIS

Conflict in Science-Fiction

In this chapter we discussed how difficult it is to address the "human vs. environment" conflict because of the technological and aesthetic limitations of television as a medium. However, the resurgence of science-fiction dramas has reintroduced this struggle to the small screen. Choose your favorite sci-fi drama and discuss how it addresses the "human vs. environment" conflict. Then speculate as to why you think this conflict works (or doesn't work) well within the sci-fi format.

CONFLICT IN SCIENCE-FICTION

References and Resources

Ang, I. (1985). *Watching Dallas*: *Soap Opera and the Melodramatic Imagination*. London: Methuen.

Bacon-Smith, C. (1986). Spock among the women. *The New York Times Book Review*, November 16, pp. 1, cont. 26.

Blair, K. (1979). The garden in the machine: the why of *Star Trek*. *Journal of Popular Culture, 13,* 310–20.

Boddy, W. (1984). Entering the *Twilight Zone*. *Screen, 25,* 98–108.

Boyd-Bowman, S. (1984). *The Day After*: representations of the nuclear holocaust. *Screen, 25,* 71–97.

Carpenter, R. (1967). *I Spy* and *Mission: Impossible*: gimmicks and a fairy tale. *Journal of Popular Culture, 1,* 286–290.

Caughie, J. (1980). Progressive television and documentary drama. *Screen, 21,* 9–35.

Charland, M. (1979). The private eye: from print to television. *Journal of Popular Culture, 12,* 210–215.

Cloud, D. L. (1992). The limits of interpretation: ambivalence and the stereotype in *Spenser: For Hire*. *Critical Studies in Mass Communication, 9,* 311-324.

Deming, C. J. (1985). *Hill Street Blues* as narrative. *Critical Studies in Mass Communication, 2,* 1–22.

Dennington, J. & Tulloch, J. (1976). Cops, consensus, and ideology. *Screen Education, 20,* 37–46.

Finch, M. (1986). Sex and address in *Dynasty*. *Screen, 27,* 24–42.

Flitterman, S. (1985). Thighs and whiskers: the fascination of *Magnum, P. I. Screen, 26,* 42–58.

Greenberg, H. R. (1984). In search of Spock: a psychoanalytic inquiry. *Journal of Popular Film and Television, 12,* 52–65.

Hanke, R. (1990). Hegemonic masculinity in *thirtysomething*. *Critical Studies in Mass Communication, 7,* 231–248.

Hoffer, T. W. & Nelson, R. A. (1978). Docudrama on American television. *Journal of the University Film Association, 30,* 21–28.

Jenkins, H. (1988). *Star Trek* rerun, reread, rewritten: fan writing as textual poaching. *Critical Studies in Mass Communication, 5,* 85–107.

Loeb, J. C. (1990). Rhetorical and ideological conservatism in *thirtysomething*. *Critical Studies in Mass Communication, 7,* 249–261.

Mander, M. (1983). *Dallas*: the mythology of crime and moral occult. *Journal of Popular Culture, 17,* 44–50.

Marshak, S. & Culbreath, M. (1978). *Star Trek*: *The New Voyages*. New York: Bantam Books.

McGrath, J. (1977). TV drama: the case against naturalism. *Sight and Sound, 46,* 100–105.

Millman, J. (1993). *NYPD Blue* is on target. San Francisco *Examiner*, 7 November, pp. D-1, D-6.

Nochimson, M. (1992-93). Desire under the Douglas firs: entering the body of reality in *Twin Peaks*. *Film Quarterly, 46,* 22–34.

Pringle, A. (1972). A methodology for television analysis with reference to the drama series. *Screen, 13,* 117–128.

Schwichtenberg, C. (1981). *Charlie's Angels* (ABC-TV). *JumpCut, 24/25,* 13–15.

Schwichtenberg, C. (1984). *The Love Boat*: the packaging and selling of love, heterosexual romance, and family. *Media, Culture, and Society, 6*, 301–311.

Seiter, E. (1983). Men, sex, and money in recent family melodrama. *Journal of the University Film and Video Association, 35*, 17–27.

Stein, H. F. (1977). In search of *Roots*: an epic of origins and destiny. *Journal of Popular Culture, 11*, 11–17.

Tucker, L. R. & Shah, H. (1992). Race and the transformation of culture: the making of the television miniseries *Roots*. *Critical Studies in Mass Communication, 9*, 325–336.

Tyrrell, W. B. (1977). *Star Trek* as myth and television as mythmaker. *Journal of Popular Culture, 10*, 711–719.

Vande Berg, L. R. (1993). *China Beach*, prime time war in the postfeminist age: an example of patriarchy in a different voice. *Western Journal of Communication, 57*, 349–366.

Zimmerman, P. R. (1985). Good girls, bad women: the role of older women on *Dynasty*. *Journal of Film and Video, 37*, 89–92.

Zoglin, R. (1990). Like nothing on earth: David Lynch's *Twin Peaks* may be the most original show on TV. *Time*, April 9, p. 96–97.

CHAPTER 8

GAME SHOWS

I apologize for insulting your intelligence. From now on I promise to stick to comedy.

—*Jackie Gleason*

That's how the Great One himself greeted the CBS Friday night audience tuned-in to his game show, *You're In the Picture*, on January 27, 1961. What next happened was a television rarity, one not likely ever to be repeated. A program was cancelled, not because of sponsor disenchantment or low ratings, but because its star was embarrassed by it. This prime-time game show had premiered the week before and featured comedian Gleason. There was also a panel of celebrities who'd put their faces through the holes of an amusement park souvenir photo scene and were required to guess what the scene depicted.

On the night of the 27th, the series' second episode, the stage was bare. In the center sat a somber Jackie Gleason, nestled in an arm chair. He spent the program's half hour apologizing to his viewers for the foolishness that he had subjected them to the week before.

There are more than a few viewers and critics who wish that other game show hosts were as considerate of their viewers. But game shows have endured, enjoying success, surviving scandal, and currently revelling in something of a mini-boom. They are older than soap operas, remarkably profitable for their pro-

ducers and broadcasters, and immensely popular with a sizable audience, many of whom, however, refuse to admit their addiction.

Overview

Among the most parodied forms of television, the game show has long been a medium staple, coming over from radio. We will examine game shows' migration from radio to television, the impact of the Quiz Show Scandal on the game show format and we will see how well-intentioned government regulation helped increase their presence on the schedules of local stations and networks. We will discuss the reasons for and advantages of their apparently simple formats and visual look and we will discover how the very same factors that are transforming all television genres are doing the same thing to television game shows.

The Beginning to the Scandal

Like most other television forms, game shows began on radio. The radio forerunners of the game show were quiz, amateur, and interview or man-in-the-street shows. In addition, almost every radio station had some sort of "give away" promotion during ratings periods in order to introduce new advertisers.

The quiz show was introduced to the network radio audience in 1924 by Time magazine. It sponsored *The Pop Question*, a news quiz in which panel members fielded questions about current events. *Major Bowes and His Original Amateur Hour* premiered on the NBC radio network in 1935, and is considered the first nationally broadcast amateur hour program.

Amateur talent would perform on stage for the evening radio audience, but before they could begin their acts, they were interviewed by Major Bowes. These conversations were played strictly for laughs by the Master of Ceremonies (known as the MC). Two other hints of game shows to come were featured in Bowes' amateur hour. Winners were determined by the spin of a carnival wheel-of-chance and losers were dispatched by a bong of the gong.

The first interview or man-in-the-street program was NBC's *Vox Pop*. When it premiered in 1932 it was called *Sidewalk Interview* and its format revolved around humorous man-in-the-street conversations. Participants, however, were rewarded with gifts for being good sports.

It was in 1936, though, that all these elements came together in broadcasting's first real game show, a program in which contestants from off the street or out in the audience could compete in a game of skill or chance in order to win money or merchandise. NBC struck first with *Uncle Jim's Question Bee*. A simple show, audience members were invited on stage to answer quiz questions posed by the host, Jim McWilliams. Later that same year, CBS unveiled *Professor Quiz*. Similar to Uncle Jim's show in that audience members answered questions posed by a host—in this case Professor Craig Earl—it was different in that it moved, week to week, to different towns and cities to quiz the populace.

The questions were simple, common-knowledge queries; the gifts were small amounts of cash, usually only five dollars. Yet these shows were instant hits. Within five years there were fifty quiz shows on the air. Within fifteen years there were two hundred quiz shows on network and local radio. Some early game shows were so popular, in fact, that they survived into the television era. NBC's *Information, Please* premiered on radio in 1938 and departed for CBS television in June of 1952. 1938 also saw the birth of NBC's *Kay Kyser's Kollege of Musical Knowledge.* It made it to television in 1949, was hosted by band leader Kyser and then by Tennessee Ernie Ford, and lasted until September of 1954.

Game shows made the transition from radio to television with remarkable ease. There were several reasons for the smoothness of this transition, not the least of which was the existence of dozens of very popular radio quizzes that brought with them their built-in audiences. The *Kollege of Musical Knowledge* and *Information, Please* were only two cross-over shows. More familiar, however, are programs like *Truth or Consequences, People Are Funny, Queen For A Day, Twenty Questions, This Is Your Life, Strike It Rich,* and *You Bet Your Life.* All of these began on radio, developed large and loyal followings, and then moved to television.

Also facilitating the games' move to television were the new medium's novelty value, the technical limitations of early live television, and the scientific nature of its development.

Quiz and panel shows where a host or MC posed questions to respondents may have made for good radio listening, but it was not a particularly visual enterprise. The fact that this exchange could be seen at all, however, assured its success. Because it was new, people would watch anything on television, even one person asking another questions. Curiosity, too, played a part. People were anxious to see what their favorite radio quiz show personalities looked like when they were playing their games.

The simple format of the quiz was beautifully

suited for early television. Bulky cameras, hot lights, restrictive stages and sets, inexperienced personnel running new and unfamiliar equipment, and small operating budgets all demanded simple productions. What could be simpler to televise than one person asking another a question?

Motion pictures were developed by showmen and entrepreneurs, and early movies demonstrated their flair. Television, however, was developed by scientists who either worked at universities or in close contact with those institutions. The quiz (people matching wits with other people) was a logical format for information-oriented professors in need of something to broadcast on the new medium that they were developing.

This does not mean, however, that all early television quiz shows were simple or visually uninteresting. *Kay Kyser's Kollege of Musical Knowledge* featured the Frank DeVol Orchestra outfitted like pre-WWII college freshmen; the band leader Kyser attired in professor's robes; musical questions presented to contestants by the band and guest stars; and a panel of three bearded judges wearing tailcoats and seated behind a judge's bench who would pass on the correctness of an answer by speaking their words in perfect unison. Most early television quiz shows, however, were somewhat simpler in format and less ambitious in style.

DuMont was the first to bring game shows to network television. In 1946, it premiered *Play the Game*. Hosted by a New York University professor, Dr. Harvey Zorbaugh, it presented celebrities playing charades and asked viewers to call in their guesses as to what the stars were attempting to represent. Interestingly, the program first ran on NBC's experimental station in New York in 1941. When it reappeared on the DuMont network of two stations in 1946, the show was produced by ABC personnel. That network wanted its people to get hands-on production experience but had no completed television facilities of its own. ABC simply bought network time from DuMont.

Games shows did well on television in its early days, the late 1940s, and some of the conventions that we see now were developed then. The "lock out button" was introduced in 1948 on CBS's *Winner Take All*. It allowed the first contestant who thought he or she knew the right answer to lock out the response of the competition by pushing a button. Continuing champions, a staple of contemporary game shows, also had their television genesis on *Winner Take All*.

It was the 1950s, however, that were to see game shows become the dominant prime-time television genre and it was that same decade that would see their fall, precipitated by the quiz show scandals.

In 1955, the year that The *$64,000 Question* premiered, there were twenty three audience participation—or game—shows on the networks' prime-time schedules. Game show ratings were astronomical. *The $64,000 Question*, for example, had a rating of 57.1 and a share of 84.8 one evening. Advertisers stood in line to sponsor new quiz shows. *I Love Lucy's* ratings slipped as its NBC competition, *Twenty One*, gained popularity. Quiz show winners became celebrities and talk show hosts, and some were featured on magazine covers. Prizes rose higher and higher. The *$100,000 Big Surprise* and *Break the $250,000 Bank* were introduced to dwarf *The $64,000 Question* and *The $64,000 Challenge*. These latter two shows then altered their rules to allow contestants to win more money than the amount indicated by their titles. In 1958, bluecollar worker Teddy Nadler won $264,000 on *The $64,000 Challenge*, until 1980, the largest amount ever won on a television game show (Nadler's winnings have been surpassed by those of twenty-four year old Navy fighter pilot Lt. Thom McKee who won $312,700 and eight cars in nine weeks of success on the syndicated game show *Tic Tac Dough*).

Then the bubble burst. In 1957 a contestant on *Twenty One* complained to reporters that he had been instructed to lose his match to a contestant who was, the show's producers had told him, more popular with viewers and

Ratings

who promised to deliver higher ratings. Other losing contestants from other shows complained as well and *Look* magazine published a story about quiz show rigging and abuses, naming several of the most popular programs as offenders. But there was no proof of misdeed.

None, that is, until 1958 when a contestant, waiting to compete on NBC's *Dotto*, discovered a notebook containing all the evening's questions and answers among the belongings of another contestant who was, not coincidentally, doing quite well that night. A grand jury was convened in New York to investigate the riggings and issued its report in 1959 and then, in the U.S. Congress, a House of Representatives' committee conducted its own examination of the fixings.

These investigations left little doubt. Producers and sponsors fixed the quiz shows to retain popular contestants and dispatch unpopular ones, to artificially build suspense in order to keep viewers coming back week after week to see how the champion or their favorite fared, and to artificially keep scores close on a given evening to insure that the audience remained for a full thirty minutes of viewing.

Soon, even the most popular shows, including several that were not rigged, were in trouble. All the quiz shows suffered guilt by association and by 1960 they were gone from prime-time all together.

Dead in the evenings, the now-named *game* shows became boffo during the day. Dropping "quiz" from the name was designed to distance the new generation of game shows from their disgraced predecessors. In addition, because fixing was now illegal, quizzes became too difficult for the contestants to play. A lot of people not knowing the answers to a lot of questions made for bad television. So quiz shows—which required intelligence and/or rigging—were replaced by game shows—which required little more than warm bodies.

The Comeback

Throughout the 1960s game shows flourished on the late morning and early afternoon network schedules. But as that decade drew to a close, the renaissance waned, the networks began to replace them with reruns of their own evening situation comedies. In fact, in 1967, CBS cancelled every one of its game shows. Network people claimed that they were being offered fewer and fewer good game shows and turned to reruns as a result. Game show producers argued that the move to morning showings of *I Love Lucy* and *The Real McCoys* was purely financial, the networks felt that they could save production expenses by re-running their own properties.

Regardless of who was correct, game shows were forced to find additional outlets beyond ABC, CBS, and NBC. And while a few did prosper on the networks during that period, for example *Hollywood Squares* on NBC and *The Newlywed Game* on ABC, syndication for sale to local stations became the game show's salvation. The genre found assistance in its battle for survival from an unexpected and reluctant source, the FCC.

In May of 1970, after ten years of study, the FCC passed Rule 73.658(k), better known as the *Prime Time Access Rule*. The commissioners were attempting to instill some variety into local stations' evening fare, feeling that their schedules were too dominated by network programming. The commission initially considered a rule that would have required stations to program half of every evening with non-network material, but finally settled, to the advantage of game shows, on a compromise—the half hour that immediately preceded prime-time would be set aside for local, or non-network, access. The rule applied to network affiliates in the top fifty markets and required that they fill that half hour with programming of their own choice, as long as it was not originated by one of the three commercial networks.

The FCC envisioned the half hour as an oasis of local and regional diversity. Local stations would expand news coverage, or air discussion programs or documentaries of local interest, and in general give television exposure to ideas that were being ignored in prime-time by networks forced to program for a national audience.

Those visions never materialized. Broadcasters were faced with the difficult task of programming seven additional half hours each week. Many stations did not have the expertise or the financial ability to undertake their own independent productions. Many simply saw the rule as a chance to reap large profits.

The rule that had been intended to foster regional diversity and variety had just the opposite effect. With a series of half hours, one a night, always at the same time, most stations decided to *strip* that slot in their schedule. That is, they would run an episode of the same program five, six, or seven nights a week in that time period. *Stripping* offered many advantages to the broadcasters. It reduced scheduling problems—the same program was shown every day. It allowed for easier, less expensive promotion—rather than promoting several different shows, one commercial or newspaper ad could promote the entire week's offerings. Stripping also encouraged habit viewing. Viewers had no trouble following the program schedule—at the same time every night they could tune in and see the show they've followed all week.

Stripping, encouraged by the nightly half hour created by the Prime Time Access Rule, was ideal for game shows. Games are relatively inexpensive to produce. It cost the producers of a game show about thirty to fifty thousand dollars to produce five syndicated episodes at the time of the Prime Time Access Rule. One episode of a syndicated half hour situation comedy, however, would cost $130,000 to make. Therefore, they were less expensive for local stations to buy. With continuing encounters by continuing contestants, games lent themselves quite well to daily viewing. Games were popular. A year after the rule went into effect, *Let's Make A Deal*, already on ABC's daytime schedule, was being syndicated in

forty-three of the fifty top markets. Of the five leading syndicated programs that were filling the access half hour that year, three were remakes of game shows that had at one time or another aired on the network—*To Tell The Truth, Truth Or Consequence,* and *What's My Line.* Nine of the top twenty syndicated offerings in the access half hour were game shows. So much for regional diversity and returning a half hour of television time to local television.

The games made a comeback on network television as well. One of the CBS game shows cancelled in 1967 was *Password.* Its production company, Goodson-Todman, convinced ABC, consistently last in the daytime ratings race, to revive it on their network. Coupled with its 1969 signing away of *Let's Make A Deal* from NBC, ABC's 1972 resurrection of *Password* moved it up to number two in the daytime ratings. This dual game show blow dropped NBC to number three, costing it over $100 million in lost advertising revenues that year alone.

CBS was impressed at the game shows' ratings power and their success in syndication and jumped back into the breech with a remake of the old *The Price Is Right,* a game that had aired on ABC and NBC in the 1950s and 1960s, and called it *The New Price Is Right.* Games were back on all three networks in full force. Once-cancelled games made national comebacks—*Match Game, The New Treasure Hunt*—and new ones were developed—*The $100,000 Pyramid* (it began as *The $10,000 Pyramid* but had to update its name because of inflation), *High Rollers, Family Feud, The Gong Show.* The renaissance was complete.

Today, though, that renewal has taken on a somewhat different character. Game shows are absent from the networks' daytime schedules (there were six each day in 1980) and they no longer appear in network prime-time. They live primarily in the syndication market and on cable channels like USA, Lifetime and the Family Channel. For example, *Jeopardy!* is syndicated to over 190 markets and *Wheel of Fortune* appears in over 200.

Game shows are popular with local programmers for obvious reasons. They are relatively inexpensive to secure, easy to strip, and are popular. In her book, *TV Game Shows*, Maxine Fabe (1979) totalled over seven hundred different local, network, and syndicated game shows that have made it to television since 1948.

Format

The reason for the low production costs are obvious as soon as we sit down to watch. Sets are static, although often very elaborate. Once they are designed and built—each game show uses only one set—the only expenses are the salaries of the production crew and talent and the cost of some of the prizes.

Hosts are paid well, celebrity guests are usually paid minimally. Most celebrities who appear on games are "between jobs" and happy for the exposure. But what about the prizes? They must be expensive.

They are, but they're generally free to the game shows. Games shows give away prizes in three categories—small, medium, and large priced prizes. Almost all game shows give away small prizes like cosmetics, packages of food, and cleaning goods. The programs receive cash payments for mentioning these products on the air when they give them away. They use this money to buy expensive, large prizes like cars, boats, and vacations.

The people who hunt up the gifts for the game shows are sometimes called *Schlockmeisters*. The best ever is reputed to be Paul Mosher who procured gifts for thirteen and a half years for NBC's game shows. He brought in over seven million dollars worth of gifts in that time and often had big gift manufacturers paying cash to the shows to take their products because he so skillfully negotiated their prices down to a level where the money owed for the on-air announcements was higher than the new product price.

Cash prizes, on the other hand, offer more disadvantage than advantage. Obviously, it is less work to secure cash than gifts and there is no need to plug manufacturers if a show awards cash prizes, an important matter on games that depend on speed like *The $100,000 Pyramid*. This program gives away over a million dollars a year, an advantage in attracting viewers who enjoy big money games, but something of a disadvantage for a producer who wants to keep his or her costs down.

The real disadvantage of cash prizes is that money runs out. Merchandise for prizes is always available, it can be purchased with promotional announcements. Game shows that depend on cash prizes sometimes give away more than they have budgeted. When this happens, the producers will go to that special set of questions or categories that is intentionally difficult. If you ever see a particularly obscure category on *Pyramid* (Things in a neurosurgeon's black bag), they've probably given away too much money that week. One time, on CBS's 1950s *Two For the Money* that strategy backfired. Contestants were asked to name words in a given category in a given period of time. One week the show was well over budget, so the contestants were told that they would win money for each word that they could come up with that ended in "th." The producers were certain that this was difficult enough to insure a small pay-off. What they did not consider was that one of the competitors would say "fourth" and the second would respond with "fifth" and that they would continue right on down through all the number rankings that ended in "th."

In addition to prizes, the other important elements in the game show format are the *host, contestants, audience*, and of course, *the games* themselves.

Hosts in the 1950s and 1960s tended to be serious looking types like Allen Ludden, Mike Wallace, Art Fleming, John Daly, Robert Q. Lewis, and Bud Collyer. Those were the days of quiz games and intellectual types seemed appropriate as hosts for skill-oriented games. In addition, most of these men were older than contemporary game show hosts because they had begun as announcers or hosts in radio and good-voiced radio types were thought to be the best MCs for the new medium's skill games.

But the new breed of game hosts—Alex Trebek, Dick Clark, Geoff Edwards, Bob Eubanks, Wink Martindale, Pat Sajak, Jim Lange—tend to be stylish, ever smiling, sexy men.

The one thing you will not see a game show host be is female. While there very often are "lovely assistants" like the famous Vanna White, there may be difficult to overcome cultural reasons that no women are used as hostesses of games. Unfortunately, strong, take-charge women, those who can say "all right, that's enough fun, let's play!" still tend to frighten some segments of the audience (at least that's what most game show producers think). And there may be an even deeper cultural bias against women as game show hosts. In our society, wealth and resources are traditionally controlled by men, and until more women assume that role, they may not be given the opportunity to control wealth and resources on television game shows.

Game show hosts are always affable, pleasant, smiling people. They are the attractive men whom sponsors hope will be invited into the homes of women between the ages of eighteen and forty (another reason why male hosts dominate). That pleasantness, however, is not as important a characteristic of a host as the ability to take charge, to run the game according to the proscribed format, with the proper pace, and within the allotted thirty minutes.

Contestants are almost always ordinary people, folks with whom the television audience can identify. Despite the impression of contestants as people-off-the-street, however, they are actually selected very carefully and must meet stiff requirements before they can appear. They have to be emotional (passivity looks bad on television, especially in a game show that is supposed to be exiting) and they must have some skill at the game to be played. To determine the qualifications of potential contestants, they must go through one or more lengthy interviews and practice games.

Contestants are on the screen eighty to ninety percent of the time that the game show airs, so their selection cannot be too careful. Bad contestants mean bad ratings. Only five percent of all the people who ever reach the interview stage—two to three hundred per week per game show—ever appear on the air. The staff of *Family Feud*, for example, interviews three hundred families every week and selects only eight for the air.

The audience is quite important to the game show format as well. It adds to the excitement, shouts encouragement, and sometimes, as in *Love Connection*, participates in the game. A hallmark of the game show is the appearance of spontaneity and a lively audience strengthens that impression. In fact, a televised game is not a game unless there are spectators. To insure that there is an audience in the first place, most game shows depend on *head hunters*, services that, for a dollar or so a head, fill the show's seats. The head hunters provide the game show with a specific type of audience as well. Specific programs need specific audiences—young adults for *Love Connection*, women in their late twenties and early thirties for *The New Price Is Right*, and so on. It is most important that all seats be filled, of course, but beyond that requirement, the composition of the audience is crucial.

The excitement in contemporary game shows depends heavily on the reaction of the audience. It's particularly important for the contestants who are typically inexperienced video performers. So the right audience for the specific show is crucial. As a result, the unspoken target of the head hunters' craft is the elderly. Not that the head hunters look *for* them, they look for people who will fill seats *instead* of them. Older, retired folks have the time to file into game show studios, but they are not the audience that responds enthusiastically to the contemporary games.

To insure that the audience does respond enthusiastically, all game shows utilize *warm-up men and women*. Before the host and contestants appear, the audience warm-up man or woman performs on stage and walks through the audience, telling jokes, talking to people, and getting them excited. While styles of warm-up differ, the aim of the warm-up person is the same: to create rapport and goodwill with an audience and transfer it to the show. They work to turn the audience into participants—not just spectators—because the more they encourage the contestants, the better the show will be.

The games that are actually played on game shows vary from contests of skill to forums for humiliation. Gone in the wake of the quiz game scandals are the quiz shows—programs that featured information and knowledge games. They encouraged cheating and were often too difficult for the folks at home to play along. *Jeopardy!*, a hard quiz game show that was cancelled by NBC in 1975, is now, in syndication, the last of that breed and a favorite among college students and professional people.

Other game formats have had varying success, some have vanished, often for the better. One is the charade game. *It's Your Move* and *Celebrity Charades* are two that have made recent (Eighties) television appearances. The game in these programs was for contestants to guess a charade's solution.

Stunt games seem to come and go. *Beat the Clock* and *Truth or Consequences* are two programs that required contestants to perform odd stunts in order to win prizes. There have been comedy games (Groucho Marx' and later, Bill Cosby's *You Bet Your Life*, Johnny Carson's *Who Do You Trust?*), musical games (*Name That Tune*), word games (*Password*), money games (*The Price Is Right*), children's games (*Quiz Kids*), talent games (*So You Wanna Lead a Band*), intellectual games (*College Bowl*), family games (*Family Feud*), sports games (*Sports Challenge*), gambling games (*The New High Rollers*), down and out or sympathy games (*Queen For A Day*), people games (*To Tell The Truth*), and celebrity games (*Hollywood Squares*). Clearly, there are other forms that games shows have taken over the last forty years, especially with over seven hundred having made it to the screen in that time. One thing is certain, however, those hundreds of shows would never have been aired if the genre was not popular with viewers.

Yet where soaps and situation comedies are often the object of critic and viewer derision, game shows are often the object of their disgust. *Panorama* called them "television's thriving theater of humiliation." *TV Guide* predicted that future generations would look at our game shows and judge them "some form of public punishment to humiliate social violators."

The Popularity of Game Shows

Good or bad, people watch them and the question always asked is "Why?"

Vicarious greed is the most common answer, but there is some evidence that avarice may not be that important a factor. *What's My Line?* aired nationally for seventeen years. The most it ever awarded a contestant was fifty dollars. *Jeopardy!* rarely awards more than $1,500 and a home version of the game. Some viewers, many perhaps, enjoy the huge prizes and large amounts of cash on some game shows, but it may not be greed that fuels that pleasure. Instead of appealing to viewers' greediness, a kinder view may be that games satisfy the Cinderella in people. Viewers enjoy watching someone cash in, make it big. The Horatio Alger fantasy has been and still is an important part of our culture.

Game shows do appeal to the particularly American fantasy of getting something for nothing, however. Game show contestants are like the land rushers of *Oklahoma*, reaching riches, not through hard work or intellect, but by guts, quickness, and the luck of the draw. Viewers enjoy their unrealistic chase for riches.

Another reason for the popularity of game shows is the *competition*. There are and have been some silly games, but many are exacting and challenging. Even when they are not, viewers can play along, cheer for favorites, guess answers, or predict responses, all in the no-fail, no-lose security of their homes. Good game shows, like good television sports, are active, involving, and exciting. They are as spontaneous as television can be, and they are a kibitzer's delight. In fact, three board game-based programs on the Family Channel—*Trivial Pursuit*, *Boggle*, and *Shuffle*—even have 900 telephone numbers to permit viewers to interactively participate.

An important aspect of the game shows' excitement is their *simplicity*. Designed for daytime and early evening schedules, they must be simple enough that a busy audience can follow the action even though its attention is divided between home and the screen.

The *daily drama* of game shows is also partly responsible for their popularity. They are un-rehearsed soap operas of sorts. Viewers know the rules and relationships, they relate to the players (who have been carefully selected to generate that empathy), they know and trust the host. They are familiar with him, the regular panelists if any, and the returning contestants. Lt. Thom McKee's success on *Tic Tac Dough*, for example, was closely followed and reported by the major wire news services and chronicled in *People* magazine alongside the JR Ewing shooting and the exploits of the soaps' biggest stars.

Many viewers also enjoy seeing *celebrities* interact in these more or less familiar game situations. Programs like *Hollywood Squares* offered little in the way of vicarious greed (the cash prizes were generally quite small) and contestants rarely continued beyond a week's time. Its great success (fourteen years on the network, tremendous syndication profits, numerous Emmies, prime time specials) was attributed solely to its humanization of the stars, its presentation of celebrities "being themselves." The fact that the stars were coached on the questions that they would receive prior to each show was unimportant. Millions of viewers found continuing satisfaction in watching "Hollywood's finest" in a non-acting setting.

Trends in Game Shows

A final reason offered for the success of game shows can be seen as a relatively recent trend—the audience's desire to see *other people humiliated*.

Humiliation has long been a part of the game show formula. Even the earliest radio games like *Uncle Jim's Question Bee* featured the host's gentle chiding of microphone-shy or losing contestants. Many of television's most famous games put contestants in situations in which they would inevitably embarrass themselves. *Beat The Clock*, for example, had competitors perform zany races like carrying eggs in tablespoons in order to win prizes. Many of the medium's most obscure games did the same thing. Do you remember NBC's 1975 offering, *Diamond Head*? Don't worry, no one else does either. It required people to dive for money that erupted from inside a paper-mache volcano. In these programs, however, the humiliation of contestants was a humorous by-product of an otherwise straight-forward, albeit silly game.

With the passing of the big money games and contests of skill and intellect, the humiliation game gained strength. Chuck Barris' introduction of *The Dating Game* in 1965 is considered the beginning of the game designed specifically to humiliate its contestants. His 1976 debut of *The Gong Show* is credited with raising the humiliation game show to new lows.

In *The Dating Game* three members of one sex were required to answer provocative questions posed by a member of the opposite sex in order to win a blind date and prizes. In 1966, Barris followed this success with *The Newlywed Game*. It required newly married couples to reveal their innermost and private sexual and personal activities for daytime and evening ABC audiences. *The Gong Show's* contestants paraded their silly talents before a panel of celebrity judges and the television audience. Losers were dispatched by the enthusiastic hitting of the ubiquitous gong and winners received $516.32. The more bizarre the act, the greater the likelihood that it would reach the air.

Continuing in the tradition of "Television's Thriving Theater of Humiliation," were shows like *Three's A Crowd, Let's Make A Deal, The Cheap Show* and *Buns.* Today, shows like *Love Connection, Family Feud, Shop 'til You Drop,* MTV's *Lip Service* and the Family Channel's *That's My Dog* carry on this unfortunate tradition, although the humiliation is much more subtle, prompting the contestants to be as silly through the nature of the competition rather than building the degradation into the game itself. Many games, however, for example *Press Your Luck* and *$100,000 Name That Tune,* nevertheless expect contestants to "ham it up."

The second trend in game shows is the mini-boom in popularity that they are experiencing on several of the cable channels. As an easy and inexpensive way to produce programming to help fill a schedule, they are attractive to the cable channels for the same reasons they were to the early broadcast networks. Their ease and inexpensiveness make them fine vehicles to reach specific or narrow demographic groups. *Lip Service* on MTV targets urban teens and hip-hop and rap music fans. *That's My Dog* on The Family Channel aims at pet owners. Lifetime, which "brand identifies" itself as a "women's channel," offers *Supermarket Sweep* and *Shop 'til You Drop.* And kids have their own game shows on Nickelodeon, *Family Double Dare,* for example.

SHAW

Genre analysis forms the basis of the Shaw essay on game shows. But you'll see that he finds it necessary to recount some history and economics to support his thesis. This is not uncommon in television genre studies. Can you speculate as to why?

What does he mean when he talks about game shows as a "fringe genre?" Does this little inside joke (the double meaning of fringe) add or detract from your appreciation of his work?

Shaw uses two variables that contribute to the form's "foundation of suspense," the basis of competition and the dominant orientation of the performance, to prove his argument that game shows are a "value-laden system of cultural expression." What does he mean by these two variables? Does he convince you that this seemingly empty genre is in fact what he says it is? Why or why not?

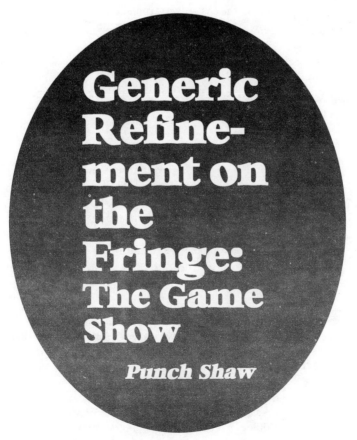

Generic Refinement on the Fringe: The Game Show

Punch Shaw

Although figuring prominently in prime-time schedules of the 1940s and 1950s, the game show today is a staple of TV's daytime and early evening schedules. In making the transition from prime-time attraction to fringe institution, the game show has become one of television's most enduring and least endearing formulas. To many critics and commentators, game shows represent the wasteland view of television. Along with televised professional wrestling, the game show often stands as a particularly damning example of what is almost always described as "mindless entertainment." But in the haste to condemn the formula, media critics have often underestimated the game show's status as genre, that is, its place as a value-laden system of cultural expression.

Many historical accounts (Anderson, 1978; Barnouw, 1982; Brown, 1986; Fabe, 1979; Sterling & Kitross, 1978) have identified two crucial political or legal incidents as having altered the evolution of the game show. The first involved the famous quiz show scandals of the late 1950's, scandals that have been credited with both leading to the prime-time demise of the game show and changing the sponsor-program relation-

---

Dr. Shaw is Assistant Professor of Radio-Television, Southern Illinois University at Carbondale, IL.

Reprinted with permission of the Southern States Communication Association.

ship that network TV inherited from radio.[1] The second was the passage of the FCC's Prime Time Access Rule (PTAR) in 1971, a regulatory event that many believe inadvertently encouraged increased game show production.[2]

Although the scandals and the PTAR certainly helped shape the history of the game show, the most decisive influences on the genre's relatively secure position on television are economic. Game shows are, and always have been, inexpensive to produce. As a rule, this production economy translates into tremendous bargains for both broadcast stations and advertisers. Even though other programming types generally attract larger audiences, the relatively low cost of acquiring syndicated game shows permits television stations to run them in access slots with little financial risk. On network television, a typical thirty second spot on a soap opera costs twice as much as a similar spot on a game show. While soap operas average better rating in all age categories, the difference in advertising rates is not simply a function of the different in audience size: the "cost per 1000" (CPMs) (the rate paid by advertisers for each 1000 viewers) is considerable cheaper on game shows. In other words, for the same dollar a manufacturer can generally reach more people by advertising on a game show than by advertising on a soap opera. Thus, both in syndication and on daytime network schedules, the popularity of the genre is not as important as its profit potential. Basic economic conditions on the fringe, then, have contributed to the health and longevity of the genre.

Major Characteristics of the Formula

But economics, alone, do not explain the success of the game show. As a system of cultural expression, the game show has been engaging television audiences with a consistency rivaled only by the soap opera and the situation comedy. The game show is, after all, a game. The pleasure of watching *Wheel of Fortune* (syndication), for example, is akin to the pleasure of observing any other contest. Whether it be a football game or a political campaign, the element of suspense inherent in any game sustains spectator interest and activates intense audience identification. In the case of the typical game show, this suspense is fairly uncomplicated. Created in quick pulses—each question in *Jeopardy* (NBC, 1964–1975; syndication), each new word in *Password* (CBS, 1962–1967; syndication)—the suspense builds until the outcome is clear.

Rather than passively reflecting social reality, competition via the game show becomes a vehicle for promoting, negotiating, and discussing relevant values and ideals associated with American life. As a fringe genre, the game show is a very powerful form of expressing what Fiske and Hartley (1978) call the "core needs . . . which underlie a free-enterprise, competitive, though liberal, society in which winners are rewarded, and losers are protected, not humiliated." Therefore, in understanding the popularity of *Wheel of Fortune,* we must recognize that spinning the wheel and guessing the word puzzle may, in fact, not be as decisive to the success of the show as the "purchasing" of prizes from the product showcase. In other words, a certain genius emerges in the reward phase of *Wheel of Fortune:* contestants never receive cold cash, even the surplus is handled with "gift certificates." Instead of promoting the accumulation of capital, then, *Wheel of Fortune* celebrates consumption, a value that, of course, resonates with the advertising message integrated into the flow of the program.

To approach systematically the diverse programs associated with the game show, I will organize the genre according to two major variables related to what Welch (1958) calls the formula's "foundation of suspense": (1) the basis of competition; and (2) the dominant orientation of the performance.[3] In some shows, knowledge is the basis of competition; in others, luck and the logic of the game govern the competition; and in still other shows, a competitive framework becomes the means of showcasing special talents or skills. The particular basis of competition is, however, modulated and filtered by the second decisive variable, the perfor-

---

1. The degree to which the scandals led to sponsors' getting out of the business of program production may be overestimated. The phasing out of the one-sponsor show on network television was a gradual process that actually began with Sylvester "Pat" Weaver's tenure as head of NBC programming in the early 1950s (Gross, 1979). The one tangible change attributable to the scandals was the passage in 1960 of an amendment to the Communications Act of 1934, Section 509, which makes deceptive practices on television punishable law.

2. When the FCC passed the Prime-Time Access Rule (PTAR) in 1971, it intended to encourage the local production of public affairs programming. Although revised slightly over the years, the PTAR essentially requires the 7 p.m. to 8 p.m. EST time slot be filled by local affiliates with non-network programming. Contrary to the noble designs of the FCC, most television stations devoted the time to inexpensive syndicated programming which often took the form of the game show (Brown, 1986). The PTAR came at a time when the game show needed a boost: in 1969, the networks did not add a single new game show to their schedules, and, in 1970, they added only one.

3. See Kaminsky (1985) for another way of organizing the genre based on Frye's analytic methods.

mance dynamic that overlays the competition. In some cases, the performance is oriented around a host; in others, celebrities constitute the prime orientation of the competitive performance; and, of course, in some shows the center of attention is the head-to-head performances of ordinary people who act as the players/contestants.

Exemplified by a type of prime-time television show popular in the 1950s, the quiz show is perhaps the purest example of a game of knowledge. Having "educational" overtones, competition in the quiz show is based on extensive or at least specialized knowledge; rather than simply "playing" a game, the contestants face a difficult "test." Beginning with ancient radio shows like *Professor Quiz* (CBS, 1936-1941), the history of the game of knowledge pre-dates the age of television. One radio program debuting on CBS in 1940 is of particular relevance to the quiz show's future via TV. Called *Take It or Leave It* (CBS, 1940–1950), the program gave the top prize to the player who correctly answers "the $64 question." Of course, the stakes were raised when the idea was modified for television to become *The $64,000 Question* (CBS, 1955-1958). With an incredible average rating of 47.5 in its debut season, *The $64,000 Question* was so popular that contestants who succeeded in winning the top prize often achieved celebrity status. Dr. Joyce Brothers, one such early winner, has even converted her success on the show into a long career as a celebrated "expert" (Brooks & Marsh, 1981).

Today's games of knowledge differ from the classic quizzes of the 1950s in that the questions are less demanding and often constitute only part of the competition. For example, in *Tic Tac Dough* (NBC, 19560–1959; syndication) contestants answer relatively easy questions to meet the primary basis of the competition, winning a game of tick-tack-toe. *Jeopardy* is one of the few current shows to both challenge contestants with relatively difficult questions and provide immediate cash rewards for correct answers. In most games of knowledge, the "quiz" is merely a preliminary step to gaining access to the "game" involving the major prizes. Here, mastering the logic of the game is more important than possessing expert knowledge. In other shows, like *Family Feud* (ABC, 1966–1974; syndication) or *The Price is Right* (NBC, ABC, CBS, 1954–present) or *The Newlywed Game (*ABC, 1966–1974; syndication), the basis of competition is not expert knowledge, but some other form of knowledge: common sense in *Family Feud;* consumer sense in *The Price is Right;* or interpersonal knowledge in *The Newlywed Game.*[4]

Games of logic reward those who master "the rules" of the game. In these, chance often plays a major role in the competition. Perhaps the most popular game of logic and chance in the history of the genre is *Wheel of Fortune.* But by far the most bizarre programs in this tradition are those shows which treat justice and law as games of logic: F. Lee Bailey's *Lie Detector* (syndication) and Judge Wapner's *People's Court (*syndication). In *Lie Detector,* the typical program featured people accused of violating the law who approached Bailey in hopes of being vindicated by his polygraph. Rather than compete against another player on the "wheel of fortune," these "contestants" competed against the "machine of truth." In *People's Court,* parties with actual pending litigation agree to have their cases decided by a television court. The circumstances are real in each case brought before Judge Wapner, but when placed in the context of television entertainment, the complexities of law and justice are often reduced to simple vaudeville.

In the talent showcase, the basis of competition moves from knowledge or logic to performance. This sub-genre has a grand tradition that dates back to radio's *Major Bowes' Amateur Hour* (NBC, CBS, ABC, 1935–1952). Its television forefather is *Ted-Mack's Original Amateur Hour* (Dumont, ABC, CBS, NBC, 1948-1960) which thrived on entertainers who underscored the "amateur" in the program's title. Chuck Barris' infamous parodies, *The Gong Show* (NBC, 1976–1978) and *The $1.98 Beauty Contest (*syndication), laid bare the darker side of competition oriented around performance by making the show into an arena for public humiliation. Today, the talent showcase is represented by shows like *Dance Fever (*syndication) and *Star Search* (syndication) that feature slick production values and relatively professional performances.

In host-centered game shows, the orientation of the performance can be more important to the success of the show than the basis of competition. Here, the contestants and the game only function as a pretext for the performance of the host. Perhaps the purest example of this type of game show is *You Bet Your Life* (NBC, 1950–1961), a quiz show which served primarily as a forum for the talents of Groucho Marx. Although contestants answered questions for cash and uttering the "secret word" would bring a Groucho-like stuffed duck from the rafters bearing a $101 prize, the primary duty of the contestant was to act as a straight per-

---

4. Williams (1974) has identified programming such as *The Newlywed Game a*s "conventionalized speculative mimings of various levels of personal relationships."

son for Marx.[5] Edgar Bergen, Jack Parr, Basil Rathbone, Vincent Price, Rod Sterling, and Walter Cronkite also served as game show hosts during the 1950s and 1960s. Perhaps the most important host of this period was a young man named Johnny Carson. His game show career began with *Earn Your Vacation* (CBS, 1954), continued with *Who Do You Trust?* (CBS, 1958-1963), and ended in 1962 when he became host of the *Tonight Show* (NBC, 1954-1992).

Although no stars of Groucho or Carson's stature host games shows today, some semi-host-oriented contests, like *Family Feud,* have enjoyed recent success. Achieving notoriety as the host of *Family Feud,* Richard Dawson did not dominate the competition to the same extent as Marx. The opening of the show centered on Dawson's performance during the obligatory kissing routine associated with his ritual introduction and Dawson's performance again dominated the closing of the show. During the middle of the show, the attention shifted from Dawson to the performance of the competing families playing the game.

The celebrity-oriented show acts as a bridge between host-oriented and contestant-centered variations of the genre. In focusing on the celebrity performance, these shows foreground the participation of well-known people who play or assist contestants in playing the game at hand. Its origins lie in the celebrity panel shows of the 1950s typified by *What's My Line?* (CBS, 1950–1967), *I've Got a Secret* (CBS, 1952–1967) and *To Tell the Truth* (CBS, 1950–1967). *Hollywood Squares* (NBC, 1966–1980; syndication), which continues in syndication more than fifteen years after its debut, is the most successful of recent celebrity-centered

game shows. Other current shows in this tradition, most notably *Password* and *The $20,000 Pyramid* (CBS, ABC, 1974-present; syndication), balance the performances of celebrities and contestants by placing a show business personality in partnership with a layperson during the conduct of the competition.

Although almost all game shows are contestant-oriented to some degree, *contestant-centered shows* are those that focus primarily on the performance of the common people who act as players rather than on the host, set, celebrities, or the complexity or difficulty of the game. Perhaps this type of show is represented best by *The Price is Right* and *Truth or Consequences* (NBC, 1954–1964). By making the game secondary to the actions and reactions of the contestant, both shows cued the audience to identify with the typical, familiar people who generally played the games. Through this identification, the shows encouraged audience members to participate vicariously in the thrill of winning and the fulfillment of consumption fantasies. The facts that *The Price is Right* has recently been reactivated in syndication, and that the equally simple and consumption-oriented *Wheel of Fortune* ranked first among all syndicated programs in 1985, speak to the enduring power of this performance orientation in the game show formula.

Conclusion

In concert with institutional and economic analysis, approaching the game show genre according to the basis of the competition and the orientation of the performance allows us to isolate and describe ways the game show has both changed and remained the same over the years. With our analytic scheme we

can appreciate how early radio and TV game shows established many of the conventions that still govern the genre, note shifts in the basis of competition away from games rewarding expert knowledge, and recognize the current dominance of contestant-centered shows.

But we must be careful in interpreting these findings. For instance, we cannot simply say that the shift away from the rewarding of expert knowledge in the game show represents a devaluation of such knowledge in our society. Such an interpretation, in assuming that game shows represent a direct reflection of social reality, misses the complexity of how popular TV genres function as expressive forms and ignores other factors that may have contributed to this shift, factors like the quiz show scandals. In fact, the classic quiz show's emphasis on expert knowledge played an important role in the scandals. Producers discovered that locating bright and engaging contestants who were able to answer these questions was difficult. Consequently, many producers conducted "rehearsals" in which favored contestants would be primed with correct answers and schooled on how to make their on-air performance more fetching (Anderson, 1978).

The trends identified in our analysis, then, speak of subtle generic refinements designed to accommodate and exploit the game show's secure niche on the fringe of broadcast television. The factors that have made the genre so successful for so long are not likely to change significantly. With both fringe economics and FCC regulation working in its favor, the game show will probably continue as a

---

5. Marx's popularity as the host of *You Bet Your Life* resulted in the show's placing in the top ten of the Nielsen ratings in six of its eleven seasons (Brooks & Marsh, 1981).

stable genre in a changing medium.

References

Anderson, K. (1978). *Television Fraud: The History and Implication of the Quiz Show Scandals.* Westport, CT: Greenwood Press.

Barnouw, E. (1982). *Tube of Plenty: The Evolution of American Television* (revised ed.). New York: Oxford University Press.

Brooks, T. & Marsh, E. (1981). *The Complete Directory to Prime Time Network TV Shows: 1956–Present.* New York: Balentine Books.

Fabe, M. (1979). *TV Game Shows.* New York: Doubleday & Co.

Fiske, J. & Hartley, J. (1978). *Reading Television.* London: Methune.

Gross, L. S. (1979). *Telecommunications: An Introduction to Radio, Television, and the New Technologies.* Dubuque: W. C. Brown.

Kaminsky, S. (1985). *American Television Genres.* Chicago: Nelson Hall.

Sterling, C. & Kitross, J. (1978). *Stay Tuned: A Concise History of American Broadcasting.* Belmont, CA: Wadsworth Publishing Co.

Welch, P. (1958). The Quiz Programs: A Network TV staple. *Journal of Broadcasting, 2,* 317.

Williams, R. (1974). *Television: Technology and Cultural Form.* London: Fontana.

Chapter Exercise

Design Your Own Game Shows

Design and name a game show (use the provided elements) for each of the following venues:

1. A broadcast station during the fringe time-slot; and

2. A cable channel of your choice during prime-time.

	BROADCAST/FRINGE	CABLE/PRIME-TIME
Contest		
Host		
Contestant(s)		
Audience		
Your own added feature		
Your own added feature		
Your own added feature		

Once you have thoroughly described your two game shows, explain why you designed them the way you did. How do the programs differ from one another? Why do they work well in these two venues at these specific times? Will your shows encompass any of the components (vicarious greed, competition, simplicity, daily drama, celebrity participation and / or seeing other people humiliated) that are typically attributed to game shows' popularity?

References and Resources

Anderson, K. (1978). *Television Fraud: The History and Implication of the Quiz Show Scandals.* Westport, CT: Greenwood Press.

Brown, P. H. (1980). Television's thriving theater of humiliation. *Panorama, 1,* 61–65.

Brown-Guillory, E. (1988). Integrating television game shows and reader-response criticism. *Exercise-Exchange, 34,* 42–43.

Fabe, M. (1979). *TV Game Shows.* Garden City, NY: Doubleday Dolphin.

Welch, P. (1958). The quiz programs: a network TV staple. *Journal of Broadcasting, 2,* 317.

Zoglin, R. (1992). Game shows get gamier. *Time,* September 28, p. 70.

CHAPTER 9

SOAP OPERAS

While serving time in the penitentiary, convict Miranda Marlowe discovered her teenage daughter Bilan was still alive. Miranda had to abandon Bilan as an infant because the infamous Mr. Big had murdered the baby's father and she feared for Bilan's life. Tom and Margo promised Miranda they'd try to find Bilan. At the same time, Mr. Big was searching for Bilan because she may yield a clue to her dead father's missing treasure. He had his men tail Tom and Margo to the Island of Drasue where Bilan was found in a jungle village.

—Plot synopsis from *As The World Turns*

Soap Opera Magazine wasn't making up this plot from the well-known soap opera for its "Remember When" (1993, p. 22) feature. And in the world of soap operas, things can get even stranger. In 1986 hundreds of fans called local television network affiliates to complain that coverage of the the space shuttle Challenger explosion had interrupted their daily dose of stories. Currently, fans can call a 24-hour soap hot-line for recaps and predictions. They can attend any of several tours of soap opera personalities that travel the country. They can read one or more of the nearly twenty national fan magazines and newsletters devoted exclusively to soap operas and their stars. They can listen to the radio stations in nearly every town that review the plots of the previous day's soaps (several times each day) for the benefit of those unlucky fans who may have missed their favorite show and forgotten to set their VCRs. And they can read their local newspaper's weekly television schedule supplement that includes a column on soaps with titles like "Daytime TV," "Soap Opera Scene," and "Speaking of Soaps."

Despite the seemingly hokey story lines in soap operas—those mid-day domestic dramas—fan devotion is not only common, but quite intense. But just as common are questions about why that dedication exists. The production quality of the daytime soaps is decidedly low budget; the sets tend to be cheap and flat—unsophisticated by prime-time standards. The plots are never-endingly confused and seemingly unrealistic; they are almost free of the action and adventure that characterize evening drama.

Overview

In this chapter we will examine the large and loyal following of television's serialized daytime dramas, the soap operas. The popularity of this genre will be discussed in terms of its narrative conventions—its recurring fantasy themes and its internal and external forms of reality. We will also look at how these conventions are facilitated by the soaps' particular production methods and their format (movement, characterization, and setting).

The Loyal Many

The soap opera audience has been estimated to be anywhere from twenty million people a day to seventy million a week. The audience may be even larger than these estimates suggest. It's been said that soaps are like Big Macs—a lot of people eat them but won't admit it.

The Nielsen ratings show that fifty-five percent of all the women in this country will watch at least one soap in a given week. Sixty-two percent of the total soap opera audience is female, aged eighteen to forty-years old. Fifteen percent are male (*All My Children* is the favorite with men, drawing a thirty percent male audience). The remaining twenty-three percent of the viewers are women younger than eighteen and older than forty.

The soap opera audience is not only large, it is devoted and involved sometimes to the point of irrationality. Eileen Fulton, the now reformed shrew-like Lisa Shea Coleman of *As the World Turns*, was physically attacked on a New York City street by a fan who resented her wicked ways. When Julie Williams on *Days of Our Lives* was considering an abortion, she was flooded with mail, including photographs of terminated fetuses, in an attempt to convince her to forego the procedure. Fans have been known to buy wedding dresses and set up receptions in their homes so they can "attend" the wedding of a favorite character. *Another World* is the all-time record holder in the leave-'em-at-the-altar category—Alice Matthews and Steve Frame cancelled weddings four times, prompting one viewer to write to the producers, complaining, "Why don't you let them get married? Four times I've bought a new dress for the wedding. Four times I've bought champagne."

Not everyone, however, is enamored with the soaps. Commentator David Susskind once said that they were "beneath intelligent notice" and other observers have denounced them as foolish, wasteful, sordid and demeaning.

Nonetheless, few television genres demand the kind of fan support that the soaps enjoy even though they have plot lines like the following:

Marlena: Damned for the sins of her twin. Don: Determined that Sam gets what she deserves! (*Days of Our Lives*);

M. J. Married Tom: A dream wedding ruined by a honeymoon nightmare. (*The Guiding Light*);

Beau proposes to Annie—will she go to bed with him now? (*As the World Turns*);

Jake and Paulina get a bit cozy in the storeroom. (*Another World*).

These plot lines can read like promotional blurbs for Gothic romance novels. So why do soap operas draw such a large and devoted fan following?

The Popularity of Soap Operas

The question of the soaps' popularity has been raised ever since they appeared on radio in the 1930s. At that time, evening entertainment programs like *Amos 'n' Andy*, *The Goldbergs*, and *True Romance* were popular. And because radio back then was the full-time mass medium equivalent to what television is today, stations began experimenting with entertainment programs during the day.

The predominantly female audience for daytime radio suggested that that entertainment take the form of romantic drama. The fact that it was a relatively constant, day-in-day-out audience made the serial drama a possibility.

The first two daytime serials premiered on the national radio networks in the first years of the 1930s. They were not soap operas, however. *Vic and Sade* was a rural, white version of CBS's evening *Amos 'n' Andy*. *Clara, Lu, 'n' Em* featured three women supposedly sitting around a kitchen table, gossiping about themselves and their neighbors.

The true pioneers of soap operas, however, were a school teacher named Irna Phillips; two advertising professionals, Frank Hummert and his future-wife, Anne Ashenhurst; and a radio writer, Charles Robert Douglas Hardy Andrews. They attempted several local station soaps, with little success, but soon after *Clara, Lu, 'n' Em* and *Vic and Sade* appeared, the group settled on a new, improved formula—angst and heartache in the afternoon—one that still exists today. On October 10, 1932 the first real soap opera premiered on a national radio network. It was Hummert, Ashenhurst, and Andrews' *Betty and Bob* on NBC. Phillips, too, soon put together a successful daytime drama. Her *The Guiding Light* premiered on radio in 1937 and is still on the air (now on television) nearly sixty years later. Three of her other creations, *As the World Turns, Another World*, and *Days of Our Lives* still share the air with *The Guiding Light*.

The radio soap operas were daily fifteen-minute dramas—twelve minutes of dialogue sandwiched between an introduction ("As you remember, Karen told Sarah that Robert had proposed . . . ") and a closing ("Will Karen overlook Robert's humble origins and criminal past? Tune-in tomorrow").

The daytime serials' sponsorship left them with the name soap opera even though the very first soap, *Betty and Bob*, was sponsored by a cereal manufacturer, General Mills. One commercial would follow the introduction and a second would precede the closing. Frequently a sponsor's name would be worked into the story itself. *Oxodol's Own Ma Perkins* was well known for the characters' outspoken use of Oxodol products in the conduct of their everyday lives.

Today, there are ten daily television soaps. But in the 1930s and early 1940s there were as many as sixty soaps a day on the national radio networks as well as an unknown number of locally produced serials. Even allowing

for the fact that they were only 15 minutes long in those days (as opposed to 60 now), their numbers were clearly impressive.

Soaps came to television in 1950, the first was *The First Hundred Years*, but they fared poorly in the beginning. Television was new and unfamiliar, radio was still the dominant mass medium and fan devotion to their favorite radio soaps died hard. But by 1960, when the last of the radio soaps disappeared, television soaps were firmly entrenched.

From the perspective of the networks, the main reason that soaps became and have remained mainstays in their television schedules is that they are remarkably profitable. A popular soap opera, *Days of Our Lives*, for example, will typically earn its network, in this case NBC, three times its production costs. While most prime-time programming—at best—breaks even in its first run, well established soaps average a 250% profit, thus financing the airing of the more expensive evening fare. In the early 1970s, for example, when CBS was the undisputed king of the soaps, its daytime programming—soaps and game shows—accounted for seventy-five percent of that networks' annual net earnings. The other two networks showed similar, although slightly lower figures because of their lower ratings.

Prime-time programming is significantly more expensive than soaps. Prime-time allows for fewer commercial minutes per hour than does daytime, and there are simply more daytime than prime-time hours in which the networks can sell time. Equally important, the daytime audience is a remarkably homogeneous one, eighty-five percent female, sixty-two percent in the all-important eighteen to forty year old group that spends its money on soap, toothpaste, frozen vegetables, trash bags, and laundry detergent. Daytime television reaches a lot of women with frequency and efficiency. A soap like *The Young and the Restless* may have a Nielsen rating of 8.4 (puny by prime-time standards) but that represents nearly eight million households; households where the purchase of soap is typically entrusted to the female.

In all, soaps are good business for the networks. As most industry financial experts concede, network television operations wouldn't show much profit without successful daytime programming.

The reasons that the soap operas have remained popular with viewers, however, are somewhat more complex. One often-cited reason is their humorous or "camp" value. The inexpensive sets and the outlandish situations make for fine fun and many parodies such as television's *Soap* and the big screen's *Tootsie* and *Soapdish*, for example.

People also enjoy soaps because of their informational value. The producers of *All My Children* used Nina Cortlandt's bout with diabetic retinopathy to inform viewers of the need for diagnosis and the ease of treatment associated with that sight-robbing disease. *All My Children* also presented several episodes that encouraged women to have pap tests to detect the presence of uterine cancer.

Another reason that is offered for the popularity of soaps is that viewers are bored, they simply want entertainment and escapism during the day. The soaps offer an attractive diversion for people who spend their daytime in their homes.

Most discussion of the popularity of soap operas, however, centers on the nature of their realism. One group of critics and fans argues that they are successful because they offer fantasy. Another group says that they do well because they offer reality.

In *The Soap Opera Book,* Manuela Soares (1978) details the soaps' recurring fantasy themes that she feels are responsible for their appeal. It is this television form's unrealistic elements—the high incidence of amnesia, the overpopulation of doctors, two-year pregnancies—that give it its unique character; a special character, she argues, that meets an important need for the viewer—the need for fantasy.

Soaps offer the *fantasy of everyday romance.*

Characters *live* romance rather than *have* romances. They romance every day; there are no ruts in their lives. Viewers whose lives are in ruts or those who worry about their lives possibly falling into one (this includes everybody, according to Soares), need this everyday romance fantasy for reassurance, to know that for them, too, romance is just around the corner.

Soaps offer the *fantasy of romantic sex.* Sex is portrayed quite unrealistically—always in a romantic context. There is little casual sex and little non-committal sex. There is an emphasis on emotional language, on romantic talk. When, for example, *General Hospital's* Luke Spencer raped his girlfriend, "It was," he was quoted, "a rape like no one had ever put on TV before. No hitting, no slapping, no screaming. It would be all sensual." Some critics contend that it was a totally romantic, unrealistically portrayal of a serious crime but it was perfectly consistent with the genre's romantic fantasy approach to sex. In fact, the fantasy is powerful enough that Anthony Geary, the actor who portrayed Luke Spencer, found himself revered after the televised rape. One woman in St. Louis even went as far as to present him with a foot-high trophy bearing the inscription "To Luke—America's Most Beloved Rapist."

Soap operas present a *romantic fantasy of children.* Children are seen when they return from the hospital soon after birth—child-bearing is romantic. We also see teenagers in the soap opera world—teenagers complicate lives and romances, and complication is the stuff of soaps. Children between one and fifteen, however, represent drudgery. Soares called them "objective responsibilities." We rarely see these children; they have no place for the viewer engaged in fantasy.

Soaps also present the *fantasy of the newly discovered parent, the amnesia fantasy, fantastic representations of pregnancy and death, and the fantasy of the small town.*

We have all fantasized about having different parents than our actual mothers and fathers—

"What would it be like to be a movie star's daughter? I wonder if I'm adopted?" Parents losing track of their children and/or children suddenly discovering new parentage actually rarely ever occurs in real life. But it happens almost weekly on the soaps. Laura Vining is the long-lost daughter of Lesley Faulkner on *General Hospital*. Brian Kendall is the son of Patricia Kendall and Tony Lord (although Tony doesn't know it) on *One Life to Live*.

Amnesia is a rare phenomenon everywhere but on daytime television. Kim Dixon on *As the World Turns* had it. *Days of Our Lives'* Amanda Peters did too, as did Mickey Horton who, while in that unfortunate state, married Maggie Horton (and he later regretted it). We have all fantasized about starting over as a new person, someone with no past, and the soaps' portrayal of amnesia reinforces that fantasy.

Most real-life pregnancies are predictable, uneventful, nine-month events. But as mothers-to-be go through the changes and the overall process, they often fantasize about the baby that they are carrying—"Is it a boy or a girl? Will it be healthy? Will the delivery be easy?" Soap operas offer fantastic pregnancies—miscarriages caused by guilt or births fatal to the mother because she wanted the baby for the wrong reason. Pregnancy is a romantic rather than a physical condition on soap operas; that's why there can be two-month and two-year terms. As a result, rarely is there a regular, nine-month, uncomplicated pregnancy.

Death on soaps is consistent with our fantasies of death as well—"I'll go out in a blaze of glory. My death will be significant, noted, or notable." We subconsciously hope that our deaths will be purposeful, that we will not die for nothing. On soap operas there is always a reason for a character's death—to free a living character to marry her true love, to rid the show of an unpopular character or to write-out a character who wants to leave the series.

Almost all of television's successful soap operas have been set in small towns—Somerset, Bay City, Oakdale, Pine Valley, Rosehill. The states remain unidentified. There are exceptions, such as *Ryan's Hope* in New York City, *Texas* in Houston, and *Santa Barbara* in California. But it is the stereotyped perceptions of these states that are used to provide character and scene contexts. It is hard to imagine ethnic pub owners living in small towns or rural America; it's also difficult to have big-talking, oil-rich Texans in any place but a big-talking, oil-rich city like Houston; nor can you have rich California-beach community people in any place but a California beach community (all three of these soap operas, incidentally, are no longer on the air).

Americans have a traditional love affair with the small town. We "return to the basics," "get back to the land," "find our roots." New York City is the epitome of what is evil in America; Muncie is symbolic of what is cherished.

The soaps give us support and affirmation, they lie to us with their unrealistic portrayals of the very things about which we fantasize. Many of their fans contend that the soaps remain popular *because* of this lack of realism.

There are other soap opera fans, however, who disagree. They claim that the success of the soaps is due to their realism which gives their writers the opportunity to be creative and true-to-life. Plots can be developed with infinite care because there is no clock to watch like in prime-time. Plots are considered *realistic* because they feature familiar, "real" (authentic) people dealing with real problems with real results. These soap characters remain week after week. They grow up, change, marry, fail, and pay for their errors. Fans argue that the plot lines found on soaps (which include amnesia, pregnancy, death, and the Coleman's on *As the World Turns* encountering new-found children) are much more realistic drama than prime-time *Viper* bolting around the country crushing organized crime and foreign subversives before the last commercial. In addition, soaps can present subjects in the daytime that might not necessarily appear at night because the daytime audience is virtually all adult.

We should look at soaps, then, in terms of two types of reality. One is *external reality*. That is, how realistic is the story when compared to the actual world. The second is *internal reality* (or what Newcomb, 1974, p. 171, called a "technical type of reality"). That is, how realistic is the story when compared to the world of the soap opera.

The existence of these two realities accounts for the divergent views of the soaps' success. While it is true that soaps may have little external reality (plots feature few minority or poor people yet many amnesia epidemics and fifteen-month pregnancies), successful soaps all demonstrate a remarkable sense of internal reality. People are always punished for their transgressions; they learn from their encounters. This internal reality tells us that in a world like the one portrayed on the soaps (even if it's not much like our own), certain truths are maintained. Lying is bad, honesty is good. Fidelity breeds good children, healthy pregnancies, strong families. Alcohol and pills damage relationships and are for weak people.

The lack of external reality is unimportant because it is the characters and their actions in the world in which they operate that create the drama in soap operas. The drama in soaps depends on relationships, not action. So, if the sudden appearance of a long-lost illegitimate daughter who has just recovered from a bout with amnesia is needed to catalyze a given relationship, that daughter will appear. Such an occurrence may be unrealistic in terms of external reality, but the interactions that are engendered will no doubt be quite realistic.

It may be that the combination of fantasy and internal reality is what makes soaps so popular. Our need for fantasy, for escape from our daily worlds and into our dreams, is met. Our need for reassurance that familiar, real people face real problems in real ways and either succeed or fail, is also met.

Format of the Soaps

Soaps are free to offer us the kinds of fantasy and reality that they do because of their unique format and production techniques. In a medium where most stories are told in neat thirty and sixty-minute packages, the soap opera stands alone. It can present unsolvable problems because there is no need to solve them before the last commercial. The soap opera can present complicated, multifaceted characters and fantastic occurrences because it has a virtually unlimited amount of time to explain them. Imagine *The Untouchables'* Eliot Ness racked with indecision and confusion, confronted by his long-lost illegitimate daughter who has just recovered from a bout with amnesia, while he is locked in machine gun battle with Al Capone. That may be a bit much for even Eliot to handle in sixty minutes.

Another characteristic that allows soaps their special kind of fantasy and reality is their flexibility which is the product of their unique production methods. Expensive prime-time filmed drama is produced all at once. That is, work is done on all of the episodes until a season's worth is completed. A particular episode may be in the can for months before it reaches the air. As a result, problems, solutions, and characters have to be timeless. There is little room for flexibility and there is a good deal of security in conservatism. A newly introduced character, for example, must be presented in such a way that the audience will immediately like him/her. If the character is too complex, the audience may reject the character, but there is no way to remove him/her from the already completed programs nor is it possible to alter the characterization.

Soaps, however, are produced according to a twelve-month outline: the show's *bible*. The bible maps out a general picture of where the events should be at various points in the year. Characters are charted by the week to insure that someone does not marry his sister by accident.

Once the bible is set, the story is filled out by the show's writers. They prepare daily plots and send them along to dialogists who write the dialogue. They receive the daily plots about six weeks before a given episode is to be videotaped and they have two weeks to write the cast's lines. The completed script is then passed on to that episode's director. Because of the time demands of a daily dramatic program, most soaps have two or three directors who alternate the series' production among themselves. While the director is planning the shooting strategy, the actors receive their scripts. They usually have only one day to learn their lines (because they have to learn new lines every day). They are aided, fortunately, by each episode's three rehearsals on the day of the taping and by a teleprompter or other cueing devices.

Each episode is normally produced in one day as was the case with live soaps before the invention of videotape. An episode usually reaches the screen the day after it is taped.

With this daily production (and not incidentally, a lack of concern for satisfying audiences in the future syndication market), the soaps have almost unlimited flexibility. An unpopular character can quickly be dispatched, or to test a character's popularity, he or she can be written out of the script for a few days to gauge fan reaction. One famous example is Laura Spencer (raped by and then married to Luke on *General Hospital*) dying at sea in 1981 (her contract with the soap having expired) and reappearing in Port Charles in 1983, claiming that her death was a hoax (she had failed to make a hit in prime-time and *General Hospital* wanted her back) only to be dispatched again and then once more making a much celebrated return in 1993.

Soaps can also use the short production schedule and daily tapings to raid and/or thwart the competition. Soap opera writers closely watch the ratings and the other soaps. If a competitor is improving its ratings with the introduction of a new character or situation, writers can steal the idea and quickly incorporate it into their own show. Likewise, if a new twist is unpopular and it is reflected in the ratings, it can be written out of the story. As for thwarting the opposition, specific events can be written into a soap to counter big doings on the opposing show. *Loving* even went as far as to use a new character (played by big-named star Morgan Fairchild) to revamp its whole show and introduce its new name, *The City*.

The Soap Opera Formula

Like other television fare, soap operas adhere to an established formula. One aspect of that formula relates to action. There is very little physical action on soaps; the action is carried by the dialogue. The confines of the set inhibit physical action somewhat, but the main reason that there is little action is because soap operas deal with relationships, not adventure. Action simply is not that important.

Because there is limited physical action, the soap has its own forms of *story movement*. Newcomb identified two (1974). Soaps have *lateral movement*—the effects of the plots and subplots move laterally, across the community of characters and the "action" occurs when we see the reaction of the players as the effects move through the community.

There is also *vertical movement*—the effects of the plots and subplots move vertically, above the community of characters and the "action" occurs as new characters are added to the existing community in order to accommodate the new doings.

Another ingredient of the soap formula is *characterization*. Most soaps center around upper middle class families and people. They tend to be well dressed, well educated, and good looking. They are usually professional people—doctors, lawyers, nurses, police. This allows for exciting crises. The daily job pressures of orthodontists and insurance actuaries do not make for great drama. Just as important, drug addiction and infidelity among well-to-do people has a fascination that is missing when similar misfortunes strike poorer folks.

Soap operas are also characterized by *archetypes*, standard character-types that exist on all soaps. There are usually a young and vulnerable romantic heroine, old fashioned villains, the attractive rival for a mate's affection, the suffering antagonist, the former playboy or playgirl, Mr. Right, Ms. Right, the "bitch," the "bastard" and others. Although they fit archetypical categories, they are not the flat, one-dimensional characters sometimes seen in prime-time drama. Their character-typing allows for easy identification; we know right away who the bad woman is or who the benevolent mother is. Characters are free, however, to deal with relationships in non-predictable ways. They can grow and change within their given character type or evolve into a completely different one. *As the World Turns'* Lisa Coleman was every bit as evil as *All My Children's* Phoebe Tyler. But over the years, Lisa learned from her failings and mellowed. She evolved into a "good woman" and a loyal wife to her husband.

Rodina, Cassata and Skill (1983) identified five primary and seven secondary specific character types. The primary ones were:

1. **The chic suburbanites** are characters who are well-educated, upper-middle class, male or female, aged 20 to 34. They are typically single or divorced, hold professional jobs and are upwardly mobile and concerned about image and status (Erica Kane on *All My Children*).

2. **The subtle singles** are much like the chic suburbanites, but are more concerned with ties to family and friends. They are less selfish and more responsible (Ross Marler on *The Guiding Light*).

3. **The traditional family person** characters are married, hold a variety of jobs from professional to blue-collar to homemaker. They vary much more than the above types in age, and see home as the center of everything (Alice Horton on *Days of Our Lives*).

4. **The successful professionals** are usually middle-aged and upper-middle class. They are typically single or divorced because of career pressures and although

they are basically good people, they are lacking somehow because they have let work become so important (Fletcher Reed on *The Guiding Light*).

5. **The elegant socialites** are middle-aged upper-class women who are civic-minded and cultural, but for the wrong reasons. They flaunt it because they have it (Alexandra Spaulding on *The Guiding Light*).

The secondary character types appear less frequently and less centrally in soaps because they simply do not fit the fantasies that make soaps so appealing to their fans:

1. **The self-made businessperson** characters are wealthy, ruthless, and see those around them as either friends or foes, nothing in between.

2. **Contented youth** characters are pretty normal high-school and college-aged people who maintain ties to their families and their values.

3. **Troubled teens** are the opposite of contented youths; they are into drugs, sex, alcohol and trouble.

4. **Happy homemakers** are women of strength upon whom the family can depend.

5. **Dissatisfied homemakers** are the opposite of happy homemakers. Their dissatisfaction causes trouble for all.

6. **Retired homebodies** are pleasant, responsible older folks who dispense wisdom and love to their families.

7. **Frustrated laborers** are either young with no firm direction yet in their lives or are older, bored and dissatisfied with their lot.

Setting follows the soap formula as well. Because the action is dialogue-bound and involves relationships between people, most settings are indoors. The sets themselves tend to be symbolic of the characters and action on screen. Mary Ellison on *As the World Turns* has a simple, middle class kitchen and a wrongly married couple take their honeymoon in a sleazy room dominated by an immoral-looking round bed covered with red satin sheets.

Sets also tend to be relatively simple, lacking much of the realistic detail present in prime-time drama. A soap opera hospital room, for example, looks under-equipped when compared to one on *ER*. Set detail is not important because it is the characters and their interactions that carry the soaps' drama; setting is secondary.

Of course, one of the more obvious formula elements in soaps is their *serial*, or continuing nature. And while there are practical reasons for this lack of closure (daily telecasts, recurring characters, no future sales in syndication packages, etc.), there may also be reasons imbedded in what Nochimson called the feminine nature of their narrative. She wrote:

> *As the Hollywood film tends toward a masculine narrative because its syntax is dictated by the aesthetic of closure, soap opera tends toward a feminine story because its syntax is dictated by the resistance to closure.*
>
> *From this it follows that soap opera is valuable as a site from which we may gain perspective on the true and the beautiful as gendered constructs. Truth in the Hollywood film is the truth of linearity, the truth of mastery and control. Truth is domination: Rhett Butler carrying Scarlet O'Hara up the stairs. Truth is singular: the chaotic feminine multiple perspectives of the Hall of Mirrors in* The Lady from Shanghai *resolving to the pristine monocular vision of the hero. Truth is Oedipal: Superman's either/or choice in* Superman II *between emotional fulfillment with Lois Lane on the one hand and the continued strength and viability of the United States of America on the other. These narratives reflect what is normally accepted as truth. In contrast with that of soap opera, however, Hollywood's truth is a reductive form of normalcy.*

> *In soap opera, truth is the multiple-perspective of the unclosed line, of mutuality and intimacy. In soap opera there are* truths *(1992, p. 193).*

Stay Tuned . . . Soaps Today and Tomorrow

One relatively recent change in soaps has been their move toward youth. When *The Young and the Restless* premiered in 1973, its use of young people and young themes revolutionized the soaps. It rated very highly with the important eighteen to forty-year old female audience, so the other soaps quickly began introducing youthful characters and youthful crises—drugs, teenage pregnancy, new marriage, and so on.

Another important trend in soaps is the upgrading of their look. Some industry insiders call it "going Hollywood." Videotape allowed the soaps to leave the live studio, although outdoor taping did not come until 1978. Now, for example, when *The Guiding Light's* Roger Thorpe kidnapped his former wife in Santo Domingo, viewers were taken there to see it happen.

Videotape has also improved the pace and timing of soaps. Through the 1970s, soaps were videotaped using a method called "live tape." That is, they were taped without interruption, like a live play. As the 1980s opened, more and more soaps began to follow the lead of *General Hospital*, the first soap to tape out of sequence in the same way that a film drama is produced. The post-taping editing makes for a cleaner, faster-paced episode.

Sets, too, have become more elaborate with the videotape-created mobility. Swimming pools, opulent discotheques, fine restaurants and other settings (*General Hospital's* Luke and Laura were married aboard a yacht) are beginning to appear alongside the folksy kitchen and living room. Taping out of sequence allowed the setup of shots in these more elaborate settings that were impossible in live and live tape production.

Just as soaps have moved out of the studio, so too have they moved out of daytime. This "soapification" of prime-time can be seen across a variety of program types.

Prime-time schedules offer and have offered drama and comedy that look suspiciously like soap operas—*Dallas, L.A. Law, Dynasty,* and *Knot's Landing* for example. In fact, NBC introduced *Texas* in 1980 with the expressed intent of moving it to prime-time once it became established and successful (it didn't). The networks apparently felt that prime-time programming flavored with popular soap opera conventions—archetypical characters and domestic disaster, for example—could succeed. In the cases of *Dallas, Dynasty, Falcon Crest, L.A.Law,* and *Soap,* to name a few, they were correct.

The success of miniseries like *Roots, Tales of the City, Shogun, Rich Man, Poor Man, Lonesome Dove,* and others can be attributed in part to their soap opera qualities. They resemble soap operas more than they resemble traditional prime-time drama. They feature growing, changing characters, unsolvable problems, realistic failures and successes, and vertical and lateral plot movement. In a sense, they are epic soap operas.

The soaps' influence can also be seen in the prime-time domestic comedy of today and the recent past. Programs like *Mary Tyler Moore;* the Norman Lear comedies, *M*A*S*H, Barney Miller;* and others were or are produced like soap operas. They have continuing, evolving characters like soaps (remember the scandal of Mary Richards spending the night at a man's house? Roseanne's kissing Mariel Hemmingway in a gay bar?). They deal with problems similar to those on soaps (Edith's rape, Archie's drug addition), and they demonstrate the willingness to serialize—to continue a story for two or more weeks (a common occurrence on *Cheers, The Wonder Years,* and *Seinfeld.*)

This soapification of prime-time, if nothing else, should help silence the soaps' critics. If soap operas are so bad, a daytime drama fan can rightfully ask, why are the programs in prime-time looking more and more like their daytime cousins?

Another trend in soaps is their declining numbers and continuing loss of audience to other daytime fare, especially talk shows. In 1969, before cable ate into the network audience and allowed the explosion of syndicated talk shows (Chapter 14), ten soap operas had higher ratings than *The Young and the Restless.* There are only ten soaps total on the networks today, and *The Young and the Restless* is now the form's top-rated show. Yet, it still attracts 1.5 million fewer households every day than does *The Oprah Winfrey Show.*

RABINOVITZ

Rabinovitz makes the assertion that "meaning is not textually inherent but a result of a reader's relationship with a text and the cultural and temporal 'sediments' attached to or 'encrusted' onto any popular text." This assertion marks her work as fundamentally reader-oriented analysis. Her goal, then, is to examine the "cultural discourses" between soaps, magazines, the fashion industry, and audience members as they combine to produce "bridal fantasies."

What does she mean when she says "media discourses activate a range of meanings while closing down others?" Are you surprised to see such an assertion in a piece of reader-oriented criticism?

How does she relate such arcane facts as ratings and production costs to her primary thesis? What does she mean by "foregrounding?" Who are her "subversive readers?"

When *One Life to Live's* resident siren-vixen, Tina Lord Roberts, walked down the aisle in the spring of 1988, the wedding vows she recited were a soap opera heroine's succinct declaration of ambivalence about impending marriage. Speaking to her groom-on-the-rebound Max Holden, she said, 'I take thee, *Cord,* uhh, I mean *Max*'. The symbolic value of naming at this especially privileged moment makes her statement rife with ambivalence—is she simply unsure about which man she wishes to marry? Or does her misnaming reflect an underlying uncertainty over monogamy and the end of romantic courtship with two men? Or is she resisting marriage as the end of her independence and right to her own sexuality? Even though the statement, emphasized in a closeup, is itself enough to establish productive meanings, it did not have to carry the full weight of the scene. In a subjective fantasy sequence that provided a classic case of 'overdetermination', Tina began the ceremony imagining that she was marrying her 'ex', Cord Roberts.

Her 'mistake" replaced a smiling Cord with Max as the groom. Max, responding to what Tina kept insisting was a simple slip of the tongue, stopped the wedding.

Meanwhile, soap superstar Erica Kane of *All My Children* (ABC, 1970—) delayed her walk down the aisle in order to discuss with a friend whether or not she really wanted to go through with the marriage. After keeping the groom, the guests, and the audience waiting for as long as possible (two days in real time, several hours in 'soap time'), she returned to the wedding scene. But the disruption made for a less than perfect storybook ceremony. Although weddings interrupted by a change of heart are a regular feature of many daytime soap operas, these particular examples are richly suggestive of the important position that marriage holds in daytime serial narrative as well as the potential multiplicity of its meanings. Television scholars agree that in soap operas, 'Marriage is not a point of narrative

Reprinted by permission of Oxford University Press as published in *Screen*, Autumn, 1992, Vol. 33 by L. Rabinovitz.

and ideological closure because soap operas interrogate it as they celebrate it. Building that threat into the celebration opens marriage up to readings other than those preferred by patriarchy.'[1]

Such moments are integral to larger considerations of soap operas as narratives of distinct feminine address. Soap opera's distinctive narrative patterns have been identified as feminized modalities—their open-endedness and continuity, their multiple and cyclical storylines, their reliance on repetition, excess, disruption, and deferment. Soap operas have also been discussed in terms of how they construct sexual difference differently—in other words, by fetishizing relationships rather than the body; by generating pleasure through continuous deferments; by foregrounding traditionally feminine skills of verbalizing emotions and interpersonal relationships as legitimate, powerful tools for social control; and through a characteristic programming 'flow' which mirrors the rhythms and routines of domestic activities and the sexual division of household labour.

Such genre definitions originated in the early 1980s as feminist critics began to identify textual features that allowed soap operas a 'feminine space' for producing pleasurable responses while maintaining women's pleasure in the service of patriarchy. Two impor-

tant models were Tania Modleski's argument that daytime dramas are a feminine address organized around the rhythms of the white middle-class homemaker's work and Charlotte Brunsdon's analysis of how a soap opera constructs a feminine address that draws on a range of gendered cultural discourses.[2] Modleski and Brunsdon also make two important assumptions that furthered more general discussions about female television spectatorship as something distinctly different from female movie spectatorship: actual viewers should not be discussed in the abstract as an idealized spectator, nor should the relationship between the viewer and the television screen be modelled after the cinematic ideal of an intense and concentrated relationship in a darkened room.

While their analyses have played important roles in a history of feminist television criticism, it is also important to point out their differences from each other. Modleski's concerns are primarily organized by what material markers signify the text, an arena largely defined by literary and critical theory.[3] Brunsdon located textual meanings through their organization and regulation in wider cultural discourses. She activates a move from an appreciation of soap opera primarily as the textual space that addresses distinct feminine pleasures to soaps' social functions as an insti-

tutional site that engages struggle over cultural meanings. Lidia Curti's recent discussion of the fascination which soap operas hold as the confluence of the image, the female spectator, and desire infers support for the direction of this move:

Those who fall into the temptation of thinking of women's television, of the screen space materially occupied by women, as a space for women, have been accused of falling into 'the seductive trap of the image', of taking its sheer presence as a triumph or at least as a mark of presence of a subjective position, of the independence of desire.[4]

The assumption here, as proposed in reading formation studies, is that meaning is not textually inherent but a result of a reader's relationship with a text and the cultural and temporal 'sediments' attached to or 'encrusted' onto any popular text.[5] In the words of Angela McRobbie, a text becomes meaningful to readers only 'within the discourses through which it is mediated to its audience and within which its meanings are articulated'.[6] While various culture critics from Janice Radway to David Morley have attempted to analyse this dimension of experience through ethnographic audience research, I prefer to examine the cultural discourses organized through economically overlapping and converging institutions in the televi-

1. John Fiske, *Television Culture* (New York: Methuen, 1987), p. 181.

2. Tania Modlesky, *Loving With A Vengeance: Mass-Produced Fantasies for Women* (New York: Methuen, 1982); Charlotte Brunsdon, 'Crossroads: notes on a soap opera, *Screen*, vol. 22, no. 4 (1981), pp. 32–37. The discussions as well as the modifications of their arguments are already well documented. See, for example, Annette Kuhn, 'Women's genres', *Screen*, vol. 25, no. 1 (1984), p. 25; Ann Gray, 'Behind closed doors: video recorders in the home', in Helen Baehr and Gillian Gyer (eds), *Boxed In: Women and Television* (London: Pandora, 1987), pp. 38-54.

3. Modleski, *Loving With A Vengeance*.

4. Lidia Curti, 'What is real and what is not: female fabulations in cultural analysis' in Lawrence Grossberg, Cary Nelson and Paula Treichler (eds), *Cultural Studies* (New York and London: Routledge, 1991), p. 146.

5. For example, see Tony Bennett 'Texts/readers/reading formations', *Literature and History*, vol. 9, no. 2 (1983), pp. 214-27; Tony Bennett and Janet Woollacott, *Bond and Beyond: The Political Career of a Popular Hero* (New York Methuen, 1987). For examples specifically about soap opera, see Robert C. Allen, *Speaking of Soap Operas* (Chapel Hill: University of North Carolina Press, 1985); Jane Feuer, 'Reading *Dynasty:* television and reception theory', *The South Atlantic Quarterly,* vol. 88, no. 2 (1989), pp. 443–60.

sion, print media, and fashion industries.[7] Such an examination is not a mere 'preference' since the ways that industrial and media discourses activate a range of meanings while closing down others is integral to how we theorize or develop concepts of contemporary cultural production and practices. By analyzing daytime television's representation of the wedding ritual as a formation in wider cultural practice, I can suggest how in the late 1980s and early 1990s female desire and pleasure have been culturally produced through consumption and use for at least some groups of spectators.

A contemporary set of relations among spectators, the apparatus of video-recorder technology, and the discursive intertext among television soaps, fan magazines and production companies currently defines the parameters of the television industry's discourse on soap operas as a media genre. The A. C. Nielsen Company, which produces commodified information about audiences for the US television industry, reports that at least fifty-eight per cent of television homes in the United States have video recorders.[8] The figure signifies a change not only in how we watch soaps but who watches daytime serial dramas. Television's demographers likewise assert that soap operas are no longer the exclusive

domain of the adult, white female housewife, who characterized the target audience in the 1950s through the 1970s; today's soap operas may draw on the average thirty per cent male viewers, forty-four per cent female viewers who work part- or full-time outside the home, and approximately twenty per cent non-white viewers.[9] *All My Children's* producers estimate that their show is taped and watched daily by more than half of its total audience, a factor that they believe critically contributes to their especially high rating demographics among women who work outside the home, African-Americans, and adult males. Indeed, trade and general circulation periodicals alike regularly report that soap operas top all other categories of broadcast material for VCR home taping.[10]

The industry, however, expresses greater concern for the downward changes that have simultaneously occurred in the overall numbers of viewers currently being measured. The proliferation of cable stations and video recorders has generated a greater number of entertainment outlets for any given time period, and the ratings companies link a more dispersed audience to a decrease in the number of network viewers during all times of the day. In addition, ratings companies and the television industry posit that there are more

daytime viewers who watch television outside the home and are hence not accounted for by current methods of measuring viewership. The result, according to *Soap Opera Digest,* is that "daytime dramas are no longer the powerhouses of revenue they once were."[11] Soap operas, in other words, are no longer the major source of advertising income for networks that could formerly generate predictable and sizable demographics of women from eighteen to forty-nine.

In the face of these reported economic circumstances, the television industry tries to lure increasing numbers of target women back to soap operas while not giving up the numbers and diversity of the audience that they generate. Their tactics include: advertising soap operas in newspapers, magazines and television; using marketing tie-ins (such as call-in hotlines like ABC's 'Soap Talk' which reported more than half a million callers in its first week); producing press materials for newspapers (particularly weekly plot summaries); and co-operating with fan or supermarket magazines steeped in star discourse.[12] In this latter category, soap opera magazines now dominate the fan-magazine market, and industry leader *Soap Opera Digest* has a circulation of four million readers. One report says that the combined market for soap operas and soap opera

6. Angela McRobbie, 'Settling accounts with subculture: a feminist critique' in T. Bennett, G. Martin, C. Mercer and J. Woollacott (eds), *Culture, Ideology and Social Process: A Reader* (London: Batsford Academic and Education Ltd. 1981), pp. 113–23.

7. Janice Radway, *Reading the Romance: Women, Patriarchy, and Popular Culture* (Chapel Hill, University of North Carolina Press, 1984); David Morley, *The Nationwide Audience* (London, British Film Institute, 1980).

8. A. C. Nielsen, 'TV homes', January 1988, quoted in *TV Basics 1988–89: The Television Bureau of Advertising's Report on the Scope and Dimensions of Television Today* (New York: Television Bureau of Advertising, 1988), p. 2.

9. Judith Waldrop and Diane Crispell, 'Daytime dramas, demographic dreams', *American Demographics,* vol. 10, no. 10 (1988), p. 30.

10. See, the example Ben Brown, 'Booming TV-taping puts soaps first', *USA Today,* 4 May 1984, p. A-1; David Crook, 'Soaps make a big splash with home video tapers', *Los Angeles Times,* 8 May 1984, part VI, p. 1; 'The most-recorded list', *Channels,* February 1988, p. 112, is exemplary of the repetitive listing of soap operas as the most recorded programmes in North America.

11. Alan Leigh, 'Hotline: Hollywood', *Soap Opera Digest,* vol. 13, no. 9 (1988), p. 80.

12. The figure regarding ABC's 'Soap Talk' is from Waldrop and Crispell, 'Daytime dramas', p. 31.

publications exceeds 40 million.[13] In addition, the shows' narratives themselves respond to outside factors with story cycles that climax in 'sweeps weeks' or are organized around the four annual periods when ratings are measured to set advertising rates.

During the four sweep periods, plots speed up, become less multiple and interrupted, and offer dramatic courses of action and resolution. For example, they may intermix genres. In May 1988, *One Life to Live (*ABC, 1968—) mixed the soap opera narrative with the western and science fiction in its self-styled *Back to the Future/Shane* time travel plot set. In May 1987, it evoked the fantastic with its out-of-the-body travel to the after-life plot. In February 1988, *All My Children* mimicked the made-for-television-movie with its two-hour 'movie-within-a-soap' entitled 'Erica: The Movie', wherein Erica Kane confronts the men and highlights of all ten of her past romantic liaisons in a continuous narration set within a dream (reminiscent of *All That Jazz*). In these instances, the producers draw upon associations with other popular culture texts and genres, their own star discourse of past and present cast members, and their desire to exceptionalize sweeps week episodes with highly romanticized costumes, exotic settings and location footage that contrasts the everyday look of the soap opera.

Since soaps during sweeps aim to deliver greater numbers of female viewers to advertisers, the industry predictably employs the biggest commodity spectacle of women's gendered roles—the wedding. In the 1987–88 season alone, *Soap Opera Digest* counted twenty-nine weddings that occurred in and around sweeps weeks (and that does not include weddings, like Tina's, that were never finished).[14] My own count for a single sweeps week in February 1989 was ten weddings although not all the weddings were completed. The rhetoric of the fan magazines supports the privileged status of these events: "Weddings may be a big deal in real life, but they're an even bigger deal on the soaps."[15] Put even more simply by another magazine writer: "Weddings represent the apex of human experience on soap operas. You can go no higher on the scale."[16] Even when television scholars choose memorable soap opera examples for close textual analysis, they have a propensity to remember a sweeps week wedding episode as Sandy Flitterman-Lewis did in her recapitulation of the 1986 *General Hospital* (ABC, 1963—) wedding.[17]

Spectacular weddings were a new distinctive feature of US television soap operas in the 1980s. From the 1950s through the early 1970s, television weddings were 'simple affairs'. They were studio based and occurred in a family's living room, the home of the justice of the peace, or the small chapel of the always essential hospital workplace. The emphasis of camera shots and editing remained on the couple and their relationship, whether it was two people who had overcome adversity to express their mutual love or whether the bride had co-erced the groom to the altar through a faked pregnancy. The wedding ceremony, itself set in familiar surroundings that were not separate from other narrative lines, functioned as both closure and crisis in ongoing plot developments. Before the 1980s, there was little fanfare prefiguring the wedding and no advance publicity outside the serials to encourage viewer curiosity about the wedding and its meanings.

Although weddings became 'bigger' events throughout the 1970s, it was Luke's and Laura's wedding on *General Hospital* in sweeps week of November 1981—the early years of the Reagan era and the season succeeding Prince Charles's and Lady Di's media-saturated wedding—that shifted the representation and function of soap opera weddings. The advent of Portapak video equipment now made location shooting both swift and economical. With a large crew on location at a replica of a Norman French chateau, *General Hospital* producers went all out to stage an extravagant fantasy wedding, complete with movie star Elizabeth Taylor in attendance as a mysterious wedding guest. The episodes received an unprecedented avalanche of press and television publicity before they were broadcast, and local news stations even did reports on college students watching and responding to the wedding on 16 November, thereby providing additional advertising for the 17 November conclusion.[18] Luke's and Laura's wedding episodes of *General Hospital* remain to date the industry's most frequently cited

13. Jerome Shapiro, quoted in Waldrop and Crispell, 'Daytime dramas', p. 29.

14. Meredity Brown, 'Editor's note, *Soap Opera Digest*, vol. 13, no. 20 (1988), p. 10.

15. Diva Von Dish, 'The best and worst wedding dresses', *Soap Opera Digest*, vol. 14, no. 22 (1989), p. 130.

16. Stella Bednarz and Robert Rorke, 'What you'll never see at a soap opera wedding', *Soap Opera Digest*, vol. 14, no. 12 (1989), p. 34.

17. Sandy Flitterman-Lewis, 'Psychoanalysis, film and television', in Robert C. Allen (ed.). *Channels of Discourse: Television and Contemporary Criticism* (Chapel Hill: University of North Carolina Press, 1987), pp. 196–204.

18. I had never in my life watched *General Hospital* but I knew about and watched Luke's and Laura's wedding due to extensive media coverage in Chicago.

example of the single most watched hours of daytime serials: sixteen million people tuned-in each day.[19]

General Hospital's widely proclaimed success convinced other producers that such lavishly staged spectacles routinely promoted before broadcast date could improve ratings in the sensitive weeks when they mattered most. *Days of Our Lives* (NBC, 1965—) executive producer Al Rabin said, 'Fairy-tale perfect ceremonies and pricey receptions are the rage on daytime television . . . . Without the pomp and circumstance, viewers would be clicking off their dials.'[20] Daytime soaps now construct multiple plot developments and even occasionally halt or defer all other plots around a single or double episode in sweeps periods. They regularly spend between $300,000 and $750,000 for these 'special' episodes, figures that belie the traditional myth of minimal expenditures in daytime productions. As *Soap Opera Digest* describes the phenomenon, 'The producers like to pump up the fantasies of their viewers and turn this simple ritual into an extravanganza'.[21]

For example, *Santa Barbara* (NBC, 1984—) itemized $20,000 for one wedding's flowers and $13,400 for casting a hundred extras as wedding guests in another ceremony. Scheduled to coincide with Andy's and Fergie's real-life wedding in 1986, *Days of Our Lives*

gave viewers an on-location English wedding. The half-million dollar budget for Bo's and Hope's ceremony included a custom-designed bridal gown for $20,000 and $7,000 worth of flowers. *Days of Our Lives'* most expensive wedding, however, was a more recent $750,000 extravanganza set on-location in Greece.

If I am highlighting the production budgets here, it is not simply to marvel over the price tags but to dramatize that the shows themselves emphasize certain lavish costs for remote sequences in their own publicity, in general interest magazines like *TV Guide*, and in the fan magazines. The repetitive identification of production costs always specifies items that contribute to and enhance the illusion of spectacle. The feature stories rarely mention labour, transportation or equipment costs—production expenses that do not 'show' on the screen. In contrast, bridal gowns, costumes, flowers, regal limosines and carriages, food displays, and other sumptuous visual trappings and sets are described in detail. The publicity both exceptionalizes the sweeps episodes as costlier and more spectacular than 'everyday' soap operas while it also influences the marketplace by defining the event through the very commodities that prospective brides are elsewhere encouraged to purchase.

Fan magazines especially fore-

ground this association between the spectacle on the screen and the real-life weddings. Entire magazines like *Soap Opera Wedding Album* and *Soap Opera Digest Wedding Special,* and articles in *Soap Opera Digest* such as 'The ten most breathtaking gowns', 'A shopper's guide to soaps' and most elegant wedding dressed', 'How to dress like a soap opera bride', 'TV weddings: the inside stories', 'I must have that dress!' and 'Wild wedding' are representative of regularized coverage of soap opera weddings as idealized commodity packages.[22] The fan magazines even explicitly link the onscreen weddings to the real-life weddings of the actor-stars who participate in both by featuring colour photographs of each wedding side-by-side.[23] A *Soap Opera Digest* reporter summarizes her magazine's ideological perspective: 'Sure, the sex, scandal and backstabbing are great. But, let's face it, what really interests many soap viewers is one of the most important aspects of life: clothing.'[24]

Such fan magazines are aimed at exactly the same female demographic group that consumes such publications as *Bride's Magazine, Southern Bride, Elegant Bride and Modern Bride.* Whereas bridal magazines are more like thick merchandizing catalogues that offer slim prose material but are chock-full of colour advertise-

19. For example, see Mary Alice Kellogg, Soaps: happy 25th, G.H.', *TV Guide,* vol. 36, no. 13 (1988), p. 18.

20. Mary Beth Sammons, 'How much do TV weddings cost?'; *Soap Opera Digest Presents: Best Soap Weddings,* vol. 1, no. 35 (1988), p. 44.

21. Von Dish, 'The best and worst wedding dresses', p. 130.

22. 'The ten most breathtaking gowns', *Soap Opera Digest Presents Best Soap Weddings,* vol. 1, no 35 (1988), pp. 452–52; Terry Collymore, 'A shopper's guide to soaps most elegant wedding dresses, vol. 17, no. 12 (1992), pp. 20–8; Mary Beth Sammons, 'How to dress like a soap opera bride', vol. 13, no. 25 (1988), pp. 20–4; 'TV weddings: the inside stories', vol. 15, no. 17 (1990), pp. 15–23; Mary Beth Sammons, 'I must have that dress!', vol. 13, no. 10 (1988), p. 140-4; Mary Beth Sammons, 'Wild wedding', vol. 15, no. 17, (1990), pp. 24–8.

23. A good example is 'Stars' real-life weddings', *Soap Opera Digest,* vol. 12, no. 13 (1987), pp. 28–40. Even the weekly tabloid press participates in this practice of comparing soap-opera stars' television weddings to their offscreen ones. 'Which is the fairy tale wedding and which is for real?' *The National Enquirer Special: 100 Superstar Weddings,* vol. 3, no. 2 (1992), p. 3.

24. Sammons, 'I must have that dress!, p. 140.

ments, soap opera fan magazines present themselves primarily as 'easy' reading or 'browsing' material with brief large-print articles, few advertisements, and colour reserved largely for star photographs. Although fan magazines generally do not employ the characteristic direct address prose that bridal magazines use to exhort and chasten the individual bride-to-be, their coverage of soap opera weddings often does use direct address as punctuation, and they feature colour fashion photography which mimics the high-gloss, full-page advertisements of wedding gowns in *Bride's Magazine*. Colour wedding photos are either of the bride and groom—caught both formally and 'candidly'—or are full-length portraits of the bride outfitted, posed, and lighted to emphasize her glamour while she looks directly at the viewer.

Fan magazines have even gone so far as to acknowledge the intertextual relations among fan magazines, bridal magazines and soap operas, suggesting that each one stimulates the purchase of the other two: 'First and foremost, forget the bridal consultant. Just flick on that dial and tune into the wonderful world of soap operas, where wedding attire has always been a fashion show'.[25] One fan magazine article quotes the editor of a bridal magazine saying, 'I know that costume designers look in magazines for soap opera wedding gowns. The gowns are inspired by the magazines. The bride then goes back to

the magazine to find something similar.'[26] The relationship is especially enunciated through individual dresses. Employing the characteristic second-person address of a bridal magazine, one fan magazine article stated, 'It may be just coincidence, but look in the recent issues of bridal magazines. Is that or is it not the Nina wedding look?' (referring to *All My Children's* daring, strapless, black velvet, and white satin wedding gown shown in December 1986).[27] Indeed, one magazine subsequently reported that the dress caused a 'rush' on black velvet gowns in 'department stores across America'.[28]

Like the bridal magazines that address women with pictures of gowns and accessories for sale in today's lucrative consumer bridal market, the fan magazines offer plenty of advice on wedding dress purchases. One article interviews *Loving's* (ABC, 1983—) costume designer who tells the story of a visiting fan: 'She quizzed me about everything from where I bought Ava's bridal dress to what kind of shoes she was wearing, and what Ava wore after the wedding, how they did her makeup . . . . [She] really wanted to be Ava on her wedding day.'[29] Another article cajoles, 'If *All My Children's* Nina can go strapless in black velvet, you certainly can, too'.[30]

The idea that women want to model their weddings on those of the soaps figures throughout the stories. According to one fan magazine author, *Guiding Light* (CBS,

1952—) received five hundred telephone calls about Reva's bridesmaids' dresses: 'Every young girl across America wanted that dress'.[31] Another production company quoted in a fan magazine said, 'Most of the calls [we get] are from middle Americans like people from Kansas City'.[32] Put another way by *All My Children's* costume coordinator," 'Soap opera characters get to be a princess every day of their lives. In real life, you're only allowed one day.'[33] All these articles base their art of persuasion not on the bridal market's explicit argument about doing what is fashionable this season but on stories about other women's desires to identify with soap opera stars. In effect, they reassure that desire for celebrity glamour can be fulfilled with the right purchases and that such desire is culturally sanctioned because there is already a community of viewers who rely upon television weddings as a video catalogue of prospective fantasy wedding packages.

But such stories always contain a contradictory note. The very same articles also promise that real-life women cannot attain their fantasy ideal through the simple purchase of the right clothes. *Days of Our Lives* costume designer Lee Smith tells how she always responds to requests about the show's gown patterns, and then she assures the reader, 'I think many of [the fans] want their real-life wedding to look exactly like what's on TV. But you've also got to take into account

25. Sammons, 'How to dress like a soap opera bride', p. 20.

26. *Bride's Magazine* editor Barbara Tober, quoted in Irene Krause, Kathryn Walsh and Hildee Zwisk, 'The making of a TV wedding', *Soap Opera Wedding Album: Daytime TV's Greatest Stories,* no. 21 (1988), p. 8.

27. Sammons, 'I must have that dress!', p. 144.

28. Krause et al, 'The making of a TV wedding', p. 7.

29. Sammons, 'I must have that dress!', p. 144.

30. Sammons, 'How to dress like a soap opera bride', p. 20.

31. Krause et al, 'The making of a TV wedding', pp. 7–8.

32. Sammons, 'I must have that dress!, p. 144.

33. Sammons, 'How to dress like a soap opera bride', p. 24.

that the women we're dressing here are all extremely beautiful. It's a little more than just the clothes.'[34] Elsewhere, the owner of a Brooklyn bridal salon that outfits actresses from *All My Children* and *As the World Turns* (CBS, 1956—) says:

As soon as the soap opera bride walks down the aisle, we're swamped with brides who want to look just like the stars . . . . The major problem we have is that these real-life girls have a fantasy of the dress and what they think they can look like if they have exactly what some star was wearing. Unfortunately, we've often just got to be honest and say, 'You are short and not so svelte as the star'.[35]

The stories both evade and repress how the soap operas fantasy is constructed in and through lighting and camera angles, multiple takes and rehearsals, post-production and editing, a large behind-the-scenes labour crew and thousands of dollars. They instead displace the impossibility of achieving that fantasy onto the 'real-life' women, who are figured as inadequate when physically compared with the 'extraordinary' stars.

Of course, the contradiction feeds back into the relentless bulk of advertising that propels both the magazines and shows, promising greater personal beauty if one buys hair colour, make-up, diet pills, and other cosmetic self-improvement aids. While it has long been argued by advertising historians like Jackson Lears that advertising stimulates desire and promises pleasure while it also frustrates that pleasure in order to keep consumers buying continuous supplies of the product, it is important to articulate

here how that cycle is maintained in soap operas through a larger, more complex set of relations than simply the fiction and its interladen commercials.[36] These soap opera weddings, as managed and framed through their discursive relationships to larger industrial and cultural institutions, do not so much imply the importance of a shared cultural understanding of wedding rituals as the importance of mediation itself on behalf of viewers who are chastened and taught proper consumer responses amid the multivocalities otherwise frequently celebrated in the soap opera genre.

Soap opera weddings' intertextual claims on the fashion system and publishing industries seemingly implicate the worst fears of cultural critics who argue that the effects of commodity culture are totalizing. The soap opera wedding's conflicted and contradictory expression of a woman's desire for self is not only duplicated and proliferated in the intertextual discourse but also through the consumer behavior on which the discourse is dependent. We do maintain the ability, however, to respond oppositionally to soap opera weddings, for example as subversive readers (and here I am thinking of possible applications of Jane Feuer's and Mark Finch's recent work on gay readings of *Dynasty)* or as deconstructionists of commodities and commodity culture.[37] But these examples that argue against the totalizing effects of commodity culture are only partial or incomplete strategies for addressing social and economic inequalities in capitalism.

What is at stake in the act of such subversion or analysis as a means of resistance—and not within a politics of reifying our own pleasure—is how pleasures in popular culture are hegemonically constructed. In our recent historical haste to rationalize our scholarly investment in the fictional soap opera text and in our desire to mediate the soap opera genre for feminist purposes, we too often neglect how pleasure is subjects to and regulated through the interests of commodity consumerism.

My thanks to Lynn Spigel for her contribution to my revision of this article.

---

34. Sammons, 'I must have that dress!', pp. 143–4.

35. Ibid., p. 144

36. T. J. Jackson Lears, 'From salvation to self-realization, advertising and the therapeutic roots of consumer culture, 1880-1930' in Richard Wightman Fox and T. J. Jackson Lears (eds), *The Culture of Consumption: Critical Essays in American History, 1880–1980* (New York: Pantheon Books, 1983), pp. 1-38.

37. Feuer, 'Reading *Dynasty:* television and reception theory'; Mark Finch, 'Sec and address in *Dynasty*', *Screen,* vol. 27, no. 6 (1986), pp. 24–43.

GAITHER

Most people will confront television criticism in publications like *T.V. Guide* and other mass-circulation publications like their daily newspaper. In a sense, this makes journalistic or popular criticism equal to if not more important than academic criticism in influencing the relationship between a "typical" viewer and the medium. The Gaither essay, a seemingly breezy fan-o-gram for *Melrose Place*, demonstrates that a critic can deal with things like genre issues, narrative, and characterization, even when trying to keep the column light and funny.

In this brief piece we see the journalistic television critic as entertainer, to be sure, but also as reporter, illuminator and educator.

The tag-on section of this critique, the fun-poking at *Beverly Hills, 90210,* was no doubt necessitated by critic Gaither's need to fill a specified amount of space. But what do you think of such "silliness" when it comes to television criticism? Does it reinforce the common assumption that television is beneath serious attention? Does it draw readers into the world of television analysis where they might encounter more important discussions? How would you have used your "extra" space if you were writing a regular, weekly TV column for a daily paper?

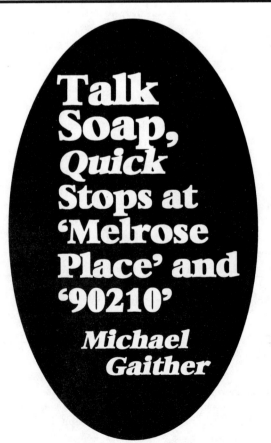

Talk Soap, *Quick* Stops at 'Melrose Place' and '90210'

Michael Gaither

INTERACTIVE television, high-tech's most recently stated buzzword, promises us a hand-held device which will allow television viewers to play along with game shows and sporting events.

This could be applied to TV soap operas, as well: consider "Interactive Melrose Place." Each week the audience sits at home and tries to guess who'll sleep with whom during the next hour.

Of course, anyone who's seen "Melrose Place" probably already does that. The characters on the show are about as "interactive" as you can get away with at 9 p.m. on a Wednesday night . . . even for the FOX network.

Initially a spin-off of "Beverly Hills 90210," "Melrose Place" started as a straight 60-minute drama. Each episode juggled three sub-plots, then resolved them before the hour was up. It was nothing terribly exciting. The show then tried experimenting with episodic stories that carried on for weeks. TV viewers were obviously hungry for a soap opera, and "Melrose Place" began to gain a following.

I wasn't much of a fan at this point—I still can't forgive myself for that brief spell in which I became a "90210" fan—so I didn't pay much attention to "Melrose." But last month I talked with Josie Bissett, Thomas Calabro, and Laura Leighton, the actors who play (respectively) sweet Jane, her evil ex-husband Michael, and her bad seed sister Sydney on the show. I figured I'd better start watching again and catch up.

Reprinted by permission of the Santa Cruz County Sentinel.

I watched it for a few weeks and now, sad to say, I'm a regular viewer.

They got me. I hate when that happens.

"Melrose" fans know that Michael and Jane started out as the show's only married couple. Then Michael had an affair. He and Jane split bitterly. Michael's new girl-friend was killed when she and Michael were in a car wreck (Michael was driving drunk, but convinced Matt to falsify his blood records at the hospital to cover his butt.) About the same time, Sydney figured this out and blackmailed Michael into marrying HER. Then Jane discovered Sydney's black-mailing and in turn tried to black-mail Michael and Sydney.

Like I said, this is a soap opera.

It's also turned Jane, Michael and Sydney into one of the strang-est relationships on TV since the Old Darren-Samantha-New Darren triangle on "Bewitched."

Thomas Calabro's Michael Mancini has changed the most since the show began: as he puts it, "That's me—slimeball." But now that Michael's a creep, he's "Ten times more fun to play."

Calabro explains Michael's bad and good quite simply: "What's bad is that he's evil. What's good is that millions of people like watch-ing him."

And the thing with Sydney? "Like any other relationship, that evolves," said Calabro. "At first he saw her mostly as a tool. As time goes on he finds qualities in her that he finds very admirable, espe-cially her single-mindedness."

The character of Sydney Andrews is interesting in that it's a lot more complex than the other witch of "Melrose," Amanda (Heather Locklear). Amanda comes across as purely manipulative. Sydney seems a little more com-plex.

Leighton agreed: "She's caught up in her childhood insecurities, reaching for some sort of power or control, and she's not sure how to get the respect she wants.

"I love the fact that everyone gets so opinionated about the show, taking the side of certain characters and hating others . . . it's great!"

When "Melrose Place" first started, even Bissett admits that it was a bit tame for soap opera: "In the beginning it was a little boring. Michael and Jane were the sweet married couple, but it was getting a little boring with Jane always say-ing, 'Honey, come have sex with me!' Since Jane and Michael's di-vorce the show has become more interesting."

Unfortunately for Bissett, her character Jane—which is probably the most interesting one of "Melrose Place"—has been given nothing to do except get dumped on by Michael and Sydney. (The fan in me speaks again, argh!)

How long can she play the vic-tim? Bissett said, "That's what hard with this character. People will screw me over and I'll forgive them, again and again. I'd like her to be a survivor, but she's written as the victim a lot."

I asked her if Jane will ever reach a breaking point? "I hope so. I get a little revenge in some stuff we're shooting now. I know everyone wants to see it."

Hmm. I can see it now: "Interac-tive Melrose—Jane's Revenge." Beats the heck out of "Super Mario Bros."

Meanwhile, back on "Beverly Hills, 90210," the rumor mill is decidedly undecided as to whether Shannen Dougherty will return next season as Brenda Walsh.

Initially, producer Aaron Spell-ing refused to renew her contract because of her attitude, lack of punctuality, and bad press (a num-ber of well-publicized barroom brawls either helped or hindered her teenybopper image. You figure it out.)

But lately, Dougherty has been given the spotlight in a number of episodes. (She was even arrested . . . art imitates life?) If there's no Brenda next year, there are a num-ber of spin-offs where she'd be suc-cessful. Here are some suggestions:

"Brenda and Butt-head"—Dougherty joins up with Beavis and sidekick and does what the rest of us have always wanted to do: Slap these two animated cre-tins silly.

"Married With Brenda"—Dougherty's ex-husband Ashley Hamilton says this show won't last more than six months.

"NYPD Brenda"—Looks like her photograph in Playboy caught producer Stephen Bochco's atten-tion.

"Shan Can Cook"—PBS learns that not only can Shannen Dougherty swing a mean right in a Hollywood bar, but she can beat up an entire TV crew on a low-key cooking show, as well.

"The Adventures of Brenda County Jr."—This FOX western takes a feminist turn when Dougherty joins the cast as the wild west's first female bounty hunter—and she gets to beat up people every week.

Michael Gaither is a Sentinel correspondent.

Chapter Exercises

Identifying Soap Opera Character Types

In the box below provide a list of ten characters (past or present) from popular daytime soap operas. In the space provided categorize them in terms of which primary or secondary character type you think they best represent. Explain your choice. If you are not a daytime soap opera fan, watch one for this exercise and consult with a fan for any needed context.

CHARACTER NAME AND PROGRAM TITLE	CHARACTER TYPE
1.	
Why?	
2.	
Why?	
3.	
Why?	
4.	
Why?	
5.	
Why?	
6.	
Why?	
7.	
Why?	
8.	
Why?	
9.	
Why?	
10.	
Why?	

Identifying Soap Opera Conventions

In this chapter we introduced the conventions commonly used by soap operas (they, in fact, *characterize* the genre). In the space provided, compare and contrast a daytime soap-opera with a prime-time soap in terms of these stylistic conventions.

	DAYTIME	PRIME-TIME
Fantasy themes		
Internal Reality		
External Reality		
Lateral Movement		
Vertical Movement		
Setting		
Lack of Closure (Serial)		
Primary Characters		
Secondary Characters		
Plot Lines		

References and Resources

Alexander, A. (1985). Soap opera viewing and relational perceptions. *Journal of Broadcasting and Electronic Media, 29,* 295–308.

Are soaps only suds? (1943). *New York Times Magazine,* March 28, pp. 19, cont. 36.

Allen, R.C. (1985). *Speaking of Soap Operas.* Chapel Hill, NC: University of North Carolina Press.

Barbatsis, G. & Guy, Y. (1991). Analyzing meaning in form: soap opera's compositional construction of "realness." *Journal of Broadcasting & Electronic Media,* 35, 59–74.

Buerkel-Rothfuss, N. L. & Mayes, S. (1981). Soap opera viewing: the cultivation effect. *Journal of Communication,* 31, 108–115.

Buckman, P. (1985). *All for Love: A Study of Soap Opera.* Salem, NH: Merrimack.

Butler, J. (1986). Notes on the soap opera apparatus: televisual style and *As The World Turns. Cinema Journal,* 25, 53–70.

Cantor, M. G. & Pingree, S. (1983). *The Soap Opera.* Beverly Hills, CA: Sage.

Carveth, R. & Alexander, A. (1985). Soap opera viewing motivations and the cultivation process. *Journal of Broadcasting and Electronic Media,* 29, 259–273.

Cassata, M. & Skill, T. (1983). *Life on Daytime Television: Tuning in American Serial Drama.* Norwood, NJ: Ablex.

The code of sudsville. (1972). *Time,* 20 March, p. 94.

Compesi, R. J. (1980). Gratifications of daytime serial viewers. *Journalism Quarterly,* 57, 155–158.

Demeuth, P. & Barton, E. (1982). Soaps get in your mind. *Psychology Today,* July, pp. 74-78.

Derry, C. (1983). Television soap operas: incest, bigamy and fatal disease. *Journal of the University Film and Video Association,* 35, 4–16.

Downing, M. (1974). Heroine of the daytime serials. *Journal of Communication,* 24, 130–137.

Elsaesser, T. (1972). Tales of sound and fury: observations on the family melodrama. *Monogram,* 4, 2–15.

Estep, R. & MacDonald, P. T. (1985). Crime in the afternoon: murder and robbery on soap operas. *Journal of Broadcasting and Electronic Media,* 29, 323–331.

Feuer, J. (1984). Melodrama, serial form and television today. *Screen,* 25, 4–16.

Fine, M. G. (1981). Soap opera conversations. *Journal of Communication,* 31, 97–107.

Galperin, W. (1988). Sliding off the stereotype: gender difference in the future of television. In E.A. Kaplan (Ed.). *Postmodernism and Its Discontents: Theories, Practises.* London: Verso.

Gilligan, C. (1982). *In a Different Voice.* Cambridge, MA: Harvard University Press.

Gledhill, C. (1988). Pleasurable negotiations. In D. Pribram (Ed.). *Female Spectators: Looking at Film and Television.* New York: Routledge.

Goldsen, R. (1976). Throwaway husbands, wives and lovers. *Human Behavior,* 35, 64–69.

Hobson, D. (1982). *Crosswords: The Drama of a Soap Opera.* London: Methuen.

Intintoli, M. (1985). *Taking Soaps Seriously.* New York: Praeger.

Kaplan, F. I. (1975). Intimacy and conformity in American soap opera. *Journal of Popular Culture, 9,* 622–625.

Katzman, N. (1972). Television soap operas: what's been going on anyway? *Public Opinion Quarterly, 36,* 200–212.

Keeler, J. (1980). Soap: counterpart to the 18th century's quasi-moral novel. New York *Times,* March 16, p. 34.

Kinzer, N. S. (1973). Soap sin in the afternoon. *Psychology Today,* August, pp. 46–48.

Kreizenbeck, A. (1983). Soaps: promiscuity, adultery and "New Improved Cheer." *Journal of Popular Culture, 17,* 175–181.

Kuhn, A. (1982). *Women's Pictures: Feminism and Cinema.* London: Routledge.

LaGuardia, R. (1983). *Soap World.* New York: Arbor House.

Landry, R. J. (1984). The soaps: then and now. *Variety,* January 11, p. 170.

Larson, S. G. (1991). Television's mixed messages: sexual content on *All My Children. Communication Quarterly, 39,* 156–163.

Lemay, H. (1981). *Eight Years in Another World.* New York: Atheneum.

Logan, M. (1994). Do Suds Need More Sleaze? *TV Guide,* May 14, p. 33.

Lopate, C. (1977). Daytime television: you'll never want to leave home. *Radical America, 2,* 33–51.

Lowry, D. T., Love, G. & Kirby, M. (1981). Sex on the soap operas: patterns of intimacy. *Journal of Communication, 31,* 90–96.

Martin, W. (1986). *Recent Theories of Narrative.* Ithica, NY: Cornell University Press.

Matelski, M. J. (1988). *The Soap Opera Evolution: America's Enduring Romance with Daytime Drama.* Jefferson, NC: McFarland & Company.

McAdow, R. (1974). Experience of soap opera. *Journal of Popular Culture, 7,* 955–965.

McManus, J. (1991). Afternoon delight. *Mediaweek,* February 18, pp. 21–22.

Miller, N.K. (1986). *The Heroine's Text.* New York: Columbia University Press.

Modleski, T. (1984). *Loving with a Vengeance: Mass Produced Fantasies for Women.* New York: Methuen.

Modleski, T. (1979). The search for tomorrow in today's soap operas: notes on a feminine narrative form. *Film Quarterly, 33,* 12–21.

Newcomb, H. (1974). TV: *The Most Popular Art.* New York: Anchor Doubleday.

Nixon, A. E. (1970). Coming of age in Sudsville. *Television Quarterly, 9,* 61–70.

Nochimson, M. (1992). *No End to Her: Soap Opera and the Female Subject.* Berkeley, CA: University of California Press.

Porter, D. (1977). Soap time: thoughts on a commodity art form. *College English, 28,* 782–788.

Remember when. (1993). *Soap Opera Magazine,* August 3, p. 22.

Rodina, M. L., Cassata, M. & Skill, T. (1983). Placing a "lid" on television serial drama: an analysis of the lifestyles, interpersonal management skills, and demography of daytime's fictional population. In M. Cassata & T. Skill (Eds.). *Life on Daytime Television: Tuning in American Serial Drama.* Norwood, NJ: Ablex.

Schemering, C. (1985). *The Soap Opera Encyclopedia.* New York: Ballantine.

Seiter, E. (1982). Promise and contradiction: the daytime television serials. *Screen, 23,* 150–163.

Seiter, E. (1981). The role of the woman reader: Eco's narrative theory and soap opera. *Tabloid, 6,* 36–43.

Showalter, E. (1981). Feminist criticism in the wilderness. *Critical Inquiry, 8,* 179–205.

Spence, L. (1984). Life's little problems . . . and pleasures: an investigation into the narrative structures of *The Young and the Restless. Quarterly Review of Film Studies, 9,* 301–308.

Soares, M. (1978). *The Soap Opera Book*. New York: Harmony Press.

Wakefield, D. (1976). *All Her Children*. New York: Avon.

Waters, H.F. (1990). New varieties of soap: teens and gays push the limits of the genre. *Newsweek*, February 26, p. 60.

Wiley, G. (1961). End of an era: the daytime radio serial. *Journal of Broadcasting*, 5, 97–115.

CHAPTER 10

NEWS AND REALITY-BASED TELEVISION

They've got another news director telling his staff that he didn't want stories on the Pope's visit—he wanted stories—plural—on Madonna's Sex Book. It's the ratings, stupid. And they've got us putting more and more fuzz and wuzz on the air, cop show stuff, so as to compete not with other news programs but with entertainment programs (including those posing as news programs) for dead bodies, mayhem, and lurid tales. They tell us international news doesn't get ratings, doesn't sell, and, besides, it's too expensive. "Foreign news" is considered an expletive best deleted in most local station newsrooms and has fallen from favor even among networks. Thoughtfully-written analysis is out, "live pops" are in. . . . Hire lookers, not writers. Do powder-puff, not probing interviews. Stay away from controversial subjects. Kiss ass, move with the mass, and for heaven and the ratings' sake don't make anybody mad. . . . Make nice, not news.

What radical, ivory-tower critic said these things to the Annual Convention of the Radio and Television News Directors Association in Miami in 1993? Some dreamer idealist who believes that television news should be about service, not only profits? No, it wasn't an out-of-touch egg head; it was CBS Evening News anchor Dan Rather. And he should know. Earlier that same year his own network's Paula Zahn commented on the air to her *This Morning* co-host Harry Smith as Rather delivered a live report on Hurricane Emily, "Harry, I don't want to take away from the severity of what you two were talking about, but please pass along to Dan he looks great in his jeans today" (Today's..., 1993, p. 4A). Yes, Dan looks great, so does almost everyone and everything on screen in television news.

Why, then, is so much contemporary comment on television news negative? The answer is complicated, as we'll see, but so few critics have little good to say about television news because news is different from all the medium's other forms by virtue of the fact that it is not necessarily (supposed to be) designed to entertain. A very entertaining soap opera will win high ratings and financial success for its producers, its advertisers, and the network and stations that carry it. An exciting televised football game can show the potential of television in its purest form and it will win high ratings and financial success for its producers, its advertisers, and the network and stations that carry it. But entertaining and exciting news, while it might win high ratings and financial success for its producers, its advertisers, and the network and stations that carry it, may not be very good for the public or our democracy. In other words, television news can be wonderful television, but can it then still be wonderful news?

Overview

We will attempt to answer this question by returning to broadcast news' roots on radio, follow its move to television, and then discuss how it has changed as the medium has matured. We will examine why news works so well as television but we will spend the greater portion of this chapter detailing the negative critical opinion that haunts the form. Finally, we will talk about the future of the genre and, of necessity, this will take us into the realm of the so-called "reality" shows like *Cops* and *Hard Copy*.

Broadcast News Develops Its Form

During the first decade of radio, news was either once-a-week commentary or special coverage of important events like disasters and big criminal trials. Radio was thought of as entertainment, not as an information medium. In 1930 NBC began regular weekday evening news reports, and within two years these 15 minute broadcasts were a regular part of the national network radio scene. But the newspaper industry took offense to radio's intrusion into their domain and pressured the networks into limiting their broadcasts to two a day, one at 9:30 a.m. and another at any time after 9 p.m., in order to protect the morning and afternoon editions of city newspapers. This *Biltmore Agreement*, signed in 1933, did not apply to local stations, however, so news exploded onto their schedules. Sterling and Kittross (1990, p. 175) report that in 1938 "one-tenth of broadcast programming was news; with special events coverage added, radio devoted one-sixth of its programming to news and public affairs; and more news and special events programs originated locally than were supplied by national networks." The imme-

diacy and reality of the new medium's reports made news and radio a good match, one that became even more important to listeners and filled even more hours on the air as America entered WWII.

Broadcast news, characterized by the wartime reporting of CBS's Edward R. Murrow, became not only an important, but an *expected* part of broadcasters' service to their audiences. So, it was simply understood that news would find a prominent spot in the schedules of the new television networks. On February 17, 1946, NBC began television's first regularly scheduled news program, airing *The Esso Newsreel* (sometimes *The Esso Reporter*) three evenings a week. Like the DuMont, ABC and CBS offerings that were to soon follow, this was a 15 minute newsreel program accompanied by commentary from an unseen studio reporter. In 1948 NBC replaced the *Esso Newsreel* with the *Camel Newsreel Theatre*, now broadcasting Monday through Friday. A year later, announcer John Cameron Swayze moved from behind the newsreel footage to in front of the camera, becoming television's first anchorperson, and the *Camel News Caravan* was born.

The network news format with which we are now familiar soon emerged. In 1963, the evening newscasts of the Big 3 (DuMont had failed in 1954) expanded to 30 minutes, began a six-nights-a-week schedule in 1969, settling into its current seven-nights-a-week a year later. Since that time, their frequent efforts to expand to 60 minutes a night have been consistently thwarted by local affiliates unwilling to give up the lucrative slot adjacent to the national news.

The Sixties, with assassinations, war, space shots and political and cultural turmoil also saw the proliferation of newscasts throughout the morning and daytime hours on both the network and local levels. Equally important, this decade proved to be something of a "Golden Age" for television documentary, a form almost dead on commercial television today.

Documentaries

Documentaries, regularly scheduled social dramas drawn from the events and issues of the day, were a staple from the beginning of network television as they were the perfect embodiment of the power of journalism wedded to film. CBS's *See It Now*, produced by journalistic legends Edward R. Murrow and Fred Friendly, premiered in 1951 and established the form by focussing on social conflicts and their resolution. In 1959 it was replaced by *CBS Reports* and in 1960, NBC and ABC both unveiled their equivalents, *NBC White Paper* and *ABC Close-Up*. The form flourished. NBC, for example, averaged 11 documentary hours a year from 1950 to 1961. From '62 to 66 it averaged 38. Today it is rare if NBC, ABC and CBS together broadcast more than five documentary hours a year in prime-time.

Several factors combined to kill the challenging, topical documentary:

1. **The audience changed.** The social consciousness of the Sixties disappeared in the Seventies.

2. **Television changed.** As competition for advertising revenues grew, news was increasingly called upon to turn a profit; controversy was the death of profit.

3. **The world changed.** Civil Rights, the Viet Nam War, feminism, drugs, decay of the cities, assassinations, Watergate, all the issues that cried out for lengthy and detailed investigation were also very complicated and "messy." That meant that they might be controversial (see above) which meant that they might challenge audiences (see above that).

Three very controversial documentaries at the beginning of the Seventies sealed the documentary's doom. 1971 saw the broadcast of CBS's *Selling of the Pentagon*, which questioned the military's spending of millions of tax dollars on their own public relations. The Pentagon, conservative members of Congress and defense industry groups screamed.

1972's *Pensions: The Broken Promise* was an examination of abuses in various industries' pension funds, an issue that was then before Congress. Faced with a complaint from a conservative media watch-dog group, the FCC ruled that the program had been "accurate" but "not balanced." Bad pension funds were bad, the network claimed; what good could be said about bad pension funds? The ice was getting more slippery in the documentary business. Finally, in 1973, NBC ran *What Price Health?* examining rising health costs. The attack from the AMA was withering. The audience didn't want documentaries much anymore. The programs turned little or no profit and were becoming increasingly controversial. All this led to the final blow to documentaries...

4. **Lack of advertiser support.** Even the bravest company saw little value in being associated with a potentially troublesome program.

In 1968 CBS, realizing that the camera and reporter were integral parts of the story, decided to turn this fact to its best advantage and unveiled *60 Minutes*. *CBS Reports* was cancelled, and the other regularly scheduled documentary programs soon followed it into broadcast history.

It is not accurate, however, to say that there are no challenging documentaries on television today. PBS's embattled (by conservative voices in Congress) *Frontline* offers weekly films by independent documentarians; the cable channels, especially CNN and HBO, make periodic use of the form; and even commercial networks like ABC, which aired in 1994 *Turning Point: Coverup at Ground Zero* examining the "downwinders," people in the path of the nuclear fall-out from the government's Nevada bomb tests in the 50s and 60s, can be counted on to do an occasional penetrating report (although they do tend to be aired during "black week," the four periods each year in which no ratings are taken).

Documentaries aside, news proved to be popular and profitable on television, a fact not lost on local broadcasters and cable entrepreneurs. In addition to the networks' evening newscasts, their prime-time news magazines (*20/20*, *48 Hours*) and week-end interview shows (*Face the Nation*, *Meet the Press*), almost every local television station offers some form of local news (for many, it is their most profitable programming) and cable now offers two CNN channels, a Weather Channel, C-SPAN, and a Public Broadcasting System that, despite growing financial and political pressure, persists in many markets in making the fullest use of the medium's journalistic potential.

Why the Bad Press?

If the television schedule is so full of news, why is there so much negative criticism of the genre? The answer has to do with the special nature of news and its role in our democracy. The press, which of course includes television news, *is the only industry protected by name in the Constitution*. It enjoys this privileged position under the First Amendment because a democracy is governed by the people, and those people can best govern only if they have access to the freest and fullest news possible. The forces of profit and duty collide in all journalism, but nowhere more visibly and importantly than in television news. Anchor Rather addressed this issue in that controversial 1993 speech:

> *Our reputations have been reduced, our credibility cracked, justifiably. This has happened because too often for too long we have answered to the worst, not to the best, within ourselves and within our audience. We are less because of this. Our audience is less, and so is our country....[Edward R. Murrow] recognized that news operations couldn't be run as philanthropies. But, he added (quote), "I can find nothing in the Bill of Rights or the Communications Act which says that [news divisions] must increase their net profits each year, lest the Republic collapse."...Private profit from television is fine, but there should be a responsibility to news and public service that goes with it.*

The devil, however, is in the details. Where do those who collect, produce, and distribute television draw the line between profit and service? There are many critics who argue that even the question itself is irrelevant because television news, by its very nature, cannot produce anything remotely close to the kind of journalism required for the maintenance and prosperity of our democratic society. Recognizing that nearly 70 percent of the American public "turns to TV as the source of most of its news,...54% ranks it as the most believable news source" (Broadcasting..., 1993, p. xxi) and that news is what newspeople say it is, Edward J. Epstein is one of these critics. In *News From Nowhere* (1973) he detailed his experience as an inside observer at the networks' news operations. His analysis was convincing but troubling. In essence, he argued, what appears on the screen is the product of "concerns" that logically drive the coverage and shape the reporting of the news. These aren't bad things, these are not the product of laziness, they are simply the facts of life in television news. The problem, though, is that few have anything to do with providing the audience with the fullest information on which to make important decisions. The three sets of concerns he identified are:

1. Organizational Concerns

- Network policy. Different news operations have rules that guide their operation, for example, no live broadcast of demonstrations.

- Skill of the "group." Some organizations simply strive to be and/or are better than others.

- Concern for variety and pacing. Because a news show is still a "show," it must not have too much of any one thing, or get too bogged down in a detailed discussion of some story.

- Use of expected or routinized events. The easiest, quickest and least expensive events to cover are those that are pre-planned (like press conferences, openings of new amusement parks) and different news organizations depend on these stories to varying degrees.

- Drive for originality. It is the goal of most organizations to "scoop" the competition, to beat them and be Number 1, but this is often tempered by...

- News consensus. It is much worse to be scooped, so most nightly news programs look remarkably the same (the image of the row of monitors overlooking a television newsroom is almost a cliché, but what's on these screens is typically the opposition's broadcasts).

- Generalizability. The national networks must satisfy a national audience, so there cannot be too many stories from Washington and New York; there has to be some evidence that other parts of the country are being covered.

- Investigative reporting. Different news organizations make different levels of commitment to investigative reporting.

2. Political Concerns

- Interaction with the FCC. There is the regulatory expectation of balance and service to the public.

- Affiliate pressure. Those who must clear time refuse to clear an additional half hour, get angry when profitable entertainment programming is pre-empted, and make constant demands for "non-offensive" reporting, a vague standard for a national news broadcast that is viewed in Los Angeles as well as McEwen, Tennessee and Fabens, Texas.

- Reliance on government officials. Broadcasters rely on Congress and the courts for their regulatory atmosphere, but more immediately, journalists need access to those in power and access comes most readily from friends.

3. Economic Concerns

- Ratings. Or as Rather said (1993), "fear of ratings slippage if not failure, fear that this quarter's bottom line will not be better than last quarter's—and a whole lot better than the same quarter's a year ago."

- Availability of pictures. Television is a visual medium, so stories with video make it to the screen more often than those without.

- Where a story occurs. Stories that happen where there is an available news crew are cheaper to cover than those that require the sending of a team.

- When a story occurs. Things that happen at night get covered in the morning paper, so these stories are too old for the evening news. Things that happen early in the day have a better chance of making it to the air (plenty of time to shoot, edit, write and rehearse the story).

- Pooling. In order to save money covering static events like a Space Shuttle blast-off or a Senate Committee Hearing, the networks will "pool" resources—one provides cameras and crew, one electricians, one switchers and directors—so the picture on all the outlets is the same, but the anchors and reporters are from the individual networks. The issue here is whether or not viewers are being offered several different perspectives (journalism's traditional "multitude of tongues") or, because in television the picture drives the story, only one.

Think about these concerns; they are logical, rational, and seemingly benign. Yet many critics (Iyengar & Kinder, 1987, Noelle-Neumann, 1984, Turow, 1983, Bennett, 1988, and Tuchman, 1978, to name only a few) argue that they inevitably produce more coverage of Lorena Bobbitt and the Hollywood Madam than they do of complex, non-visual, but important stories. These critics might ask: How much of our tax money might have been saved if the abuses that led to the S&L scandal and subsequent bail-out had been more thoroughly covered? Where was television journalism when Americans were being fed plutonium?

The broadcasters' response, from both local and national news operations, is that too much is expected of them. They often offer the *mirror analogy* or the *spotlight analogy*. In other words, television news is only a mirror of society, it simply reflects the world as it is; or, all television news can do is cast a spotlight on the events of the day; it is up to citizens to recognize that depth and detail are difficult in television and they must look to other media to complete *their* responsibilities as citizens. Critics of television news tend to dismiss these views, arguing that television is a *funhouse mirror*, expanding some things out of true proportion, making other things disappear altogether. And that if television is a spotlight, it illuminates a strange and narrow collection of activities. These arguments are most forcefully presented by those engaged in ideological criticism, especially critics watching news with a neo-Marxist or cultural studies eye (Chapter 5). Bennett (1988), for example, argues that the economic and industrial systems that underlie television news produce anything but a true picture of the society by pointing to four common practices that distort news content:

1. **Personalized news:** people in television news believe that audiences relate better to individuals than to groups or institutions, so most news stories center around people. He wrote, "The focus on individual actors who are easy to identify with positively or negatively invites members of the news audience to project their own private feelings and fantasies onto public life" (p. 27). Personalization of the news helps viewers find relevance in remote or complex events. But at what price? The larger social world becomes a big soap-opera: Michael Jackson's personal life gets more attention than healthcare reform and the budget deficit is blamed on "welfare queens."

2. **Dramatized news:** Like the medium's other genres, news must attract and hold its audience, and one way to do this is to make it dramatic. The following confession from respected television journalist

Daniel Schorr (1992, p. 5C) makes the point well:

I found (in the mid-1960s) that I was more likely to get on the CBS Evening News with a black militant talking the language of "Burn, baby, burn!" than with moderates appealing for a Marshall Plan for the ghetto. So, I spent a lot of time interviewing such militants as Stokely Carmichael and H. Rap Brown.

In early February 1968, the Rev. Martin Luther King, Jr. came to Washington....I came to his news conference with a CBS camera crew prepared to do what TV reporters do—get the most threatening sound bite I could to ensure a place on the evening news line-up. I succeeded in eliciting from him phrases on the possibility of "disruptive protests" directed at the Johnson Administration and Congress.

As I waited for my camera crew to pack up, I noticed that King remained seated behind a table in an almost empty room, looking depressed. Approaching him, I asked why he seemed so morose.

"Because of you," he said, "and because of your colleagues in television. You try to provoke me to threaten violence and, if I don't, then you will put on television those who do. And by putting them on television, you will elect them our leaders. And if there is violence, will you think about your part in bringing it about?"

3. **Fragmented news:** Because of concerns for variety and pacing, television newscasts are made up of brief, capsulated reports of a lot of different, unrelated events; there is little effort, in the name of "objectivity," to link them. Making connections requires that reporters put their stories into a broader context, requiring speculative, maybe even controversial linkages. So "the news" ultimately adds up to little more than a collage of reports and pictures. Critics have referred to the

product as "mind candy," presented in a "contextual void," producing "popular amnesia."

4. **Normalized news:** Stories about challenges to the status quo, for example disasters, social movements, and protests, are reported in a way that "normalizes" them. Officials and other elites are allowed to give explanations and information. Anything less might damage access to important sources, challenge and possibly even activate audience members, and most feared of all, scare off advertisers. During the 1991 Gulf War the same small corp of military experts was interviewed and re-interviewed. And no broadcast of an airplane disaster is complete without mention of how, rest easy worried viewer, the FAA is on the case.

Social scientists Iyengar and Kinder (1987) challenge the mirror and spotlight analogies from the perspective of television's *agenda-setting* influence, that is, the power, not to tell us what to think, but what to think about. The way news is presented, they argued, shapes national discourse and, therefore, national policy. If the news gives the impression that a story is important, violent crime for example, it becomes important for those who watch. The medium's demands for vivid presentations focus attention on specific situations and individuals, not on the larger issue at hand. Visual or dramatic stories placed at the top of a news broadcast appear to have more importance than those, possibly more complex but also more significant, placed later. Because television news' brief, fragmented, snapshot reports constitute "those bits and pieces of political memory that are accessible" (Bennett, 1988, p. 114), for even the most motivated citizens, they *prime* viewers' thinking by drawing attention *to* certain aspects of political life and *away from* others. These issues, therefore, become important parts of the public's agenda; making them, of necessity, important parts of their leaders' agendas. It's been widely reported, for example, that President Bill Clinton re-wrote his 1994 State of the Union Address to emphasize crime after constant television coverage of the abduction and death of teenager Polly Klaas from her suburban California home moved the issue to the top of the people's agenda. He went as far to evoke her name in his call for tougher penalties for criminals.

ABC's *Day One* was among the best of the breed of newsmagazines that offered in-depth examinations of important stories. Here correspondent Forrest Sawyer visits the site of a bloody Vietnam War battle with a retired American general and three North Vienamese war veterans for a 1993 broadcast.

The Case for the Defense

The mirror and spotlight defenses are difficult to support, especially in light of the self-examination offered by insiders like Rather and Schorr. But that doesn't mean that television news cannot be good television and contribute to the effective conduct of our society. We've already mentioned individual broadcaster effort to air challenging documentaries, and PBS's *MacNeil/Lehrer NewsHour* consciously works to overcome many of the problems identified by critics like Epstein and Bennett by devoting entire programs to no more than three stories. The Big 3 evening newscasts, too, are granting more time to fewer stories each night and often devote a segment on each of an entire week's broadcasts to one issue. News magazine programs like *60 Minutes*, *Dateline NBC*, and *PrimeTime Live* often offer serious journalism, and *Nightline* is fre-

quently the national ratings winner in its late-evening time slot. Certainly these successful programs occasionally offer stories about Madonna's bodyguards and intrigue in competitive figure skating, but more often than not, they take the high journalistic road.

Local news, once characterized by "anchors named Skip and Cindi-with-an-*i*, reading scripted ad-libs from a TelePrompTer, weather forecasters in earmuffs throwing snowballs at the camera, (and) self-appointed protectors of the downtrodden feigning rage because some capitalist has charged an elderly indigent $1800 for a used TV set" (Cartwright, 1984, p. 98), has become in the Nineties more sober and responsible and has re-attracted audiences lost in the previous decade. Admittedly, this transformation came only after audiences, tired of the happy-talk sideshows that often passed for local news and stations, realized that the

The local newscast of KNTV-TV "The San Jose NewsChannel" is co-anchored by Maggi Scura and Doug Moore and was awarded best newscast by the Associated Press and by the Northern California RTNDA in 1993. It serves as a good example of quality in local television news.

large number of viewers excited to the potential of news by the 1991 Gulf War and 1992 Presidential election coverage could be profitably tapped.

The Future of Television News

This audience re-interest in television news is threatened by the very conditions that helped spawn it. The proliferation of news magazines, for example, is the product of declining network audience and revenue. News is cheaper to put on the air than entertainment fare and it draws good demographics, so *60 Minutes* gets cloned. But competition among the "news-mags" can lead to more reporting of sensational stories (*20/20* filmed an exorcism on a 16 year old girl in 1991) and other problems also emerge (the faked explosion of a GM truck on *Dateline NBC* is one of the most obvious examples.)

Technology, too, has helped renew interest in television news. Light, portable electronic news gathering (ENG) equipment and the growing availability of satellite access make the reporting of news from distant places easier and cheaper than ever before. As we've said above, the Gulf War and Presidential elections turned audiences back on to television news and a large part of that excitement was generated by the amazing technology utilized by CNN and the networks. This creates several potential problems, however. For one, these available and relatively inexpensive technologies now allow local stations to send reporters to the scene of far-off stories. These reporters are typically not as well-trained and experienced as the network reporters who generally cover those beats; consequently, their coverage often has less news than ratings value. Second, these technologies have allowed even the big commercial networks to close bureaus in many foreign and even domestic news centers because it's now cheaper for them to buy tape from any of several suppliers. That means that there are fewer of those well-trained and experienced network reporters we just mentioned covering those beats. The coverage that results can lead to what U.N. Ambassador Madeleine Albright called the "CNN effect." That is, dramatic pictures from overseas, for example shots of dead children from Bosnia unaccompanied by the context and background that come from regular thorough reporting, can fuel American public opinion and, subsequently drive American foreign policy.

Changes in the economics of television and advances in technology have also combined to create what many see as the biggest threat to the future of television news: the so-called reality programs.

The Reality Programs

We've already read what Dan Rather thinks of these "entertainment programs...posing as news programs," shows like *A Current Affair*, *Hard Copy*, *Inside Edition*, *Cops*, *Rescue 911* and the many Geraldo Rivera broadcasts. What does Watergate hero Carl Bernstein think? He wrote (1992, p. 4C), "We have been moving away from real journalism toward the creation of a sleazoid infotainment culture....In this new culture of journalistic titillation, we teach our...viewers that the trivial is significant, that the lurid and loopy are more important than real news." He doesn't think much of these programs born out of satellites' ability to simultaneously deliver nightly syndicated programming to every market in America and low-cost videotape technology that makes every mom and dad with a video camera a potential Murrow or Rather.

Quick! Who was the American Ambassador to the United Nations in 1993/94 when NAFTA was passed, GATT negotiated, Bosnia burned, North Korea threatened, Mexico rebelled, South Africa abolished apartheid, and the United States formally recognized Viet Nam? Her name appears a only few lines back. Quick! In 1993/94 who were Tonya Harding, Heidi Fleiss, Joey Buttafuoco, Marla Maples, John Bobbitt, Amy Fisher, and Lorena Bobbitt? You knew them all, but not from the television tabloids. From the "real news," you say. That was Rather's point in the opening quote. What *is* the real news in today's television?

Why the Fuss?

Knowing what really is happening "out there" is essential in a democracy. For decades, much respected anchorperson Walter Cronkite would close his evening news broadcast on CBS with, "And that's the way it is, April 27, 1963." But it wasn't. That's the way it was inasmuch as CBS could distill that portion of an entire days happenings all around the world that its cameras happened to catch into the 20 or so minutes of news left over after the commercial time was deducted from the half hour program.

Actually, Cronkite never intended for his generic, sign-off phrase to define news as some sort of divine edict of the Truth. However, *news is what newspeople say it is.* What events happen each day that aren't covered and, therefore, by definition aren't news? What do we really know about the world around us and does it really matter how television reports it to us? BBC and Swedish Radio correspondent Roger Wallis and one of this text's co-authors turned to Plato's Allegory of the Caves, written 400 years before the birth of Christ, to answer these related questions:

Plato's characters are human beings who have been chained in a cave since childhood and are chained to its walls so they cannot turn their heads and, therefore, can only look straight ahead. Behind and above them sits a blazing fire that casts the prisoners' (own) shadows and those of the people that pass between the flame and them upon a far wall. "Like ourselves," Plato says, "they see only their own shadows, or the shadows of one another....To them the Truth would be literally nothing but the shadows of the images."

Like the prisoners in the cave, we too come to know the world beyond the boundaries of our actual experience through the shadows of light and dark beamed into our homes. And if it is true that we know the world (even if only in part) through the pictures of it brought to us by broadcast news, then we need to understand those forces that shape the shadows that shape the perceptions that very often shape our interactions and behaviours in that world (Wallis & Baran, 1990, p. 2).

DOWLING

The author lays out his perspective in this piece of rhetorical criticism at the start when he asserts that genre is "more than coincidental." But in an interesting maneuver, he treats terrorism as a news genre in and of itself and proceeds to explain how the "inflexible and unquestioned" criteria of newsworthiness that now permeate television news' own genre demands serve those who resort to terrorism.

Do you agree with his arguments that terrorists are actually television news producers? What does he mean by this? Does he support this assertion well?

Dowling sets up a puzzle for his reader. He demonstrates that terrorists owe their existence to the media but then argues that their goals are ultimately frustrated by television. Can you reconcile this dilemma?

Do you agree with those who argue that television should simply stop covering terrorist acts? What might the results be?

As you've no doubt noticed in the academic critical essays you've read so far, and just as Chapter 5 argued, most academic criticism, even that firmly rooted in one critical approach, often borrows from other approaches. Can you identify bits of narrative analysis and reader-oriented criticism in this essay?

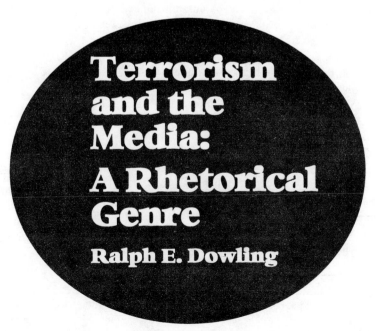

Terrorism frequently has rhetorical ends. Critics of rhetoric have a duty to examine terrorism to determine what contributions they can make to understanding it and to evaluating proposed responses to the terrorist threat. Burgess (6), Scott and Smith (25), Campbell (7), and others have argued that refusing to study essentially rhetorical acts on the normative basis that they are irrational or immoral is contrary to the goals of scholarly inquiry. As Burgess lamented, "these judgments send coercion into rhetorical ... oblivion in the face of its increased use in resolving public controversy" (6, p. 63).

Only certain terrorist activities, however, fall within the domain of rhetorical acts. Hacker (14) has identified three distinct types of terror-

Ralph E. Dowling is Assistant Professor in the Department of Speech Communication, Ball State University.

Dowling. "Terrorism and the Media: A Rhetorical Genre." *The Journal of Communication* 36 (1): 12–24 (1986).

ists:[1] criminals, who are motivated by the possibility of monetary gain (see 6); crazies, who seek personal glory, to overcome massive insecurity, or to wreak revenge on the world that scares them to death; and crusaders, who are the focus of this article. Crusaders practice terrorism for political ends, defined by the Task Force on Disorders and Terrorism as "violent criminal behavior designed primarily to generate fear in the community . . . for political purposes" (22). Echoing this definition, Jenkins (16, p. 115) ruefully concluded that "the use of terrorist tactics will persist as a mode of political expression, of gaining international attention, and of achieving limited political goals." My purpose is to identify the situational demands influencing political terrorists, the recurrent forms of a terrorist genre, the rhetorical purposes of terrorists, and the probable results of proposed responses to terrorism.

A genre is more than the coincidental repetition of forms; the recurring forms must be strategic responses to the situational restraints and the purposes of the rhetors (see 8, esp. pp. 19, 21). Genres "will emerge most clearly," according to Simons, "when rhetorical practices are most constrained by purpose and situation. . . . Should purpose and situation be highly constraining . . . we should be able to predict much of what rhetors will say before they say it" (26, p. 42).

Terrorists seek to change the world, yet they lack the power to do so. Unwilling to work within the institutions they seek to overthrow, they deny themselves the conventional tools of political power. Indeed, terrorists' use of violence must not be confused with an intent on their part to seek conventional military victory. Aware of their absolute impotence as armed forces, "terrorists do not try to take and hold ground or physically destroy their opponents' forces. While terrorists may kill . . . the objective of terrorism is not mass murder. . . . Terrorism is theatre" (15, p. 235). Too small or weak to obtain a military victory, terrorists are forced to use violence rhetorically. According to Laqueur, "the terrorist act by itself is next to nothing, whereas publicity is all . . . The real danger facing the terrorist is that of being ignored" (18, p. 62).

Terrorists, news people, and media experts "share the assumption that those whose names make the headlines have power, that getting one's name on the front page is a major political achievement" (18, p. 57). Gerbner and Gross (12, p. 368) opined that "representation in the world of television gives an idea, a cause, a group its sense of public identity, importance, and relevance. No movement can get going without some visibility." Modern terrorists seek access to the media by committing acts that closely fit news agencies' definitions(s) of news: being timely and unique, involving adventure or having entertainment value, and somehow affecting the lives of those being informed of them (17, pp. 158–159).

Those who seek media access have a history of properly responding to the requirements of newsworthiness, of creating "pseudo-events" (4). Mander (19, pp. 31–32) ranked the common ones: "Press conferences got coverage at once. Rallies brought more attention than press conferences. Marches more than rallies. Sit-ins more than marches. Violence more than sit-ins." Wanton violence attracts coverage and has priority over less dramatic pseudo-events.[2]

Terrorists engage in recurrent rhetorical forms that force the media to provide the access without which terrorism could not fulfill its objectives. The genre, which Bell (3) has called the "terrorist spectacular," has three optimum requirements:

A terrorist-spectacular first should be staged in an ideologically satisfactory locale with more than adequate technological facilities. Munich was ideal— No Justice for Palestine, No Peace for the World, not even at the Olympics, and several thousand journalists and cameramen on the spot. . . .

Second, the terrorist drama must offer the reality or prospect of violence. Unlike conventional television serials, the violence is real and the outcome uncertain . . . .

The third component . . . is movement—the change of scenery that allows the cameras to follow the actors from one site to the next— coupled with the passage of time. The Croatian hijacking in 1976 managed to include New York, Chicago, Montreal, London, and Paris, with Rekjavik in Iceland thrown in. The Croatian spectacular ran for thirty hours (3, pp. 48-49).

The terrorist whose acts include these elements transcends mere access to the media. Such a terrorist is no longer subject to editorial judgments; rather, the news agencies become his or her pawns. Journalistic responses are inevitable

---

1. Several scholars have discussed the political and rhetorical implications of the label "terrorist," who is empowered to bestow it, how they are empowered, etc. These are critical questions, but their answers are not relevant to the issues discussed here.

2. The vulnerability of U.S. media to terrorism—and six rival explanations for it—can be found in Schmid and de Graaf (24, pp. 68-76). See also Molotch and Lester (21, pp. 108-109) for a consistent analysis.

because the newsworthiness criteria are inflexible and unquestioned. When the critics charge journalists with inciting terrorism, journalists will "continue to insist that, as always, they simply covered the news" (3, pp. 47–48; see also 24, pp. 68-69, 71–75). The news, however, is created and staged by terrorists seeking media access.

A Rand Corporation study of 63 terrorist incidents between 1968 and 1974 found that terrorists "achieved a virtually one hundred percent probability of gaining major publicity whenever that was one of the terrorists' goals. And it nearly always was" (3, p. 49). Compare this with Rutkus's (23) finding that Presidents Johnson, Nixon, and Ford received simultaneous network time to address the nation 44 times by requesting such time on 45 occasions. The President of the United States, arguably the most powerful person on earth, has had slightly less success than terrorists in obtaining media access. The clearest explanation for this amazing success is provided by Bell:

> These new transnational gunmen are, in fact, television producers constructing a package so spectacular, so violent, so compelling that the networks, acting as executives, supplying the cameramen and the audience, cannot refuse the offer. Given a script with an uncertain ending, live actors . . . and a skilled director who choreographs the unfolding incident for maximum impact, television is helpless (3, p. 50).

The viewing/reading public encourages this coverage, and news organizations must fill the demand or lose their audience and thus their reason for existing. Within the limits set by newsworthiness, decorum, and the integrity of news ex-

ecutives, these news organizations must give the public what it wants—and it wants dramatic entertainment. Altheide notes that, "with few exceptions, viewers seldom watch the evening news in order to learn about topics experienced independently of news channels. Rather, people watch the news because that is where newsworthy events are presented" (2, p. 25; see also 24, pp. 69–76). Thus, the audience watches the news because it provides the newsworthy entertainment the audience craves. The attitudes of news agencies and their audiences guarantee terrorist coverage.

It is erroneous to assume that the purpose of terrorists and terrorism is the ideological conversion of the masses (cf. 9, p. 3), although they may have some impact on their own cohorts.[3] Violent terrorist spectaculars do little to enhance the ethos of terrorists in the eyes of the mass audience. If persuasion is believed to be their goal, terrorism becomes paradoxical, because "the spectacular massacres appear fruitless displays by men and women frustrated beyond reason . . . horror on horror's head that gains not power, but publicity that, in fact, is counterproductive" (3, p. 47). And even if the mass audience could ignore the negative ethos generated by the forms of the genre, the terrorists would be unable to persuade the masses, because the ideologies they espouse are alien to the audience's experiences and beliefs.

The inability or unwillingness of terrorists to work within the institutions they seek to supplant is strong evidence of this ideological gap. Terrorist groups do not raise funds to print and disseminate literature. They do not frequently trouble themselves to export media presentation of their ideologies; when they have made such attempts,

their ideological statements have been so scathing, polarizing, and rife with inexplicable argot that they could not have been aimed at any audience but the "community of the blessed" (see 5).

The dismissal of ideological conversion as a goal of terror does not deny that terrorists purposefully convey rhetorical messages. Rather, they send messages by performing violent spectaculars and not by enacting the discursive forms that would be used if they were trying to persuade us of the rightness of their cause.

Messages to insiders. By conducting a successful terrorist spectacular, the terrorist can persuade the loyal minions that, "even if their aspirations are not closer to reality, they can at least still act on events" (3, p. 50). The importance of this message to improving terrorists' morale must not be underestimated. Denied the ability to transform their utopian dreams into social realities, terrorist groups must be satisfied with lesser accomplishments. Laqueur (18) argues that terrorist groups are motivated by "a free floating activism that can with equal ease turn right or left. Terrorism . . . is not a philosophical school—it is always the action that counts" (18, p. 60). Such ideological ambivalence casts further doubt on the suggestion (9) that ideological conversion is a major purpose of terrorism.

Another goal of terrorism is to demonstrate to terrorists that they are worthy and, in the process, to claim a sort of moral victory. In their study of confrontation as rhetoric, Scott and Smith (25) discuss how, "by the act of overcoming his enemy, he who supplants demonstrates his own worthiness, effacing the mark, whatever it may be—immaturity, weakness, subhumanity—that his enemy has

---

3. There is limited evidence that the media audience of terrorists tends to perceive both terrorists and their cause as more important than non-audience members (30).

set upon his brow" (25, p. 4). Any concession by the stronger authorities becomes a terrorist victory—including the airing of ideologies, grievances, or demands.

Lacking the final victory they seek, terrorists also can claim at least a limited victory when they succeed in gaining any concession(s) in exchange for releasing hostages or agreeing not to detonate explosives: when authorities are forced to release "political" prisoners, feed the poor, guarantee immunity from prosecution, provide transportation to safe havens for political exiles, or allow the publication/broadcast of ideological statements or lists of demands. Terrorists can persuade themselves that their heroism, determination, and rightness of cause ensure them of eventual victory over the enemy who lacks the "stomach for the fight."[4] According to Scott and Smith, radicals may "work out the rite of the kill symbolically. Harassing, embarrassing, disarming the enemy may suffice, especially if he is finally led to admit his impotence in the face of the superior will of the revolutionary" (25, p. 4).

The evidence supports terrorists' claims of victory. Despite the authorities' best efforts, 79 percent of all members of terrorist teams have escaped alive and unpunished (3, p. 49).

Messages to outsiders. The first step in the terrorist strategy is to make outsiders aware of their existence. To ensure our awareness, terrorists must gain and hold our attention. The level of awareness is a function of the terrorists' adherence to the genre. In evaluating some of the recurring types of terrorism, Jenkins identifies this hierarchy of quality:

> *Hostage incidents seem to have greater impact than murder, barricade situations more than kid-*
> *napping. Hostage situations may last for days, possibly weeks. Human life hangs in the balance. The whole world watches and waits. By contrast, a death, even many deaths, are news for only a few days. They lack suspense and are soon forgotten (16, pp. 59-60).*

Jenkins goes on to argue that the Croatian hijacking of an airliner in 1976, which fulfilled all of the characteristics of the genre, is better remembered today than the sudden deaths of 73 caused by a bomb placed aboard a Cubana airliner just three weeks later. Patty Hearst and the SLA, the PLO and Israeli commandoes at Entebbe (later the subject of a television docudrama), Black September killers and Israeli athletes in Munich, South Moluccans and Dutch school children, and Hanafi Muslims in B'nai B'rith headquarters in Washington, D.C., have become universal memories through successful enactment of the terrorist genre.

Adherence to the terrorist genre also explains why government officials and private citizens have often erroneously commented on increases in terrorism during years that actually witnessed absolute decreases in both the number of incidents and the damage inflicted. Laqueur attributes the discrepancy between reality and perception to the dramatic character of the smaller number of incidents (18, p. 64). All of this indicates that the genre is a description of reality as well as a prescription for success.

Other variables influence terrorists' success in gaining awareness. Since many world events compete for the finite time and space available on news channels, "timing is important. Terrorist violence is easily submerged by higher levels of conflict, individual acts of violence lose their meaning in a war" (16, p. 119). Terrorists must also take care

not to split our attention with simultaneous incidents, lest the impact of their deeds be diminished. Laqueur provides several examples of terrorists who succeeded in gaining attention:

> *Only a few years ago, newspaper readers in the Western world were led to believe that the German Baadder-Meinhof group, the Japanese United Red Army, the Symbionese Liberation Army, and the British "Angry Brigade" were substantial movements that ought to be taken very seriously. Their "communiques" were published in the mass media; there were earnest sociological studies on the background of their members and their motivations; their "ideology" was analyzed in tedious detail. But these were groups of between five and fifty members and their only victories were in the area of publicity (18, pp. 59-60).*

Terror obviously does not produce traditional Aristotelian ethos. Terrorists, instead, seek to be perceived as credible terrorists, capable of producing great fear, representing the courage and commitment of their followers, and stymieing law enforcement. Unwilling to risk being perceived as criminals or crazies, crusader terrorists distance themselves from the riffraff of terrorism:

> *For the terrorists, the path to legitimacy is through one's reputation for resilience, for self-sacrifice and daring, for brutality, and, above all for effective discipline over words and actions . . . . It is the credibility that violence produces, whenever it appalls, that renders terrorism horrifying yet powerful and, if successful, self-legitimating (31, pp. 278-279).*

This credibility theoretically allows terrorists to create "an emotional state of extreme fear in target groups" (1, p. 102). All of the authorities on terrorism agree that ter-

---

4. A discussion of the intrapersonal functions served by some radical rhetoric can be found in Gregg (13).

rorists seek to create fear; what is the purpose behind their goal?

Contemporary terrorism has not achieved the long-term goals of its practitioners. There is no Palestinian homeland, no free Croatia, no liberation of South Molucca, no end to British domination of Northern Ireland, and no sign of radical transformations in the structure of Western society. The creation of a climate of fear is the only terrorist strategy that might directly contribute to such goals. Dobson and Payne described this strategy:

> The philosophers of terror have assumed that one of their principle aims, the creation of a climate of repression in liberal societies, would become easier. They hoped by this repression to achieve what they call the alienation of the masses which then prepares the way for revolution. But in Europe and the United States the theory has not worked out. . . . The police state, a step on the road to revolution, has failed to emerge (10, p. 208).

The creation of mass fear as an inducement to repressive responses places the liberal regime at a disadvantage. Liberal regimes enjoy popular support because they allow a great deal of freedom. The citizens of such a state presumably will be unsatisfied with the authorities if freedoms are sacrificed in an attempt to clamp down on terrorism. In his instructions to terrorists, Carlos Marighella made this strategy clear:

> The war of nerves or psychological warfare is an aggressive technique. . . . The government is always at a disadvantage since it imposes censorship on the mass media and winds up in a defensive position. . . . At this point it becomes desperate, is involved in greater contradictions and loss of prestige (20, pp. 104-105).

The provocation of repressive responses by authorities can serve other purposes as well. Terrorists may provoke violent responses from the authorities to counter the negative reactions aroused by their own violence (25). The Israeli-Palestinian conflict yields one example. An investigative report on the Palestine Liberation Organization conducted by ABC-TV (29) hypothesized that one of the major goals of Palestinian terror is to promote violent responses from Israeli authorities that will be violent enough to anger Israel's allies, erode domestic support for the Israeli government, and demonstrate that the Israelis are not the "good guys" in this conflict. This goal seems to have been accomplished to some extent, as violent responses from Israel have been provoked, despite the inevitable loss of innocent lives and predictable arousal of international condemnation. And among nations that have not traditionally supported Israel, a more dramatic development can be observed: the rise of the PLO from near-total obscurity to a legitimized political group.

The terrorists' belief that fear can be produced has some foundation. But, perhaps because their ideology demands it, terrorists seem unable to accept the fact that the responses of a liberal government may actually reflect the desires of the people. Since greater fear produces greater willingness to rely on authority, the public will not likely be alienated by reasonable responses from officials. As Gerbner and Gross suggest,

> Ritualized displays of any violence (such as crime and disaster news, as well as mass-produced drama) may cultivate exaggerated assumptions about the extent of threat and danger in the world and lead to demands for protection. What is the net result? A heightened sense of risk and insecurity is more likely to increase acquiescence to and dependence upon established authority, and to legitimize its use of force than it is to threaten the social order (12, p. 391).

Thus, terrorists will not succeed unless they can provoke the authorities into taking actions contrary to popular will. This they have not done. Terrorists have been noticeably ineffectual in the United States. Prior restrain on the media is still taboo—live coverage of terrorist spectaculars goes on unabated. The Bill of Rights is intact. The only significant response has been the annoying but uncontroversial screening of passengers in airport terminals.

Terrorists seeking to induce fear in the United States also may have ignored the way U.S. viewers respond to news coverage. The obvious failure of their strategy might be attributable to audience response patterns to the most popular and credible sources of news in the United States—the television networks. Sperry explains:

> As the keystone of each network's evening programming, television news attempts to build and hold its audience by lifting elements of that mythic formula which is the basis of its entertainment programs. Av Westin, former president of ABC news, says that he expects an audience to come to his news program asking "Is the world safe and am I secure?" There is clearly a link between that question and the answer provided by a news structure that plot events along the lines of a hero story: The world at peace is disrupted by some event (say, an act of terrorism). That event, which becomes the evil, is named and, if possible, analyzed and understood. It is then attacked by some leader, the hero figure, often a representative of the people (28, p. 135).

The relevant issue, then, is the effect such a presentation has on viewer responses to terrorist violence. Sperry's description of audience responses bodes ill for the terrorist strategy of creating fear. She believes that, "by structuring an event as a plotted story, involving all the drama of filmed confrontation . . . the television newsman deliberately invites his audience to respond to the news in the same way that it responds to entertainment programming" (28, p. 141; see also 24, p. 69). If this is true, terrorism cannot succeed in creating fear.

Sperry's theory explains the failure of terrorism without denying its successes. The memorable successes of terrorists seeking to arouse our awareness of their existence are memorable in the same fashion as a good novel, play, movie, or television program. The failure to create sufficient fear is due to the lack of immediacy in the violence found in entertainment. Our fear ends when the movie, or the news, is over; the only lasting effect of such fear is the memory of having been thoroughly entertained. The fear becomes a small, unidentifiable component of the "heightened sense of risk and insecurity" that Gerbner and Gross hypothesize as the net result of real and fictional televised violence. Sloan recognized the psychological distance maintained by the audience:

> To a public both fascinated and repulsed by the carnage they often witness on the evening news, terrorism is something to be observed, not experienced. Skyjacking, kidnapping and assassination attempts are often perceived to be a deadly game between authorities and terrorists while the victims mutely await their uncertain fates (27, p. 1).

The failure of terrorists to incite repressive countermeasures is an important one, whatever its causes. Combined with their inability to persuade or conquer us, this failure makes terrorism an impotent means of attaining long-term objectives. In Fromkin's words, "terrorism only wins if you respond to it in the way that the terrorists want you to . . . . The important point is that the choice is yours. That is the ultimate weakness of terrorism as a strategy" (11, p. 23).

Terrorism succeeds only in transmitting the desired messages to insiders. The world cannot be changed by means of terrorist spectaculars. The fact that the terrorists must satisfy themselves with fleeting and ultimately meaningless victories does not, however, diminish the relevance of discussing proposed solutions. We are not charged with preventing terrorists from realizing their utopian dreams. In fact, if terrorists seek desirable ends, we should help them find other means of attaining them.

Our most pressing duty is to mitigate the carnage terrorists have yet to produce. There are growing fears that terrorist violence might one day escalate beyond current levels of destruction, graduating to weapons of mass destruction or to sabotage aimed at killing hundreds of thousands rather than scores of people. The evaluation of proposed solutions requires, and is currently lacking, an understanding of the rhetorical purposes of terrorists and of the social context in which they operate. Terrorists owe their existence to the media in liberal societies. A media spectacular could be staged in the Soviet Union, but it would not be covered by Tass or Izvestia. Laqueur asserts that the real question "is not whether terrorism can be defeated—even a third rate dictatorship has shown that it can be put down with great ease" (18, pp. 61-62). Dictators can stop terrorism by denying access to the media, by trampling human rights in rooting out terrorists before the fact, and by executing terrorists without regard for the lives of hostages or bystanders.

In liberal societies, however, "as long as terrorism exists, there will continue to be clashes between the perceived need for increased social control and the protection of individual liberties" (16, p. 123). All authorities on terrorism regard prior restraints on the media and enactment of repressive law enforcement measures as unacceptable prices to pay for solution of the threat proposed by terrorism.

Some suggest that the news media should agree that no coverage will be given to terrorist spectaculars. After all, these advocates reason, if the media give birth to these terrorists, they can eliminate them by reversing their actions. Perhaps the biggest problem with such a voluntary ban is that it very quickly would become a battle of wills between the determined terrorists and the reluctant complying media. We can easily predict the winner of such a battle if Bell's gloomy scenario—that "potential television terrorist frustrated by the imposition of any such ban might well devise a more awesome media event that would force coverage—an escalation of horrors" (3, p. 50)—becomes a reality.

This disadvantage is not the only drawback to such a ban. The proposal fails to consider that terrorism sends a powerful message to insiders regardless of the coverage received. Terrorists can reassure themselves that they are heroic, that they have the ability to act, and that they can beat the authorities for a short period of time. If such insider-directed messages are as important as they appear, such a voluntary ban does not eliminate the utility of violence.

Others suggest that contextual coverage is the solution. The media would be asked to downplay spectacular coverage and to provide the audience with information about the size, strategies, and goals of terrorist groups. This proposal, too, fails to consider the messages sent by violence to insiders. The proposal also fails to realize that "the quality of the coverage is quite immaterial to the terrorist's purpose; only the intensity and quantity of coverage matter" (3, p. 50). The only potential benefit of contextual coverage would be to provide additional insurance against the possibility that terrorists might someday create a level of extreme fear. If we know terrorists are impotent, we should not fear them. If we know they are seeking fear and repressive countermeasures, we should be far less willing to play the dupe by offering the desired fearful response.

Yet another group of observers would ask the media to provide terrorists with free access to present whatever messages they desire. The most glaring inadequacy of this proposal is its failure, like the others, to account for the messages conveyed by the actual violent deeds that could not be conveyed by words. Jenkins believes that, since "the use of terrorist tactics has won them publicity and occasional concessions," the value of violence will suffice to preclude the abandonment of terrorist tactics (16, p. 115). Since terrorists are unable to persuade us, we cannot be sure that they would accept the offer.

Given the important rhetorical purposes served by the terrorist spectaculars, we must conclude that the prevention of terrorism cannot be realized through voluntary restraint or self-regulation by the news media. The most common approaches to terrorism prevention are erroneous because they are based upon false assumptions about the motivations that give rise to terrorism and about the rhetorical purposes served by violent actions. This identification and analysis of terrorism as a rhetorical genre may provide a more realistic direction for evaluating proposed solutions.

References

1. Alexander, Y. "Terrorism, the Media, and the Police." *Journal of International Affairs 32*, 1978, pp. 101-113.
2. Altheide, D. L. *Creating Reality: How Television News Distorts Events.* Beverly Hills, Cal.: Sage, 1976.
3. Bell, J. B. "Terrorist Scripts and Live-Action Spectaculars." *Columbia Journalism Review,* May-June 1978, pp. 47-50.
4. Boorstin, D. J. *The Image, Or What Happened to the American Dream.* New York: Atheneum, 1962.
5. Booth, W. C. "The Scope of Rhetoric Today: A Polemical Excursion." In L. F. Bitzer and E. Black (Eds.) *The Prospect of Rhetoric.* Englewoods Cliffs, N.J.: Prentice-Hall, 1971, pp. 93–114.
6. Burgess, P. G. "Crisis Rhetoric: Coercion vs. Force." *Quarterly Journal of Speech 59,* 1973, pp. 61-73.
7. Campbell, K. K. "Criticism: Ephemeral and Enduring." *Speech Teacher 23,* 1974, pp. 9-14.
8. Campbell, K. K. and K. H. Jamieson. *Form and Genre: Shaping Rhetorical Action.* Falls Church, Va.: Speech Communication Association, 1977.
9. Decker, W. and D. Rainey. "Terrorism as Communication." Paper presented at the Speech Communication Association Convention, New York, 1980.
10. Dobson, C. and R. Payne. *The Carlos Complex: A Study in Terror.* New York: Putnam, 1977.
11. Fromkin, D. "The Strategy of Terrorism." In J. D. Elliot and L. K. Gibson (Eds.) *Contemporary Terrorism.* Gaithersburg, MD.: International Association of Chiefs of Police, 1978.
12. Gerbner, G. and L. Gross. "Living with Television: The Violence Profile." In H. Newcomb (Ed.) *Television: The Critical View* (2d ed.). New York: Oxford University Press, 1979, pp. 363-393.
13. Gregg, R. B. "The Ego-Function of the Rhetoric of Protest." *Philosophy and Rhetoric 4,* 1971, pp. 71-91.
14. Hacker, F. J. *Crusaders, Criminals, Crazies: Terror and Terrorism in Our Time.* New York: Norton, 1976.
15. Jenkins, B. "International Terrorism: A Balance Sheet." In J. D. Elliot and L. K. Gibson (Eds.) *Contemporary Terrorism: Selected Readings.* Gaithersburg, Md.: International Association of Chiefs of Police, 1978.
16. Jenkins B. "International Terrorism: Trends and Potentialities." *Journal of International Affairs 32,* 1978, pp. 115–123.
17. Johnpoll, B. "Terrorism and the Mass Media in the United States." In Y. Alexander and S. M. Finger (Eds.) *Terrorism: Interdisciplinary Perspectives.* New York: John Jay, 1977.
18. Laqueur, W. "Terrorism Makes a Tremendous Noise." *Across the Board,* January 1978, pp. 57–67.
19. Mander, J. *Four Arguments for the Elimination of Television.* New York: Morrow-Quill, 1978.
20. Marighella, C. "Minimanual of the Urban Guerrilla." In J. Mallin (Ed.) *Terror and Urban Guerrillas.* Coral Gables, Fla.: University of Miami Press, 1971.
21. Molotch, H. and M. Lester. "News as Purposive Behavior: On the Strategic Use of Routine Events, Accidents, and Scandals." *American Sociological Review 39,* 1974, pp. 101-112.

22. National Advisory Committee on Criminal Justice Standards and Goals. Task Force on Disorders and Terrorism. *Disorders and Terrorism: Report of the Task Force.* Washington, D.C., 1976.

23. Rutkus, D. "Presidential Television." *Journal of Communication 26(2),* Spring 1976, pp. 73-78.

24. Schmid, A. P. and J. de Graaf. *Violence as Communication: Insurgent Terrorism and the Western News Media.* London: Sage, 1982.

25. Scott, R. L. and D. K. Smith. "The Rhetoric of Confrontation." *Quarterly Journal of Speech 55,* 1969, pp. 1–8.

26. Simons, H. W. "Generalizing about Rhetoric: A Scientific Approach." In K. K. Campbell and K. H. Jamieson (Eds.) *Form and Genre: Shaping Rhetorical Action.* Falls Church, Va.: Speech Communication Association, 1977, pp. 33–50.

27. Sloan, S. "International Terrorism: Academic Quest, Operational Art, and Policy Implications." *Journal of International Affairs 32,* 1978, pp. 1-5.

28. Sperry, S. L. "Television News as Narrative." In R. Adler and D. Cater (Eds.) *Television as a Cultural Force.* New York: Praeger, 1976, pp. 129-146.

29. "The Unholy War." An Investigative report by ABC News (G. Rivera, reporter) on "20/20." April 2, 1981.

30. Weimann, G. "The Theater of Terror: Effects of Press Coverage," *Journal of Communication 33(1),* Winter 1983, pp. 38-45.

31. Weisband, E. and D. Roguly, "Palestinian Terrorism: Violence, Verbal Strategy, and Legitimacy." In Y. Alexander (Ed.) *International Terrorism.* New York: Praeger, 1976.

STEELE

Author Steele uses humor as her attention-getting opening and then quickly proceeds to her critical thesis: Why do television reporters persist in calling on the same talking heads for their reports? Using the example of the 1991 Gulf War, she makes the case that this is an important question, for both television news and the public. Does her light-hearted introduction help or hurt her critical effort?

What does she mean by operational bias? By illusion of depth? How does one influence the other? How do Epstein's "concerns" that shape the news relate to operational bias?

Steele quotes one news producer who complained that she had difficulty finding enough talking heads. This critic's reasonable solution is to add "experts in ethics, history, language, and theology." What operational bias in television news kept her from suggesting the following talking heads:

1. ordinary people on the street;

2. people opposed to the conflict; and,

3. Iraqi citizens living in the U.S.

If you were a network news producer, would you have given air-time to these view points? Why or why not?

Can you find traces of sociological academic television criticism in this essay? Would you be surprised to know that *Columbia Journalism Review*, for which this article was written, is a publication geared toward practitioners and scholars of journalism and mass communication?

During the war in the Persian Gulf it became common for humorists to mock the battalions of Middle East "experts" who appeared on television night after night to make predictions and supply analysis. From the comment of the general's wife depicted in a *New Yorker* cartoon ("Oh, he's pretty depressed—he's the only retired general the networks haven't called") to Andy Rooney's spoof of the "professor of old rocks and stones" on *60 Minutes*, the retired generals, policy experts, and "news consultants" became easy targets of such friendly fire.

While humor at the expense of television's ubiquitous experts ran the gamut from satire to derision, the analysts also attracted their share of serious media criticism. Critics and viewers alike found something unsettling in the ease with which the experts shaped the events of the war into sound bites for the evening news.

Many of the articles about television's use of all these experts debunked the experts' predictions. Focusing on how many of the predictions had been off-target, they ignored what should be a more significant question for students of the

TV's Talking Headaches

When covering a crisis, the networks call on experts—but show little expertise when it comes to choosing and using them

Janet Steele

media: Why did reporters persist in asking the experts for predictions in the first place?

Coverage of the gulf war provides a good opportunity to examine the issues of objectivity and operational bias—a term I use to describe the emphasis television news organizations place on players, policies, and predictions, on

what will happen next as opposed to what lies behind what has already happened.

The Experts

Television's use of experts in its coverage of this war differed from ordinary news analysis in two ways: the producers had the opportunity to plan ahead, and the extended news coverage gave experts more time to speak their minds. Every network news producer I spoke to emphasized the planning that went into his or her organization's coverage of the war. Between Saddam Hussein's invasion of Kuwait on August 2, 1990, and the first allied air strikes against Iraq on January 16, 1991, television researchers compiled books listing the regional experts and their specialties. At CBS, for example, researchers began in October to cull newspapers and magazines for the names of Middle East experts. By December they had assembled a bulging briefing book that included the names, addresses, and phone numbers of experts who had already demonstrated their media savvy by appearing in print.

Once the war began the experts had more than the usual eight or nine seconds to make their points. According to CBS producer Diane Wallerstein, the biggest problem was finding enough "talking heads" to fill up the air time. To guarantee

Janet Steele is an assistant professor in the department of rhetoric and communication studies at the University of Virginia, in Charlottesville. This article is adapted from a paper Steele wrote as a guest scholar at the Media Studies Project of the Woodrow Wilson Center in Washington, D.C.

Reprinted from the *Columbia Journalism Review*, July/Aug © 1992.

the availability of the experts required to help fill that time, each of the networks had three or more under contract. Though actual figure are hard to come by, *Newsday's* Vern Gay estimates their pay as having been between $500 and $1,000 per day. Paid consultants were often asked to provide the names of other experts or to evaluate the qualifications of those who had already been tapped. Thus the networks created a self-perpetuating cycle.

A relatively small group of unofficial sources dominated television coverage of the gulf crisis. In the eight months of regularly scheduled network news programming that I examined, 188 individuals appeared on television an average of 4.5 times for a total of 843 appearances. Experts from the Brookings Institution and the Center for Strategic and International Studies made up 102 of those appearances, accounting for 12 percent of the total. Most of the others were either retired military personnel or scholars from other think tanks. In many instances they were both. The news organizations used relatively few independent, university-based scholars to explain or interpret the news.

Most of the experts who appeared repeatedly on television were affiliated with institutions located either in New York or Washington. All of the producers I spoke to said that they were willing to book the leading expert regardless of where he or she was located (provided that, as one put it, the expert didn't live in "Podunk"). In spite of these declarations, my data suggest that all of the networks tended to rely on the familiar local faces.

The New York and Washington think tanks have a symbiotic relationship with the networks. Producers find in them a ready supply of media-savvy experts, and television exposure gives the think tanks

the publicity they need to procure foundation grants and corporate donations.

If the war created the opportunity for extended news analysis, it also raised a unique set of problems. Of these the most significant was American ignorance of the Middle East—an ignorance shared by many broadcast journalists. There seems to be a myopia among all Americans about the diversity of peoples and cultures in the middle East. As Stanford University historian Joel Beinin has written, "Would you ask a historian of France to comment on a crisis in Portugal on the grounds that they are both European countries?" Though his answer to this rhetorical question was obviously no, during the war Beinin (a historian of Egypt, Palestine, and Israel) was frequently asked to comment on events in Iraq—a country he had never visited.

This lack of basic knowledge of the region was compounded by the fact that many "Middle East analysts" have political biases. Most of the experts used on television were either former public officials closely associated with the administrations they had served or scholars affiliated with organizations seeking to promote certain policies in the Middle East. Their political biases were, for the most part, apparent.

The biases of the second group of experts—those affiliated with policy-oriented think tanks—were more difficult for viewers to assess. The names of many of the think tanks are similar enough to be virtually indistinguishable to the public, and their political agendas are murky at best. Even those think tanks that are not overtly ideological may have political agendas. For example, scholars from the Center for Strategic and International Studies appeared in my sample of experts a total of forty-four times. The CSIS was presented as just another prestigious think tank, al-

though, as Howard Kurtz reported in *The Washington Post Magazine,* it is a "markedly conservative organization that forms a sort of interlocking directorate with the Washington establishment." According to Kurtz, 10 percent of CSIS's funding comes from the Pentagon and other federal agencies, with significant financial support coming from defense contractors such as Boeing, General Dynamics, Rockwell, Honeywell, and Westinghouse. Such ties to the military industrial complex undermine CSIS's claim to independent status.

The networks' reliance on experts from CSIS illustrates what I have called the operational bias of television news, a bias that shapes news coverage yet does not conform to the conventional framework of left versus right. What the think-tankers, former public officials, and retired military personnel who appeared on television over and over again had in common was a technical expertise and a desire to shape policy. Meanwhile, rather than using these experts to provide background, context, or analysis, television journalists asked them to generate a never-ending supply of predictions. In just one of dozens of similar examples, on February 5, 1991, ABC anchor Peter Jennings asked "news consultant" Anthony Cordesman the following series of questions—all of which were concerned with either strategy or tactics or what was going to happen next.

What is the best the U.S. can hope for from the B-52 campaign against the Republican Guard? . . . Can the Iraqis confuse the U.S. on the ground? . . . What did the Pentagon mean by saying it could put companies out of action if 30 to 50 percent of them are destroyed? . . . Can you move out and around during a B-52 attack? Or do you have to stay dug in all the time? . . . Can the Iraqis get themselves back together again a couple weeks after taking this kind of attack?

Obviously, the American people want and deserve answers to questions like the ones Jennings posed. The safety of American troops, the reliability of U.S. equipment, the determination and moral of the enemy are all issues of vital concern in wartime. The problem is that these were the *only kinds* of questions that the news organizations asked—or, indeed, were prepared to ask. The operational bias meant that all divisions of every news organization were concentrated on strategy, tactics, and what was going to happen next. The pool reports, news footage, Pentagon briefings, and expert analysis were all focused on illustrating, expanding, and explaining what CBS News producer Wallerstein referred to as "the picture of the moment."

During the war, journalists also pressed the experts to provide answers to an endless series of unanswerable questions like, "Is Saddam insane?" Lack of credible information in no way deterred the experts from commenting. For example, on January 5, 1991, the *CBS Evening News* included a report from Mark Phillips on "speculation on what's going on in the mind of Saddam Hussein:"

Mark Phillips—The analysts see him not as a madman, but as something worse.

Jerrold Post (George Washington University "political psychologist")—This is a judicious political calculator who is by no means irrational, but dangerous to the extreme. From early on this man has been obsesses with dreams of glory, with the goal of becoming the preeminent strong man in the Arab world.

Phebe Marr (National Defense University)—The word "dignity" is a word that Saddam uses very frequently. In my view he's got a Rodney Dangerfield complex—he wants the world's respect.

Geoffrey Kemp (Carnegie En-

dowment for International Peace)—The mind set, as some people have said, is straight out of *The Godfather*. This is a Mafia don who understands his own power arrangements and his own principles and his own values very well, but has an awful difficulty relating to what goes on in the rest of the world.

In short, the most important service the experts provided was assistance in creating an atmosphere of gravity and authority on television news programs. By making predictions and attempting to answer the unanswerable, they did little more than supply television viewers with what Steven Waldman in a *Washington Monthly* piece has called "the illusion of depth."

Expertise

In academia, a scholar claiming to be an expert on the Middle East would—at the minimum—have an ability to speak Arabic, have spent time in the region, have completed a significant body of primary research on the area, and be well read in the secondary literature of the field. Surprisingly, none of these considerations are important to television producers. In answer to the question of what makes a good expert, NBC's Mary Alice O'Rourke explained that the best experts have "a lot of contacts," can work the phones, and can "tell you what's going on." This is important, because "things happen fast."

Although some of the network news producers with whom I spoke found it difficult to explain their selection of expert sources, producers for *Nightline* and *The MacNeil/Lehrer NewsHour* could clearly articulate the qualities they believe make one an expert. For Michael Mosettig of *MacNeil/Lehrer* the most important qualities are "sufficient authority" and the experience of having "operated out in the real world." Mosettig expressed a preference for getting "the players" first. In his words, *MacNeil/Lehrer* consciously

"avoids university seminars on the air."

Nightline's Richard Harris agreed that firsthand experience is important in defining expertise, and pointed out that, since its inception, *Nightline* has "gone after people who make policy." Harris, whose title is guest booker, emphasized that the contacts an expert maintains make up an important aspect of his or her expertise. Unlike what Harris termed "book experts," *Nightline* often prefers individuals like Judith Kipper, the "world's greatest networker." Harris's defense of Kipper is revealing in that it articulates a set of criteria for expertise that is dramatically different from its academic counterpart. Though Kipper has spent time in the Middle East, she does not speak Arabic and has written nothing of consequence on the region. Yet Kipper is, by television standards, an expert because, while lacking "good book knowledge," she has had the important "on-ground experiences."

Interestingly, Harris's description of Kipper makes her sound like a kind of super-journalist. Not only does her contractual relationship with ABC News allow the network to use her as a highly paid, part-time correspondent, but the arrangement also permits the organization to contract for her services in lieu of taking on the financial burden of a full-time employee—an important consideration in an era of severe budget cuts.

Meanwhile, experts who do have real expertise—be it military, regional, or political—were not used effectively in television's coverage of the Persian Gulf war. The operation bias means that experts were almost never asked to put events in a broad historical context. While the first responsibility of television journalists is obviously to provide viewers with news of the latest events, news devoid of context is also biased. A person who watched nothing but the nightly news would have a view of the gulf war in which Saddam Hussein was a madman who without any provocation or explanation seized the helpless country of Kuwait. With one or two exceptions, there were no stories that presented the background of the crisis in a meaningful way. The issues were framed as a struggle between the forces of good and evil in the world, which were also the terms established by the Bush administration.

Experts, if used thoughtfully, can add real depth to news coverage. But in order for them to do so, the networks must refine their understanding of "expertise" and use experts in a responsible manner—to provide real background, context, and analysis.

At the very least, they should properly identify expert sources, including an acknowledgement of any particular biases or conflicts of interest. During the gulf war, television news organizations were inconsistent in the way they identified the experts. For example, retired Pentagon and National Security Council aide Anthony Cordesman (who may have been the most ubiquitous expert of them

all, with fifty-six appearances in my sample) was presented variously as "Georgetown University professor," "military analyst," "defense analyst," "national security analyst," and "ABC News consultant." Cordesman is in reality an adjunct professor at Georgetown University, meaning that he teaches there part-time. It is thus misleading to call him a "Georgetown University professor," which implies a life devoted to teaching, research, and scholarship, rather than to the shaping of public policy.

Like the experts, think tanks were not properly identified. As has already been noted, many policy experts affiliated with think tanks are former public officials. It is misleading to present such individuals as neutral experts rather than as partisans for their former employers. Frank Gaffney of the Center for Security Policy, who appeared eight times in my sample, is a case in point. As a former deputy assistant secretary of defense in the Reagan administration, he has a clear point of view—one that was not properly identified. There is nothing wrong with using opinionated experts who will take a strong position on the issues. The problem

arises when an opinionated expert is presented as a neutral one; this is unfair to both the expert and the public.

The networks need not only to be more candid about the experts they use but to use a greater variety of them, as well. As Jay Rosen has observed in *Tikkun*, technical expertise was the only kind of expertise used in covering the gulf war. By allowing experts in ethics, history, language, and theology to add their voices to the discussion, television would expand the discourse from a simple left-right dichotomy of policy experts to an examination of the issues in all of their complexity. Thus, at a time when producers were complaining of the problem of filling air time, it would not have been difficult to examine the relationship between Iraq and Kuwait from the perspective of the last seventy years rather than the last seventy days.

By decontextualizing the news, broadcast journalists strip events of their meaning. In this informational vacuum, is it any wonder that Americans resort to anti-Arab stereotypes and explain world events as a simplistic confrontation between good and evil?

CALERO

Senior San Jose State University Radio-TV-Film major Solon Calero has written a review of Spanish-language network Telemundo's coverage of the 1993 Mayan rebellion in the Chiapas region of Mexico that bears several unmistakable signs of ideological criticism. Invocation of neo-Marxism, frequent references to the network's financial and political self-interest, and a sub-theme of us vs. them make clear that his essay is politically informed. This author makes no claim of neutrality or fairness, but this is not uncommon in ideological writing. How do you think critic Calero would explain this "oversight?" Would you accept this explanation?

Unless you watch Telemundo, it is unlikely that you will be familiar with the specific broadcasts that Calero references. Therefore, you are at the critic's mercy because he is doing the picking and choosing. Do you believe that he has presented enough evidence to support his serious charges? What might you have done differently?

Telemundo Normalizes the News From Chiapas

Solon Calero

On December 31, 1993, a phantasmagoric event occurred in Mexico. The ghost of Emiliano Zapata, the legendary hero of Mexico's 1910 revolution, was resurrected. According to the apocalyptic images telecast by Telemundo, the most important Spanish language television network in the USA, 300 armed peasants, led by a very suspicious left wing intellectual, were threatening the political security of a country that appeared to be one of the most stable nations of Latin America. The ghost of Zapata, reincarnated in comandante Marcos and his followers, suddenly erupted from the Lancandon rainforest, located in the southeastern state of Chiapas, and began their fight against a political system that had ignored them for more than a century. According to

Telemundo, the Zapatista National Liberation Army intended to sabotage the honeymoon that the Mexican government and the Clinton administration were enjoying in the wake of the passage of the NAFTA treaty.

Pictures of revolucionarios armed with machine guns, hunting rifles, and in some cases toy pistols were presented to the Spanish speaking audience in Telemundo's evening newscast (Noticiero Telemundo) to alert it that another revolution might start in that region. In that same evening edition, the cameras of Telemundo showed on several occasions the bodies of six rebels, dead in the central market of one of the towns affected by the insurrection. Their hands had been tied, and each had been killed with a bullet in

Written in 1994 by Solon Calero, Radio-TV-Film Major at San Jose State.

the back of the head, apparent victims of summary executions. This scene was presented by the reporter as the natural response of the Mexican National Guard to control the subversives. Coverage of the Chiapas events, as is often the case in reporting by Telemundo, lacked any significant explanatory background that would have made the story more contextually readable for the Spanish-speaking audience. Clearly, Telemundo's obsession with visual stories that distort the real meaning of the information it broadcasts demonstrates that its own economic and ideological interests are more important than its "good" intentions to inform honestly the Hispanic audience about important events that directly affect the course of its history and its culture.

In order to understand why this powerful Spanish network has come to deal so poorly with important issues like the insurrection in Chiapas, it is necessary to provide some background about how Telemundo functions in the USA. This network operates in the United States and Puerto Rico through its own stations and affiliates. According to the bilingual newspaper, *El Observador*, the evening telecast (Noticiero Telemundo) is viewed by approximately 85.4% of the Hispanic households in the USA. In addition, Telemundo already transmits its newscast and many other programs to several Latin American countries and is seeking to expand its market throughout all Latin America.

Now, why is it so important for the Latino community to pay attention to and demand more from what is presented as news on Telemundo?

One answer rests in media analyst Everette. E. Dennis' observation that it is now critical for the people of any culture to confront what is produced in TV newsrooms: "Their reputation and our intelligence depend on it." If this is true,

it is essential that we evaluate the role played by Telemundo in the controversial Chiapas insurrection. Telemundo, in fact, is the most important source of information that the Latino community has in the USA. Therefore, for the sake of our intelligence, more than for the reputation of Telemundo, we, latinos, should be alert to what it presents as news.

Its distortion of news content is the product of specific economic interests that Telemundo has with its future Latin American markets and with its big audience in the USA. A good example of distortion of content is the characterization made of comandante Marcos, leader of the Zapatistas. The visual analogies of him with Fidel Castro and the Sandinistas were more than evident. Comandante Marcos always appeared in close up, smoking a pipe and wearing the black ski mask that has become his trademark. After many years of successful ideological manipulation through the mass media, for the majority of Latinos Fidel and the Sandinistas represent evil, communism, and the forces that oppose progress. Telemundo has been a strong supporter of NAFTA and of Mexican president Salinas's economic policies. Consequently, Telemundo's portrait of comandante Marcos and his followers, a group of Mayan Indians, is clearly stereotyped. The Zapatistas not only opposed the NAFTA treaty, they are also fighting for political reform and economic justice in Mexico. Obviously, for Telemundo these "outrageous demands" mean the possible Cubanization of Mexico (La Revolución). At the same time, this kind of civil strife clashes with Telemundo's interests in expanding its market in Latin America.

The reasons for and the political implications of the Zapatista's revolt never were addressed by Telemundo. The only information

provided by this network was that the Zapatista National Liberation Army had seized several towns and villages and declared its intentions to overthrow the government of President Carlos Salinas de Gortary. Dramatic scenes of people crying were presented as the primary supporting evidence. Why was and is Telemundo not willing to deal with issues such as allegations that the Mexican army committed rights violations against the Indian population? Why has it never addressed the issue that there is much to be done in terms of political and social reform in Mexico? Clearly, the answer to these questions is that such reporting challenges the political system of which Telemundo is a strong supporter and beneficiary. As a result, the information provided is biased and lacks the necessary background (historical or sociological) that an event of this magnitude requires.

Many days after the uprising, when political negotiations were under way, Telemundo presented only the official version of the issues. What is taking place, in neo-Marxist terms, is Telemundo's "normalizing" of the news. This crucial story about a major challenge to the Mexican status quo was reported "officially." It was President Salinas' opinion about these events that Telemundo featured. Comandante Marcos' interpretation of the situation, however, was never considered by Telemundo. It appears as if normalization of the Chiapas revolt was an important need for the business community as well. According to several different reports aired by Telemundo, Mexican and American business people were not very concerned about the events in Chiapas. To them, the uprising would have little impact on the pursuit of business interests between the two nations. All is well. Those who are really interested in the well-being of Mexico will conduct business as usual. This view not only reflects the arrogance of the business communities on both sides of the border, but it further demonstrates Telemundo's commitment to normalized news.

Many other important aspects of this event were not covered and explained to the audience. For example, Salinas' efforts to create a modern, free-market economy in Mexico generated great hostility in Chiapas, where the large Indian community has been exploited for decades by big landholders and ignored by the government. NAFTA only added to their anger: it calls for the elimination of subsidies to traditional Mayan farming communities. There is no doubt that events in Chiapas derive from poverty and the inability of the political system to deal with the fundamental problems of Mexican society. The revitalization of the Mexican democracy does not depend exclusively on NAFTA, as Telemundo seems to believe and would have us believe as well. This is a much more complex problem, one that requires a different more thoughtful journalistic approach.

Telemundo must rise to the challenge. To date, its handling of the events in this remote state of Mexico demonstrates that its obligation to inform impartially the Hispanic audience is not being met. It also sends a clear message to that community. That is, that Telemundo's obsession with visual stories, without real content, proves that is own economic and ideological interests are more important than the right of the audience to be well informed. Furthermore, the main concern of Telemundo is to expand its market throughout Latin America and to maintain its tight alliance with the status quo. Consequently, it is our responsibility as viewers to be alert to the pictures and information we receive from them.

Chapter Exercises

Be a Political Campaign Media Manager

In the space provided below, adopt the role of a campaign manager and describe the political candidate whose campaign you will run (e.g., the political office he/she is seeking, personal characteristics, gender, cultural background, political beliefs, etc.).

CANDIDATE DESCRIPTION

Now, using the concerns and pressures that shape television news judgements and values (as forwarded by Epstein), plan a media strategy that takes advantage of these to insure your candidate's successful election to office. Not all may apply to your strategy, but use as many as you can.

ORGANIZATIONAL CONCERNS
Network policy —   **Skill of the "group"—**   **Concern for variety and pacing —**   **Use of expected or routinized events —**   **Drive for originality —**   **News consensus —**   **Generalizability —**   **Investigative reporting —**

POLITICAL CONCERNS

Interaction with the FCC—

Affiliate pressure—

Reliance on government officials—

ECONOMIC CONCERNS

Ratings —

Availability of pictures—

Where a story occurs—

When a story occurs —

Pooling—

Encouraging Common (Unfortunate) News Practices

How does the campaign you've prepared help television broadcasters produce the following kinds of news that Bennett says are common practices in television journalism?

TELEVISION NEWS PRACTICES
Personalized news
Dramatized news
Fragmented news
Normalized news

Evaluate the Impact of Your Campaign

Presume you've done a fine job....Your candidate has been elected. In the box below, note your thoughts on what you believe your campaign has added to or detracted from the political process.

POST-ELECTION REFLECTION

References and Resources

Arlen, M. (1977). The prosecutor. *The New Yorker*, November 23, pp. 166–173.

Baker, R. W. (1993). Truth, lies, and videotape: *PrimeTime Live* and the hidden camera. *Columbia Journalism Review*, July/August, 25-28.

Barnouw, E. (1983). Documentary: *A History of the Non-Fiction Film.* New York: Oxford University Press.

Barnouw, E. (1975). *The Tube of Plenty: The Evolution of American Television.* New York: Oxford University Press.

Baughman, J. L. The strange birth of *CBS Reports* revisited. *Historical Journal of Film, Radio, and Television, 2*, 28–38.

Bazalgette, C. & Paterson, R. (1980) Real entertainment: the Iranian Embassy siege. *Screen Education, 37*, 55–67.

Bennett, W. L. (1988). *News: The Politics of Illusion, 2nd edition.* New York: Longman.

Berkowitz, D. (1993). Work roles and news selection in local TV: examining the business-journalism dialectic. *Journal of Broadcasting & Electronic Media, 37*, 67-81.

Bernstein, C. (1992). Feeding the "idiot culture." San Jose *Mercury News*, June 21, 1C, 4C.

Bluem, A. W. (1965). *Documentary in American Television: Form, Function and Method.* New York: Hastings House.

Broadcasting & Cable Yearbook 1993. (1993). New Providence, NJ: R. R. Bowker.

Bruck, P. (1982). The social production of texts: on the relation production/product in the news media. *Communication-Information, 4*, 92–124.

Campbell, R. (1987). Securing the middle ground: reporter formulas in *60 Minutes. Critical Studies in Mass Communication, 4*, 325–350.

Cartwright, G. (1984). Bad news. *Texas Monthly*, February, 98-100.

CBS News. (1980). *60 Minutes Verbatim.* New York: Arno Press.

Curtin, M. (1992). The discourse of "scientific anti-communism" in the "golden age" of documentary. *Cinema Journal, 32*, 3-25.

Dahlgren, P. (1981). TV news as a social relation. *Media, Culture, and Society, 3*, 291–302.

Davie, W. R. & Lee, J. S. (1993). Television news technology: do more sources mean less diversity? *Journal of Broadcasting & Electronic Media, 37*, 453–464.

Epstein, E. J. (1973). *News From Nowhere: Television and the News.* New York: Random House.

Epstein, E. J. (1975). *Between Fact and Fiction: the Problems of Journalism.* New York: Vintage.

Fallows, J. (1996). *Breaking the News: How the Media Undermine American Democracy.* New York: Pantheon.

Flander, J. (1992). NBC's Tim Russert: the insider. *Columbia Journalism Review*, September/October, 40–42.

Funt, P. (1980). Television news: seeing isn't believing. *Saturday Review*, November, pp. 30-32.

Gans, H. J. (1980). *Deciding What's News: A Study of CBS Evening News, NBC Nightly News, Newsweek and Time.* New York: Vintage Books.

Gibson, W. (1980). Network news: elements of a theory. *Social Text*, 3, 88–111.

Grossman, L. K. (1996). CBS, *60 Minutes*, and the unseen interview. *Columbia Journalism Review*, January/February, 39–51.

Hackett, R. A. (1984). Decline of a paradigm? Bias and objectivity in news media studies. *Critical Studies in Mass Communication*, 1, 229–259.

Hartley, J. (1983). *Understanding News*. London: Methuen.

Hartley, J. & Fiske, J. (1977). Myth—representation: a cultural reading of *News at Ten*. *Communications Studies Bulletin*, 4, 12–33.

Henry, W. A. (1986). Don Hewitt: man of the hour. *Washington Journalism Review*, May, 25-29.

Iyengar, S. & Kinder, D. R. (1987). *News That Matters: Television and American Opinion*. Chicago: University of Chicago Press.

Kaplan, E. A. (1977). The documentary form. *Jump Cut*, 15, 11–12.

Katz, J. (1993). Covering the cops. *Columbia Journalism Review*, January/February, 25–30.

Kendrick, A. (1969). *Prime Time: The Life of Edward R. Murrow*. Boston, MA: Little, Brown and Co.

Kervin, D. (1985). Reality according to television news: pictures from El Salvador. *Wide Angle*, 7, 61–71.

MacArthur, J. R. (1992). *Second Front: Censorship and Propaganda in the Gulf War*. New York: Hill and Wang.

MacDonald, J. F. (1985). *Television and the Red Menace: The Video Road to Vietnam*. New York: Praeger.

Madsen, A. (1964). *60 Minutes: The Power and the Politics of America's Most Popular TV News Show*. New York: Dodd, Mead, & Co.

Massing, M. (1991). Is the most popular evening newscast the best? *Columbia Journalism Review*, March/April, 30–35.

McKinley, R. (1983). Culture meets nature on the *Six O'Clock News*: American cosmology. *Journal of Popular Culture*, 17, 109–114.

Mohr, H. (1971). TV weather programs. *Journal of Popular Culture*, 4, 628–633.

Moore, D. (1978). *60 Minutes. Rolling Stone*, January 12, pp. 43–46.

Mould, D.H. (1984). Historical trends in the criticism of the newsreel and television news, 1930-1955. *Journal of Popular Film and Television*, 12, 118–26.

Noelle-Neumann, E. (1984). *The Spiral of Silence—Our Social Skin*. Chicago: University of Chicago Press.

Rather, D. (1993). Call it courage. Remarks before the Radio and Television News Directors Association Annual Convention, Miami, September 29. New York: CBS News.

Schleuder, J. D., White, A. V. & Cameron, G. T. (1993). Priming effects of television news bumpers and teasers on attention and memory. *Journal of Broadcasting & Electronic Media*, 37, 437–452.

Schorr, D. (1992). True confessions of a lifetime TV journalist. San Jose *Mercury News*, May 17, 1C, 5C.

Silverstone, R. (1983). The right to speak: on a poetic for television documentary. *Media, Culture, and Society*, 5, 137-154.

Sterling, C. H. & Kittross, J. M. (1990). *Stay Tuned: A Concise History of American Broadcasting*. Belmont, CA: Wadsworth.

Today's quote. (1993). *San Jose Mercury News*, September 20, 4A.

Traub, J. (1985). That (too long?) one-hour news show. *Columbia Journalism Review*, January/February, 41-43.

Tuchman, G. (1978). Television news and the metaphor of myth. *Studies in the Anthropology of Visual Culture*, 5, 56–62.

Tuchman, G. (1978). *Making News: A Study in the Construction of Reality*. New York: Free Press.

Turow, J. (1983). Local television: producing soft news. *Journal of Communication, 33,* 111–123.

Wallis, R. & Baran, S. J. (1990). *The Known World of Broadcast News: International News and the Electronic Media.* New York: Routledge.

Walters, L. M. & Hornig, S. (1993). Faces in the news: network television news coverage of Hurricane Hugo and the Loma Prieta Earthquake. *Journal of Broadcasting & Electronic Media, 37,* 219–232.

Watson, M. A. (1988). The golden age of the American television documentary. *Television Quarterly, 23,* 57-75.

Weiss, P. & Zuckerman, L. (1987). The shadow of a medium. *Columbia Journalism Review,* March/April, 33–39.

White, D. (1974). Television non-fiction as historical narrative. *Journal of Popular Culture, 7,* 928–933.

Wolf, N. (1993). Are opinions male? *The New Republic,* November 29, 20–26.

CHAPTER 11

MUSIC TELEVISION

Every now and then a TV series comes along that is so monumentally bad, so palpably derivative, so incredible that it beggars the mind. The last such show was Gilligan's Island. *Last night NBC topped that one with a numbing new half hour called* The Monkees.

—Bernie Harrison

This 1966 (p. A20) review of *The Monkees* by the Washington *Evening Star's* television critic suggests two things about music and television. First, the two had come together long before MTV and, second, this union is almost always unwelcomed by the critics.

Overview

After initial criticism, however, typically comes serious analysis (if not praise) as critics eventually see the product of this marriage as more than simply the sum of the parts—as a different genre of television in and of itself. We'll examine the beginnings of music on television and some early "rock videos." Then we'll discuss the emergence of MTV, the revolution in music video that it spawned, and the early criticism of this new form of television. Finally, we'll present examples of some contemporary analyses of music television that assume its aesthetic, economic and cultural importance. As Denisoff (1988, p. 1) wrote, "MTV is the third major breakthrough in music broad-

casting, the first being when Todd Storz gave birth to 'Top Forty' radio in 1955 and the second being the advent of 'free form' or 'progressive' rock at KMPK in San Francisco in 1967. The early broadcasting innovations molded the state of rock music exposure for nearly twenty years. Then came MTV."

Music on Television

Music and moving visuals have been paired ever since the latter existed. The very first silent films, as early as 1895, were accompanied by piano or organ music and later silent films sometimes would enjoy full orchestral accompaniment. Sound movies were introduced to the public in the Twenties and, as might be expected, music was featured—what better sound to use to show off the potential of this development. But with very few exceptions, the music came *after* the pictures. Shore (1984, p. 20) writes, "Rock videos as we know them represent a break with the long history of music and visuals. Generally speaking, until recently, music for opera, musical theatre, movie musicals, and film soundtracks, was created *after* or at best concurrently with, the story and visuals. It was not until rock 'concept' videos came along that the story and visuals were created after, and as a complement to, the music."

With sound still subordinate to pictures, music easily made the move from radio to television. What worked on the older medium was sure to work even better on the new: musical performers were not only heard, but shown performing on a host of variety and popular music programs. Some of the earliest were *Face the Music, Your Hit Parade, Upbeat,* and *The Big Record. The Big Record* was the first television program to showcase rock and roll acts, although those presented tended to be safe, adult-approved, middle-of-the-road teen idols. It survived until 1958.

By this time, though, serious anti-establishment rock, people like Elvis Presley, Buddy Holly, Bill Haley and the Comets, and Jerry Lee Lewis, had grabbed kids' attention. However, raucous rock and mainstream television were not yet a good match. Every time Elvis or Jerry Lee would appear on the small screen, adults from parents to church leaders would cry that this "jungle music" was the first step toward damnation. Despite the fact that the rock performers of the time were uniformly white, the fear of race was never far from the surface (Kaplan, 1987). Television, though, could not ignore this youth music (it meant too much money), so it attempted to tame it. Ed Sullivan's waist-up-only broadcast of Elvis "the Pelvis" is the most famous early example. There were countless others, including having neat, establishment-looking young ladies and gentlemen sing smarmy versions of the rockers' hits.

And then there was *American Bandstand,* first aired locally in Philadelphia in 1952 and then moving to ABC in 1957 with its new young host, Dick Clark. This program, primarily a dance show that featured an occasional artist lip-synching his or her latest hit, was also squeaky-clean and adult sanctioned (even to-

day, compare it to the not particularly outrageous *Soul Train*). The "British Invasion" of the mid-Sixties, though, turned even more kids on to rock; and ABC in 1964 premiered its copy of the BBC's *Ready Steady Go!*, calling it *Shindig!* This was a music program (not a dance show) and presented hip artists (Sam Cooke and the Everly Brothers were on the premiere) and hip regulars like the Righteous Brothers and Bobby Sherman. It was such a hit that the network expanded it from 30 to 60 minutes a show and even aired it twice a week. NBC took notice, and in 1965 presented its own hour-long *Hullabaloo,* complete with minimally-clad go-go girls dancin' up a storm in cages suspended above the set.

Shore (1984) points to the existence of these television programs (and two other ABC shows, Clark's daytime *Where the Action Is* and *Malibu U*) as the impetus for the making of the first promotional rock films: "bands began making promotional films to be sent to the TV shows whenever they were too busy or too far from the studio to make a personal appearance. American TV, more rooted in the straight performance idea, rarely, if ever, showed them. British and European rock shows did" (p. 30).

The Monkees, so loathed by critic Harrison, is also important in music television's transformation from straight performance to concept videos. Yes, it was a rip-off of the Beatle's *Hard Day's Night* and yes, the "band members" were not musicians, but this was not a program that presented artists making (or lip synching) their music for an audience, this was a show in which "the story and visuals were created after, and as a complement to, the music."

Then Came MTV

Despite appearances today, rock is supposed to be rebellious music (Frith, 1981). Music on television in the Seventies meant *Don Kirshner's Rock Concert* and Wolfman Jack's *Midnight Special.* However, music on the big screen (at the movies) did stay truer to those rebellious values: *Easy Rider* where rock music *is* the narrator; *Tommy* the pin-ball wizard; the Band's *Last Waltz* (directed by Martin Scorsese); and Led Zeppelin's *The Song Remains the Same*. No lip synching and no string sections. It was rock music and rock images for rock fans, fans who were having their visual as well as their aural expectations met.

The only problem was that rock in general was becoming dull and predictable. Rock critic Denisoff (1988) labeled 1979 "the great depression" of the rock music industry. "A form of 'catch-22' began to plague the recording industry. Sluggish sales meant less money to spend on advertising new releases, and the absence of advertising helped ensure low sales figures" (Lewis, 1990, pp. 22–23).

Enter MTV founder Bob Pittman, a one-time program director for NBC's owned-and-operated FM radio stations. Pittman envisioned a cable television music channel as not only an advertising medium, but as an aid to the music industry, serving it in a number of ways (from Wolfe, 1983, p. 42):

1. Claiming that cable was not serving the 12 to 34 year old audience, he formatted MTV to attract this important record-buying demographic group.

2. Arguing that "the only sure-fire way to break in new acts is through TV," Pittman promised to "expose a whole new genre of artists" by committing MTV to new music, meaning music by new acts. He saw MTV as the equivalent of a national radio network.

3. The result, he reasoned, would be that in building interest in the music that appeared on MTV, the channel would benefit record companies, record stores, and local radio stations that carried that music.

In spite of some resistance from a few labels, it was not difficult to persuade the record companies that in exchange for the video clips provided to MTV for free, they would be receiving millions of dollars of free advertising

on a 24-hour a day, 365 day a year contemporary medium that was far more efficient than concert tours and radio for promoting their releases.

On August 1, 1981 MTV began its very first telecast with the Buggles' *Video Killed the Radio Star*. And while there is some disagreement on the nature of MTV's impact on radio, there is no question that it helped salvage the troubled music business. The record companies certainly did want their MTV.

Between 1979 and MTV's premiere, record sales were down 40% industry-wide. Yet within two months of the channel's opening, *Billboard* was able to report, "Does video music on cable tv sell records and tapes? The early returns on MTV, the 24-hour stereo cable music channel from Warner Amex...suggest strongly that it does. A spotcheck of record retailers in such markets as Tulsa, Syracuse, Des Moines and Wichita—all markets with relatively high pay tv/cable penetration that have added MTV—indicates that the new Warner concept has an impact on album purchases" (McCullaugh, 1981, p. 1). That same publication, two years later, quoted a buyer for several big record stores, "MTV and other music programs have been very helpful in opening up a lot of record sales to groups who wouldn't ordinarily get sales—especially new wave groups....It adds excitement to the big acts as well" (Golden, 1983, p. 28). The New York *Times* enthused, "Nothing has rekindled interest in pop as much as music video" (Parales, 1983, p. 13C).

As suggested above, however, not all saw MTV's benefit to radio. *Billboard* agreed with Pittman, "It leads the local radio stations to move more adventurous programming on the air" (Golden, 1983, p. 28). Pittman himself believed that radio had pretty much abandoned young rock fans in favor of the non-record-buying Album Oriented Rock (AOR) and "oldies" station crowd (Wolfe, 1983). But many radio programmers saw differently: One radio manager in a *Billboard* guest editorial (Paiva, 1983, p. 10) argued that "The money spent on rock videos goes to help support radio's direct competition, cable video, and it comes right out of radio. Radio is being paralyzed by the lessening of available advertising dollars (when) record companies pour money into a competing medium." Another radio executive was quoted, "MTV is blatantly robbing AOR radio of its audience, and programmers who don't recognize it are just naive" (Sacks, 1983, p. 66).

Within three years, MTV was in 24.2 million homes and carried on 2,900 cable systems. In 1982 it earned advertising revenues of $7 million. Two years later, in 1984, it took in over $50 million. The "MTV style" quickly spread to other television genres, changing the look of commercials and even the news. Great for the record industry, a boon to record stores, a new outlet for new music, good for radio (maybe, maybe not), but what about the music itself? It was not long before critics began to question the logic of having rock (the rebellious voice of youth) promoted on a commercial channel through the use of what amounted to little more than three minute long, very sophisticated commercials. The obvious issue became the impact of the (commercial) visual on the sound.

Selling Out?

In 1983 *Rolling Stone's* Steven Levy authored a long essay entitled, "Ad Nauseam: How MTV Sells Out Rock & Roll." Writing, "MTV is inescapable. Even if you have never watched it, its catalytic effect on the rock industry has probably affected what songs you hear, maybe what records you buy. And its significance goes deeper. MTV is a stunning paradigm for our time and may be a heady portent for our future" (p. 33). He proceeded to captured the essence of the many criticisms of the new channel (and by extension, the new form of television):

1. **The loss of community.** Rock has always been young people's music, the expression of their values and the rejection of their parents'. The music that became popular was their music. Pittman himself explained the change to Levy, "In the Sixties, politics and music fused. But there are no more political statements. The only thing rock fans have in common is the music, that's the coalition that MTV has gathered" (p. 78). But many critics argued that the artificiality of MTV's market research-based play list even made talk of a common music "coalition" seem hollow. "We believe (MTV) was the most researched channel in history," one of its executives boasted to Levy (p. 33). The channel's survey researchers still make over 5,000 phone calls a week. The problem, say the critics, is not research *per se*, but that factors *other than the music* itself are shaping rock and roll.

2. **Changing definitions of quality**. What happens when rock and roll is replaced by commercials? Must artists and bands look good rather than sound good? An RCA Records vice-president told *Time*, "Personal appearance has always been a factor, but since the advent of videos it has become crucial." Another executive from CBS Records said, "Cyndi Lauper had the vocals as well as the visuals, or she wouldn't have been signed" (both in Cocks, 1983, p. 62). Could a potentially great band with something to say in its music be denied its "shot" because of bad advertising, that is, an unattractive video? Could mediocre acts become stars and therefore shape rock because of good advertising, that is, a great video? Would Bob Dylan have made it in the MTV age? Joe Cocker? Lou Reed? Explain Adam Ant and Milli Vanilli. Levy tried. He wrote, MTV's "purpose was not to provide the best, most challenging music possible, but to ensnare the passions of Americans who fit certain demographic or, as Pittman puts it, 'psychographic' requirements—young people who had money and the inclination to buy things like records, candy bars, video games, beer and pimple cream" (p. 34).

3. **Racist and sexist programming.** What happens to those who don't fit the pre-

ferred psychographic? They get ignored or they get marginalized. Several studies of MTV (e.g., Brown & Campbell, 1986) scientifically demonstrated what was plain to the eye: African-Americans were invisible and women were denigrated, dehumanized and demeaned. Lewis wrote (1990, p. 72), "MTV created the conditions for cultural struggle by establishing a new, effective promotional device for music artists, industries and audiences and then representing the musicians, music, and music consumers in narrow and biased ways." The MTV answer was "It's the format," failing to understand that it should have been the music. For African American/Blacks, it meant that of the over 750 different videos shown in MTV's first year and a half, only about twenty featured African American/Black performers. When these artists would submit videos, they would be rejected as "not rock and roll." Yet Phil Collins' video of his re-make of the Supremes' *You Can't Hurry Love* apparently was rock and roll enough. For women it meant, according to former MTV producer Sue Steinberg, "violence to women. Women being pushed away. Spike heels and dark stockings. The emphasis on certain images contributes to the illusion of violence and sexism. They seem to see how far they can go. And it's getting worse" (Levy, 1983, p. 76).

4. **Erasing or blurring distinctions between cultures.** A recent echo of Levy's criticism of MTV comes from William Sonnega (1995). He argues that, in its drive to maximize international profits, MTV, while offering representations of numerous and different cultures, "morphs" or blends them into the homogeneous look or "culture" of MTV. He wrote, "The values, structure, and content of the culture MTV creates are deeply inscribed in European or North American models of multicultural representation rather than intercultural critique" (p. 51). In other words, MTV presents what *it* thinks other cultures are like, not what those cultures themselves think they are.

The Pictures in Our Heads

Although these complaints are still heard today, there have been two important changes in the music television scene since MTV's early days. First, MTV's success spawned numerous competitors and spin-offs, for example its own VH1; Black Entertainment Television's (BET) *Video Soul* and *Video Vibrations*; the Nashville Network (TNN); *Night Tracks*; HBO's *Video Jukebox*; and *Night Flight*. More outlets meant more variety and more variety meant that music (or video) of all types is now amply represented—if not by MTV, at least by music television. Second, MTV itself, in response to this competition and its attendant negative financial impact, broadened the scope its programming content. Cynics could argue that its *MTV Jams* is less about presenting contemporary African American/Black music and more about appealing to the primary buyers of rap music: White suburban teenagers. But the fact remains, MTV has expanded its playlist and the types of programs it airs, from *Beavis and Butt-head* to game shows to half-hour comedy.

Another criticism, initially raised concerning MTV but now offered of all music television, has to do with the pictures in our heads. Critics argue that merger of picture and sound robs listeners of the freedom, even the ability, to construct their own experiences and meanings from the music. Quick! *Addicted to Love* by Robert Palmer. What thought came to mind?

The problem, according to many critics is that "one of the signal virtues of music is its power to evoke deep, wordless sensations—effects that vary from one hearing to the next. Video decides what your fantasy will be" (Gelman *et al.*, 1983, p. 98). Music, especially rock as traditionally understood, is supposed to be personal, important, central to the creation of the listeners' experience not only of listening, but to the times in which that listening occurs. The association of someone else's vision or fantasy renders that meaning-making less personal, it makes it someone else's experience.

The counter argument is that the visual and the music are inseparable, that the experience of modern rock *is* the experience of both. Who would deny the power of Pearl Jam's *I'm Alive* or Nirvana's *All Apologies* or Billy Joel's *We Didn't Start the Fire*? The critical response, however, is that although these might seem like exceptions, most videos are created with the genre's commercial rather than artistic goals in mind, and the resulting experience is market-research based, shallow, anything but personally meaningful.

Music Television's Generic Characteristics

Regardless of where you stand in this debate, it is inarguable that music and television have come together to create a new form of television. And like the medium's other primary genres, it is characterized by its own grammar and style.

One way to examine that style is to categorize music video into its different stylistic or production categories. One obvious style of video is the *performance video*, basically a videotape reproduction of the artist or band playing for an audience. Red Hot Chili Peppers' *Under the Bridge* is a well known example.

Related to the straight performance video is the *personal address video* where the act performs directly to the camera and, visually, for the viewer. Robert Palmer's *Addicted to Love* and Salt 'N Pepa (with En Vogue's) *Whatta Man* are popular examples, as is virtually any video ever made by Prince.

There are also two types of videos that tell a story. These *narrative videos* can be divided into *performer as self* and *performer as actor*. In the former, the artist performs her or his music as part of the narrative, Bruce Springsteen, for example, playing out a concert date in *Dancing in Dark* and selecting an adoring fan to dance with him on stage or Snoop Doggy Dogg throwing a party with his friends in *Gin and Juice*. In the performer as actor, even if the artist

performs a song, he or she is a character in a story, not a musical performer, for example when Michael Jackson and his date are pursued by Zombies on a dark street in *Thriller*.

The final two styles of video are both *art videos*. One can be called *art as narrative* video. In these, video and computer techniques dominate the visuals, but at the same time support the song's lyrics. Michael Jackson's *Black and White*, with its famous face transformations, is one example. The other can be labeled *art as art video*. Here the visual techniques have nothing to do with the lyrics of the tune. Peter Gabriel is one artist who has mastered this form; his ground-breaking *Sledgehammer* is a classic of this form.

A last note on video styles; like all television today, the lines between categories are becoming increasingly thin as audiences become more sophisticated and demanding. The Springsteen video mentioned above is a good example. For all intents and purposes it is a performance video. He and his band are playing to a sold-out house and we see shots from the audience's point-of-view and from behind the performers. Camera people scurry about the stage to record the performance, the lights swirl, the smoke spreads. But it's really a piece of fiction. One scripted with actors.

Kaplan (1987) approached the music television genre from a variety of critical perspectives (e.g., narrative, gender and ideological analysis), in identifying five types of music video:

1. **Romantic videos** in which the images are "linked in a narrative chain that reproduces the song lines about love, loss, reunion. But it is a weak narrative chain, the main focus being on the emotions of loss or reunion rather than on the causes or effects of such loss" (p. 59). Toni Braxton's *I Shall Never Breathe Again* and Guns and Roses' *Since I Don't Have You* are obvious examples.

2. **Social conscious** videos make social issues their focus and tell stories that are in reaction against the "establishment." John

Cougar Mellancamp's *Authority Song* and the Stray Cats' *Look at that Cadillac* both question the powers-that-be.

3. **Nihilist video** usually features heavy metal bands, typically in concert, doing their best to shock the uninitiated; for example AC/DC's *For Those About to Rock, We Salute You*. The editing and camera motion are fast, sharp and jarring. Those nihilist videos which do not show bands in performance, for example Ozzy Osbourne's *Shot in the Dark*, present stories based in an alien, disorienting world. Either way, they are angry, iconoclastic, and/or challenging.

4. **Classical video** occurs in two forms. The first is "classic" in that it retains "the voyeuristic/fetishistic gaze toward woman as an object of desire" that feminist critics say is common in traditional Hollywood film. That is, its classic-ness comes from its reliance on the "classic rock" male ideology and perspective. David Lee Roth's *Just Like a Gigolo/I Ain't Got Nobody* even uses a Hollywood musical motif.

The second type of classical video is classic in that it replicates Hollywood's traditional genres, for example Jackson's *Thriller* is a mini-horror film.

5. **Post-modernist video** where uncertainty and self-reflexivity reign, or as Kaplan (p. 63) wrote, this type is characterized by

"its refusal to take a clear position vis-a-vis its images, its habit of hedging along the line of not communicating a clear signified....Each element of the text is undercut by others...[they] are disturbing in not manifesting a position from which they speak." She offers Motley Crue's *Too Young to Fall in Love* as an example and gives this explanation:

The trio—bizarrely dressed in tight leather pants, studded leather straps over bare chests, leather boots, and wearing their hair very long and straggly—(is) involved in a James Bond-style oriental crime plot. With much macho maneuvering and improbable sword play, they rescue the beautiful young oriental girl from the clutches of her stolid fat captors. But it is impossible to tell whether or not this video intends to comment upon, and thus critique, the clichéd Bond conventions. Is it merely employing them for its own ends? Are we supposed to find interest in the contrast between the Bond mise-en-scene and the Motley Crue stars in their outlandish attire? Does the video merely want us to delight in the stars' wonderful bodies so highlighted by their clothes, and in their dazzling macho feats?

Kaplan reminds her readers that elements of these forms often intermingle, that certain types seem to be more prevalent at different times in the life of music video, and that like music television itself, these types develop and change.

FRY & FRY

The authors make it very clear at the outset that their goal is to combine genre analysis and audience orientation as a device to frame their structural analysis of music videos. They explicitly make the point that structural analyses should not be conducted independent of creator and reader concerns. Do you agree with this argument or not? Why?

At one point they write, "characteristics within the text encourage certain interpretations and discourage others." In what earlier essay was this same argument offered? What significance does it hold for the critic?

Fry and Fry use two other genres (drama and commercials) to help support their premise. Do you find this helpful or confusing? How might they have structured their argument using music video alone?

What is meant by "montage structures?" By "denotation?"

These authors conclude their analysis with a discussion of the relationship between "habitual use" of television texts and genre. What is that relationship? Do you find their arguments here persuasive? What does this interaction between audience's use of television content and genre have to do with structuralism? Do you feel that this relationship may exist for some genres more than others?

Assuming that the meaning of a film or television program resides within the text, genre critics typically have examined textual forms in insolation from the process of textual production and audience decoding and interpretation. Advancing the concept of genre, however, requires a critic both to position the concept within the larger concerns of mass communication research and to define the

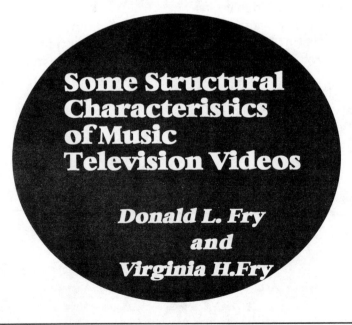

Some Structural Characteristics of Music Television Videos

Donald L. Fry
and
Virginia H. Fry

characteristics of mediated content which allow for the differentiation among textual forms. This essay will not only offer a theoretical link between genre and audience interpretation, but also propose a structural analysis of television texts which isolates generic characteristics important in the audience member's encounter with them.

To reconceptualize

Donald L. Fry is an Assistant Professor of Mass Communication at Emerson College in Boston, MA 02116. Virginia Fry is an Assistant Professor of Communication at Babson College in Babson Park (Wellesley), MA 02157-0901.

An early version of this paper was presented at the Speech Communication Association Convention in Chicago, 1984.

Reprinted with permission of the Southern States Communication Association.

genre as an interaction between text and audience members requires beginning with the function the text serves for them. Elsewhere we have argued that media texts form a matrix of potential meanings and that audience members draw from textual and nontextual sources in selecting a meaning or set of meanings from the matrix.[1] Meaning, then, is less a characteristic of the text *per se* than of the signification processes of audience members. This perspective explains audience interpretations which vary dramatically from those intended by the text's encoder.[2] While the audience is active in the signification process, the text establishes boundaries within which the audience may function. Clearly, characteristics within the text encourage certain interpretations and discourage others.

These textual characteristics contain the significance of genre. Eco has contended that audience members cannot realize the full potential of a media text but, instead, must draw selectively from socially stored constructs to signify the text.[3] In other words, audience members produce interpretations of texts based on their stored social knowledge which leads them to connect particular textual characteristics with certain predictable interpretations. Tex-

tual characteristics "open up" for consideration certain dimensions of the textual potentiality while closing off other aspects. The skillful encoder can develop texts which encourage some interpretations, while discouraging others. Elsewhere Eco has argued that denotative and connotative markers within the text function to guide audience interpretation toward a preferred meaning.[4] Since Eco's use of these concepts is somewhat different than many scholars, some elaboration is necessary.

When an audience member first encounters a media text, s/he initially recognizes its form (this is a music video, this is a soap opera, and so forth) and its characteristics (this is a Billy Idol video, this is The Edge of Night, and so forth) based on social knowledge about such texts. This "denotation" establishes the parameters for further inferences, or "connotations," about the meaning of the text. Connotations are, then, the audience members' inferences from and extensions of the initial and primary denotations. Though such inferences extend the denotation, the denotative identification of the text always guides the signification process.[5]

From this theoretical perspective, a genre is a denotative marker which informs the audience member about the form and character-

ization of the text. Thus, a text's genre plays a significant part in its interpretation. From this perspective, genre is a focal point in an interactionist approach to the study of mass communication. We will return to this issue later when we discuss some implications of generic structure on the audience/text interactions.

To integrate the concept of genre into an interactionist perspective towards mass communication, we must determine genre categories by delineating structural characteristics of various media texts. Other research has demonstrated the importance of the text's structure on the interpretation process. Kress and Hodge, for example, have argued that the grammatical structure of texts is significant in interpreting them because the structural characteristics carry embedded assumptions about the world which structure audience perceptions. While grammatical structures function as connotative not denotative markers, Kress and Hodge highlight the importance of textual structures in interpretation.

Porter has suggested expropriating the concept of montage to delineate among various forms of television programming.[6] Though montage analyses have been used in various forms to discuss the structural characteristics of visual

---

1. Donald Fry and Virginia Fry, "A Semiotic Model for the Study of Mass Communication," in *Communication Yearbook 9*, ed. M. McLaughlin (Beverly Hills: Sage Publications, 1985) 443–462.

2. Umberto Eco, "Towards A Semiotic Inquiry into the Television Message," in *Working Papers in Cultural Studies,* No. 3 (1972) 105; also see Stuart Hall, "Encoding/decoding," in *Culture, Media, Language: Working Papers in Cultural Studies,* ed. Stuart Hall, D. Hobson, A. Lowe, and P. Willis (London: Hutchinson and Co. Publishers, 1981) for a discussion of a similar issue.

3. Umberto Eco, *The Role of the Reader,* 1st Midland Book ed. (Bloomington: Indiana University Press, 1979) 23.

4. Umberto Eco, *A Theory of Semiotics,* 1st Midland Book ed. (Bloomington: Indiana University Press, 1976) 84–85.

5. Stuart Hall, Ian Connell, and Lidia Curti, "The Unity of Current Affairs Television," *Working Papers in Cultural Studies,* No. 9 (1976); and Hall, "Encoding/decoding," discuss at some length the issue of intended meaning and intended audience.

6. Michael Porter, "*The Grande Syntagmatique:* A Methodology for Analysis of Montage Structures of Television Narratives," *The Southern Speech Communication Journal,* 47 (1982) 330–341; Michael Porter, "Applying Semiotics to the Study of Prime Time Television Programs," *Journal of Broadcasting,* 27 (1983) 69–75.

images in film,[7] with the exception of Porter's work they rarely have been applied to television. The systematic use of montage to determine generic categories in television programming has potential for several reasons. First, such an approach allows the critic to focus on the visual component of the medium which is central in television. Second, and more importantly, because montage is a function of structural relationships within the text, it is a definable denotative marker which allows for the differentiation among generic forms.

We draw our conception of montage from Eco's general definition which identifies montage as one of many codes and subcodes which systematically organize television messages. "Codes" are defined as systems of conventions or rules which couple signs and semantic units to establish the structural organization of both. Television messages have three basic codes: iconic, linguistic, and sound. Dependent subcodes derive from each code. Iconic codes are visual and, thus, montages are one of their subcodes. Eco contends that the montage subcode "sets combinatory rules for the image . . . both in the composition of the shots and in their sequence."[8]

We will apply Porter's adaptation of montage analysis to define television genres to assess whether this approach can increase our understanding of genre within the interactional orientation outlined above. In the following analysis, the montage typology developed by Metz[9] and the metric montage defined by Eisenstein[10] will be used to analyze three types of television texts: Music Television videos, commercial advertisements, and standard prime time dramas. If, as Porter has suggested, montage is a useful means of defining television genres, clear differences should appear across these different forms.

Method

A sample of music videos was selected from those broadcast on the MTV cable channel. A VCR was set to record MTV programming for fifteen minutes every two hours for a forty-eight hour period. After non-video material (advertisements, etc.), duplicated videos, and partially recorded videos were excluded, a sample of fifty-seven was available for analysis.[11] The sample of thirty-six advertisements was drawn from prime time commercial television using a similar technique. Data on prime-time

dramas were drawn from Porter's results.[12]

Two trained coders coded the montage structures (see below) in each video and advertisement. In cases of coder disagreement, a third coder was used. Total agreement on the video montage structures occurred in 82.5% of the cases; total agreement on the number of shots per video occurred in 91.2% of the cases. Each video was also timed to permit the calculation of the metric montage structure for each. Total agreement of advertisement montage structures occurred in 95.1% of the cases; total agreement on the number of shots per ad occurred in 98% of the cases.

The videos and advertisements were coded and evaluated through the use of two types of montage structures. The first is based on the typology developed by Metz.[13] His cascading chart progressively breaks down autonomous film segments into their independent constituent units. The primary basis for this division centers on the visual treatment of temporal and spatial relationships. The first discrimination occurs between autonomous shots, which are constituted by a single shot, and syntagmas, which are constituted by more than one shot (see Figure 1). The

7. See for example Christien Metz, *Film Language: A Semiotic of the Cinema,* trans. M. Taylor (New York: Oxford University Press, 1974); R. Arnheim, *Film as Art* (Berkeley: University of California Press, 1957); and Sergi Eisenstein, *Film Forms* (New York: Harcourt Brace Jovanovich, Inc., 1949).

8. Eco, "Towards a Semiotic Inquiry," 113.

9. Metz, *Film Language,* 148.

10. Eisenstein, *Film Forms.*

11. The following is a list of the fifty-seven videos analyzed: Blind Vision, Modern Love, Lawyers in Love, It's Inevitable, Missed Again, Everyday I Write the Book, Church of the Poison Mind, Don't Pay the Ferryman, Twisting By the Pool, She Blinded Me With Science, Love To Two Times, Hotel California, Slipping Away, Love Is A Stranger, One Thing Leads To Another, Stand Or Fall, Sara, Wishing, Fool For The City, Baby's In The Mountains, Rock It, Practicing First Aid, Heart & Soul, Dancing With Myself, I'm Still Standing, Hot Rockin, Don't Forget To Dance, Screaming In The Night, Lucky Ones, Pop Music, Our House, Burning Up, Dr. Hekyll & and Mr. Jive, My Town, I Melt With You, Suddenly Last Summer, Pass The Deutchie, Something To Grab For, Synchronicity II, Brass In Pocket, 1999, Take Another Picture, All Night Long, Come On Feel The Noise, If I Had You Back, Tom Sawyer, Major Tom, Maniac, True, Lonely Is The Night, Sexy & 17, Burn Down The House, Prime Time, Red Red Wine, and Sharp Dressed Man.

12. Porter, "Applying Semiotics."

13. Metz, *Film Language,* 148.

autonomous shots are one of the eight segments in the typology. Syntagmas are subdivided into achronological (undefined temporal and spatial relationships) and chronological (defined temporal and spatial relationships) syntagmas. Achronological syntagmas are divided further into parallel and bracket syntagmas, the second and third segments of the typology. Parallel syntagmas weave together, normally for symbolic impact, two or more alternating motifs which have no direct temporal or spatial relationship. A commercial example is the Snickers candy bar advertisement which juxtaposes someone talking about how the candy bar satisfies hunger with visual images of the candy bar itself. Because no clear temporal or spatial relationship exists between the two visual images, the advertisement employs a parallel syntagma. Bracket syntagmas provide samples of an event or situation which are meant to represent that which is typical, without establishing clear temporal or spatial links between the sampled aspects. The Levis' 501 jeans commercials depicting a series of temporally and spatially unrelated images displaying the type of people who wear Levis' jeans is a good example. Chronological syntagmas are further subdivided into descriptive and narrative syntagmas. Descriptive syntagmas, the fourth element of the typology, are clusters of shots with clear temporal and/or spatial relationships serving only to describe an environmental context. The music video "My Town" which visually describes the return of the musician to his home town through spatially and temporally connected images of his drive into the town is a clear case. Narrative syntagmas are segments which temporally and spatially propel a narrative.

Narrative syntagmas subdivide into alternate syntagmas and linear narratives. Alternate syntagmas, the fifth in the typology, interweave several distinct temporal progressions to create the impression of simultaneity of occurrences (e.g. shots of the pursued and shots of the pursuer in a chase sequence). Linear narratives are linear progressions of a single occurrence. Such narratives are divided into scenes, a continuous flow of action without temporal or spatial breaks, and sequences, discontinuous temporal or spatial ordering. Scenes are the sixth type of segment. Finally, sequences are subdivided into episodic and ordinary sequences, the last two segments of the typology. Episodic sequences string together brief scenes, usually separated by optical devices such as dissolves or

Figure 1
Metz's Typology of Autonomous Film Segments

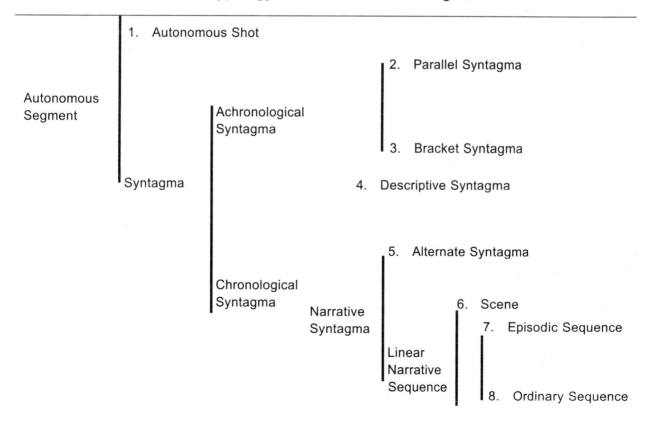

fades, which have a strict chronological progression. Ordinary sequences are constituted by unorganized temporal discontinuity, that is, events in the temporal progression are excluded so that moments having no bearing on the plot can be eliminated. An example is a shot of a character at the bottom of a stairs followed immediately by a shot of the character at the top of the stairs.

The remaining montage structure arises from that posited by Eisenstein. A metric montage is constituted by the length of shots across the film or video. This montage structure can be used to display the visual pacing of the text.

Results

The metric montage provided clear distinctions among the three types of television texts. Porter reported an average shots per minute of 9.95 (in fact, the findings ranged from a low of 7.5 to a high of 12.6),[14] which was noticeably lower than the music videos and commercials (see Table 1). Shots per minute for music videos averaged 19.94; commercial advertisements had the highest shots per minute, averaging 28.33.

Some shots-per-minute differences existed among the videos in our sample. Those differences suggested the possibility of three distinct definable types, or sub-genres, of music videos: concert, conceptual, and combinational. The distinction among these three types was based on whether the visual aspects focused (1) on the concert performance of the singer or group, (2) on conceptual images unrelated to the actual performance of the music, or (3) on a combination of concert and conceptual images. Concert videos had an average shots per minute of 17.91, conceptual videos averaged 20.38, and combination videos averaged 22.90. While shots per minute variations made the visual pacing of concert videos more like that of drama, conceptual and combinational videos were more like commercials. Despite these differences, however,

certain things were clear. First, as one moves from television drama through music videos to commercials, the visual pacing increased; and, second, in terms of visual pacing, music videos and commercials were more similar than either was with drama.

Application of Metz' typology provided two types of data. First, simply assessing the total number of independent segments which appear in a video or a commercial (this data was not readily accessible through Porter's research) was possible. The average number of independent segments for music videos was 2.74, with concert videos averaging 1.2 and conceptual videos averaging 3.86. While the number of segments ranged as high as eight, a relatively large percentage of videos (42%) was constituted by only one segment. In comparison, commercials averaged 1.48 segments each. In fact, though these results were somewhat less valuable than the more detailed analysis below, they do demonstrate ef-

TABLE 1

Montage Structures by Commercials, Music Video Type, and Television Drama

	Mean Montage Segments	Mean Shots per Minute	N
MTV	2.74	19.94	57
Concert	1.20	17.91	15
Combination	1.79	22.90	14
Conceptual	3.86	20.38	28
Commercials	1.45	28.33	36
Television			
Drama	*	9.95	18

* Shots per minute for television dramas were calculated from data reported by Porter. Number of segments per program has not been reproduced for television drama due to the great disparity of program length when compared to commercials or music videos.

14.   Porter, "Applying Semiotics," 73.

fectively the relatively high visual complexity of conceptual videos.

In analyzing the types of autonomous segments which constituted the three types of television texts, a relatively clear pattern emerged. Porter found a dominance of scenes (continuous flow of action without temporal or spatial breaks) in the eighteen dramatic episodes he analyzed.[15] Autonomous shots and alternate syntagmas made up most of the small remaining percentage (see Table 2). Music videos were somewhat similar to television drama: 51% of the segments were scenes, but other segment types appeared with great frequency. Parallel syntagmas made up 18% of the total segments in the videos. Porter reported no instances of this segment in television dramas. Alternate syntagmas followed with 11% of the total. Commercials demonstrated the widest range of segments. Bracket syntagmas (samples of an event meant to represent that which is typical) were the most frequently appearing segments, making up 23.3% of the to-

tal. Scenes constituted 20% of the total segments with parallel syntagmas and autonomous shots at approximately 15%.

Two distinct montage characteristics differentiated among the three types of texts: scenes and achronological syntagmas. The relative importance of scene varied from dominant in drama, to moderately important in music videos, to unimportant in advertisements. Though achronological syntagmas (parallel and bracket syntagmas) did not appear in television drams, this structure played an important role for both music videos (25% of total segments) and advertisements (39.3% of total segments). The subgenre of music videos varied along these lines as well. Concert videos were dominated by scenes and rarely used other syntagmas. Both conceptual and combinational forms were more likely to manifest achronological syntagmas, although scene also played some role in their visual structure. The pronounced presence of achronological syntagmas in both music videos

and commercials indicated that both tended to handle time and space in similar visual ways, a tendency which further differentiated these two genres from television drama.

Discussion

The study of genre can become central in exploring the creation of meaning by audience members, but only if genre is tied to the signification process, a process which encompasses both the text and audience member. We have argued that a necessary part of understanding the interaction between media texts and audience members is the process of denotation.[16] One approach of studying denotation is to isolate structural characteristics in media messages which affect the signification process of audience members. Both the metric montage and Metz's typology differentiate among the three textual forms solely on the basis of their denotative visual characteristics.

TABLE 2

Percentage of Metz's Montage Types by MTV Videos, Commercials and Televised Drama*

	Drama	MTV	Commercial
Scene	76%	51%	20%
Parallel Syntagma	0%	18%	16%
Bracket Syntagma	0%	7%	23.3%
Autonomous Shot	11%	6%	16.6%
Alternate Syntagma	8.5%	11%	6.6%
Descriptive Syntagma	0%	1%	10%
Ordinary Sequence	4%	5%	6.6%
Episodic Sequence	0%	1%	0%

* The percentages for television drama were calculated from results presented by Porter.

15. Porter, "Applying Semiotics," 72.

16. Fry and Fry, "A Semiotic Model"; see also Jenny Nelson, "Soaps/Sitcoms: Television Genre as Situated Discourse," in *Semiotics 1984,* ed. John Deely (Lanham, Maryland and London, England: University Press of America, Inc., 1985). 137-145.

The analyses we present place television drama and commercial advertisements at polar extremes based on their denotative visual characteristics. Music videos fall somewhere between these two. In essence, music videos are hybrids, an amalgam of the distinguishing characteristics of both forms. While some videos are similar to dramas and some are much more like advertisements, as a group their distinctiveness arises from their hybrid nature. Their power may lie in that fact. Although they are neither drama nor advertisement, when taken together, the three music video sub-genres present viewers with some of the structural characteristics of both. That blend constitutes their distinctiveness as a genre.

The hybrid structural characteristics of music videos can be accounted for, in part, by the fact that they perform the functions of both dramatic and commercial genres. Music videos serve both an entertainment and promotional function. Viewers recognize advertisements, as a genre, as overtly selling a consumable product. The product logo is prominently displayed and product features and benefits are highlighted. Music videos do much the same thing in a very similar way. This function explains the use of achronological syntagmas, particularly in conceptual and combinational videos. Both parallel and bracket syntagmas effectively highlight the performers by juxtaposing them with some style (as in a particular mode of dress such as Michael Jackson's glove) or activity. Often this juxtaposition links performances and activities which are unconnected either temporally or spatially. The video is not "telling a story" in the traditional narrative form; instead, the video presents completed images which are positioned visually to assert that

this musical group stands for, or represents, this style of dress or has this orientation towards women, parents, etc. A video displays a signer's or group's logo (in this case the person's or group's style of dress). Commercial advertisements also often use this technique. The Levis' 501 jeans commercials display a series of apparently unrelated people walking or dancing in an urban area. These temporally and spatially distinct images suggest the connection between a style of behavior and the wearing of Levis' jeans.

On the other hand, the function of television drama is distinctly different. These programs neither intend to promote a particular actor or group of actors (at least as a product to be purchased) nor attempt to sell a particular consumable item. Instead, they aim to engage the audience and hold its attention over a determined period of time. A more common visual form, the scene, effectively serves this function. The dominance of scene in concert videos suggests this primary entertainment functioning.

At the beginning we suggested the possibility of formulating a theoretical link between genre and audience interpretation. We presented a speculative discussion which made the audience's recognition and extension of denotative markers crucial. Textual identifiers (denotative markers) become important only if we reason that audience members are capable of recognizing and extending those markers in interpretation. The montage structures which differentiate among genre are textual identifiers which allow audience members to differentiate among generic forms. Non-textual factors, of course, also affect an audience member's interpretation of genre. Although most audience members probably agree

in classifying various messages as belonging to a particular genre based on their recognition of key distinguishing denotative structures, not all of them will necessarily attribute the same meaning or significance to various genres. While one viewer may conclude that music videos are meaningless nonsense (based on the conceptual video's employment of achronological syntagmas), another viewer may be engaged by the video's lack of linear structure. While the audience's familiarity with repetitive and conventional textual forms is the basis for genre identification, non-textual factors certainly influence the meaning such texts will hold for particular audience members.

Although the montage structures we have isolated differentiate among the three television texts, montage alone may not be sufficient to define various genres. Of the three primary codes (linguistic, sound and iconic) suggested by Eco,[17] montage structures focus on the iconic. Subsequent research must integrate the visual structures of a text with its other dominant codes. One way to approach that task would be to analyze the correspondence among the various dominant codes, rather than focusing only on the linguistic, the sound or, as in this study, on the visual. As only one example, close observation reveals that music videos have a careful correspondence between the visual pacing (as measured by the metric montage) and the rhythm of the music. This correspondence makes these videos distinct, although the technique is emerging in commercial advertisements.

In conclusion, we would like to return to an issue raised earlier in the essay. Genre can and should be considered a central part of the signification process functioning in

---

17.   Eco, "Towards a Semiotic Inquiry," III.

mass communication. Audience expectations for certain television genres will set parameters for meanings which audience members will create. An audience member's reaction to a music video probably will be definably different from a reaction to television drama. Certainly, although many factors contribute to this difference, one factor is the expectation an audience member has for a particular genre.

Not only does genre contribute to the specific meaning an audience member creates from a media text, but it plays a significant role in determining our habitual monitoring of the media. Often we do not desire particular pieces of information as we use the media. In some cases our use of media may have little to do with the content *per se*.[18] Our expectations about particular genres contribute to our ready and habitual use of media texts to gratify various needs. The audience member's expectations also allow him/her to monitor the media in a relatively low-involved state. As the audience develops expectations for a particular genre, paying close attention becomes less and less important. Because the structural characteristics become predictable, only limited attention is necessary to follow the text. This habitual reaction to textual genres can contribute to the low-involvement effects of advertisements posited by Krugman.[19]

18. For one of many discussions of this issue see *The Uses of Mass Communication* ed. Jay Blumler and Elihu Katz (Beverly Hills: Sage Publications, 1974).

19. Herbert Krugman, "The Impact of Television Advertising: Learning Without Involvement," *Public Opinion Quarterly,* 29 (1965) 349–356.

LELAND

Critic Leland takes on the role of illuminator/teacher and uses the MTV program *Beavis and Butt-head* as the departure point for an examination of not only the youth-oriented music network, but of youth-oriented television programming in general. He is naturally drawn into a form of academic sociological criticism as he invokes the state of contemporary education, differing generational levels of achievement, and even the economy to support his thesis.

Do you agree with his argument that for a certain large segment of the audience (primarily the "Generation X" viewers), "stupidity, served up as knowing intelligence, has become the next best thing to smarts?" What does he mean by this? Can you offer television examples other than those he mentions that support this view?

Incidental to his primary thesis but still present in this essay are discussions of "television commenting on television," (called "intertextuality," see Chapter 5) and of texts containing multiple layers of meaning. Many critics see these as recent developments in television. What audience and medium factors contribute to these phenomena? Do you see them as steps forward or retrenchment for television content?

Critic Leland obviously believes that television has a significant impact on its viewers. The essay's title is one hint and the attention he devotes to the apparently easy to dismiss *Beavis and Butt-head, The Simpsons, Married . . . with Children* and the like is another. Do you think he has sufficiently demonstrated the possibility of television effects? Do you feel that criticism of this type simply accepts the presence of effects as a given? Do you accept that link? Why or why not?

It is television at its most redeeming. A whale swims gracefully across the screen as the narrator mourns its imminent destruction. Watching in their living room, two boys, about 14, are visibly moved. Their eyes widen, their nostrils twitch uncomfortably. One boy's lips stiffen around his wire braces. The only hope, the narrator says, "is that perhaps the young people of today will grow up more caring, more understanding, more sensitive to the very special needs of the creatures of the earth." It is rich moment, ripe with television's power to make remote events movingly immediate. The boys can watch idly no longer. Finally one turns to the other and asks, "Uh, did you fart?"

The boys are Beavis and Butt-head, two animated miscreants whose adventures at the low end of the food chain are currently the most popular program on MTV. Caught in the ungainly nadir of adolescence, they are not nice boys. They torture animals, they harass girls and sniff paint thinner. They like to burn things. They have a really insidious laugh: *huh-huh huh-huh.* They are the spiritual descendants of the semi-sentient teens from "Wayne's World" and "Bill and Ted's Excellent Adventure," only dumber and meaner. The downward spiral of the living white male surely ends here: in

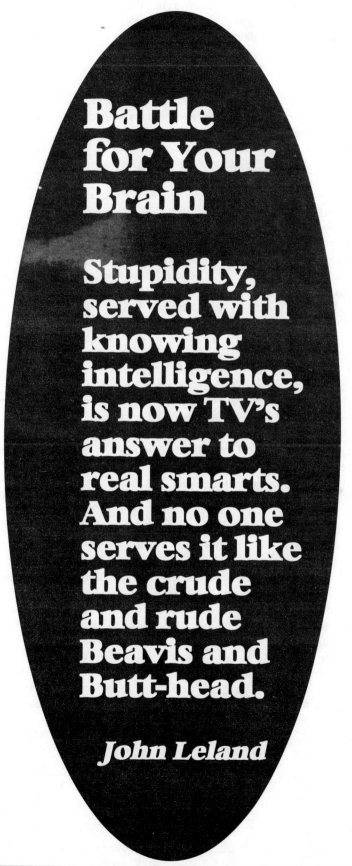

Battle for Your Brain

Stupidity, served with knowing intelligence, is now TV's answer to real smarts. And no one serves it like the crude and rude Beavis and Butt-head.

John Leland

a little pimple named Butt-head whose idea of an idea is, "Hey, Beavis, let's go over to Stuart's house and light one of his cat's butt."

For a generation reminded hourly of its diminished prospects, these losers have proven remarkably embraceable. "Why do I like 'Beavis and Butt-head'?" asks Warren Lutz, 26, a journalism major at San Francisco State. "You're asking me to think, dude." Created by beginner animator Mike Judge, 30, for a festival of "sick and twisted" cartoons last year, Beavis and Butt-head have become a trash phenomenon. T-shirts, hats, key rings, masks, buttons, calendars, dolls are all working their way to malls; a book, a comic book, a movie, a CD and a Christmas special are in the works. David Letterman drops a Beavis and Butt-head joke almost nightly; later this fall the pair will become a semiregular feature on his program. As their notoriety reached Fort Lewis College in Durango, Colo., archeology students have started calling Jim Judge, Mike's father, Dr. Butt-head. "Whenever any . . . 8- to 12-year-olds find out I'm related to Beavis and Butt-head," he says, "I become a god to them."

From *Newsweek*, Oct. 11, 1993. Newsweek, Inc. All rights reserved. Reprinted with permission.

Beavis and Butt-head, whose world divides into "things that suck" and "things that are cool," are clearly the new morons in town.

They are also part of a much wider TV phenomenon, one that drives not just stupid laughs but the front-page battle now being waged for control of Paramount Pictures (page 54). It is the battle to play road hog on the Information Highway . As cable technology continues to expand our range of viewing options, the old boundaries of propriety and decency no longer apply. Beavis and Butt-head join a growing crowd of characters who have found a magic formula: nothing cuts through the clutter like a slap of bracing crudity. Nothing stops a channel surfer like the word "sucks."

Stupidity, served with a knowing intelligence, has become the next best thing to smarts. Letterman's signature "Stupid Pet Tricks" bit, now 11 years running, introduced a new voice to television: ironic, self-aware, profoundly interested in the ingrained dumbness of the tube. Instead of dumbing down, it made smart comedy out of the process of dumbing down—and it clicked. Barry Diller successfully built Fox into the fourth network on a shockingly lumpen cartoon family, the Simpsons, and an even more lumpen real one, the Bundys of "Married . . . With Children." Nickelodeon's cartoon "The Ren & Stimpy Show," the highest-rated original series on cable, follows the scatological adventures of a Chihuahua and a cat, sometimes not getting much farther than the litter box. The network's new contender, "Rocko's Modern World," wallows down a similarly inspired low road. Its first episode, in which a home-shopping channel called "Lobot-o-shop" pitched items like tapeworm farms for kids, beat "Ren & Stimpy"in the ratings. And the widely loved and hated radio host Howard Stern has taken his act to

E! Entertainment Television. "There's a purity to [this] kind of ignorance," says "Beavis and Butt-head" writer David Felton, at 53 MTV's oldest staff member. "Going back to the basic point where thinking begins. And staying there."

But they are not just any losers, this lineage of losers. They are specifically our losers, totems of an age of decline and nonachievement. One in five people who graduated from college between 1984 and 1990 holds a job that doesn't require a college education. If this is not hard economic reality for a whole generation, it is psychological reality. Loser television has the sense to play along; it taps the anxiety in the culture and plays it back for laughs. Homer Simpson works in a nuclear power plant. Al Bundy sells shoes. Beavis and Butt-head work at Burger World and can't even visualize the good life. In one episode, as an act of community service, they get jobs in a hospital. Sucking on IV bags, planning to steal a cardiac patient's motorized cart, they agree: "It doesn't get any better than this, dude."

The shows also all share a common language. When "Beavis and Butt-head" producer John Andrews, 39, needed to put together a writing staff, he first called Letterman head writer Rob Burnett for suggestions. "Most of this stuff is done by over-educated guys who grew up reading Mad magazine, National Lampoon, and watching 'Animal House' and 'Saturday Night Live'," says Matt Groening, creator of the Simpsons. "Scripts are based on what comes out of the collective memory of the writers, which is mostly memories of sitting in front of a TV set growing up." More than just throwbacks to the intelligently dumb television of the Three Stooges and Ernie Kovacs, the current shows are broad immersions in pop culture, satirical and multitiered. They address an audience that can view reruns of

"Gilligan's Island" and "I Dream of Jeannie" half as camp, half as the fabric of shared experience. "The smarter you are, the more you see single events on different levels simultaneously," says Fernanda Moore, 25, who likes "The Simpsons," "Ren & Stimpy" and "Beavis and Butt-head." A doctoral candidate at Stanford, Moore is the daughter we all crave and perhaps fear. "Dumb people I know," she says, "aren't self-referential."

Of course, this is only one way to watch the shows. Lars Ulrich, drummer in the band Metallica, was delighted one day to spot Beavis wearing a Metallica T shirt. Yet he was also alarmed. "I would have to say—as little as I want to say it— that I think there are people like that. I'm not sure dumb is the right word. I would go more in the direction of the word ignorant." Either way, as the channels open up, the ship of fools is now sailing at full capacity.

At MTV's offices in New York last week, the ship was running through some rough waters. MTV from the inside is a Marshall McLuhan rec room, a place where precociously creative young people invent cool ways to frame ugly heavy-metal videos. In the production area of "Beavis and Butt-head," these young people had a problem. "I don't know," said the show's creator, Mike Judge, in a voice hauntingly close to Butt-head's (Judge does the voices for most of the characters). The staff was watching an unfinished episode in which Bill Clinton visits Beavis and Butt-head's high school, and something just didn't feel real. As MTV political reporter Tabitha Soren introduced the president to the assembly on screen, Judge's face just lost its air. "Do you really think she could hear [Butt-head] fart from across the gym?" he asked. It was a pressing question; the show was set to air in less than a week. The staff was hushed. Finally someone offered, "If it was a big one she could." Judge considered. "No way."

The fast success of the show, along with the rapid production pace, has been a shock to Judge. Since he moved to New York from Dallas in February, he says, he hasn't met anyone except the people he works with. His office at MTV is spare, the walls empty except for a few pictures of Beavis and Butt-head and a snapshot of his daughter, Julia, almost 2. In his locker is a stuffed Barney dinosaur, a bottle of Jack Daniel's and a Gap jacket. "You know what's weird?" he says, with a gentle Southwestern accent. "Every now and then I'll say, 'Well, that's pretty cool,' and I can't tell if that's something I would have said before or if I'm doing Butt-head." In a file on his desk, he keeps a drawing of a black Beavis and Butt-head, renamed Rufus and Tyrone. At the moment he has no plans for them. For all their anti-P.C. offensiveness, Beavis and Butt-head have yet to cross the line into race humor. "Actually," says Kimson Albert 22, one of four African-American artists on the show's staff, "the creator and producer are the most P.C. people."

Judge grew up in Albuquerque, N.M., by his own description "just the most awkward, miserable kid around." He played trumpet in the area youth symphony and competed on the swim team and made honor roll at St. Pius X High School. For kicks, he and his friends used to set fires, just to see how many they could keep going at once and still be able to stomp them out. Three years ago, after working at a couple of unhappy engineering jobs, Judge bought himself a $200 animation kit. His first short, "Office Space," aired on last month's season premiere of "Saturday Night Live." His third, completed in January 1992, introduced the characters Beavis and Butt-head. It was about torturing animals. He called it "Frog Baseball."

"I was a total animal lover," he says. "When I did the storyboard, I didn't want people to see what I was working on. I thought, 'I don't want to show this to anybody; why am I doing this?'" Even now Judge looks back on "Frog Baseball" with mixed feelings: "I never thought that's what I'd be known for."

Gwen Lipsky, 34, is MTV's vice president of research and planning. When she tested "Beavis and Butt-head" before a target audience last October, she noticed something peculiar. "The focus group was both riveted and hysterical from the moment they saw it. After the tape was over, they kept asking to see it again. Then, after they had seen it again, several people offered to buy it from me." Almost without exception, she says, the group members said Beavis and Butt-head reminded them of people they knew. "Interestingly, the people in the focus group who seem the most like Beavis and Butt-head themselves never acknowledged that the characters are them."

Susan Smith-Pinelo, 24, knows them well. A graduate of Oberlin, she is an artist working at what "Generation X" writer Douglas Coupland calls a McJob, as a receptionist at the Sierra Legal Defense Fund. "People laugh at Beavis and Butt-head, Wayne and Garth," she says. "Our organization can relate to this lunatic fringe of teenagers who have fallen out of society, live in a world of TV . . . it's kind of sick, but we like to laugh at them and say, 'I'm not a loser'."

Dick Zimmermann is not a twentysomething and is not amused. A retired broadcasting executive from Larkspur, Calif., Zimmermann, 44, won a state lottery worth nearly $10 million in 1988. Early last summer, while channel surfing, he caught Beavis and Butt-head in the infamous cat episode—touchy ground for anyone involved with the show. Even

today it makes Judge uneasy. "They never did this thing with the cat," he says defensively. "They just made a joke about it: what if you put a firecracker in Stuart's cat's butt." Five days after the show ran, when a cat was found killed by a firecracker in nearby Santa Cruz, Zimmermann put up a $5,000 reward and went to the press. The cause of death, he told Larkspur's Independent Journal in a front-page story, was "Beavis and Butt-head." Opening a hot line, he mounted a one-man campaign against the program. "I admit that shows like 'Cops' are obviously very violent," he told NEWSWEEK, "but at least there is the element of good triumphing over evil. The thing about 'Beavis and Butt-head' that caught my eye was the total lack of redeemability. [They] engage in arson, petty theft, shoplifting, auto theft, credit-card fraud, cruelty to animals and insects—not to mention their attitude toward women."

The infamous cat episode will never air again. Three other episodes are also out of circulation, and the show has softened considerably this season. All involved are particularly sensitive because the show runs in family hours: at 7 and 11 P.M. weekdays, and in the afternoon on Saturdays. "The sniffing-paint-thinner we probably shouldn't have done," Judge concedes. "But I'm new to this. I thought of this show as going on at 11, no one's ever going to see it. I think it should run once at 11. We have toned it down."

Gwen Lipsky contends that young kids don't watch the show, that 90 percent of the audience is over 12. But part of the show's appeal is that, yes, these are dangerous, irresponsible messages. "They'll do stuff that we want to do but don't have the guts to do," says Alex Chriss, 14, who dropped his karate class to watch "Beavis and Butt-head." "On one episode they stole a monster truck and ran over a hippie guy singing save-the-earth songs. We go around mimicking them—not what they say, but how they say it."

Of course, such mimicry is not always harmless, and it is here that we probably need some parental caution. Beavis and Butt-head don't have it; confronted with an image of a nuclear family at the table, Butt-head asks, "Why's that guy eating dinner with those old people?" But other children do. Bill Clinton likes to watch "American Gladiators" with Chelsea; they enjoy the camp value together. And there are lessons to be learned, even from television that prides itself on not doling out lessons. "The whole point of [Beavis and Butt-head] is that they don't grow up," says Lisa Bourgeault, an eighth grader at Marblehead Middle School in Marblehead, Mass. "That's what's hip and cool. But we will."

Let's hope so. As our former vice president once put it, with an eloquence few scripted TV characters could match, "What a waste it is to lose one's mind, or not to have a mind." To which, like Beavis and Butt-head, we can only reply, "Huh-huh. Huh-huh. Cool."

HEITZ

San Jose State University Mass Communication graduate student Jenny Heitz uses often-made complaints of sexism in MTV videos as the basis of her study of women's images on several forms of the music channel's programming.

Can you find hints of narrative and gender (in this case, feminist) analysis in her essay?

Heitz raises the issue of multiple readings of the apparently sexist Aerosmith video, *Crying.* Do you agree with her argument that a video that offers "sexist images" can disrupt its own meaning with an "empowering narrative?" This raises the question inherent in much contemporary criticism, that is, "where is meaning made?" Thinking specifically about MTV-style rock videos, how would you answer this question?

This critic concludes her analysis with the concession that MTV is an advertising medium and because sex sells, it will continue to present the type of sex that it thinks will sell best. Do you see this as resignation on the part of the author? If not, what is her goal in interjecting this bit of reality into her writing?

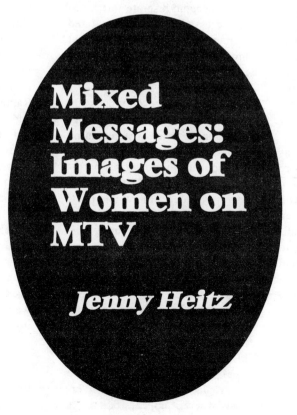

Imagine a beautiful blonde woman, out on what seems like the perfect date. She's dressed as prettily as a bride, she's treated politely, fed good food and seems to enjoy the dancing. The trouble is, she's dead and her body's been stolen from the morgue. This scene is from the most recent Tom Petty and the Heartbreakers video, and by the end of it, even her malleable corpse cannot satisfy her kidnapper, who dumps it into the ocean. MTV gives this particular image of women heavy airplay.

MTV has existed for over a decade now, and from its inception is has been lambasted for the exploitative, sexist content in the videos it broadcasts. Critics from such disparate sources as MS. magazine and Rev. Don Wildmon's National Federation for Decency have come down hard on MTV videos. In a 1990 MS. article, writer Kathi Maio wrote, "Ironically, MTV has a 'Stereotypes Suck' promo campaign (meant to foster racial harmony). Yet that very popular cable network promotes damaging stereotypes of women in almost every video it airs. In most, women are portrayed as passive scantily clad sex objects. But then you notice videos in which those same garter-belted cuties are shown behind bars or in chains."

Near the time Maio wrote these harsh words, MTV announced a format revamping, which included the introduction of new specials, an ex-

Written in 1994 by Jenny Heitz, Radio-TV-Film Major at San Jose State.

panded (and very successful) "Rock the Vote" campaign, messages encouraging kids to abstain from drugs, and mini-documentaries which stylishly explored taboo subjects like homosexuality and safe sex.

Regarding women, MTV has presented several interesting and thoughtful pieces about sexuality. Using interviews with teenagers, snappy video footage, and alternative background music, specials like The Seven Deadly Sins (literally about the biblical seven sins) and the enormously successful and parodied Real World have explored serious issues for women. On Real World, for example, one of the seven roommates, Tami, gets pregnant and decides to have an abortion. Camera crews document her feelings on the subject, as well as the reactions of her mother and of two pro-life roommates. Tami is shown before and after the operation, and her situation is presented realistically and non-judgmentally.

But while Real World may be showing women as complete, intelligent beings making decisions about their lives, in the world of Beavis and Butt-head, women are pure leering material. Ignore the fact that Beavis and Butt-head are hopeless imbeciles who, if they were human, could not get a date in a million years. The point remains that, on their show, women are there strictly for their enjoyment and entertainment and can be turned on and off at will with their cartoon remote control. Beavis and Butt-head aren't interested in talking to women, only in viewing them from the safety and anonymity of the living room sofa. And where a show like Real World is entertaining, its target audience is the twentysomethings who can relate to the series' twentysomethings. Any positive messages regarding women that might appear on the music channel fly right over the head of B&B's target 14 year-old:

he's too busy watching Beavis and Butt-head discuss female anatomy.

Beavis and Butt-head is actually a mix of an MTV in-house cartoon and the channels' usual music video lineup. All of MTV's programming implements the fast cutting, quick-as-lightning editing style made popular by music videos, but Beavis and Butt-head uses the actual videos themselves, cut to fit the show's format. Thus, in a typical episode, the viewer is treated to not only some of the more outrageously sexist videos in the MTV library, but also to the most exploitative elements present in them.

What a B&B episode does, quite effectively, is take all the context and meaning out of music videos. They no longer have a reality of their own, they are instead merely part of the adolescent world of Beavis and Butt-head. So, sexist images which may have made at least some sense within the context of the complete video suddenly become discrete images of half-dressed girls or brutalized women, complete with constant immature commentary from cartoon characters but absent a storyline.

There are, however, videos that do have a storyline, occasionally a compelling one. One example of a video containing sexist images but an empowering narrative is Aerosmith's Crying. It is a narrative video rather than a postmodern collage of images, and it tells the story of a young girl getting over an unhealthy and obsessive love affair. Throughout the video, she is dressed fairly provocatively, but not exceedingly so. In order to recover from her relationship, she gets a tattoo, pierces her bellybutton, and eventually beats up a thug who tries to steal her purse. The last scene takes place on a freeway overpass, where it appears that she's about to commit suicide. Her lost

love begs her to get down, but she jumps. The trick is, she's wearing a bungee cord, and as she bounces back up, she flips her ex-lover the finger.

The storyline of Crying may be melodramatic, but subtlety is difficult to get across in a four or five minute video. What's empowering about this video is that the heroine grows and changes in a positive way. She doesn't kill herself, she doesn't end up in an alley doing drugs, and she doesn't let other guys take advantage of her. Sure, getting a tattoo and a navel ring may, in many circles, be a less than positive response to lost love, but the video's point is that she comes through these experiences a stronger and better person.

The girl in Crying is empowered at the end of the video, due in large part to a level of character development which is usually missing in most rock videos. To reinforce this character development, Aerosmith uses the same girl in another of their videos, creating a continuing character, again, something quite rare in the music video world.

This is not to imply, however, that a narrative format guarantees female character development. Rapper Snoop Doggy Dogg's Gin and Juice follows the actions of a kid in South Central L.A. who throws a party while his parents are out. Its female characters are mere ornaments for Snoop. They comb his hair, ride in his car, fist fight over him on the front lawn and march single file into a bedroom, followed eagerly by Snoop. Variations on this theme are played out often in male rap videos, with images of women reserved for sex, waiting in cars, and generally having no personality.

Crying and Gin and Juice demonstrate that the women in MTV videos often present contradictory images. But nowhere is this more the case than in the videos for female musicians. During the 1980s,

MTV was credited with the success of female rockers like Pat Benatar and Joan Jett who used the music channel for exposure. Unfortunately, a lot has changed since then. With the popularity of grunge and metal, there seem to be fewer solitary female rockers on MTV, and the ones who do get airplay seem to exploit themselves rather blatantly, sending out unmistakable mixed signals in terms of sexism. For instance, the African-American girl group En Vogue has a video, Free Your Mind, but the only thing being freed in it are breasts, legs, and butts, flashed over and over again on a modeling runway. This video shares these contradictory elements with Madonna's Express Yourself, which features the star in bondage, immobilized. It seems likely that even the Material Girl herself would have difficulty adequately expressing anything (beyond screaming) shackled to a bed.

Another female group, the rap duo Salt-N-Pepa, teamed up with En Vogue to produce Whatta Man. At first glance, Whatta Man seems fairly original, for once a video which objectifies the male body. A closer examination, however, reveals some curiously ambiguous images. The man is shown writhing on a bed over and over again, dressed up in white frilly underwear and a stuffed lacy bra. The female performers themselves, while rhapsodizing about "whatta man," are clad in the skimpiest of clothing and are playing it up for the camera. Watching Whatta Man, we get the strange sensation that this isn't a woman's video at all; it is instead a bunch of women performing for a male audience.

Sadly, even female musicians who have strong statements to make have difficulty avoiding this trap. One of the most outspoken female rappers, Queen Latifah, articulates a very powerful message about gender relations in her latest video, U.N.I.T.Y. "Don't call me a bitch or a ho," Latifah demands of her fellows. She is an active, vibrant, demanding presence in this video, but the irony is that many of her demanding messages are delivered from a cage, hung 2 feet above her male tormentors. Is Latifah preaching down to them, or is she merely in the cage for her own protection and peace of mind?

Ultimately, MTV does not exist to relay humanist messages of tolerance and understanding to its viewers. Rather, it's an advertising medium designed to sell records and boost the recording industry, 24 hours a day. Even MTV's in-house programming, some of it excellent, is still just a part of the channel's endless music industry informercial.

One truth of advertising is that sex sells. The strange thing about MTV videos, though, is that we rarely see sex, that mutually agreed upon coupling of two people. Rather, MTV videos show sexual objectification, with women as toys in lingerie, as victims, as corpses, as two-dimensional beings whose existence revolves around men. MTV is really a man's world, and with few exceptions, the women in videos are there to address men, discuss men, display for men, and bask in the male gaze. Even the growth which occurs in Aerosmith's Crying has a man as its catalyst, and while videos often show men hanging around together, bonding, there are precious few videos which show women doing the same thing. There are plenty of videos which have no women in them at all, but hardly any which exclude men. Furthermore, MTV appears to have become a sort of Top 40 video channel, playing a very small selection of videos in heavy rotation , so the same sexist images are flashed again and again.

Journalist and critic Bill McKibben wrote of MTV in The Age of Missing Information, "I didn't, I suppose, spend as much time as I could have thinking how offensive this was. You can feel a little grubby watching it, but you watch —it knows what buttons to push." Yes, MTV knows what buttons to push for a male audience, but even with its few redeeming female video images, there is little to entice a woman to watch. And if McKibben felt "a little grubby" watching this exploitation, perhaps he can understand why women feel like they've been mud wrestling in a pasture for a long, long while.

Chapter Exercises

Identifying Video Types

Identify examples of Kaplan's five types of music video on MTV, VH1, BET, and the Nashville Network. List the video's title, artist and a note or two on why you made this choice in the space provided below. When a video is composed of two or more types, choose what you think is the dominant category, but note the presence of the additional type(s).

**MTV
MUSIC TELEVISION VIDEOS**

Romantic video

Social conscious video

Nihilist video

Classical video

Post-modernist video

**VH1
VIDEO HITS 1 VIDEOS**

Romantic video

Social conscious video

Nihilist video

Classical video

Post-modernist video

BET BLACK ENTERTAINMENT TELEVISION VIDEOS
Romantic video Social conscious video Nihilist video Classical video Post-modernist video

TNN THE NASHVILLE NETWORK VIDEOS
Romantic video Social conscious video Nihilist video Classical video Post-modernist video

Finding Video Types

Do certain types of videos appear more often on some of these channels than on others? In the box below, count the number of times each appears in a typical hour of each channel's typical music video programming. Speculate on your findings.

MUSIC VIDEO CONTENT ANALYSIS				
Types of Videos	**MTV**	**VH1**	**BET**	**TNN**
Romantic video				
Social conscious video				
Nihilist video				
Classical video				
Post-modernist video				
Total				

References and Resources

Allan, B. (1990). Musical cinema, music video, music television. *Film Quarterly, 43,* 2–14.

Altman, R. (1987). *The American Film Musical.* Bloomington, IN: Indiana University Press.

Aufderheide, P. (1986). Music videos: the look of the sound. *Journal of Communication, 36,* 57–78.

Barol, B. (1985). Women in a video cage. *Newsweek,* March 4, p. 54.

Barthes, R. (1977). *Image/Music/Text.* Trans. Stephen Heath. New York: Hill and Wang.

Brandt, P. (1982). At last . . . enough women rockers to pick and choose. *Ms.,* September, 110–116.

Brown, J. D. & Campbell, K. (1986). Race and gender in music videos: the same beat but a different drummer. *Journal of Communication, 36,* 94–106.

Cocks, J. (1983). Sing a song of seeing. *Time,* December 26, pp. 53–64.

Colley, I. & Darries, G. (1980). *Pennies From Heaven*: music, image, text. *Screen Education, 35,* 63–78.

Cretcher, J. (1983). Hard up was hard to do: the production of a rock video. *American Cinematographer,* September, 56–59.

Cubitt, S. (1985). Box pop. *Screen, 26,* 84–86.

Dannen, F. (1987). MTV's great leap backward. *Channels,* July/August, 45–47.

Denisoff, R. S. (1988). *Inside MTV.* New Brunswick, NJ: Transaction Books.

Feuer, J. (1982). The *Hollywood Musical.* London: Macmillan.

Frith, S. (1981). *Sound Effects: Youth Leisure, and the Politics of Rock 'n' Roll.* New York: Pantheon Books.

Frith, S., *et al.,* (Eds.). (1993). *Sound and Vision: the Music Video Reader.* New York: Routledge.

Gelman, E. *et al.* (1983). Rocking video. *Newsweek,* April 18, 96-98.

Golden, M. (1983). Retailers see music TV boom as a boost to record sales. *Billboard,* September 10, p. 28.

Goodwin, A. (1992). *Dancing in the Distraction Factory: Music Television and Popular Culture.* Minneapolis, MN: University of Minnesota Press.

Harrison, B. (1966). On the air: *The Monkees* hits new numbing low. Washington *Evening Star,* September 13, p. A20.

Holdstein, D. H. (1985). Music Video: Messages and Structures. *Jump Cut, 29,* 13–14.

Hustwitt, M. (1984). Rocker boy blues. *Screen, 25,* 89-98.

Jerome, J. (1984). They film the songs, they film the songs. *GQ,* March, 90, 98–100.

Kaplan, E. A. (1986). History, spectatorship and gender address in music television. *Journal of Communication Inquiry, 10,* 3–14.

Kaplan, E. A. (1986). Sexual difference, pleasure and the construction of the spectator in music television. *Oxford Literary Review, 8,* 113–23.

Kaplan, E. A. (1987). *Rocking Around the Clock: Music Television, Postmodernism, and the Consumer Culture.* New York: Methuen.

Katz, C. (1982). The video music mix. *Videography*, May, 28–35.

Kinder, M. (1984). Music video and the spectator: television, ideology, and dream. *Film Quarterly, 38,* 2–15.

Laing, D. (1985). Music video—industrial product, cultural form. *Screen, 26,* 78–83.

Levine, E. (1983). TV rocks with music. *New York Times Magazine*, May 8, pp. 42, cont. 55-59.

Levy, S. (1983). Ad nauseam: how MTV sells out rock & roll. *Rolling Stone*, December 8, pp. 30–37, cont. 74–79.

Lewis, L. A. (1990). *Gender Politics and MTV: Voicing the Difference.* Philadelphia, PA: Temple University Press.

McCullaugh, J. (1981). MTV cable spurs disk sales of artists aired. *Billboard*, October 10, p. 1.

Paiva, B. (1983). Putting $$ where they count. *Billboard*, June 8, p. 10.

Parales, J. (1983). Pop record business shows signs of recovery. *New York Times*, November 28, p. 13C.

Sacks, L. (1983). MTV seen aiding AOR stations. *Billboard*, May 28, p. 66.

Shore, M. (1984). *The Rolling Stone Book of Rock Video.* New York: Rolling Stone Press.

Sonnega, W. (1995). Morphing borders: the remanence of MTV. *The Drama Review, 39,* 45–61.

Ward, B. (1985). Music video grows up. *Sky*, April, 80-91.

Wolfe, A. S. (1983). Rock on cable: on MTV: music television, the first video music channel. *Popular Music and Society, 9,* 41-50.

CHAPTER 12

TELEVISION SPORTS

$1,300,000 for 30 seconds

That's what NBC charged for commercial time on its broadcast of the 1995 Super Bowl football game from Phoenix. But it was worth it. The game's 46.1 rating and 72 share meant that 138.5 million viewers tuned-in for all or part of the broadcast. Yes, sports on television is big business and big money; television sports do have that in common with the medium's other genres. But beyond the similarities, there are differences between sports and television's other familiar forms that raise fascinating questions for the critic. As the editors of *Channels* wrote, "In recent years sports and television...have not merely affected one another but have *transformed* one another. Television technology has fundamentally changed the way Americans watch sports....Television, in one guise or another, will continue to mediate sports for the American public. As television technology has evolved, so has our experience of the games we see on the screen" (TV's new rule book, 1986, p. 45).

Overview

In this chapter we will examine how sports came to television, the economics that supported and then threatened this union, how sports and television have changed each other, why certain sports are better suited for the medium than others, and what role the viewer plays in the ever-expanding presence of athletics on television.

The Evolution of Televised Sports

The history of sports on television is the history of sports on network television. Television sports director Harry Coyle reminisced about these beginnings when he said, "Television got off the ground because of sports. Today, maybe, sports need television to survive, but it was just the opposite when it first started. When we (NBC) put on the World Series in 1947, heavyweight fights, the Army-Navy football game, the sales of television sets just spurted," (Luciano & Fisher, 1988, p. 254). Coyle told a different interviewer, "Early fans were easily satisfied, just seeing a picture made them go ape" (Talen, 1986, p. 50).

With only 190,000 sets in use in 1948, the attraction of sports to the networks in those days obviously was not advertising dollars. They were banking on the future of the medium, so they aired sports to help boost demand for the new medium (which would eventually pay off in advertising revenues). But because NBC, CBS and DuMont manufactured and sold sets, their more immediate goal was to sell more sets. Sports did indeed draw viewers, and although the stunning acceptance and diffusion of television cannot be attributed solely to sports, only two years later, in 1950, the number of sets in use in the U.S. reached ten and a half million (Kraus & Davis, 1976, p. 9).

Technical and economic factors made sports attractive to the fledging medium. Early television cameras were heavy and cumbersome and needed bright light to produce even a passable picture. So boxing and wrestling, contested in a confined, very well-lit space and baseball and football, well-lit by the sun and played out in a well-defined, predictable space, were perfect subjects for the lens. Equally important, because sporting events existed already (i.e., no sets to build, no actors to hire), they were cheap to produce, a primary concern when the audience was small and not generating large advertising revenues.

Although the first televised sporting event was a college baseball game between Columbia and Princeton in 1939 covered by one camera along the third base line, the first network sports broadcast was NBC's *Gillette Cavalcade of Sports*, premiering in 1944 with the Willie Pep vs. Chalky White featherweight championship bout. Soon, sports became a fixture on prime-time network programming, often accounting for one third of the webs' total evening fare. But in the 1950s, as television's other genres matured and developed their own large and loyal (and approximately fifty percent female) followings, sports began to drift out of network prime-time, settling into a very profitable and successful niche on weekends. This, too, would change, like so much else in television, with alterations in the technology and economics of the medium (remember the lessons of Chapters 3 and 4).

Gillette Cavalcade of Sports stayed on the network air for 20 years, but in the mid-1960s, televised sports had become so expensive that individual advertisers could no longer afford to sponsor major events by themselves. So the same magazine-style advertising that helped transform televised drama from its Golden to its modern age, changed sports. The number of hours of sports on network television exploded as the audience grew and the multiplying ranks of spot-buying advertisers chased them. This mutually beneficial state of affairs persisted until well into the 1980s when the "steadily increasing supply of advertising dollars...diminished, and the networks (were) hit where it counts—in their closely watched profit margins. The era of spectacular growth and easy money (had) come to an end, and the three networks, as well as the sports leagues, (were) forced to moderate their expectations" (TV's new . . . , 1986, p. 45).

It was in the 1980s that the economics of televised sports began to unravel.

Exploding rights fees. In 1970 the networks paid $50 million to broadcast the National Football League (NFL), $2 million for the National Basketball Association (NBA) and $18 million for major league baseball. In 1985 those figures had risen to $450 million, $45 million and $160 million respectively. What fueled these rises? The public's interest in professional sports grew during this span of time, in part as a result of more and better television coverage. But equally important, the networks saw the broadcasting of big time sports as the hallmark of supremacy in broadcasting. Major league sports meant major league broadcasting—not an unimportant issue for the networks now challenged by VCR, the newly empowered independents, and cable. Making matters even worse for the Big 3 was that some of these cable channels were themselves carrying sports (WGN, WTBS, and HBO, for example), and one, ESPN, did *nothing but* sports. Sure, CBS, NBC, and ABC could argue, but who cares about Australian Rules Football?

Dwindling audiences. Rising rights fees, in and of themselves, are not bad. But when accompanied by falling ratings, they were disastrous. From 1980 to 1984, broadcasts of professional football lost 7% of their viewership (12% among men 18 to 34 years old) and baseball lost 26% of its viewers, showing a 63% decline among young males. The network alternatives took many of these viewers. One financial analyst commented, "If people aren't going to watch sports on television, advertisers won't pay to reach them" (Easton, 1986, p. 47). In addition, sports on those competing channels further diluted the sports audience that did remain.

Increases in the cost of advertising time. To make up for falling revenues on all its programming as they began to lose audience to the alternatives, the networks began to raise the price of advertising time on its sports shows to cover the huge rights fees it was locked into paying the sports leagues. Advertisers balked. Not only were they unwilling to pay higher prices for smaller audiences, but the once attractive male audience was becoming less desirable as working women came to control even larger amounts of consumer capital. So rather than pay what they saw as inflated rates for a smaller and now less prized set of viewers, many advertisers bought commercial time away from sports altogether, feeling that they could reach their target audiences more efficiently through other types of shows. Car manufacturers turned to prime-time drama to reach women, who were increasingly making car-buying decisions; beer makers were turning to MTV to get young women and young men.

The overabundance of sports on television. In order to make the most of their expensive contracts with the major sports leagues, the networks began broadcasting more sports. But "spots on sports shows would be easier to sell if there were fewer of them on the market. The three networks together showed 1,500 hours of sports in 1985. That is double what they put on in 1960. With about 8 minutes of commercials an hour, the addition of a relatively few hours of programming can have noticeable effects on the supply-and-demand balance of the ad market" (Goodwin, 1986, p. A15).

The alternatives. Not only were the networks themselves responsible for the oversupply of advertising time, but as already mentioned, about this time WTBS, WGN, and HBO began national, cable-fed sports programming. Add to this ESPN. Launched in 1979, by mid-1980 it reached 4 million homes. By 1986, it was in 37 million households. The glut of sports on television was abetted even more by the courts, where colleges, wanting access to broadcast riches, successfully challenged the NCAA and sometimes their very own conferences to be free of what they thought were restrictive television contracts and broadcast revenue sharing agreements. College basketball and football, once decentralized, began appearing all over the television dial in a complex array of syndication packages and school-centered or conference-centered television networks.

The history of sports on television may have been the history of sports on network television, but the current and future states of the genre certainly are not. There are more televised sports today than ever before and they continue to draw a large audience, but it is an audience that is fragmented among the many available choices. Sports on television, then, is decreasingly likely to be national network originated. Despite the Super Bowl's annually growing audience and increases in the price of a 30 second spot, it remains a television anomaly, unique as a television and cultural event. This Roman-numeralled clash aside, the ratings for individual television sports programs in general continue to decline in this decade. The 1993 World Series, for example, had a cumulative rating for all its games of slightly more than 16, besting only the 1989 Series interrupted by the Loma Prieta earthquake. Game 1 of the '93 contest between Toronto and Atlanta was the lowest rated World Series game ever recorded by Nielsen. When CBS's four year, $1.06 billion deal with major league baseball ended with that Series, the best network deal that the league could make was an arrangement with both ABC and NBC that tied baseball's income to the amount of advertising sold, forcing the sport into the business of selling advertising time for the networks (and therefore, for themselves). Hockey's ratings on its ABC and ESPN/ESPN2 telecasts, never big, also are in decline, from 0.9 in 1992 to 0.8 in 1993. The pattern is the same for football, basketball and the Olympics.

This does not mean, however, that people aren't watching sports on television, they just aren't watching the big marquee events in as large numbers as they once did. Now cable channels and local stations have joined the networks as primary outlets for sports programming.

The Popularity of Sports for Broadcasters

Sports would not be all over schedules of the networks, independent stations, and cable channels if broadcasters did not find them attractive and profitable programming. Their appeal has several dimensions:

1. **Audience demographics.** Except for the big ticket events like the NCAA Championships, the Super Bowl, the World Series, the NBA Championships and the major college football bowl games, televised sports generally produce smaller audiences than prime-time network programming. Of course, for independents and cable channels sports contests may often draw their *biggest* viewership. But regardless of the size of the audience for a sports telecast, it is its composition that is important—it is demographically attractive to advertisers who want to reach males, 18 to 49 years old. Certain sports also bring with them even more narrowly defined audience segments. Watch a bowling match, a game of golf and an auto race, look at who advertises on these broadcasts and it should become immediately clear that a particular demographic is being targeted (and at advertising rates usually well below those charged on more general-interest programming).

2. **Inexpensive programming.** As we saw above, when the new technologies began to divide the television audience, huge rights fees to big sports leagues became a burden for the networks. But for cable channels, local broadcasters and even for certain events on the networks, sports are often cheaper to buy and air than much first-run programming. This is why we see so many regional sports networks like the Boston Red Sox Baseball Network, team-centered and conference-centered ad hoc networks (groups of stations that come together in a network for specific programming like the Pac-10 Football Network or the Big East Game of the Week), and ballgames or boxing matches on cable channels like HBO, WTBS, WGN, and TNT.

3. **Weekend attraction.** Sports is the only programming that can attract any kind of audience on a weekend day.

4. **Free promotion.** The newspapers, radio stations, even television stations that are in competition with a broadcaster who is airing that weekend's big game all provide free advertising in the course of their usual sports coverage.

The Popularity of Sports for Viewers

Ultimately, the reason that sports are popular with broadcasters is that they are popular with viewers. Even the 1993 "low rated" World Series drew fourteen and a half million households a game, on average. The NHL's tiny 0.8 rating per game still means three quarters of a million homes. And, as you'll see in the example of journalistic criticism that concludes this chapter, it is sports, in this instance NFL football, that can still declare a broadcaster "BIG TIME!" But why are these contests of skill, originally designed to test the abilities of the participants and then to delight those who attend, so popular from a distance, on an illuminated iridescent screen?

Familiarity. Viewers identify with *their* team, their favorite players, those warriors who carry the the good name of their city, college, conference, hair color, nation, ethnic heritage, or whatever, into battle. Sports offer *real* heroes and villains (as opposed to the fictional characters of televised drama and comedy). Fans become familiar with them and their teams, following them, learning about them, living and dying with them, or, in the immortal words of *ABC Wide World of Sports*, experiencing with them the "joy of victory and the agony of defeat."

Immediacy. Sports on television is live television, it is history in the making, it is being "up close and personal" (again, thanks to ABC) as possibly momentous events unfold.

Personal satisfaction. Ask yourself why you watch *The Simpsons*, or if you prefer, *Deep Space 9*. Now, ask yourself why you watch sports, especially your favorite teams or players on television. To pass time is no doubt one reason that comes to mind, but you could have said that about Bart Simpson, *Seinfeld* or *DS9*. To thrill in the victory of a favorite, to let loose with an exciting game or to learn more about the teams, players or games on the set are three possible satisfactions that are obviously specific to sports on television.

Sports As Good Television

No doubt a fourth reason why people watch televised sports is that they often make great television. Carlton Fisk's famous 1975 World Series homer, the American hockey victory over the Soviet Union team at the Lake Placid Olympics and the camera's sad attention in the last quarter of the 1994 Super Bowl on Thurman Thomas whose miscues had led to a fourth straight Buffalo Bills defeat are only three examples of the wonder that can be sports on television. But just what does make an individual sporting event "good television?" As Talen (1986, p. 50) writes, "All sports are not created equal. The most popular sports on TV are those best served by the medium's limitations." What she means is that even if

there are 20 cameras and 40 microphones at an event, what the viewer receives is still one picture and one set of sounds. Together these must convey a sense of what is happening in the actual contest. Talen (p. 50-51) offers the example of *Monday Night Football's* long-time director, Chet Forte, who claims, "'It's impossible to blow a football game'" and continues,

Football works as a flattened sport. Its rectangular field fits on the screen far more readily than, for example, golf's far-flung woods and sand traps. The football moves right or left on the screen and back again. Its limited repertoire—kick, pass, and run—sets it apart from, say, baseball, where the range of possibilities for the ball and the players at any given moment is enormous. "The reason it's easier to cover," says CBS's top football director, Sandy Grossman, "is because every play is a separate story. There's a beginning, a middle, and an end, and then there's 20 or 30 seconds to retell it or react to it."

There are, in other words, certain characteristics of the different sports that make them better dramatic and visual matches for television, and in doing so, render them more popular with audiences. There are eight obvious ones; we'll list them, briefly describe each and give a quick example. Later you can apply your own standards in judging what you think makes a sport well or poorly suited for television.

1. **Fixed starting point.** The camera, and therefore the fans' attention, is repeatedly redirected to a specific starting point for each new play, serve, or pitch. This is what CBS's Grossman above called a "separate story." Therefore, football and baseball are better than hockey and soccer in providing a discrete starting point.

2. **Continual crisis.** Tension can be sustained and viewer interest maintained if something crucial can occur at any moment. Any pitch can result in a home run or a fine running catch by the center fielder. Any pass can produce a touchdown or an interception. In contrast, the

first three quarters of a basketball game serve only to set up the last three minutes and much of soccer's action happens at mid-field, yards and yards away from the goal.

3. **Natural breaks.** Baseball has innings, football has time-outs and quarters. Those covering and those watching the event can get into a rhythm that allows for the more-or-less natural insertion of commercials and runs to the refrigerator. Soccer has continuous action, so, too, does hockey which makes commercial insertion more complex.

4. **Big ball.** Cameras and viewers have to be able to follow the object of interest on the field and on the small screen, respectively. Basketballs and footballs are big while hockey pucks and golf balls are quite small.

5. **Visual variety**. Television is a visual medium; it lives by the pictures it offers its viewers. Baseball and football offer spectacle, big, full, beautiful stadiums, lovely playing surfaces, the blimp, cheerleaders (football) and the bullpen (baseball). Whereas, tennis has a small rectangular court and bowling has a skinny lane of wood.

6. **Physical action.** Nothing adds to visual variety like physical action, people moving and competing. Basketball is ballet above the rim. In football there are incredible tests of strength and aggression. Golf, on the other hand, offers a much smaller amount of physical action as players in strangely colored clothes walk around and, on occasion, swing a metal stick.

7. **Personal side**. Fans follow players as well as teams and the camera is well versed in the close-up. Roone Arledge of ABC called this "sports as soap opera." Baseball gives us the tight shot of the pitcher's anxiety as he holds the runners on first and third or zooms in on the

concentration in the basketball player's eyes as he shoots two from the charity stripe with the game on the line. In hockey it's much more difficult to provide close-up, personal video images because the players wear helmets and skate at 30 miles an hour.

8. **National interest.** Of course, television prefers sports with wide interest because it assures more viewers and ad revenue; but this is also a plus for sports fans as well. How many of us have watched a game between two teams that we don't typically follow, because the outcome might impact our home-town favorites or because we want to see that scrappy second baseman we've read so much about? Quick! Name two hockey players other than Gretzky and Mario Lemieux.

You'll no doubt quarrel with our examples. For example, what becomes of visual variety (and the blimp) when even baseball and football are broadcast from domed stadiums? These broadcasts might be considered much less enjoyable for those at home. And doesn't hockey's constant physical action compensate for its lack of continual crisis?

The Double Edge of the Sports/ Television Union

This chapter opened with the comment that televised sports were different and alike enough from the medium's other forms to raise some interesting critical questions; and now, after discussing the genre, we can revisit the issue. The similarities between televised sports and other forms of television are obvious: concern for ratings, the need to attract the correct or best demographics, issues of production and other costs, the ascendance of "stars" and personalities (John Madden = Dan Rather, Michael Jordan = Roseanne Arnold?), and the impact of the new technologies. But it is the differences that are most interesting.

Most significantly, unlike soap operas and situation comedies, sports exist apart from television. Major league baseball, for example, was born before even radio was invented and developed its rules, traditions, nature and character apart from television. Moreover, sports are played in front of and *for* paying customers. This produces two important questions. First, what have sports lost and gained from their wedding to television? Second, what have fans lost and gained?

The gains might be obvious. The leagues and athletes have prospered. More and more teams and tournaments are played in more and more cities and fill more and more television screens. Television has helped create tremendous interest and excitement for the public, turning the Super Bowl, for example, into something akin to a national celebration.

The losses, however, might be less obvious. For example, trying to explain dips in television ratings and attendance at games in the 1993 NFL season, sports reporter Bud Geracie wrote,

> *Terry Bradshaw says that although Dallas is "as good as any team that's ever played, the league as a whole isn't fun to watch." Is this a temporary lull in the action, or a permanent condition? Is this NFL season the product of fluky misfortunes, or is it the beast born of parity....The NFL wanted parity—and took measures to achieve it—and you can't argue with the logic or the success of the concept. The NFL wished to maximize the number of teams in play-off contention late in the season, thereby maximizing fan interest, TV ratings, revenues and the rest. This is what the NFL bosses sought, and this is what they got. What they seem to have lost in the process is the big game. "There are no big games between 5-4 teams vying for wildcard spots," said Bob Costas of NBC (1993, p. 5E).*

Sports Illustrated (The last . . . 1994) detailed another negative result of the sports/television relationship—the destruction of traditional conferences. In February of that year, four schools, Texas, Texas A&M, Texas Tech and Baylor, bolted the 80 year old Southwest Conference to join the Big Eight in order to

cash in on ABC's promise to "pay the expanded league between $85 million and $90 million over five years with the potential for $10 million more" if the new football super-conference developed a play-off. *SI* responded with the words of Texas Christian (one of the jilted schools) alum and track coach, Bubba Thornton:

> *What the Southwest Conference was about was small towns and big cities, Texans against Texans, wives and girlfriends dressing up, bragging rights, the Methodist preacher talking Sunday morning about beating the Christians, all the things that keep you going. We were about tradition all these years instead of instant gratification and egos. This decision will come back to haunt us (p. 14).*

Your own list might be different, but here are several other "concessions" that fans and the games themselves have made to television: 1) games moved to awkward times of day to satisfy television schedules but that ignore fans who've bought tickets; 2) giant video screens in arenas and stadiums; 3) TV time-outs; 4) free agency; 5) pro teams moving to better "markets;" 6) wild-card games; 7) expanded playoffs; 8) the 40 second clock in the NFL; 9) the designated hitter in the American League; 10) over-expansion in the professional leagues; 11) salary caps; 12) player strikes; 13) umpire and officials strikes; 14) recruiting abuses as college teams chase television riches; 15) the playing of World Series games at night in freezing October weather (Game 7 of the 1994 Series was scheduled for October 30); 16) electric lights in Wrigley Field.

The future of sports on television is certainly one that promises more contests on the screen and more transformation of both the games and the medium. It's widely accepted, for example, that one of the reasons that the networks paid such heavy rights fees to the professional sports leagues throughout the Eighties was to keep them away from pay-per-view, and for now they have been successful. But virtually every cable system in America offers at least boxing on a pay basis and Sports Channel is, for all intents and purposes, pay television. What will happen to competitiveness, franchise stability, and scheduling as individual teams become star attractions? What will happen to the look of the broadcasts and the nature of the games that are played if advertising is no longer the basis of program support? What will changes in the economics of the sports-television marriage mean to the teams, the medium and to the fans? What technological innovations (in covering the games and in distributing them) will we see and what might be their impact? The instant replay, slow motion, reverse angle, and video chalkboard are now so much a part of our reality of the game that we feel uncomfortable when attending a sporting event in person because we feel information-deprived. And if pay-per-view is to succeed, it will no doubt be dependent on DBS or, more likely, fiber-optics technology. Both exist already. Are you plugged in yet?

NEAL-LUNSFORD

In this essay Neal-Lunsford combines historical and genre analysis to paint a detailed portrait of how sports first came to network television. As such, he is fulfilling the critical role of historian/ recorder. Once he introduces his critical question, however, he begins "a brief history of television." Do you think that this helps or impedes the flow of his argument? What obligation does the critic have to ensure that all his/her readers share sufficient background to fully appreciate the analysis that is to follow?

This critic does more than record names, dates, and places. In several spots he takes his investigation into the realm of the medium's impact on how the games it covers are played. This is an important critical issue. How does he use it? Does it enrich his overall thesis; or is it an interesting note to move the reader to think for a moment about the sports/television marriage; or is it an important part of his analysis that he leaves unfulfilled or poorly documented?

Do you have to be a sports fan to enjoy this piece? If not, what devices does this critic use to keep his readers' interest?

Neal-Lunsford details a period in television history in which sports were commonly found in prime-time. What put them there in those early days? What eventually banished them to weekends? Do you find his evidence sufficient on these issues? Can you offer one or more alternative explanations?

On December 13, 1988, CBS obtained the network broadcast rights for major league baseball. The price: $1.08 billion for an exclusive four-year contract.[1] Early in 1989, the cable sports network ESPN paid $400 million for the exclusive right to air major league baseball on cable.[2] NBC's 1991–94 contract with the National Football League called for the network to pay the league $188 million per year for national broadcast rights. CBS paid $267 million per year for its football telecasts, while ABC, which airs Monday Night Football, paid the NFL $249 million per year.[3] This income from the broadcast networks supplied professional football with nearly 60% of its revenue during the early 1990s; for professional basketball and baseball, the figure has been closer to 30% of total revenue.[4]

Such high prices for programming are not limited to the so-called "major" sports, such as basketball, base-

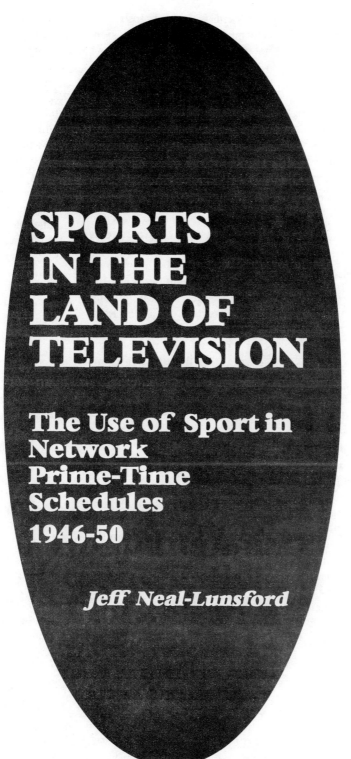

SPORTS IN THE LAND OF TELEVISION

The Use of Sport in Network Prime-Time Schedules 1946-50

Jeff Neal-Lunsford

ball, and football. CBS paid $243 million for the broadcast rights to the 1992 Winter Olympics, later selling a portion of those rights to the TNT cable network. NBC paid $401 million for the more popular Summer Games.[5] Other sports events, such as the Indianapolis 500, Kentucky Derby, Rose Bowl, and Masters golf tournament have also cost broadcast and cable networks many millions of dollars in rights fees. Such large outlays of cash signal the importance of televised sports programming to the networks and also the large profits that can be earned by airing sporting events. The networks' generosity has also made organized sport highly dependent on television revenue. Without television, no team could hand out multi-million dollar contracts to players such as Dwight Gooden, Joe Montana, or Michael Jordan. In the sport-television relationship, television, with its deep pockets, has become the dominant partner.

While it is true that sport today comprises an

---

1. William O. Johnson and William Taaffe, "A Whole New Game," *Sports Illustrated*, 26 December 1988, 34–42.

2. "ESPN Gets to Play Ball for $400 Million." *Broadcasting*, 9 January 1989, 43.

3. Richard Huff, "NFL Wraps TV Deals with CBS, NBC Pacts," *Variety*, 14 March 1990, 43.

4. Ibid., 26.

5. Johnson and Taaffe, "A Whole New Game," 35.

Reprinted with permission of *Journal of Sport History*.

important part of the networks' overall programming schemes, most sports telecasts can be found only on weekend afternoons. Televised sports attracts a heavily male audience which can not compete, in terms of sheer numbers, with the large and more heterogeneous audiences for prime-time programming.[6] The logic is simple: Advertisers for prime-time programs demand large audiences; therefore, television programmers try to attract as many people as possible by airing programs that appeal to a broad audience. Outside of prime time, this logic changes somewhat; the daytime audience is largely composed of women, thereby attracting advertisers who want to reach a female audience. On weekends, it is the male audience that holds sway, which results in a heavy concentration of televised sport.

It was not always this way. For a brief period comprising the first five years of network television programming, no ground rules had been established. The television industry, in its infancy, had no experience with which to guide itself; there were no television ratings, no demographic breakdowns of the audience. In this time of uncertainty and experimentation, prime-time programmers found themselves drawn to sports as a way to attract an audience to their new medium. For a short time this strat-egy worked as televised sports lured many people to watch television, first in taverns and restaurants, and then in their own homes. From 1946 to 1950, it was sports which held the upper hand in its relationship with television as the networks relied heavily on sports to fill out their prime-time schedules in those first few years.[7]

A Brief History of Television

Prior to World War II radio dominated the airwaves. RCA and others had conducted experiments as early as the 1920s with a new medium, television, but only slowly developed an economical and efficient television transmission and reception system. In 1939, RCA president David Sarnoff, eager to begin regular television broadcasts, had arranged with the Federal Communications Commission (FCC) for NBC to televise several events from the New York World's Fair.[8] In addition, a mobile production truck began televising various events in the New York City area, sport being a prominent subject of the telecasts. This mobile unit provided the first sports telecast, a Columbia-Princeton baseball game, shot with one camera stationed near the third-base line. It was not an aesthetic success. A later telecast from Ebbets Field, for a Reds-Dodgers doubleheader, was improved somewhat by the addition of a second camera. The mobile unit also covered boxing and wrestling cards on an irregular basis, all for an audience which numbered in the hundreds. CBS also experimented with sports telecasts in 1939, including the first televised boxing match, in which Lou Nova took on Max Baer at Yankee Stadium.[9]

By the early 1940s both NBC and CBS, competing to develop a market for their television receivers, were broadcasting a limited schedule of programs to the small number of set owners in New York City from their newly-built television stations. The start of World War II, however, suddenly halted the development of television, as technological expertise and raw materials were channeled into the war effort. Once the war ended, television became a top priority for broadcasters and advertisers, although not all were convinced that the new medium would succeed. One imposing obstacle was that television sets cost almost as much as a new car. Others in the industry, secure in their financial and popular success, simply felt that nothing could ever supplant radio as the entertainment medium of choice.

In 1946 NBC became the first network to establish regular television programming, followed shortly by DuMont, a short-lived television network headed by Dr. Allen

---

6. Jerry Schosberg, "Who Watches Television Sports?" *American Demographics*, February 1987, 45–49, 59. A survey by the Simmons Market Research Bureau found that men comprised the majority of the audience for all of the top twenty televised sports.

7. Those "first few years" are a somewhat frustrating time period study. One problem is that the networks and local stations of the era had no idea that what they were doing would someday be regarded as significant. As a result, most of their records and film libraries are now believed to reside in landfills in New Jersey and other places. Government documents provide little because the FCC was not concerned about programming, instead directing its energies toward such problems as frequency (the "*freeze*" and a standard for color television). Richard Keller of Emporia State University aptly summarizes the problem in "Sport and Television in the 1950's: A Preliminary Survey," included in the 1982 North American Society for Sport History newsletter. As Kelly put it. "Not even God knows much about television sports during the 1950s."

8. Erik Barnouw, *A History of Broadcasting in the United States* (Vol.2) *The Golden Web* (New York: Oxford University Press. 1968), 126–127.

9. "Sports Shows. Radio vs. Video," *New York Times*, 13 June 1946.

DuMont, a pioneer in experimental television broadcasting.[10] The other national radio networks, CBS and ABC, were, for different reasons, slower to enter the television arena. ABC, created in 1943 when NBC was forced by the government to spin off its "blue" radio network, lacked a New York television station from which to originate network programming.[11] CBS did have a New York station, but held off on developing a television presence because it wanted its experimental color system accepted as the industry standard, rather than the color system developed by RCA, NBC's parent company. The FCC ultimately chose NBC's color system because it was compatible with the black-and-white system then in use, unlike the CBS system, which would have required viewers to buy new sets. While CBS waited four years for the FCC to make a decision regarding color, it lost time in establishing regular network television programming.[12] For ABC, the problem was money; the network had little to spend on television.

By 1948 ABC and CBS had followed NBC's lead and established their own network programming schedules. Although the FCC issued a temporary freeze on the construction of new television stations in 1948, network television began to spread westward via coaxial cable. By 1949 the midwest was linked to the networks, and in 1951 the link reached the west coast. In a short time television had gained a firm hold on the nation's consciousness.

For some at the radio networks, television was simply an extension of radio; for others it was a new and unexplored visual world. For all, it was an uncertain business in which no one had any experience in identifying which shows would succeed and which would fail. What was certain, however, was that television needed programming, and lots of it. The network schedule of the late 1940s and early 1950s reflected both uncertainty about programming strategy and the scarcity of programs. The networks, in their attempts to lure an audience, aired a wide variety of program genres, including such variety programs as *Your Show of Shows* and *Texaco Star Theater*, crime dramas such as *Man Against Crime*, a long list of anthologies including *Goodyear Television Playhouse* and *Kraft Television Theater*, and quiz shows such as *Majority Rules* and *Think Fast*. Advertisers, rather than buying a commercial or two within a program, as is the practice today, bought entire blocks of time on the networks during the 1940s and 1950s, which resulted in such early programs as Chevrolet *Tele-The-ater*, *In the Kelvinator Kitchen*, and *Mohawk* [Carpet] *Showroom*. Amidst all this programming variety, sports programming was not neglected. In their early years, the networks looked to sports as an essential component of prime-time programming.

Sports was given a chance in prime time because no one knew what kinds of programs the public wanted to watch, which made the early years of network program-

ming a time of great trial-and-error. With no prior experience of audience research to guide them, programmers put lots of shows on the air and hoped some would find an audience. Since sport had long been a popular staple on radio, it seemed to be a natural for television. As broadcasting historian J. Fred MacDonald points out, a parallel exists between the early programming strategies of radio and television in which both media used the "excitement of sport contests" to attract the male audience.[13] For those advertisers whose products were primarily purchased by men, such as tires, cigarettes, and beer, advertising on sports programs appeared to be a logical strategy. Said sportswriter Red Smith, in reference to baseball telecasts, "The sport of Father Chadwick and Al G. Spalding has been taken over by John Barleycorn and Lady Nicotine, who are not going to let it go as long as it sells products."[14]

Sports also provided a convenient and relatively cheap source of programming. The infant networks, all based in New York City, had an easy access to a multitude of local sports teams and events. Especially important were the numerous arenas that dotted the city, providing an ongoing schedule of boxing and wrestling cards. Perhaps most important of all, the networks believed that sports programming led directly to the sale of television sets. As long-time NBC director Harry Coyle reminisced in 1988, "What some people forget is that television got off the ground because of

10.   Tim Brooks and Earle Marsh, *The Complete Directory to Prime-Time TV Shows, 1946–Present* (New York: Ballatine Books, 1981), xiii.

11.   Sterling Quinlan, *Inside ABC: American Broadcasting Company's Rise to Power* (New York: Hastings House, 1979), 6–7.

12.   Barnouw, *The Golden Web,* 243.

13.   J. Fred MacDonald, *Don't Touch That Dial!: Radio Programming in American Life From 1920 to 1960.* Chicago: Nelson-Hall, 1979), 9.

14.   Benjamin G. Rader, *In its Own Image: How Television Has Transformed Sports* (New York: Free Press, 1983), 58.

sports. Today, maybe, sports need television to survive, but it was just the opposite when it first started. When we put on the World Series in 1947, heavyweight fights, the Army-Navy football game, the sales of television sets just spurted."[15] Considering that NBC and DuMont (followed in 1951 by CBS) were all in the business of manufacturing television sets, one of their primary goals was obvious: If it sells sets, put it on. As the networks quickly discovered, sports did indeed sell sets.

1946: Birth of the Networks

In 1946, the first year of network prime-time programming,[16] only NBC and DuMont had regular schedules, and then just barely. There was just barely an audience as well. In 1946, only 8,000 television sets had been sold to a public concentrated in the New York City area.[17] The two networks were on the air only an hour or two per night, and not at all on Saturdays.[18] Sports, or boxing, to be more exact, represented a significant part of the network schedules (see Figure 1).[19]

As can be seen, the prime-time sports schedule for 1946 is sparse, but so was network programming as a whole. DuMont and NBC col-lectively aired only nine hours and 30 minutes of prime-time programming per week; of this, sports programs comprised three hours and 45 minutes, or nearly 40% of all programming. Prime-time sports in this year was represented mostly by a single NBC program, *The Gillette Cavalcade of Sports*. The program was not owned by NBC, but by Gillette, a razor blade manufacturer.[20] It was a program ideal for early television, considering the medium's level of technical development. Broadcasting equipment of the time was bulky and difficult to maneuver. Television cameras needed large amounts of light in order to produce a watchable picture, and picture clarity was a problem even under good conditions-long shots of objects tended to reduce those objects to unidentifiable specks. *The Cavalcade* solved these problems and made television engineers happy by televising boxing matches. Boxing lent itself to the existing state of television technology because it took place in a small indoor area which could be provided with the large amount of light needed by the cameras. The relatively small size of the ring enabled cameras to shoot close-ups of the participants, which helped overcome the picture's fuzziness.[21] Like the television engineers, Gillette was also happy with boxing. It was cheaper to produce than a studio program, with production costs running about $2,500 per program.[22] In addition, the structure of the sport, with three-minute rounds separated by one-minute intermissions, provided ample opportunity for the company to advertise its wares.

Another plus for the show, at least in its early years, was that while few homes had television, many taverns did. Large numbers of males gathered in their neighborhood saloons to watch the fights, thus bringing together Gillette's target audience in a place that did not have the distractions of home, where wives and children might want to watch something other than boxing.[23] Gillette must have been pleased with *Cavalcade* in any event-the show did not leave the air until 1964, after having presented over 600 nights of boxing, in addition to such events as the Orange Bowl and the World Series.[24] Gillette was not alone in its happiness with televised boxing—a 1946 NBC telecast of the Joe Louis-Billy

---

15. Ron Luciano and David Fisher, *Remembrance of Swings Past* (New York: Bantam Book, 1988), 254.

16. *"Prime Time"* was originally defined as 7 to 11 P.M. (eastern time) until 1971, when the FCC ruled that stations in the top fifty markets could air only three hours of network prime-time programming per night. By industry convention, prime-time hours then became 8 to 11 P.M.

17. *Historical Statistics of the United States—Colonial Times to 1970, Bicentennial Edition, Part 2* (Washington, DC: U.S. Bureau of the Census, 1975), 796.

18. Marc Eilot, *American Television: The Official Art of the Artificial* (New York: Anchor Press, 1968), 127–130.

19. As the contemporary viewer well knows, television schedules are "subject to change." The schedules presented here (all eastern time) represent the programming that occupied a particular time slot. These schedules were derived from the following sources: Tim Brooks and Earle Marsh, *The Complete Directory to Prime-Time TV Shows, 1946–Present* (New York: Ballantine Books, 1981); Mitchell E. Shapiro, *Television Network Prime-Time Programming, 1948–1988* (Jefferson, BC MaFarland, 1989); Eliot, *American Television*.

20 Until the 1960s it was common practice for advertisers to obtain the rights to sports events and then pay a network or local station to carry the events. It took the networks several years to establish their own separate sports divisions: prior to that sports operations were a part of the networks' news divisions.

21. Ron Powers, *Supertube: The Rise of Television Sports* (New Uork: Coward-McCann, 1984), 243.

22. "Program Product Chart." *Television*, February 1949, 16.

23. Powers, *Supertube*, 52–53.

24. Ibid., 53.

Figure 1. Network sport in prime-time: 1946							
	Sunday	Monday	Tuesday	Wednesday	Thursday	Friday	Saturday
A B C							
D U M O N T							
C B S							
N B C		9–11 P.M. Gilette Cavalcade of Sports			9–9:15 P.M. Fight Film Filler 9–11 P.M. Gillette Cavalcade		

Conn heavyweight championship fight inspired the Washington Post to declare: "Television looks good for a 1000 year run."[25] More important to the networks, the Louis-Conn bout garnered praise from the Leo Burnett advertising agency, which declared that the fight was "another achievement by the industry to bring forcibly to the attention of the public the practical value of television."[26] At a time when advertisers and their agencies were largely unconvinced of television's future, this was a significant endorsement of television's potential as an advertising medium.

In addition to *Cavalcade*, NBC also presented a fifteen-minute fight film filler following the variety show *Hour Glass*, its main offering on Thursday nights. In an era prior to the development of videotape, such filmed programs were an economical way for the networks to fill air time since they could be run again and again.

1947: Gillette and Boxing

As the sales of television sets increased to 14,000 units in 1947,[27]

25. Erik Barnouw, *A History of Broadcasting in the United States (Vol. 3) The Image Empire* (New York: Oxford University Press, 1970). 244.

26. "Vodeo Status Confused, Agency Finds," *Broadcasting,* 112 August 1946, 32.

27. *Historial Statistic of the United States,* 796.

NBC and DuMont still had the prime-time airwaves to themselves. The two fledgling networks, however, offered the viewer little more programming than in the previous year.[28] Weekend programming, in fact, nearly stopped altogether save for a few special programs presented on NBC. In all, network prime-time programming expanded by three hours to an average of 14 hours and 45 minutes per week: of this, sports programming accounted for three hours and 45 minutes, or 25% of the total prime-time programming. While this represents a decrease from the networks' inaugural year, sports programming still represented a substantial part of the networks' programming schedules. Critics noticed this and praised the sports programming efforts of the networks and local stations. One preview of the 1947 season cited sporting events as "television's most professional entertainment" and noted the growing popularity of Gillette's *Cavalcade* with the television audience.[29]

The Gillette Company recognized early on that televised sports would be an ideal vehicle for selling razor blades to their male target audience. In 1944, when television wasn't much more than a rumor, Gillette signed a contract with Madison Square Garden to sponsor weekly fight contests, continuing a tradition of sports sponsorship that had begun years earlier in radio.[30] For the most part, Gillette's partnership with televised sports proved to be beneficial for everyone involved. Gillette saw its share of the shaving products market rise from 16 percent in the 1930s to more than 60 percent in the late 1950s.[31] In turn, Gillette's success led to large expenditures on sports programming, which gratified those viewers hungry for boxing, baseball, and football. Certainly the networks were the beneficiaries of Gillette's increasingly large advertising budgets. While many advertisers remained leery of television's power to sell products, Gillette supplied the networks with both desperately needed programming and the income to develop additional programs. Gillette's power in this regard was made most evident in 1959. Faced with the cancellation of its *Cavalcade of Sports* on NBC, Gillette moved almost all of its advertising budget to ABC, the weakest and most poor of networks. As a result, ABC suddenly found itself $8 million dollars richer, an amount more than the combined profits of its radio and television operations for all of 1959.[32] Armed with this new and potent war chest, ABC moved quickly to wrest the important NCAA football rights from NBC and began to establish its own sports programming, most notably the long-running *Wide World of Sports*. Thanks in large part to Gillette's infusion of cash, ABC was able to begin constructing the framework that would eventually allow it to dominate network sports programming.

In the 1947 television season, Gillette's *Cavalcade*, still relying heavily on boxing to fill its air time, remained as the only prime-time sport program (see Figure 2). The first fifteen minutes of the Monday night Cavalcade were replaced by the *Esso Reporter*, but the Friday *Cavalcade* was expanded by 30 minutes. The Thursday fight film filler was dropped, which left the *Cavalcade* on the air for the same amount of time as in 1946.[33] The Friday *Cavalacade*, which featured boxing from Madison Square Garden, was a hit with barroom audiences throughout New York City. Gillette would pay for this success when the Garden demanded a then-astronomical $200,000 for the weekly boxing rights during the 1948 season.[34] Early on, sports promoters were learning that television could be a potential gold mine.

While boxing continued to be popular with television viewers, the relationship between television and boxing would soon become strained. The popularity of televised boxing kept fans in front of their television sets and away from the boxing arenas. Live attendance dropped sharply; particularly hard hit were small boxing clubs, and even the prestigious Madison Square Garden saw its gate steadily decrease as the sales of television sets increased.[35] The live attendance problem made negotiation between television and sports interests more difficult. DuMont, for example, was able to renew its contract to cover boxing and wrestling at New York City's Jamaica Arena, but only at what was described as a "considerable increase in fee."[36]

Even at this early stage of

28. Brooks and Marsh, *Directory to Prime Time TV Shows*.

29. Bruce Robertson, "Autum Expansion Is Seen for Video," *"Broadcasting,* 26 August 1946, 15.

30. Rader, *In its Own Image,* 42.

31. Bert Randolph Sugar, *The Thrill of Victory: The Inside Story of ABC Sports*. (New York: Hawthorn Books, 1978), 47.

32. Ibid., 47–49.

33. Eliot, *American Television,* 130–33.

34. Jack Gould, Radio News, *New York Times,* 11 March 1948.

35. Rader, *In its Own Image,* 45.

36. Jack Gould, The News of Radio, *New York Times,* 25 August 1947.

	Sunday	Monday	Tuesday	Wednesday	Thursday	Friday	Saturday
A B C							
D U M O N T							
C B S							
N B C		9–11 P.M. Gillette Cavalcade of Sports			9–11 P.M. Gillette Cavalcade of Sports		

Figure 2. Network sport in prime-time: 1947

television's history it soon became apparent that the power of the medium not only affected the audience for a sport, but also influenced how the sport was played. In the case of boxing, promoters quickly learned that brawlers appealed more strongly to the viewing audience than boxers who relied on finesse. Fights between power punchers were more filled with action, and there was always the possibility of a sudden and exciting KO. Realizing this, promoters sought sluggers for televised bouts, leaving finesse fighters in the background as boxing interests strove to make their product more appealing to the television audience.[37] In a short time, the power of television would permanently alter the "sweet science."

In 1947, however, it was sports that held sway in its relationship with television. Television executives saw sports as an effective means to increase the sale of television sets, which would not only

---

37. Robert W. McChensey, "Media Made Sport: A History of Sports Coverage in the United States," in *Media, Sports and Society,* ed. Lawrence A. Wenner (Beverly Hills: Sage, 1989), 60–61

increase revenues for the manufacturing and research and development arms of NBC, CBS, and DuMont, but would also increase the available television audience. With an increased audience, the networks hoped, would come increased interest from advertisers in the form of stronger advertising commitments to the new medium. CBS president Frank Stanton underscored the importance of sport in announcing an agreement between CBS and the Ford Motor Company for a new sports series. According to Stanton, not only would the income from the Ford series enable the network to develop better techniques for televising sports, but would also enable the network to produce better overall programming. In addition, Stanton saw sports as providing "a wealth of the finest kind of program material for development of the kind of television everybody wants-color television."[38] This latter point was vital to CBS, then locked in a struggle with NBC to develop a standard for color television.

In 1948 television set sales jumped from 14,000 to 172,000.[39] Despite the slow westward progress of the coaxial cable, television stations were popping up across the country. New stations, whose applications had been approved before the FCC's licensing freeze took effect, went on the air in such cities as Omaha, Tulsa, Salt Lake City, Seattle, Phoenix, Kansas City, and Los Angeles.[40] Without a direct cable connection to the networks, these stations either bought programming from syndicators or had programs sent to them from the networks on film or kinescopes.

In this year CBS and ABC aired their first prime-time network schedules, and sports was an important component for both networks in their initial programming efforts. As shown in Figure 3, all four networks relied heavily on sports as a prime-time programming vehicle in 1948.[41] While program schedules in the early years of television were especially volatile, the addition of CBS and ABC increased the amount of weekly programming to 83 hours. Sports programs accounted for nearly 27 hours of the total, or nearly one-third of the networks' programming schedules.[42] The number of hours of boxing alone available to viewers more than doubled, from less than four hours to more than eight hours.[43] As one observer put it, "the passionate affair between television and professional fighting turned into an orgy" as both the networks and local stations found boxing to be profitable and easily produced.[44]

In spite of boxing's popularity as TV fare, it was basketball that dominated the network programming schedules in the winter of 1948, at least for a brief time. Professional basketball circa 1948 was described as a "small-time, penny ante sport, because it attracted so many small-time penny ante operators."[45] This was the era just prior to the formation of NBA, when semi-pro leagues such as the Basketball Association of America and the National Basketball League fought for dominance. Professional basketball in the 1940s and early 1950s was a slow game with an uncertain following. In particular, the lack of a successful team in a major media market such as New York hampered the development of fan support.[46] To compound the problem, blacks were excluded from the professional game, not only depriving the leagues of a significant pool of talent, but also alienating part of the potential audience. The leagues themselves were shaky affairs, with teams frequently folding or moving to different cities.

In spite of these problems, all of the networks except DuMont regularly aired basketball games, mostly on Saturdays, when three games were often aired simultaneously. The networks, with little previous programming experience to guide them, risked failure in dedicating nine-and-a-half hours of their collective schedule each week to professional basketball. They quickly learned that basketball was not a wise choice for prime-time programming, as it proved to be much less popular than boxing. The game

---

38. "Ford will Sponsor CBS Sports Video," *Broadcasting,* 5 August 1946, 18.

39. *Historial Statistics of the United States,* 796.

40. "Television Magazine's Status Map," *Television Magazine,* March 1950, 16–17.

41. During the 1948 season CBS aired movies and sports events in the 8:30–11:00 P.M. time slot on Thursdays, but existent schedules do not include what was shown on any particular night.

42. Brooks and Marsh, *Directory of Prime Time TV Shows,* 854.

43. Eliot, *American Television,* 141–147.

44. Rader, *In its Own Image,* 41.

45. Douglas A. Noverr and Lawrence E. Ziewasz, *The Games They Played: Sports in American History, 1865–1980* (Chicago: Nelson-Hall, 1983), 183–184.

46. Barnouw, *The Image Empire,* 146.

46. Barnouw, *The Image Empire,* 146.

Figure 3. Network sport in prime-time: 1948						
	Sunday	Monday	Tuesday	Wednesday	Thursday	Friday	Saturday
A B C				9–11 P.M. Wrestling from Washinton D.C.			7:30–7:45 P.M. Sports with Joe Hazel 9–11 P.M. Basketball
D U M O N T			9–11 P.M. Boxing	9–11 P.M. Boxing from Jamaica Arena	9–11 P.M. Wrestling/ Football	9–11 P.M. Wrestling from Jamaica Arena	
C B S		9–11 P.M. Basketball		9:30–10:45 P.M. Boxing from Westchester	8:30–11 P.M. Movies/ Sports	7–7:15 P.M. Your Sports Special 8–8:05 P.M. Sportman's Quiz	9–11 P.M. Basketball
N B C		9:15–11 P.M. Boxing from St. Nicholas Arena	9–11 P.M. Wrestling from St. Nicholas Arena		7:45–7:50 P.M. Sports-Woman of the Week	9:45–11 P.M. Gillette Cavalcade of Sports	8:30–11 P.M. Basketball

was not yet ready for network exposure, although the development of the NBA and the emergence of such star players as George Mikan and Bill Russell would later make pro basketball a much more popular sport.[47]

College basketball games scored better with audiences than the professional games.[48] A factor that no doubt helped was that television sets and stations were still concentrated in the east and provided a ready audience for such eastern college powers of the late 1940s as Holy Cross, NYU, and CCNY. Even so, both professional and college basketball disappeared from prime time after only one year. Later, representatives from both college and professional basketball would take steps to ban their games from television, convinced that telecasts on local stations would hurt live attendance.[49]

The concern over the effect of televised sports on live attendance

---

47. Barnouw, *The Image Empire*, 145.

48. Brooks and Marsh, *Directory to Prime-Time TV Shows*, 65.

49. Rader, *In its Own Image*, 67–75.

was shared by executives in professional baseball, basketball, and football as well. R. C. Embry, president of both the professional basketball and football teams in Baltimore, discontinued broadcasts of the Bullets' home games, citing a 25% decline in attendance.[50] Baseball executives were especially concerned about the impact of television. Said Washington Senators owner Clark Griffith, "Television doesn't show you enough. You can't follow the play. If it ever becomes good, I'll throw it out."[51] In a similar vein, baseball commissioner Ford Frick wanted camera coverage of baseball to be strictly limited. "The view a fan gets at home," Frick said, "should not be any better than that of the fan in the worst seat of the ball park."[52] In an eerily accurate prophecy regarding an attempt by minor leagues baseball to limit baseball broadcasts in 1948, television critic John Drebinger proved both Griffith and Frick wrong when he concluded that any attempt to limit baseball telecasts would fail because "the majors seem unable to resist the lush profits that the expansion of television promises to yield."[53] A song written by a baseball writer and presented at a meeting of the New York chapter of the Baseball Writers Association, illustrated one of the prevailing attitudes of the day toward television. It was sung to the tune of Take Me Out to the Ball Game: "Take us home to the ball game/Take us home to the wife/ Get us our slippers, they're just the

style/Plug in the gadget and spin the old dial/Then we'll root for plenty of action/If a tube blows out, it's a shame/But no matter what happens we'll never go out/To the old ball game."[54]

Another sport to first hit the network schedules in 1948 was professional wrestling. ABC and DuMont both featured wrestling on their prime-time schedules, ABC because it had not yet developed much programming, and DuMont because wrestling was cheap to produce, and, like boxing, lent itself to the available television technology. This was important to DuMont, as the network was struggling financially in its efforts to keep up with NBC and CBS, who were able to fuel their television efforts with the profits from their radio networks. Many of these wrestling programs originated at such venues in the New York area as Jerome Arena and Sunnyside Gardens. Some of the wrestlers who toiled in those arenas rapidly became famous; grapplers such as Gorgeous George, Nature Boy, and The Mighty Atlas became household names.

Wrestling, like boxing, attracted a large barroom audience. What really made wrestling popular with advertisers, however, was that most estimates, however reliable, found women to be the most avid home wrestling viewers. Attracted by the scantily clad and well-muscled grapplers, the female audience was not so much interested in wrestling technique as it was in watching

their heroes pose and preen under the hot television lights. One eastern wrestling promoter, waxing optimistic, estimated that women comprised 90% of the home audience.[55] Such estimates made wrestling an appealing vehicle for retail advertisers who traditionally aimed their advertising messages at women, who were responsible for spending much of the average household budget.[56]

Perhaps the most significant aspect of wrestling's appeal is that it is as much an art form as a sport, or, as one scholar describes it, "a ritual dance in which accident has been precluded."[57] In New York, legislators examined wrestling, with its easily identified "heroes" and "villains" dressed in velvet robes, masks and other strange attire, and enacted a law requiring every professional match to be listed as an exhibition, not as a contest.[58] Television programmers were unconcerned about wrestling's status as a sport; all they knew or cared about was that wrestling attracted viewers. For their part, wrestling promoters and the wrestlers themselves proved eager to accommodate their activities to the small screen. Televised wrestling matches were filled with greatly exaggerated wrestling moves, a more polished sense of showmanship, and ongoing storylines which heightened the continuing struggle between the forces of good and evil. And even though the fan at home might perceive the matches as uncontrolled mayhem, wrestling promoters took

50. "Baltimore Five to Halt Telecasting of Contests," *New York Times,* 13 June 1948.

51. Luciano and Fisher, *Remembrance of Swings Past,* 254.

52. Marc Gunther and Bill Carter, *Monday Night Mayhem* (New York: Beech Tree Books), 16–17.

53. John Drebinger, "Minors Seek to Limit Baseball Broadcasts and Telecasts," *New Tork Times*, 10 December 1948.

54. Arthur Daley, "When the Ringside Becomes the Fireside," *New York Times Magazine, 27* March 1949.

55. "It Pays to Sponsor Television Corn," *Business Week,* 7 October 1950, 25–26.

56. "Women Buy 55% of U.S. Goods, Study Indicates," *Advertising Age,* 26 January 1950, 36.

57. Michael Sorkin, "Faking It," in *Watching Television,* ed. Todd Gitlin (New York: Pantheon Books, 1986), 164.

58. "It Pays to Sponsor Television Corn," 25.

special care to ensure that the matches did not exceed the time slots between commercial interruptions.[59]

Television helped perpetuate the carnival atmosphere of wrestling by allowing the announcers to throw away any semblance of objective reporting and become part of the antics themselves. DuMont's Dennis James, for example, provided sound effects to match the action in the ring.[60] If a wrestler had an opponent in a hammerlock, James would draw his fingernail across an inflated balloon in imitation of a cry of agony. To reproduce the sound of breaking bones, James would employ a rubber dog bone, which, when bent, emitted a sharp cracking noise. Wrestling, then as now, left no stone unturned in its attempts to entertain.

In addition to wrestling, several short-form sports programs made their debut in 1948. *Sportswoman of the Week*, a fifteen-minute show on NBC, featured tennis champion Sarah Cooke playing host to outstanding women athletes. *Your Sports Special*, also a fifteen-minute program, featured sports reporter Carswell Adams and former major league umpire Dolly Stark in a sports news and interview show. *Sports with Joe Hasel* was a fifteen-minute weekly summary of sports news on ABC. CBS aired a five-minute show, *Sportsman's Quiz*, which posed questions about hunting, fishing, conservation, and other outdoor topics. The questions were asked by Bernard Dudley and answered by Don Baker, with the help of such visual aids as drawings or diagrams.[61] These cheaply-produced programs were created mainly to fill air time on the networks' schedule. None of them lasted very long.

Prime-time programming from the four networks increased in 1949 from 83 to 88 hours, but the amount of sports on the networks dropped considerably, from nearly 27 hours a week in 1948 to less than 15 hours a year later (see Figure 4).[62] Sports programming now comprised less than 17% of prime-time. Nation's Business, early in 1949, pointed out the reason for the decline: "Up to now, sports have been popular on television largely by default. The few variety shows already on the air have pushed sports into a weak No. 2 spot and dramatic programs are coming up fast on the pole. When the Jack Bennys, Bob Hopes, and Bing Crosbys and, heaven help us, soap operas turn to television, sports will be relieved of the dilemma of deciding whether or not to telecast."[63] The Hooper ratings, long used to measure radio audiences and now used for television, supported this opinion. The ratings of the top shows for 1948 included such programs as *Texaco Star Theater*, *Arthur Godfrey's Talent Scouts*, *Toast of the Town*, and *Howdy Doody*.[64] The fact that no sports programs were included in the list was an ominous sign of things to come for the producers of prime-time sports. Advertisers, having learned from radio to associate themselves with the highest-rated shows, soon began to withdraw from sports programming. The networks, which had begun to depend on prime time for the bulk of their revenues, now looked at sports with less optimism than in the recent past. The Hooper ratings, and more significantly, their financial implications, would soon signal the end of sports on prime-time television.

Indeed, as the networks, particularly CBS and NBC, infused their schedules with such enormously popular programs as *The Amateur Hour, We, the People*, and *Break the Bank*, televised sports became almost something of a programming burden in prime time to both the networks and program sponsors. Only DuMont and ABC, both struggling to match the efforts of NBC and CBS, still relied on sports to attract an audience. As the sales of television sets reached nearly a million units in 1949, the networks began to realize that sports was not the only programming genre that would inspire the public to pay $400 to $500 for a set.[65] In the mind of the networks, Milton Berle's star now outshown that of Gorgeous George. Even more important to the networks' bottom line, Berle's popularity led to the sale of many more television sets. This marked a significant change in the television-sports relationship. No longer did television need sports to sell sets, as it did just a few years earlier. New and better salesmen, in the form of such highly popular shows as *Texaco Star Theater* and *Philco TV Playhouse*, had arrived on the scene.

59. Gerald W. Morton and George M. O'Brien, *Wrestling to Rasslin: Ancient Sport to American Spectacle* (Bowling Green, OH: Bowling Green State University Popular Press), 47–49.

60. "Dog Bones and Flying Mares," *New Yorker,* 18 September 1950, 23–24.

61. Brooks and Marsh, *Directory to Prime Time TV Shows,* 703.

62. Eliot, *American Television,* 141–147.

63. Stanley Frank, "Main Event: TV vs. SRO," *Nation's Business,* March 1946–49.

64. Radio and Television, *New York Times,* 30 December 1948.

65. *Historical Statisitics of the United States,* 796.

	Sunday	Monday	Tuesday	Wednesday	Thursday	Friday	Saturday
A B C			10–11 P.M. Tomorrow's Boxing Champions	9:30–11 P.M. Wrestling from Chicago	10–11 P.M. Roller Derby	10–11 P.M. Roller Derby	9–11 P.M. Roller Derby
D U M O N T		9:30–11 P.M. Wrestling				9–9:30 P.M. Fishing and Hunting Club ——————— 10–11 P.M. Boxing from Chicago	10–11 P.M. Wrestling from Chicago
C B S				10–10:45 P.M. This Week in Sports	9:30–11 P.M. Boxing from Sunnyside Gardens		
N B C						10–11 P.M. Gillette Cavalcade of Sports	

Figure 4. Network sport in prime-time: 1949

As television historian Ron Powers has pointed out, the reasons for the decline of sports during prime-time are several.[66] First, advertisers were concerned that while televised sports appealed mainly to men, market research indicated that women controlled family viewing choices as well as consumer spending. Program length also played a role in the networks' growing dissatisfaction with sports on television. Unlike dramas or variety programs, there was no way to predict when a sports event would end, which made scheduling difficult. Where once the networks depended on sporting events to fill large amounts of time, this was now a drawback. In addition, snobbery played a role. Was it not better to offer audiences sophisticated musical programs, such as the moderately popular *Kay Kyser's Kollege of Musical Knowledge* or the *Fred Waring Show* than to dignify the often more popular sweating and

---

66. Powers, *Supertube*, 52–53.

grunting of the forebears of Hulk Hogan? With this in mind, it is not surprising that sports programs began to be shifted to weekends and other non prime-time hours.

In 1949 the weekly supply of network wrestling programming dropped from seven hours to four, with most of that supplied by the ill-fated DuMont network, which was still struggling to fill out its schedule.[67] Boxing was still relatively popular during prime-time, but the ratings were beginning to fall. The various short-form programs from 1948, such as *Sportsman's Quiz,* all disappeared, the victims of low viewership. CBS tried again with a new fifteen-minute show, *This Week in Sports.* This program featured highlights of the past week's activities in sports as well as short profiles of well-known sports personalities. In the same vein, DuMont introduced a short-lived half-hour program, *Fishing and Hunting Club,* which featured sports interviews and demonstrations.[68]

ABC, trying to catch up in prime-time programming with its more prosperous and star-laden competitors, continued to experiment with sports programming. The network caught lightning in a bottle, at least briefly, when it brought Roller Derby to network audiences. At one point in 1949 Roller Derby was seen four hours a week during prime-time on ABC as it became the network's most popular show.[69]

The 1949 official program of Roller Derby describes the "sport" (a spectacle more akin to professional wrestling than to an athletic competition) in this way: "In the past decade, two impacts have hit the American public—the atom bomb and the Roller Derby—and it appears the latter will have the most permanent effect."[70] History has not justified the optimism of Roller Derby's promoters, but for a brief time, it caught the fancy of the viewing audience. Today, Roller Derby can still be seen, but only on the fringes of syndicated television.

If there are similarities between Roller Derby and professional wrestling, part of the reason stems from the fact that both were introduced to television by sports entrepreneur Dick Lane.[71] A Roller Derby contest consists of two five-person teams (there are both men's and women's teams) skating in packs around a banked track. The goal of the game is for the "jammer" of a team to lap the pack and pass the opposing team's blockers, thus scoring points. Punching, wrestling, and hair-pulling are supposedly illegal but occur on a frequent basis. It is the sport's apparent violence, in fact, that forms part of its appeal. Lane himself observed the similarities between wrestlers, Roller Derby skaters, and their fans: "[V]iolent? Oh, my God yes, they were violent. Especially the fans. They were like the wrestling fans. I'd look at them out there in the seats sometimes, screaming and yelling and throwing things, and I'd say to myself, 'My goodness-they must eat their young.'"[72]

While Roller Derby was popular with its fans and with television viewers, television critics weren't quite so kind. One such critique, dripping the sarcasm, had this to say: "On every hand the evidence is conclusive that the hours of toil which the scientists spend in developing television were not wasted. Never before has roller skating meant so much."[73] The critic needn't have worried. The novelty of Roller Derby soon wore off, and by 1951 it was confined mostly to local stations.

In addition to its popularity, Roller Derby represented a needed source of cheap programming for ABC. Like wrestling and boxing, Roller Derby took place indoors in a relatively small and brightly lit area, making it easy to televise while enabling cameras to provide more close-ups than was feasible with such stadium sports as football or baseball. This was still an important consideration in 1949 as television engineers strove to improve the clarity of the picture.

1950: The Decline of Prime-Time Sports

In 1950 prime-time programming sprang into full bloom as ABC, CBS and NBC offered complete prime-time schedules several days a week. Only the DuMont network, losing the battle with its more prosperous competitors, failed to air four hours of prime-time programming each night. Although television had not yet eclipsed radio as America's favorite entertainment medium, it was closing fast. By mid-1950 over 7.5 million television sets were in use, and some television shows were receiving higher ratings than *Lux Radio Theater,* radio's top-rated program.[74] In five short years the television audience had grown from a few thousand to millions of viewers.

67. Powers, *Supertube,* 45.

68. Brooks and Marsh, *Directory of Prime-Time TV Shows,* 254.

69. Ibid., 644

70. "Roller Derby: An An Industry Made by Television," *Business Week,* 4 June 1949, 22–23.

71. Powers, *Supertube,* 48.

72. Ibid., 49.

73. Jack Gould, "The Roller Derby," *New York Times,* 6 May 1949.

74. Telestus, *Broadcasting,* 25 September 1950, 8.

The vast majority of these viewers watched television at home, not in barrooms, a development which would greatly affect the programming efforts of the networks as a rapidly growing audience segment of women and children had to be taken into account.

Combined, the networks' weekly offerings in prime-time jumped from 90 to 109 hours. As Figure 5 indicates, however, sports programming showed a further decline in this year, dropping to 12 hours and 30 minutes, or 11% of the total schedule.[75] Gillette's *Cavalcade of Sports*, once the mainstay of NBC's sports schedule, was now on only 45 minutes a week (15 minutes of its time slot was taken by a film filler, Greatest Fights of the Century). Outside of the *Cavalcade*, prime-time wrestling telecasts were down to three hours a week, as were boxing programs, which just two years before comprised over eight hours of the networks' weekly prime-time schedules. Boxing and wrestling fans were anything but deprived, however, as local stations began to air their own boxing and wrestling shows. There was even an hour less per week of Roller Derby on ABC as the popularity of the games began to fade and the network strove to bring other types of programming to its schedule. At NBC and CBS, sports was still an important schedule component, but not during prime-time, where the two networks were now duplicating on television their earlier dominance of radio. Sports was now relegated mostly to daytime slots on weekends. At DuMont and ABC, where programming attempts had not yet

yielded much success, sports was still important in prime-time, but as much for its production economy as for its ability to attract a large audience.

Professional football made its first appearance in prime-time during the 1950 television season, although complete games were not telecast.[76] ABC aired two half-hour football highlight programs which showed edited versions of various games, focusing on outstanding plays. *The Game of the Week*, featuring highlights of major college games, aired on Tuesday nights and *Pro Football Highlights,* which concentrated on the New York Giants, aired on Friday evenings.[77] Neither show was successful and did not return for a second season, although *Pro Football Highlights* was later picked up by DuMont for the 1952 season.

A major hinderance to scheduling pro football games on television was that in contrast to its great popularity today, the professional game of the early 1950s was a minor sport with a relatively small following. Even newspapers were loathe to cover the pro games, preferring to cover college football, which was a success in stadiums across the country and on Saturday afternoon television. Telecasts of complete professional games would not appear until 1953 on DuMont.[78] NFL football on television, as we know it today, would have to wait for a decade, and the arrival of television-minded NFL commissioner Pete Rozelle, before it made an impact on network television.

The financially strapped DuMont network (the 1954 season would be its last) found an eco-

nomical way to program two hours on Saturday nights with Madison Square Garden. DuMont simply arranged with New York's famous arena to present, live, whatever event was being staged there.[79] Although the program lasted only a few months, it became a forerunner of such sports anthology shows as ABC's Wide World of Sports, televising a variety of such sports events as rodeos, track meets, and horse shows, as well as more prestigious events such at the NIT basketball tournament.

Nineteen-fifty marked the end of a brief era in television. In 1951 sports all but disappeared from prime-time, with the exception of two wrestling programs and a football highlights show on DuMont. Network sports programs moved to weekends, and boxing, wrestling, baseball, and basketball would become featured attractions seen mostly on local, not network, television. Sports had been used well by the networks, but the programming emphasis was changing to such genres as sitcoms and dramas. The networks, now aware of their ability to draw vast numbers of viewers, began their almost single-minded quest to continually increase the size of their audience. Larger audiences meant higher ratings, which in turn meant higher advertising revenues. With millions of viewers and many millions of dollars of revenue at stake, television had ceased to be an experiment and had become a rapidly growing industry. After a brief heyday, sports had been eclipsed in drawing power in the critical prime-time hours and could no longer deliver the large audiences needed

---

75. Eliot, *American Television,* 148–154.

76. McChesney, "Media Made Sport," 62.

77. Brooks and Marsh, *Director to Prime-Time TV Shows,* 543.

78. Ibid., 260.

79. Ibid., 660.

	Sunday	Monday	Tuesday	Wednesday	Thursday	Friday	Saturday
A B C			8–8:30 P.M. Game of the Week ———— 10:30–11 P.M. Roller Derby	10–11 P.M. Chicago Wrestling	10:30–9 P.M. Roller Derby	8:30–9 P.M. Pro Football Highlights	9–11 P.M. Roller Derby
D U M O N T		9–11 P.M. Wrestling from Columbia Park			9:30–11 P.M. Boxing from Dexter Arena		9–11 P.M. Madison Square Garden
C B S				10–11 P.M. Blue Ribbon Bouts			
N B C						10–10:45 P.M. Gillette Cavalcade ———— 10:45–11 P.M. Greatest Fights	

Figure 5. Network sport in prime-time: 1950

by advertisers. This alone was enough for the networks to eliminate sports from their prime-time schedules.

Sports and Television Today

In 1949 CBS paid $100,000 for the rights to televise the Rose Bowl. Baseball rights could be had for $1000 per game. College football was a bit more expensive at $3,000 per game.[80] These prices would quickly become a fond memory for the networks. In 1983 NBC signed a three-year deal to air the Rose Bowl—at $2.33 million per year.[81] The price of professional football rights in the 1990s reached hundreds of millions of dollars, and the baseball rights package at CBS cost more than a billion dollars. Sports today has become a major component of television programming for broadcast networks, local stations, and cable networks. For the most part, however, televised sports takes place outside of prime-

---

80. Frank, "Main Event: TV vs. SRO," 84.

81. Klatell and Marcus, *Sports for Sale,* 35.

time.[82] ABC has had success with *Monday Night Football* in prime time, although its ratings have declined in recent years.[83] ABC has also attempted to televise major league baseball in prime time, which turned out to be something of a ratings disaster.[84] Aside from *Monday Night Football*, sports in prime-time on the broadcast networks is confined to such major events as the World Series, NCAA football bowl games and Final Four basketball tournament, the NBA finals, and the Super Bowl. Unlike the early years of network programming, television programmers have learned, to a certain degree, how to attract the widest possible audience for their offerings. They have discovered that aside from special events, sports programming in prime-time is not a viable programming alternative, not when higher ratings and more revenue can be earned from sitcoms, dramas, movies, and the like.

While television was new, sports telecasts were an essential element in establishing the fledgling medium. In 1948, television critic Arthur Daley outlined what he called the "inestimable value" of televised sports.[85] First, when television had no identity of its own to sell to the public, sports provided a ready-made cast of well-known stars to attract an audience. Even better, these stars needed no rehearsals and no scripts, with the possible exception of the professional wrestlers. Second, sports helped to spur the sales of television sets and stir further interest in the new medium. Starting out in bars, clubs, and restaurants, sets quickly began to appear in private homes as television began its westward migration across the country. Third, in a time when television programs were restricted to low budget productions, televised sports not only allowed the networks to shoot on location, thus avoiding the high expense of building studio sets, but also filled large amounts of time on the networks' sparse schedules. Without the crutch of sports to lean on, the development of network television may well have been much slower.

Despite its disappearance from prime-time, sports has continued to grow and thrive on television. The emergence of cable networks in the past decade has increased the amount of televised sports and changed the programming landscape to a significant degree. Since cable is not received in all homes, cable networks usually must settle for smaller audiences than do the broadcast networks. Because of this, such cable networks as TNT and ESPN, and superstations such at WTBS, WGN, and WWOR have found sports programming to be viable prime-time fare. For the sports viewer equipped with cable, sports programming can be had 24 hours a day. It is no longer necessary to rely solely on the broadcast networks for sports coverage. Basketball, baseball, football, wrestling, boxing and a multitude of other sports can be seen once again in prime-time.

Technological developments have also affected sports on television. Better cameras can see farther and in less light than those used in television's early years, thus allowing such widely dispersed sports as golf and even sailing to be telecast. Miniature cameras are now routinely installed in race cars, affording a view that previously could be seen only by the driver. Instant replay has not only allowed viewers to enjoy outstanding or controversial plays again and again, it has also become, in the case of pro football, an integral part of how the game is conducted as field officials consult with replay officials to determine whether or not certain calls should stand. Other developments such as videotape and slow motion replays have shown fans a view of games that could not be seen with the naked eye. As the technology has grown more advanced, television coverage of sports has grown much more sophisticated.

Television has also grown to become an integral part of the way in which sports is conducted. Many sports have adjusted their rules to accommodate television. The "TV time out" in basketball is a good example of this. Starting times for games are now routinely adjusted to better fit television schedules. The enormous amounts of money paid by broadcast and cable networks have also had a significant impact on the economics of both professional and amateur sports. Television is not just a purveyor of sports to the viewing audience, it is an active participant in the conduct of sporting events.

In contrast to today, the early years of network prime-time programming can be described as years of programming innocence, when no one really knew what would work, and, just as importantly, what wouldn't. As a result, the networks experimented with sport as a programming vehicle, but as the great radio stars took their acts to television, and as ratings services such as Hooper and Nielsen began to more

---

82. Susan Tyler Eastman and Tim Meyer, "Sports Programming: Scheduling, Cost, and Competition," in Wenner, ed., *Media, Sports, and Society,* 97–119.

83. Johnson and Taaffe, "A Whole New Game," 40.

84. Ibid.

85. Authur Daley, "Sports Help to Fill the Bill," *New York Times,* 13 June 1948.

accurately count the audience, prime-time sports fell by the wayside as the networks narrowed their programming focus to maximizing the size of the audience in order to increase advertising revenues. As network television focused its efforts on increasing audience size, the predominantly male audience attracted by sports telecasts could not compete with the larger and more heterogeneous audiences of the variety shows, dramas, and game shows. When the networks realized that *Blue Ribbon Bouts* and *Wrestling from Columbia Park* could not equal the drawing power of Uncle Miltie, Arthur Godfrey, and *Our Miss Brooks*, an adventurous era in broadcasting came to an end.

WULF

Critic Wulf's imaginary John Madden play-by-play of Fox Television's defeat of CBS is not only an interesting opening, but it makes clear that his primary audience is sports fans. But as you read on in this *Sports Illustrated* essay you'll see that he assumes much television knowledge on the part of those readers. Ratings fragmentation? Network? Affiliate? Shannen Doherty? Ratings lead-in? Is this an assumption that might be safer to make when talking about television sports fans as opposed to fans of television's other genres? Why or why not?

What aspects of journalistic television criticism are present in these few well-written pages?

What is your opinion of the Fox move? Given the evidence Wulf lays out, will Fox's high-priced gamble pay off? Given what you know about television and its audience, would you have advised this network to make the deal? Why or why not?

"Here's the replay. From the left of your screen, you can see Murdoch coming on the blitz. He's drawing a bead on Tisch, who thinks he's got all the time in the world, but nobody's picked up Rupert, and—boom!— he blindsides Tisch and strips the ball. Hey, that guy Murdoch didn't get to be in the Fortune 500 for nothing."

That's how John Madden of CBS might have described the play by Rupert Murdoch that stunned the television sports industry last Friday. Fox, Murdoch's six-year-old network, grabbed the rights to televise NFC games, as well as the 1997 Super Bowl, away from CBS by offering the NFL

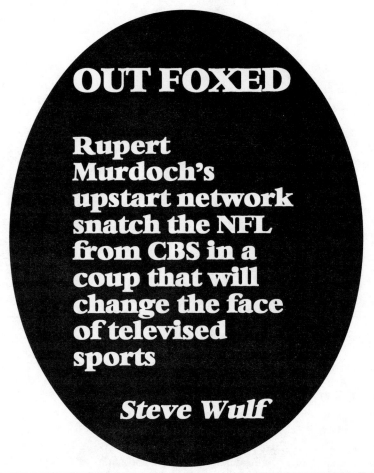

OUT FOXED

Rupert Murdoch's upstart network snatch the NFL from CBS in a coup that will change the face of televised sports

Steve Wulf

$1.6 billion over four years, which was some $100 million a year more than CBS chairman Laurence Tisch was willing to spend. Boom!

And bust for CBS, which on Monday lost out to the incumbent, NBC, for the rights to televise AFC games. Despite a last-minute phone-lobbying campaign by Madden himself, the owners chose NBC and its four-year, $880 million offer over CBS's 13th-hour billion-dollar bid. Nearly as upset as CBS was the NFL Players Association, whose members' pay is derived largely from TV dollars. Even as NBC was trumpeting its victory, the NFLPA was threaten-

The following article is reprinted courtesy of *Sports Illustrated* from the Dec. 27, 1993 issue, ©1993, Time Inc. "Outfoxed" by Steve Wulf. All rights reserved.

ing to hold up the deal. But if the arrangement stands, it would mean that for the first time since 1956, fans will not be watching NFL games on CBS on Sunday afternoons.

For Fox the NFC package means instant credibility. From his vacation home in Vail, Colo., a jubilant Murdoch told SI's Jill Lieber on Sunday night, "We're a network now. Like no other sport will do, the NFL will make us into a real network. In the future there will be 400 or 500 channels on cable, and ratings will be fragmented. But football on Sunday will have the same ratings, regardless of the number of channels. Football will not fragment."

Fox won the battle by offering more than just money. Dallas Cowboy owner Jerry Jones, a member of the NFL's TV committee, told SI's Peter King, "CBS has given the league 38 years and great tradition, and we preferred the incumbent. We handicapped Fox: they had to be significantly better. But they were. The type of commitment they gave us, we felt, was above and beyond dollars. They said, 'We'll take this entity, the NFC, and build our network around it.' It's a tremendous commitment on their part, and we just couldn't look past it."

As for Madden, don't worry, Mr. and Mrs. Big Fan, he won't be out of a job for long. "We will certainly make an offer to John," says Murdoch. "He will bring us even more credibility."

As it turned out, the day of infamy for CBS was Dec. 7, Pearl Harbor Day, when Fox made a presentation to members of the TV committee at the GTE Conference Center in Dallas. Speaking for Fox were David Hill, an Australian who is the president of Murdoch's soccer-oriented Sky Sports channel and who is also married to a devout Denver Bronco fan; Lucie Salhany, the chairman of Fox Broadcasting;

and Chase Carey, executive vice-president and chief operating officer and a man not to be confused with Fox's unlamented former late-night talk-show host. Murdoch had tried twice before without success to buy into the NFL, in 1987 and again in '90. But this time the Fox contingent offered to make the NFL the centerpiece of the network. The committee members were shown a tape of a Sky Sports telecast of a First Division soccer game in England, and, says Jones, the quality of the production compared favorably with that of any NFL game on U.S. television. The committee also heard about Fox's plans for year-round NFL programming, including a children's show, and international opportunities. According to Jones, "They talked about using our players on the network a lot, maybe even on their shows." Great! Shannen Doherty meets Leon Lett.

Fox was suddenly very much in the game. Out of loyalty the NFL told CBS and NBC that the league was taking Fox seriously. But, says one source close to the negotiations, "I don't know if CBS was complacent or just slow, but they weren't as astute as NBC. So the NFL began to steer Fox more toward the NFC."

Three days after the Dallas meeting, the Fox people made eye-opening offers for both conferences, but they preferred the NFC with its larger markets, nine straight Super Bowl championships and 20% higher ratings, and they underscored that preference with a staggering bid. Says Murdoch, "CBS, we knew, was grudgingly prepared to go over $300 million [a year]. But we didn't know how much. Would they go to 320? 350? So I said, 'Let's go for the knockout bid. The $400 million.'"

Last Thursday, CBS was told how much the NFL (which had already agreed on a new Monday-night package with ABC and a Sunday-night cooperative with ESPN

and TNT) wanted for the NFC. In order to keep the NFC, CBS did not have to match the Fox offer, but it would have had to offer far more than the $265 million it was already paying. "There is no question," says Murdoch, "that if CBS had been $20 million lower than us, the NFL would have taken CBS." The league gave CBS 72 hours to make an offer. But on Friday, the network told the NFL that it would pass. Murdoch, who was on his way to New York's Kennedy Airport, got the news over his car phone.

At that point the AFC, often derided by CBS personnel, still appeared to be a loose ball. In fact, a negotiating team from the NFL had already reached a tentative agreement with NBC, although the decision would not be official until the TV committee's conference all on Monday. That two-day delay led CBS to believe that it had one final opportunity to make a bid. Suddenly the boys at Black Rock, CBS headquarters in midtown Manhattan, wanted it. Hell, they needed it. But late Monday afternoon the NFL rejected CBS's bid, even though it exceeded NBC's by $30 million a year. "At no time before last Friday did CBS say they were interested in the AFC package," explains NFL vice-president Joe Browne. "After saying no to the AFC for weeks, they became interested after losing the NFC to Fox. By then, frankly, the interest was too late. Their offer was too late."

Dick Ebersol, the president of NBC Sports, says that Murdoch established the price for each conference, and it was left to NBC and CBS to rise to the challenge. But only one did. "It became clear to me," says Ebersol, "that whichever network acted first and came north of 210 million for the AFC, or 300 for the NFC, would get football. CBS never responded until it was over. In Murdoch we have someone with a different rationale for being in sports television. This marks the end of the three-network dance for rights to major sports."

It will take a while for the dust to clear and for Madden to put a new logo on his bus, bit it's fairly easy to sort out the winners and the losers in this new world.

The Winners:

- **Fox.** Some people think Murdoch was crazy to spend that kind of money on the NFC. Crazy like a fox. The deal not only puts Fox in the same league as the Big Three but is also a preemptive strike against the fifth and sixth networks planned by Time Warner (which publishes *Sports Illustrated*) and Paramount Communications. Says Kevin O'Malley, senior vice-president for programming at TNT. "That's what prompted the Fox deal: to foreclose on the competition. It's worth $400 million a year to Murdoch to preempt Time Warner ad Paramount."

The NFL will also increase the value of each of the 139 stations that carry Fox. And Murdoch hopes that Sunday-afternoon football will do for Fox's Sunday night ratings what it did for CBS's post-NFL lineup. "If our 7-to-11 p.m. ratings are a couple of points higher," he says, "that's worth a lot of money to us."

- **The NFL.** At the outset of negotiations, both CBS and NBC made it clear that they had lost money on the previous contracts and did not intend to do so this time around. But that was before the hungry Fox entered the picture. The Fox deal also addresses a concern of newer owners such as Jones and Denver's Pat Bowlen, namely that the league has become too staid. Fox's younger audience appeals to them, and so does the global reach of Murdoch's empire.

- **The Richer Teams.** Under the

league's new collective bargaining agreement with the players, a salary cap will begin next year that will be based on 66% of each club's designated revenues. Until the Fox deal came along, teams like the Buffalo Bills and San Francisco 49ers were fretting that they would not be able to keep their squads intact with only $30 million available for salaries. But the Fox-NBC windfall will raise that amount to nearly $34 million. Says 49er general manager Carmen Policy. "Now there's a light at the end of the tunnel for us."

- **The Players**. The higher cap will mean bigger salaries for stars and more job security for marginal veterans.

The Losers:

- **CBS**. Before NFL Today aired on Sunday, CBS Sports president Neal Pilson gathered the troops to give them a pep talk. "He told us not to worry," says someone who was at the meeting, "that we still had plenty of sports, like the Masters and the U.S. Open in tennis. At one point Terry Bradshaw raised his hand and asked, 'Does the Masters have a pregame show?' That broke everybody up."

For the most part, though, the mood at the CBS Broadcast Center on Sunday was grim. A lot of people will be out of jobs. Without the NFL, CBS Sports has little more left than the Masters, the U.S. Open, the upcoming Winter Olympics, a few college football bowl games and college basketball's Final Four. In the last year alone CBS has lost out on Major League Baseball, the 1996 Atlanta Summer Olympics and now the NFL. They may have to bring back refrigerator racing on Sundays. Nobody at CBS is blaming Pilson, though. The point man on the NFL talks was executive vice-

president Peter Lund, and he was following Tisch's orders. Pilson was only the messenger.

Another cause for concern over at CBS is what will happen to its vaunted Sunday-night lineup. Will as many people watch 60 Minutes and Murder, She Wrote if Madden and Pat Summerall aren't promoting Mike and Jessica during the Sunday-afternoon NFC game? "It's funny," says one former CBS Sports employee. "CBS spent all that money on baseball and the Winter Olympics a few years ago, and it's helped take them to the top. Now Fox is using the same strategy against them. You live by the sword, you die by the sword."

A CBS executive was even more blunt. "This wasn't a rights-fee negotiation," he said. "This was a hostile takeover by Fox."

- **Smalltown, U.S.A.** Of Fox's 139 stations, 120 are on the weaker UHF band. While most of those stations are on cable, and Fox claims that it can blanket 95% of the U.S., there might be a few isolated areas that will no longer receive NFC games.

- **The Poorer Clubs**. Bill Parcells was kind of hoping to get some of those ex-49ers for his New England Patriots.

There are skeptics who think that Murdoch will lose his custom-made shirt over the NFL deal; one estimate has him losing $500 million over the next four years. Says Murdoch, "I've seen those outrageous numbers. We'll lose a few million in the first year, but even if it was 40 or 50 million, it would be tax deductible. It was a cheap way of buying a network."

There are also those who don't think that Fox will be able to mobilize quickly enough to provide quality NFL coverage beginning next fall. But thanks to network cutbacks, there are many seasoned producers, directors and on-air talents that Fox will be able to hire for a lot less than those people were earning before.

And if Murdoch wants a Jimmy the Greek type, who among us can ever forget the episode a few years back on Fox's The Simpsons when little Lisa Simpson made a fortune for Homer with her NFL picks?

On Sunday, during CBS's telecast of the 49er-Detroit Lion game, Madden was describing what happens when a back goes in motion out of a full-house backfield. "At that point," he said, "the guys on defense are yelling, 'They broke the house! They broke the house!'"

Fox broke the NFL's house of the last 38 years. But who knows? Maybe the league's new home will be in a better neighborhood.

CAMPBELL

San Jose State University Radio-TV-Film senior Keith Campbell, obviously a baseball fan, uses a series of famous names to grab his readers' attention. His hope is that this honor roll will invoke the same memories in his readers as it does for him. Is this as good an opening for Campbell's essay as Wulf's was for his? What do they have in common? What makes them different?

You've read (in Chapter 1) that criticism can be subjective but that it should not be personal. But this is clearly a personal essay. Campbell's only support for his thesis is the invocation of the spirit of baseball. He calls on his readers to share his love for the game. Do you find his case persuasive? Do you think some readers (for example, baseball fans) might have one reaction and non-fans another? What could he have done differently to persuade even non-fans to his position? Should he have made that effort?

Is this critic's evaluation baseball-specific? That is, can the same argument be made for television's demythologizing of football (college and pro) and basketball? Why or why not? Does your answer have more to do with television's coverage of those sports or with the nature of the sports themselves?

Cobb, Shoeless Joe, Cy Young, Dizzy, The Babe, Gehrig, DiMaggio, Mickey, Willie, Yaz, the list of baseball legends could go on for pages and pages. "Say it ain't so Joe." Casey at the Bat. The Babe pointing to center field, then hitting the ball into its bleachers. Baseball, the national pastime. Major League Baseball and the players were larger than life. But where are the legends of the 1980s? Television brought unimaginable wealth to team owners as well as to players, but what price has been paid for that extensive television coverage of baseball? That television money has affected Major League Baseball is obvious. Players' salaries are rapidly spiralling to unbelievable heights. The owners commanding the best cable television markets attempt to buy pennants through

---

Written in 1993 by Keith Campbell, Radio-TV-Film Major at San Jose State.

free-agency. Players are transient, moving from team to team, playing for the highest bidder. However, it is the nature of television itself that has had the greatest affect on the fan's perception of baseball. Television has shrunk the great expanses of the ball park and in doing so eliminated the fan's frame of reference. It has over exposed both Major League Baseball and the players. Before television intruded, only the game's participants could cross the magical white lines separating baseball from the commonness of everyday life. Television has robbed the game of its legendary status and removed the players from their heroic perch. Television has demythologized the game of baseball.

In other genres, the text is imbued with characters, story lines and symbols which create mythical narratives teaching and confirming society's values. For example, policemen are portrayed as knights in shining armor. They capture criminals, proving once again that good defeats evil and all is well in our society. Ironically, with television coverage of Major League Baseball just the opposite has been true. Baseball did not need television to artificially create its myths. Prior to television, baseball was full of heroes and legends. Each game was a contest between the home town heroes and the visiting villains, all of whom were imposing, almost godlike figures. Rather than create mythical figures and symbols, television has helped eliminate the myth, not just from televised baseball games, but from all of Major League Baseball.

Before television intruded on our national pastime there were two ways to see a Major League Baseball game. One was to personally attend a contest. Fans were allowed to enter the world of the players, as long as they stayed on their own side of the white lines. The other way to see a game was through the greatest contributor to the mythol-ogy of baseball, radio. Fans listened to the radio and saw the game through their own imagination. Audiences took cues from the radio announcers to create images of impossible diving catches, exploding fastballs and mammoth home runs. Yet television provided fans with a third way to watch baseball; on a small box. Unfortunately, while the baseball parks of both reality and the mind are huge, on the television screen they are tiny. Fans lose their frame of reference. On television the beauty of the majestic, towering home run is lost while fans attempt to find the tiny ball as the screen switches from one camera shot to the next. Fans can no longer see the long run made before the outfielder's lunging catch or the amount of ground the shortstop quickly covers to make the backhanded stop. On television a routine catch looks almost the same as the great catch. Since television reduces the fan's ability to see the great play, a new emphasis has been placed on players' mistakes. Instead of Richardson's legendary catch of the McCovey line shot which ended the 1962 world series, we now have Bill Buckner missing a ground ball to end the Boston Red Sox season.

Through network, local and cable television, fans can watch baseball nearly every day of the Major League Baseball season. To see a game is no loner special. Television has brought baseball right into the fan's living room. When a fan can watch over 5000 at bats in a single season, what is magical about any one particular at bat, be it a record setting strikeout or a rookie's first home run? Television has not only presented the fan with the ability to view many games, but it has also placed the fan on the field for those games. No longer is the field the player's domain. The fans do not imagine what happens on the field anymore, television shows them the reality. The fans can see the emotions of the players as they are reduced to human levels after striking out or making an error. Television has allowed viewers to follow the players into the dugouts where they see them looking anything but heroic as they throw bats, helmets and glove. As salaries of these now all too human players have escalated, the fans' reactions to them have changed. No longer are the hometown players honored as heroes competing in a mythical contest against the awe-inspiring villains of the visiting team. Players are now perceived as greedy, often unlikable men who are not deserving of the salaries they earn. In the past, fans may have booed the enemy on the visiting team, but now fans boo the hometown players who are not capable of living up to their large contracts.

"Gibson has his lead off first. The pitch to Scioscia is lined deep to left center. Bonds and Van Slyke are racing back, racing, racing, and it's Van Slyke who makes a stumbling, remarkable catch, falling to the warning track but holding the ball! Gibson, around second, is in trouble. Van Slyke is up and throws a strike to Jay Bell who whirls, and with crucial accuracy duplicates Van Slyke's perfect peg to double up Gibson by a wide and humiliating four or five feet! Scioscia hit the ball as wide and deep as the August sky and has come away with only the dust of a double play to show for it!" What fan doesn't remember hearing a great call by a baseball radio announcer? While this great call by Vin Scully allowed listeners to clearly see the play in their own minds, each would imagine it differently. Individual listeners would replay it in their minds, the catch and throw becoming more and more fantastic-the stuff of legend. Almost everyone has read a good book and then been disappointed upon seeing the movie based on that book. The setting, character, and the entire ambience of the story are not quite the same as the reader had imagined. Watching baseball on television brings the same frustration. Television makes most plays look routine, therefore they can never compare to the plays seen live, let alone to plays seen only through one's imagination. When a great play does occur, television replays it over and over again, analyzing its every aspect. Nothing is left to the imagination, there's no opportunity to build the play into greatness, it has become routine and common through overexposure. While television shows and tells fans what has occurred, radio describes the action and lets the fans see it through their own mind's eye.

Great players cannot become legends on their own, nor can the owners or the media build a player up to legendary status. It takes the fans' imagination to create a heroic and legendary baseball player. Television has robbed baseball of its heroes and taken away the game's mythical feeling. Baseball is no longer the unquestionable national pastime. Its realm is constantly besieged by professional basketball and football. Pete Rose, Jose Canseco, Wade Boggs, Dale Murphy, Mike Schmidt and Fred Lynn all were or are great players, but none are legends. Television has invaded the baseball players' dominion, reduced the field's majestic proportions and presented the fans with a view of players that has revealed their all too human natures. The television industry has recently advised Major League Baseball that the ratings for baseball games have been low and subsequent television contracts must be for substantially less money. Perhaps along with this fee reduction will come less televised baseball and a return to baseball at its best. Live at the stadium with all of the sights, sounds, and smells or as seen through the imagination, those are the places where legends are created.

Chapter Exercise

Judging Sports as Good and Bad Television

Determine for yourself, using your own values as a viewer and critic, which sports make good television and which sports don't. Be prepared to defend your opinions. Place an "X" in each box where you think the sport fulfills the demands of television. When you've finished, total the "Xs" for each sport to determine which are good and not so good television.

	Baseball	Football	Tennis	Basketball	Hockey	Golf	Auto Racing	Bowling
Fixed Starting Point								
Continual Crisis								
Natural Breaks								
Big Ball								
Visual Variety								
Physical Action								
Personal Side								
National Interest								
TOTALS								

References and Resources

Bryant, J., Brown, D., Comisky, P. W. & Zillman, D. (1982). Sports and spectators: commentary and appreciation. *Journal of Communication, 32,* 109–119.

Chandler, J. M. (1988). *Television and National Ssports: The United States and Britain.* Urbana, IL: University of Illinois Press.

Easton, T. (1986). Caught in a squeeze. *Channels,* April, 46–49.

Geracie, B. (1993). In the NFL, it's the schedules that count. San Jose *Mercury News,* November 22, pp. 1E, 5E.

Goodwin, M. (1986). TV sports glut pulling plug on advertisers. Austin *American-Statesman,* January 26, pp. A1, A15.

Hocking, J. E. (1982). Sports and spectators: intra-audience effects. *Journal of Communication, 32,* 100–108.

Kraus, S. & Davis, D. K. (1976). *The Effects of Mass Communication on Political Behavior.* University Park, PA: Pennsylvania State University Press.

The last football show. (1994). *Sports Illustrated,* March 7, p. 14.

Luciano, R. & Fisher, D. (1988). *Rememberances of Swings Past.* New York: Bantam Books.

McKay, J. (1973). *My Wide World.* New York: Macmillan.

McKeon, R. (1993). Pro hockey. San Francisco *Examiner,* December 26, p. C–8.

O'Neil, T. (1989). *The Game Behind the Game: High Pressure, High Stakes in Television Sports.* New York: Harper & Row.

Patton, P. (1984). *Razzle Dazzle: The Curious Marriage of Television and Professional Football.* Garden City, NY: Dial Press.

Powers, R. (1984). *Supertube: The Rise of Television Sports.* New York: Coward-McCann.

Rader, B. G. (1984). *In Its Own Image: How Television Has Ttransformed Sports.* New York: Free Press.

Spence, J. (1988). *Up Close and Personal: The Inside Story of Network Television Sports.* New York: Atheneum.

Smith, C. (1987). *Voices of the Game: The First Full-Scale Overview of Baseball Broadcasting, 1921 to the Present.* South Bend, IN: Diamond Communication.

Talen, J. (1986). How the Camera Changes the Game. *Channels,* April, 50–55.

TV's new rule book. (1986). *Channels,* April, 45.

CHAPTER 13

COMMERCIALS

Commercials are not filmed on Earth; they're filmed on the Commercial Planet, where everything is different; where fast-food-chain employees really are happy to serve you; where there is some meaningful difference between Coke and Pepsi; and where "light" beer does not taste like weasel spit.

—*Dave Barry*

Humorist Barry (1993, p. 23) is wrong; the commercials we see on television are, in fact, filmed on Earth. But they're produced in a very special atmosphere, one where money, time, aesthetics, government regulation, creativity, truth, and the audience combine to encourage what many critics would call the very worst of contemporary television or, what many others would argue, is the very best.

Good or bad, they are on the air in unprecedented numbers and they are the life-blood of commercial television: In 1993 television billings for stations and networks amounted to $12.5 billion (national network and national syndication), $5.6 billion (national non-network), and $5.6 billion (local). "The average 30-second prime-time network television announcement now costs $100,000 (spots on a top-rated series cost $325,000; low-rated spots average about $50,000) . . . Thirty-second announcements on individual TV stations range from $20,000 in top-rated specials in major markets to as low as $10 in the second-hundred markets" *Broadcasting . . .* , 1995, p. xxi).

Overview

We will examine how the viewer is the one who eventually pays these huge sums. From the medium's first days, the audience has been exposed to increasing amounts of commercial time per hour and even more individual spots per commercial break. We'll revisit the quiz show scandal and examine other industrial, economic, regulatory and technological changes that have encouraged/allowed this to happen; but, we'll also look at how these very same factors changed the content of those spots, often for the better (as far as the viewer is concerned), but maybe for the worse for the sponsors.

Commercial from the Start

In the early days of radio, it was assumed that the medium would find its financial support in the manufacture and sale of receivers. Stations went on the air primarily so people would have something to listen to if they bought a set. The problem with this plan soon became obvious...once every listener had a radio, sales of receivers would drop, and the stations would have no way to make the money they needed to stay afloat. The solution was as close as the local news stand: advertising. In 1922, despite the fretting of Commerce Secretary Herbert Hoover that "so great a possibility for service" could be drowned in "advertising chatter" (Steinberg, 1980, p. 190), WEAF in New York City began accepting commercial sponsorship (called toll broadcasting) for its programming.

By the time commercial television came along in the late 1940s, it was just that...commercial. The networks were in place, the mechanism for the sale and purchase of time was established, the ad agency-broadcaster relationship was well established, and a large number of programs and stars carried their sponsors with them when they moved from radio to television. Just as important, a new kind of audience existed, one bursting with money and leisure as a result of WWII's transformation of American society—working women, suburban lifestyles, and a work force that was primarily industrially, rather than agriculturally, based. No more working seven days a week from sunrise to sunset. No more labor that required you to pour all of your money back into the land. In contrast, factory and office workers lived a nine-to-five, five-days-a-week existence. They had time left over at the end of the work day (leisure time) and extra money to spend after the necessities were satisfied (expendable cash).

These workers needed to spend their money somewhere, so the plants and factories that had been humming under war-related manufacture now made the new consumer products for those folks to buy. But how would people learn about the cornucopia that awaited them? Commercial television. Whetmore (1992, p. 417) wrote, "Commercial television came along just after World War II and has since helped change our attitudes about everything from mouthwash to credit cards. Television—a heavily used, intimate, trusted, emotionally

stimulating, and visually compelling medium—is *perfectly* suited to carry advertising."

In television's early years, sponsors, not networks, controlled the medium and selected programs to be produced and aired (Chapter 8). An advertiser would produce or buy a program from an independent producer and the networks served as national sales agents for their affiliated stations. The networks would clear time with the stations and collect money from the advertiser based on the operating costs of each station.

But by the mid-Fifties, the networks were actively maneuvering to remove the advertiser from any position of power. Realizing that even greater profits lay in the production and owning of programming and not (necessarily) solely in their distribution, the networks began producing a number of programs themselves. An early example was NBC's *Today* which premiered in January of 1952.

The 1959 Quiz Show Scandal (Chapters 3 and 8) killed off the last of the sponsor-produced programs on the networks (remember CBS President Frank Stanton's promise to "be masters of our own house").

Now that they did not own their own programs, advertisers found it impossibly expensive to sole-sponsor a network production. They quickly learned that it was more efficient and profitable to spread their commercials across several programs and, thus, reach substantially more viewers. The networks were happy to cooperate, selling advertising time in 60-second segments in what they called magazine-style advertising. This produced not only great profits for the networks, but because there was now more competition for viewer attention and recall among advertisers whose messages populated a single program, the nature of the ads themselves changed. *Creativity* came to television advertising.

No longer in possession of the luxury of sole-sponsorship, advertisers discovered that they needed to develop selling strategies to make their occasional commercials stand out among the abundance of others. In addition, because several advertisers would now be after the same audience, many commercials would be selling the same or a similar product during a particular program. Because many products advertised were essentially the same in quality and cost (e.g., cosmetics, candy, cigarettes, and household cleaners) the goal of much of this early advertising was *brand awareness*. Brand identification through catchy slogans and jingles became the order of the day. The airwaves were filled with commercials comparing one brand with another through demonstrations and testimonials. Commercials during this time were highly *product-oriented*. This would change, however, as the quantity of commercials on television once again increased, this time due to government regulation.

In the late 1960s the efforts of a young attorney-consumer advocate, John Banzhaf, led to the removal of cigarette commercials from the airwaves. The ban, effected in 1971, had an immediate impact. At the time, cigarette companies were television's biggest advertisers. American Tobacco alone was spending over $46 million a year on the medium. With this important cash-cow absent, the networks soon discovered that there were not enough advertisers who could afford to buy 60-seconds spots on a popular prime-time program.

Lowering the price of advertising time was a logical solution, but production costs for their entertainment programming made this an impossibility for the networks. In 1953, for example, a one hour episode of *Studio One* cost CBS $30,000 to produce. In 1975, *Gunsmoke* cost the same network $230,000 per hour. The solution: Split the 60-second spots into more affordable 30-second segments. Now even more advertisers had access to the potent medium and, not incidentally, the networks could make more money by selling two 30 second spots at more than the price of one full 60, making each minute of advertising more profitable. The networks avoided financial disaster but advertisers now found their commercials amidst twice as many competing messages. In 1965, *every* network television commercial was a full 60 seconds (although 23% were piggybacked, that is, a single sponsor presented two products in the same minute). In 1975, only 6% were a full minute long.

Not only did the number of commercial announcements grow, the number of commercial minutes allowed on television also increased. In 1967, for instance, there were an estimated 100,000 commercial minutes on the networks; in 1974, network television presented 105,622 commercial minutes; That's 5,600 *additional* minutes on the three commercial networks alone. More recently, during the Reagan administration, the FCC granted broadcasters permission to increase the number of prime-time commercial minutes to eight per hour (that's 13% of your viewing time spent on watching commercials).

From the mid-Fifties to today, the amount of money spent on television advertising has exploded. In 1956, a total of $1.25 billion in television advertising time was sold. In 1976, $6.7 billion; 1986, $22.6 billion, and as you saw at the top of this chapter, in 1993, $23.7 billion (Biagi, 1992 and *Broadcasting . . .* 1995).

The Evolution of Contemporary Television Commercials

In the Eighties, these trends accelerated. The price of commercial time continued to rise, television's income from advertising continued to grow, production costs continued to escalate, the number of commercials on the air continued to increase, the television time allowed for advertising continued to expand and, as a result, the length of commercial spots continued to shrink. Fifteen and even ten second spots became a popular and affordable way to advertise, although there were more and more commercials filling the breaks between program segments, producing that bane of advertisers, *clutter*. Stark (1985, p. A24) commented on this situation:

The switch to 15-second commercials seems to be nothing more than a complicated story about the inner workings of the broadcast industry, another tale of the pursuit of the almighty dollar. But it's more important than you might think. Because commercials influence the fabric of television, they, in turn, influence the fabric of everything else. When ads change, it's a sign that television is changing, as well as the culture.

Genre and Production Characteristics

The change he's talking about is even more dramatic and consequential than the transition from single-sponsorship announcements to product-oriented advertising that followed the networks' take-over of programming. It is the shift from product-oriented to *image-oriented* commercials. Pritkin (1979) explained it this way, "Since most products aren't special, most advertising does all that so-called image stuff....There's no information about the product, there's only information about the kind of people who might be inclined to use the product" (p. 43). Draper (1986, p. 16) offered excerpts from a *60 Minutes* interview with ad agency chairman George Lois to explain image advertising:

> *Advertising to me is poison gas. I put a commercial on the air, I spray it and I make people fall down. I make people say "I want that product." Not because the product is so much more wonderful than another product, but because they want to be involved in buying that product, they want to be involved in owning it.*

Lois' explanation of how television advertising works suggests that the viewer is an active participant in the process. This is something that image advertisers have understood for a long time. Marketing researcher Solomon, for example, wrote that advertisers should place their messages' emphasis "on the importance of products in 'setting the stage' for the multitude of social roles people must play (lover, gourmand, executive, athlete, and so on)....Consumers employ product symbolism to define social reality and to ensure that be-haviors appropriate to that reality will ensue....Product symbolism is often consumed by the social actor for the purpose of defining and clarifying behavior patterns associated with social roles" (1983, p. 16).

But how do television commercials accomplish this task? According to television critic Price (1978), commercials play to the unconscious, working very hard to make the "unreal" seem real. He argued that these fabrications are effective because they work like dreams.

There are, in fact, several production practices used in making television commercials that arguably are employed to make them seem like dreams. Before we list several, we offer Draper's comment that these techniques are "so imaginative that (they) often amount to misinformation, and at times to plain lying" (1986, p. 16). As you read this section, decide for yourself.

Time Compression. Dreams actually last for only a few seconds each. But when we awake it seems as if the dream lasted a long time and contained an extraordinary amount of information. Similarly, commercials seem to take up more time than their 10, 15, 30 or 60 second allotment and contain an amazing amount of information. Time compression, created by New York University marketing professor James MacLachlan, electronically erases minuscule segments of blank space within and between words on a commercial's voice track. The tape recording is then spliced back together without altering its clarity, and the visual portion of the commercial is accelerated to match the condensed sound. Thus, 45 seconds of information can be fit into a 30 second commercial. Tests have suggested that, like our retention of dreams, those who watch the fast-paced, information-packed ads average 36 percent better remembrance of the commercial content (although there is still some debate about time compression effectiveness).

Volume Compression. We remember many dreams because they often contain intense and extremely vivid images. Many commercials are designed to similarly assault our senses, often by being louder than the programs that house them. By means of volume compression, variations in sound intensity in a given passage of speech or music are evened out, so that nearly every syllable or note is broadcast at, or very near, the maximum permissible levels.

Physio- and Psycho-Acoustics. Besides compression, other phenomena—some physiological, some psychological—can influence our perception of loudness and are frequently manipulated by advertisers. For example, pitch can influence loudness. Because our ears are more sensitive to some frequencies than others, a siren or whining voice can sound much louder than other sounds at the same intensity. By the same token, psychological factors can come into play, whereby two commercials of equal volume can seem different if one presents pleasant information (i.e., puppies, children, flowers) and the other presents annoying, obtrusive information (i.e., headaches, arguing, hemorrhoids). Many successful advertisements, such as Alka-Seltzer's "I can't believe I ate the whole thing" and Sega's screaming-faces campaigns, are based on this premise.

Distortion. Often it's the most bizarre or surrealistic parts of dreams that we tend to remember. What is most disturbing about these images is that they are essentially based on real and familiar people and places, but appear in a highly distorted context. Distorting reality has become a highly popular, though high-risk, advertising strategy. We see close-up, strange-angle, hand-held camera shots of nothing but men's butts clad in Dockers, children being flown out of the galaxy via an enormous bubble blown from the newest brand of chewing gum, Chanel No. 5's version of a Salvador Dali lithograph, complete with men transforming into inanimate objects.

Infomercials. The strategy in these 30 minute commercials is not to replicate dreams, but to duplicate news and talk programs. These commercials never *actually* claim to be news and information fare, they just strongly sug-

gest that they are by using the conventions (sets, editing, anchors or hosts) of the more objective forms they copy. The example of journalistic criticism that follows offers additional insight.

Regardless of your feelings about these technical aspects of a commercial's production, it is difficult to argue with the fact that spots are becoming increasingly creative as they struggle to stand out among the clutter. Critic Price is correct, very often the best things on television are the commercials, but as Vivian (1991, p. 263) warns, creativity does not guarantee success: "Harry McMahan studied Clio awards for creativity in (television) advertising and discovered that 36 agencies that produced 81 winners of the prestigious awards for advertisements had either lost the winning account or gone out of business."

Part of the problem or, if you prefer, the challenge for television commercial makers goes well beyond clutter and the need to stand out. It's technology. The television remote control allows viewers to *graze* through the many channels available to them when a commercial interrupts the program they're watching; *zip* through commercials, that is, fast-forward through them in videotaped programming; or *zap* commercials out altogether by pausing the VCR as the the program is recorded (Massey & Baran, 1990). In fact, fast-forwarding (zipping) isn't even necessary now that many newer VCRs have the ability to detect the electronic *black frame* that separates commercials and programs. Once detected, the machines automatically zap the ad. In response to these increases in viewers' power, advertisers have attempted a number of strategies to keep them glued to the commercials:

1. **Familiar faces, familiar voices.** Tom Selleck narrates for AT&T, Jerry Seinfeld stands-up for American Express, Candice Bergen is charming for Sprint. Dennis Hopper descends deeper and deeper into insanity for Nike shoes. These are the faces and voices of performers that we enjoy seeing and hearing even if it is on a commercial.

2. **Games and contests.** Collins (1988) mentions *pods* wherein " the TV networks . . .present trivia questions or puzzles before the first commercial in the pod is aired and then present the answers at the end of the pod" (p. 13). "You Make the Call" on major league baseball and NFL broadcasts are good examples. Other strategies touted by the National Association of Broadcasters are prize games such as sweepstakes based on Social Security numbers and a bingo-type game using advertised products instead of numbers called TV WINGO (Making the call . . . , 1986).

3. **Recurring stories.** Viewers watch a romance develop between a delightful man and pretty woman over several individual commercials and several cups of Maxwell House Coffee. Viewers shriek (with joy? horror?) with each installment of the Energizer bunny campaign.

4. **Sensation television.** Pioneered "by the 'three Ms'—Madison Avenue, MTV and *Miami Vice*. Rock music, close-ups, bright colors, random violence and diminished use of language and plot are all...designed to snap viewers out of their trances and break through the clutter. The point is not to force the audience to think, but to cut through the clutter" (Stark, 1985, p. A24). Taco Bell, Sega, United Airlines, at any given time any viewer can add a dozen sponsors to the list of those who use their 30 or 15 seconds to wash our senses in sight and sound.

Controversy in Television Advertising

The diminution of word and plot in today's advertising is not without its critics. On a general level, it runs counter to the idea that advertising creates the informed, discriminating consumers necessary to an economic system driven by true competition. Draper (1986, p. 15) argues that, in fact, information-free advertising leads to monopoly:

Perfect competition requires highly standardized products, many buyers and sellers, and "perfect information." Every buyer knows what every seller proposes to charge for every product and feature. Price competition, the inevitable result, forces sellers to use their resources efficiently. Consumers benefit doubly—first, because all their products are as cheap as possible and, second, because the sum of society's wealth is greater than it would be in an imperfect market . . .

The theory of monopoly concedes that advertising deflects consumers from the rational aim of buying in the cheapest market and makes them, instead, want a certain brand, irrespective of cost. (Since the company that produces the brand is the only one than can do so, it has a "limited monopoly.")

How else can Nike demand and get $180 for a pair of basketball shoes and Evian make a profit selling water at 2 dollars a bottle?

A more specific criticism arises because many people believe that because commercials are ahead of the medium's other forms aesthetically and creatively, they set the tone for all the medium's other genres. Do we really want our news to have commercials' flash, speed and lack of depth? Some say that it already does (Chapter 10). As Stark (1985, p. A24) warns, "In the media age, tonight's television audience is tomorrow's electorate." Increasingly, political campaigns (and the task of governance itself) look more and more like the "three Ms."

Not unrelated is the complaint that television ads, in their attempt to touch our emotions while avoiding our intellects—and do it in 15 seconds amid the clutter of competing commercials—inevitably cheapen and demean the important parts of human existence that they portray. What is the commercial representation of motherhood? The wisdom to buy a $1.89 bottle of Downy. What is its distillation of family? Of success? Of attractiveness? Does the night *really* belong to Michelob? This is an excerpt from an editorial by Philip Harper (1989, p. 10B):

The commercial is titled "Freedom," and it was shot entirely on location at the Berlin Wall.

As people pass through a checkpoint, presumably from East to West, the camera captures their uncertainty and wonder. There is a real breath-holding quality to the scene? Will they make it to the other side? And, if they do, will what they find there live up to expectations?

Tension and emotion build.

Then, before you can say, "Ich bin ein Berliner," out come the bottles of Pepsi Cola. Uncertainty becomes utter contentment; freedom, it seems, never tasted so good. . . .

To equate physical thirst for a soft drink with the soul's thirst for freedom is obscene. It also makes capitalism appear every bit as frivolous and vulgar—every bit as corrupt—*as Marxists have always said it was.*

There are many other complaints that follow television advertising. For example, should advertising to children, people who presumably do not possess mature reasoning skills, be allowed? As one member of Action for Children's Television asked a Senate subcommittee, if we don't allow live salespeople to enter our homes to sell our children products, why do we allow the most sophisticated salespeople of all to do it for 12 minutes every hour every Saturday morning?

American television allows beer and wine commercials despite growing scientific evidence that they lead to increased consumption on the part of under-age drinkers. Ads for fruit-flavored and fruit-colored wine coolers have drawn particular attention. Yet American television shrinks away from advertising condoms, despite growing scientific evidence (and the great success of drinking and driving and anti-smoking public service campaigns) that demonstrates that these spots can promote safe sex.

Ultimately, we have to understand that the reason television advertising draws so much attention and criticism is that it is ubiquitous and seems to work.

BROWN

In this essay critic Brown combines gender (feminist), semiotic and structural analysis to produce a challenging critique of a specific Pepsi television commercial. Her discussion is peppered with terms that typically appear in gender analysis. But rather than explicitly define them, she provides meaning for them through their use in the context of her writing. What is meant by "dominant cultural codes?" "feminine reading?" "feminine discourse?" "patriarchal text?"

Many terms from narrative analysis and semiotics also appear. What is "foregrounding?" "moment of purchase?" "codes?" What does it mean to say that "narrative is a system of exchange?"

Brown's analysis is especially valuable if you agree with her argument that "femininity . . . is an ongoing process." What does she mean by this? What does television advertising contribute to this process? Does she do a convincing job of demonstrating this point using this one Pepsi ad?

Brown concludes with an argument similar to that of student critic Heitz (Chapter 11, "Mixed Messages . . . "), who also employed feminist analysis. The issue is oppositional reading. In concluding her primary thesis that this particular commercial "invites a feminine reading," she writes, "As a television commercial, it necessarily uses the code of advertising, yet it does so in a way that interrogates the patriarchal nature of that code as it uses it." How does this commercial do this? Do you think that its producers knew they were "interrogating" the patriarchal nature of advertising's codes? So, we return to one of criticism's central questions, where is meaning in television made?

The Ferraro Pepsi commercial[1] contextualizes the term "feminine" within the scope of intertextual reading practices and locates it within the media's coverage of Ferraro's Vice-Presidential campaign, a campaign whose "story" in the media conformed closely to Peter Brooks' (1976, 11–12) characterization of classic melodrama:

> *the indulgence of strong emotionalism; moral polarization and schematization; extreme states of being, situations, actions; overt villainy, persecution of the good, and final reward of virtue; inflated and extravagant expression; dark plottings, suspense, breathtaking peripety.*

The melodrama of the Ferraro campaign, as narrated by the media, reveals the struggle of the press, interacting with events and campaign rhetoric, to deal with the terms "feminine" and "masculine" in Ferraro's public position.

As time goes on, our heroine struggles against adversarial forces. The complexity of her position, the double bind of the oxy-

THE DIALECTIC OF THE FEMININE:

Melodrama and commodity in the Ferraro Pepsi commercial

Mary Ellen Brown

moron "public woman," is clear from the beginning. She and her running mate must not appear to be mates in any other sense. Congress and the press find flaws in the family's financial statement. Through the serial episodes of the daily news we see her cope with, and succeed in laying to rest for the moment, the fears that her husband's financial dealings will ruin her political career. We see her face her opponent in public televised debate. She holds her own. Her opponent, true to his melodramatic positioning as villain, hits "below the belt." His comment on "kicking ass" sends the media into a furor. Miraculously, the media remains sympathetic to Ferraro, but it is a close call. As the election draws near, the press speculates on hidden support for the Mondale-Ferraro team-but it fails to surface. The final chapter is the election and defeat—or is it? The press is kind to her in defeat, sensing that the story is not yet over: more episodes are to follow. Tune in tomorrow.

The narrative of Geraldine Ferraro as "almost powerful woman" continues in the 1985 Pepsi commercial featuring Ferraro and her two daughters. Ferraro is here repositioned as wife and mother and

Reprinted from *Communication* ©1987, Vol. 9, pp. 335–354. With permission from Gordon and Breach Science Publishers S.A.

also (and only incidentally) candidate for Vice-President of the United States. As Charlotte Brundson and David Morley (1978, p. 25) put it:

The 'naturalness' of common sense cannot be separated from the commonsensical definition of woman through their 'natural' and 'timeless' roles of wife and mother, roles which correspondingly define

them as the 'bearers' and repository of a basic/natural wisdom which is founded on their taken-for-granted separation from political life.

Through the intertextuality of

THE GERALDINE FERRARO PEPSI AD

Video	Audio
	D1: /"Looking for a job, Mom?"/(Seagull noises in background)
1. XLS: Sunlit, Victorian sun porch. One woman at a table in lounge chair (extreme back lighting), reading a newspaper. Another walks in in pants, younger, apparently serving something.	
2. CU: Newspaper picture of man (too fast to see who, but looks political).	GF: /"Very funny."/
3. XCU: GF (Figure 1)	
4. MS: Legs coming in a screen door (in long skirt).	D2(Laura): /"Well, I am."/
5. CU: Laura coming in door (face).	D1: /"What's it this week, Laura, marine biology?"/
6. XXCU: Daughter 1. Parts of face (locked down camera so face moves within the frame-side view-last show, eyes). (Fig. 2).	
7. XXCU: GF. Newspaper in front of her mouth, we see her eyes.	GF: /"Aren't we still hoping to be a star of stage and screen?"/
8. XCU: Pepsi being poured into glass. Woman's hand picks up glass from the top and pulls it upward.	D2 (Laura): /"Come on, Mom,/(Sound of ice cubes clinking.)
9. XCU: Laura drinking it (cut on the movement).	/It's a tough choice."/
10. XXCU: GF. Face, eyes and mouth.	GF: /"Sure it's tough when you can be anything you want to be."/
11. MCU: Skirted woman taking seat at the table (Shot from under the table.)	Male VO: /"When you make a choice, what's right is what feels right,/
12. XLS: Sunlit porch (same as shot 1). The three woman are now sitting around the table.	/"Diet Pepsi."/
13. CU: Diet Pepsi can-glass goes through the bottom of frame right to left (shot from above and side).	GF: /"You know, there's one choice I'll never regret."/
14. XXCU: GF. Face (side view, one eye screen right; edge of newspaper screen left).	D2 (Laura): /"Politics?"/
15. XXCU: Laura. Face (mouth to eye) sways back and forth slightly (Figure 3)	GF: /"Unh-unh. Being a mother."/
16. XXCU: GF and daughter. (GF screen right, daughter screen left; two eyes at first). (Figure 4)	Male VO: /"Diet Pepsi-the one calorie choice of a new generation."/
17. CU: Pepsi can. Side view.	

Super in: The one calorie Choice of A New Generation (Camera Angles: CU = close up; XCU = extreme close up; LS = wide angle or distance shot; M = middle, medium) hegemonic discourse, Ferraro is returned to the home—or is she?

The problem I shall address is whether the making of the Pepsi commercial has destroyed Ferraro's "meanings" for women or whether the "Ferraro-for-women" of the campaign can still be read against the patriarchal grain of the television commercial. A commercial is typically a masculine text—the framing provided by the inevitable male voiceover evidences this—but while this may make a feminine reading difficult, it does not, in itself, make one impossible. In my analysis of this Pepsi commercial I shall try to demonstrate how the text works to reposition Ferraro safely within patriarchy, but that "hegemony is leaky" and that there are elements in it which not only make a feminine reading possible, but actually invite one.

This commercial is, like any test, open to multiple readings. Conservative women can use it to reposition women in the home; progressive women to assert women's right to choose. It does not subvert or deny patriarchy in a revolutionary way, but it can be seen as resistant, for it does negotiate a larger and more active space for men within the system. It moves to redefine the family in a more constructive way for women than representational systems which glorify the young female body in the expectation that the woman will disappear from public view after she has been safely married. It also redefines female roles within the family by extending the nature of the choices open to women. We must not claim too much for it, but in a small way, this commercial can be seen to encourage a shift in society's definition of femininity in a direction that favors women and helps to weaken the patriarchal grip both on the nature of the definition and on the gender that has the power to make it.

As Roland Barthes, in *S/Z* (1979), has used Girodet's paint-

ing *Endymion Sleeping* and Balzac's short novel *Sarassine* to elaborate the writerly test with its multiplicity of signifiers, codes, and meanings, so will I attempt to play upon this test, the Ferraro Pepsi ad, using some of the insights gained from S/Z to enter the text as Barthes would at the

> *entrance into a network with a thousand entrances; to take this entrance is to aim, ultimately, not at a legal structure of norms and departures, a narrative or poetic law, but a perspective (of fragments, of voices from other tests, other codes), whose vanishing point is nonetheless ceaselessly pushed back, mysteriously opened: each (single) test is the very theory (and not the mere example) of this vanishing, of this difference which indefinitely returns, insubmissive (p.12).*

At the same time that the test is insubmissive, I will seek to show that the woman-in-the-text is also insubmissive. This text, although heavily burdened with the weight of dominant cultural codes, does not entirely submit to the domination of the female term.

Feminine Discourse

In the development of feminist theory, the initial assumption is that the basic division among humans is between males and females and that this division orders most, if not all, aspects of social existence. In society, conventions develop in ways which serve the interests of whatever ideological sex/gender system is in power. For example, Gayle Rubin (1975, p. 159) uses the term "sex/gender system" to refer to the domain of sexual or gender relationships within social contexts. Rubin describes a "political economy" of sex in the following way:

> *Hunger is hunger, but what counts as food is culturally determined and obtained. Every society has some form of organized economic activity. Sex is sex, but what counts as sex is equally culturally determined and obtained. Every society also has a sex/ gender system—a set of arrangements by which the biological raw material of human sex and procreation is shaped by human, social intervention and satisfied in a conventional manner, no matter how bizarre some of the conventions may be (p. 165).*

Various cultural forms within a society, then, interact with the sex/ gender system. Our society, given its heterosexual basis, uses the female body to sell products. Buying is based on perceived choice, desire and want, and consuming is often made to seem pleasurable in the advertisements by its intimate connection with sex, frequently expressed by images of the female body. The word "feminine" in the context of family bears a different set of connotations than it does in terms of sexuality and the body in the areas of psychoanalytic or semiotic criticism.

"Femininity" in this use is defined not by a completed moment in the history of the individual psyche but by an ongoing process. It is therefore susceptible to modification, even contradiction: for as social conditions change, so do the constructions of the feminine that they produce. In the same way, texts are already produced, and popular texts in a patriarchy must necessarily be inscribed with the patriarchal voice, but this does not mean that women have to read these texts or respond to them in ways that conform to the dominant ideology. Women *are* able to influence the meanings of patriarchal texts: they can read them in a feminine way. Thus, when I speak of feminine discourse, I speak of discourse which is understandable to women because they have lived in a female body in this culture. It is the French feminists who have recouped the word "feminine" for women. They have linked the word with feminine psychoanalytic theory and with feminine discourse, particularly writing and the body. The body, when claimed, or reclaimed, by women for their own pleasure, and ultimately *jouissance,* becomes a powerful political tool. It functions in two ways. First, the knowledge of bodily pleasure created by women for themselves is a denial of desire in male terms around which much dominant discourse is narratively constructed. Second, it is a source of independence for women around which a political feminine is constructed and can be further developed. (See, for examples, Mitchell and Rose (1982), Cixous (1976) and (1981), and Mulvey (1975).)

An example of how girls and women can use dominant media and cultural forms for their own pleasure and as their own cultural capital is provided in Angela McRobbie's article "Dance and Social Fantasy" (1984). In it, she analyzes how girls and women use dancing and the representations of dance in movies like *Flashdance* to construct meaning for themselves. In *Flashdance* the women are performing for men and the male gaze dominates, yet the narrative is like that of the Woman's Film; female bonding and female independence are pivotal themes. The structuring of dance for the male gaze, however, does not in itself deny girls and women pleasure completely. McRobbie hypothesizes that the process of looking at women performing from a female point of view entails and interrogation of the form and the pleasure—and pain—involved. She does not suggest that women's uses of such hegemonic renderings of dominant culture

serve to subvert that culture, but that they open some dominant ideological popular texts and practices to multiple readings by subordinate or oppositional groups, who can thus find a voice or space for themselves within the dominant ideological frame of patriarchy.

Recent feminist scholarship has emphasized the importance of mother-daughter relationships in feminist critical theory and practice. Marianne Hirsch (1981) states the position unequivocally:

> *There can be no systematic and theoretical study of women in patriarchal culture, there can be no theory of women's oppression, that does not take into account woman's role as a mother of daughters and as a daughter of mothers, that does not study female identity in relation to previous and subsequent generations of women, and that does not study that relationship in the wider context in which it takes place: the emotional, political, economic, and symbolic structures of family and society (p. 201).*

This significance of negating or making invisible the biological power of women to reproduce not only the species but daughters who inherit this power is evidenced within a variety of representational discursive systems. The struggle to contain female reproductive power is clearly available in some melodramatic texts. One characteristic of the Woman's film, here defined as "discourse *addressed* specifically to women" (Doane 1983, p. 68—emphasis mine), is that apart from the discourse of desire, there emerges another discourse—a discourse about mothers and daughters (see Williams, 1984). Perhaps this discourse is more tentatively managed by patriarchal film form than other discourses because it is a discourse which the male cannot know. Certainly, it could be con-

tended that there is privileged conversation among women about childbirth, which is so powerful that the process of birthing and its discourse have been taken over by the medical profession and characterized as a sickness. The relationship between mother and daughter is obviously important to women and is a frequent theme in the Woman's Film. Two classic Woman's Films provide good examples. In *Now, Voyager* (1942), Charlotte Vale's satisfaction at the end of the film is gained through her relationship to Tina, her symbolic daughter. In *Stella Dallas* (1937), Stella's excesses are punished by the loss of her daughter. In both films the relationship between mother and daughter is seen as empowering the daughter as well as giving a sense of identity to the mother. The Ferraro commercial foregrounds the mother-daughter relationship and Ferraro verbalizes the power of choice to her daughters, but like many of its melodramatic predecessors, the absent male serves as a counterpoint which frames and attempts to control the discourse. Such frames or controls Barthes calls codes.

The Commercial

In using the five codes devised by Barthes in *S/Z*—the referential/cultural code, the hermeneutic code, the proairetic code or code of action, the semic code, and the symbolic code, we need to conceptualize narrative not as a system of meaning, but as a system of exchange or an economy. In the economy of the text, the reader "exchanges" the narrative for meanings that enable her or him to make sense of the culture. A code, as Barthes uses the word, is a bridge between culture and meaning, between reader and text. Thus it does not convey a particular meaning, but is rather the means by which readers make meaning. It effects an exchange between a text and areas of shared cultural experience, and conveys not raw "reality," but already encoded representations of it: "reality" becomes what is regularly, routinely, represented in the codes of a culture. So "reality," as it is conveyed by the codes of any one text, is already part of the network of meanings that constitute culture. Thus the code of advertising functions by using the structure of one system to give meaning to another system.

The point at which the translation from one system to another takes place is the advertisement. Most advertisements propose to differentiate between products that are essentially the same. The Pepsi ads, for example, seek to differentiate Pepsi Cola from other soft drinks, but particularly from Coca-Cola. Since taste cannot be conveyed in a commercial, Pepsi's differentiations rests on the connection the ad makes with an image drawn from outside the work of advertising. Coca-Cola ads have traditionally linked Coca-Cola with Americana:

> Coke is the heartland, the nuclear family . . . it's nature. It's a small town in the Midwest. In a Saturday Evening Post cover by Normal Rockwell. Coke is nostalgia; it's the past (St. Louis Post Dispatch, May 6, 1985, p. E-1).

The Pepsi ads link Pepsi with the future, with the new generation, in this case with the political woman. There is no need for her to be seen drinking or holding a Pepsi; the juxtaposition of Ferraro's image with Diet Pepsi within the same advertisement puts them in apposition in the grammar of the ad. The ad translates what Ferraro "means" to the product, Diet Pepsi. Her position in the system of signs signifying political woman makes her image useful as linguistic currency.

Linda Williamson (1978) speaks of the content of the form in advertisements. Looking at the concept semiotically she replaces form and content with signifier and signified thereby changing the emphasis of the terms. Signifiers are things; form is invisible. Signifieds are ideas; content is material (18). Form and content are oppositional, but bound together as sign, signifier, and signified, they are inseparable. This distinction is important in looking at the Ferraro ad because although Ferraro, the person, attempts to control the discourse of the ad by assuming its authorship, once her image becomes a part of the linguistic currency of the code of advertising, she loses much of that control. However, the meanings generated for each reader by the evoked Ferraro melodrama or by the symbolic code of motherhood (to name one) remain powerful. Part of the struggle for control of the discourse goes on outside the commercial; however, the struggle also takes place in the "content of the form" or the sign system of the code of advertising.

A positive reading of the commercial for women is made difficult by the presence felt and heard in the male voiceover. Doane (1980) attests to the power of the voice without the body. The voiceover, according to Doane, bypasses the characters and establishes a complicity between itself and the spectator. It possesses knowledge and the "unquestioned activity of interpretation"; lacking a specific time and space, it is beyond criticism. In this ad the male voiceover is a powerful bearer of the patriarchal frame of the code of advertising within which the feminine discourse struggles to assert itself. Both melodramatically and in terms of the cultural/referential code of advertising the absent male is indicative of the female's lack of economic power. Male power functions through economic power in advanced capitalist societies. Ferraro's husband's economic problems are one of the complications of Ferraro's intertextual public melodrama, and the absent male in the commercial manifests itself in the economic register of advertising conventions. But the feminine discourse of mothers and daughters struggles against advertising conventions. Advertisers, however, lose control over the unadvertised messages, the connotations, deposited "neither gaudily nor surreptitiously, but 'just there' quietly" in what Blonsky (1982, p. 78) calls "wild semiosis." These are the elements which make a feminine reading possible. Specifically, in this commercial they are the use of the voice, the use of Geraldine Ferraro herself, and the use of the eyes and the look.

We see the hermeneutic code or the search for truth at play at the beginning of the commercial in the delay of the answer to the question, who are these people? The importance of Ferraro's voice is evident in the opening shot. An extreme long shot, it eludes immediate identification of the characters as well as our identification of the commercial as a commercial. The first shot of Ferraro does not assure her identification either. In it, an extreme close up, the bottom part of her face is shielded from our view by the newspaper she is holding. The commercial contains no music as an auditory clue that this is a commercial; however, the grainy voice, which we know from Ferraro's campaign, is a hermeneutic clue. Thus Ferraro—the person and public figure—is evoked to give meaning to the verbal and public discourse that she lost the election, hence we understand the joke about her looking for a job. Once we realize that this *is* the Ferraro Pepsi commercial, the hermeneutic question becomes, how is it that we understand its construction of meaning?

Action in the ad is almost nonexistent. As the three women—mother and daughters—gather on a sun porch to chat as they read the newspaper, one daughter jokes with her mother as the other, Laura, comes indoors discussing career options. Pepsis are poured and sipped as the voiceover links career choice to the choice of Diet Pepsi. Mother and daughter embrace as Ferraro tells the young women that the choice she will never regret is being a mother. Diet Pepsis are shown as the voiceover names Diet Pepsi as the choice of a new generation.

But of course we have only come in on the tail end of the narrative. From this tiny bit of the story, "fat and hungry with American narratives" (Blonsky, 1982, p. 74), the reader knows that the story begins when Gerri Ferraro, the kid from Brooklyn, is nominated the first female candidate for Vice-President in this country. The final test—the election and defeat—brings us finally to the denouement, the moment of the commercial, the moment when despite her public defeat, goodness and morality win out. She rests here with her daughters. She has not been defeated as Stella Dallas was defeated—by the loss of her daughter, the loss of self—in this final scene, for this week.

In the proairetic code, this bit of narrative completes the cycle for the moment. As Blonsky puts it:

A proairetism is a bit in a sequence, a lock-step of acts each of which lead ineluctably to the next and at last to term. The proairetic code would accrete instances, fascinate with the next, *forcing from us the 'and then? and then?' of the child. U.S. cultural, political, amorous, professional doings are at the same time semiotic activities. They are narrative whose segments constitute the egos we are (p. 74).*

The audience, the reader, makes sense of her "reality" in relation to her participation in the ongoing narrative, both within and around the commercial. But as with all ongoing serial melodramas, a new plot emerges even as this one ends.

The commercial itself as a kind of meta-melodrama has become a source of a new problematic—is it morally right for a person with an understanding of her own symbolic value for women to place herself, her story, and her image into the visual and oral economy of commodity fetishism, the conventions and signifying systems of which usually objectify women? In the 1930s and 40s stars like Bette Davis exercised some control over their scrips and interviews in fan magazines and the popular press (La Place, 1985). Ferraro's position is similar: she is not only a public figure who is a woman and a mother, but she also has attempted to control the discourse. The question then becomes will she succeed to the extent that her readers want her to. Perhaps the better question would be, what would constitute her symbolic success for her readers—her audience?

The ad can only be conceptualized as success if we allow it its multiplicity of meanings. Although Geraldine Ferraro does not call herself a feminist and is not active in feminist groups, she has obvious symbolic value for women by virtue of her public position. In addition, personal acts are interpreted as political acts for her. The *New York Times Magazine,* for example, in describing her statement on abortion, said that "a national candidate for office for the first time spoke in the first person about abortion" (September 30, 1984). Thus when we look at the Ferraro commercial we are concerned with referential/cultural codes by which previous "meanings-of-Ferraro" are brought to bear on it by the reader and by which the reader enters into the economy of the commercial. We are concerned with the characters, the semic code, in terms of Ferraro

the *person,* Ferraro the *character,* and Ferraro the *figure* of the mother in the commercial. The semic code is the major means by which characters (or objects or places) are encoded. It works by grouping signifiers around either a proper name or another signifier that functions as if it were a proper name. These signifiers, which provide another signifier with a semantic value, Barthes calls "semes." Such semes require repetition to attach themselves to a proper name to turn it into a character. Here, the proper name is not spoken, but the visual image and voice substitute for it. The semes are pre-existent, intertextual—the commercial depends on the shared referential/cultural code to bring with it the semes of Ferraro as political woman, as successful woman, as progressive woman, as socially integrated ethnic: these repeated semes, and others, are her history, her meaning as a media character already familiar to the reader of her melodrama.

Geraldine Ferraro and her daughters Laura Zaccaro and Donna Zaccaro are, in fact, characters in a narrative. Yet these are not fictive characters—they are people—endowed with moral freedom and motives. Thus the semes available for these characters come, in part, from semiotic information available in the commercial and from the reader's previous knowledge of these characters in other media texts which have constructed them as "real people." They are actors in their own docu-drama in which they enact not their "real" lives, but an impersonation of those lives. Their own dialogue seems to control their images, yet the fact that we see them also gives them temporal and spatial position not evidenced in the male voiceover. He is known only intertextually from other ads; here the reader knows nothing about him and very much (everything) about the women. The women are investigated, discovered, uncovered, segmented, and reassembled. Yet the reader, unlike the spectator in classical narrative film, is not sutured into the narrative by shot/reverse shot formations, but kept outside, an intimate observer so closely placed to the image that reader and image could embrace. The close-ups are microscopic, investigatory; the reader is the investigator. The semes inherent in the public woman, the Geraldine Ferraro of the respectful long shot, are placed in the home in terms of the setting of the ad and are projected into the viewer's personal space in terms of the camera shots. The code of advertising treats her image and those of her daughters in the conventional manner: the images are fragmented, fetishized. In them the woman becomes, as Barthes describes, a collection of body parts for men:

> *Divided, anatomized, she is merely a kind of dictionary of fetish objects. This sundered, dissected body . . . is reassembled by the artist . . . into a whole body, the body of love descended from the heaven of art (p. 123).*

These visual conventions are common in television advertisements—particularly the Pepsi ads which rely almost entirely on the play of signifiers and ellipses to create the Pepsi image.

Through Barthes' symbolic code we can see the possibility of the generation of new meanings within the conventional frames of the advertisement. The symbolic code is composed of anti-theses, binary oppositions which are represented as both eternal and inexplicable, yet they are central to the organization of the cultural order. Barthes considers the most important of these to be between male and female. Cary Nelson (1985, p. 54) lists the following cultural transformations of this basic opposition, gleaned largely from the works of de Beauvoir, Cixous, Le Doeuff, and

Rich (the male term is, typically, the first in each pair):

> *Masculine/feminine; active/passive; presence/absence; validated/excluded; success/failure; superior/inferior; primary/secondary; independent/dependent; unity/multiplicity; organized/scattered; intellect/imagination; logical/illogical; defined/undefined; dependable/capricious; head/heart; mind/body; subject/object; penis/vagina; firm/soft; sky/earth; day/night; air/water; form/matter; transcendence/inurement; culture/nature; logos/pathos.*

Among the binary oppositions in the Ferraro commercial are those between "mother" and "career" and "passive" and "active." The usual cultural association among these four terms is mother-passive and career-active, but the narrative here indicates that although career and active remain linked, mother is also an active choice. Likewise the binary relationship of make-active and female-passive is brought into question. The relationship here becomes male-active and female-active. Thus inscribed into the text of the commercial is the meaning, or sense, that the symbolic field exceeds the biological difference—that, as Silverman (1983, p. 217) puts it, "the phallus designates a cluster of privileges which are as fully capable of finding their locus in a female subject as in a male." Silverman is referring to S/Z, but here in the Pepsi ad the signified is Geraldine Ferraro the public woman presented to a reader who clearly knows the bearer of the unmentioned proper name is the first woman Vice-Presidential candidate in this country. Her history and its meanings challenge the positioning of women as helpless commodities, objects of exchange whose only function is to sell other commodities. Women readers who see

Ferraro as an active, progressive woman functioning to advance the position and change the meaning of womanhood in our society can find moments of purchase within this ad where their previous meanings of Ferraro can be used to activate a feminine reading that opposes the dominant patriarchal one. First, Ferraro herself becomes a moment of purchase, not only because of her history, but also because of her face, whose wrinkles and "imperfections" set it in opposition to those "faces" conventionally used to construct meanings of "attractive femininity" with which to sell commodities. Second, her voice brings with it the meaning of the public power which it gained during her campaign and whose "rough" edge contracts it significantly with the smooth "sexy" female voices conventionally used in ads. Third, the use of eyes and the look strengthen the semiotic position of women in the ad. Erving Goffman (1976) has characterized the look of woman in advertising as "licensed withdrawal." He argues that this is an important sign of subordination, for the unfocused gaze suggests that women can only operate in the interior world of daydreams and imagination, whereas men, whose gaze is focused on their immediate environment, are signified as having executive power over the environment. In this ad, the extreme close-ups of the women's eyes consistently show these eyes as focused, active, and purposeful.

These moments of purchase open up the text to make a feminine reading possible, even though it has to struggle against patriarchal hegemony. Unlike most television, commercials are made for repeated viewings, and these moments of purchase become clearer on subsequent viewings, particularly to those women whose initial pro-Ferraro stance is offended by the patriarchal commercialism of the ad. As spectators to the objectification of women by the code of advertising, female readers may still be positioned within the female body as a result of their previous relationship to cultural meaning systems. As Berger points out:

> Women watch themselves being looked at. This determines not only most relations between men and women but also the relation of women to themselves. The surveyor of woman in herself is male: the surveyed female. Thus she turns herself into an object— and most particular an object of vision: a sight(1972, p. 47).

Thus it is possible to understand McRobbie's (1984) reference noted above to the pleasure—and pain— that women may feel as they view this ad. Ferraro and daughters— persons, characters, figures—and the audience compete for control of the discourse of the ad with the meaning systems evoked by the code of advertising. Such a referential or cultural code is never an isolated phenomenon in any text. Cultural codes are inserted into discourse when an author produces a narrative as her or his natural expression, what Barthes calls the novelistic code. Cultural codes, then, are spoken by novelistic codes or, in this case, televisual codes. Enveloping both cultural and televisual codes and absorbing the naiveté of the previous two is the ironic code which is the code of the reader. It attempts to speak the author, become a supra-authorial position, and involve the reader as an accomplice of the discourse. Thus the speaking by an authorial voice of a referential code is subsumed in the act of reading—made into the process of cultural exchange—the production and distribution of meaning. It is the reader, then, who manages the multiplicity of meanings which are presented to her, who balances her live social meaning with the representational "com-

mon sense" meaning which she sees and hears.

Conclusion

At her peril, considering the conventions and codes used in the ad, Ferraro has inserted her name into the economy of cultural codes. Ferraro, in the Pepsi commercial, attempts to speak a reordering of the symbolic code of binary oppositions which constitutes woman as passive if man is active, woman in the home if man is outside, woman as mother if man is worker. As a television commercial, it necessarily uses the cool of advertising, yet it does so in a way that interrogates the patriarchal nature of that code as it uses it. This critical interrogation of patriarchy opens up a space within which the discourse of the feminine may be heard in its own voice, under and against the gruffer, loud voice of the male, but unmistakably there for the reader/viewer with ears to hear it. It is, as always, up to the reader of the commercial to complete the exchange, and to "buy," not Pepsi as the male wants her to, but her own voice.

The ad is clearly a man's text, a product of patriarchal hegemony. It does not evade the fetishizing look of the camera as Mulvey (1975) demands, but it does raise the issue of women's relationship to the language of the commercial and the use of women's bodies in representational forms. It can be seen to use female body parts differently. In the character of Ferraro, the gaze, face, and voice of women are differentiated from the conventional constructions of patriarchy. They invite a feminine reading, as does the power of the mother-daughter relationship in the commercial. The foregrounding of the notion of choice works similarly, particularly when we remember that the choice is not between commodities, as the male voice would have us believe, but between careers, that is between socially located definitions of the feminine. The

choice between "politics" and "mother" is a choice of meanings of woman, and, more importantly, the choice is woman's. What *is* chosen is less significant than the fact that it is *woman* who has the power to choose.

Notes

1. The Ferraro Pepsi commercial was one of three produced in 1985 for Diet Pepsi by Batten, Barton, Durstine and Osborn, Inc. (New York).

References

Barthes, Roland, *S/Z,* (New York: Hill and Wang, 1979).

Berger, John, *Ways of Seeing,* (London: Pelican, 1972).

Blonsky, Marshal, "Politics of the image: The body is advertising," *Social Text,* Vol. 6 (1982), pp. 73-85.

Brooks, Peter, *The Melodramatic Imagination,* (New Haven: Yale University Press, 1976).

Brundson, Charlotte and David Morley, *Everyday Television: 'Nationwide',* (London: British Film Institute, 1978).

Cixous, Hélène, "The laugh of the Medusa," *Signs: Journal of Women in Culture and Society,* Vol. 1, (1976), pp. 875–893.

Cixous, Hélène, "Castration or decapitation?" *Signs,* Vol. 7, (1981), pp. 41-55.

Doane, Mary Ann, "The voice in the cinema: The articulation of body and space," *Yale French Studies,* Vol.60, (1980), pp. 33-50.

Doane, Mary Anne, "The woman's film: Possession and address," in Mary Ann Doane, et al. (eds.), *Re-vision: Essays in Feminist Criticism,* (Los Angeles: American Film Institute Monogram Series, 1983).

Goffman, Erving, *Gender Advertisements* (New York: Macmillan, 1976).

Hirsch, Mary Ann, "Mothers and daughters," *Signs,* Vol. 7, (1981), pp. 200-222.

La Place, Marie, "Bette Davis and the ideal of consumption," *Wide Angle,* Vol. 6, (1985), pp. 34-43.

McRobbie, Angela, "Dance and social fantasy," in Angela McRobbie and Mica Nava (eds.), *Gender and Generation,* (London: MacMillan, 1984).

Mitchell, Juliet and Jacqueline Rose, *Feminine Sexuality: Jacques Lacan and the école freudienne,* (London: MacMillan, 1982).

Mulvey, Laura, "Visual pleasure and narrative cinema," *Screen,* Vol. 26, (1975), pp. 6-18.

Nelson, Cary, "Envoys of otherness: Difference and continuity in feminist criticism," in Paula A. Treichler, et al. (eds.), *For Alma Mater: Theory and Practice in Feminine Scholarship,* (Urbana: University of Illinois Press, 1985).

Rubin, Gayle, "The traffic in women: Notes on the 'political economy' of sex," in Rayna R. Reiter (ed.), *Toward an Anthropology of Women,* (New York: Monthly Review Press, 1975).

Silverman, Kaja, *The Subject of Semiotics,* (New York: Oxford University Press, 1983).

Williams, Linda, "Something else besides a mother: Stella Dallas and the maternal melodrama," *Cinema Journal,* Vol. 24, (1984), pp. 2-27.

Williamson, Judith, *Decoding Advertisements: Ideology and Meaning in Advertising,* (London: Marion Boyars, 1978).

CHESTER & MONTGOMERY

In this *Columbia Journalism Review* essay, the authors engage several aspects of journalistic television journalism: reporter, attention caller, educator, illuminator. But most centrally, their stance is that of watch dog.

They draw a distinction between "infomercials," "advertorials," and even those PLCs that masquerade as talk shows to focus on those 30 minute commercials that adopt the look of news programs.

Why do these critics see this as of particular concern to viewers and the television industry? Are they fair in presenting the "opposing view" of those who produce these PLCs and to those who air them? Should they be?

What do you think of the Lifetime channel spokesman's claim that broadcasters are "more concerned about whether the product being sold exists and works as described, and less concerned about how the program (the PLC) is formatted?" As a television critic, do you see this as a reasonable position for broadcasters and cablecasters to take?

TV's hidden money games

COUNTERFEITING THE NEWS

Jeffrey Chester
and
Kathryn Montgomery

You're turning the dial on your television set when you're suddenly struck by a gripping scene. A masked man is breaking into a woman's house in the middle of the night. Inside, the woman awakens with a start. While the intruder crawls through her window, she sits up in bed, listening apprehensively. As the eerie music rises to a piercing shriek, the woman screams in terror. The attacker leaps. The frame freezes.

In the next shot, you see a TV newsroom. Upbeat theme music plays. The title appears: "Special Report: Preventing Violent Crime." The camera zooms in on the anchor at his desk. "Welcome," he says.

"Our topic today is how to protect yourself from becoming a victim of violent crime." Promising to provide "tips on how to protect yourself, interviews with top experts in crime prevention, and live demonstrations on the use of the latest self-defence technology," the putative newsman tells his viewers, "Knowledge is your best defense against violent crime."

It looks like an informative news program; in fact, it is a slick thirty-minute commercial. Though it offers some information and advice to its audience, its single purpose is to sell the Nova XR 5000 stun gun, a weapon that uses electric shock to temporarily disable an attacker.

This advertisement is only one among dozens of "program-length commercials" (PLCs) now appearing on TV screens around the country. They are the latest version of the "infomercial" or "advertorial." Many of them are showing up late at night or early in the morning on TV stations and cable channels. New cable networks, such as TWA's The Travel Channel and Teleworld's World Access Television, are being created that will rely almost entirely on PLCs. A growing number of these commercials are disguising themselves as news.

Program-length commercials are a throwback to the days when shows

---

Jeffery Chester is a Los Angeles-based reporter who specializes in telecommunications policy. Kathryn Montgomery teaches film and television at the University of California at Los Angeles. Her book *Target: Prime Time* will be published next year by the Oxford University Press.

Reprinted from the *Columbia Journalism Review,* May/June ©1988.

like *Great Moments in Music* and *100 Paintings* presented themselves as fifteen-minute cultural programs when they were actually mail-order ads for records and art reproductions. Complaints from viewers ultimately caused the Federal Communications Commission to ban such commercials in the early 1970s. Four years ago, however, during the commission's comprehensive deregulation of the television industry, the FCC lifted the ban. There are still rules that require broadcasters to identify PLCs as ads. (Some cable networks, however, are not subject to these rules.) But the required disclaimers usually flash on the screen for only a few seconds, at the beginning or end of the programs, making them easy to miss as viewers switch from channel to channel.

All of these commercials include the standard mail-order pitch that has been the staple of direct-response advertising for years. Only now, instead of having just thirty seconds to stimulate viewers to call in their orders, marketers have a solid half-hour to hour to do the job.

PLCs blend information and entertainment with advertising as a strategy to hold viewers' attention. "Something special happens when you advertise for thirty solid minutes and make it entertaining so people don't turn you off," says Brian Anderson, senior vice-president of Marcoa DR Group Inc. (part of BBDO Worldwide), and president of the Electronic Media Marketing Association.

With many of these shows the intent is obvious. Some are modeled after the successful talk-show formats of Donahue and Oprah Winfrey, but with the goal of encouraging viewers to buy self-improvement or how-to-get-rich-quick tapes and books. Shows like Can You Be Thinner? and Think and Grow Rich combine audience participation with pep talks, testimonials, and statements by experts.

The more insidious PLCs are those that employ the conventional trappings of newscasts to confuse viewers into thinking that what they're seeing is bonafide news. The PLC for the Nova stun gun, for example, combines documentary footage, dramatized scenes of crimes being committed, and "news" reports to create anxiety while lending credibility to the message of the program. "According to U.S. Justice Department statistics," the man posing as an anchor tells us, "chances are one in three that someone in your home will become the next victim of a violent crime in the next twelve months." To illustrate these dangers, the show presents a police recording of a woman telephoning the police as she is being attacked. The last thing heard on the tape is her anguished scream. Then the line goes dead.

A list of safety tips appears on the screen as the actor/anchor reads them. The pitch first appears disguised as objective journalism. "Our investigators," explains the anchor, "searched for the most effective nonlethal weapon available. They found one device, and only one, that is used by more than four-hundred police departments and thousands of civilians around the world. It's called the Nova XR 5000, commonly known as the stun gun. We contacted its manufacturer, Nova Technologies, and they sent us the following promotional tape." Portions of the tape are then shown.

Twice in the course of the half-hour program an anchor announces a commercial break with the familiar words, "We'll be right back," suggesting there is a distinction between the sixty-second stun-gun commercial that follows and the program, when in fact the whole program is a commercial message.

Consumer Challenge is a PLC that purports to be an investigative broadcast. Joseph Sugarman, creator of the show and president of JS&A, a direct-marketing company based in Northbrook, Illinois, explained to us how he came up with the idea. "When we looked at TV and asked what programs were the most popular," Sugarman said, "we selected *60 Minutes, 20/20*, and game shows. We decided it would be more interesting to do an interview-and-investigative-reporter type of approach." The show began airing last summer and, Sugarman says, it continues to be seen on twenty or thirty stations and cable systems.

Like the Nova stun-gun PLC, *Consumer Challenge* is set in a TV newsroom where an "anchor," flanked by two "investigative reporters," announce: "Today on *Consumer Challenge*: Can a pair of sunglasses actually make you see farther, clearer, and sharper? That's exactly what these [print] advertisements claim. They've been popping up in hundreds of magazines. . . . Because [they] have been attracting customers throughout the United States, *Consumer Challenge* intends to find out if these claims are true. Or is this another consumer rip-off?" (The ads were actually written by Sugarman and placed in several magazines.)

Throughout the show, pains have been taken to make it appear as if the reporters are objectively investigating JS&A's BluBlocker sunglasses. One "investigative reporter" proudly explains how she was able to go "right to the top" of the JS&A company to speak to its president, Joseph Sugarman. In the taped interview, Sugarman declines to comment on his product's claims. Instead, he suggests that the reporter take the sunglasses out in the street and ask people to try them on. The program then provides testimonials, interviews with an optometrist and a "leading marketing consultant," and more Sugarman.

By the end of the half hour, the two "investigative reporters" are giving their own personal testimonials for the product. During the wrap-up, one of them explains that he tried to do a "well-balanced report" but that it had been "hard to find anyone who had anything really negative to say" about BluBlockers. The show ends with an announcer telling viewers: "Look for our next *Consumer Challenge*, the show that challenges the products of our time to make you a better, more-informed consumer in the future." (Other *Challenged* products include a line of vitamins and a game that supposedly enhances one's intuitive powers.)

Legal Action Hotline looks like a typical public affairs program during which guests discuss issues of public importance. Three attorneys are seated around a host, talking about how people can exercise their legal rights. Much of the discussion focuses on what to do if you're injured in an auto accident. For legal advice, viewers are urged to call a toll-free *Legal Action Hotline* number. What they don't know is that the only names the operators will supply are those of attorneys who have paid to be listed. All of the *Legal Action Hotline* TV guests are also paying members of the referral service.

Legal Action Hotline has been airing on TV stations in San Francisco, Los Angeles, and San Diego. The program has been so successful, says producer Steve Cannon, that he intends to expand the series this spring, creating a national edition as well as local versions in the top twenty-five TV markets.

The producers of the news-format PLCs spurn any suggestion that their use of that format is unethical. Keith DeGreen, executive producer of the Nova stun-gun program, explains that "we were very careful not to imply we were an independent news agency. But we thought having a newscaster sit at a desk made as much sense as anything else." DeGreen bristles at the idea that some people might confuse his show with a bona fide news program. "Are we to abandon a direct look into the camera because

news programs use the same format?" he asks.

Michael Levey, who wrote, produced, and directed a later version of the stun-gun PLC, says, "The intent of the show is to get to the consumer. We're in the business of producing shows that sell the product."

Joseph Sugarman also rejects criticism that his *Consumer Challenge* show is misleading, though he does not deny that some viewers may be confused: "People will walk away from the show and say, 'I saw this program on a product,' much the same way people might mistake an ad in a newspaper that is made to appear as a news story."

Airing PLCs is very tempting to stations and cable networks. For one thing, as Jack Fentress, vice-president of Petry National Television, points out, they "provide income in time periods when income would have been limited, or nonexistent, in the past." More important, since station operators don't have to pay for program material in the half-hour slot occupied by a PLC, they stand to make a lot more money—in some instances, up to 400 percent more—than they could by buying, say, a syndicated rerun of an old sitcom and selling thirty-second spots. This makes PLCs appealing to the growing number of independent stations that are finding it tough just to stay afloat. With a soft advertising market and escalating costs of syndication, PLCs are becoming a bargain-basement programming staple.

While some stations turn down PLCs because they believe these shows hurt ratings and can ruin a station's image, producers, for the most part, have little trouble getting their programs shown. "As long as [the producers] are qualified sponsors, there's an impetus to sell them airtime," says Larry Pate, program director at WALA, an NBC affiliate in Mobile, Alabama. Although Pate says he does examine the PLCs before they air, he be-

lieves "this should not be an issue where broadcasters decide what to put on. It's an issue of whether consumers will tolerate the program and purchase the product." Marion Meginnis, program manager at WBTV, a CBS affiliate in Charlotte, North Carolina, is more wary of PLCs. "These kinds of shows make me nervous," she says. "Stations don't have to take everything that comes down the pike."

One would think that programs like *Consumer Challenge* or the stun-gun show would ring alarm bells for broadcasters. *Consumer Challenge*, for example, was shown on Lifetime during a late-night block of time the health-oriented cable network sells to advertisers. When asked why Lifetime let such a blatantly misleading show appear on its network, Lorne G. Williamson, Lifetime's director of standards and practices, admitted that often broadcasters are "more concerned about whether the product being sold exists and works as described, and less concerned about how the program is formatted."

Because of the potentially confusing nature of PLCs, however, Lifetime came up with its own disclaimer policy. As Williamson explains, "We now require an announcement at both the beginning and end of the show identifying that it's a paid ad, and that all the claims and representations are the sole responsibility of the sponsor."

But complaints are beginning to mount. Todd Magel, a reporter with KCCI-TV, a CBS affiliate in Des Moines, came home late one night and found *Consumer Challenge* airing on KDSM, an independent TV station. He tipped off Iowa's attorney general, Thomas Miller, who, after an investigation, filed a lawsuit against JS&A last October. Miller alleged that the show and the related print ads were "deceptive, false, and misleading."

When the Iowa attorney general began inquiring into his operation,

Sugarman added a slightly longer disclaimer. After the lawsuit was filed, Iowa TV stations dropped *Consumer Challenge*, although the program can still be seen there on some national cable networks. Sugarman has refused to comply with Iowa's demand that he stop airing the program nationally. The suit is still in progress.

"Any TV station which accepts paid advertising that can confuse the audience about its own news product is shooting itself in the foot," says Jeffrey Marks, chair of the Ethics Committee of the Radio-Television News Directors Association and news director for the Maine Broadcasting System. "We don't want any confusion about what comes from a news set. News executives ought to be screaming about this when their TV stations accept this kind of material." But Marks also points out that, in some ways, TV news has made itself vulnerable to imitation. He cites the trend toward airing more soft news in order to attract viewers and increase ratings. "We've made the news interesting to a lot of people and raised the production values," he says, "so in a sense news became as glitzy as commercials. Now the reverse is happening."

But broadcasters are quick to defend the right of stations to air PLCs. Jeff Baumann, general counsel of the National Association of Broadcasters, for instance, believes that "a PLC can convey a lot of information to consumers. The FCC recognized that in the early 1980s when it repealed guidelines prohibiting them. These are often very popular programs. What we've done is to let the consumer vote whether or not he accepts them."

John Kamp, director of public affairs for the FCC, agrees. He believes that PLCs serve some of the same functions as classified ads in newspapers and magazines. "Under existing rules," he says, "there's no such thing as excess commercialization." But Kamp admits that PLCs posing as news raise a seri-

ous question that the FCC may have to examine.

Others take a stronger position. John Wicklein, formerly news and public affairs program officer for the corporation for Public Broadcasting and now director of the Kiplinger public affairs reporting program at Ohio State University, calls such commercials a "fraud on the public" because they are "deliberately designed to mislead viewers into thinking they are legitimate news and public affairs programs." He charges that stations which run them are prostituting themselves. His recommendation is that the FCC or the Federal Trade Commission should require these programs to "announce every three minutes that this is a commercial message prepared by the sponsor."

Henry Geller, a Washington, D.C.-based communications attorney and a former FCC staff lawyer, sees the news-oriented PLCs as a serious public policy question. "It is one thing to weave a commercial in and out of an entertainment show," he notes. "In that case a viewer has the option of watching it or not watching it. But if he thinks that he is being informed, and he's in fact being propagandized for a product in a program disguised as news and information, then that is inherently deceptive, and it is something both the FCC and the FTC ought to take up as an issue."

The FTC, which is mandated to investigate fraud and misleading and deceptive advertising, is "aware of the situation," says commissioner Andrew J. Strenio, Jr. However, he adds carefully, "Following agency rules, I can neither confirm nor deny the existence of any investigation. And my comments don't constitute conclusions about the facts about any particular situation. Moreover," he cautions, "this topic may raise some serious First Amendment issues." He is, he says, "very concerned about allegations that consumers are being misled about the sponsorship and purpose of programs that purport to be 'critical

reviews' of the very products that actually are being promoted." The commissioner adds, "As a former journalist, I am especially sensitive to the risk that unless they're identified accurately, actors posing as correspondents may destroy the credibility of legitimate reporters."

Whether consumer pressure and state and federal investigations will lead to additional regulations is not yet clear. In a recent address, FCC chairman Dennis Patrick warned broadcasters to "beware the regulators." In his view, broadcast deregulation has created "more interesting consumer-response programming than ever before," and he notes that consumers now have a "smorgasbord of choices." But if present trends continue, this smorgasbord may include more and more programs that blend news and information with commercial copy. For example, *The Wall Street Journal* recently reported that the Financial News Network had aired a six-part series on personal finance which in reality was a three-hour commercial for The New England, a Boston-based insurance and financial-services company. Well-known network, nespaper, and magazine reporters appeared, lending credibility to the program.

The proliferation of program-length commercials should be seen in the context of a larger, more disturbing trend: the cutting back of public service programming in order to serve the bottom line. News-oriented PLCs are now part of TV schedules that no longer have room for documentaries, investigative reports, and public affairs programs.

"We need to make a distinction between the marketplace of ideas and the ideas of the marketplace," says Nicholas Johnson, a former FCC commissioner who is currently teaching at the University of Iowa's law college. "In the absence of regulation, the marketplace produces the ideas that serve the marketplace."

Chapter Exercises

Visuals and Information in Commercials I

Choose three commercials, one for a service (airline, restaurant, etc.), one for an inexpensive consumer product (soap, beer, etc.), and one for a durable consumer product (PC, car, etc.). In the appropriate spaces below, count how many different cuts (changes from one visual image to another) there are in each and count the number of statements of consumer-oriented information that also appear in each.

PRODUCT	NUMBER OF CUTS	NUMBER OF STATEMENTS
SPOT #1		
SPOT #2		
SPOT #3		

Visuals and Information in Commercials II

Repeat this counting exercise, but now choose only one product type and analyze commercials for it that are aimed at different demographic groups. Comment on your results.

COMMERCIALS FOR	PRODUCT TYPE: _____	
	NUMBER OF CUTS	NUMBER OF STATEMENTS
Target Group #1		
Target Group #2		
Target Group #3		

References and Resources

Baran, S. J., Mok, J. J., Land, M. & Kang, T. Y. (1989). You are what you buy: mass-mediated judgments of people's worth. *Journal of Communication, 39,* 46–54.

Baran, S. J. & Blasko, V. J. (1984). Social perceptions and the by-products of advertising. *Journal of Communication, 34,* 12–20.

Baran, S. J. (1987). Automobile "positioning" and the construction of social reality. In S. Thomas (Ed.). *Culture and Communication: Methodology, Behavior, Artifacts, and Institutions.* Norwood, NJ: Ablex.

Barry, D. (1993). Die, you scum! *West Magazine,* October 3, p. 23.

Biagi, S. (1992). *Media/Impact: An Introduction to Mass Media.* Belmont, CA: Wadsworth.

Broadcasting & Cable Yearbook 1995. (1995). New Providence, NJ: R. R. Bowker.

Collins, G. (1988). For many, a vast wasteland has become a brave new world. New York *Times,* March 20, p. 13.

Draper, R. (1986). The faithless shepherd. *The New York Review,* June 26, pp. 14–18.

Ewen, S. (1976). *Captains of Consciousness.* New York: McGraw-Hill.

Flitterman, S. (1983). The real soap operas: TV commercials. In E. A. Kaplan (Ed.). *Regarding Television—Critical Approaches: An Anthology, American Film Institute Monograph Series, vol. 2.* Frederick, MD: University Publications of America.

Fox, S. (1986). *The Mirror Makers: A History of American Advertising and Its Creators.* New York: Vintage.

Gillian, D. (1982). *Advertising as Communication.* London: Methuen.

Greenberg, B. S. & Brand, J. E. (1993). Television news and advertising in schools: the "Channel One" controversy. *Journal of Communication, 43,* 143–151.

Harper, P. (1989). The exploitation of the wall. San Jose *Mercury-News,* December 18, p. 10B.

Kaplan, E. A. (1985). A post-modern play of the signifier? Advertising, pastiche and schizophrenia in music television. In P. Drummond & R. Paterson (Eds.). *Television in Transition,* London: British Film Institute.

Lovdal, L. T. (1989). Sex role messages in television commercials: an update. *Sex Roles, 21,* 715–724.

Maas, J. (1986). *Adventures of an Advertising Woman.* New York: St. Martin's Press.

Making the call on pods. (1986). *Advertising Age,* March 24, p. 17.

Marchand, R. (1986). *Advertising the American Dream: Making Way for Modernity, 1920-1940.* Berkeley, CA: University of California Press.

Massey, K. K. & Baran, S. J. (1990). VCRs and people's control of their leisure time. In J. Dobrow (Ed.). *Social and Cultural Aspects of VCR Use.* Hillsdale, NJ: Earlbaum.

Myers, P. N. & Biocca, F. A. (1992). The elastic body image: the effect of television advertising and programming on body image distortions in young women. *Journal of Communication, 42,* 108–133.

Ogilvy, D. (1986). *Ogilvy on Advertising.* New York: Vintage.

O'Toole, J. (1986). *The Trouble With Advertising.* New York: Random House.

Price, J. (1978). *The Best Thing on TV: Commercials.* New York: Viking Press.

Pritkin, R. (1979). Charlie Haas on advertising. *New West*, November 5, p. 40–46.

Ruble, D. N. et al. (1981). Gender constancy and the effect of sex-typed television toy commercials. *Child Development, 52*, 667–673.

Schudson, M. (1986). *Advertising, The Uneasy Persuasion: Its Dubious Impact on American Society.* New York: Basic Books.

Solomon, M. R. (1983). The role of products as social stimuli: a symbolic interactionism perspective. *Journal of Consumer Research, 10*, 319–329.

Stark, S. (1985). TV quickens the quick-sell. Boston *Globe*, October 27, pp. A1, A24.

Steinberg, C. S. (1980). *TV facts.* New York: Facts on File.

Twitchell, J. B. (1996). *Adcult USA: The Triumph of Advertising in American Culture*. New York: Columbia University Press.

Vivian, J. (1991). *The Media of Mass Communication*. Needham Heights, MA: Allyn and Bacon.

Whetmore, E. J. (1992). *American Electric: Introduction to Telecommunications and Electronic Media.* New York: McGraw-Hill.

Williamson, J. (1978). *Decoding Advertisements: Ideology and Meaning in Advertising.* London: Marion Boyars.

Wood, S. C. (1990). Television's first political spot ad campaign: Eisenhower answers America. *Presidential Studies Quarterly, 20*, 265–283.

CHAPTER 14

TALK SHOWS

Talk shows are getting old. I've asked the same questions for 21 years. We've done lesbian nuns. We've done the mothers who marry their sons.

—Joan Rivers

Talk show hostess-turned Shopping Channel pitchwoman Rivers (1994, p. 4A) is only half right: Maybe talk shows as she defines them are getting old, but the genre is undergoing a remarkable re-birth as the very same forces that are reshaping the television medium in general are fueling this genre's new Golden Age.

Talk shows, people more or less sitting around chatting in front of cameras and (sometimes) an audience, abound on contemporary television, as do questions about their impact on viewers, politics, and the culture that they seem so perfectly (some would say unfortunately) to reflect. We have to admit that this is an interesting and even strange genre when a story like this appears in the daily paper: "A slapping, kicking fight between serial killer Richard Ramirez's fiancee and a woman who has developed a 'relationship' with him since he has been in jail was deleted from the (*Sally Jessy Raphael*) show. The so-called California 'Nightstalker' was convicted of committing 13 murders in the mid-1980s" ('Sally' . . . , 1994, p. 4A). When the three major Presidential candi-

dates in the 1992 election use talk shows to circumvent the traditional press and speak directly to the people, we have to admit that this is an important genre. But when on his *Late Show* David Letterman sends his mother Dorothy to interview Hillary Rodham Clinton (architect of President Clinton's overhaul of the American health system) at the 1994 Winter Olympics, we have to ask what happens when the line between entertainment and news blurs. And this is only one of the issues surrounding talk shows that concerns critics.

Overview

We'll look at several other issues as well, but first we'll examine how the talk show form began on television and eventually took shape. We'll meet some of the early innovators and those, like Johnny Carson, who have virtually come to define the genre—or at least one of its forms. There are many types of talk shows, from the early morning light talk and information programs to the late night celebrity interview and entertainment shows. Technology and money, as we've seen several times, have changed television, and the various forms of talk shows have not been immune to this change. The resulting transformation and proliferation of talks that we see today will be discussed as will several views on their meaning in and value to our culture.

A Staple From the Start

Talk shows came easily to television in the medium's first days for many of the same reasons that quiz shows did, but unlike the games, they did not move from network radio to network television. The Golden Age of network radio was before World War II. Prior to that conflict (and the coming of television), ours was a nation of distinct regions. Entertainment may know no boundaries or borders, but public affairs and opinion did. So talk on the radio was primarily local. When network television began, then, there were no nationally well-known talk programs and hosts to move from radio as was the case with the medium's other recognizable formats. Most television talk shows had to begin from scratch. But like quizzes, there was something about televising talk that made it well-suited for the fledgling medium: It was easy to produce in an era of very hot lights and very heavy equipment; it was cheap to produce in the days before advertising dollars began their steady flow into the networks' coffers; it filled time when the nets had yet to develop their stables of shows; and, it was novel, audiences could now see the people talking to them, and all the better if the voice (and now face) belonged to a celebrity. Also like the quiz shows, talk shows were a logical early form of content because of the scientific roots of the medium. What else would engineers and professors find interesting but public affairs and information programming?

Ross (1993, p. 22) wrote, "Television began with a man sitting at a desk, talking. The desk, at first, was a matter of necessity—early T.V. cameras were massive and immobile, so their subjects needed a visual motive for staying put." And NBC understood this well, putting moderator Martha Roundtree, Lawrence E. Spivak and other panelists, and the program's visitors behind desks for its *Meet the Press*. One of the few talks to move over from radio, it premiered on November 6, 1947 and is not only network television's longest running talk show, but it is the longest running program of any kind in the medium's history. The format was simple, four journalists interviewing a newsmaker (sometimes two). But there was no shortage of desks or talk as the networks worked to bring *public affairs conversation* to their audiences. Within a few years CBS presented *Face the Nation* and ABC offered *Issues and Answers*.

Of course, not all the early talk shows were of this brainy ilk. There were also the *late night, light conversation, comedy variety shows* that eventually led to the form's classic incarnation, *The Tonight Show*. In fact, it was television's very newness that led to their development. In May of 1950 NBC debuted *Broadway Open House*, hoping that this nightly 11:00 p.m. show would serve three functions important to its new television network: introduce radio stars and shows coming over to television, parade new talent before the camera to see who had it and who didn't, and to promote its prime-time program schedule. Hosted on alternate nights by Morey Amsterdam (later to find fame on *The Dick VanDyke Show*) and Jerry Lester, the show featured guests who would "drop in," sometimes perform, and maybe talk about their new show on NBC. The MCs and a crew of regulars would also perform light comedy skits.

But of course, there were also the *early morning talk and information shows*. Their tone and character were set by the initial host of the first of these programs, *Today*. That man was Dave Garroway, who came to the network in 1952 from Chicago where he'd been a local television talk show host. He was low-key and unhurried, as was the show's format. It featured brief news reports, celebrity interviews, weather reports, homey conversation, and frequent time checks. Both the host and format were perfect for a program watched by people scurrying about to get their days going. For two decades NBC's *Today* was the pre-eminent talk show of the networks' a.m. schedules, but it was not the only one during that time. Opposite it CBS scheduled *The Morning Show*, first with Walter Cronkite and then, in 1956, with Will Rogers, changing its name to *Good Morning!*

Talks in syndication were at their most popular in the Sixties and early Seventies and tended to be somewhat different from their network cousins. *The Merv Griffin Show* and *The Mike Douglas Show* were examples of *celebrity interview talk shows*, featuring hosts that sang a tune or two and then sat down, chair to chair, with one or a few "stars" for a bit of very light chat. These shows were typically aired in the late afternoon and were often criticized for their fawning manner toward show-biz royalty.

The Dick Cavett Show is an example of the *in-depth talk shows* that also succeeded in syndication. Where its host had fared poorly in ABC's challenge to the *Tonight Show*, his wit and intellect were perfectly suited to one-on-one insightful conversations with not only stars, but with newsmakers as well. NBC, seeing Cavett's success and recognizing that there might be a late night audience for talk in those tumultuous times of Vietnam and civil rights unrest, brought this format to network television, hiring local news anchor Tom Snyder to host its 1:00 to 2:00 A.M. in-depth talk show, *The Tomorrow Show*. Often controversial, often penetrating, Snyder drew an estimated nightly audience of three million people.

In the Sixties, when the nation was confronting the notion of "alternative lifestyles" as it never had before, another form of talk show was born in syndication. In this format, a host would interview seemingly regular people who "would reveal sex lives or family relationships that differed from the prevailing mores of American society, and they would respond to questions from (the host) and the studio audience, which was specially selected to include people familiar with the topic. Viewers would call in to offer their experiences.

Designated experts would transmute this raw material into sociological profundity" (Golden, 1988, p. 18). Phil Donahue, a radio talk show host, began his television talk show in Dayton, Ohio and intentionally avoided the society chit-chat of *Merv Griffin* and *Mike Douglas*. *Donahue* was the first and, for years the most popular of these *psychic chatter programs*, and although it may be the most tame of what we now call *confessional talk television*, it was even more "normal" back then, not yet having to face the challenge of *Geraldo*, *The Oprah Winfrey Show*, *Montel Williams* and *The Sally Jessy Raphael Show*. As Golden (1988, p. 19) wrote, "*Donahue's* early, controversial shows on atheists and homosexuals pale before the contemporary parade of self-mutilators, multiple personalities, and people who think Elvis is alive and shopping in their grocery store."

The Titan of Talk

Today, talk shows seem to have over-run television, and the comings and goings of the shows and their hosts make front page news. Who will replace Carson? Chevy Chase fails! Joan Rivers, Alan Thicke, Dennis Miller and Pat Sajak, too! Will Letterman go or stay? Nazis beat up Geraldo! How did Oprah lose all that weight?

But from the start, talk's defining talent and program were Johnny Carson and his *Tonight Show*. As Zoglin (1992, p. 63) wrote, "The history of Carson's years at the *Tonight Show*, is, to a large degree, the history of television. In 1972, after 10 years in New York City, he moved the program to Burbank, reflecting an industry-wide migration from the East to the West Coast. In 1980 the show was cut from 90 minutes to an hour, creating a tighter entertainment package out of the more free-flowing gabfest that had become, in some ways, a relic of an earlier TV era."

A typical Carson show would draw a rating of 8, but a dominating share, accounting in most years for nearly 20 percent of NBC's annual income. But the *Tonight Show* did not begin with Carson at the desk. In 1954, Steve Allen took over as host of the new NBC entry which had already been a local New York show for a year. Allen was intelligent and sophisticated (he was a composer, pianist, author of both poetry and prose, and politically active), and the show bore his stamp. It was fast, often impromptu, and combined music, interviews, and imaginative sketches featuring the host and his regular cast members, Bill Dana, Don Knotts, Steve Lawrence, Eydie Gorme, and Andy Williams. In 1956 Allen moved on to the less demanding weekly *Steve Allen Show* and *Tonight* passed into the able if controversial hands of Jack Paar in 1957.

The name of the program was changed to *The Jack Paar Show* but still contained many of the characteristics of Allen's *Tonight*. Zany sketches remained, as did the intelligent conversation and interviews. Paar's distinction, however, was that he was a highly emotional and, not unlike Allen, a highly political man. He would occasionally cry on camera if moved by a guest, engage in angry on-air feuds with newspaper reporters and even Ed Sullivan, and broadcast from the Berlin Wall (he even tried to trade farm equipment for prisoners taken in the 1961 failed Bay of Pigs invasion in Cuba). Emotional and principled, Paar tearfully stormed out of one broadcast, angry that NBC censors had cut a joke about a "water closet" (times *have* changed).

Paar and NBC split in early 1962 and the network quickly signed a young game and variety show host who'd been successful in the daytime on both ABC and CBS. While they waited for his ABC contract to expire, several guest hosts warmed the seat of the re-named *Tonight Show*. Among them were Groucho Marx, Jerry Lewis, Jimmy Dean, and Joey Bishop.

But on October 2, 1962, Marx introduced the audience to Carson, and Johnny would own the desk and chair for 30 years. He was cool where Paar was hot. Where Allen opened each show at his piano, Carson opened with a monologue. Where both Paar and Allen had regular troupes of actors for their sketches, Johnny went it alone as Art Fern, Carnac the

Magnificent, and Aunt Blabby. Where Paar negotiated for prisoners, Carson hosted the wedding of Tiny Tim.

The Tonight Show Starring Johnny Carson became a television institution and a cultural phenomenon. To be granted the "Carson Nod" was to be assured show business success. Comedian Robert Klein told *Time*, "He'll help a young comedian by saying 'Funny stuff' or 'Boy, that's funny' or by laughing a lot. The audience practically takes its signal from him" (Zoglin, 1992, p. 64). But to be the butt of Carson's jokes often meant political doom. A Washington newsletter publisher said of him, "If you've made the Carson show three or four nights in a row, you better start to worry. Nothing undoes a candidate more certainly than if he or she is the object of unremitting ridicule in the monologues" (Zoglin, 1992, p. 64). For his three decades, Carson's opening monologue has been a remarkably accurate barometer of the public's mood. Kaplan expounded on the political importance of the talk show, especially Carson and his heir, Dave Letterman, when he wrote:

This is a nation run by talk, with an agenda set by talk—and television. Why does Jesse Helms go crazy protesting Dan Rather when Rather's power to interpret the news is nothing as compared to Carson and Letterman? When you want to know where we're going there's only one fast road map, and it's under the talk show desk. The television joke guides the nation. And whoever owns it controls more than just the arena of the laugh—that person controls the American playing field of values. What Reagan did, ostensibly, was control America's frame of reference. But hasn't Carson, and won't Letterman? The playing field is the rectangle of the television screen (1988, p. 75).

Possibly, though, it is another Carson innovation that will have the most lasting effect on the evening talk show genre, that is, his self-reflexivity. Carson frequently wondered aloud to his audience how he, an adult, could be making millions of dollars doing something as silly as telling jokes and talking to movie stars. This turning the form on itself became the core joke of the man that followed Carson in the NBC late night schedule, David Letterman

Letterman and the Rest

When Carson left the *Tonight Show* the network installed frequent guest host Jay Leno onto the throne. A disappointed and angry Letterman took $42 million from CBS for a three year commitment and moved his hip band, stupid pet tricks, and top-10 list to a time slot opposite Leno and the show he'd assumed for years he'd eventually host (Carter, 1994). Obviously a profitable move for Letterman, was it a good move for CBS? The network was able to charge $30,000 per 30 second spot on Dave's show, compared to amounts of half that on the rotating series of crime dramas that previously filled the slot. In his first three months with CBS, Dave and the 5.3 million homes that tuned in nightly helped lead that network to its first profitable financial quarter since 1985. How did he do against Leno? Dave: 5.9 rating/16 share. Jay: 3.9 rating/13 share. Even Ted Koppel's *Nightline* beat Leno. Advertisers were moving with Dave, too. CBS reported new sponsors Levi's, Carnival Cruise Lines, Ford, Mazda, Paramount and 20th Century Fox. What did CBS know about Letterman that NBC failed to see?

Letterman had taken the television institution and cultural phenomenon that Carson had created and refined (or reduced) it to its essence. Of course the window scene of Hollywood behind Johnny was fake. So Letterman would make viewers admit it by throwing failed jokes through the phony window scene of New York to the sound of breaking glass. Johnny would have as guests an elderly couple who'd won a square dancing contest in Nebraska. Letterman would have stupid pet tricks. Johnny had semi-regular sketch player Carol Wayne, blond bombshell. Letterman had Chris Elliott, blond nut-case. Johnny had Doc Severinson and his orchestra playing *Spinning Wheel*. David had Paul Schaffer and his band blasting *Foxy Lady*. Johnny was the Bea-

ver. Dave was Eddie Haskell. The late night talk show audience was younger, hipper, more cynical, less impressed with Hollywood celebrity. Ross wrote,

If Carson closed out the story of the National Hosts, then it's hard to find a place for David Letterman. He came on stage as an insincere endnote to the Carson phenomenon, a cynical extension of a faded form. He had no trace of Carson's transcontinental, Vegas-tinged suavity. . . . He is the model of the new television personality, less intent on universal adoration than on a kind of maladjusted—and ironic—realism. . . . Late Night, *in the early and mid-'80s, was* The Tonight Show *gone to seed. Every component in its daily lineup— set, guests, sidekicks, recurring characters, funny animals—was a deliberate inadequate echo of Carson's show-biz juggernaut (1993, p. 23).*

In other words, where NBC *substituted* Jay Leno for Johnny Carson, CBS *replaced* Johnny Carson and his *Tonight Show* with Letterman. Or, as Arsenio Hall (Brady, 1994, p. 30) said, "Leno today is like, well . . . I have an aunt 57 years old, and she thinks Leno is wonderful."

Technology gave rise to the other major players in late night talk, *The Arsenio Hall Show* and *Nightline*. Satellite makes the familiar *Nightline* format possible, as host Koppel interviews news makers and pits verbal opponents against one another. When big stories are breaking, *Nightline* very often wins the time slot, even over Letterman, but typically, because it and Leno's show more or less share the same audience, it is usually number two or three.

Habitually number four in the late night race was Arsenio Hall's program. He, too, benefitted from technology's (especially cable's) boost to Fox and the independents (see Chapter 3). After Joan Rivers washed out on Fox's attempt to battle Johnny Carson, comedian Hall was hired to complete the last several weeks of the show's run. Paramount was impressed, and in January of 1989 launched his talk show into syndication on over 200 stations. Until it went off the air in 1994, *Arsenio Hall* was hip, topical (President

Clinton played the saxophone and talked to the audience in the 1992 campaign on his show), and entertaining. It was a young person's version of Johnny's old show rather than a version of any kind of Letterman's.

Cable has also given the public HBO's *The Larry Sanders Show*. Although a 30 minute comedy, it is more like *Letterman* than any of Dave's nightly competitors. It is television staring back at itself, self-reflexively and self-consciously. When the *The Larry Sanders Show* is "on the air," viewers see the familiar "look" of videotape. When the plot takes the action "off the air," and moves it behind the scenes, viewers confront filmed action, designed to convey reality. *The Larry Sanders Show* is about *The Larry Sanders Show*. Each episode of the real show begins with the opening of the fictional program. Where Letterman tells his viewers, "Listen, this is a truly silly way for me to make a living and for you to spend your time, but we're here, so let's party," Garry Shandling, alter ego of Larry Sanders, says, television talk is "not so false, that it's like watching professional wrestling. But, look, it's artificial from the get-go because nine times out of ten, the host has already said hello to the guest in the hallway, yet when the guest sits down, they go, 'So nice to see you! Haven't seen you in a long time.' So the lie begins" (Mitchell, 1993, p. 108). It may be comedy, not talk, but *Sanders* and *Letterman* ultimately make the same point: The audience, not the star behind the desk, makes meaning and pleasure from this familiar form.

Confessional Talk Television

Too familiar, many critics might say, is the dominant form of television talk, the confessional talk show. As 1994 opened, there were 17 nationally syndicated confessional talks, from the well known *Oprah* (19 million viewers a day), *Sally Jessy* (11.7 million), and *Montel Williams* to the less familiar *The Chuck Woolery Show*.

Cable and the independents opened up television schedules for these programs and the $1.4 billion a year barter syndication market helps to sustain them. But that doesn't explain a) why people appear on these shows to confess the strangest of personal histories and b) why people watch.

There are two answers to the first question. The cynical one is that some people will do anything to get on television, even allow themselves to be captioned WAS TURNED OFF BY SEX (*Geraldo*) or SLEPT WITH TWO GAY MEN TO CONCEIVE BABY (*Sally*). A kinder response is that the people who appear may have something important to convey to the viewers, may just want to instill tolerance for their alternative lifestyles, may want to shed light on important social problems, or may want regular people to know that there are others even more miserable than they. This explanation may have rung true in the simpler days of the early *Donahue*, but today, especially during sweeps ratings periods, it sounds hollow. SUED EX-LOVER FOR CONTRACTING GENITAL HERPES. POURED LIGHTER FLUID ON SON, SET HIM AFIRE, NOW BLAMES MEDIA FOR MAKING HIM A "MONSTER." FATHERED A DAUGHTER WITH HIS LESBIAN ROOMMATE. This is hardly the stuff of understanding and compassion. Sonya Friedman of CNN's *Sonya Live* says, "The talk shows deal with disillusion and destruction. They are the freak shows of American television" (Bass, 1993, p. 15A). Participants are likely to be deeply troubled people. And where these talk shows have been credited with opening up the public dialogue on previously forbidden issues like child abuse and domestic violence, they very often undercut their (stated) aim by featuring the most extreme, titillating cases.

The second question, why people watch, is more difficult to answer. They have replaced soaps as viewers' genre of choice for daytime angst, so one answer may be that audiences need to see people humbled to be assured of their own superiority. Another answer may be that audiences are becoming increasingly desensitized to the bizarre, that they want to see the weirdest of sideshows simply because they've become voyeurs. Neither speaks well for the public. A third possibility is that, no matter how horrible the guests or their transgressions, they can be humanized and controlled by the hosts and their shows. The message is "no matter how out of control this sick world gets, there are those (Oprah, Montel, Jessy) who can help you hold it together."

But what's the big deal anyway? It's only television, everyone knows it's not real, these kooks come out of the woodwork to get on TV to try to shock us. Much critical attention has recently been directed to this question.

The Problem of Television Talk

The Elayne Rapping essay that follows this section makes a compelling case for the importance of the talk shows to public discourse. And if we limit our discussion to those talks that at least try to appear serious, *Larry King Live* (where vice-president Al Gore had it out with Ross Perot over NAFTA in 1993), *The McLaughlin Group*, and even Rush Limbaugh's show, it is not hard to agree with her. The problem that troubles many critics, however, manifests itself in the blurring of the line between fact and fiction, entertainment and news, confession and policy discussion. Was it serious or play, entertainment or news, when Presidential aspirant Bill Clinton appeared on *Arsenio*, resplendent in bluesman's shades, blowing his sax? Was it serious or play, entertainment or news, when Presidential aspirant Bill Clinton appeared on the more sedate *Donahue* and refused to answer questions about his sex life? Was it serious or play, entertainment or news, when Letterman's mom interviewed the President's wife, Hillary Rodham Clinton, at the 1994 Winter Olympics? Who won the Perot/Gore NAFTA debate on *Larry King Live*, the debater with the best command of his facts and issues or the one with the greater facility with television? These questions suggest several not unrelated criticisms of today's various types of talk shows:

1. **Blurring of news and entertainment.** When a President appears on a celebrity-oriented talk show, is it news or entertainment? In a society where growing numbers of citizens already neither trust nor respect their elected leaders, can we afford leaders more intent on notoriety and celebrity than on conveying important ideas and policies? Watergate investigative reporter Carl Bernstein argues,

For more than 15 years we have been moving away from real journalism toward the creation of a sleazoid infotainment culture in which the lines between Oprah and Phil and Geraldo and Diane (Sawyer of CBS) and even Ted (Koppel) . . . are too often indistinguishable . . . in which public discourse is reduced to ranting and raving and posturing. We now have a mainstream press whose news agenda is increasingly influenced by this netherworld. Now the apotheosis of this talk-show culture is before us. I refer to Ross Perot, a candidate created and sustained by television, launched on Larry King Live, *whose only substantive proposal is to replace representative democracy with a live TV talk show for the entire nation (1992, p. 4C).*

Can CBS, ABC, NBC and CNN ignore Tonya Harding, Heidi Fleiss and Michael Jackson's alleged "skin markings" when the talk shows do not?

2. **The demeaning of candidates, politics and public discourse.** How can democracy be served when "candidates stampede like English soccer hooligans to appear on *Larry King*, MTV and other infotainment chat fests with soft-ball interviewers, soft-focus lighting and direct access to the public?" (Whalen, 1993, p. 16). What distinguishes President Clinton's appearance on *Arsenio* from Madonna's? What differentiates a Vice-President offering his "Top 10" on *Letterman*, ending with "Buttafuoco," from the talk show host himself? Is Vice-President Gore a "liar," as Perot claimed in their famous NAFTA debate? Is Perot's son making millions at the public's expense, as Gore charged? Television talk shows, dependent on grabbing and holding the audience's attention (and grab-

bing and holding ratings), may not be the best place for America to debate its important concerns.

3. **The debasement of important social contracts.** A fair trial is a basic right in America. Yet "Monday, 12 'impartial' mock jurors on Geraldo Rivera's talk show will decide whether to indict (Joey) Buttafuoco for statutory rape of 16-year-old Amy Fisher in the summer of 1991 and conspiracy to shoot his wife, Mary Jo, last May" (Forrest, 1993, p. 2A). Buttafuoco was eventually sentenced to a real prison for statutory rape. But this mock trial is only a condensed televised version of the trial-by-talk show suffered by any person unfortunate enough to be caught up in a titillating story instantly blown to gigantic proportions by a talk show-fed media frenzy. Standards of fairness, never mind evidence, completely vanish as rumor and speculation are passed on as the talks compete with the tabloid TV shows and one another. Long before Tonya Harding had her day in court in March of 1994, the Olympic skater's ex-husband, fitness trainer, and ex-body guards (the actual hit men) had already testified on the talks, all implicating her, free from the challenge of cross-examination or the threat of punishment for perjury.

4. **The trivialization of important issues.** By devoting one day's show to PRIESTS WHO HAVE SEX WITH CHILDREN, the next to the lack of availability of affordable child care for working mothers, and the next to I AM HITLER'S LOVE CHILD, the talk shows blur the line between major social problems and the trivial. Whether you agree or disagree with the need to legally recognize same-sex unions, many cities and states are now debating legislation to do just that. TRANSVESTITE WEDDINGS is not a topic destined to shed light on the issue for either side of the debate.

5. **The personalization of public discourse.** Television, especially television talk shows, seems to have great difficulty presenting complex issues in interesting, attention-holding ways. (Yes, it can be done, as a quick scan of PBS and CNN and even some network news programs will attest, but this, unfortunately, does not appear to be an industry standard.) So the talk shows "personalize" the issues. The need for safe, affordable, quickly available organ transplants becomes MADELYN NEEDS A KIDNEY; ESTRANGED FATHER WANTS TO SELL HER HIS. Audiences are encouraged to understand the complex world through "the prism of personal feelings, rather than through intellectual ideas or scientific information. . . . This self-absorption spills over into politics, where many voters are more concerned with how they feel about a political candidate than with how that candidate stands on important issues" (Bass, 1993, p. 15A).

The Future of Television Talk

The spate of late night talk show failures argues that that audience is sufficiently mined. Leno has his niche, Letterman has his, and *Nightline* has its own, too. Many cable and syndicated challengers have tried and failed in the last few years. Still, 500 channels multiplied by 24 hours a day means that there is much room for low cost, demographically targeted talk. *Up Late With Ron Reagan* and Jenny Jones' *Girls Night Out* are two examples of the new generation of semi-entertainment/semi-information talk shows that hope to fill some of the available time.

The "re-cycling" of the same guests and same themes by the confessional talk shows may force this particular form to become more thoughtful and down to earth in its choice of topics, but as Golden (1988, p. 56) writes, this is unlikely "as long as there are people like Nedra Weston. Weston . . . told *Geraldo's* audience that she is so afraid of becoming pregnant that she and her husband have intercourse only during her menstrual period" on that program's WOMEN WHO DON'T WANT SEX installment.

Ultimately, talk shows will not only survive but thrive because the same forces that operated to make them early television standards have come together again. New technology means new channels that have to fill time. New channels need inexpensive, easy to produce programs with formats that are easily identifiable to viewers. We can offer no better characterization of television talk shows.

TIMBERG

Critic Timberg expressly states his thesis at the outset of his essay and then methodically sets out (through personal observation and interpretation, selection of appropriate pieces of dialogue, and germane quotes from the writings of others) to support it. His primary argument is that both the Carson and Letterman shows offered a "familiar implied narrative, a variation of the Horatio Alger story."

Before you read his evidence, how willing were you to accept his position that these programs are narratives in and of themselves, possessing a "storyline (that) proceeds through a series of tensions?" How can a talk show composed of stand-up comedy routine, light chatter, and an occasional comedy sketch be a narrative—a story that speaks the culture's beliefs and values?

If this author had not expressly positioned his criticism as narrative analysis, his use of expressions such as the "structuring of *The Tonight Show* expresses . . . " and "the presentation of Letterman's performance articulates . . . " would clearly have identified it as such.

What is the relationship between what Timberg calls "ritual space" and the narrative, or storytelling function of these two shows? Before you read this essay, had such connections ever occurred to you as you watched either or both Carson and Letterman? Has this knowledge changed how you now watch these shows? Your level of enjoyment and/or understanding? Shouldn't all good criticism have this effect?

Near the end of his analysis, Timberg interjects a bit of reader-oriented analysis when he discusses "TV's shadow side." How does he use this idea as evidence for his own narrative analysis? Why does this brief section qualify as reader-oriented analysis?

Timber's formal conclusion is that these programs are "not narratives in any traditional sense." Has he sufficiently supported this finding? If so, what marks the Carson and Letterman shows as narratives? But what makes them non-traditional?

A man from America's heartland comes to the city, making his way through its absurdities and frustrations with feckless humor. The exemplary middle American portrays himself as square, basically innocent, though somewhat ironic and irreverent. Straddling the worlds of common sense and show business, he becomes a national jester, commenting on the idiosyncracies of both coasts, wondering at and mocking them, a surrogate for millions of Americans.

This familiar role can be traced back to the "Yankee" character in early American theater and the "Toby" character in tent repertory theater.[1] With the arrival of television, the character took to the new medium. Johnny Carson exemplifies the first generation of Yanks in the new world of the electronic media, arriving just in time to poke fun at the conformist world of the late 1950s and 1960s. As the politics of accommodation became the politics of confrontation in the satire of *Saturday Night Live*, and as Carson achieved clear ascendance in the show business establishment as the "king of late night comedy," a new Yankee

TELEVISION TALK AND RITUAL SPACE:

CARSON AND LETTERMAN

Bernard Timberg

character emerged. The ironic stance of David Letterman captured the voice of his generation in the 1980s, but only in the context of a series of show business and post-film era televisual traditions which had been accepted in the previous two decades.

The Tonight Show Starring Johnny Carson and *Late Night with David Letterman* offer viewers not only a familiar character, but also a familiar implied narrative, a variation of the Horatio Alger story. Both shows are organized as ritual quests for a certain kind of social knowledge and experience that has brought the star/host fame and glory. The story-line proceeds through a series of tensions between the host's control and lack of control of this ritualized quest, between his seemingly meaningless fun with fleeting topicality and the enduring social values he represents as a champion of common sense.

The themes of the late night talk show are not simply communicated to viewers through words. As in a play, the setting frames and defines the words and actions of the characters. Television performances have some of the formal elements of drama, even in the pre-

Dr. Timberg is Assistant Professor of Theater Arts and Speech, Rutgers University, Newark, New Jersey.

1. For recent discussions of the roots of the Yankee character and its presentation in 19th century American theater see Meserve (1977 and 1981). See Glassen (1979) for a scholarly discussion of the "Toby" character.

Reprinted with permission of the Southern States Communication Association.

sentational forms of news, game shows, and talk shows. But the camera captures and organizes these theatrical elements. Thus, any analysis of the ritual space of a television program must consider both the structuring of the performance and its immediate physical environment and the secondary mediation of the performance as it is transformed from live to television event.

This essay explores the formal organization of images that appear on the television screen in the late night television talk show. My thesis is that the character of the star/host and the aesthetic history and social function of the show dictate the form of the fringe talk show: Carson emerges from a pre-television era stage tradition which his show reflects. Letterman is from a generation so thoroughly familiar with TV that it needs to play with the medium to maintain interest. This essay, then, examines the shift that occurred from Carson to Letterman as the Yankee character learned not only to exploit but to play with the medium of television.

Structuring The Star Hosts' Performance

Like the openings of most television programs, the first few moments of a talk show set the stage, the tone, and the mood for what follows. The characteristic elements of the talk show's implied narrative are established in worlds, as well as in the staging, camera work, and set design that present the star-host to the public. In the case of the Tonight Show, the opening alternates between parody and celebration. We have, in sequence, the musical fanfare and introduction of the band and guests, followed by Ed McMahon's stentorian bellow: "Here's Johnny!" Then the vertically striped curtains part

and McMahon with the audience shouts "Hey-yo!" As enthusiasm builds, Carson emerges, pleased but a bit embarrassed by the hoopla. Carson's demeanor during the welcoming ovation might be characterized as mock heroic: though clearly a star receiving celebrity treatment, he does not place himself above the audience nor beneath them as a fool or comic butt of jokes. As Everyman, Carson suggests he is directly on beam with the sensibilities of his viewing public.[2]

As Carson walks toward it, the camera remains absolutely frontal at a fixed focal length. We see no movement in the frame except for the host. When Carson arrives at center stage, the camera remains in the same formal medium shot, wide enough to take in his entire upper torso, arms, and hands. Carson makes mock obeisance left and right, attempts to silence the crowd, and, after a few asides to his cohorts on stage, begins his monologue. We see his familiar gestures as he nervously touches his tie, pulls at his sleeves, clasps his hands together or thrusts them behind his back.

Although static, the camerawork, which follows the visual and temporal logic of the opening, is suited to Carson's personality and stance from several perspectives. Like the camerawork, Carson's physical presence is formal, reserved, buttoned-down, vertical; the only relief is his nervous gestures. As Tynan (1978, p. 47) notes, Carson "holds himself like the midshipman he once was." The camera fixes and contains the bursts of energy and gesture that dart from the perimeter of Carson's body: the static camera and rectangular *mise en scene* situate him in a two-dimensional frame; the vertical stripes in the curtain behind echo

this stiffness, verticality, and reserve.

The fixed camera also isolates Carson spatially to underscore his reputation as a loner and emphasize his firm control of the proceedings. A man who has long resisted invasions of his emotional privacy, Carson seldom fraternizes with colleagues or guests before the show (Tynan, 1978, p. 51). His barbs at McMahon and Severinsen, his seismographic responses to the studio audience, and his mock disparagement of his writers' material are all delivered in steady, unrelenting camera isolation. We see McMahon and Severinsen in separate shots (cutaways) when Carson addresses them directly. But we never see over-the-shoulder or crossover shots that include the two with Carson in the same frame. Moreover, during the opening, we never see the studio audience.

From Carson's first verbal encounters with McMahon and Severinsen throughout the monologue, the camera's undeviating focus on him enhances his control. That control is summed up at the end of the monologue when he delivers the closing verbal cue ("we'll be right back") as he brings in the music that precedes the first commercial with an imaginary golf swing, silencing the band peremptorily with an abrupt gesture. He, not the band leader, conducts the musical flourish.

Letterman's journey of discovery and experiences of incredulity ("unbelievable" was for a long time his favorite word) center on what happens in New York and originate from the same studio and the same stage where Carson got his start as a late night talk show host twenty years ago. Letterman with executive producer Jack Rollins (whose company manages and produces films for Woody Allen, among oth-

---

2.   Quotes and other detailed observations on the production of the *Tonight Show* are derived from a week I spent on the Burbank set in June of 1984 and from video tapes of shows broadcast between 1983–1985.

ers) assembled a production team for *Late Night* that included an announcer from *The Ernie Kovacs Show*, three writers from *Saturday Night Live*, a musical director who had worked on both *Saturday Night Live* and *SCTV*, a producer who had worked for Mike Douglas and David Frost, and an experienced television director who had been associated with the innovative 1960's parody *That Was The Week That Was* (Timberg, 1984, February 16; 1984, March 4; 1984, March 18).[3] In gathering talent with experience in other important fringe comedy shows, *Late Night* tapped into traditions established by the *Tonight Show* while updating and making them relevant to a young audience versed in the hip humor of *Saturday Night Live* and *SCTV*. Making *Late Night* into a laboratory for self-reflexive comedy, this team recapitulated zany stunts that had characterized Steve Allen on the *Tonight Show* and used outlandish props, situations, and video techniques reminiscent of or directly borrowed from Ernie Kovacs.[4]

Where the structuring of the *Tonight Show* emphasizes the stability and isolation of its host, the presentation of Letterman's performance expresses mobility and interconnectedness, themes that are articulated in the pans, tilts, and dissolves of *Late Night's* pre-recorded standard opening which show various views of New York at night. In this introductory montage sequence, the words "Late Night with David Letterman" appear on the top of a taxi, on a billboard, stencilled in the street, on a sign outside the Holland Tunnel, and in a flashing neon sign before a dissolve to the final shot that zooms in to a close up of a bright window in darkened Rockefeller Center. In contrast to the graphics of the *Tonight Show*, which are two dimensional and compartmentalized in an artist's rendering, *Late Night's* graphics are three-dimensional, photographic, and situated in the world outside the studio. In the *Tonight Show*, graphics function as signs marking transitions to and from commercial interruptions; in *Late Night*, graphics integrate and link the inner space of the studio to the world outside.[5]

After the montage, the opening of *Late Night* resembles the first moments of the *Tonight Show*: it also includes a musical fanfare, a grand entrance, and a monologue punctuated by the host's banter with other cast members. But the opening does not use the rigid camerawork of Carson's introduction; instead, a series of camera angles and movements do more to connect than isolate.

Letterman initially appears in a wide establishing shot, taken from an elevated vantage point that includes the entire set, some of the audience, and a large studio monitor. From the very beginning we are reminded of Letterman's presence as media image. Rather than emerging from parted curtains, Letterman casually wanders into view from an off-stage area behind the mock skyline of New York. In contrast to the flat, full-stage lighting of the *Tonight Show*, pools of light and dark on *Late Night* give a sense of depth to the space commanded by Letterman. Admittedly, the camera work that establishes Letterman's entry is largely formulaic: typically the opening establishing shot is followed by a dissolve to a closer shot of Letterman passing in front of the band which, in turn, leads to a medium shot of Shaffer and then a zoom back from the band into a series of dissolves back and forth between Letterman and Shaffer. But this formulaic interlacing of Letterman's entrance with shots of the band further integrates Letterman into his environment. By the time the host launches his monologue, the graphics, sound, camera work, and camera switching patterns of the show have already well established the interconnectedness of the studio world.

During the monologue, Carson and Letterman establish different relationships with the camera and, by extension, with the viewing audience. As Carson performs his familiar stand-up routine, he swivels his head rapidly from left to right, to both wings of the stage and to the studio audience. He acknowledges the camera in only the most fragmentary ways during the monologue; eye contact with the camera is rare and fleeting; his connection with the viewing audience remains, for the most part, a presumed one, with the studio audience substituting for the one at home. These strategies reinforce a feeling that we are sitting in on a staged performance.

Letterman, on the other hand, often opens by addressing the camera directly with a personal comment like, "Hello, I'm David Letterman. What a fine set of human beings we have here today." The effect is a dialogue through the lens of the camera. The feeling of

---

3. These personal interviews were recorded on or around the *Late Night* set.

4. The writers of *Late Night* and Letterman have visited the Museum of Broadcasting to get ideas from tapes of old shows created by Ernie Kovacs and Steve Allen. Curator Ron Simon, with the help of some of the writers and researchers on Letterman's staff, put together a reel of Kovacs-influenced bits from *Late Night* for the Museum of Broadcasting's retrospective on Kovacs in the summer of 1986.

5. Quotes and other detailed observations on the production of *Late Night* are derived from personal visits to the New York set between 1983 and 1985, as well as from video recordings of show aired during that same period.

personal engagement he establishes is paralleled by the relaxed, sweeping gestures of his arms. Although some of Letterman's gestures (the way he claps his hands together, for instance) echo Carson's and even Jack Benny's, Letterman's gestures are less frequent, less frenetic, and less abrupt.

In general, Letterman seems more at home with the camera, willing to play with it, explore it, and see what it can do. Of course, Carson is not unaware of the camera. He knows how to play to it precisely. He is, in fact, a master of mugging to the camera. But while Carson establishes contact with the camera at discrete moments as he introduces and ends various segments of the *Tonight Show*, Letterman maintains almost constant contact with his camera and viewing audience during the often turbulent flow of *Late Night*.

Controlling: The Ritual Space

Along with the compartmentalization, formality, and reserve that characterize Carson's relationship with the camera comes a high degree of predictability in camera composition and switching. Because Carson's show normally maintains a straightforward shot/reaction-shot pattern, a strange angle or unfamiliar composition is a surprise. After all, Carson's ritual performance is based on control, on reserve, on smooth routine. Therefore, the *Tonight Show* is characterized by Carson's implicit and explicit direction of every aspect of the show. This control is also evident in the transitions from one phase of the show to the next: certain things happen at certain times every night. The movement into the next phase is always explicitly set up, cued, or announced in some way.

Letterman's loosely choreographed performance contrasts with the predictability of the standard talk show. On *Late Night*, sponta-

neity is built into the direction and camera work of the show: director and crew are always ready for shifts of format or design, last minute changes, or sudden actions that veer off the main course of the program. In contrast to the *Tonight Show's* structured, calculated camera work, Letterman's cameras are much freer. Often the cameras roam through the studios with Letterman or go backstage.

Exploring the environment of the studio with the mobile camera is, indeed, characteristic of Letterman's modus operandi. The viewer associates Letterman with these forays into the studio, the network lobby, or, by way of film or videotape, into New York City itself. The camera is a sidekick, traveling companion, and friend. When it goes, as it frequently does, camera subjective, we can see what Letterman sees. In the bits using the "sky-cam" (a mobile camera mounted on a winch overhead), the "monkey-cam" (a camera mounted on a monkey), and the "hat-cam" (a camera mounted on Paul Shaffer's cap), camera digressions even mock the current infatuation with technology for its own sake. Such camera techniques keep both the crews and the home audience loose, reinforcing the anything-can-happen atmosphere of *Late Night*.

But not only these planned moments play with the camera work and switching patterns on *Late Night*. Every night, the director and crew are sensitive to unplanned moments; running gags or riffs develop out of nowhere and may require a break in the switching routine. For example, when a carelessly tossed cigarette comes to Letterman's attention and causes him to interrupt his monologue with an outraged appeal for neatness, a camera swings immediately into an unusual extreme close-up of the offending stub. In almost every program, incidents, remarks, or pieces of comic business threaten to trap

Letterman in his own digressions. Together these spontaneous incidents provide the sparks that leap the gaps and meld the rehearsed elements of *Late Night*.

One major stylistic difference, then, between Carson and Letterman is the degree to which they actively flirt with chaos and are willing to loosen the boundaries of their control of the program. These differences are perhaps most visible in the hosts' relationship with sidekicks, musicians, and visiting guests who share the ritual space of the talk show.

As Carson commented to Tynan (1978, p. 88): "When people get outrageous, you have to capitalize on their outrageousness and go with it. The only absolute rule is: Never lose control of the show." Although Carson normally maintains firm control of the interview, guests like Robin Williams or Don Rickels have successfully broken the rules of the *Tonight Show's* decorum. Part of the pleasure of viewing these memorable encounters comes from the conflict between Carson's obvious delight in the chaos of the moment and his desire to regain control. Clearly, Letterman does not exercise the same firm control during interviews.

Perhaps the most distinct contrast in styles, however, is in the host-sidekick relationship. Carson and McMahon have been performing variations of their routine for more than twenty-six years, longer than most show business marriages. McMahon unobtrusively deflects Carson's barbs, at times slyly sabotaging him with a practiced hand. Audiences realize on some level that this interplay is part of the bond, the trust and security, that has kept them together for so long. We also understand that Carson is the "top banana," the "boss" who initiates and dominates their comic interactions.

Letterman's relationship with Shaffer is less formal and less controlled. Shaffer's enthusiasm and silly ideas often represent surface fawning and subsurface revolt. In his open collars and leather jackets, with his cheshire cat smiles and mannered gestures, Shaffer dutifully plays the second banana role as he simultaneously undermines it. Shaffer is both a parody of McMahon and a hybrid of the qualities McMahon and Severinsen possess as sidekicks.

Generally, the interchange between Shaffer and Letterman at the beginning is brief, with Shaffer saying something adulatory about what a great man Letterman is, what a great host, etc. Shaffer's repartee with Letterman here serves the same purpose as McMahon's or Severinsen's with Carson. But, sometimes Shaffer keeps the show from getting off the ground or temporarily derails it.

The show aired September 18, 1983, is an example. The opening segment had already run long before Shaffer's ecstatic digression praising the evening's musical guest, Roni Spector or the 1960s' singing group, "The Ronettes":

I'll tell you what she meant to me. It was back in '63 or so, when 'Be My Baby' hit. She was like a voice just stretching out, reaching me in Canada, a little kid there in the North, saying, 'Come down, come to New York, come and get involved in the business.'

Politely, at first, Letterman tries to damped Shaffer's enthusiasm. After delivering a topical joke, Letterman backs off from the camera, delivering the line that automatically covers his movement to the desk, "Say hello to Paul Shaffer." As the camera switches to Shaffer, Letterman catches himself, remembering, "Well, you've already said hello to Paul . . . [pause] . . . Say hello to Paul, again." While Letterman takes his seat, Shaffer, covering the transition with an eerie grin, adds, "Thank you. I'm the kind of guy you can never say hello to more than enough." While Letterman and the audience try to understand his meaning, Shaffer interjects another comment: "David, last night Ed McMahon coined a very important word for our show. You remember what it was?" Letterman, taking on the role of straight man, asks, "What was that?" "One of the categories of talent was 'spokesmodel,'" Shaffer answers. Letterman interrupts "Yes, a beautiful, successful, young spokesperson for a product," Shaffer continues. "Can I be the spokesmodel for this show?"

At this point, Letterman is anxious to get to the planned material. Shifting his note cards for the first event of the evening (cross-country phone calls), he tries to defuse the exuberant Shaffer with a perfunctory, "Did you have a good day?" but Shaffer responds with an elaborate account of his musical preparations with Roni Spector. Letterman struggles for several moments to muzzle his musical director politely, finally giving up in exasperation with an abrupt, "Look, Paul, we have a show to do." More than five minutes into the show, Letterman regains enough control to launch the first comedy bit of the evening.

The interchange between Letterman and Shaffer illustrates several things: the loose structuring of the *Late Night* opening; the ad-lib quality of Letterman's relationship with Shaffer; the way Letterman's dependence on Shaffer for expansion and supporting material puts his control of the proceedings at risk; and, Letterman's ability to shift into and out of the role of straight man. Although this kind of out-of-control episode also occurs on the *Tonight Show* when McMahon steps out of his usual role, stubbornly holding his ground or pursuing a point Carson wants dropped, on *Late Night* such spontaneous situations are more frequent and clearly designed to disturb the timing and course of the program to humorous effect.

The Social Role of the Talk Show Host: Continuities

Under Carson's control, the fringe talk show became the form of television that most consistently and humorously talked about itself. Letterman takes Carson's ironic stance to an extreme. For both Carson and Letterman, the gestures that unmask their shows' machinery reinforce the theme of the talk show host as Everyman hero who does not belong to the world of tinsel and glitter. Each time Carson refers to his writers or behind-the-scenes staff, each time Letterman makes a pointed reference to the phony skyline of New York in the set behind him, viewers share this in-joke: as Letterman reiterates, "Remember, folk, this is just TV."

In the star-host's role as moderator of potential chaos and reinforcer of mainstream social values, even a raised eyebrow can indicate that a guest or joke has gone over the line of cultural acceptability. But the social, cultural, or political messages that emerge from the potpourri in a nightly talk show are never straightforward ones; they are open to varied interpretations and responses. As Arlen (1981, pp. 317–319) has pointed out, the frantic sociability of the talk show ritual has a shadow side, a flight from silence, loneliness, and fear of others. The surface humor of television sociability skirts the emptiness at the center of all the talk. Even so, Letterman has come closer than any other contemporary television comedian to casting light on TV's shadow side. Steve O'Donnell, *Late Night's* head writer, attributes Letterman's often cynical stance toward the contrivances of his own show to a paradoxical relationship with television:

It's all part of that queer relationship Dave has with TV and show business and celebrities. He likes them and he doesn't like them. He loves TV and he hates TV. TV to him is wonderful—but at the same time it's one of the stupidest, crassest, dehumanizing loads of horseshit that ever was. (Timberg, 1984, March 8).

The talk show host plays many roles: comedian and commentator on society; surrogate questioner of celebrities, experts, and oddballs; master of ceremonies for the rites of the show and centerpiece for his staff's comedic strategies and jokes; and familiar face, voice, and companion to millions of people enjoying the riskless intimacy of their evening hour before the tube. The different roles of the talk show host have encouraged a series of thematic oppositions which we see from their first moments in front of the studio audience. The host is in control of the program, but always in danger of losing control. The host is an Everyman figure, a regular person penetrating the heart of the matter and puncturing the pomposity of Hollywood celebrity, and she/he is also a celebrity, the regal ruler of late night comedy in network TV. For this reason, the ovations and cries of greeting the star-host receives are problematic. Why all the fuss for a regular person? But as an indication of approval, popularity, and power, the reaction is welcomed. The talk show host enjoys the show business popularity, but she/he must appear to maintain his/her equilibrium, the sense of his/her roots, as if she/he had not arrived there, because the audience's identification with him/her as one of their own has established this success.

The talk show host must be aware of new fads, fashions, technologies, of the twists and turns, allures and fascinations of big city and national culture, while viewing these developments from the commonsensical view point of the average citizen. In Carson's middle-age Midwesterner transplanted to the West Coast and in David Letterman's gap-toothed, collegiate new boy in the city, we have the talk show host as cultural balance point between the old and the new, a compass point and processor of what appears on the cultural horizon. When, to take one small example, Letterman hangs himself upside down from the heels in a faddish, anti-gravity contraption, sarcastically commenting about it at each moment of self-imposed silliness, he is not only spinning off the joke of the moment, he is in some sense the personal balance point of the culture's interface with new concepts of health, body, and exercise.

The *Tonight Show* and *Late Night* are not narratives in any traditional sense. They are mixed presentational forms, forums for a series of talk and performance events. Yet a cohesive narrative is implied in the proceedings. A fresh-faced boy comes out of the Midwest; he discovers the city. Uprooted from his home, he is in search of America. His curiosity, humor, and determination to know are his tools for understanding and mediating the America he finds. He reads the newspaper, meets people (celebrities, people at the peak of visible success), travels around the city (and the country) in his quest. He becomes a success. He is exposed to all that the city, the country, and the entertainment industry have to offer, but he remains the same: same humor, same perspective, same rituals of greetings to his friends and followers. He and his viewers are aware that his success is based upon a transparent fascination with trivia. The home audience is an accomplice in the host's mocking rediscovery of America, consuming happily the junk food for thought he brings them nightly. In this process the audience extends it sense of self, its collective identity, through the ritual spaces of the late night talk.

In this sense, although the action of the narrative is cyclic, the talk show host is as much a representative of the people as an elected official. She/he corresponds to the main character in a fairy tale sent upon a mission or quest. She/he is the mock heroic knight sent out every evening to wend a way over the surfaces of a consumer culture, to slay the dragons of the culture's fears and fantasies, to rub shoulders with its dreams of power, knowledge, and success, and through humor, to reduce to human scale and make things livable for those bombarded with unsystematic images of everyday American experience. In these ways and for these reasons, the talk show host is a very specific kind of star and cultural hero.

References

Arlen, M. (1981). *The Camera Age: Essays on Television.* New York: Farrar, Straus, Giroux.

Glassen, J. (1979). *Tent Repertory Theater: The Rosier Company.* Unpublished doctoral dissertation, Michigan State University.

Meserve, W. (1977). *An Emerging Entertainment: The Drama of the American People From the Beginning to 1828.* Bloomington: Indiana University Press.

Meserve, W. (1981). *Heralds of Promise: The Drama of the American People in the Age of Jackson, 1928–49.* Westport, CT: Greenwood Press.

Timberg, B. (Interviewer). (1984, February 16). Interview with Barry Sand, Producer, *Late Night.* Personal cassette recording collection.

Timberg, B. (Interviewer). (1984, March 4). Interview with David Tebet, Vice President of the Carson Group in charge of *Late Night.* Personal cassette recording collection.

Timberg, B. (Interviewer). (1984, March 8). Interview with Steve O'Donnell, Head Writer, *Late Night.* Personal cassette recording collection.

Timberg, B. (Interviewer). (1984, March 18). Interview with Jack Rollins, Executive Producer, *Late Night.* Personal cassette recording collection.

Tynan, K. (1978, February 20). Fifteen Years of the Salta Montale. *The New Yorker,* pp. 47–98.

RAPPING

The *Progressive* is a magazine well known for its publication of thoughtful analyses of political and cultural issues presented from a liberal, or "progressive," point of view. Critic Rapping makes very clear in her opening that she shares this liberal perspective and that it has typically led her to criticize not television, but television's wasted potential. Once that bias is noted, she proceeds to defend television viewers as "not stupid; they are cynical . . . not passive and unconcerned; they are in despair." The heart of her essay, therefore, examines television talk shows as a means of involving the cynical and desperate in their democracy to a greater degree, and in doing so, help television fulfill its potential. At first this would seem to be a formidable task, given the low esteem in which talk shows and their audiences are often held. How does she overcome this handicap? Why does Rapping label much of this criticism (from both Left and Right) as elitist? What would she have thought of the elite cultural critics we met in Chapter 2?

This author has special disdain for her liberal friends. What does she mean when she says liberals "don't necessarily think about changing the *structure* of debate to include those with less cultural capital but, too often, want merely to get rid of the Far Right pundits (McLaughlin and Pat Buchanan, for example) and replace them with our guys?"

What value does she place on the daytime talk shows like *Oprah* in her vision of talk shows as vehicles of inclusion? Do you agree with her position here?

How well has critic Rapping integrated such seemingly different forms of television talk—evening news shows, political talk shows, infomercials, MTV, staged issue summits, daytime talks, C-SPAN—into her argument?

How do you feel about this critic's conversational, personal style of writing television criticism? For example, does her recitation of how she and her family watch *The McLaughlin Group* help her overall thesis or get in its way? Would you have used such evidence in your own criticism?

When I was a student at the University of Chicago, Milton Friedman, the notorious freemarket ideologue, was fond of insisting that capitalism was "a wonderful idea that had never been tried." He meant, of course, government interventions and tamperings of one kind or another had, from the start, prevented the "invisible hand" of free-market competition, the utopian magic he so devoutly believed in.

My skepticism about his theories—and the right-wing policies they have always justified—have only deepened with age. But over my years of watching and analyzing the media, I have come to empathize with his frustration at seeing what he considered a miraculous mechanism for furthering the public welfare exploited and derailed from its potentially progressive path by a bunch of self-serving, short-sighted opportunists and hacks.

That's how I feel about television—a miraculous invention whose potential for furthering and enriching the democratic process has not only never been tapped but has, from its institutionalization in the 1950s, been systematically perverted and short-circuited to fit the callous needs of commerce and established power.

While pundits on the Left and Right continue to cross swords over the whys and wherefores of the sorry state of mass media and popular culture, there is rarely any disagreement about a common premise: that television is the en-

TELEVISION AND DEMOCRACY

Elayne Rapping

emy of civilization—whether because it is controlled by capital (according to the Left) or an agent of the culturally debasing forces of "mass society," hellbent on destroying the "true" culture of the old aristocracies (according to the Right).

I am increasingly puzzled about the political thrust of these attacks. Most people, educated and illiterate, young and old, wealthy and impoverished, are fully aware of the bad news about the media. Most even know what the problem is: corporate profiteering and, in one way or another, government control of speech.

They are not stupid; they are cynical. They are not passive and unconcerned; they are in despair about what to do about the problem. They don't want or need more horror stories of media stupidity, greed, and prostitution to the powerful. They need—are in fact screaming for—change. They want someone to convince them that it is possible to make the media serve

the public good and to give them a few ideas and examples of how it might be done.

Which brings me back to Milton Friedman and his mourning for a good idea never tried. It has often occurred to me over the years that among the naysayers and doommongers of the Right and Left, there is nary a voice to be heard asking the constructive question: How might this amazing technology—capable of bringing continuous information, discourse, culture, and public ritual to the entire world, in myriad forms and for many purposes, for the first time in human history—be mobilized to serve democratic ends?

I am moved to raise this idealistic, to many perhaps naive and addle-brained question now because it is what people all over the country are suddenly, angrily, demanding to know. Among other welcome public rumblings, audiences have begun to talk back in irate voices to the guys on the little screen, yelling, in unanimous roars, "Get real or shut up!"

The responses have been confusing and contradictory. Most immediately and obviously, last year's Presidential campaign shifted from traditional "serious" media venues to more popular, less respectable ones:

We got Ross Perot's big-bucks infomercials and egomaniacally manipulative "town meetings"—out of Frank Capra by way of George Orwell (Ominous.)

We got Bill Clinton debating his parental-consent policies with teen-

Elayne Rapping, Professor of Communications at Adelphi University, regularly contributes cultural commentary to *The Progressive*. She is the author of *The Movie of the Week*, recently published by the University of Minnesota Press.

Reprinted by permission from *The Progressive,* 409 E. Main Street, Madison, WI.

agers on MTV and running the sensation-craving Phil Donahue off his own show, with the help of a rebellious audience bored with salacious tales of sexual fondling while the country burned. (Encouraging.)

And we got Jesse Jackson and Catherine Crier hosting talk shows on CNN in which all-black and all-female panels debated the big issues from gender- and race-oriented perspectives. (I don't quibble with affirmative action.)

While all this went on, the Nielsen people (not to mention a bewildered George Bush and the cast of *Saturday Night Live*) paid tribute to another strange phenomenon; the growing, almost cult-like popularity of *The McLaughlin Group*, a Sunday morning "unrehearsed," thirty-minute free-for-all on current events, featuring a gaggle of journalists freed up to flaunt their true political biases and identities. Which, of course, ranged safely and predictably from liberal Democrat Eleanor Clift of *Newsweek* to Reagan/Bush Republican Fred Barnes of *The New Republic*.

While *The McLaughlin Group* is unique in its sudden cachet, especially with youth, it is hardly alone. The passion for loosened-up political debate and argument, free from the snooze-inducing drones of "official" spokespeople and formats, has spawned any number of hybrid talk/commentary/shouting-match shows in which various combinations of pundits, "newsmakers," and phone-in viewers go at each other with barroom abandon and verve.

What's going on? Quite a lot, I believe, some hopeful, some not. But to get at it, we need to turn away from the knee-jerk reactions of most Left and Right media watchers who are committed to seeing no good whatsoever on television. We need to look instead to the early theorists of American democracy, with an eye toward my previous question: How might the great power of telecommunications be used to further the workings of democracy?

Because there is no doubt in my mind that what audiences, in their often confused, haphazard, and badly formulated ways have been screaming for, and what networks and politicians, in their confused, haphazard, and badly formulated ways, have tried to at least seem to give them, has everything to do with democracy. People want to understand and participate in the workings of their own government. And they are right to sense that it is—at least partly—television that has been thwarting them and television that can help.

As Thomas Jefferson understood so well, there are two things crucial to democracy; universal political education (a combination of information and informed, focused debate) and universal cultural and political inclusion. These two things are essential because they make it possible for all people, no matter their class or status, to understand what is going on and to begin to participate first in public discourse and then, most importantly, in the processes of civic life.

The reason audiences revolted against the Rathers, Brokaws, and Jenningses, the traditional *Newsmaker Sunday* and *Meet the Press* formats, is that they are not inclusive in this democratic sense, and they are not educational except in a very narrow sense, for a narrow branch of the populace. They speak about and to the concerns of a small body of influence-peddlers who already have political capital. The Beltway know-it-alls, as recent events make clear, have nothing to say to most Americans because they are not talking concretely about poverty, panhandlers, and the price of eggs. They are, instead, talking about the minute workings of the inner loops of policy and deal makers; the system whereby a very few, mostly rich, white men in government and media control the conversations and

mechanisms by which decisions are made. Everyone knows this, although some of us are more articulate and clear about it than others.

Because I share the public outrage, I have been looking at the new, more popular formats emerging in response to the crisis of authority in government and media with more sympathy than many of my friends on the Left and in the academy. I think it is encouraging that our political discourses and processes have become more entertaining, more energetic, more popular, because it means that public issues are, in some way or other, being talked about and argued about instead of being ignored. And that, for me, is a necessary if not sufficient condition for popular empowerment.

I know the problems with the new McLaughlin/Larry King/Donahue/MTV-style political talk all to well. Because we leftists are not included in the political potpourri, and because the sophistication and depth of even conservative arguments are lost in the switch from small print to big pictures, the "correct lines," the "right answers" will never be heard—at least in their pure, unadulterated forms. And that worries me as much as it worries you.

Unfortunately, however, this cannot be the first thing on our agenda at a time like this, a time of such profound ignorance and apathy, especially among the young. We need, before we worry about getting *our* ideas and representatives on the air, to make sure that somebody not already tied to an interest or position is actually watching. We need, as Jefferson would have been the first to see, to get people interested, involved, and concerned enough to seek out the more sophisticated facts and arguments. We need to take them, when they get them, first to the voting booth and then to meetings and demonstrations. And that, at the moment, has more to do with structure and style than with which "heads" get to "talk."

Let me explain by looking at two much-maligned examples of "the new television"—*The McLaughlin Group* and Bill Clinton's televised two-day economic summit meeting last December. These two formats succeeded in grabbing the attention and involvement of a large number of the very people who had, until recently, been so bored and cynical and disaffected from politics that they preferred *Jeopardy* to the evening news.

The arguments against McLaughlin—most thoroughly spelled out in Eric Alterman's interesting new book, *Sound and Fury: The Washington Punditocracy and the Collapse of American Politics*—are obvious and valid. McLaughlin, who dominates and controls the proceedings like some Beltway version of Archie Bunker, is a bigot and bully, a political hack for the Right. Not, obviously, my kind of guy. As for his show, it is stagy and bombastic. It allows only established views to surface, thus limiting debate to hegemonic boundaries and, as Alterman says, it "trivializes" and "infantilizes" discourse by reducing issues to a game-show level of one-to-ten ratings on policy matters and winner-loser prediction contests.

I agree with Alterman about a lot of things, but I disagree with his conclusions about the show's debilitating role in political life. While Alterman is generally assumed to be "of the Left," his arguments—like many on the Left and the Right—are in fact elitist, and therefore, conservative rather than progressive. Indeed, while his jacket blurbs come from prominent leftists, he has, on *Crossfire* and C-SPAN, been at pains to refuse this label, insisting that, on "many issues," he is "a conservative." I think he is right, and I would like to explain by raising the issue of what it actually

means to be "Left" or "progressive" in practice (as opposed to mere ideology) because there is today much confusion about this.

Alterman's critique of public discourse is conservative, as many leftists—in these days of little activism and much institutionalized political rhetoric—have become objectively conservative. We don't necessarily think about changing the structure of debate to include those with less cultural capital but, too often, want merely to get rid of the Far Right pundits (McLaughlin and Pat Buchanan, for example) and replace them with our guys.

This is the grain of truth behind the right-wing attacks on "political correctness" at places like Harvard and Yale. The influence of "Left" theorists at prestigious universities generally has little to do with empowering those for whom the Left historically has claimed to speak. Rather, as our critics argue, it too often works merely to demand that those already relatively privileged Left intellectuals be given even greater status and influence in relation to our right-wing counterparts. In that sense, it is a battle about turf among the already culturally propertied.

I am not suggesting we are wrong to demand Left inclusion in high-level debates. Of course we should be included, and of course that would push the envelope of hegemony in the right direction. And I am certainly not arguing that Dan Quayle and Dinesh D'Souza and Camille Paglia are right to insist that "we" have anything like a dominant voice in the academy, the media, or anywhere else. That is ludicrous. Of course we are marginal, and of course we need to be fighting for our positions in the canon wars and talking-head tussles. But that is not the most important thing we need to be doing.

To be truly progressive (as opposed to ideologically leftist), we need to join the majority of people

in their frequently inarticulate demands that they, too, be included in the public debate and in the political process itself, even if what they say is not always what we might like to hear—not, in fact, "politically correct."

And that means paying attention to the formats they *do* attend to and asking why. The reason most people don't watch PBS or read *The New York Times*, no matter who is quoted or interviewed, is that they don't hear their own concerns addressed in language they can relate to, by people with whom they can identify, in a form and style they can understand and even enjoy. Ross Perot understood that and manipulated it shamefully. But others—from Jesse Jackson to Abbie Hoffman to Fidel Castro to Bill Clinton—have also understood it and have offered at least somewhat more constructive hints on what to do about it. So, take a less obvious example, has Oprah Winfrey.

The daytime talk shows, as I have argued before in these pages, allow the otherwise invisible and powerless to speak for themselves about their private experiences and values and to tell experts and anchors to shut up and listen. So they are politically refreshing.

I would not make exactly the same argument about issues of economic and foreign policy, which do indeed require knowledge and sophistication about the workings and precepts of our political, legal, and economic institutions—in a word, education. That is, again, the point behind Jefferson's insistence on the link between education and democracy. If a citizen doesn't know what the Bill of Rights is, for example, there is no point in expecting him or her to develop a progressive critique of the FCC rules on the use of the airwaves. This is something I have learned the hard way, in teaching about mass media.

Which brings me to the much-hated McLaughlin show, one of

present-day youth's more upscale, intellectually challenging entertainments. They watch it because it is fun, and because it makes politics seem exciting and interesting, as though—and they find this hard to adjust to—it actually mattered! And they learn from it. Not the "right" things, by my standards, but more than they bothered to find out before, about how government operates—by whom and according to what rules. And that, depressing as it may be for those who believed we were on the verge of revolution twenty years ago, is a necessary first step toward empowerment.

I also think we overestimate the power of television and the extent to which pundits' opinions hold sway in the minds of viewers, especially seasoned viewers. As audience-response theorists know, reading against the grain or talking back to TV texts is a common practice. When it happens in group settings, it creates a situation which television, according to the doom-mongers, was supposed to have made obsolete: It turns the privacy of our living room into a public space where political debate occurs.

My family and I, for example, watch McLaughlin with great relish on the rare Sundays when we're together, and argue with each other and the cast about issues raised by them, and we're certainly not limited to their narrow, knee-jerk opinions. I'm sure this happens everywhere. That's why the show is popular. It does revive a lost but exciting parlor game—political argument.

Of course, you may say, my children are unusual in their ability to see beyond the political bound of pundit-speak and resist being duped by it. Maybe. But this is where the issue of education and inclusion in the political process, and television's role in furthering it, comes in.

To get people to know or care about matters of national urgency, enough to figure out what the rules are and how they are rigged against us, you have to get them interested enough to pay attention and hopeful enough to believe that their attention and consideration will, potentially, let them into the game. And watching McLaughlin is an obvious place to start that process because—by whatever means—it has got people watching, talking, and arguing.

Which brings me, finally, to Bill Clinton's highly staged, highly symbolic, highly centrist economic summit, another use of television I found encouraging and progressive more for its form and style than its dominant political thrust. Yes, I know all the political caveats against this one, too. I read *The New York Times* and the left-wing press. I know he's a slick operator working to sell us on his (inadequate) long-range economic strategy because the economy won't pick up in time for reelection campaigning. Thus the hard-sell, no-holds-barred telethon. I know he brought in a lot of people of different shapes and colors for show but, in the end, Wall Street and Harvard will prevail.

Well, yes. He is the president, after all, and he's determined, if he can, to ram his policies down our throats now that he's been elected. That's his job. Still, the uses to which he put television are structurally innovative and progressive advances which will serve us well as citizens.

For one thing, Clinton put forth his ideas in some detail, a rare event in recent history, to be sure. Unlike his last several predecessors, he acted as though being a policy wonk, a man who reads and thinks, was a cool thing. He presented ideas seriously and was careful to make them clear and brief enough to be grasped, and to include a wide variety of people and interests in the conversation. Symbolic? Certainly. Much of politics and culture is symbolic. It's supposed to be.

I watched the two-day economic summit for a good long stretch of time last December. I was mesmerized, but then, I'm a confessed C-SPAN addict. The next day, however, I spoke to a colleague, a literary scholar who was quick to admit that much of the policy talk, brief and tailored to TV as it was, went over his head. Still, he said it was the first time he had any inkling at all of what economists and CEOs even talked about, much less how it affected him. My students tended to agree. Why? Because what they saw was a group of people who did, in fact, look more like them than usual—in gender, ethnic and racial variety, and age—talking and being listened to and answered, by the highest officials of the Government, all in language they could follow and relate to.

While the news reporters predictably centered on sound bites by the economic theorists and Cabinet appointees we always see on the news, my students remembered and were intrigued by very different moments. They were dazzled by the articulate statements of delegates from such grassroots groups as ACORN and 9 to 5, which deal with low-income housing and clerical working conditions and the like; by the Head Start staffers who explained, concretely, what worked and what didn't in educating inner-city kids; by the disabled people—one of whom spoke from a wheelchair with the help of a breathing machine she had depended upon for thirty-eight years—who recounted their accomplishments as activists.

This wasn't just a Reganesque setup to pander to the soap-opera crowd. These were people who were indeed poor, oppressed, female, Asian, Latino, black what-have-you, telling America what they were doing, organizationally, to effect change for themselves and telling the President what he should learn from their experiences. They were people whose faces and works have generally been invisible on television-just as, until the Hill/Thomas hearings, the existence of large numbers of black professional women was a well-kept media secret.

I am not, I repeat, addressing the specific policies pushed in these meetings, any more than I am endorsing the views of the members of *The McLaughlin Group*. I know that the head of IBM will be talking to Clinton all year long, while the head of 9 to 5 has had her five minutes of airtime. But she was there, speaking for female clerical workers and being called by her first name by the President-elect, and that meant something to my female students, many of whom have worked as clericals.

The summit was educational in several ways; more people from more walks of like, concrete language instead of the jargon and methodology of "experts," a model of leadership respectful of ideas and able to use them with skill.

No, that's not enough. And no, most of our guys weren't there. And no, President Clinton is not going to listen much to the ones who were there anyway.

But a lot of people who have been out of the loop and out to lunch for years were there, both on screen and in their momentarily politicized living rooms. And that, in an age when the television screen has become the central arena in which political debate and education take place—a non-negotiable done deal—is significant and encouraging. To argue otherwise is, I think, to underestimate the long-term, positive potential of both television and the electorate and to ignore the challenge to think creatively about both.

TRACY

San Jose State University senior television student James Tracy uses David Letterman's success as the departure point for his judgment on the performance of the other well known late night talk show hosts. His comparison of Letterman and Johnny Carson sets the stage by explaining what commonalities exist between the two that establish Letterman as the contemporary standard-bearer. He then uses their differences as the yardstick against which the modern challengers are measured. This is an interesting approach to the issue, one that pulls the reader into the debate before the critic lays out his arguments.

Do you agree with Tracy's assessments of Leno, Hall, and O'Brien? Might different readers (in terms of age, for example) come to much different conclusions? If so, what, besides age, might influence individual viewers' reactions to these hosts?

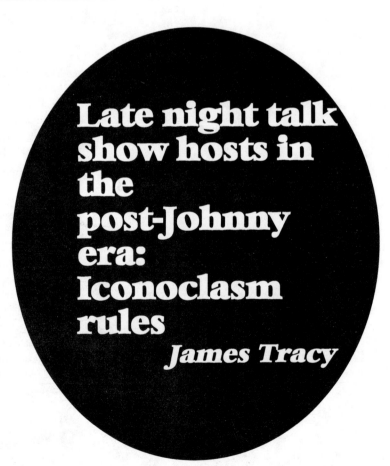

Late night talk show hosts in the post-Johnny era: Iconoclasm rules
James Tracy

In twelve short years David Letterman has ascended to the peak position of the celebrity talk show heap and, proudly waving the banner of iconoclasm, has plopped himself down on its illustrious throne. But how did he get there? And why is it that we love him so damned much?

Success and good ratings are nothing new for Letterman, beginning in the early 1980s when his different brand of television talk show was transposed from a faltering morning venue to eventual replacement for Tom Snyder's *Tomorrow* which followed *The Tonight Show with Johnny Carson*. Within a few years Letterman had carved a niche

for himself in the late night. His appeal was with the 18 to 34-year-old segment of the population; the same group who had tuned into *Saturday Night Live* and made it an unprecedented success during the mid to late 1970s. As with *Saturday Night Live*, Letterman offered his viewing audience music, comedy and in addition, a ground-breaking celebrity interview style.

To appreciate and be entertained by Letterman we first have to understand him and his wit. A generation cultivated on *Mad Magazine*, *National Lampoon*, *Second City Television*, and *The Not Ready For Prime Time Players* was more

Written in 1994 by James Tracy, Radio-TV-Film Major at San Jose State.

than ready for Letterman's slant on the world. For them his ironic, none-of-this-is-real approach was the perfect balance to Ronald Reagan's equally artificial "Morning In America."

In contrast, Johnny Carson had become a languid anachronism: the opening act to Letterman. Nevertheless, the two NBC talk show hosts had in common a tongue-in-cheek persona which enabled them to make the most of their sometime mediocre show-starting monologues and exchanges with celebrity guests. Each knew when his material was stagnant and each had the ability to follow up with ad libs or facial contortions that somehow made it all work in his favor.

The departure of Carson from *The Tonight Show* elevated competent stand up comic and frequent guest host Jay Leno to the star spot. Leno had been active on the comedy circuit in Los Angeles at the very time that Letterman was learning the rudiments of the trade, himself a novice from his native Indiana in search of work on television. Letterman sensed Leno's keen awareness of the absurd in the ordinary and converted it to his own routine, winning the recognition of television talent scouts and breaking into television, initially with appearances on Mary Tyler Moore's comeback show. Throughout Letterman's career he remained a constant admirer of Leno and demonstrated this by making him a regular guest on *Late Night.*

Unfortunately, Leno's performance on *The Tonight Show*, often uncomfortable if not tedious to view, demonstrates his unadjusted grasp of the modern talk show format. Where Letterman and Carson are at ease and natural, Leno is ever prepared to play "the nice guy." The viewing audience knows by now just how the nice guy approach plays out in practice: predictable and plain. This sets the tone of *The Tonight Show* and consummates its bland continuity.

Conversely, Letterman is both entertaining and challenging, even when there is an anticipated lull in the show. Contrary to public prediction, his transition from NBC to an earlier time slot on CBS did nothing to diminish his keen wit and satire. When recently interviewing a noticeably lackadaisical movie star, Letterman asked what the actor did in his spare time. The guest said that he slept a great deal, to which Letterman quickly retorted, "It looks like your ready for a nap right now!" It is exactly that poignant sarcasm which serves to spice up the interview portion of the Letterman show that otherwise might remain sluggish and dull.

Another late night player, Arsenio Hall, is also satisfied to play "the nice guy" next to his guests. He may be more engaging than Leno, but not by much. In fact, the two may be even more comparable if Leno were to begin using street jargon like "In the house!" or "Y'all stay tuned!" Arsenio could reciprocate by protruding his chin and speaking in the semi-nasal Yankee twang characteristic of Leno: the two are homogeneous, where Letterman is beyond such categorization.

Finally, NBC replaced Letterman's vacated late night slot with *Night Shift With Conan O'Brien.* O'Brien's attempts to emulate Letterman have disappointing if not embarrassingly poor results. Especially because their shows target the same 18 to 34 year old audience, O'Brien's ineptitude provides further evidence of Letterman's unique talent.

One of his recent pranks was replacing the four letter words used in everyday conversation with his own cuss word, "crunk." Letterman could have easily pulled this off because his audience knows that he knows that they know it's all bull-crunk. But O'Brien's stunt is somehow sabotaged by his own awkward naiveté and boyish façade. When a joke bombs, rather than smile vaguely, a la Dave, O'Brien reverts to a new low: he actually does push ups for the audience.

Another late night challenger may soon appear. Infamous radio talk show mogul Howard Stern has expressed interest in doing late night television. Yet he may be more at home with pay-per-view than mainstream television, given his bawdy nature. A recent interview with Stern in *Rolling Stone* found him assailing both Leno and Letterman with the most acrimonious scorn. He (perhaps accurately) equated Leno and his performance on *The Tonight Show* to the pathetic rambling of a wounded deer in the wilderness, refusing to lay down and die. He then compared Letterman to a big, bloated elephant. Stern might be a bit kinder to his peers were he to be granted a shot at network television. But if not, it would only be fair for him to thank Letterman for paving the way for iconoclasm in the post-Johnny era.

Chapter Exercise

Comparing Talk Shows

List the conventions/components of your favorite talk show from each of the three following categories. Then analyze them and explain why the programs provide these variations on the talk show format.

TALK SHOW COMPARISON			
	Late Night	Afternoon Syndicated	Network Weekend
Host?			
Set?			
Topics?			
Guest?			
Monologue?			
Audience Demographic?			
Studio Audience?			
Interaction With Studio Audience?			
Music / Band?			
Sponsors/ Advertising?			
Other?			

References and Resources

Bass, A. (1993). TV talk shows said to trivialize serious issues, troubled guests. San Jose *Mercury News*, October 21, p. 15A.

Bernstein, C. (1992). Feeding the "idiot culture." San Jose *Mercury News*, June 21, pp.1C, 4C.

Brady, J. (1994). In step with Arsenio Hall. *Parade Magazine*, February 13, p. 30.

Carter, B. (1994). *The Late Shift: Letterman, Leno and the Network Battle for the Night.* New York: Hyperion.

Forrest, S. (1993). Lawyers protest *Geraldo* mock trial. San Jose *Mercury News*, January 23, p. A2.

Golden, D. (1988). Oprah, Phil, Geraldo, Sally Jessy. *Boston Globe Magazine*, July 10, pp. 17, cont. 49.

Kaplan, J. (1995). Are Talk shows out of control? *TV Guide*, April 1, pp. 10–15.

Kaplan, P. W. (1988). David Letterman's stick shift: Can the anti-Quayle steer us through the nineties? *Rolling Stone*, November 3, pp. 70–75.

Koeppel, D. & Griggs, R. (1991). All talk, no action. *Mediaweek*, January 28, pp. 20–24.

Kurtz, H. (1996). *Hot Air: All Talk, All the Time.* New York: Times Books.

Mankiewicz, F. (1989). From Lippmann to Letterman: the 10 most powerful voices. *Gannett Center Journal*, 3, 81.

Mitchell, S. (1993). Reality, but not quite. *Spirit*, November, pp. 34, 104.

Rigby, J. (1994). A man's guide to TV Talk Shows. *Playboy*, August, pp. 90–92.

Rivers, J. (1994). Today's quote. San Jose *Mercury News*, January 9, p. 4A.

Rosen, J. (1992). Discourse. *Columbia Journalism Review*, November/December, pp. 34–35.

Ross, A. (1993). The politics of irony. *New Republic*, November 8, pp. 22–31.

'Sally' cuts fight. (1994). San Jose *Mercury News*, February 1, p. 4A.

Schaefer, R. J. & Avery, R. K. (1993). Audience conceptualizations of *Late Night With David Letterman. Journal of Broadcasting & Electronic Media, 37*, 253–273.

Timberg, B. (1994). *Titans of Talk.* Austin, TX: University of Texas Press.

Tomasulo, F. P. (1984). The spectator-in-the-tube: the rhetoric of *Donahue. Journal of the University Film and Video Association, 36*, 5-12.

Waters, H. F. (1990). If it ain't broke, break it: TV's sudsiest soap? The post-Pauley *Today* show. *Newsweek*, March 26, pp. 58–59.

Whalen, J. (1993). Back talk. *Metro*, January 6, p. 16.

White, M. (1992). *Tele-Advising: Therapeutic Discourse in American Television.* Chapel Hill, NC: University of North Carolina Press.

Zoglin, R. (1992). And what a reign it was: in his 30 years, Carson was the best. *Time*, March 16, pp. 62–64.

Zoglin, R. (1991). Running off at the mouth. *Time*, October 14, pp. 79–80.

EPILOGUE

You may know Quinn Martin programs like *The Fugitive, The F.B.I., Streets of San Francisco,* and the original *Untouchables.* Much like the prolific producer of these classic television programs, we felt we should "bring it all together" at the end and provide some closure with an Epilogue, a recap of what we've tried to accomplish with this text. This is one way for you to check to see if you missed anything during your reading, or even more importantly, what you may have learned *beyond* your reading (hopefully, incited *by the reading*).

First, **we introduced you to criticism and critical theory** and we showed you that there are many, many different ways to evaluate not only the medium as a whole, but even individual programs. We tried to emphasize the purpose and importance of the critical act: To cause us all to stop and *think about* what we (and others) are watching which can lead to better understanding, a more fulfilled experience and/or an improved television.

Then, **we discussed the process of criticism, that is, how to do it**. We provided you with two general formats in which to express your critical views in order to share them clearly and completely with others. In this way, your important personal opinions and experiences can enter the "cultural conversation" instead of being dismissed as a frustrated complaint or griping. You don't want your ideas disappearing in the wind.

We are not proposing that these critical formats give your viewpoints more "relevance." Rather, we are suggesting that there is a difference between complaining about (or praising) a situation and actually doing something about it or making your opinions

count. An organized, thoughtful critical response (that can be useful to yourself and others) *is doing something* about it; it is making your opinion count.

In order for your viewpoint to be well-informed, **we detailed the structure of the television industry that produces the "texts" that are evaluated in criticism**. Again, we provided some general information (an overview, if you will) of the industry and specific program types. Plus we included a bibliography at the end of each chapter. We wanted you to understand how the system works as it exists today so that you can determine how it can work for you or allow you to discover where it can be improved.

What we hope is that you will take this information as a starting "first step." We want you to realize how much information is out there for you to use. We urge you to seek out those elements which you find interesting in order to learn and to develop your own, original ideas.

Finally, using identifiable genres as our basis of organization, **we introduced you to the act of criticism.** We provided examples of analyses utilizing various established critical approaches. But again we emphasize that these approached are not the only way to engage in criticism. Instead, we presented these critical approaches as *tools* that critics can use to "get at" issues or to answer questions. We acknowledge that no critical perspective is better than the other; it is simply that some approaches are better suited to answer specific questions than others. Of course, this all depends on how the approaches are used by individual critics.

This is one reason why we organized the book as interactively as was possible with exercises and questions. Our hope is that you will continue to *use* the book as you watch television and engage in criticism. Write all over the book and notice how your perceptions change. (You might as well use the book. With technology rapidly and constantly changing the medium of television, frequent new editions of this book are inevitable so the sell-back price won't be worth pampering the pages). Just as you watch a program over and over again, and each time you watch you "see" something different than before, we want you to examine and re-examine your critical responses, approaches and perspectives as you learn and change because of your education and life experiences. By becoming familiar with the established critical approaches, we hope that you will be able to use them for your own purposes—mix and match them or develop an approach of your own based upon your knowledge of what is already being done.

This is where the student papers come into the formula: With every new edition of this book, we will be searching for your individual uses of established critical approaches or your innovative development of a new approach. We believe that anyone who views television *can and should be* a critic. And we want to provide a venue for such participation that can be shared with many others (see the Preface for details about submitting your work to us.)

As we've stated throughout this book, our goal is to open you up to new ways of understanding television's content, to guide you to become more critical viewers, and to give you the tools you'll need to be better writers of television criticism and better "readers" of our culture's dominant literature: television programming.

We hope you enjoyed the show.

INDEX